SRI LANKA
A Survey

SRI LANKA

A SURVEY

Edited by
K. M. DE SILVA

The University Press of Hawaii
Honolulu

Library of Congress Catalog Card Number 77-73917
ISBN 0-8248-0568-2

Simultaneously published by C. Hurst & Co. (Publishers) Ltd.,
London. A publication of the Institute of Asian Affairs, Hamburg.
Manufactured in Great Britain

CONTENTS

MAPS

TABLES

Contents

Page

viii
Contents

Page

PREFACE

This book owes its existence to a week-end I spent in Hamburg in October 1973 as the guest of Dr. Werner Draguhn, Director of the Institute of Asian Affairs in that city. While showing me round the Library of his institute he remarked on the lack of a scholarly study of contemporary Sri Lanka. He added that the Institute of Asian Affairs was interested in sponsoring such a volume. Two conditions were laid down; that the editor and all the contributors should be Sri Lankan scholars; and that, for technical reasons which had to do with the budgetary provisions for the production of the book, all the articles and the editorial work had to be completed by the end of 1974. The first of these conditions was attractive enough, but the second was a daunting prospect and I accepted his invitation to serve as editor of such a volume with some hesitation for I was not certain whether the deadline could be met.

In preliminary discussions with colleagues at Peradeniya it was evident that there was much enthusiasm for the project. A more formal planning session in early January 1974 indicated that it was a viable proposition, that is to say, there was a group of Sri Lankan scholars whose academic credentials were beyond question, and who could not only write the chapters of the volume as planned but be relied upon to keep the deadline of December 1974. Once work began, however, we ran into difficulties. More than one of our authors left the Island in the course of 1974, some for good—the *diaspora* of the Sri Lanka intelligentsia—and others on sabbatical leave. As a result, I, as editor, had to cope with the formidable business of communicating with authors spread over every continent save South America. One of our authors made a valiant effort to complete his assignment in Nigeria but had to give it up for lack of library facilities—relating to Sri Lanka—there. Two others, however, sent us their chapters from Western Australia and New Zealand respectively. Our optimism with regard to the deadline for the project was justified, for all but two of our authors were able to meet it, most of them with weeks to spare.

ix

This volume is as comprehensive as we could make it in the short space of time available to us. We are conscious of the fact that some themes have not been treated as fully as they ought to have been. Nevertheless, hiatuses and all, this is the first comprehensive review of Sri Lanka since Independence and one which is not limited to an analysis of the politics of the country. Indeed we have had in recent years a number of most competent volumes on the island's politics, and for that reason we have given the present book a different emphasis: on history, geography, demography, education, religion, literature and the arts, but above all, the economy has been treated in depth for the first time since the mid 1960s.

In producing this volume we have incurred many debts. It is a great pleasure to express our appreciation of the help received from Dr. Werner Draguhn and the Institute of Asian Affairs in Hamburg. He initiated the process from which this book emerged, and gave his enthusiastic support at all stages in its production while the Institute gave generous financial support. Above all they gave the editor complete freedom in planning the book, the choice of authors, and the content of the chapters. Our publisher Mr. Christopher Hurst took a deep personal interest in the book and his sympathetic understanding of the problems of the editor and the authors of the chapters went much beyond the call of duty. And finally there is our team of authors. All but one of them have been undergraduates at the University of Sri Lanka, Peradeniya (and the odd man out narrowly missed that privilege for he was at Colombo just before the University moved to Peradeniya in 1952), and all of them have been teachers here. They have been remarkably productive under very difficult circumstances without ever lowering their high standards of scholarship. By their work on this volume they have demonstrated that scholarship can not merely survive but thrive in and prevail over the inhospitable terrain that confronts the academic community of this country at present.

K. M. DE SILVA

Peradeniya, Sri Lanka
March 1976

INTRODUCTION
by K. M. de Silva

Once again we are free. It is true that no people can live on memories alone; it is equally true that their history often provides a source both of strength and inspiration, to guide them in the future. It is only against the background of the past that the present and the future can be viewed in their correct perspective.

These words of S. W. R. D. Bandaranaike were spoken on 10 February 1948 at the ceremonial opening of the first sessions of parliament in Srī Laṅkā after the attainment of independence.

Few of Srī Laṅkā's statesmen and politicians stopped to ask themselves when it was that a Sinhalese had last ruled over the island. When they did think about it at all they turned to the Kandyan kingdom — the last of the independent Sinhalese kingdoms — which had been ceded to the British in 1815, and they were not disinclined, like a whole generation of reformers and nationalists, to look upon themselves as the successors, if not heirs, of the Kandyan kingdom. And in doing so they missed the point that what D. S. Senanayake — the country's first Prime Minister after independence — and his associates had inherited from the British was much more than the Kandyan rulers had ever controlled, for these latter ruled over a landlocked kingdom whose littoral was under foreign rule.

The last Sinhalese king to rule over the whole island had been Parākramābahu VI in the fifteenth century (1415-67). But set against the background of several centuries of turmoil, instability and weakness, this was quite exceptional, and did not amount to any decisive reversal of a trend. One had to go further back into the past, to the second half of the eleventh century and the first half of the twelfth for a period when Sinhalese rulers had had effective control over the resources of the whole island, to Vijaya Bahu I, Parākramābahu I and Nissaṅka Malla. But theirs had been, in effect, an interlude of indigenous rule sandwiched between two phases of South Indian control. It is just as well then that statesmen and politicians did not go through this process of historical investigation for it would have provided occasion for morbid reflections on the fragility of the Srī Lankā polity of the past. The moral of the story was sombre enough: control over the whole island by a Sinhalese ruler, was somewhat of a rarity and novelty. No wonder then that Bandaranaike, in 1945, seconding the resolution for acceptance of the Soulbury Constitution, had thought it necessary to warn his countrymen against any excessively sanguine expectations:

We are not facing the future, Sir, in a spirit of exultation or jubilation. There is no cause for that. We are too conscious of the difficulties that will face us in the years to come . . .

D. S. Senanayake to be sure was more optimistic. He realised that his was a difficult inheritance. But to a much greater extent than the bulk of his colleagues and associates in the national leadership, he understood the implications of the fact that Srī Lankā was a plural society and his policies for the transfer of power and in the early years of independence were framed on that realistic basis.

Srī Lankā indeed has been, as Samaraweera's chapter 1 in this volume shows, a plural society from the earliest centuries of its long history. The elements of plurality have been largely ethnicity and religion and, in recent times, caste as well. Through the centuries the components of pluralism have kept increasing and not least under British rule. Nevertheless the outstanding characteristic of the communal structure in Srī Lankā is the overwhelming numerical predominance of the Sinhalese. In 1948 this was as high as 71% and in the earlier years of British rule it may have been higher still before the immigration of Indian plantation workers began and increased the number of Tamil-speakers. Tensions and complications had developed in the twentieth century because the patterns of economic development and social change in British times had given some of the ethnic and religious minorities certain advantages, if not privileges, of which the majority Sinhalese and Buddhists were increasingly resentful.

With the rise of the nationalist movement there was a tendency for the Sinhalese to equate their own ethnic nationalism with a wider all-island one, to assume that these—Sinhalese nationalism and Srī Lankā nationalism—were one and the same. In support of this they advanced arguments based on history and immemorial tradition. But it was a short-sighted and unrealistic attitude because the Tamils, the most numerous and articulate group among the minorities, passionately rejected this identification of the sectional interests of the majority with the wider all-island focus of Srī Laṅkā nationalism. The Christians (among the Sinhalese and Tamils) and more particularly the Roman Catholics were equally apprehensive and resentful of the common tendency to equate Sinhalese national-ism with Buddhism. The Tamils, for their part, developed an inward-looking ethnic nationalism of their own, though this, like the cognate process among the Sinhalese, lacked cohesion and even a touch of authenticity till language became, after independence, the basis of these rival nationalisms. With the near approach of the transfer of power the minorities became "particularly apprehen-sive of the actions of what [they regarded] as a permanent and un-assailable [Sinhalese] majority", and they felt themselves "forever debarred from obtaining an adequate share in the responsibilities of government. . ." [2]

The other version of nationalism, a Ceylon or Srī Laṅkā national-ism which emphasised the common interests of the island's various ethnic religious groups, had as its basis an acceptance of the reality of a plural society and sought the reconciliation of the legitimate interests of the majority and minorities within the context of an all-island polity. Its most influential advocate at the time of the transfer of power was D. S. Senanayake. And in 1948 this version of nationalism seemed a viable alternative to the narrower sectional-isms described above, and held out the prospect of peace and stabi-lity in the vital first phase of independence. It was based on a double compromise: the softening of Sinhalese dominance by the establish-ment of an equilibrium of political forces which emphasised moderation, and an emphasis on secularism, a refusal to mix state power and politics with religion, even though the concept of a special responsibility for Buddhism was tacitly accepted. The con-stitution devised for the transfer of power and the political structure at independence reflected this balance or equilibrium of forces. But—as we shall see—the stability of this balance was only appa-rent and was easily upset, even though this did not seem likely in 1948.

As regards the economy, much more so than with the political structure, the mood of the day was singularly sober and realistic. The crux of the problem was that foreign income which "directly or indirectly constituted the bulk of the national income began to fall rapidly", while there was a rise in the cost of imports. This was reflected in the country's balance of payments, which fell con-sistently from "a handsome surplus in 1945 to a heavy deficit in 1947". "For a country which practically lives by foreign trade," an authoritative contemporary economic survey pointed out, "no economic indices could be more significant. It represented a fall in national income and a march towards greater poverty and insecurity".[3]

D. S. Senanayake's government inherited an undiversified export economy dependent principally on three crops: tea (in terms of export earnings the most important), rubber and coconut. The weakness of the economy lay in the fact that these exports were subject to wide fluctuations, a reflection of world economic conditions.

One of the most striking features of this economic structure was the absence of an industrial sector independent of the processing of tea, rubber and coconut for export, and the engineering and mechanical requirements of these processes. Nevertheless there had been since 1931, and more particularly since the outbreak of the Second World War, some state-sponsored industrial ventures. None of these proved of more than marginal significance, and on the whole little progress had been made. Private enterprise was reluctant to embark on industrial ventures in the absence of firm support from the government. Though the new government declared that the country cannot "depend on agriculture alone to provide the minimum standard we are aiming at for our rapidly increasing people", this was merely lip-service to the almost religious faith among the intelligentsia in industrialisation as the panacea for Srī Laṅkā's economic problems.

Traditional agriculture — subsistence farming — lagged far behind the efficient plantation sector in productivity due to the long-term impact of a multiplicity of factors. Srī Laṅkā could not produce the rice needed to feed a growing population: the bulk of the country's requirements in rice and subsidiary foodstuffs was imported and accounted for more than half the imports.

Looking ahead in the years after independence the Senanayake regime placed its hopes on the achievement of self-sufficiency in rice and subsidiary foodstuffs. ". . . [increased] production particularly in the matter of home-grown food," it declared, "will be given a place of supreme importance in the policy of the Government. . .."[4] The principal means of achieving this objective was the rapid development of the dry zone, the heartland of the ancient irrigation civilization of Srī Laṅkā. Thus in this enterprise one discerned too the search for inspiration from the past and the traditional sources of legitimacy of Srī Laṅkā's rulers.

All in all, however, there was no great emphasis on far-reaching changes in the economic structure inherited from the British. This latter had taken firm root in the period of British rule, and the process of introducing changes in it was more difficult than it seemed, while any hope of dismantling it was beyond the realms of practical politics. For "the export of estate produce enabled the people of [Srī Laṅkā], or a large part of them, to be fed and clothed . . ."5 Besides, the system itself was still viable and its potential for expansion was, if not undiminished, at least reasonably good. It was also true that the political leadership of the day was reluctant to make changes in an economic system with which its own interests were identified. The result was that in the economic structure, as in the political, there was an emphasis on the maintenance of the *status quo.*

There were other problems as well, and of these much the most important was the rapidity with which population was expanding. A knowledgeable commentator on the country's affairs gave a warning in 1949 of the economic implications of the fact that the island's rate of natural increase of population had reached "the astonishing rate of about 3.3 per cent per annum". "There can be no doubt", he added, "that this is the fundamental problem of the economy of [Srī Laṅkā]..."6

Moreover, Srī Laṅkā, poor though it was, enjoyed a much higher standard of living than India, Pakistan and Burma, and the national finances seemed adequate to maintain the welfare measures to which the country had grown accustomed in the last years of British rule. It was not yet evident that the burgeoning costs of these welfare measures were an insupportable burden for a developing country and an economy whose principal feature was its dependence on the vagaries of the world market.

The fact is that, as regards the economy, the mood in 1948 though subdued and earnest, was not unduly pessimistic. There were, on the contrary, high hopes for economic achievement. For the country's assets were not unimpressive: although the population was increasing rapidly, it was—compared to that in other countries in South Asia—well fed and literate; the government of Srī Laṅkā was the largest landholder in the country, controlling no less than 3.25 million acres of land (the bulk of this land was waste forest and required the provision of roads and electricity to be rendered productive). The administration was competent, and the island was well equipped with social and economic overheads; above all, there were the large sterling balances accumulated during the war.

Nevertheless the economic legacy left behind by the British was just as ambiguous as, and perhaps even more so than the political one. The chapters of this volume will attempt a broad and dispassionate assessment of how the governments of independent Srī Laṅkā have coped with these.

REFERENCES

1. Chapter 3.
2. *Report of the Commission on Constitutional Reform* (The Soulbury Report), London, 1945, p. 50.
3. B. B. Das Gupta, *A Short Economic Survey of Ceylon*, Colombo, 1949.
4. Quoted in H. M. Oliver, *Economic Opinion and Policy in Ceylon*, Duke University Press, 1957, p. 50.
5. W. I. Jennings, *The Economy of Ceylon*, Oxford University Press, 2nd. ed., 1951, p. 40.
6. ibid., p. 4.

PART I

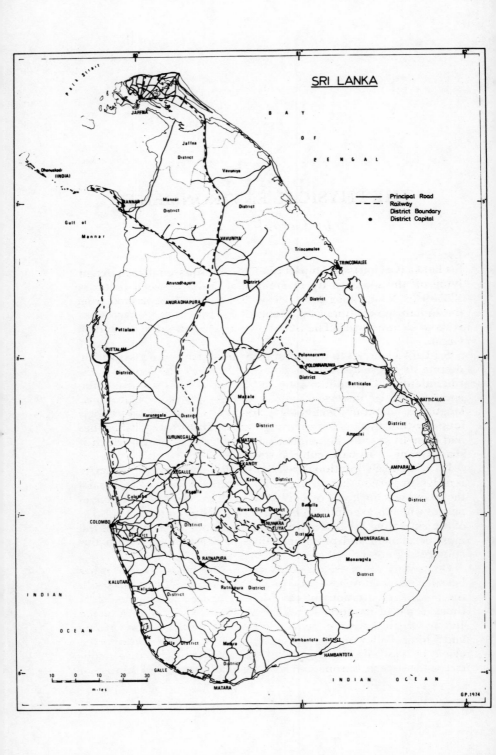

1

THE PHYSICAL ENVIRONMENT

by Gerald Peiris

Location

Srī Laṅkā (Ceylon) is a compact island 25,332 square miles in extent lying off the southern tip of Peninsular India between latitudes 5°55'-9°51' N. and longitudes 79°41'-81°53' E. It is separated from the Indian sub-continent by a strip of sea which, at its narrowest, is about 25 miles wide. The island is centrally located in the Indian Ocean.

Srī Laṅkā belongs to the cultural region of Southern Asia which, despite its internal diversity, possesses features that lend it a distinct identity. Common origins and common cross-cultural influences could be discerned among the complex of institutions, languages, literature, technology, arts, crafts, customs and beliefs found within this region. Throughout its history the island has had close links with the neighbouring sub-continent with which it shares many of its basic cultural traits.

In Srī Laṅkā's locational relationships, however, its insularity is no less important than its proximity to India. For over 2,500 years, the island was the home of a civilization of its own, the distinctiveness of which is exemplified in many facets of its culture. The strip of sea separating Srī Laṅkā from India has indeed been one of the most permanent and prominent lines of demarcation within the cultural region of Southern Asia.

On account of the island's centrality in the Indian Ocean, it has been for many centuries a focal point of sea routes. It had links with the ancient civilizations of the Mediterranean, and in medieval times, some of its ports were major commercial emporia of the Indian Ocean that were frequented by trading fleets from Arabia and China. Following the discovery of the Cape sea route to the orient by Vasco da Gama in 1498, Srī Laṅkā came into direct contact with western Europe and soon became a centre of European

3

activity in the East. The opening of the Suez Canal in 1869 enhanced the strategic importance of Srī Laṅkā in relation to the main oceanic highways linking Europe with Australia and the Far East.

Location is, of course, fundamental to the physical environment which forms the subject of this chapter. Lithological, structural, topographic, climatic and biotic attributes of the island are basically the derivatives of its location.

Physiography

Lithology and Structure. Geologically, Srī Laṅkā is a southern continuation of the Indian Deccan Massif. Geologists have postulated that Srī Laṅkā and Peninsular India along with the other landmasses that are peripheral to the Indian Ocean and the South Atlantic were once parts of a single large continent which began to fragment during mid-Jurassic times. These fragments are said to have drifted apart until about late Cretaceous times to form the present continental outlines. The formation of the narrow strip of sea which now separates Srī Laṅkā from India is believed to have occurred as recently as the Miocene epoch. Hence, there are many similarities between Srī Laṅkā and the adjacent parts of the Deccan, not only in lithology and structure but also in the unusual abundance of thorium-bearing minerals which, according to Pichamuthu[1], is a peculiarity that these areas share with Madagascar.

Much of the island of Srī Laṅkā is of great geological antiquity (Chart I). Apart from about one-tenth of its surface which has narrow belts of Jurassic, Miocene, Pleistocene and recent rocks of sedimentary origin, the rest of the island is composed of highly metamorphosed crystalline rocks. It has been contended in some recent writings [2] that these metamorphosed rocks are not, as was earlier believed, all of pre-Cambrian age; but that their origin could be placed in two geological periods separated from each other by a time-span of some 1,000 million years, one in pre-Cambrian and the other in post-Cambrian (early Palaeozoic) times. Due perhaps to the tentative nature of the evidence upon which this contention has been based, most local geologists have continued to refer to the crystalline rock complex of Srī Laṅkā as pre-Cambrian rocks.

Until about the 1950s, geologists regarded the crystalline rock complex of Srī laṅkā as falling into two groups: (*a*) the Khondalite Series, which occupies a zone about 50-100 miles in width extending from the southwest through the central parts of the country towards the northeastern coast, and (*b*) the Vijayan Series, forming two zones that lie on either side of the Khondalite Series. The Vijayan rocks were then visualized as forming a "basement" or a "synclinal basin" upon which the Khondalites rest. This simple picture has undergone considerable modification during the past two decades. While the earlier twofold division is still held to be valid in certain respects, some geologists of our time have favoured the recognition of a major sub-division in the Khondalite Series called the South Western Group. This group is said to represent a specific period of metamorphism which affected only the southwestern parts of the country and, possibly, parts of South India, and to possess distinct structural and lithological characteristics such as the presence of granitic pegmatites and granitic gneisses. The South Western Group along with the rest of the Khondalite Series is now more commonly referred to as the "Highland Series".

The earlier postulate that Khondalites rest on a Vijayan basement, which implies the latter rock series to be older than the former, has also been refuted by Vitānagē and Cooray who have contended that the Vijayans have been formed by the granitization and migmatization of rocks of the same assemblage as the Highland Series. These writers have shown that the boundaries between the two rock series are represented by narrow discontinuous transitional zones which possess lithological and structural features that characterise both series. A recent attempt by Katz[3] to revive with fresh evidence the older concept of a Vijayan basement has been criticized by Berger[4] who has questioned the validity of the evidence and the reasoning on which Katz's contentions have been based.

The Highland Series is an assemblage of highly metamorphosed sedimentary rocks. Its petrological diversity has confounded systematic sub-division and mapping. Among the main rock types belonging to this series are the Khondalites proper (garnet-silli-manite-schists, so named after their principal area of occurrence in India), crystalline limestone, dolomite, quartzites and quartz schists and granulites and gneisses. Charnokites too are extensively found throughout the series. The structural trends of the Highland Series rocks are in a general north-south direction, manifested more distinctly in its northern parts than in the south. Variations in strike direction commonly found in the latter areas could be attributed to differential tectonic pressures which have acted on this part of the Highland Series rocks and to their own varying responses to such pressures. A small outlier of the Highland Series occurs within the eastern segment of the Vijayan Series. This has been named the 'Kataragama Complex'.

The Vijayan Series consists of various types of granites, gneisses and migmatites. The absence within this series of certain minerals (e.g. sillimanite and graphite) found in abundance in the Highland Series distinguishes it lithologically from the latter. The structural

Table 1   THE MAIN GEOLOGICAL FORMATIONS OF SRĪ LAṄKĀ

Era	Period	Formation
CENOZOIC -70 to 0 m.y.	Recent Pleistocene	By-products of weathering and riverine, coastal and beach deposits
	Miocene Oligocene	Limestones (Jaffna penisula and north-west coast)
	Eocene	Sandstones (Mirihāgalkanda beds)
	Pleocene	
MESOZOIC -225 to -70 m.y.	Cretaceous Jurassic Triassic	Sandstones, artoses, grits and shales (Tabbowa, Andigama and Pallama)
PALAEOZOIC -600 to -225 m.y.	Permian Carboniferous Devonian Silurian Ordovician Cambrian	Granites and gneisses of the south-west Group
PRECAMBRIAN Older than -600 m.y.		*Vijayan Series* Gneisses, Granites, schists, etc. *Highland Series* Khondalites, crystalline lime- stones, dolomite, quartzite, quartz, granulites, gneisses and charnotites, etc.

This chart is based on Cooray, op.cit; Crawford and Oliver, op.cit. and P. Vitānagē, 'Post-Cambrian uplifts and Regional Neotectonic Movements in Ceylon', *Proceedings of the 24th International Geological Congress,* Section 3, Montreal (1972), pp. 642-52.

trends of the Vijayan rocks are also more varied and more irregular than those of the Highland Series rocks. Certain broad regional variations in the Vijayan Series have been recognised in several writings. Well banded black and white gneisses are typical of the eastern segment of the Vijayan Series while its western segment is

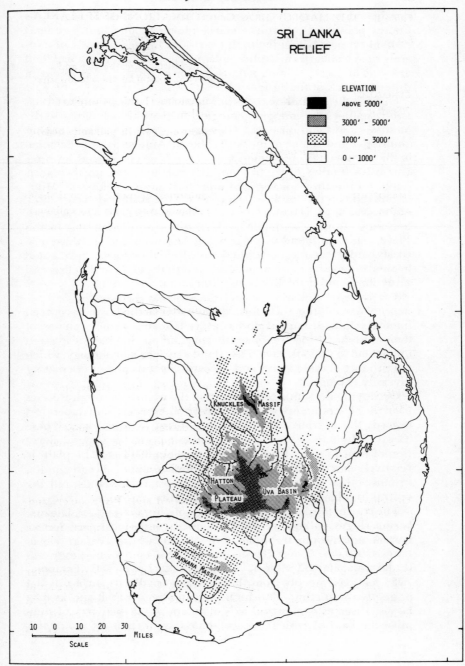

SRI LANKA
RELIEF

ELEVATION

ABOVE 5000'

3000' – 5000'

1000' – 3000'

0 – 1000'

KNUCKLES MASSIF

HATTON
PLATEAU   UVA BASIN

RAKWANA MASSIF

10   0   10   20   30
                         MILES
        SCALE

dominated by pinkish gneisses and granitic rocks. However, as Cooray points out[5], there is a marked homogeneity in the mineral content of rocks belonging to this series. A limited number of minerals such as quartz, microline, plagioclase, biotite and hornblend are said to occur in monotonous regularity in the rocks found in different parts of the series.

Outside the crystalline rock complex of Srī Laṅkā, there are relatively smaller and younger geological formations belonging to the Mesozoic and Cenozoic eras.[6] They are (a) the non-marine Jurassic sandstones and shales found at Tabbowa, Andigama and Pallama in the northwest (b) the limestones of the Miocene period forming a strip 10-20 miles in width along the northern and northwestern coasts (c) the tiny outcrop of lower Miocene sandstone at Minihāgalkanda on the southeastern coast (d) the scattered occurrences of Pleistocene gravels and laterites in the western and southwestern lowlands (e) other sedimentary formations also belonging to the Pleistocene age found in parts of the northern and northwestern coasts, and (f) the recent residual and alluvial deposits represented by sandstones and sand, mudstones and shale, and coral debris and alluvium found in the low-lying littoral of the country.

Relief. Most of the rock formations described above have been intensely folded, faulted and ruptured during certain phases of their existence. Processes of weathering and erosion have also acted upon them in various ways. The island's surface morphology, which is a product of these forces and processes, is thus one of fascinating diversity (Figure 2).

Occupying the south-central parts of the island is a rough isoceles triangle of mountains whose northern apex veers and tapers off towards the northeastern coast in a series of low ridges. These 'Central Highlands' are circumscribed by a plain, the general elevation of which ranges from sea level to about 300 feet. The plain is relatively narrow and rugged in the southwest but is broad and flat in most other parts. The rugged southwestern lowlands and the central highlands are within the Khondalite rock zone.

The core of the central highlands is a plethora of peaks, plateaux, basins, ridges, valleys and escarpments. Its innermost parts form a narrow north-south trending high plateau whose average elevation is 6,000 — 6,500 feet. Though some of Srī Laṅkā's highest peaks (Pidurutalāgala, 8,282 feet; Kirigalpotha, 7,837 feet; Totapola, 7,733 feet) rise steeply from this plateau, usually its surface is flat or gently undulating. This high plateau along with its peaks may be visualised as the vertical axis of an anchor-shaped area of summits, the base of which is represented by a chain of mountains stretching for a distance of over 45 miles from Adams Peak (7,341 feet) in the west to Namunukula (6,679 feet) in the east. This anchor is bounded on the south by an almost unbroken escarpment (named, the 'Southern Mountain Wall') parts of which form near vertical precipices of over 4,000 feet.

On either side of the high plateau are two dissected areas of relatively lower elevation. On account of the general accordance of summits in these areas, they too could be regarded as plateaux representing remnants of former erosion surfaces. The plateau on the west, the Hatton Plateau, is deeply dissected and has a northward tilt. This tilt is reflected in the progressive decrease in the height of its summits from about 5,500 feet in the south to about 4,000 feet in the north. In the Hatton Plateau there is a series of well-marked southeast-northwest trending anticlines and synclines (Ramboda anticline, Pundalu Oya syncline, Medacoombra axis, Hatton syncline, Wanaraja anticline and Norwood syncline) most of which correspond to the alternating ridges and valleys that dominate this part of the country. Their structural and topographical counterparts are found in the adjacent areas to the north and west, and less markedly, in the Welimada Plateau in the east.

The Welimada Plateau—also referred to as the 'Uva Basin'—lies to the east of the central high plateau roughly at the same elevation as the Hatton Plateau. Gentle rounded forms are typical of the topography of this area. It is traversed, however, by some deep valleys and gorges.

The central parts of the island's mountain mass described above descends abruptly in almost all directions to a series of peripheral plateaux and ledges that stand at an altitude of about 1,200-1,600 feet. Such plateaux and ledges are best exemplified in the area around Kandy and in a narrow zone in the south that stretches along the foot of the Southern Mountain Wall. These areas of intermediate height along with the more elevated plateaux which they encircle form what is known as the 'Central Massif'.

Separated from the Central Massif by broad and low-lying valleys are two other elevated areas having marked structural and topographical similarities to the former area. The one on the southwest, the 'Rakvāna Massif', has several peaks that reach heights of over 4,000 feet. The plateau that surrounds these peaks lies at an elevation of about 3,000 feet. The 'Knuckles Massif' which lies to the northeast of the Central Massif has been described as a complex of ranges resulting from a large recumbent fold. Several craggy peaks that rise to elevations of over 6,000 feet, precipitous escarpments and deep valleys characterise the topography of this highly dissected area. The eastern margins of the Knuckles form a well-defined ledge which corresponds to the plateaux of intermediate elevation found in the peripheral parts of the Central Massif.

The Central Massif together with the Rakvāna and Knuckles Massifs form the Central Highlands of Srī Laṅkā. The plain which surrounds these highlands in its northern, eastern and southern parts is an area of low relief. The flatness of these parts of the plain, however, is broken by a myriad rock butts and rounded mounds that rise occasionally to elevations of over 1,000 feet above its thick mantle of surface sediments. These are the erosional remnants of an area levelled down over aeons of uninterrupted denudation and weathering.

The southwestern parts of the coastal plain is featured by a more varied topography. A series of alternating ridges and valleys that run parallel to the coast gives this area a dissected appearance. The ridges here increase in elevation and persistence with increasing distance from the coast to merge imperceptibly with the central mountain mass.

With the exception of the Mahavāli river whose head-streams cut across the grain of the central mountains to form an annular pattern of flow [7], the island's rivers flow radially from the highlands to the sea. The upper reaches of many larger rivers are found in the inner high plateau of the Central Massif. The long profiles of these streams have sharp discontinuities that often correspond to the main topographical discontinuities within the highlands. Thus the borders of the anchor-shaped area of summits as well as the margins between the elevated plateaux of the Central Highlands and its peripheral plateaux of intermediate elevation abound with cascades and cataracts. Once the rivers enter the lowlands, they flow in open valleys that culminate in broad flood-plains, estuaries and deltas.

The island's sea front takes a variety of forms. Sand dunes, sand bars and spits, lagoons and marshes which represent the results of excessive deposition by the sluggish rivers and streams that traverse the coastal plain and by sea waves, features the western, southern and eastern coasts. Here, in certain tracts, the coast line is advancing. The sea front of the Jaffna Peninsula and the northwest is characterised by many elongated sand spits and broad sandy beaches, and, in a few localities where the horizontally laid Miocene limestone strata are exposed to erosional action of waves, by low cliffs. In the northeast and the southwest, where the coast cuts across the strike of the rock strata, rocky headlands, bays, off-shore islands and cliffs are commonly found. Some of these coastal stretches are marked by excessive sea erosion and a retreating coast line.

Geological Evolution. The general physiographic layout of the island was visualized by Adams[8] as consisting of three erosional surfaces (or, peneplains) sharply defined from one another by major topographical discontinuities. These erosional surfaces were regarded by him as being represented by the coastal plain, the intermediate plateaux and ledges, and the high plateau of the centre, which as shown earlier, are distinctly defined from one another.

Taking cognisance of the "senile" landscape found in the elevated heartland of the central mountains, Adams postulated that the three peneplains represent surfaces of erosion produced by successive uplifts of the island *en masse*. According to Adams, the "youthful" features that characterise the boundary zones which separate the peneplains from each other are the results of changes in base-level associated with such uplifts. Thus, in this conception, the highest peneplain in the centre is the area with the longest history of sub-aerial denudation.

Adams' views were refuted by Wadia.[9] While accepting the general scheme of three peneplains, Wadia claimed that the coastal plain has the most senile landforms, and is therefore the oldest erosional surface of the island. He promulgated the alternative hypothesis of "circumscribed block uplift" to explain the evolution of Srī Laṅkā's surface morphology. This hypothesis attempted to show that the central highlands were formed by two successive "telescopic uplifts" of the central parts of the island.

Leiter[10] and Kularatnam[11] regarded the conception of three peneplains as too simple an interpretation of the island's surface morphology. They saw the central highlands as a "fault complex". Kularatnam whose hypothesis is based on an analysis of topographical maps and a visual interpretation of the drainage pattern, perceived the central highlands as a series of erosional surfaces lying at different elevations and at varying angles of inclination. These surfaces, he said, are separated from each other by escarpments and shear zones that are the products of multiple block-faulting.

The hypotheses of Adams, Wadia and Kularatnam have suffered from the inadequacy of geological evidence to support the basic premise common to them that the major relief features of Srī Laṅkā are the products of large-scale vertical crustal displacement. Micro-regional investigations have shown that, with a few exceptions, the island's main topographical discontinuities do not correspond to structural discontinuities of the type associated with massive faulting and fracturing. For example, the spectacular Southern Mountain Wall which, according to the earlier postulates is an enormous boundary fault, has been shown in fact to be a product of differential erosion.

Thus, recent literature tends to place relatively less emphasis on faulting as a factor in the evolution of the major landforms of the country. Greater attention is being paid both to the study of current processes of geomorphic change as well as to correlative analysis of local features in the context of diastrophic changes that affected the *Gondwana* proto-continent of which the island was a part. The current view, in a highly simplified form, is that several waves of intense folding and crumpling of the crust in pre-Cambrian (and, possibly, in early palaeozoic) times, subsequent small-scale crustal displacement and deformation, and prolonged differential weathering and erosion account for the present surface morphology of Sri Laṅkā

Climate

The climate of Srī Laṅkā is basically controlled by its location within the tropics, its proximity to the Indian sub-continent, its insularity and the presence within it of a centrally located mountain mass.

The tropical location of Srī Laṅkā ensures a uniformly high temperature, but maritime influences consequent upon its insularity make it free from thermal extremes that are characteristic of continental interiors. Mean monthly temperatures in the lowlands of Sri Laṅkā fall between 78^0 and 85^0F. with little seasonal and moderate diurnal variations. In the central highlands, however, there is an orographically induced lowering of temperature to monthly means that range from about 55^0F. to 70^0F. in the highest parts of the country.

In the absence of marked thermal differences, rainfall becomes the conspicuous parameter in seasonal and spatial variations in climate.

Rainfall Seasons. An understanding of the main seasonal variations of rainfall in Srī Laṅkā may be obtained by reference to the large scale weather forming factors influencing the area in which the island is located. The primary atmospheric circulation pattern within the tropics consists of three circulatory systems. Briefly, they are the Doldrums or the Inter-Tropical Convergence Zone and the Northern and Southern Trade Winds. The former is a belt of calm or variable winds lying astride the thermal equator and distinct on synoptic charts during most parts of the year, while the latter are remarkably constant air streams which, in the lower atmospheric layer, flow from the sub-tropical high pressure areas towards the Doldrum zone. These circulatory systems pendulate northwards and southwards with the seasonal migrations of the sun and bring

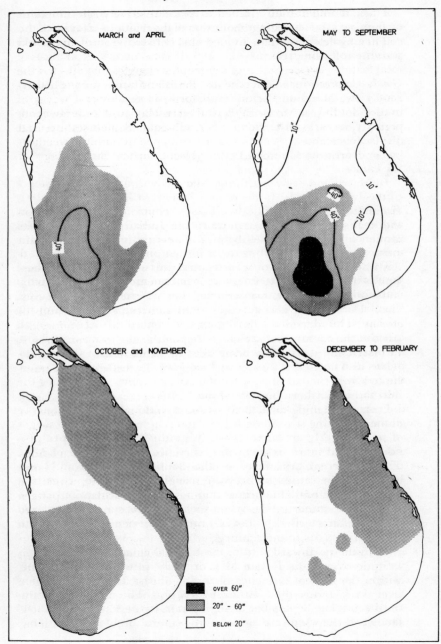

SEASONAL DISTRIBUTION OF RAIN

the island under their influence alternatively at different times of the year, thus bringing about seasonal variations in rainfall.

Thambyahpillay[12] has divided the climatic year of Srī Laṅkā into the following seasons:

(i) Convectional-Convergence Period (March to mid-April),
(ii) Pre-Monsoon Period (mid-April to late May),
(iii) Southwest Monsoon Period (late May to late September),
(iv) Convectional-Cyclonic Period (late September to late November),
(v) Northeast Monsoon Period (December to February).

In March and early April, the island comes under the influence of the Inter-Tropical Convergence Zone (ITCZ). Convectional air circulation associated with the ITCZ produces during this time of the year a more or less constant daily weather sequence. This sequence[13] is characterised by bright clear mornings that permit a vertical ascent of air leading to the formation of rain clouds by mid-day or early afternoon over the central parts of the country. These clouds then move out towards the maritime areas developing often into intense thunderstorms during late afternoon and evening. Cool clear weather is restored at night after the dissipation of the storms. Thunderstorms during this season could occur over all parts of the country but are more frequent in the southwest where, in March and April, they bring over 20 inches of rain (Figure 3a). It has been noted that this diurnal sequence of weather can be interrupted from time to time by frontal activity which occurs along the fluctuating northern borders of the ITCZ.

From about mid-April, the typical convectional weather sequence of the preceding season tends to be interrupted by periodic surges of southwesterly air currents which gradually become more pronounced and more frequent in occurrence in the month of May. These "preliminary waves of the Southwest Monsoon"[14] are believed to be caused by pressure troughs that develop over heat centres of the Indian landmass and by periodic disruptions of the ITCZ over southern Asia. When such surges occur, highly varied weather characterised by heavy rains is experienced in the south and central parts of the country.

With the northward shift of the thermal equator to about 25° N latitude over India in late May or early June, Srī Laṅkā comes within the zone of influence of the Southeast Trades which blow over the island as the Southwest Monsoon. The monsoon persists until about late September, bringing rain to the southwestern lowlands and the windward slopes of the central highlands, but blow-

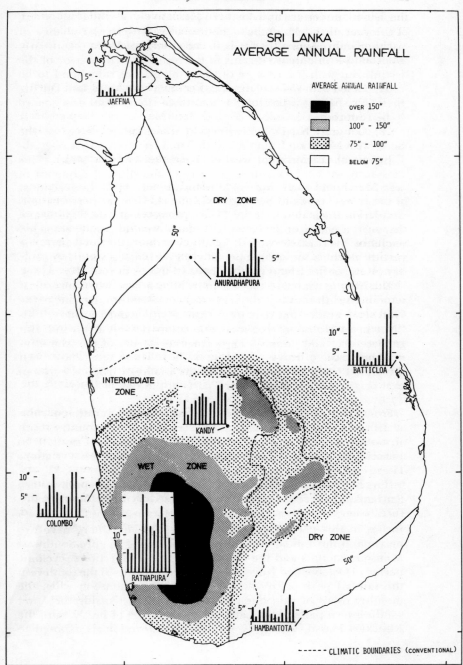

ing across the eastern and northern plains as a dry wind (Figure 3b). The onset of the Monsoon — though a less spectacular change of weather in Srī Lankā than it is in most parts of India — is usually associated with enhanced rains in the southwestern interior of the island. But with the passage of time, monsoonal rains tend to be interspersed with spells of dry weather of varying duration. During these dry spells it is possible for the convectional weather sequence to be restored.

October and November witness the oscillating retreat of the Southwest Monsoon from the South Asian environs and a re-establishment of convectional weather conditions in Srī Lankā. This season, however, lacks the regularity of the diurnal sequence of weather which was a feature of March and early April. Convectional weather now tends to be modified often by frontal perturbations and tropical cyclonic activity. The cyclones that affect the island during this period could bring about torrential rains and prolonged spells of overcast skies and squally weather. In November, the month in which the occurrence of such cyclones is most frequent, almost the entire island receives over 10 inches of rain (Figure 3c).

During the winter of the northern hemisphere when terrestrial wind belts shift southwards, Srī Lankā comes within the zone of the Northeast Trades and remains within it until about February. This "Northeast Monsoon" is a weak and comparatively dry wind. But in December and January the northeastern parts of the island invariably receive heavy rains (Figure 3d). These rains have been attributed to the movement across the island of tropical cyclones that originate over the southern parts of the Bay of Bengal.

Distribution of Rain. Variations in the intensity and duration of rains at different times of the year in different parts of the country result in a wide range of spatial variation in the total annual rainfall. In general, the effects of local topography are seen in these variations (Figure 4).

The highest rainfalls are recorded in those parts of southwestern Srī Lankā that are topographically exposed to the incoming moisture laden air masses. Monthly totals of rain rarely fall below 5 inches in this part of the country. The lowlands here have two maxima in the annual cycle of rain, one during the pre-Southwest Monsoon months and the other during the convectional cyclonic period of October and November. In the highlands of the southwest, the rainfall peak occurs during the summer monsoon when the monthly totals of rain often exceed 20 inches. Outside these wet southwestern parts of Srī Lankā is another area of heavy rain, the Knuckles Massif, which, by virtue of its elevation, is exposed to rain bearing air streams in most parts of the year and hence receives a seasonally well distributed rainfall of over 100 inches.

The average annual rainfall in the eastern and northern parts of the island is less than 75 inches. Here, unlike in the southwest, there are marked wet and dry seasons, the wet season being the convectional-cyclonic period and the early part of the northeast monsoon season (September-January) and the dry period, the season of the Southwest Monsoon. The areas of lowest rainfall are in the southeastern and northwestern parts of the coastal plain where, in the absence of topographic barriers that induce passing air streams to shed their moisture, the mean annual rainfall is below 50 inches and drought prevails over a greater part of the year.

Variability and Effectiveness of Rain. The actual amount of rain received during a given period of time in any part of the country varies considerably from the average conditions described above. Farmer [15] has shown that this variability of rain is greater in the drier parts of the country than in the wet areas as of the southwest, and in each area greater during the dry seasons than in the wet seasons. Expressed statistically, the deviation from the arithmetic mean of rainfall in the northern and eastern parts of the country, a large proportion of whose annual rainfall is derived from tropical cyclones, is greater than such deviation in areas of higher average rainfall. This implies that in the former areas, there is a relatively low "mean expectancy" of rain.

The amount of rain alone could rarely provide a satisfactory index of the effectiveness of rain which, from the point of view of plant life and human activity, is of paramount importance. Effectiveness of rain can only be assessed in relation to a defined ecological criterion. Defining "effective rainfall" as "the proportion of rainfall necessary under given conditions of evaporation to maintain the moisture content of the surface soil above wilting point", Cooray [16] examined the spatial variations in effective rain at different times of the year. He has shown that while the southwest quadrant has effective rain throughout the year, over the rest of the island, rainfall is ineffective for periods ranging in duration from one to six months of the year.

Combining the criteria of variability of rain and the effectiveness of rain, Farmer [17] has estimated the "approximate reliability of effective rain" at several places located in the drier areas of the country. His computations show that in these areas, while there is a high probability of effective rain in the months of November, December and January, their rain during the southwest monsoon season is least likely to be effective. The probability of their receiving effective rain during inter-monsoon periods, according to Farmer, appears to be evenly balanced with the probability of not receiving such rain.

Areal differences relating to the amount of rain as well as to its seasonality, reliability and effectiveness lend credence to the conception of a "wet zone" and a "dry zone" of Srī Laṅkā. The southwest quadrant of the island is the wet zone where the rainfall is heavy, seasonally well distributed and reliable and effective throughout the year. Over the rest of the island, the rainfall is relatively low, largely restricted to the period from October to January, less reliable and less effective than in the wet zone.

As a result of the spill-over of population from the crowded wet zone to the dry zone which has accompanied recent developments in irrigation and colonization in the latter area, the change in landscape encountered as one moves away from the southwest lowlands towards the dry zone is perhaps less spectacular today than it was some years ago when it was described by writers like Cook[18] and Farmer.[19] Further, in certain sections of the central highlands such as the Uva Basin, a "transitional zone" with its own climate peculiarities has also been discerned.[20] Hence, in many contemporary writings, the border areas between the wet zone and the dry zone are recognised as constituting a distinct "intermediate zone". Of Srī Laṅkā's total land area of approximately 16 million acres, about 65 per cent is regarded as falling into the dry zone. The wet zone and the intermediate zone are reckoned as constituting 23 per cent and 12 per cent respectively (Figure 4).

Physical Resources

Land and Soil. Estimates of extents under different types of land use based on aerial surveys conducted in 1956, adjusted where possible for more recent changes, show that in the island as a whole about 10 per cent of the area is under non-agricultural uses and homestead garden, 25 per cent is under sedentary agriculture, developed pasture and cultivated forests, and a further 15 per cent is under shifting cultivation. Forests, grass-lands, scrubland, swamps, marshes and inland water bodies account for the remaining 50 per cent of the total area.

In terms of land-use a clear contrast could be observed between the dry zone and the wet zone. The wet zone has nearly 80 per cent of its area under some form of utilisation, whereas about 70 per cent of the dry zone is unutilized or only marginally used for shifting cultivation.

In the wet zone, the utilisation of land for agriculture may be said to have reached near saturation. Apart from relatively small extents

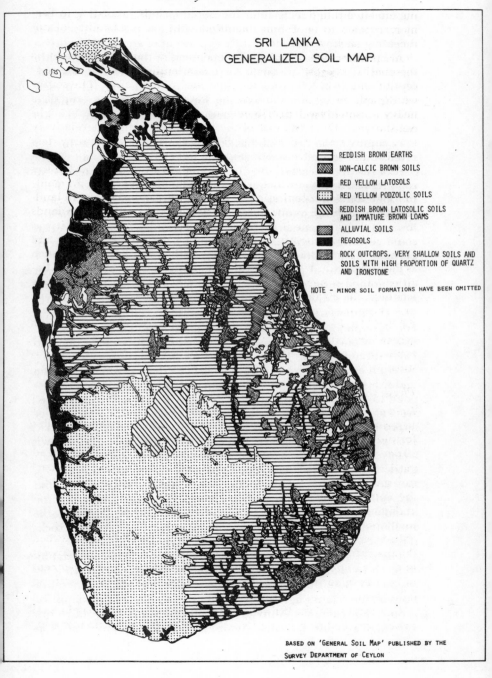

SRI LANKA
GENERALIZED SOIL MAP

REDDISH BROWN EARTHS
NON-CALCIC BROWN SOILS
RED YELLOW LATOSOLS
RED YELLOW PODZOLIC SOILS
REDDISH BROWN LATOSOLIC SOILS
AND IMMATURE BROWN LOAMS
ALLUVIAL SOILS
REGOSOLS
ROCK OUTCROPS, VERY SHALLOW SOILS AND
SOILS WITH HIGH PROPORTION OF QUARTZ
AND IRONSTONE

NOTE - MINOR SOIL FORMATIONS HAVE BEEN OMITTED

BASED ON 'GENERAL SOIL MAP' PUBLISHED BY THE
SURVEY DEPARTMENT OF CEYLON

obtainable through reclamation of coastal marshlands and, possibly, by careful terracing of some uncultivated hill slopes of the interior, there is little scope here for future expansion of area under cultivation. Forests which occupy about 9 per cent of the total area within the zone are barely adequate for conservation purposes. Indeed, several authorities have advocated not only the careful preservation and enrichment of existing forests but also the re-afforestation of some land presently under cultivation within the wet zone.

In contrast, the dry zone has considerable potential for further extension of agriculture and settlements. Here, only about 30 per cent of the area is under regular use. According to certain recent estimates an aggregate extent of approximately 30 per cent of the dry zone is unsuitable for agriculture due to the presence of various problems relating to soil or terrain. Thus, about 40 per cent of the dry zone, or approximately 5 million acres of agriculturally "good class" unutilised land, is still available for further expansion of permanent agriculture.

The agricultural potential of the land depends to a large extent on edaphic conditions of which there is considerable macro- and micro-regional diversity within Sri Lankā. The more striking macro-regional differences in soils could be related to climatic variations. For example, the Red Yellow Podzolic Soils of the soil classification by Moorman and Pānabokkē [21] which broadly correspond to Laterites and Lateritic Loams of an earlier classification by Joachim [22] cover an estimated extent of 82 per cent of the wet zone, while the Reddish Brown Earths (of Moormann and Pānabokkē which correspond to Joachim's Non-Lateritic Red and Reddish Brown Loams) are the predominant soil group of the lowland dry zone. Other important soil formations (as named by Moorman and Pānabokkē) such as the Reddish Brown Lateritic Soils and Immature Brown Loams found in hilly areas of intermediate elevation, the Non-Calcic Brown Loams that occur in patches in the eastern lowlands, the Red Yellow Latosols of the northwestern coastal belt, and strips of Alluvial Soil found adjacent to the lower courses of the island's rivers are edaphic variations that could by and large be attributed to local peculiarities in topography and parent rocks (Figure 5).

The soil classifications referred to above are based on edaphic differences of a general nature over relatively large areas. In a few instances, these differences provide a basis for broad generalizations on the relative agricultural potential of some of the major soil groups. For example, Alluvial Soils, if well drained, could be of a very high agricultural value. Again, Red-Yellow Latosols and Non-

Calcic Brown Loams have a very low inherent fertility and very poor water retention qualities. More often, however, conditions within each major soil zone are so diverse that they overshadow in importance the macro-regional differences which alone are given coverage in general classifications of soils. While it would not be feasible here to attempt a description of the diversity found within each soil zone, it is necessary to take note of two factors fundamentally responsible for much of the micro-regional heterogeneity of the soils in the country.

Soil formation, as recognised by Milne[23] in his "Catena concept", follows a definite pattern according to the topography of the site, whenever the parent material and climate do not change appreciably over an area. Developing upon Milne's concept. Morison[24] has shown that a three-fold pattern associated with topography runs across the main phyla of generic and morphological classification of soils.

Applying a theme implicit in this concept that chemical and physico-chemical properties of the soil vary over different sites in the soil catena, it is possible to draw the conclusion that in areas of marked relief, diversity in soil properties is likely to be greater than in areas of low relief. Accordingly, in some of the main soils that occur in areas of rugged terrain (such as Red Yellow Podzolic Soils, Reddish Brown Lateritic Soils and Immature Brown Loams) the thickness of the A-horizon varies according to site from 0 to 15-20 inches. The texture (relative proportions of sand, clay and silt), structure (fine grained to granular or blocky), colour and chemical composition too exhibit marked diversity.

The second factor of importance is the cultivation history of the soil. Especially in tropical areas where conditions necessary for the rapid formation of humus and the rejuvenation of the soil are absent, the failure to appreciate changes that result from the disruption of the ecological balance consequent upon the removal of natural vegetation causes rapid depletion of the soil. Effects of such adverse processes are evident in many parts of the country, especially in those areas that have been under plantation crops during the past 150 years. In these areas, repeated clearing, planting and clean weeding for a succession of crops has frequently resulted in severe erosion and the formation of truncated soils where the A-horizon is completely absent and the B-horizon is now exposed to a secondary cycle of weathering.

Water. The following estimates have been made of the volumes of average annual rainfall and surface run-off of water in Srī Laṅkā:

Table 2. RAINFALL AND SURFACE RUN-OFF

	Estimate I (IBRD, 1952)	Estimate II (Walker, 1962)	Estimate III (Arumugam, 1969)
Average annual rainfall (in million acre-feet)	102	107	89
Average annual run-off (in million acre-feet)	32.7	35	41.6
Ratio of run-off to rainfall (%)	32	33	47

The surface run-off in the island falls into the catchment areas of over one hundred rivers. Many of these rivers are small and ephemeral. In fact, only five of them have catchments of over 1,000 square miles. About 75 per cent of the mean river discharge is accounted for by twelve major rivers.

In the utilization of the surface run-off for irrigation, its uneven distribution between the wet zone and the dry zone is significant. Rivers flowing entirely through the wet zone which covers about one-fourth of the island's total area account for over half the total discharge. Hence, in the dry zone where the rainfall itself is variable and seasonally "ineffective", the surface run-off is a scarce resource providing a limited potential for use in irrigation.

The amount of river water which could be economically utilized for irrigation has not been accurately assessed. Physically, there is the possibility of diverting some of the major wet zone rivers to the drier parts of the country. Diversion of water from rivers bordering the dry zone to the northern plain has in fact been done since ancient times. According to current plans of irrigation development, it is the river Mahavāli which is considered to offer the greatest scope for expansion of area under irrigation in the dry zone through river diversion.

A recent estimate has placed the long-term mean annual flow of rivers in the dry zone, including the waters of the Mahavāli, at around 18.2 million acre-feet of which the total "useful storage" amounts to about 11 million acre-feet. From this, the existing irrigation complex of the dry zone (as in 1967) requires an estimated 5.7 million acre-feet of water per annum. Thus, as estimates stand at present, the unutilized potential for useful storage in the dry zone is in the region of 5 to 6 million acre-feet per annum. The extent of land which could be irrigated and cultivated with this volume of water would depend upon water duties for different crops and cropping patterns. However, taking into account data available on rates of water utilization and anticipated changes in patterns of land utilization, it could be assumed that the future potential for increasing the area under irrigated agriculture in the dry zone — on a rough estimate — does not exceed 1.5 million acres.

As a source of generating power, rivers are of tremendous importance to Srī Laṅkā, particularly because the country is poorly endowed with fuel minerals. In the early 1950s it was estimated that the local rivers could be harnessed to produce about 500 mw. of electric power. A subsequent estimate listed thirty possible hydro-power generating sites and estimated their aggregate power potential as 1,400 mw. These theoretical estimates have been made superfluous after the drawing up of the Mahaväli river basin development programme during the late 1960s to which the country is now committed; and, with estimates presently available of the power potential at sites specifically earmarked for development within the next few decades, the overall hydro-power potential of Srī Laṅkā may be placed at around 700-800 mw. This potential is believed to be adequate to meet the projected demand for electricity in the country till about the year 1990.

In irrigation and in power generation, the principal uses of the country's river water (domestic and direct industrial consumption have been estimated to account for less than 0.5 per cent of the water available, and river navigation is unimportant as a mode of inland transport) there are certain natural handicaps. One of these is that local rivers have wide fluctuations in flow, creating problems, in irrigation, of obtaining the water when it is most needed, and in power generation, of equalizing output. In the wet zone, there are two phases of high water discharge in the annual cycle — one, during April, May and June and the other during October, November and December. The dry zone rivers have a high discharge from about November to January. Unfortunately, the low water phases — February-March and August-September — are substantially the same for the whole island. This implies that to harness the rivers for irrigation and power generation, relatively large storage reservoirs and, therefore, a large capital expenditure, is invariably required.

Another problem in utilising river water is the high rate of erosion and silting. In many parts of the country, the surface flow is both rapid and substantial. This is coupled with the fact that there has been considerable indiscriminate clearing of land for cultivation, and also, inadequate soil conservation, leading to severe erosion and consequently to rapid silting of river beds, reservoirs and channels.

The irrigation potential of the surface water is becoming increasingly expensive to harness. Attention is hence being paid to probing the possibility of utilising sub-surface water resources. Traditionally, this source of water supply has been unimportant in agriculture except in the Jaffna Peninsula where the presence of Miocene limestones with a high water holding capacity has made possible extensive well irrigation. Recent investigations carried out through deep test drilling have shown that tapping of sub-surface water of sedimentary rock formations elsewhere in the country is an economically feasible proposition. The hard crystalline rocks that are found over a greater part of the country are usually poor reservoirs of groundwater, except where such rocks are highly fissured and jointed or deeply weathered. It has been suggested that in certain localities within the hard rock areas where the soil mantle is thick and where the water-table is perennially close to the surface, there is sufficient groundwater which, if tapped systematically, could form an important supplementary source of irrigation.

Forests. The climax vegetation in most parts of Srī Laṅkā is forest. The island's wet zone has Tropical Evergreen Forests in the lowlands and Sub-Tropical Evergreen Forests in some of its elevated areas. The lowering of temperature which accompanies the increase in elevation in the interior of the island induces changes in species of the forest flora. Forest trees at high altitudes also tend to be sparse and stunted. In certain parts of the highlands, forests are replaced by grasslands. The dry zone with its highly seasonal pattern of rain is covered for the most part by Semi-Evergreen Monsoon Forests. In the driest areas within this zone, these forests give way to a stunted, shrubby, xerophitic vegetation.

The extensive clearing of forests for settlement, agriculture and extraction of forest resources over a long period of time has reduced the climax vegetation of Srī Laṅkā to a small fraction of what it would originally have been. The Sinharāja forest and the Peak Wilderness of the southwestern interior represent the only substantial remnants of the original evergreen forests of the wet zone. The Semi-Evergreen Monsoon Forests found today in most parts of the dry zone are probably a secondary vegetation which has developed after many centuries of repeated clearing for sedentary and shifting cultivation.

About 6 million acres or 37 per cent of the total land area has been classified as forest. Of this, an extent of about one million acres are forest reserves. Planted or enriched forests account for about 150,000 acres.

The great diversity of flora which is a characteristic of Tropical Evergreen Forests and Semi-Evergreen Monsoon Forests makes the extraction from them of useful timbers difficult. Yet, the forest resources of Srī Laṅkā are by no means meagre. In the wet zone Evergreen forests species such as *Doona congestiflora* (locally named tiniya), *Dipterocarpus zeylanicus* (hora), *Cullenia ceylonica* and *Cullenia rosayroana* (kataboda) and *Cyathocalyx Zeylonicus* (kekila) occur in sufficient profusion to make their large scale commercial extraction economically feasible. A few valuable hard woods like *Periscopis mooniana* (nedun) also occur in these forests. The monsoon forests of the dry zone have, in scattered occurrence but considerably quantity, some of the world's most valuable timbers such as *Chloroxylon swietenia* (satinwood), *Diospyros ebenum* (ebony), *Swietenia mycropyla* (mahogany) and *Berrya cordifolia* (halmilla). The greatest potential in forestry, however, seems to lie in systematic afforestation and forest enrichment. Teak *(Tectona grandis)*, Mahogany and various types of Eucalyptus and Albezzia have in fact been used locally in successful afforestation programmes.

The annual natural increment of forests of Srī Laṅkā, taking into consideration all species, has been estimated to range between 4 and 16 cubic feet per acre in the dry zone and 16 to 95 cubic feet per acre in the wet zone. The annual rate of extraction at present is said to represent only a tiny fraction of these rates. Furthermore, certain timbers which occur in abundance in Srī Laṅkā's forests are not in use at present due either to an absence of a tradition of their use or to a lack of knowledge of techniques of processing to make such timbers suitable for use. If these conditions are changed, forests could become an economically important resource in the country.

Minerals[25]. Srī Laṅkā has a wide variety of economically useful minerals. Although the reserves of many economic minerals of the country still remain unassessed, it is believed that in minerals such as gemstones, graphite, ilmenite, limestones, quartz, mica, industrial clays and salt, the resource potential is considerable. Of fuel minerals, the only known resource is the low grade peat found in the swamps of Muthurājawela, north of Colombo, where the total reserve is said to be about 50 million tons. There is, of course, the somewhat remote possibility of petroleum being discovered in association with the Cenozoic formations of northwestern Srī Laṅkā where prospecting was being carried out in 1973-4. As for minerals that form the basis of major metallurgical industries like iron and steel, ferro-alloys, aluminium and copper, only iron has been found in quantities that are economically significant. The only commercially extractable non-ferrous metals known hitherto are titanium, monazite and zircon contained in the beach sands of certain parts of the island.

Extraction of minerals is relatively unimportant to the country's economy at present. Cement, ceramics, glass, salt, bricks and tiles are the only modern manufacturing industries in the country that are principally based on local mineral resources. High value minerals, extracted in small quantities, are exported invariably in unprocessed or semi-processed state. During the five-year period preceding 1972, such mineral exports accounted for only about one per cent of the total value of exports from Srī Laṅkā.

Srī Laṅkā has been famous since ancient times for the abundance and variety of its precious and semi-precious stones. Various types of high value gemstones such as cordundum (sapphire and ruby), chrysoberyl, spinel, beryl and topaz and also, a variety of semi-precious stones like moonstones, garnet, zircon, tourmaline and feldspar are among the gemstones for which Srī Laṅkā is renowned. Of the gemstone areas so far discovered, those parts of the south-western interior within the upper catchment of the Kaluganga appear to be the richest. This has been the traditional area of gem-ming in the country. Outside this area, gems have been found in many localities in and around the central highlands. With the ex-ception of moonstone and some tourmaline and garnet that occur *in situ* in semi-weathered parent rock, the local gemstones are found in association with alluvial deposits. Gem bearing layers of coarse sand and gravel occur sporadically as pockets, streaks and lenticles of limited extent at or near the surface for chance discovery by the fortunate prospector. Extraction of gems has continued to be a small-scale non-mechanized industry whose recorded output has increased substantially during the past few years to make gemming the pre-eminent mining industry in the country at present.

Graphite (crystalline carbon) deposits of high quality are found in the western, southwestern and north-central parts of the country. Pichamuthu[26] described them as the biggest and the most produc-tive graphite deposits in the world. In the principal areas of gra-phite mining — Bogala, Kahatagaha and Kolangaha — usually, the graphite veins are thick and sharply defined and are therefore easy to mine. Until 1973, graphite mining was the most important mineral extraction industry in the country.

Ilmenite (the source of titanium) and monazite (a source of certain rare earth metals and radio-active elements) are two minerals that have a wide distribution in the island. Their primary occurrence as accesory minerals in gneisses, granites, granulites and crystalline limestone is unimportant from the point of view of commercial exploitation. The chief sources of extraction are the concentrates of these minerals that occur as beach deposits in several localities. The richest deposits of ilmenite are found along a four-mile coastal strip adjacent to Kokkilai lagoon in the northeast. Commercially extracted beach sands here have an average ilmenite content of over 50 per cent. These sands also contain small proportions of rutile and zircon. Smaller ilmenite deposits are found elsewhere along the western and eastern coasts. Since 1968 when the extraction of ilmenite began, production has increased progressively, and the annual value of its exports during the past three years has been between Rs 4-5 million.

Monazite sands occur along the west coast, principally at Beruwala, Kaikawela and Kudiramalai. The appearance of monazite concentrates in the beach sands of these areas is seasonal and coincides mainly with the early part of the southwest monsoon. Although the thoria content of Srī Laṅkā's monazite is often as high as 10 per cent, and is hence comparable to the best monazite concentrates in the world, the smallness and the seasonality of occurrence of individual deposits have made its extraction difficult.

Limestones found in Srī Laṅkā are of three types[27] —the sedimentary (Miocene) limestones of the Jaffna Peninsula and the northwest, coral limestones found along the southwestern sea front, and crystalline limestones of the Highland Series. Miocene limestone of high purity are extracted for cement manufacture. Crystalline limestone in its pure form and coral limestone are used for the small-scale manufacture of chemical lime.

Dolomite (calcium, magnesium carbonate) occurs in several localities within the central highlands, especially in areas of intermediate elevation that border the Central Massif. The largest and the most accessible occurrences are at Uda-Neriella near Ratnapura and in the Kundasale-Digana area northeast of Kandy. In the latter area, dolomite is quarried and ground for use as a fertiliser component.

Mica and magnesite are among the minerals that are often found in association with dolomite and limestones of the Khondalite Series. The former is economically insignificant due to its sporadic distribution. A large surface exposure of magnesite, a mineral used mainly for the manufacture of special purpose cements and as a filler material, occurs at Randeniya which is situated at the southern margins of the Central Massif.

Apatite is an important economic mineral that has been discovered recently in Srī Laṅkā. Small crystals of this mineral found embedded in crystalline limestones that occur near Mātalē have been described by Cooray.[28] More recently, large extractable crystals of apatite have been found in the central parts of the northern plain at Eppāwala. The reserve here is reported to be substantial and is expected to form an important source of phosphate for the country.

Among the mineral resources of Srī Laṅkā are several minerals that form the main ingredients in the manufacture of clay products and glass. Kaolin (or white clay) of which the largest known deposit in the country is in the swampy area southeast of Colombo is the main raw material for the growing ceramic industry of the country. Veins of pure feldspar occur in the Knuckles Massif and the adjacent area to its north, and are mined at Rattota and Elahera. Outcrops of high quality vein quartz occur in many parts of the central highlands and are extracted in small quantities at Pusella near Ratnapura. Quartz sands that are relatively free from impurities and suitable for the manufacture of glass are found in abundance along the coastal stretch north of Negombo. To this list may be added alluvial clays obtainable from low-lying riverine tracts in many parts of the island. These clays are extensively used in the manufacture of such products as pottery, bricks and tiles.

Reference has already been made to the availability of iron ores in Srī Laṅkā. Until about the early years of the present century smelting of these ores was a small-scale industry in some rural areas of the country. The principal reserves of iron ore are the scattered surface deposits of limonite and hematite that are largely confined to the southwestern parts of the island (of which the largest known occurrences are in the vicinity of Ratnapura, at Dela, Noragolla, Opatha and Poranuwa), and the sub-surface veins of magnetite found at Wilagedara and Panirendawa in the northwestern interior. In the southwest, the ore deposits are reported to vary in size from about 10,000 to 150,000 tons and to have an average iron content of 53-54 per cent. It has also been estimated that the total exploitable reserve here is about 2.2 million tons. Ore deposits of the northwest are believed to be larger and richer in iron content. The Panirendawa deposit alone is said to contain about 5.6 million tons of magnetite. Although the relative smallness and the scattered nature of occurrence of Srī Laṅkā's iron ores make their commercial extraction difficult, it has been argued that their mining and processing could be done within economically profitable limits of cost.

The potential which exists at several coastal localities in the drier parts of the country for the manufacture of common salt may be mentioned among the mineral resources of Srī Laṅkā. Where the sea water is trapped in lagoons or artificial pools, evaporation results in the formation of solid pans of salt. At present the most important salterns in the country are found at Hambantota, Elephant Pass and the Puttalam lagoon.

A comprehensive inventory of Srī Laṅkā's mineral resources should include sands, gravel, laterite and various types of hard rock that are extensively used as constructional material. These are plentifully available in almost all parts of the island and have been in use since ancient times.

REFERENCES

1. C. S. Pichamuthu, 'The Precambrian of Ceylon' in Kalervo Rankema (ed.) *The Pre Cambrian*, Vol. 3 (1967), Interscience Publishers, pp. 97-121.
2. P. G. Cooray, *An Introduction to the Geology of Ceylon*, National Museums of Ceylon Publication, Colombo (1967), p. 83; A. R. Crawford and R. L. Oliver, 'The Precambrian Geochronology of Ceylon', special publication of the Geological Society, Australia, 2 (1969), pp. 283-306.
3. M. B. Katz, 'The Precambrian Metamorphic Rocks of Ceylon', *Sonderdruck aus der Geologischen Rundschau Band*, Vol. 60 (1971), pp. 1523-49 (hereafter, S.G.R.B.)
4. A. R. Berger, 'The Precambrian Metamorphic Rocks of Ceylon', *S.G. R.B.*, Vol. 62 (1973), pp. 342-6.
5. P. G. Cooray, op. cit., p. 67.
6. For descriptions of these mezozoic and cenozoic formations see Cooray, op. cit.; E. J. Wayland, 'The Jurassic Rocks of Tabbowa', *Ceylon Journal of Science*, Vol. 13 (1925), pp. 195-208 (hereafter *C.J.S*); J. S. Coates, 'The Geology of Ceylon', *C.J.S. (Section B)*, Vol. 19 (1935), pp. 101-91; L. J. D. Fernando, 'The Geology and Mineral Deposits of Ceylon', *Bulletin of the Imperial Institute*, Vol. 16 (1954), Nos. 2-4, pp. 303-25.
7. For a detailed study of the Mahavali river where "river capture" has been suggested to explain its "anomalous pattern of flow", see K. Kularatnam, 'The Drainage Pattern and Denudation Chronology of the Mahavali Ganga Basin', *University of Ceylon Review*, Vol. 20, (1962), pp. 84-95 (hereafter *U.C.R.*)
8. F. D. Adams, 'The Geology of Ceylon', *Canadian Journal of Research*, Vol. 1 (1929), pp. 425-551.
9. D. N. Wadia, 'The Three Superposed Peneplains of Ceylon', *Records of the Department of Mineralogy (Ceylon)*, Professional Paper No. 1 (1945), pp. 25-32.
10. N. Leiter, 'Denudation Chronology and the Drainage Pattern of the Central Massif of Ceylon', *Bulletin of the Ceylon Geographical Society*, Vol. 11 (1947), pp. 64-9 (hereafter *B.C.G.S.*).
11. K. Kularatnam, 'The Face of Ceylon', *Proceedings of the 9th Annual Session of the Ceylon Association for the Advancement of Science*, Part II (1954), pp. 113-23.
12. G. G. R. Thambyahpillay, 'The Rainfall Rhythm of Ceylon', *Climatological Research Series* I (1955).

13. Thambyahpillay, op. cit., 164-8; see also Thambyahpillay, 'Thunderstorm Phenomena of Ceylon', *U.C.R.*, Vol. 12, No. 3 (1954), pp. 164-75.
14. Thambyahpillay, 'The Burst of the Southwest Monsoon: the new perspective' *U.C.R.* Vol. 17, Nos. 1-2 (1959), pp. 18-40, especially pp. 19-21.
15. B. H. Farmer, 'Rainfall and Water Supply Conditions in the Dry Zone of Ceylon' in R. W. Steel, C. A. Fisher (eds.), *Geographical Essays on British Tropical Lands*, London (1956); *Pioneer Peasant Colonization in Ceylon*, London (1957), pp. 22-8; and 'Ceylon' in O. H. K. Spate and A. T. A. Learmonth, *India and Pakistan:a General and Regional Geography* London, 1967, pp. 786-824, especially pp. 793-5.
16. P. G. Cooray, 'Effective Rainfall and Moisture Zones of Ceylon', *B.C.G.S.* Vol. 3, No. 2 (1948), pp. 39-44.
17. B. H. Farmer, 'Rainfall an Water Supply Conditions in the Dry Zone of Ceylon', op. cit.
18. Elsie K. Cook, *Ceylon: its Geography, its Resorces and its People* (Revised ed.), London (1951).
19. B. H. Farmer, *Pioneer Peasant Colonization in the Dry Zone of Ceylon*, London (1957).
20. W. S. M. Domross, 'The Rainfall Pattern of the Uva Basin', *The Ceylon Geography*, Vol. 20 (1966), pp. 74-81.
21. F. R. Moorman, and C. R. Pānabokkē, 'Soils of Ceylon', *Tropical Agriculturalist*, Vol. 117 (1961), pp. 161-172 (hereafter *T. A.*).
22. A. W. R. Joachim, 'Soils of Ceylon', *T. A.*, Vol. 101 (1955), pp. 161-72.
23. G. Milne, 'Catena Concept', *Soil Research*, Vol. 4 (1939), pp. 183-94; 'Catena Concept', *Journal of Ecology*, Vol. 35 (1947), pp. 192-265.
24. C. G. T. Morison, 'Catena Concept and the Classification of Tropical Soils', *Proceedings of the 1st Commonwealth Conference on Tropical and Sub-Tropical Soils*, (1948), pp. 124-8.
25. The following account of the mineral resources of Srī Laṅkā is based principally on Corray (1967), op. cit.; Pichamuthu, op. cit.; and Fernando, op. cit.
26. Pichamuthu, op. cit., p. 117.
27. D. B. Pattiaratchi, 'Limestones', *The Ceylon Geographer*, Vol. 18, Nos. 1-4 (1964) pp. 21-6.
28. P. G. Cooray, 'A Carbonate Bearing Flure-chlor-hydroxyapatite from Matale, Ceylon', *The American Minerologist*, Vol. 55 (1970), pp. 2038-41.

2

HISTORICAL SURVEY

by K. M. de Silva

The island of Srī Laṅkā was known in ancient times by a variety of names suggestive of wealth, riches and prosperity — the 'Land without Sorrow' to the Chinese and the 'Isle of Gems' to the Tamils of South India; the 'Isle of Delight' to the merchants of Arabia; to the Sinhalese themselves it was Laṅkā dīpa 'the Resplendent Isle'; and Laṅkā was the name by which the island was known in the great Indian epic the *Rāmāyana*. The earliest European account of Srī Laṅkā, written about twenty years after the death of Alexander the Great, came from Megasthenes, a Seleucid envoy to India, who spoke from hearsay about its elephants, gold and jewels. Pliny is believed to have personally interviewed the Sinhalese envoys to Rome during the reign of Claudius, and Ptolemy's *Geographia* contained a description of Srī Laṅkā, identifying *Anurogrammum Regium* (Anurādhapura) as its capital. And Fa-Hien, the Chinese monk who visited the island in the fifth century A. D., described it as a land where "the [climate] is temperate and attractive, without any difference of summer and winter. The vegetation is always luxuriant. Cultivation proceeds whenever men think fit: there are no fixed seasons for it."

Proximity to India brought Srī Laṅkā within easy range of a diversity of influences from the sub-continent over much of its history. The narrow stretch of sea which separates it from the sub-continent was adequate, however, to ensure that the civilization which evolved in Srī Laṅkā developed characteristics which made it more than merely a variant of an Indian prototype, or hybrid, but something distinctive or autonomous, though the Indian element was never totally obliterated.

Ancient Sri Lanka
For the study of the island's early history there is a unique source of

historical information, the *Mahavaṁsa* (compiled possibly about
the sixth century A.D. but probably later) and its continuation the
Cūlavaṁsa. Composed by *bhikkhus*[1], permeated naturally enough by
a strong religious bias, and encrusted with miracle and invention,
these chronicles nevertheless contain a surprisingly full and
accurate account of the island's early history. They compare well
with chronicles written about the same time in France ánd England,
and have no rival in India.

Both legend and linguistic evidence indicate that the Sinhalese
were a people of Aryan origin who came to the island from Northern
India about 500 B.C. The exact location of their original home in
India cannot be determined with any degree of certainty. The
founding of the Sinhala race is treated in elaborate detail in the
Mahāvaṁsa with great emphasis on the arrival of Vijaya (the legen-
dary founding father of the Sinhalese) and his band in the island.
Their advent is made to coincide with the *parinibbāna* (the passing
away of the Buddha) in a deliberate attempt to emphasise the historic role of the island as a bulwark of Buddhist civilisation.

It was in the dry zone of Srī Lanka that the early settlements arose.
These were riverine in character, and rice was the staple crop. The
earliest colonists were dependent on the Northeast Monsoon to
cultivate a single annual crop of rice. The climate was rigorous if
not harsh, the rains seasonal but not reliable. With the expansion
of the settlements the great problem was to provide insurance
against not infrequent droughts. As a solution to this problem the
ancient Sinhalese developed a highly sophisticated irrigation
system,[2] in which technological skills of an extraordinary nature
were demonstrated. Two general solutions were applied together:
irrigation by means of channels cut from rivers, and the construction of tanks or reservoirs. The construction of these canals or channels exhibited an amazing knowledge of trigonometry, and the
design of the tanks a thorough grasp of hydraulic principles. The
dams had broad bases which could withstand heavy pressures, and
at suitable points at the end of the embankment there were outlets
for the discharge of water. The method of regulating this escape of
water from the tanks was highly ingenious. Sinhalese engineers
had discovered the principle of 'valve tower' or 'valve pit' more
than 2,000 years ago.

Large-scale irrigation works were first constructed by the beginning of the first century A.D. using the water of the Mahaväli Ganga
and other rivers whose sources lay in the wet zone. Increasing sophistication in irrigation technology over the next five centuries
saw an extension of these activities to cover the water resources of
the dry zone, and to the development of two major complexes of

irrigation works, one based on the Mahävali and its tributaries and others drawing on the waters of the Malvatu and Kalä Oyas. These complexes were developed and elaborated further in subsequent centuries. And by the end of the eighth century irrigation facilities were adequate not merely for the opening of extensive tracts of land for cultivation but also for a more intensive cultivation of land.

Two important cores of Sinhalese civilisation developed and control of these gave the Sinhalese rulers the resources to extend their sway over the whole island. The two cities of Anurädhäpura and Polonnaruva were located in these; they became in time, and in succession, the capitals of the whole Sinhalese kingdom. There was a third core in the dry zone of the south, the present Mägampattu where the climate was more severe and the rainfall much less reliable. This region — called Ruhuna — was settled by the ancient Sinhalese nearly as early as Anurädhäpura itself, and a well-developed irrigation system was established there. Ruhuna periodically asserted its independence from the main centres of Sinhalese power in the north-central regions of the island, or served as a refuge for defeated Sinhalese kings or rival claimants to the throne, but it was as frequently controlled from Anuradhapura and seems never to have rivalled it in economic power or population resources.

The introduction of Buddhism to the island influenced and moulded every aspect of the life of the people. Its impact was quite as decisive in its own way as the development of irrigation technology was in economic activity. According to the *Mahavamsa*, the introduction of Buddhism to Srī Lankā occurred during the reign of Dēvānampiya Tissa (307-267 B.C.) a contemporary of the great Indian Emperor Asoka whose emissary Mahinda (Asoka's son according to some authorities and brother according to others) converted Dēvānampiya Tissa to the new faith. But it is possible that traces of some form of Buddhism might well have existed in the island before the time of Dēvānampiya Tissa, and that the *Mahāvamsa* dramatised the conversion of the former to suit the requirements of its author in his reconstruction of the historical evolution of the island in accordance with the framework he had in mind.

Nevertheless it was from the time of Dēvanampiya Tissa that Buddhism became the bedrock of the culture and civilisation of the island. And Anurädhäpura itself became a great centre of Buddhist civilisation.

During the reign of Dēvānampiya Tissa a branch of the sacred bo tree (*ficus religosa*) at Buddhagayā, under which the Buddha attained enlightenment, was brought to Srī Laṅkā by Saṅgamitta, a Buddhist nun believed to be a daughter of Asoka, and planted at Anurādhāpura. This tree still survives — indeed it is the oldest historical tree in the world — and is the object of veneration. In 300 B.C. he built the elegant Thūpārāma *dāgāba* or *stupa* to house two relics of the Buddha, his right collar-bone and his alms-bowl, both of which Dēvānampiya Tissa is said to have obtained from Asoka.

In time the Thūpārāma came to be overshadowed, in size at least, by four other major *stupas* at Anurādhāpura; the Ruvanvälisāya or the *Mahā Stupa* built by Dutthagāmani, the Mirisavätiya also from the time of Dutthagāmani; the Abhayagiri *stupa* built by Vaṭṭagā-mini Abhaya (87-76 B.C.) and enlarged by Gajabāhu I in the second century A.D. — the Abhayagiri surpassed even the Ruvanvälisāya in size; and the Jētavanārāmaya, built by Mahāsen (275-301), was comparable in bulk with the Third Pyramid of Gizeh.

The Mahāvihāra monastery (which had the Ruvanvälisāya for its *dagaba*), established upon the introduction of Buddhism in the reign of Dēvānampiya Tissa, was the historic centre of Theravada Buddhism in Srī Laṅkā. In the reign of Vaṭṭāgamani Abhaya, one of the great events in the annals of Buddhism and in the religious history of the world, took place at Aluvihara near Mātale when the *Tripitaka*, the teachings of the Buddha, which until this time had been transmitted orally, were committed to writing for the first time. This became the orthodox version of Theravada Buddhism, and added greatly to Srī Laṅkā's prestige in the Buddhist world. It was to make copies of certain of these scriptures that Fa-Hien, the Chinese pilgrim monk, came to the island in 411 A.D. and stayed two years.

Ironically it was Vaṭṭāgamani Abhaya who endowed the Abhaya-giri Vihara which eventually became the centre of a sect with strong Mahayanist leanings, and bitterly opposed to the orthodox Maha-vihara.

By the time the *Mahāvamsa* came to be written, Buddhism was much the main influence in shaping the outlook of the masses of the people. It was not merely an ethic or a philosophy — a set of ideas — but a way of life, a design for living. Equally important, Buddhism — as the state "religion" — became the indispensable bond between the ruler and the people whom he governed. This connection between religion, culture, language and national identity has continued to exert a powerful influence on the Sinhalese.

In the early years of the island's history centrifugal tendencies held sway, with the main centres of agricultural settlement under the control of semi-independent rulers. But with the expansion of population, an aspiration to all-island sovereignty emerged. Anurādhāpura developed into the capital of the kingdom. There were two distinct features in these trends: (*a*) an increase in the power of the King, the ruler at Anuradhapura and (*b*) the problem of control over the outer provinces from the capital which was just as intractable in a small island like Sri Lanka as it was in the vast Indian subcontinent.

In theory the king was an absolute ruler, but custom and tradition acted as formidable constraints on his absolutism. From the earliest times the ruler was entitled to a share of the land revenues, and to call upon his subjects to render gratuitous service on public works. Part of the agricultural surplus at his disposal was used to pay the officials of the realm who were allocated grants of land and land revenue. Similarly grants of land were given to Buddhist monasteries, some of which came to control extensive landholdings. Thus the system of land control, in its own way, acted as a restraint on the ruler's absolutism. While the ruler of the realm exercised certain rights over land, private individuals and institutions — such as monasteries — could purchase and alienate land. It would be evident from this discussion that the ancient Sinhalese kingdom had many of the attributes of a feudal polity. Two of these are of special importance: the comparative weakness of central authority, and the importance of land as a determinant of social and economic relationships. Thus the Sinhalese kingdom was not a highly centralised autocratic structure but one in which the balance of political forces incorporated a tolerance of centrifugalism characteristic of most feudal polities. Land and the rights to land were shared by a wide number of individuals and institutions and held under a wide variety of tenurial obligations. This pattern of landownership and royal revenue changed little throughout the centuries of Sinhalese kingship.

Although powerful rulers succeeded in unifying the country, such periods of effective central control over the island were rare, and no ruler succeeded in devising an institutional structure capable of surviving when royal power at Anuradhapura was weakened especially at times — not infrequent — of disputed succession. Nor could it be said that the administrative resources available to the king were adequate to ensure permanent control over the outer provinces — the control of Ruhuṇa from Anurādhāpura was always a formidable problem given the nature of the island's topography.

While central control of the provinces was weak, it had the advantage that instability at the centre did not necessarily extend to the outer provinces. The administrative infrastructure, especially at the village and district level, appears to have been strong and resilient enough to cope with periods of turmoil during power struggles in the upper reaches of the administrative structure at the capital, or during foreign invasions. These were, in a sense, more enduring than the central government institutions. It is this which explains one of the paradoxes of the history of Srī Laṅkā in ancient times, that so brittle and unstable a political structure could have developed the magnificent irrigation system that was the glory of Sinhalese civilisation. No doubt the maintenance of this system in good repair, quite apart from its expansion, required a sophisticated machinery of administration under central control. But it was the permanent institutions rooted among the people at village level which ensured the survival of the system during the periods of turmoil which were a regular feature in Srī Laṅkā's ancient history. Thus Srī Laṅkā in ancient times was a hydraulic society without the rigorous authoritarian and heavily bureaucratic structures which Wittfogel, the theorist of hydraulic civilisations,[3] regarded as the key features of such a polity.

One other important feature of Srī Laṅkā's social structure needs mention at this point. While Sinhalese society shared with European feudalism the obligation to service as a condition of holding land, whether from secular or religious authorities, there was one vital difference that in Srī Laṅkā the nature of that obligation was also determined by a person's position in the caste hierarchy. Caste was the basis of social stratification in Sinhalese society. As with regard to practically everything else, caste was an Indian transplant which developed its own peculiar characteristics in Srī Laṅkā (the irony of a Buddhist civilisation absorbing a caste system being perhaps the most significant of these). It is doubtful if Sinhalese society was ever actually organised on the basis of the conventional fourfold caste hierarchy of Indian society — Brahman, Kshatriya, Vaisya and Sudra. From the beginning there were castes in Sinhalese society which did not resemble Indian castes or sub-castes.

As under the Indian system, however, most castes had a service or occupational role as their primary distinguishing function, but in the Sinhalese system — in contrast to the Indian prototype — there was no religious sanction for caste. Caste groups were brought within a system of services in which hereditary status was the determinant of role and function. Caste services, however, were not always attached to land. The lower castes could be paid in cash or kind for their services. Thus the system of caste duties afforded an institutional framework through which members of different castes were brought into relationships with each other.

There is little or no reliable information in the *Mahāvaṁsa* on the indigenous population of the island at the time of the Aryan colonisation. Knowledge of the island's pre-history remains decidedly meagre even today.

Nor is there any firm evidence concerning the dates of the first Tamil settlements in the island. Tamil and other literary sources, however, point to substantial urban and trading centres in South India in the third century B.C. It is possible that there were trade relations between these centres and Srī Laṅkā at this time, and that the island's trade with the west may have been through these South Indian ports. As early as 237 B.C. two Tamil adventurers usurped the Sinhalese throne and ruled here for twenty-two years, while ten years later came a Cōḷa general Elāra who ruled at Anurādhāpura for forty-four years, earning a great reputation for justice and impartial administration.

The long — fifteen-year — campaign waged by Dutthagāmini, a Sinhalese prince, which culminated in the defeat of Elāra is dramatised as the central theme of the later chapters of the *Mahāvamsa* and is developed there into a major confrontation between the Sinhalese and Tamils. But the evidence suggests that there were large reserves of support for Elāra among the Sinhalese, and that Dutthagāmini, as a prelude to his final and decisive encounter with Elāra, had to face the resistance of other Sinhalese rivals who appear to have been deeply suspicious of his political ambitions. His eventual triumph over Elāra was not a victory of a self-conscious Sinhalese proto-nationalism over Dravidian imperialism so much as the first significant success of centripetalism over centrifugalism in Srī Laṅkā's history. With his victory Anurādhāpura became the capital of the island in a real sense, and remained so till 1017. (There was one interesting break in the fifth century A.D. when the patricide Kāśyapa, son of Dhātusēna — the builder of the great Kalāvāva tank — abandoned Anurādhāpura and imaginatively converted a solitary sheer monolith of granite at Sīgiriya, rising 500 feet from the plains, into an elegant palace surrounded by well-ordered gardens.)

It would appear that Aryan settlement and colonisation preceded the arrival of Dravidian settlers by several centuries. Srī Laṅkā has been from early in its recorded history a multi-racial society in which there was a distinct Dravidian element which could not alter the basic Aryan or North Indian character of the population. Ethnicity, however, was not an important factor in society at the time of the Dutthagāmini-Elāra conflict, and it would seem that neither the Sinhalese nor the Tamils remained racially pure. More importantly there is no reason to suppose that tension was the normal

state of affairs between them. It is more appropriate to describe
Srī Laṅkā in the first few centuries after the Aryan settlement as a
multi-racial society (a conception which emphasises harmony and
a spirit of live and let live) than a plural society (in which tension
between ethnic or other distinctive groups is a main feature).

⌊ In the fifth and sixth centuries A.D. a new factor of instability
was introduced into the politics of Srī Laṅkā with the rise of three
Hindu states in South India, the Pāndyas, Pallavas and Cōḷas. The
flourishing but very vulnerable irrigation civilisation of Srī Laṅkā's
northern plains proved a tempting target for invasion from South
India. There was a special quality of hostility in the threat from
this quarter. This emerged from the fact that these Dravidian states
of South India were militantly Hindu, and that Buddhism, which
had maintained its hold in that region up to this time, disappeared
in the face of this aggressive Hinduism. This development was not
without its effects on the Tamils in Srī Laṅkā, who became more
conscious of their ethnicity — which they sought to identify in terms
of culture, language and religion — Dravidian, Tamil and Hindu.
The Tamil settlements in the island became sources of support for
the South Indian invaders. Thus Srī Laṅkā, from being a multi-
racial polity, became a plural society in which two distinct ethnic
groups lived in a state of sporadic tension. ⌉

The Sinhalese contributed to their own discomfiture by calling
in Tamil assistance to settle disputed successions or dynastic disputes. The Kāśyapa episode is an illustration of this. Kāśyapa had
ruled at Sīgiriya for eighteen years till his brother Mugalan returned from India with an avenging army. Mugalan's reliance on an
army of Indian mercenaries proved, in the long run, to be more
significant than his victory over Kāśyapa.

In the seventh century A.D. a Sinhalese prince, Mānavamma
seized the throne with Pallava assistance, and the dynasty he established continued to rule for almost three centuries. In the early
stages the Pallava influence left its stamp not merely on the island's
politics but also on the culture of the people, being especially
noticeable in architecture and sculpture. But association, if not
alliance, with the Pallavas brought political perils in its train.

The fluctuating fortunes of the various South Indian kingdoms
were not without effect upon the Sinhalese, who were drawn into
these conflicts — voluntarily or involuntarily — as a necessary condition of their geopolitical position in South Asia. The fact is that the
Sinhalese kingdom was rather weaker than the neighbouring kingdoms of South India — and while from time to time it came completely under the influence, if not control, of one or other of them
it could still maintain its identity by trying, often with success to

play one of them off against the other or others. Srī Laṅkā was by now an integral element in the power politics of peninsular India.

By the middle of the ninth century the Sinhalese kingdom was drawn into the vortex of South Indian politics in the wake of the Pāndyans. The ascendancy of the Pāndyans in South Indian politics had immediate consequences for Srī Laṅkā in the shape of a Pāndyan invasion, the inevitable sack of Anurādhāpura, and the imposition of a substantial indemnity as the price of Pāndyan withdrawal. This was the beginning of a Sinhalese involvement in Pañdyan affairs which was to have disastrous consequences for both parties. Within a short while of the Pāndyan withdrawal, the Sinhalese invaded Pāndya in support of a rebel Pāndyan prince, and during their campaign sacked the ancient city of Madurai. In the tenth century the Sinhalese again sent an invading army to the mainland but on this occasion in support of Pāndya against the rising Cōḷa power. The Pāndyans were defeated and their ruler fled to Srī Laṅkā carrying with him the Pāndya insignia. The Sinhalese had now to face the wrath of the victors, for whom a desire to capture the Pāndya insignia was an added impetus to a retaliatory invasion of Srī Laṅkā.

Under Rājārāja the Great (985-1018) the Cōḷas, having conquered all South India, extended their control to Sri Laṅkā, attaching the *rajarata*, the heartland of the Sinhalese kingdom, to the Cōḷā empire. Anurādhāpura was sacked once more. Mahinda V, who ascended the throne in 982, was the last of the Sinhalese kings to rule at Anurādhāpura. He was taken prisoner by the invading Cōḷas in 1017, and he died in captivity in South India. Under Rajaraja's son Rajēndra (1018-35) Cōḷa power extended beyond the South Asian mainland, and posed a threat to the Srī Vijaya empire in modern Malaya and Sumatra. For seventy-five years Srī Laṅkā was ruled as a province of South India, the only such episode in its long history.

With the destruction of Anurādhāpura, the Cōḷas established their capital at Poḷonnaruva in the north east of the dry zone, and nearer the Māhavāli. For the Cōḷas the shift of the capital to Poḷonnaruva was determined by considerations of security. The river itself afforded some protection to the city, and it was in a good position to guard against invasion from Ruhuṇa — the refuge of any potential Sinhalese liberation force — since it lay near the main crossing place on the Mahāvāli which any army from Ruhuṇa must force.

The Sinhalese rulers never re-established Anuradhapura as the capital. They remembered how Anuradhapura had been sacked

again and again in the past, and how dangerously exposed it was
to invasion from India. For them Poḷonnaruva had the virtue of
greater protection against this peril.

The Poḷonnaru Kingdom

Considerations of security were not the only factors determining
the shift of the capital to Polonnaruva. The region around Polonnaruva had been developed long before the capital itself was shifted to that city. Mahāsen (274-304 A.D.) built the famous Minnēriya
tank there. Between the fourth and ninth centuries several smaller
tanks were built in that region, and these must have supported a
considerable local population. The irrigation network there was
widened in the eleventh century and after, and the city and its sur-
rounding agricultural base appear to have become nearly as large
and as densely populated as the old Anurādhāpura region itself.
Besides, the proximity to the Mahāvali, the longest river in Srī
Laṅkā, increased the economic potential of this region.

The Cōḷas were driven out of Sri Lanka in 1070 by Vijaya Bahu I.
Once again Ruhuṇa had risen to the rescue and liberation of Srī
Laṅkā. Although Vijaya Bahu regained control of Anurādhāpura, he followed the Cōḷas in retaining Polonnaruva as the
capital.

During his reign of forty years the country recovered from the
ravages of Cōḷa misrule, although the author of the *Cūlavaṁsa* does
not give him the credit due to him for his skilful campaign of liberation in which the odds against him were overwhelming, and for his
achievement in the more prosaic fields of administrative recovery
and economic regeneration. Buddhism had received a severe setback during the rule of the Cōḷas when Saivite Hinduism flourished, and Vijaya Bahu devoted his attention to organising its recovery
and restoration to its once vigorous condition.

But Vijaya Bahu left a disputed succession, and there was another
period of extensive civil war from which emerged in time the remarkable figure of Parakramabahu I. He ruled at Polonnaruva
from 1153 to 1186, unified Sri Lanka under his control, reformed
the *sangha*, helped heal the long-standing schism between the Maha-
vihara and the Abhayagiri vihara (a task which the author of the
Culavamsa regarded as being even more formidable than his political problems), built a remarkable series of irrigation works including the massive Parakrama Samudra tank (the Sea of Parakrama)
and public and religious monuments. All these helped make the
city of Polonnaruva, as impressive in its own way as Anurādhāpura
had once been, though decidedly on a smaller scale in extent and
in the size, if not variety, of its major buildings.

His reign marks the last major phase in the development of irrigation in ancient and medieval Srī Laṅkā. The irrigation works of his period represent an advance in the techniques of heavy construction. Not only were the earthworks unprecedented in scale, but the masonry of these irrigation works involved the handling of stone blocks weighing up to about 10½ tons.

He conducted an active foreign policy, sending his navy on a punitive expedition against Burma for mistreatment of a Srī Laṅkā mission, and his army to South India in support of a Pāndyan claimant to the throne. While this latter expedition failed after initial success, the Burmese mission fared better, and in general his foreign policy was active rather than successful.

Parākramabāhu is the hero of the *Cūlavaṁsa* just as Dutthagāmini was the hero of the *Mahāvaṁsa*. And, in fact, it would appear that the author of the *Cūlavaṁsa* plays down the very real achievements of Vijaya-Bāhu I to build a more favourable image of Parākramabāhu I. (The failures of the latter's foreign policy ventures are concealed.) The reign of Parākramabāhu, with all its achievements and its revival of ancient grandeur, proved to be the Indian summer of Sinhalese greatness; indeed his vigorous rule, in particular his ambitious foreign policy, may have contributed to the suddenness and completeness of the collapse which followed so soon after his death.

After the death of Parākramabāhu there was a brief decade of order and stability under Nissaṅka Malla (1187-96) during which Polonnaruva reached the peak of its development as a capital city. Its architectural features rivalled those of Anurādhāpura though they emerged during a much shorter period of time.

Among the most notable of these are: the *vatadāgē*, one of the most beautiful examples of Buddhist architecture in Srī Laṅkā; the *Saṭmahalprasāda*, which has striking Cambodian features and which on a more subdued scale looks very much like a building in Angkor Vat; the *Nissaṅka-latā-mandapaya;* the Kiri-vehera which though small is still twice the size of the Thūpārāma; the Laṅkā-tilaka vihāra which, with its colossal standing image of the Buddha, is the largest Buddhist temple in Srī Laṅkā; the lotus bath; the magnificent Gal-Vihāra, a rock-cut temple celebrated for its sculpture — the whole complex was fashioned at the command of Parākramabāhu from one enormous granite outcrop; and the colossal sculpture eleven and half feet tall carved in high relief from the granulite outcrop and traditionally supposed to be a sage, or a portrait of a ruler holding the yoke of sovereignity. The distinctive feature of these architectural remains is the mingling of Buddhist and Hindu decorative elements, a mingling which extended far beyond the mere stylistic plagiarism of Hindu forms. It provides strong evidence of the great influence of Mahayanism and Hinduism in the life of the rulers and the people.

With Nissaṅka Malla's death, there was renewed dissension among the Sinhalese, and dynastic disputes contributed to the break-up of the Poḷonnaruva kingdom. Sinhalese claimants to the throne invited South Indian and other aid in establishing their claims. But the ensuing political instability attracted South Indian invasions, by Cōḷa and Pāndya adventurers, culminating in a devastating campaign of pillage under Māgha of Kalinga.

⌐After Māgha's death in 1255, Polonnaruva and the heartland of the old Sinhalese kingdom and Ṙuhuṇa itself were abandoned. And the Sinhalese kings and people, in the face of repeated invasions from South India retreated further and further into the hills of the wet zone of the island — in search primarily of security, but also for some kind of new economic base to support the truncated state they controlled. They paid increasing attention to trade — especially in cinnamon, which was gathered wild in the wet zone forests, and exported largely through ports on the southwestern coast. In the meantime Tamil settlers occupied the Jaffna peninsula and much of the land between Jaffna and Anurādhāpura known as the Vanni; they were joined by Tamil members of the invading armies, often mercenaries, who chose to settle in Srī Laṅkā rather than return to India with the rest of their compatriots. It would appear that by the thirteenth century the Tamils too withdrew from the Vanni, and thereafter their main settlements were confined almost entirely to the Jaffna peninsula and possibly to several scattered settlements near the Eastern seaboard. ⌐

⌐The abandonment of the ancient Sinhalese kingdom of the dry zone is one of the great unsolved puzzles of Srī Lāṅkā's history.⌐ It has its parallel in the abandonment of similar points of civilisation, in dry zones in other parts of Southeast Asia, in Cambodia, Northern Thailand and the Pagan region of Burma. All these, like the Sinhalese kingdom, were highly productive with a large agricultural surplus, and all of them owed their prosperity in varying degrees to irrigation. And they collapsed at much the same time. What led to their abandonment and why were they never reoccupied?

To take the case of Sri Lanka. To attribute this dramatic withdrawal simply to the South Indian invasions, as local tradition does, ignores the repeated returns to the dry zone from the hills and the revival of the whole ancient irrigation system after each of the many invasions of preceding centuries, some of which (notably the Cōḷa invasion under Rajaraja) seem to have been as destructive as those which followed the death of Nissaṅka Malla. Was it then a matter of a change of climate, or was it a matter of soil exhaustion? Was it siltation of the tanks and channels? Each of these theories seems so attractive superficially, but none of them are tenable in the face of further and closer examination.

A civilization based on a dry zone irrigation complex presupposes a high level of organisation and a massive labour force to build the works and provide the constant maintenance that was essential. The irrigation works of ancient Sri Lanka and the monumental scale of the ancient capitals, re-emphasise the nature of the state and society which created them. But as with other civilisations of a similar nature, the institutional machinery for the maintenance of the large irrigation works on which their prosperity depended weakens in time and breaks down from internal causes, quite apart from the invasions of the sort that plagued ancient Srī Laṅkā. The cumulative effect of these invasions must have been destructive — they ate into the vitals of a society already losing its vigour with age. In Central Asia too, as in Ceylon, the irrigation societies repeatedly fell and disappeared leaving behind them water works which they were no longer able to maintain after invasions and internal decay had weakened them.

The next question is why the collapse of the ancient civilisation came in the thirteenth century, and not earlier with the Cōḷa invasion of the eleventh century? Here again, no definite answer is possible, except to suggest that by the thirteenth century the cumulative disintegration, from the various causes mentioned, had reached a point of no return. And there does seem to be another factor which may have made the thirteenth century different from any of the earlier periods of crisis—malaria. Here it must be emphasised that malaria did not cause the original abandonment of the heartland of ancient Sri Lanka. Too little is known of the history of malaria's spread to permit definite assertions about when it took root in the island, but it appears to have spread to Sri Lanka well before the sixteenth century. It has been pointed out that the *anopheles* mosquito would have found ideal breeding places in the abandoned tanks and channels, and in fact malaria has often followed the destruction or abandonment or irrigation works in other parts of Asia. Within a century of its spread to Ceylon it would have added a further insuperable obstacle to the re-occupation of the traditional homelands of the Sinhalese in the dry zone; it defeated all attempts at large-scale re-settlement till the advent of DDT. Briefly, then, malaria — coming in on the heels of invasion and thriving on disused irrigation works—played a critically important part in multiplying obstacles to re-settlement.

The Drift to the Southwest

The years 1200-1500 in the history of Srī Laṅkā constitute a period
of almost uninterrupted decline in which central power collapsed,
the ancient irrigation civilisations were abandoned, and forces of
centrifugalism triumphed. In the politics of the period there were
four main developments: the drift of Sinhalese power to the south-
west and centre, with the main thrust in the former direction; the
establishment and consolidation of a Tamil Kingdom in the North;
and the eventual emergence in the centre of the island of a separate
political entity with aspirations to the status of a separate kingdom
— the early beginnings of the Kandyan Kingdom; and the arrival
of the Portuguese. There was also a fundamental change in the
economic organisation and basis of the state in Srī Laṅkā, from an
overwhelming dependence on irrigation-based rice cultivation,
to rain-fed subsistence agriculture, and notably, trade. Cinnamon
emerged as a basic element in the ruler's revenue in the south-
west, and in the north there was, besides trade, the pearl fishery
as well.

One significant point about the drift to the southwest needs special
mention. The coastal regions of the west and north had from the
early years of the Anuradhapura kingdom supported small but
economically viable trade settlements. Through the centuries these
settlements not merely survived but expanded with the increase
in the volume of trade transacted between Srī Laṅkā and the states
of the Indian Ocean. These settlements would no doubt have attracted people from the heartland of the irrigation civilisation of the
Sinhalese. With increasing political instability at the centre of
Sinhalese power they would have had a more compelling attraction
for the people. Thus the shift of population to the southwest was
not a movement to some unknown and unexplored regions of the
island, but to familiar localities which offered not merely security
but also potential for a more than modest livelihood. Briefly, when
the collapse of the irrigation civilisation of the dry zone left the
people of those regions with no alternative but to move away, their
drift to the southwest was governed not only by an elemental search
for security, but also by the attraction of economic potential.

After the rule of the Kaliṅga king Māgha at Polonnaruva in the
thirteenth century, the next three kings ruled from Dambadeniya.
One ruler made Yāpahuva his royal residence. Both these points
were rock fortresses. Kurunägala was another site of royal power
in this quest for safety against invasion from South India. From
Kurunägala the centre of power shifted to Gampola and eventually
to Kotte near Colombo. The last Sinhalese king to rule from Polonnaruva was Parakramabahu III (1278-93) but his reign only served

to illustrate the parlous position to which Sinhalese power had been reduced; he ruled at Polonnaruva only because of his subservience to the Pandyans. But not all the Sinhalese rulers of this period were willing to accept the position and status of the ruler of a satellite state of Tamil power in South India, or to abandon the natural aspiration of a Sinhalese king to rule over the whole country even if the resources to achieve these ends were grievously limited. Parākramabāhu II (1236-71) almost achieved this: his power extended over Ruhuna, the central hills and the Vanni, and he annexed Polonnaruva. But though he defeated the Tamils in battle once, he could not establish control over the Tamil kingdom in the north of the island. More important, he held his coronation at Polonnaruva. However, this proved to be merely a symbolic gesture, for although he attempted to restore Polonnaruva to its pristine glory as a centre of Sinhalese power, he was compelled to return to Dambadeniya, which remained his capital for the rest of his reign, in recognition of the persistent danger of a Pandyan invasion of the island.

South Indian invasions were not the only peril which confronted the Sinhalese rulers. The threat of encroachments by an expanding Tamil kingdom of the north was equally real. And to confuse the situation still further there were occasional but embarrassing threats from foreign rulers from across the seas. The first of these came in the thirteenth century when Chandrabhānu, a Buddhist king from Malaya, invaded the island twice — not indeed for the purpose of conquest and territorial control, but to exploit the disturbed political conditions in the Sinhalese kingdom in order to seize the two most sacred relics of the Buddha within its domain; the Tooth Relic and the Alms Bowl. In the early fifteenth century Srī Lankā suffered the strange misfortune of a Chinese invasion (in 1410) or landing by one of the great fleets of junks which the Ming emperors despatched to the southern seas in the first half of the fifteenth century.[5]

Political instability continued to be the bane of Srī Lankā's history throughout this period. But, on the constructive side, economic activity developed on new lines. While the main occupation of the people continued to be the cultivation of rice, the rulers no longer devoted all their energies to it. For centuries, large-scale agriculture had been dependent on the provision of an elaborate irrigation network under the direction of the central administration. But the wet zone had sufficient rain and there was no need for an investment of scarce resources in irrigation. (Nor was the political instability and insecurity, so characteristic of the history of the Sinhalese kingdom in these centuries, conducive to the development of irri-

gation facilities, even if such investment had been found essential
for agriculture.)

Trade rose higher in the scale of the rulers' priorities than ever
before. Cinnamon now emerged as one of the main export commodities with the increased demand for spices in Europe after
the Crusades. There was no need to cultivate cinnamon; it grew
wild in the forests of the wet zone, and the yield from it was more
than adequate for the export trade. The larger share of the profits
from it undoubtedly went to the king who, as a result, became less
dependent on revenue from grain than the Sinhalese kings of the
past. The increasing importance attached to the cinnamon trade
was demonstrated by two developments. First, the bid of the Tamil
rulers of the north of the island — the Ārya Chakravartis — to undertake the conquest of the south-west had not a little to do with the
fact that the cinnamon resources of the island were concentrated
in that region. Secondly, the decision to make Kōṭṭē the capital of
the Sinhalese kingdom in 1415 stemmed largely from a recognition
of its value for the effective control of the cinnamon producing
areas.

The emphasis on trade at this time has one other noteworthy
point of interest. Muslim settlers in the island largely controlled
its export trade. As this trade grew in importance, they settled in
larger numbers in the coastal areas and in the ports. Gradually they
penetrated to the interior in the interests of their trade. The gradual
increase in the Muslim population added another element of
plurality to the Srī Laṅkā polity.

From a brief review of the history of the Sinhalese kingdom of
the southwest, we turn now to the affairs of the north of the island
where in the thirteenth century a Tamil kingdom had been established with the Jaffna peninsula as its core. Except for a brief period
in the middle of the fifteenth century when it came under the control of the principal Sinhalese ruler of the island, it maintained its
independent position till the beginning of the seventeenth century.
During the period of its existence as a separate state, the Tamils of
the north developed a more distinct and confident Hindu culture
that looked for its inspiration towards the rich cultural traditions
of South India. The impact of South India on the Tamil kingdom
of the north was not restricted to culture and religion but affected
its political evolution as well. The Tamil kingdom could not avoid
being drawn into the orbit of the dominant South Indian state of
the day.

As the Sinhalese power in the island of Srī Laṅkā declined, that
of the Tamils seemed to wax, and they advanced southwards to
exact tribute from the south-west and the central regions. By the

middle of the fourteenth century the kingdom of the Ārya Chakra-vartis extended as far south as Puttalam. It was poised for the conquest of the rest of the island and the establishment of Tamil supremacy over Srī Laṅkā.

That the Sinhalese resistance to those Tamil incursions succeeded was not a little due to the rulers of the north soon having to fight on two fronts, for the Vijayanagara rulers in an expansionist mood had turned their attention to the Tamil kingdom of north Srī Laṅkā. The Sinhalese kingdom with its capital at Kōttē at last threw up a ruler resourceful and dynamic enough to meet the challenges that confronted it and to prevail over them. This was Pārakrama-bāhu VI (1412-67), the last Sinhalese ruler to bring the whole island under his rule, and the first since the heyday of the Polonnaruva kingdom under Parākramabāhu I and Nissaṅka Malla in the twelfth century. He overran Jaffna in 1450. But Sinhalese control over the north was not maintained for long after his death, and Jaffna re-asserted its independence under Parārājasēkeram (1478-1519), when the politics of Kōttē returned to what was the normal state in the Sinhalese kingdom of the southwest — turmoil, instability and dissension.

The successors of Parākramabāhu VI at Kōttē were confronted not merely by the re-assertion of the independence of the Jaffna kingdom but by a wholly novel development as well when the central region began to stake a claim to an independent political role of its own. The foundation of this kingdom may be traced back to the last quarter of the fifteenth century, though a territorial unit centred on its mountainous core but with indistinct boundaries and political status has a longer history. Two factors contributed to the emergence of a separatist aspirations among the Kandyans. The first undoubtedly was the threat posed by the Tamil kingdom of the north, especially in the efforts to exact tribute from the Kandyans, and the failure of the rulers of the Sinhalese kingdom of the south-west to afford them adequate protection against this. The absorption of the Kandyan region into the Kōttē kingdom under the energetic Pārakramabāhu VI did not entirely extinguish the separatist tendencies of the Kandyans. On the contrary, it may in fact have helped transform these into a proto-nationalism. Secondly, it was undoubtedly the turmoil in the Kōttē kingdom in the late fifteenth and early sixteenth centuries that afforded the Kandyans the opportunity to assert their independence from the control of the ruler at Kōttē. Reeling under the pressures set off by power struggles in the wake of disputed successions, and prolonged political turmoil, Kōttē was in no position to re-establish its control over the Kandyans. Thus the decline of Kōttē proved to be a necessary condition for the rise of the Kandyan kingdom. The result was that when the Portuguese arrived in the island in the first decade of the sixteenth century, they found that Sri Lanka, like Caesar's Gaul, was divided into three parts.

By the third decade of the sixteenth century the Srī Laṅkā polity appeared to have reached a state of fragmentation which seemed beyond the powers of any statemanship to repair. The most striking evidence of this was provided by the disintegration of Kōttē, the main political power in the island, which came about as a result of a palace revolution in 1521 when its territories were partitioned among three rulers. Kōttē's aspirations to overlordship over the rest of the island, never really capable of fulfilment since the death of Parākramabāhu VI, now seemed a'cruel joke. The kingdom of Jaffna did not have the potential for domination over the rest of the island, and the ambitions of Kandy were limited to mere survival as an independent entity.

It is against this background that one needs to view the entry of the Portuguese into the Srī Laṅkā scene. The first Portuguese contact with the Kōttē kingdom in 1505-6 was largely accidental, and not until twelve years later did the Portuguese seek to establish a fortified trading settlement. The building of the first fort near Colombo aroused popular hostility, fanned no doubt by the Moorish traders established in the island who largely controlled its external trade, and it had to be given up.

In all their activities in Asia and Africa the Portuguese did not aim at territorial conquest so much as the control of commerce by subduing and dominating the strategic points through which it passed, by means of their naval power. At no stage did they establish a dominance over the politics of South Asia. What they did was to use their sea-power and superior technology at points of weakness or where there were sharp divisions, and they thus attained an influence which was out of proportion to their real strength. As regards Srī Laṅkā, however, they were drawn into the vortex of Kōttē's politics, in their anxiety to establish a bridgehead for control over the island's cinnamon trade. After the partition of Kōttē into three distinct political entities, the ruler at the old capital of Kōttē found himself confronted with the increasing power and influence of the ruler of Sītāvaka, Māyadunnē, who was soon in control of two of the three divisions of the old Kōttē kingdom and was pressing for domination and control over the rest. The Kōttē ruler hoped that Portuguese protection would preserve his kingdom against Māyadunnē and willingly accepted the status of a Portuguese satellite by agreeing to pay an annual tribute largely of cinnamon.

Over the rest of the century the story of the truncated kingdom of Kōttē was a history of increasing dependence on the Portuguese. The phases in this process may be demarcated thus. The first step was taken in 1540 when an embassy was sent to Lisbon to secure a guarantee that the ruler's grandson would succeed to the throne on his death. João III of Portugal solemnly crowned a golden statue of the young prince in 1543 and formally promised to safeguard the succession and protect him. The second phase began when this prince became a convert to Roman Catholicism in 1557, a step which his grandfather had steadfastly refused to take in spite of Portuguese pressure, though he had assented to the entry of Roman Catholic missionaries to Kōttē in 1543 and countenanced their activities. Dharmāpala's conversion to Catholicism was to have disastrous consequences for him. This ostentatious severance of the traditional bond between the Sinhalese ruler and the Buddhist religion was of great advantage to Māyādunnē, who now emerged as the champion of Buddhism. The subjects of the Kōttē ruler were decisively alienated, and Māyādunnē and his son Rājasinha moved in to redouble their efforts to subdue Kotte. Their relentless attacks were increasingly successful. By 1565 the capital city of Kōttē was abandoned and Dharmapāla took refuge in the fort of Colombo which was practically all that he and his Portuguese mentors now controlled. The third phase began in 1580 when he bequeathed his throne to the Portuguese King Dom Henrique, though he did not die till 1597. His grandfather had been a protégé of the Portuguese, a pliant ruler of a satellite state; Dharmapala ended as a *roi fainéant.*

Till the last decade of the sixteenth century, Portuguese power was confined to the fort of Colombo and a few coastal areas around other ports of the island. The predominant power in the island's politics was Sītāvaka.

The rulers of Sītāvaka aimed at a domination of the island's polity. One phase in this has already been referred to — the subjugation of the Kōttē kingdom which they achieved by 1565. Only the fort of Colombo was beyond their control; the rest of the southwest littoral, including the richest cinnamon-producing areas, was under their rule. At the same time they made it their objective to drive the foreigner — the Portuguese — out of Srī Lankā. Indeed, during its brief existence of about seventy years the Sītāvaka kingdom established a record of resistance to foreign rule which has never been matched in the history of the encounter between western imperialism and Srī Lankā. Māyadunnē's resistance to the Portuguese was relentless if not entirely unbroken; Rājasinha's opposition was even more passionate and consistent. More than once they nearly succeeded in driving the Portuguese out of the island; only the lack of a navy or effective naval support prevented a complete success. The second phase was their campaign to gain control of the Kandyan kingdom which began in the 1570s. On their third attempt (1581-2), they succeeded in routing the Kandyan forces and bringing that kingdom under their control. For ten years from 1581 to 1591 there was no independent kingdom of Kandy. Only the Tamil kingdom of the north remained outside the sphere of control of the ruler of Sītāvaka, if not his influence.

One of the great tragedies of Srī Laṅkā's history was that the collapse of Sītāvaka was even more dramatic and precipitate that its meteoric rise and expansion. Rājasiṅha I was only about fifty years old at the time of his death in 1593; he had eliminated almost every potential rival so that there was no effective successor to consolidate his achievements, or indeed to hold the kingdom together against its numerous enemies. Within a few years of his death, Portuguese control over the south-west littoral was extended, consolidated and stabilised. In 1591 the Kandyan kingdom regained its independence. It was now the last surviving Sinhalese kingdom.

The establishment of Portuguese control over Jaffna came about at much the same time as the collapse of Sītāvaka. Portuguese interest in the Tamil areas of the north had begun in the 1540s, and as part of the extension of Roman Catholic missionary activity in the island. The missionaries had crossed over from South India and by 1544 had made heavy inroads especially among the fisherfolk of Mannār and Jaffna. But the Hindu ruler of Jaffna reacted angrily against this process. In 1560 the Portuguese sent a retaliatory expedition which achieved some success at first but in the following year they were forced to retreat to Mannār. It was not until 1591 that another Portuguese attack on the north was launched; on this occasion the king of Jaffna was killed and a Portuguese protégé placed on the throne.

For Srī Laṅkā the crisis of the sixteenth century, which began with the partition of Kōttē, culminated at the end of the century in Portuguese dominance, if not control, over two of the three kingdoms that had existed at its beginning.

The Kandyan Kingdom and its Struggle for Survival

By the beginning of the seventeenth century the Portuguese quickly lost such dominance as they had in the Indian Ocean, with the arrival there of the Dutch as challengers to the Iberian control of the non-European world. But the first third of the seventeenth century was precisely the period when the Portuguese extended their control in the only two regions they ever penetrated beyond the range of their coastal forts — in the Zambezi river valley in Africa and in Srī Laṅkā.

In this island they had two objectives: to complete the process of control over the Jaffna kingdom; and to subjugate the Kandyan kingdom. The first was much the easier proposition and by 1619 they had annexed it. In so doing they brought to an end the independent existence of a Tamil kingdom in Srī Laṅkā. Never again did it recover its independence, and this subjugation of the Jaffna kingdom was one of the most lasting effects of Portuguese rule. The Dutch and the British after them continued the policy of treating Jaffna as a mere unit of a larger political entity.

If, at the beginning of the sixteenth century, the Kandyan ruler had been asked to specify the most potent threat to the existence of his kingdom, he would unhesitatingly have pointed his finger at Kōttē. No doubt the Kandyan kingdom regarded itself as one of the principal beneficiaries of the partition of Kōttē in 1521, but any relief at the seeming weakening of the main source of danger was short-lived, for out of the chaos of the partition emerged the vigorous and aggressive Sītāvaka kingdom, a much more serious threat to the integrity of Kandy than Kōttē had ever been.

Faced with this frightening prospect, the Kandyan ruler did what the Kōttē kings had done in similar circumstances — he turned to the Portuguese and willingly accepted the status of a satellite state. The symbols of this voluntary subordination were the presence of a small Portuguese force in Kandy, and the entry of Roman Catholic priests there. At the same time another line of approach was adopted, a marriage alliance with the ruling family of Kōttē. The Portuguese connection, like that with Kōttē, was to cause immense difficulties for the Kandyan kingdom later. But more important, neither singly nor in combination were these connections effective sources of support against Sītāvaka. As we have seen Sītāvaka turned on Kandy after she had successfully dealt with Kōttē and had reduced Dharmapāla to the position of a king without a kingdom. By 1581 Rājasiṅha I had conquered the Kandyan kingdom, and for ten years it remained part of Sītāvaka. The dramatic collapse of Sītāvaka after Rājasiṅha's death enabled the Kandyan kingdom to assert its independence once more. But with the release from Sītāvaka's domination came a new danger and a new enemy.

For two decades after regaining its independence the Kandyan kingdom was confronted by a concerted Portuguese attempt to bring it under their rule, and thus complete their domination over the whole island. The Portuguese had gained considerable influence in the ruling circles of Kandy during their friendly association with that kingdom. Through the process of conversion to

Roman Catholicism, the Portuguese had pliant protégés whose claims to the Kandyan throne were as good as those of any other aspirant, and these claims were now advanced in support of an extension of Portuguese power. At the same time they had another line of attack. As legatees of the Kōttē ruler, the Portuguese reasserted Kōttē's claim to overlordship over Kandy. The future Vimala Dharma Sūriya (1591-1604) thwarted the Portuguese by capturing and marrying the princess whom they wished to install on the Kandyan throne. His claims were now greatly enhanced, even though the Portuguese would not recognise them. The Portuguese stood forth now as heirs of Kōttē.

Vimala Dharma Sūriya and Senarath (1604-1635) re-established the kingdom of Kandy. Their aims were modest, and their vision limited. Survival was all and peace on any terms which the Portuguese would be prepared to grant. But the latter were not interested in peace with the Kandyan kingdom and were intent on the systematic destruction of parts of that kingdom through regular raids. Kandy survived at all only because the Portuguese could not muster the manpower (in terms of Portuguese soldiers) necessary for this purpose. Their anxiety to subjugate Kandy increased with the arrival of the Dutch in Asian waters. But Kandyan policy towards the Portuguese did not change. It was still one of détente. And this they did achieve to some extent by the Treaty of 1617 under the terms of which the Portuguese recognised Senarath as ruler of the Kandyans, and the latter in turn acknowledged the authority of the Portuguese to rule over the maritime districts of Srī Laṅkā. The Kandyans agreed to pay tribute to the Portuguese, and promised to deny entry to any enemy of the Portuguese.

The annexation of Jaffna in 1619 worked to the disadvantage of the Kandyans by depriving them of a potential ally and a bridgehead for communication with other rulers in South India. One result of the annexation was that the only ports which the Portuguese did not control in Srī Laṅkā were on the east coast, which was acknowledged as being part of the Kandyan kingdom. Despite this fact they soon set about gaining control of the two major ports of Batticaloa and Trincomalee; the latter they seized quite easily, and in 1628 they seized and fortified Batticaloa. While these blatant infringements of Kandyan sovereignty were taking place, Senarath would do nothing to precipitate a confrontation with the Portuguese.

By 1628, however, signs of a change in the Kandyan policy towards the Portuguese were evident. Senerath's son Rājasiṅha — the future Rājasiṅha II — anxious to take on the mantle of Sītāvaka and of his namesake, in resolute opposition to the Portuguese was largely responsible for the change. The Kandyans now resorted to a more aggressive policy, and organised incursions deep into Portuguese-held territory. The Portuguese, in turn, reverted to the old policy of attempting an armed invasion for the subjugation of Kandy. In 1630 a Portuguese expedition under Constantine de Saa set out for this purpose, but was routed at the battle of Raṅde-nivela near Vällaväya. Once again as under the Sītāvaka kings, the Portuguese were harried and pushed back to the security of their fortś. Once again, in imitation of Māyadunné and Rājasiṅha I the aim was to drive the Portuguese out of Sri Laṅkā.

The change of policy from détente to vigorous resistance was sustained over the next twenty-eight years. But in the meantime a respite came in 1623 — a temporary truce, caused by exhaustion. A Luso-Kandyan treaty signed in 1633 incorporated terms which were much the same as those of 1617, except that, curiously, they were more favourable to the Portuguese in that the latter's control over the ports of the eastern coastline was recognised. It required the threat of a renewal of war to get the Kandyans to accept the treaty. To them the treaty was a disagreeable but temporary neces-sity. And they began to look earnestly for the foreign assistance without which the expulsion of the Portuguese could not be effect-ed — the prevention of reinforcements from abroad to troops that were secure in forts located on the seafront. They found an ally in the Dutch.

Negotiations between Rājasiṅha II and the Dutch were conduct-ed over a long period but were successfully concluded in 1638. Each side hoped to use the other for its own ends. For the Dutch the pri-mary interest was in the cinnamon trade which they desired to control and, if possible, monopolise. They were assigned a mono-poly of the spice trade of the island in return for aid against the Portuguese; and they were also assured re-imbursement of the costs of the campaign against the Portuguese — a clause which was to cause interminable disputes in the future. For Rāja-siṅha II the objective was Dutch assistance in the expulsion of the Portuguese.

The treaty came into effect immediately and almost at once it led to misunderstandings and bickering between the allies. In 1639 Trincomalee and Batticaloa were captured from the Portuguese and handed back to the Kandyans, but when the ports of Galle and Negombo were taken in 1640, the Dutch retained them under their control on the grounds that the Kandyan ruler had not met their expenses. It is not without significance that while the east coast was not a cinnamon-producing area, the ports of Galle and Negombo gave effective control over some of the richest cinnamon lands in the island.

Meanwhile the diplomatic and political affairs of Europe also intruded into the conflict in Sri Laṅkā. At this time — 1640 — a native Portuguese dynasty was raised to the throne (by a very popular rebellion) after a spell of eighty years during which Portugal was under Habsburg rule. One of the immediate effects of this was to put an end to hostilities between the Dutch and the Portuguese in Europe. However this armistice did not apply to the conflict between them in the eastern seas till 1645. For a period of about seven years thereafter there was a lull during which the Portuguese in Sri Laṅkā were afforded a breathing space. During the same period relations between Rājasiṅha and the Dutch were greatly strained, and there seemed every prospect of a triangular conflict in Sri Laṅkā. However, when hostilities between the Dutch and the Portuguese were resumed in 1652, Rājasiṅha returned to support the Dutch in what proved to be the final phase in the expulsion of the Portuguese. In May 1656 the Portuguese fort of Colombo surrendered after a long and bitter siege. Jaffna, the last Portuguese stronghold, was captured in 1658, and with that Portuguese rule in Sri Laṅkā was at an end.

[One western power was eliminated from Sri Laṅkā by the intervention of another, but this latter was soon in comfortable occupation of most of the seaboard of the island once controlled by the Portuguese, and a good deal of the cinnamon-producing land though not all of it.] Under the treaty they had signed with Rājasiṅha II the Dutch were supposed to hand over the captured territories to the Sinhalese ruler, but the treaty itself was a piece of chicanery; in any case they put him off by demands that he first pay the bill presented for the cost of military operations, and the costs were inflated beyond the capacity of the Sinhalese to pay. Rājasiṅha attempted to stir up rebellion against the Dutch but failed to unsettle them; equally, Dutch efforts to penetrate beyond the boundaries of the territories which they controlled were ineffective. Eventually Rājasiṅha was hamstrung by the outbreak of a formidable rebellion against his rule in his own territories in the hills in 1664 and the two parties, the Dutch and the Kandyans, settled down to an uneasy truce which gradually became a *modus vivendi.*

For the Kandyan kingdom the substitution of Dutch for Portuguese control of the island's seaboard territories had certain definite advantages. For one thing the area controlled by the Dutch was much less than that under effective Portuguese occupation in the seventeenth century[Besides the Dutch were much less aggressive and were not generally intent on confrontation, conflict or territorial conquest. Indeed there was a long period of peaceful relations between the two powers till 1762 — in striking contrast to the turbulence and violence of the Portuguese in the years from 1597 to their departure. Moreover the Dutch kept up the legal fiction of administering the territories under their control as agents or trustees of the Kandyan ruler. Their primary, if not sole, interest lay in gaining monopolistic control over the island's cinnamon trade, and since much of the most valuable cinnamon-producing areas was under Kandyan rule, it was politic to maintain peaceful relations with the Kandyans. Indeed their diplomatic relations with the Kandyans were formally correct to the point of being obsequious, in recognition of the fact that the Kandyan ruler did have a great deal of influence with the Sinhalese people under Dutch rule. The Buddhist religion was the main link between them.

In 1739 the dynasty established by Vimala Dharma Sūriya became extinct in the male line, and the South Indian Nāyakkar dynasty came to the Kandyan throne by virtue of marriage alliances with the ruling house in Kandy. In internal policy this did not lead to any substantial change. The Nāyakkars in fact became more Kandyan than the Kandyans and this was especially so in the patronage given to Buddhism. There was a great Buddhist revival under the later Nāyakkars, and this had its influence on the low country as well. More important, the Nāyakkars posed a threat to the Dutch by virtue of their surer grasp of the mechanics of power politics in South India, and they had friends and compatriots outside Srī Laṅkā on whom they could rely. The greatest danger was the prospect of a link between the English East India Company in South India and the Kandyans, and by the early 1760s this threat had emerged in very positive form.

By this time, however, relations between the Kandyans and the Dutch had deteriorated to the point where the Dutch contemplated military action against the Kandyan kingdom. In 1762 an expedition set out for the Kandyan hills, but it met with disaster, as had the frequent Portuguese invasions of the sixteenth and seventeenth century. But a second expedition despatched in 1765 was better planned and succeeded in forcing on the Kandyans a treaty (that of 1766), which conceded to the Dutch full sovereignty over the territories they had captured from the Portuguese, and reduced the Kandyan kingdom to the position of a completely landlocked power.[6]

Two points about this extension of Dutch power are worth noting. First, it came at a time when Dutch power in the Indian Ocean was on the decline and against the background of the Anglo-French conflict for control over India. Secondly, for the Kandyans the treaty imposed on them in 1766 was unpalatable and they were scheming to have it abrogated, and to expel the Dutch with foreign assistance, English or French. Ultimately it was English intervention which was crucial in the expulsion of the Dutch from Srī Laṅkā in the last decade of the eighteenth century.

In the seventeenth and eighteenth centuries Srī Laṅkā had seen decisive changes. At this point it would be useful to consider the effect of some of these on the island's development.

The most notable legacy of Portuguese rule in Srī Laṅkā lay in the introduction of Roman Catholicism. In their zeal for proselytisation the Portuguese used force — they ruthlessly destroyed Buddhist and Hindu temples and gave temple properties over to the Roman Catholic orders — and the more conventional technique of preaching and teaching. As the religion of the establishment, Roman Catholicism would have had a potent appeal to those at the apex of the Sinhalese caste hierarchy (and probably among the Tamils as well) who aspired to high office or to the retention of their traditional position under the new dispensation — for which adherence to the established church was a necessary qualification. For the humble and the lowly, Roman Catholicism was a means of gaining the standing denied them under the traditional religions.

Under the Dutch the interconnection between religion and education continued, with the difference that the Calvinism of the Dutch Reformed Church replaced Roman Catholicism as the established religion. The Dutch set up two seminaries for "higher" education, and in general continued the schools established by the Portuguese. Religious persecution was now directed in the main against the Roman Catholics, whose harried clergy found a haven in the Kandyan kingdom in much the same way as Muslim refugees from Portuguese persecution had found a new home there in the past. Harassment of Hinduism and Islam continued though not with the same virulence as under the Portuguese. While they did not actually harass the Buddhists (for fear of offending the Kandyan ruler who regarded himself as the trustee of Buddhist rights in the island) they did not officially countenance Buddhism either. In general the Dutch encouraged the adoption of Calvinism by the people over whom they ruled — membership of the Dutch Reformed Church was a normal prerequisite for high office under the Dutch, the higher offices being confined to adherents of the Dutch Reformed Church. But Calvinism, unlike Roman Catholicism, did not develop any strong roots among the people. It is to the credit of the Portuguese that conversions to Roman Catholicism stood the test of persecution under the Dutch and the indifference of the British. Throughout the nineteenth and twentieth centuries the

Roman Catholics have constituted nine-tenths of the Christian community in the island.

[Under the Portuguese there was little or no interference with the old administrative hierarchy. Almost all the hereditary officials in the lower rungs of the hierarchy were continued in service by the Portuguese, as were many of the high-ranking *mudaliyārs*. Like the Portuguese the Dutch too used the native administrative hierarchy for their own purposes, leaving it much as they found it, except that the highest offices at the provincial level were confined to Dutchmen, but the *mudaliyārs* — the highest native officials — were not displaced so long as they made the necessary change in religious affiliation.]

In the same way the traditional service obligation of *rājakāriya* was made use of by the Portuguese for military purposes to gather conscripts for service under their hereditary officers.

Some changes were made, under Portuguese rule, in the traditional system of service obligations of the people to the government. The Portuguese preferred to use revenue farmers to collect taxes rather than rely entirely on officials for this purpose. The renters were required to pay fixed sums of money to the government. At the same time officials, whether Sinhala or Portuguese, were given land grants called *accomodessans* in the traditional Sinhalese manner, instead of salaries. The Portuguese did make an attempt to encourage *fidalgos* to settle in the island as landlord-tax collectors but not many were attracted by these offers. There was also one notable contribution of the Portuguese in the sphere of administration — in order to determine the state of the revenues, they compiled *tombos* or land registers of agricultural holdings.

Many of these trends were continued under Dutch rule. The changes they attempted in the system of land grants and land tenure did not have any far-reaching effects. Greater use was made of renters in the collection of taxes, and this was continued under their successors the British, who also maintained some of the tenurial changes introduced by the Dutch. Settlement of Dutch colonists was encouraged sporadically and with no greater success than similar colonisation experiments by *fidalgos* under the Portuguese.

"The Helen, or Bride in contest, of this isle", said Baldeus, a Dutch writer, "is the finest and purest cinnamon." The Portuguese and the Dutch monopolised the export trade in this valuable commodity. The resulting profits became the mainstay of the revenue of the territories they controlled in Sri Lanka. This marked the beginning of a fundamental change in the revenue system of the island — the dominance of the export sector over the traditional sector as a source of state revenue.]

One of the major contributions of the Dutch lay in the introduction of a plantation system. In the late eighteenth century they began cultivating cinnamon in plantations. Hitherto it had been the practice to gather the cinnamon bark from the trees that grew in the jungle. They also introduced other cash crops such as coffee, sugar, cotton and tobacco, but these were essentially minor products in comparison with cinnamon, and probably even in comparison with coconut.

The most lasting contribution of the Dutch lay in the judicial system which they established in the areas they controlled. Wherever possible, customary law was applied in their courts; the laws and customs of the Tamils of Jaffna were codified for the first time in the *Tesavalamai*, and the Muslims had their own Islamic law. In all other instances the Roman Dutch Law was used. The popularity of Roman Dutch law was such that by the first decade of the nineteenth century, when the British were in control of the maritime districts of Sri Lankā held by the Dutch, the customary laws of the Sinhalese had become obsolete.

During these centuries the traditional Sinhalese system prevailed in the Kandyan kingdom in the administrative machinery, the social structure and the economy. The changes which took place under Portuguese and Dutch rule in the littoral — these did not amount to anything very far-reaching — had little or no impact on the people of the Kandyan kingdom.

In the political sphere there were two fundamentally important developments. First, the fact that neither the Portuguese nor the Dutch succeeded in conquering the Kandyan kingdom was crucial in the emergence of a distinction between the Sinhalese of the maritime districts and those in the Kandyan areas. Indeed it could be said that the distinction was based on custom and outlook fostered by colonial rule in the one instance and the absence of it in the other. But it is important to remember that the sense of a distinct identity was not very sharp throughout these centuries. The new economic forces that had been introduced under the Portuguese and more particularly under the Dutch affected only limited areas on the littoral. There was regular migration of people between the Sinhalese of the southwest littoral and the Kandyan kingdom. Ethnicity and religious sentiment — pertaining to Buddhism — would not be confined by the artificial barrier imposed by western control of part of the Sinhalese areas, and in any case the political boundaries were never sharply defined. The Sinhalese under Portuguese and Dutch rule tended to regard the Kandyan ruler as king of all the Sinhalese.

Secondly, there was the record of resistance to western rule.

In this the Kandyan kingdom was the legatee of the Sītāvaka tradition. It is important to note, however, that a comparison between Sitāvaka and the Kandyan kingdom as defenders of Sinhalese independence would show that Sitāvaka's achievement was the more memorable of the two. For one thing Sītāvaka did not have the advantage of easily defensible frontiers; no mountain chains protected it, and the Kälani river, unlike the Mahavāli in the Kandyan areas, was navigable almost up to Sitāvaka by river craft which could transport men and arms for the Portuguese. What the two kingdoms had in common were the forests, and the men of Sītāvaka were as skilled in guerrilla warfare as the people of Kandy were to be. But the rulers of Sītāvaka were also adept in the arts of conventional warfare, the open confrontation between armies on a battlefield. Very early they had learnt the techniques of modern warfare and military technology, and more than once the rulers of Sītavāka proved to be a match, or more than a match, for the Portuguese in conventional warfare. In this sense no Sinhalese ruler of the future bore comparison with Māyadunnē and Rājasinha I as warriors; they seldom had to bear the same heavy odds as those which faced the rulers of Sītāvaka.

The guiding principle of British imperial policy in relation to India from the mid-eighteenth century was the desire to prevent the French from filling the power vacuum caused by the break-up of Mughal supremacy and order. The threat to the Dutch in the maritime regions of Sri Lankā and British interest in the island emerged from this. The island's main attraction to the British lay in its supremely important strategic position/ and the harbour of Trincomalee.

The rigorous terms imposed by the Dutch on the Kandyans by the treaty of 1766 spurred them to a feverish search for foreign assistance in expelling the Dutch from Sri Lankā. The Kandyans' passionate pursuit of a policy of revenge against the Dutch coincided with the development of the penultimate phase in the Anglo-French conflict for the control of India in the last quarter of the eighteenth century. For at this time Sri Lankā, and Trincomalee in particular, loomed large in the calculations and schemes of British statesmen. Throughout this period the British had access to Trincomalee harbour, in times of peace as well as of war, and they had no reason therefore to commit themselves to supporting the Kandyans against the Dutch. But in the last two decades of the eighteenth century British relations with the Dutch deteriorated sharply, and as a result the British were willing to change their policy with regard to Sri Lankā. Dutch relations with the French were increasingly

cordial, and with the outbreak of the French Revolution the new
revolutionary ideology found a receptive soil in the Dutch Republic
and the British needed to move swiftly to prevent the transfer of
the Dutch colonies in Asia to French control.

⟨Military action against the Dutch in Srī Laṅkā was preceded by
the renewal of diplomatic negotiations with the Kandyans in 1795.⟩
On two previous occasions in 1762 and 1782, British missions to
Kandy had failed to respond positively to Kandyan requests for
assistance against the Dutch. Now the British offered the Kandyans
a draft treaty whose clauses were much more favourable to them
than the treaty imposed by the Dutch in 1766. On this occasion it
was the Kandyans who held back — in the hope of extracting more
favourable terms. But soon the British were in command of the
former Dutch possessions in Srī Laṅkā without any substantial
assistance from the Kandyans. The British did not for a while
realise the extent of the concessions made by the Kandyans to the
Dutch by the treaty of 1766. And the Kandyans were in no hurry to
put them wise. But it was impossible to conceal this for long, and
the British, once they were aware of the clauses of the treaty, recognised the strength of their legal position as successors to the Dutch
by virtue of conquest of a coastal belt extending round the island
but in depth seldom stretching more than 20 miles into the interior.

⟨With the British conquest of the former Dutch possessions in Srī
Laṅkā, the balance of power in the island had shifted decisively
against the Kandyans. The Kandyan policy of seeking foreign
assistance to oust the European power established on the littoral
had on this occasion led to the substitution of a very powerful
neighbour for a weak one. Not only were the British the most formidable imperial power at this time but they were also in the process of expanding their possessions in the Indian sub-continent at
the expense of all rivals, indigenous and foreign, to the point where
they had emerged, by the end of the eighteenth century, as clearly
the dominant force in South Asia. More important, the success of
the Kandyans against repeated Portuguese and Dutch encroachments, and the continued survival of the Kandyan kingdom in the
seventeenth and eighteenth centuries engendered among the Kandyans a feeling of self-confidence that bordered on a complacent
assumption of invincibility. And yet the survival of the Kandyan
kingdom was due more to the inadequacy of the resources of the
Portuguese and the Dutch for the purpose of subjugating the
Kandyan kingdom than to the inherent military strength of
the latter. The British were an altogether more formidable proposition.

But there was a preliminary issue to be settled: whether the

British conquests in Sri Laṅkā should be returned to the Dutch when hostilities ceased in Europe, the main theatre of war, or whether they would be retained as a British possession. The uncertain political future of these territories was reflected in the arrangements devised in 1796 for their administration. They were placed under the Madras Government of the East India Company, who proceeded to adopt a variety of expedients to recoup from these territories the costs of the conquest and military occupation. By 1797 Whitehall had taken the decision to retain these territories as a British possession, and compelled a reluctant East India Company to share the administration with the Crown. The Company was guaranteed a monopoly of trade, the most coveted portion of which was the cinnamon trade, once a flourishing venture but now yielding a moderate profit. This system of 'Dual Control' lasted from 1798 to 1802 when at last, following the cession to the British by the Peace of Amiens in 1801, the former Dutch possessions in Sri Laṅkā became a British crown colony.

From this brief, but essentially unhappy association with Madras and the English East India Company, Sri Laṅkā gained one inestimable advantage. In future, whenever it was suggested that for the sake of economy or administrative convenience the island should be treated as an integral part of the Indian empire, the memory of these unhappy years served as a reminder of the perils involved.

In the meantime the British turned to the Kandyan problem. The disputed succession to the Kandyan throne at the death of Rājādi Rājasiṅha in 1798 afforded opportunities for interference in Kandyan affairs which the British governor, Frederick North, impetuously sought to exploit. What he had in mind originally was a scheme for the establishment of a controlling British interest in Kandy, and a policy of "limited" interference in Kandyan affairs. But, once the intrigue began, North was no more in full control of the situation than those in the Kandyan kingdom who sought to use the British for their own personal interests and against the king. What began as an attempt at limited interference soon assumed the proportion of a purposeful bid to subjugate Kandy and round off total control over Sri Laṅkā. It was with this purpose that the first British expedition against Kandy set out in 1803; it met with defeat as had so many Portuguese and Dutch expeditions in the past. The real cause of the disaster was the inadequacy of North's planning for an expedition of this magnitude.

But within a dozen years of this successful resistance to invasion, the Kandyan kingdom was ceded to the British. In 1815, largely because of divisions within the Kandyan kingdom, the British were

able to overthrow the Nāyakkar dynasty and establish their control.]
The monarchy, long established and cherished in popular sentiment, was so readily overthrown because of the alienation of nearly
all the conservative and influential elements in Kandyan society
by Sri Vikrama Rājasinha (in contrast to his Nāyakkar predecessors). But because the British owed so much to the assistance rendered in this enterprise by the aristocracy and the *bhikkhus,* the Kandyan
Convention which embodied the terms of cession upheld many of
their privileges and above all else promised support and maintenance to the Buddhist religion.

The cession of the Kandyan kingdom to the British did not stem
from some deep-rooted crisis of confidence in the institutional and
ideological structure of Kandyan society but from a political conflict which was mainly confined to the king and the aristocracy. The
substitution of British control for Nāyakkar rule had the effect of
reinforcing and deepening the commitment to the old society,
and to the institutions, secular and religious, associated with it. All
strata of Kandyan society were involved. Nostalgia for the traditional monarchical forces — the one element of the old system which
the British quite deliberately eliminated — affected far more than
simply the aristocracy. The passion for monarchical restoration
re-kindled the old Kandyan traditions of resistance to the foreigner.
And the sense of loss felt by the Kandyans at the removal of the
indigenous monarchy became, within a very short time of the establishment of British rule, a powerful and combustible political force
which needed only a spark or two to be ignited. British administrators in the Kandyan provinces, though not deliberately insensitive
to Kandyan feelings, nevertheless gave adequate cause for dissatisfaction with the manner in which the undertakings given in 1815
were being carried out, and this led in 1817-18 to a widespread
rebellion against British rule. This the 'Great Rebellion', was much
the most formidable insurrection during the whole period of the
British occupation of Srı Laṅka.

[When, after a long and ruthless campaign, the resistance of the
Kandyans was broken at last, the British were effectively rulers of
the whole·of Srī Laṅkā. For the first time since the days of Vijaya-
bahu I, Parākramabahu I and Nissaṅkā Malla, the island was under
the control of a single power/ Between them and 1818 only Parākramabahu VI of Kōttē laid claim to a similar all-island control,
but his claims to this status were more aspirations than actual
achievements. The British had achieved what Kōttē, the Portuguese and the Dutch had so signally failed to do—to conquer the
Kandyan kingdom. Thus the year 1818 marks a true turning-point
in the history of Srī Laṅkā.

The Consolidation of British Rule

The cession of the Kandyan kingdom and the suppression of the Great Rebellion made little difference to the basic pattern of British rule in Srī Laṅkā — the island was viewed as fundamentally a military station and valued for the protection it afforded the expanding British possessions in India. There was also a second notable trend in policy, a tightening of the British grip on the Kandyan provinces. The separate administrative system for the Kandyan provinces established in 1815 was continued beyond 1818, despite the suppression of the rebellion. The maintenance of two separate administrative systems was eminently justified considering the special problems of administration in the Kandyan kingdom. In the 1820s one sees a steady consolidation of British rule, largely through the road system constructed on the initiative of Governor Sir Edward Barnes. These roads, built with the help of compulsory labour under the traditional *rājakāriya* system, placed the military control of the Kandyan provinces firmly in British hands; indeed this road system sealed the fate of this region as effectively as roads sealed the fate of the Highlands of Scotland after the Jacobite threat of the '45 rebellion. The secret of Kandy's long and successful survival in face of over two centuries of attempts by western powers at conquest lay in the fact that the bulk of the country was a wilderness suited to guerrilla warfare of which the Kandyans were masters. No longer now could guerrilla tactics cut communications between garrisons or hold up troop movements.

This conception of Srī Laṅkā as a strategic entity served to inhibit reform and innovation in the administration, the economy and the social structure. The variety of the island's resources, however, would appear to have tempted early governors to indulge in some piecemeal reforms. Indeed, in the Maritime Provinces the first two decades of British rule were characterised by an urge to break away from some of the rigours of the Dutch pattern of administration. But the sum total of these modifications did not amount to a fundamental change in the system of administration which the British had inherited, nor was there any system or pattern in the innovations attempted. To a large extent near-bankruptcy of the economy prevented the adoption of measures of reform entailing substantial expenditure. The Colonial Office was opposed to financing even the most beneficient projects so long as the colonial revenues could not meet the basic expenses of administration and the armed forces; this opposition was so much stronger because Srī Laṅkā, like Cape Colony, was viewed at Whitehall mainly in terms of its strategic value in relation to India, little thought being given to the possibilities of developing or improving its natural resources.

In the 1820s Governor Barnes was associated with attempts at experimenting in a variety of commercial crops, coffee being the most important, aimed at inducing a measure of buoyancy into a stagnant economy dependent on a visibly declining cinnamon trade. Though these experiments bore fruit only a decade later, the fact that they were attempted is proof of a reformist turn of mind. Curiously, though, these experiments were in a sense a continuation of Dutch policy. It is an indication at once of the strength of the Dutch pattern of colonialism, and of the futility of attempts to break away from it as long as the basic assumptions of the successor regime were so much like those of the Dutch.

In the first three decades of British rule in Srī Laṅkā, the one consistent agent of change was the missionary. Much more than the soldier and the administrator, he was committed to the advocacy of change, the more because he had seldom to bear the consequences of impulsive attempts at evangelisation and was therefore much less concerned with the administrator's and the soldier's preoccupation with the maintenance of political stability. British missionary groups could look forward to no systematic support from the state, though individual governors gave them intermittent assistance. The reluctance of the state to afford consistent support may be explained largely by their fear that missionary activity might provoke opposition and lead to embarrassing incidents; they were always conscious of the political consequences of a disturbance of the traditional religious observances of the people. Hence the missionaries were discouraged from penetrating into the Kandyan region where the traditional culture and the Buddhist religion were at their strongest. In the maritime provinces which had been exposed to the influence of Christianity since the sixteenth century, there were fewer restrictions on missionary activity.

Economic stagnation continued to affect the country until the 1830s, when the gradual success of coffee culture revolutionised the economy. By the 1830s the British, as indisputed masters of the Indian seas, were in the process of consolidating their possessions in India, and had more time to ponder the possibilities of profitably developing the economy of the island and settling its major political problems. The appointment of the Commission of Eastern Inquiry — the Colebrooke-Cameron Commission — was evidence that the Colonial Office had decided on a new phase in the colony's development.

The Colebrooke-Cameron reforms were an integrated and in many ways radical set of reform proposals. They aimed at establishing in Srī Laṅkā the superstructure of the *laissez-faire* state. They had much in common with reforms then being introduced in British

India, but were more far-reaching in their impact and more consistent in the application of current liberalism.

As adherents of *laissez-faire* and free trade, the Commissioners were opposed to mercantilism, state monopolies, discriminatory administrative regulations and in general to any interference of the state in the economy. Thus they recommended the abolition of the cinnamon monopoly, the commanding height of the mercantilist economic structure which the British had inherited and developed. As regards *rājakāriya*, Colebrooke and Cameron were opposed to it on humanitarian' grounds — to them it savoured of feudalism and feudal oppression — but these were by no means the only considerations in their forthright insistence on its abolition. *Rājakāriya* was at once an obstacle to the creation of a land market, and to the free movement of labour, important considerations in "creating an environment conducive to the growth of private enterprise".

It is impossible in a survey as brief as this to review all aspects of these reforms. But some need particular emphasis. The Charter of Justice of 1833, based on Cameron's report, marks the beginning of the modern judicial system in the island. It established a uniform judicial system for Srī Laṅkā. There was also their valuable contribution to the island's future political development — to give it a more liberal form of government than that which prevailed before 1833. The truly remarkable feature of the Legislative Council established in 1833 on Colebrooke's recommendation, was not so much the existence of an official majority within it as the presence of unofficials. As a measure of constitutional reform, it was far ahead of anything prevalent at that time in India or other non-white colonies.

In 1833, in acceptance of Colebrooke's proposals, the separate existence of the Kandyan provinces was abolished and they were amalgamated with the Maritime provinces in a single unified administrative structure for the whole island. The provincial boundaries within the two administrative divisions — the Kandyan and Maritime provinces — were replaced by a new set of provincial units, five in all, in which only one — the Central province — was purely Kandyan. The new provincial boundaries cut across the traditional divisions and placed many Kandyan regions under the administrative control of the old Maritime provinces. In this simple but crude manner, an administrative (including judicial) and legislative unification was imposed on Srī Laṅkā, and a policy of absorbing and assimilating the old Kandyan kingdom within this structure was initiated as a means of obliterating the sense of nationality among the Kandyans.

The Colebrooke-Cameron reforms, all in all, were the first well-integrated system of reforms introduced after the establishment of

British rule in the island. They marked the first systematic and successful attempt to break away from the Dutch pattern of colonial administration and to reject its basic assumptions in favour of a more enlightened form of government.

A period of experimentation in plantation crops began in the mid-1830s, and within fifteen years the success of one of these, coffee, radically transformed the island's economy. The stimulus to this rapid expansion of coffee cultivation was provided by a steep increase in the consumption of coffee in Great Britain and Western Europe, and to a lesser extent by the protection accorded to colonial as against foreign coffee in the British market. The extraordinary success of coffee in these years should not divert attention from its failure to establish a distinct ascendancy over other crops like sugar and cotton in which European planters were investing till the mid-1840s. Capital for investment in Ceylon's plantations was very limited and this tended to concentrate on the one successful enterprise, coffee. There was another parallel development — the decline of the cinnamon industry, which had been till this period the staple of the island's export economy and very much the most prominent — and productive of revenue — of the trade monopolies controlled by the state. (The monopoly was abolished on the recommendations of Colebrooke.) Thus by the mid-nineteenth century there was every prospect that the island's economic development in the immediate future would be characterised by monoculture in its plantation sector.

The overwhelming predominance of coffee as a plantation industry was not maintained for long. By the 1860s coconut had emerged as a plantation crop with great potential for expansion. From the late 1860s tea and cinchona established footholds in the plantation districts and soon ceased to be merely experimental crops. Over the next decade they remained in the shadow of the giant coffee industry, but both had demonstrated their viability as commercial ventures, and their potential for future development into thriving industries.

During the four decades beginning in 1850 the coffee industry was in a preponderant position in the export economy. From 1830 to 1880 it was the catalyst of modernisation of the economy; indeed it generated a momentum that made possible the process of modernisation. Since the main centre of coffee production was the Kandyan provinces, the expansion of coffee and the network of roads and railways broke the isolation of the old Kandyan kingdom, and brought it into the modern sector of the economy. The plantations were the economic basis for the unification of the island, consolidating the process of unification set in motion by the ad-

ministrative and judicial reforms of 1832. The economic factor, in
this instance, provided a stronger bond of unification than administrative and political reforms. But coffee was stricken by *hemleia
vastratrix*, a leaf disease, which spread remorselessly in all the plantation districts in the decade beginning 1870. Within fifteen years
the coffee industry was destroyed, never to recover.

Nevertheless, one of the striking features of the island's economic history in the last quarter of the nineteenth century was the
remarkable resilience of the plantation economy from the near
bankruptcy to which it seemed destined when the coffee industry
collapsed. The three decades 1880-1910 mark a period of sustained
growth in the plantation sector of the economy which matched, if
it did not surpass, that achieved in the coffee era. It is in these years
that the pattern of an overwhelming dominance of three major
plantation crops — tea, rubber and coconut — in the island's economy was established and which has perhaps survived for too long
in the face of all efforts to diversify the economy and to reduce its
overwhelming dependence on them. Of these crops, tea and rubber
(and especially the latter) emerged into full bloom after the collapse
of the coffee industry. Coconut, on the other hand, had a longer
history as a plantation crop from the early years of the coffee era.
In terms of the area which it occupied, the coconut industry was
much the largest of these plantation industries by the end of the
nineteenth century.

Looking back from 1910 to 1850 there had been a remarkable
transformation of the island's economy. The modern or export
sector of Srī Laṅkā economy was much larger in relation to the traditional sector than was the case in many tropical colonies. There
is no doubt that the development of the plantations enabled the
country to achieve a modest breakthrough towards prosperity in
the nineteenth century. Its stimulus was sufficiently powerful to
give Srī Laṅkā a standard of living well ahead of the rest of South
Asia, and most of South-east Asia, with the possible exception of
Singapore and parts of the Federated Malay States.

Moreover, at every stage segments of the indigenous population
participated in plantation agriculture. Local capitalists, smallholders and peasants controlled over one-third of the acreage under
coffee. They were influential in rubber as well and predominant in
coconut, while their share of the tea industry was more modest. Thus
indigenous planters, capitalists, smallholders and peasants played
a more prominent role in plantation agriculture than their counterparts in most other tropical colonies.

Labour on the coffee plantations was predominantly (but not
exclusively) immigrant Indian. At first this immigration was sea-

sonal. The coffee plantations did not require the maintenance of a permanent supply of resident labour. Tea and, to a lesser extent, rubber did require such a permanent supply of resident labour, and as a result there developed a fundamental change in the character of the immigration of Indian labour. Immigrant labourers from India were also employed in road building and the construction of railways and harbours, and in various forms of hard, tedious and unpleasant work in the towns. By the end of the nineteenth century a plantation and urban proletariat had emerged, but cut off from the local population by language and culture — and living in the plantations or in the slums of the towns. Thus another element of plurality had been added to the island's multi-racial society, and one which was to have profound consequences for the future. Srī Laṅkā's Indian problem, in its modern form, had emerged.

This was not the sole or even the most significant of the adverse effects of the rapid expansion of plantation agriculture in the period after 1830. One of the most controversial of these latter has been the land question, the sale of land by the state to planters for conversion into plantations, and the development of a land market. Indeed the sale of land for plantation agriculture, and the legislation introduced for this purpose, became one of the most emotion-charged issues in the Kandyan areas. They were necessary instruments of the intrusion of a dynamic capitalist structure into a region of the country which had preserved the traditional economic structure in its pristine form much more than the littoral which had come under western rule earlier. It has been argued that these land sales deprived the peasants in the Kandyan areas of land which had traditionally been available to them for their own use, and that the consequence was the emergence of landlessness as a serious problem in this region. No doubt there is a measure of justice in this charge, but it is basically an exaggeration. For in the coffee era (1830-80) there was an adequate supply of land in the periphery of the villages for the potential cultivation needs of the immediate future. More important, peasants and smallholders had converted lands in their control for the production of coffee, and one-third of the acreage under coffee was held by them. Indeed it was with the development of rubber and coconut cultivation in the last quarter of the nineteenth century, and the expansion of plantation agriculture into the low country, which was more densely populated than the Kandyan areas, that the ratio of peasant and indigenous landholdings to population became increasingly unfavourable. If, at the end of the nineteenth century, this ratio was unfavourable in any part of the country, it was not in the Central province and Uva, but in the plantation districts in the low country.

⎧One of the adverse effects of the expansion of plantation agriculture was the lop-sided development of the economy, and the comparative neglect of traditional agriculture.⎦This theme is of sufficient importance to be treated as a separate topic in this discussion.

Till the middle of the nineteenth century, the colonial administration in Srī Laṅkā had shown little concern for the welfare of the peasant population. The focus of attention and interest was always on the development of the plantations. A change began under Governor Sir Henry Ward (1855-60) with regard to irrigation. Over the next fifty years a sustained, though not unbroken, effort was made to rehabilitate the dry zone through a revival of the ancient irrigation works there. As a result, there was an increase in the area under cultivation. Though this was modest and moderate in comparison with the investment involved, it was — in historical perspective — the first such extension in cultivation in the dry zone for several centuries. For the first time since the days of the Polonnaruva kings, a positive effort was made to repair and restore the irrigation facilities of the heartland of the ancient irrigation civilisation of the Sinhalese. It also marked the reversal of the tendency to neglect peasant agriculture, which had been a feature of the early years of British rule.

But the principal achievement and object of this programme of irrigation activity was to convert irregular cultivation into regular cultivation, rather than open up new areas for peasant agriculture. The irrigation programme did not amount to a formulation of a comprehensive policy on peasant agriculture. It did not touch the wet zone where, by the 1890s, peasant agriculture and plantation activity were in unequal competition. Plantation crops were regarded as being unquestionably more profitable than paddy cultivation.

There was, in fact, an increase of about 200,000 acres in land under rice production during the nineteenth century. Of this a substantial proportion was in the wet zone, where irrigation was unimportant or unnecessary.⎛Nevertheless this increase in the area under paddy cultivation, in general, represents a not insignificant achievement, considering the fact that there was at the same time an expansion of the area under plantation crops—mainly coffee, coconut and tea, but also rubber by the last decade of the nineteenth century. The expansion in paddy cultivation kept pace with the growth of population.⎦

Except in a few areas subsistence production of paddy was the norm. Paddy was not produced for the market⎛Secondly, low yields per acre were a general feature of paddy production in Srī Laṅkā.⎤

Productivity of rice lands in the island was among the lowest in Asia, and this persisted well into the twentieth century. Indeed in the whole of the dry zone only one region, the Jaffna peninsula, supported an efficient and intensive system of cultivation of food crops. But it had certain natural and other advantages, which served to delineate the factors operating as obstacles to the emergence of a similar system in other parts of the dry zone. On the whole, traditional techniques of cultivation were not changed, and few technical innovations were attempted. Paddy production seldom, if ever, attracted capitalists or large commercial firms, since the profits seemed so much more limited than in the island's main commercial crops.

Thirdly, the island was not self-sufficient in rice, and was dependent on imports. Two segments of the population had developed a taste for imported varieties of rice — the élite groups and the immigrant labourers, the latter being by far the larger of these two. They would not consume the locally produced rice, and the planters began the practice of providing them with imported rice. Thus the increase in the demand for rice which emerged with the entry of immigrant labour did not serve as a stimulus to the expansion of local production. In any case, imported rice was relatively cheap. Nor would the government of the day have thought of imposing protective tariffs in favour of local rice production if such a demand had been made — in fact, there was no such demand.

There were sporadic attempts at a more emphatic attitude of support for peasant landholdings during the second half of the nineteenth century, but at no stage were the implications of this fully spelled out. Nor, as we have shown earlier, was there any sustained attempt to develop a comprehensive policy on peasant agriculture. The attitude to many problems of peasant agriculture can only be described as unimaginative and misguided when not hard-hearted.

Throughout the last quarter of the nineteenth century and the first decade of the twentieth, there are frequent references in published official documents to famines, conditions of near-famine, chronic rural poverty, destitution, and above all to starvation in many parts of the country especially in the dry zone. Clearly, the living standards of the rural population in most parts of the country had shown no improvement after a whole century of British administration. Peace and stability, the British had undoubtedly brought, but the economic hardships of the Sinhalese peasant had not been alleviated in any substantial way.

In the early years the transformation of the economy through investment in plantation agriculture had its parallel in other spheres as well. The reformist momentum generated by the Cole-brooke-Cameron reforms did not exhaust itself for at least two decades. And every sphere of activity, political, economic and social was affected by a passion for aggressive change. Indeed these decades form a strong contrast to the last quarter of the nineteenth century when the British administration became a conservative force. It was only in plantation enterprise that the old zest and energy was maintained.

In this first phase reformist zeal was most notable in matters relating to religion. This was due to the Evangelical influence at the Colonial Office, and to men like Governor Stewart Mackenzie (1837-41) and many officials in the colony who believed in the urgency of converting the "heathen" to Christianity; and partly to the agitation of the missionary organisations for a redefinition of the relationship between Buddhism and the colonial government in the island which had been established by the Kandyan Convention of 1815. The same forces were behind an emphasis on the expansion of schools and investment in education in general.

There was less scope for the social reformers in Srī Laṅkā than in India since the indigenous religions had no glaring social abuses in any way associated with them — no *sati, thugi* or infanticide, and no ritual ceremonies of the type associated with the temple of Jagan-nāth in India. As for caste, had there been something as morally or socially repugnant as untouchability, it might have been possible to focus attention on it and compel the adoption of a positive reformist policy, but untouchability scarcely existed in the island, where the caste system — among the Buddhists — was much less rigid than the Indian counterpart. It was too amorphous to be tackled by a precise and deliberate policy. Neither the administrators nor the missionaries had a clear policy on caste beyond a vague egalitarianism.

Nevertheless, at this stage the government acted on the conviction that the caste system was obnoxious and intolerable, and was opposed to any recognition of caste distinctions. On the contrary, more than once positive declarations were made explicitly and ostentatiously directed at caste discrimination. Of these the most notable were the abolition of *rājakāriya* in 1832-3 and the firm refusal to recognise caste distinctions in the formation of juries when this became a matter of controversy in 1843. Again in appointments to posts of *mudaliyār*, the claims of men of distinction and achievement who belonged to the emerging castes such as the *karāva* and *salāgama* were recognised to the chagrin of the *goyigama mudaliyārs* who resented this breach of the monopoly they claimed over such appointments on the basis of caste privilege.

But the most striking impact of the influence of Evangelicalism and the missionaries was in the severance of the connection between Buddhism and the state. The crucial policy decisions on this were taken in Whitehall in the 1840s, despite the opposition of the Kandyans and the obvious lack of enthusiasm for this course of action demonstrated by the more cautious local administration. The "rebellion" of 1848 compelled a re-appraisal of the Buddhist policy of the British government, largely because it was recognised that it had contributed to the alienation of the Kandyan aristocracy and the *bhikkus* who, as the natural and traditional leaders of Kandyan opinion, looked upon the ostentatious dissociation of the state from Buddhism as a gross betrayal of the solemn undertaking given on the occasion of the signing of the Kandyan Convention. The dissociation marked the severance of an intimate connection between the Buddhist religion and the rulers of Sri Lankā which had lasted from the early days of the Anurādhapura kingdom. The withdrawal of the traditional patronage accorded to Buddhism, with its consequent loss of precedence and prestige, was deeply resented. The compromise settlement effected in 1852 was not a satisfactory one. Although an effective administrative machinery for the control of Buddhist temporalities was promised, it did not come about for several decades thereafter. The steady deterioration in the administration of Buddhist temporalities was one of the persistent complaints of the Buddhists, whose sense of grievance against the government was thus aggravated.

In the early 1840s the mild form of predail slavery existing in the island was abolished. The Kandyan Marriage Ordinance of 1859, which sought to end polyandrous marriages among the Kandyans, was the last notable piece of social reform in the three decades after 1833.

This reformist zeal had its influence in the political sphere as well. The British were wary of the *mudaliyārs* in the low country, and while they were permitted to retain their positions in the lower rungs of the administrative machinery, they were deprived of much of their influence. On the other hand, the British were positively suspicious of the Kandyan aristocracy whom they regarded as potentially the main source of opposition to their own rule. And the policy of using changes in provincial boundaries to break the national feeling of the Kandyans was continued beyond 1833: in 1845, when the North-western province was formed as a sixth provincial unit, this was the main argument advanced in support of the decision.

The last quarter of the nineteenth century affords a striking contrast to this period of aggressive reformist zeal. The first most notable reversal of policy was with regard to Buddhism. At this time there was a strong Buddhist revival, which two of the most dynamic governors of this period, Gregory and Gordon, sought to channel into a conservative mould. Gregory initiated a policy of active interest in and sympathy for Buddhism, by according a judicious measure of patronage to the Buddhist revival and consciously seeking to emphasise the government's neutrality in religious affairs. Gordon not only continued this policy but endeavoured to underscore the principle of a special obligation towards Buddhism.

The change in policy was equally decisive with regard to caste, and to the related problem of the *mudaliyārs* and the Kandyan aristocracy. One of the main features of the processes of social change in operation at this time was the emergence to prominence of the dynamic, aggressive and wealthy *karāva* caste. The affluent *karāvas* posed a challenge to the *goyigama* dominance of public life and were the spearhead of a political and constitutional reform movement. To be sure, their political ambitions were as narrowly limited as those of the men they sought to displace. Governor Gordon threw his influence on the side of the *goyigama* establishment against their challengers in a well-publicised reversal of the traditional British attitude of not countenancing caste prejudices.

Earlier Gregory had initiated an even more noteworthy change by boldly reversing the attitude — discernible since the Great Rebellion of 1817-18 — of being wary of the powers and privileges of the Kandyan aristocracy, whom he considered safe enough to be admitted to a junior partnership in the administration of the country. Gordon went a stage further in his indefatigable enthusiasm to bolster the claims of the chiefs to influence and power. Where Gregory had been driven by sentiment and impulse, Gordon was purposeful in his policy of aristocratic revival, disregarding the claims and demands of better educated men of other social groups and those of the emerging castes to equality of opportunity. The policy of aristocratic resuscitation was enthusiastically continued by Governor MacCallum in the first decade of the twentieth century, and once again the reason behind this was political — to build a counterweight to the more assertive sections of the educated élite who were demanding a share of political power in the colony.

Gregory's administration was notable also for one other development in administrative policy — a reversal of the earlier policy of using changes in provincial boundaries to break up the unity of the Kandyan provinces. Between 1873 and 1889 three Kandyan provinces — the North Central, Uva and Sabaragamuva — were carved out, giving expression to the fact that the Kandyan problem, in the sense of a "traditional" nationalism guided by an aristocratic leadership, had ceased to be a serious threat to the continued stability of British rule. Thus the policy that had prevailed since 1833 was abandoned — only because the political factor on which it was based had lost its validity.

By the last quarter of the nineteenth century the long history of Kandyan resistance to the British had come to an end. Between the 1880s and the attainment of independence, the Kandyans mostly took satisfaction in a new role — as associates of the British and as a counterweight to the reform and nationalist movements dominated by the western-educated élite of the low country. The leaders of Kandyan opinion seldom showed much sympathy for the political aspirations of these movements. They stood aloof and suspicious when not positively hostile.

One of the most far-reaching effects of the development of a capitalist economy on the foundation of plantation agriculture and trade was the growth of a new élite who were largely an indigenous capitalist class for whom the wealth they accumulated through capitalist enterprise became a very effective channel of social mobility. Apart from investment in plantation agriculture, the most significant avenues of profit-making were the control of graphite mining and export and the transport of coffee by carts, which was very much in the hands of the Sinhalese; but most profitable and productive was the liquor industry. The new capitalist class used the wealth they accumulated for the education of their children in British and European universities largely, and thus bolstered the élite status they had won through success in commercial ventures.

It is important to remember that the traditional élite — the *mudaliyārs* in the low country and to a lesser extent the Kandyan aristocracy — were not displaced. They were absorbed into this expanding new élite. Indeed the opportunities of acquiring a western education through the schools opened by the missionaries and the state were used to great advantage by the *mudaliyārs* in the early nineteenth century as a means of consolidating their position at the apex of the local social hierarchy. And they were among the first to convert their landholdings for commercial production of plantation crops. Thus they shared with the new men two attributes of élite status — the acquisition of a western education and participation in capitalist enterprise.

But they were soon left far behind in both these areas. Much to the resentment of the *mudaliyārs*, élite status became much less dependent on hereditary privilege and the holding of government

office. Thus élite competition became a feature of the late nineteenth century as the *mudaliyār* class found their privileged position increasingly under attack by men who were far richer and better
educated than themselves. Among the most assertive and affluent
segments of the new capitalist class were members of the *karāva*
caste, and as a result élite competition became very much a matter
of caste rivalry as well. Indeed one of the most striking developments in the social and political life of the élite in the last quarter
of the nineteenth century was the challenge posed by the *karāvas*
to the *goyigama* establishment — the *mudaliyārs* — whose claims to
primacy were based on caste privilege and hereditary status. One
other feature of this process of social change is noteworthy. The
capitalist class were largely low-country Sinhalese with a sprinkling
of Tamils and other minority groups. Kandyan representation
within it was extremely small. All these features were to have profound consequences upon the future political evolution of the
country.

As in many other parts of Asia, the origins of modern nationalism
may be traced back to the programmes of religious revivalism which
were a reaction to Christian missionary enterprise. This first phase
in the emergence of nationalism in Srī Laṅkā would cover the last
three decades of the nineteenth century. While incipient nationalist sentiment was primarily religious in outlook and content —
asserting the need for the primacy of Buddhist values and claiming
that Buddhism was in danger — political overtones in it were
visible from its inception especially in the appeal to the indigenous past as against a contemporary situation of foreign domination.

These political overtones became more pronounced in the first
two decades of the twentieth century with the growth of the temperance movement. Indeed, by the end of the nineteenth century
a sustained temperance agitation gave added momentum to the
growth of nationalist sentiment. This agitation became at once an
integral part of the Buddhist revival and an introduction — tentative and astutely restrained — to political activity, the rallying-
point of the recovery of national consciousness.

The chief centre of activity was the low country, and there
religious revivalism and temperance agitation demonstrated many
of the characteristics of modern mass nationalism (nothing on the
lines of this "religious nationalism" reappeared in Srī Laṅkā on
the same scale of intensity till after independence). Surprisingly
a movement such as this, with an appeal affecting not merely the
elite but the people at large, had little impact on the formal political
activity of the élite. On the whole, the Buddhist movement in

general lacked an institutional apparatus which might have been converted into a political organisation. No attempt was made to channel the mass emotions evoked by this temperance campaign into a sustained and organised political movement. The politicisation of the temperance movement, once its appeal to the people became evident, seemed the logical and inevitable next step, but this was never taken. Equally significantly, the mass grass-roots support achieved by the temperance agitation was secured without the assistance of such political associations or organisations as existed, the chief of which was the Ceylon National Association.

The Twentieth Century, to 1948

In the first two decades of the twentieth century the colonial administration in the island successfully withstood the pressures of the elite for a share in the administration of the country. They were in no mood to make major concessions to these demands. Faith in the permanence of the British control over the affairs of the island remained largely unshaken. It was an assumption not confined to the colonial administration but shared by influential sections of the elite engaged in political activity. Indeed at the turn of the century nobody in public life in the island could have imagined that Srī Lankā would attain the status of an independent state within five decades. Any such suggestion would have been dismissed as visionary and impractical.

The most prominent feature of nationalist agitation at this time was the role within it of the reform movement. Its keynote was an emphasis on constitutional reform as the major goal of political endeavour, an insistence on the need to reconcile Srī Lankān patriotism with loyalty to Britain, and the belief that these were complementary and not inherently incompatible. Those at the helm of the reform movement—the "constitutionalists"—steeped in the British Liberal tradition, placed their hopes in the establishment, in the course of time, of a Srī Lankā version of the British system of parliamentary government. They showed scant interest in broadening the bases of their political organizations, and were strongly opposed to techniques of agitation that would bring the masses into politics. These attitudes were influential and powerful political forces in Srī Lankā throughout the first half of the twentieth century. Although the endeavours of men in the reform movement contributed to the eventual transfer of power from British hands, many of them were not consciously motivated by a desire to shake off the bonds of colonial rule. They did not think this to be possible in their lifetime.

Some of them played an active role in the temperance movement.

There they had evoked a positive response from the people by appealing to them on an issue that was meaningful in terms of the traditional cultural and social patterns of the country. But they were not
interested in politicizing the movement, or in the efforts to forge an
ideological link between resurgent Buddhism and incipient nationalist agitation.

The Sinhalese-Muslim riots of 1915, or rather the methods used by
the colonial authorities in suppressing them and—even more—in
punishing the accused embittered most sections of the elite. While
this ought to have stimulated greater enthusiasm in organised
political activity, the immediate effect, curiously enough, was
to act as a restraint. After the riots no serious attempt was made
to revive the temperance movement on the old scale or on the
old basis. And there was no move towards a more pronounced
radicalisation of politics nor was there any significant attempt
at broadening the bases of existing political organisations,
much less any efforts at politicising the masses. True, the Ceylon
National Congress was established in 1919, but what was significant
in this was the long struggle that had to be waged before it could be
established, and the lethargy — if not active opposition — of influential sections of the elite who were perturbed by the prospects, which
such an organisation held out, of agitational politics, and feared
the potential trends towards radicalism inherent in broadening
the bases of existing political organisations. And if men like Sir
Ponnambalam Arunachalam, who led the movement for its establishment, regarded the Ceylon National Congress as the local
counterpart of the Indian National Congress, they were soon in a
small minority in its governing body. The Ceylon National
Congress was from the first an élitist organisation dominated by
conservatives.

In contrast to the first two decades of the twentieth century, the
1920s were characterised by bolder political initiatives. In retrospect, they marked the first phase in the transfer of power, when
the British, at Whitehall and in the colonial administration in the
island, began for the first time to contemplate the possibility —
indeed the necessity — of sharing power on a formal basis with the
representatives of the indigenous population. Secondly, it was in
this decade that some of the most intractable and complicated problems of contemporary Srī Laṅkā emerged, many of them either
developing out of, or complicated by, the prospect of a transfer of a
share of political power.

Before beginning a discussion of these political initiatives, it
is necessary to review some of these intractable problems. The first
of these was the economic situation which, in contrast to the first two

decades of the twentieth century, was one of stagnation and contraction if not decline . The period 1880-1913 had been one of comparative prosperity for the tropical colonies, and the plantation sector
of Srī Laṅkā's economy had shared in this. From the beginning of
the century up to the outbreak of the First World War Srī Laṅkā's
plantation sector had enjoyed a period of aggressive growth, its
most notable feature being the expansion of the rubber industry.
In the rubber boom of 1910-12, prices for rubber reached heights
which were not only astounding but which were never attained
again (the indigenous planters had a substantial interest in the
rubber industry from its very inception). At the same time, tea and
coconut held their own, although they were temporarily overshadowed by the rubber industry. This comparative prosperity
was followed by a long period of depression, from the beginning
of the First World War to the outbreak of the Second. This was the
result of a decline in the growth of world trade, first because of the
First World War, and secondly because of economic dislocation in
Europe in the 1920s and the great depression of the 1930s. Tropical
trade, in general, had grown in volume at an average annual rate
of 3.6% in the period 1883-1913; between 1913 and 1929 its growth
rate dropped to 3.1%; and between 1929 and 1955 it dropped still
further to 1.5%. The terms of trade had already turned adverse by
the late 1920s. Thus the whole period 1913-39 may be regarded as
one of great depression for the tropical colonies. The rate of growth
of their income declined, and with this there was also a decline in
the rate of growth of their productive capacity. The export sector
of Srī Laṅkā's economy reflected this trend.

  This post-war dislocation of the island's export economy in the
early 1920s was accompanied by a rise in the price of imported goods
— including foodstuffs — and, immediately after the war, shortages
of food. As a result there emerged a significant heightening of
working-class activity and trade unionism, which began to impinge
on the political situation. The urban working class of Colombo
was beginning to push its way into the political arena, and with that
came glimpses of a new and more attractive dimension in Srī
Laṅkā's politics — the appearance of a radical challenge to the conservative domination of the country's politics. A. E. Goonesinha
was the most notable figure in this new trend in working-class agitation, and his contribution to the development of the nationalist
movement in Srī Laṅkā lay in the introduction of techniques of
agitation based on the politicisation of the urban working class of
Colombo. They advocated more vigorous expression of opposition
to British rule in imitation of the contemporary policies of the
Indian National Congress. The "constitutionalists" who were in

firm control of the "official" movement for constitutional reform
were not receptive to these ideas.

If the radicalisation of the urban working class of Colombo and
its entry into political activity were emphatically invigorating
features of this period, much more intractable a problem was the
breakdown of the comparative harmony of interests and outlook
which had characterised relations between Sinhalese and Tamil
politicians in the first two decades of the twentieth century. National
unity and ethnic harmony, which the Ceylon National Congress
was expected to epitomise, proved illusory within three years of
its establishment. At this stage in the island's political evolution
under British rule, the Sinhalese and Tamils were regarded as its
two majority communities; the minorities were the smaller ethnic
groups. The situation changed fundamentally after 1922: instead
of two majority communities and the minorities, there was now just
one majority community, the Sinhalese, and the Tamils regarded
themselves — and were regarded as — a minority community. This
has remained so ever since. Nor were the Sinhalese themselves a
monolithic group. The Kandyans entered the political arena once
again, but largely in opposition to the leaders of the nationalist
movement, voicing a sense of grievance which counselled retarding
the pace of advance, and in this sense they served as collaborators
of the British.

Dissension and mutual suspicion between the Sinhalese and the
Tamils was one of the unfortunate but inevitable consequences of
the concentration of energies on constitutional reform, and the
increasing prospect of a transfer of a substantial measure of political
power from the British to the indigenous political leaderships.
Minority groups led by the Tamils were opposed to any positive
measures of constitutional progress towards responsible government, unless these included a scheme of checks and balances to
protect their interests.

The arrival of the Donoughmore Commission in the island in
1927 brought these various conflicts into the open and to a head.
With the practical certainty of a further and substantial measure
of constitutional reform in the near future, Sinhalese-Tamil rivalries were exacerbated. At the same time, the small "radical" group
in national politics led by A. E. Goonesinha asserted their independence from and opposition to be "constitutionalists". While
A. E. Goonesinha shared with the Congress leadership a desire for
self-government, he recognised — as they did not — the need for
far-reaching social reform as the concomitant of the advance towards self-government. More important, he came out in support of
universal suffrage, in which he was almost alone among those in

positions of influence and leadership in national politics. Thus the
lines were drawn between the "constitutionalists" and "radicals".
From the point of view of the island's constitutional progress
under British rule, the recommendations of the Donoughmore
Commission were of great significance. They amounted, in effect,
to an assurance of self-government as the next and almost inevitable
step, to a crossing of the great constitutional barrier towards self-
government — in much the same way as the Durham Report on
Canada initiated this process as regards the White Dominions in
the nineteenth century. Equally important was the introduction
of universal suffrage in 1931 on their recommendation. The grant
of universal suffrage was a measure which was to have the most
profound effects on the country's politics. While the full impact of
this factor was felt in the years after independence, pressures were
building up for a democratisation of Srī Laṅkā's politics in 1931-47,
when the Donoughmore Constitution was in operation.

Two themes of crucial importance in 1931-47 are reviewed below:
the impact of universal suffrage and the political and constitutional
issues involved in the transfer of power.

With the introduction of universal suffrage in 1931 the way
seemed open for the labour movement in Srī Laṅkā to assume an
independent role in politics. But it soon became clear that the
widening of the franchise made little immediate difference to
the political fortunes of the "constitutionalist" leadership. Their
strength lay in the rural constituencies, and the rural vote easily
swamped the working-class vote in the urban areas. But this did
not check the trend towards radicalisation of working-class politics,
especially in the city and suburbs of Colombo. This was evident
when Goonesinha and his Labour Party (formed in 1928) were soon
superseded in the leadership of the working-class movement by a
younger and more militant set of radicals, the Marxists. These latter
called for sterner commitment to nationalist goals where the
political objectives derived their validity not only from a sensitivity to the social and economic problems of the people but also from
being more clearly drawn in ideological terms than Goonesinha's
hazy radicalism. Despite this, however, they did not make much
greater headway against the "constitutionalists" than Goonesinha
himself.

This was partly due to the indigenous working class, despite its
increasing politicisation and militancy, being numerically smaller
than the immigrant plantation workers. Immigrant Indian labour
also formed a small but influential section of the Colombo working
class. The trade union movement on the plantations and elsewhere
among the immigrant Indians had a leadership composed of the

more affluent, educated and assertive men of their own ethnic group, and their hold on these workers was not — and has never been — successfully challenged by the indigenous working-class leaders. Thus the immigrant workers and the indigenous working class formed two distinct groups. Politically the influence of the immigrant working class was vitiated by the fact that, as an ethnic group, they were regarded as a threat to the interests of the indigenous people. Moreover, competition between immigrant and indigenous workers in the city and suburbs of Colombo became especially marked in the aftermath of the great depression of the early 1930s. As a result the working-class movement in Srī Laṅkā became sharply divided into two separate and mutually suspicious if not hostile sections, much to the advantage of the "constitutionalists".

The establishment of an electorate based on universal suffrage was among the main determining factors in the recrudescence of "religious" nationalism, i.e. nationalism intertwined with Buddhist resurgence and its associated cultural heritage. S. W. R. D. Bandaranaike sought to give leadership to this movement through his Sinhala Maha Sabha. There was no doubt about the viability of this brand of nationalism or of its appeal to a democratic electorate. But its potentially divisive effect in a plural society such as Srī Laṅkā's deterred the "constitutionalist" leadership from giving its support to such a programme with any enthusiasm. The Marxists, at this stage, were dogmatically unresponsive to the attractions of this brand of nationalism, often dismissing it as mere chauvinism.

On a different level, the introduction of universal suffrage was largely responsible for a broad impulse towards social welfare in the Donoughmore era, especially in the period of the second State Council (1936-47) when the "constitutionalist" leadership became more responsive to the social and economic facets of the resurgence of nationalism. One of the areas in which the impulse towards social welfare manifested itself was in the establishment of peasant colonisation schemes in the dry zone, with conditions of land tenure designed to prevent fragmentation of holdings. D. S. Senanayake's schemes for the restoration of the irrigation works of ancient Srī Laṅkā were among the major achievements of the Donoughmore era. There were three other areas of importance in the trend towards social welfare: education, health and food subsidies. The subsidisation of the price of wheat flour and rice began as a means of keeping the cost of living down during the Second World War, but it was continued thereafter. The desire to bring about a measure of equality in educational opportunities was the major force which

determined growth in investment in education during this period.
The concept of "free" education (which meant no more than free
tuition) as a modicum of social justice had an irresistible appeal to
the electorate. The disastrous effect of the last major malaria epide-
mic — that of 1934 — on the rural areas underlined the inadequacies
of the medical facilities in the country. The major hospitals were
located in the main towns, and the rural areas had little or nothing
by comparison. Now a programme of investment in new hospitals
in rural areas and increased emphasis on preventive medical facilities in all parts of the country had a notable impact on the people's
living conditions.

It often happens that the positive achievements of one era become
the source from which the problems of the next emerge. Improved
public health and medical care sharply reduced the crude death
rate. Though the eradication of malaria through the use of DDT
is given the credit for this, in fact not all parts of the island were
malaria-ridden, and the drop in the crude death rate had become
noticeable by 1945, a year before the DDT programme became well
established. The crude birth rate, meanwhile, remained stable and
as a result there was a phenomenal increase in population in the
years after independence. Moreover, the expanded school system
and the much greater access to education increased the number of
students aspiring to white-collar jobs at a time when the economy
was not expanding with anything like the rapidity with which
population, and the school-going population in particular, was
growing. Thus an unprecedented increase in population growth
and the rising expectations of an increasingly educated population
has created an almost unmanageable situation for Sri Lankā's
leaders in the years since independence. Moreover, by 1947 the
total expenditure on social services absorbed as much as 56.1% of
government revenues. In the late 1920s the corresponding proportion had been a mere 16.4%. The social welfare patterns of the
Donoughmore era were extended beyond 1947 — to the detriment,
it would seem, of economic growth.

It was under the leadership of D. S. Senanayake that the final
phase in the transfer of power began. There are two noteworthy
points in his negotiations with Britain on this issue. First, he was
guided by a strong belief in ordered constitutional evolution to
Dominion Status on the analogy of constitutional development in
the White Dominions. In insisting that Dominion Status should
remain the prime object of policy, and that this should be attained
in association with rather than in opposition to the British, he
placed himself in direct opposition to the views adopted in 1942 by
the Ceylon National Congress (in response to the younger policy-

makers who were becoming increasingly influential within it) that independence[7] rather than Dominion Status should be the goal of Srī Laṅkā's development. It needed all his personal prestige and tenacity of purpose to stand up against that current of opinion. Secondly, a profound suspicion of India was the dominant strand in his external policy. It was as a policy of re-insurance for the country during the early years of independence when it was not impossible that there might be a political vacuum in South Asia, that he viewed the agreement on Defence and External Affairs negotiated by Whitehall as a prelude to the grant of Dominion Status to Srī Laṅkā.

It was in his internal policy that he left the impression of his dominant personality and his moderate views. The guiding principles were: his conception of Srī Laṅkā as a multi-racial democracy; and his commitment to the maintenance of the Liberal ideal of a secular state in which the lines between state power and religion were scrupulously demarcated. Here again he placed himself in opposition to a current of opinion which viewed the Srī Laṅkā polity as being essentially Sinhalese and Buddhist in character, and which urged that government policies should be fashioned to accommodate a far-reaching transformation of the island's politics to build a new Srī Laṅkā on traditional, ideal, Sinhala-Buddhist lines. Implicit in this was a rejection of the concept of a multi-racial polity, as well as the concept of a secular state.

D. S. Senanayake, in contrast, was sensitive to minority anxieties. This was not merely a matter of political realism but it also sprang from a deep conviction of the need for generous concessions to the minorities, communal and religious in order to ensure political stability in a plural society such as Srı Laṅkā in the vital last phase in the transfer of power. One needs to draw attention, briefly, to at least three points of note in his policies on minorities. First, the guarantees against legislation discriminating against minorities, incorporated in the Soulbury Constitution, were borrowed from provisions in the Ministers' Draft Constitution of 1944 which had been introduced on D. S. Senanayake's initiative as a gesture of generosity and reassurance to the minorities. Secondly, there was his initiative in forming the United National Party. This was designed to make a fresh start in politics in the direction of a consensus of moderate opinion in national politics; it was to be a political party necessarily representing the majority community but at the same time acceptable to the minorities. Thirdly, he thwarted all efforts to abandon the concept of a secular state and the principle of the religious neutrality of the state. He succeeded in this to the extent that in 1948, despite some Buddhist displeasure over the continued prestigious and influential position enjoyed by the Christian minority (chiefly the Roman Catholics), there seemed little or no evidence of the religious turmoil or linguistic conflicts which were to burst to the surface in 1956.

In striking contrast to other parts of South Asia (including Burma), Srī Laṅkā in 1948 was an oasis of stability, peace and order. The transfer of power was smooth and peaceful, a reflection of the moderate tone of the dominant strand in the country's nationalist movement. More important, one saw very little of the divisions and bitterness which were tearing at the recent independence of the South Asian countries. In general, the situation in the country seemed to provide an impressive basis for a solid start in nation-building and national regeneration.[8]

But if the political leadership in Srī Laṅkā took pride in the smoothness of the transfer of power, it seemed oblivious to the political perils involved in making the process so bland as to be almost imperceptible. In retrospect it seems that the lack of innovation in the constitutional process by which independence was achieved in Srī Laṅkā was the crux of the problem. There was a notable difference between the constitutional and legal instruments which conferred independence on Srī Laṅkā and the cognate process in other parts of South Asia. All this seemed to indicate a qualitative difference in the nature of the independence that was being achieved when no meaningful difference in status was either intended by Britain or accepted by Srī Laṅkā's leaders.

Thus the real worth of D. S. Senanayake's achievement came to be denied because the means adopted for the attainment of independence under his leadership were not as robust or as ostentatiously dramatic as they might have been. The Indian experience seemed to provide a more emotionally satisfying example than the process by which power had been transferred in Srī Laṅkā — independence granted from above (as in Srī Laṅkā) was regarded as being much less satisfying to the spirit of nationalism than if it had been won after prolonged strife and untiring sacrifice.

More important, neither the government led by D. S. Senanayake nor its left-wing critics displayed any grasp of the sense of outrage and indignation of the Buddhists at what they regarded as the historic injustices suffered by their religion under western rule. Beneath the surface these religious emotions and the associated cultural and linguistic issues were gathering momentum, and developing into a force too powerful for the equilibrium of political and social forces established in 1948 to withstand. Its eruption to the surface nearly tore the country apart within a decade of 1948 to the discomfiture of both the U.N.P. and its left-wing critics.

REFERENCES

1. Generally translated as 'priest' or 'monk', a member of the Buddhist order.

2. See R. L. Brohier, *Ancient Irrigation Works in Ceylon*, 3 vols., Colombo (1934) and R. A. L. H. Gunawardana, 'Irrigation and Hydraulic Society in Early Medieval Ceylon', *Past and Present*, 53 (November 1971), pp. 3-27.

3. K. A. Wittfogel, *Oriental Despotism*, Yale University Press (1957); see also E. Leach, 'Hydraulic Society in Ceylon', *Past and Present*, 15 (April 1959), pp. 2-26. R. A. L. H. Gunawardana, op. cit.

4. For discussion of this theme see, R. Murphy, 'The Ruin of Ancient Ceylon', *Journal of Asian Studies*, XVI(ii) pp. 181-200. This paragraph and the four that follow are based on this article.

5. Seven large naval expeditions, under the command of Cheng-Ho, visited the ports of the Indian Ocean in both the eastern and western seas, demanding tribute and obedience to the Emperor of China. Cheng-Ho first visited Srī Laṅkā in 1405; five years later he led the expedition which captured the Sinhalese ruler, his queen and officers and took them to China.

6. What was vital was the definition which specified that the *entire* coastline to a depth of about eight miles was conceded to the Dutch.

7. Independence did not carry the lingering connotations of constitutional subordination to Britain which Dominion Status, at this time, appeared to have.

8. For a review of the economic situation at independence, see chapter 5.

3

THE EVOLUTION OF A PLURAL SOCIETY

by Vijaya Samaraweera

The plurality of society in Srī Laṅkā and the problems arising out of it have been dissected and discoursed upon by many writers in the recent past, and they have spawned considerable polemical writings in the national languages. The present essay does not propose to review this literature, nor is it concerned with the problems of a plural society and their solutions. It has a rather restricted scope: an analysis of the structure of pluralism as it took the form identifiable in contemporary times.

For the greater part, until the complexion changed with the arrival of the first of the colonial powers, social pluralism in Srī Laṅkā meant essentially the existence of the two social groups, the Sinhalese and the Tamils. The Sinhalese and the Tamils claimed descent from distinct racial stocks, from the Aryans and the Dravidians respectively, and as the claims were deeply imbedded in their consciousness, the ethnic difference was always important in the structuring of plurality in pre-colonial Srī Laṅkā, and indeed thereafter. But the ethnic difference alone was not responsible for the emergence of the Sinhalese and the Tamils as distinctive social groups, above all because neither of them ever succeeded in retaining anything like a racial purity. There were a number of other factors which helped to amplify the original ethnic differences. Among these was religion: since the Sinhalese embraced Buddhism and the Tamils largely retained their Hindu faith, religion became a divisive factor in society. Religion was to become even more crucial, since it germinated an ideology among the Sinhalese which was politically emotive and potent. This ideology was built up around the special destiny claimed for the Sinhalese and the land they inhabited as the chosen guardians of Buddhism, and it brought together — with what proved to be of profound consequence — two distinct elements, nation and religion: the unity of *Sinhaladīpa*

(Island of the Sinhalese) and *Dhammadīpa* (Island of Buddhism) was the fruit. Historians are divided as to when the ideology first appeared — recent studies place the appearance not in the second century B.C., as is usually accepted, but much later, as late as the sixth century A.D. — but its appearance was reflection enough of the development of a group identity among the Sinhalese *vis-à-vis* the Tamils. Contrary to popular thinking, the development of a group identity did not result in constant tension and conflict in society, and there is no reason to believe that the ideology constantly clouded relations between the Sinhalese and the Tamils. The ideology seemed to have surfaced only in times of crisis. Thus it was evoked in the later eleventh century against the South Indian Cōlas who had conquered much of the island, and in the post-Cōla period against divisive tendencies on the local political plane. The evocation of the ideology had its measure of success, but the impact was never to be lasting; a political entity which could be described as Sinhalese — Buddhist was rarely to be meaningful in an all-island framework. The political reality became more than apparent with the emergence in the early thirteenth century of a separate kingdom of the Tamils in the north, and after the thirteenth century there was even to be a geographical separation of the social groups because of the migration of the Sinhalese from their original settlement area in the *rajarata* (King's country) to the south-west coastal belt. Not that either of these factors brought about the total isolation of the social groups from each other — latterly the original propinquity was lost, but there was no break in the social and economic relations between the two peoples, and underlying all these was a strong cultural affinity.

Aberrations no doubt existed, but the early history of Srī Laṅkā reveals largely a picture of harmonious social relations between the Sinhalese and the Tamils. However, the collective memory of the Sinhalese especially has tended to dwell not upon the more general conditions which prevailed but on the tension and hostility which were generated at times of crisis. Thus much has been made of the invasions from South India which took place from the earliest times — were they not responsible for the destruction of the ancient polity and the migration of the Sinhalese from their heartland? — and the resistance which emerged to these from among the Sinhalese has been glorified and sanctified, while the heroes which the resistance threw up carved special niches for themselves in the popular imagination. Much of the responsibility for this tendency has been placed upon the *Mahāvamsa*, the sixth-century 'Great Chronicle which is the primary historical source for early Srī Laṅkā; its perspective, strongly Sinhalese-Buddhist, has coloured not only popular thinking over the years but also the historiography of the land until recent times. Later chauvinists were to take up from where the *Mahāvaṁsa* left off.

The impact of the rule of the first two colonial powers to govern Srī Laṅkā, the Portuguese (1597-1658) and the Dutch (1658-1796), on the relations between the Sinhalese and the Tamils was decidedly adverse. Many of the policies of the two powers were guided by the feeling that the distinctiveness of the social groups should be respected, if not for the sake of good order, at least for administrative convenience. Thus they consciously sought to maintain the customary laws. Indeed, they received institutionalised identity, especially through the work of the Dutch. Of considerable consequence was their formulation of separate codes of law for the social groups, for these introduced a new, indeed a lasting, institutional divide into society; the significance of this is revealed when it is noted that the Sinhalese kingdom in the interior had no personal laws but a territorial law. Both powers were also quick to exploit the separateness of the social groups for their political advantage. Thus the Portuguese, for example, as a rule deployed Sinhalese *lascarins* (native militia) in the Tamil areas and Tamil troops in the Sinhalese areas. To what extent such measures exacerbated the distance between the social groups cannot easily be gauged; in any event, it is unlikely that they would have remained insensitive to such measures.

The rule of the Portuguese and the Dutch saw the structure of social pluralism in the island assuming a complexity it had not possessed earlier. Thus new elements of plurality were introduced among the Sinhalese and the Tamils with the proselytisation of the missionaries who came to Srī Laṅkā following the respective flags. Of the missionaries, the Roman Catholics reaped a rich harvest of converts, aided by a deft use of material rewards and by attacks on the older religions, Buddhism and Hinduism, which were in any case weakened by the withdrawal of state patronage which was so essential for their sustenance. The success, however, was not to be lasting in that under the Dutch a great many of the converts left the church, some to newly established churches and others to the traditional folds. Nevertheless, a hard core remained, which perpetuated the characteristics which had made the Roman Catholics in the first place a separate social group. Dutch missionary activity was more restrained and less successful than that of the Portuguese. They too offered rewards for conversion and other religions were persecuted, though not uniformly. The Buddhists, for example, were less harshly treated, probably in order to placate the Kandyan king who had inherited the traditional role of guardian of Buddhist interests. The Hindus, who had no such patron, suffered in consequence. But they never faced the threat of a crushing persecution such as that to which the Roman Catholics were subjected. The attitude towards the Catholics is explicable in the circumstances of the bitter struggle which took place between the Dutch and the Portuguese for the control of Srī Laṅkā: the Dutch felt the need to eliminate the class of local collaborators with their foe.

The social presence of the Burghers stems from this period. There is an important distinction which is maintained among the Burghers, namely between the Portuguese Burghers and the Dutch Burghers. The socially inferior of the two are the former, the descendents of the Portuguese, and the Dutch who established unions with local women. In fact, the Portuguese Burghers were placed in an unenviable position, for *liaisons* with local women not only received the opprobrium of the European society but were also socially unacceptable to the local population. The Dutch Burghers had stronger claims for social acceptance, for they were the products of 'pure' Portuguese and Dutch marriages or marriages contracted by them with mixed (European-Asian) women. The maintenance of the Dutch Burghers as a social group of standing lay chiefly in the fortuitous circumstance under which they were able to transfer their allegiance from the Dutch to the British. Unlike the political transition from the Portuguese to the Dutch, the change-over from the Dutch to the British rule was accomplished without bitterness and an easy and amicable relationship was soon established between the Dutch Burghers and the new rulers.

The Muslims had been in the island from pre-colonial times but it was under the Portuguese and the Dutch that they were brought into sharp focus as a distinctive social group. By the colonial period the Muslims had achieved a dominant commercial position within the country but yet they seemed to have acted singularly unobtrusively in society, for there is no record of them coming into conflict or arousing the jealousies of the other groups. The advent of the Portuguese changed this image markedly. They were now viewed as hostile competitors, since both were competing for the same trade and the Portuguese adopted an uncompromisingly harsh policy towards them. Their successors acted with moderation, but their policy too tended to emphasise rather than blur the identity of Muslims as a social group. They continued to be singled out in economic policies. More significantly, a separate code of laws was compiled for them by the Dutch. As the governor who was responsible for the new code stated: 'The people of the Mohamedan [sic] faith were totally ignorant of what was or what was not their law and subject', and the Dutch borrowed a code of laws from Batavia to form the basis of the local code for the Muslims. If the Muslims were indeed 'ignorant' of their laws, then it is evidence enough that theirs was not a distinctive social life in pre-colonial times. It also exemplifies the importance of the institutional divides built up by the Europeans in the evolution of the structure of social pluralism in Sri Lanka.

The different social groups in the island found themselves thrown into a new arena with the establishment of British rule. A unitary state was soon created (the Kandyans having lost their independence in 1815); the strict parochial needs of the social groups or the pattern of their settlement no longer formed the key to the structuring of the administration. The physical distances between settlement areas were to be gradually removed with improvements in communications and transportation. Regional economies were to be knitted together to form an all-island economy. And the process of westernisation was to be more pervasively worked out. It is of course obvious that these changes did not take place uniformly and that there were deviations from these as well as contrary developments. Nevertheless, it is possible to argue that British rule (1796-1948) saw the establishment of a framework within which the diverse social groups could have transcended their disparateness by reaching towards a normative consensus on their mode of life. This they failed to achieve and in fact social pluralism became more obvious during this period. It is as true to say that the social groups were inherently incapable of achieving integration as to say that exogenous forces beyond their control acted as insurmountable obstacles to integration. Thus, on the one hand, the focus could be on, say, the competitiveness which emerged, albeit consciously, at the early stages among the social groups to grasp the opportunities for advancement offered by the new rulers, and latterly on their jockeying for primacy as independence from the British became a possibility. On the other hand, attention could be drawn to the policies pursued by the British which had the effect not only of marking out more clearly the boundaries between social groups but also of introducing new elements of plurality — though the creation of a homogenous society in the island was their oft-pronounced objective, indeed the very *raison d'être* of the continued maintenance of their rule in later times.

To illustrate the working out of these processes, four broad areas could be delineated for discussion: religion, education and employment, the economy and politics. In religion, a conspicuously different setting from the earlier colonial period gradually developed. The Anglican Church became the new established church, but it never received the highly privileged status accorded to previous established churches. The colonial government's policy towards the Anglican Church was always fraught with ambiguity: the supremacy of the Anglican hierarchy was constantly challenged by other denominations, and prosleytisation was to be marred by deep and often bitter sectarian conflict. The result of this was that, while a new Christian flock was founded, it was not homogeneous either in belief pattern or in behaviour. Conversion to Protestantism did not reach significant proportions. A significant aspect of Protestantism is that new converts were not immediately removed to a totally new and different social plane, but were able to retain manifold links with the bases from which they sprang. This can easily be explained. Absence of persecution was crucial. Equally important was the increasing westernisation of the society in general; religious conversion was now neither the sole nor the principal means of mobility. Because of these factors, Protestant Christians cannot be easily demarcated as a social group: they are certainly less identifiable as a social group than the Roman Catholics.

It was inevitable that among those who adhered to the traditional religions, a reaction would set in against the Christian missionaries. Apart from their deep concern with education, the work of the missionaries became highly visible and became an irritant because of the very nature of their methods. They developed a predilection for seeking out confrontations with the traditional religions, of provoking "dialogues" and "debates" with the representatives of these religions. With their concern for devising means of proselytisation which would be intelligible within the traditional framework, they came much closer within the orbit of village society than earlier missionaries. Given this background it is not surprising that conflicts arose between the older religions and the Protestants. Understandably, the first reaction to Protestantism came from the Kandyans. The Kandyan response was not strictly religious; it had much more besides, and indeed many of the elements which are characteristic of the early stages of nationalist movements—the inheritance of the Sinhalese-Buddhist ideology no doubt provided them with the emotional impetus here. The activism of the Kandyans did not last long. However, the Sinhalese littoral was to throw up a more considerable and a more lasting response. It was to be distinguished by a tremendous vitality and self-confidence, which was perhaps best exemplified in the 'victories' of the Buddhists over the Christians in the religious debates which were publicly inaugurated in the 1860s. It was also to be moved by modernising forces, though essentially imitative of the work of the Christians. The Buddhists of the low country were not to function without internal contradiction but the crucial factor is that the resurgence among them gave rise to a

self-awareness as members of a particular faith. The Buddhists
throughout the island were to remain aware of a unity, but what
came to be demonstrated at this time and in the coming years was
that beneath this was a division, between the low-country Sinhalese
and the Kandyans.

The Hindus and Muslims were slower to move towards a confrontation with the Christians. They also lacked the aggressiveness
which marked the Buddhist response. Moreover, again in contrast
to the Buddhists, only a small number among them were drawn
into a confrontation; there was not among them anything comparable to the Buddhist temperance movement which drew support
from the wider body of Buddhist society. These differences could
be explained. First, unlike the Hindus and the Muslims, the
Buddhists had inherited a proud tradition of resistance to foreign
intrusion. It is also arguable that the Buddhists felt the impact of
Protestantism much more than the others. Certainly throughout
British rule they had a serious grievance constantly in focus: the
abrogation of the 'inviolable' guarantees given for the protection
of Buddhism at the time Kandy was conquered. Above all, lacking
opportunities of drawing sustenance from co-religionists elsewhere, the Buddhists were forced to rely upon their own inner
resources; the millennial movements which became conspicuous
among them testified amply to this. The Hindus too felt the impact
of Protestantism but they had one substantial means of cushioning
it somewhat; the ability to draw inspiration from South India. This
was of great value but it was to have adverse repercussions in the
local society, for it gave rise to fears among the Sinhalese-Buddhists
that there would be a coalescence of the ethnically and culturally
connected two peoples of North Srī Laṅkā and South India. It is
perhaps no exaggeration to say that, of the older religions, Islam
was the least affected by the proselytisation of the Christians: to
the immense frustration of the missionaries, hardly any Muslims
were moved by the Gospel. Nevertheless, no doubt stimulated by
the example of the Buddhists and the Hindus, the Muslims too
were to throw up a religious resurgence.

The other major religious group, the Roman Catholics, were now
in a persecution-free climate, but were to be subjected time and
again to the overt opposition of the officials and the Protestant
missionaries. This, however, instead of acting as a restraint seemed
to spur them on. Aided by a devoted priesthood and efficient parochial organisations like schools, the Catholics were to develop their
special identity centred around their faith, and in time they became
one of the most cohesive social groups in the island.

In one way or another, all the religious groups were reacting to the presence of Protestantism by the later decades of the nineteenth century. In reacting to Protestantism, their activities were also to be marked by a spirit of competitiveness with each other. The nature and extent of the competition which emerged among the social groups under the British was much more evident in the area of education and employment than in religion. Over the years, English education became one of the critical areas in which the deep interest and feelings of the different social groups were aroused. The reason for this is primarily to be found in the premium which was placed on English education by the wider society. It brought about employment in the administration, vastly attractive not only because of its material rewards but also because of the high social status it conferred. It paved the way to wealth and access to goods and services valued by society. It also opened up the path to the political arena and political power. In all these ways and more, an education in English carried untold value in society but its availability was limited, thus giving it a scarcity value. Not only this, but it was not distributed equally; a disproportionate number from certain social groups obtained the valued education and so equipped themselves to grasp the opportunities that were opening up. Non-Christians were able to exploit the new educational facilities from the beginning, but for the greater part of the nineteenth century education was mostly the preserve of the Christians. Not that the missionaries succeeded in moulding the whole educational structure to serve their strictly sectarian interests — the crucial factor is the Christian dominance, for it evoked a response from the older religions.

When the other religious groups began to challenge the Christians in education, they did not venture to explore new educational methods or deploy new means. Their work largely followed the pattern already established by the Protestant missions. Judged purely by educational criteria, the new schools made substantial progress but they were not able to dislodge the Christian institutions from their position of primacy. This failure should not cloud the significance of the role they played in the context of social pluralism in the island. They provided the arena in which an intense competition developed to acquire the resources which were considered vital for social advancement. They were undeniably a principal channel by which a greater consciousness of group identity permeated within the respective social groups. Further, the religio-cultural bias of the education provided in these schools was largely responsible for instilling in their respective student communities inter-group prejudices, stereotype images of their own social group as well as others.

One further impact of English education merits notice, for it seems to belie the proposition that education had the effect of accentuating the boundaries between the social groups. This concerns the creation of an Anglicised group in society. This was neither unexpected nor unwelcome from the point of view of the British: as early as 1801 Sir Frederick North, the first British governor, had set as his goal the formation of a class 'attached to their country by birth, and to England by education'. On the surface, at least during the first generation, the English-educated displayed all the characteristics of an entirely new social group divorced from the traditional ethos.

Recruitment to the new class depended upon English education and not on the criteria which had hitherto determined the membership of social groupings, race, religion and caste. It is equally true to say that the English-educated, not only in the first generation but also in the generations which followed, felt much more at ease in each other's company than with the rest of the society because of a shared outlook and a common access to wealth, power and status. Little wonder that some English writers saw in the members of this group, who had adopted western dress, modes of speech and mores, a mirror-image of themselves. Nevertheless, the divorce of this group from the local *milieu* proved more apparent than real. The revivalism which caught the traditional religions in the 1860s saw the English-educated championing the cause of their respective religions against the dominance of Christianity. The caste rivalries which broke out among the Sinhalese about the same period demonstrated the extent to which the sophisticated could be moved by the narrow sectarianism of the old order. The inherent lack of unity among the English-educated was perhaps most notably exemplified at the election for the 'Educated Ceylonese' seat of the Legislative Council in 1912, when the whole class was torn asunder by caste and ethnic emotions. And, finally with the emergence in the 1920s of political organisations based strictly on ethnic grounds, the notion that the new social groups consisted of individuals who were above the old order of things and that they were fully in sympathy with each other was totally destroyed.

Because of the nebulous nature of the English-educated as a group, it would be difficult to place them in proper perspective within the context of social pluralism of Srī Laṅkā. At several levels the boundary of the group is fairly well defined, but at other levels it is blurred and tends to merge with the wider social groupings, especially where the English-educated propelled themselves into positions of leadership and drew a clientele from the respective social groups from which they emerged.

Education and employment were inextricably linked. Since an

English education was the *sine qua non* for entering both the administration and the professions, the imbalance in the acquisition of an English education by the different social groups had necessarily to be reflected also in the employment area. A recent analysis of census data makes this clear. The data on males in select professions (doctors, lawyers, engineers, land surveyors and appraisers) for the year 1921 shows that only a total of 46 per cent of them were Sinhalese though they constituted 76 per cent of the total adult male population in the island with the exclusion of Europeans. The breakdown of the Sinhalese category is equally interesting, for it shows that 42.5 per cent were low-country Sinhalese while only 3.5 were Kandyans, their percentage of the total adult males being 49 per cent and 27 per cent respectively. On the other hand the Tamils, who constituted 13.3 per cent of the total, had a strength of 31.9 per cent in the professions and the Burghers, who formed only a minute 0.7 per cent of the adult males, were equally disproportionately represented with a figure of 17.7 per cent. The Muslims, who constituted 7.9 per cent of the total adult males, were under-represented with only 1.8 per cent.

The proportions were to change but the basic picture of imbalance remained substantially unchanged until near the end of British rule. Some salient points relevant to the present discussion may be drawn from this picture. First, on the remarkable preponderence of the Burghers. With the striking capacity they displayed for adaptation at this time — they quickly acquired, for example, a proficiency in English and then adopted it as their 'mother-tongue' — they were able to become one of the more forward-looking of the social groups in the island. They were the first to enter government service and become a dominant element; and, once broader avenues opened up in employment, they were again to be the first to gain a foothold and achieve dominance — this was true of the legal and, even more, the medical profession. Throughout British rule the Burghers were to show a most intimate connection with the administration and the professions, so much so that it is no exaggeration to say that their horizon did not extend beyond these. Certainly, few of the Burghers were to join the other social groups in the exploitation of the opportunities in the economy.

One further factor may be noted about the Burghers: those who achieved distinction were the Dutch Burghers. The Portuguese Burghers were in no way able to match the advances gained by the Dutch Burghers, and in fact their position deteriorated considerably, both economically and as regards status. It was inevitable that the social distance between them and the Dutch Burghers would widen in these years.

The explanation for the disproportionate representation of the Tamils in employment has been sought in the ecology of the region in which they lived: the continuous absorption of an increasing population into the traditional occupations based upon land was highly limited, and alternate avenues had to be explored. Seizing the openings in the administration and the professions was an obvious choice. And, this was also a rational choice in view of the educational facilities provided among them from the beginning of British rule; the alacrity with which the Tamils exploited the new facilities could perhaps be gauged from the illuminating statement in the 1921 *Census Report* that 'the Tamils were ahead of the low-country Sinhalese in English literacy but they were behind them in literacy generally'. The public service became a strong tradition with the Tamils and they soon began to compete most effectively with the Burghers and they, generally succeeded in keeping one step ahead of the other social groups throughout British rule.

The relative positions of the two Sinhalese social groups in the area of employment displays an interesting contrast. Like the Tamils, the low-country Sinhalese benefited from the early provision of English education, but it was concentrated largely on the Western province at the expense of the other districts and, taken in its totality, cannot be favourably compared with the facilities received by the Tamils — which perhaps explains why the low-country Sinhalese lagged behind the Tamils in educational advancement. The low-country Sinhalese were of course aware of the rewards of an English education but there were other avenues, particularly in the economy, which carried competitive values. This is perhaps why there was not among them a total identification with English education and, leading from it, with the employment area; but paradoxically, their involvement in the economy provides a key to their increasing concern with education, in that wealth thereby accumulated was often devoted to the promotion of education in their areas. In complete contrast, the Kandyans were to show little interest in education. It is true that the Kandyans were poorly served educationally, both by the government and by the missionaries, but there seemed to have been a conspicuous lack of interest among them in education. Where attention was paid by the Kandyans to government employment, they were to be preoccupied with the traditional offices which, although carrying status and influence, were not strictly integrated into the administrative machinery of the British: thus, it is arguable that there was not only little vertical mobility among the Kandyans but also hardly any spatial mobility. This was one more ingredient which went into the making of the separate Kandyan identity.

The under-representation of the Muslims in the area of employment was understandable enough, for of all the social groups they were the least attracted by English education. This was partly because of their conservation — they were firmly wedded to the Koran and the Arabic language in education — and partly because of the continuous material rewards of their principal traditional occupation, trading. Only in the last decades of the nineteenth century did an interest arise among them in English education, but even then it affected only a small number.

When the competition arose among the social groups for places in the administration and in the professions, it was not only the disparate educational structure which counted. Of great pertinence, especially in relation to the public service — which, after all, was the more attractive sphere — was the limited nature of the openings which became available. The lower and middle levels of the administration were 'Ceylonised' early, but the extent of this soon proved inadequate to satisfy the aspirations of the educated. There was an increasingly vocal demand that the civil service, which had become the exclusive preserve of the Europeans, be entirely thrown open to the locals. The claims were not to be ignored by the British but the intake of local candidates was to be increased only gradually. With the restriction of the intake and the *visibility* a position in the civil service carried, any local recruitment tended to be interpreted not as the success of a gifted individual but as a comparative social group success — perhaps the best indicator of the competitive spirit which developed among the social groups in the areas of education and employment.

In the area of the economy, the roles seemed to have been somewhat reversed, for it was the low-country Sinhalese, rather than the Burghers and the Tamils, who formed the vanguard of the involvement of the locals in the new economic activities. The low-country Sinhalese had of course already acquired some understanding of the new economic forces, but only during British rule was there a conspicuous participation by them in the merchant and plantation capitalist structure which was being built up from the eighteenth century. There is little doubt that the traditionally pre-eminent in the low-country society benefited greatly from the new economy, but at no stage were they left unchallenged by those of the lower strata and the competition which developed is important because it had the effect of sharpening the entrepreneurship of the low-country Sinhalese as a group. The role of the new elements which came up carried a further significance in that they were less inhibited by the value-matrix of the old order than the traditional elements, and were therefore able to act as pioneers in some new spheres of the economy. It is also necessary to note the setting in which both the traditional and the newer elements among the low-country Sinhalese functioned: the dominance of the European capitalists. This proved to be crucial, for it helped to legitimise not only the economic thrust of the low-country Sinhalese as a group but also their early incursions into the political arena.

The position of the Kandyans in the economy should be juxta-posed with that of the low-country Sinhalese. The resulting contrast is striking, and provides a further clue to the evolution of Kandyans as a separate social group. In the interior, it was the low-country Sinhalese rather than the Kandyans who were to benefit from the new economic forces which became activated after the British conquest. Not that the Kandyans remained insensitive to economic stimuli; their engagement in coffee culture, for example, demonstrated that they did not lack economic initiative but they never fulfilled the early promise they displayed. Certainly, they ceased, after the 'coffee crash', to play even a marginally significant role in the new economy. In the meantime, the low-country Sinha-lese extended and intensified their economic activities in the in-terior and there is ample evidence to show that this aroused much resentment and jealousy of the Kandyans, which in turn no doubt contributed to the moulding of a separate Kandyan consciousness.

There is reason to believe that the presence of another economic element in the interior — the Indians brought over by the British to work in the plantations—acted as a greater irritant among the Kandyans than among the low-country Sinhalese. Sinhalese society had often displayed a capacity to absorb the migrants from the neighbouring sub-continent without disequilibrium: thus new castes were created in medieval times with the successful assimila-tion of migrants. The Kandyans, as heirs to this society, possessed an absorptive capacity, but the numbers of new migrants would have made the task of assimilation impossible: the level of the migration could be gauged by the fact that in the nineteenth century it added a higher percentage to the total population than was added by the natural increase. The pattern of estate settlement and the strong retention by the migrants of their original social structure and culture resulted in the creation of distinct social enclaves within the Kandyan region. This became a sore point with the Kandyans — after all, were not the Indians a major contributory factor in the dispossession of their patrimony in land? — and the increasing con-cern of the government with the improvement of the working con-ditions of the plantation labour (they were the first to receive the benefits of labour laws) and the manifest neglect of the impoverish-ed Kandyan peasant were not to help the situation at all.

It is a cliché, but nonetheless true, that the most damaging impact of the new economy is to be found in the interior. Above all, because of the expansion of the plantations, the Kandyan villages have become hemmed in without adequate room for expansion: the Kandyan battle-cry that the 'peasants are confined to the land on which their huts stand' exaggerates the picture but epitomises the deep feelings aroused over the effects of the development of the plantations. This sense of grievance was crucial to the rise of the Kandyan identity — indeed, it has been even questioned whether but for the overall effects of the plantations — including the presence of the immigrant labour, the Kandyan identity would have emerged at all, at least in the distinct form it assumed.

The role of the Tamils in the new economy was of little more than marginal importance. They were concerned with urban properties and coconut culture, for example, but neither in these spheres nor elsewhere in the economy were they to clash openly with the low-country Sinhalese. The significance of this lies in the fact that when competition arose in a different area with economic implications—in employment—it was to take great intensity: not possessing deep roots in the new economy, the Tamils were moved to guard zealously their achievement in it.

Finally, what of the Muslims? The Muslims were hardly immediately concerned with the new economy, but were nevertheless to profit from some of the changes which took place. Thus they were beneficiaries of the improvements in transportation and communications: only with the British did the truly ubiquitous Muslim trader —as reflected in the proverb, 'there is no place where the Moormen and the crow cannot be found' —emerge. The Muslim traders were central figures in both the village and the urban economy but now theirs was not an unobstrusive role. First, their economic dominance had its implications. Secondly, their social life had become more clearly structured: a social group which at an earlier stage took no advantage of the religious freedom granted by the Sinhalese kings to establish religious buildings had now entered the public domain in the practice of their religion. And, of course, they were now acting with a heightened self-awareness. How these different but related factors converged to create overt hostility against the Muslims was to be most dramatically demonstrated with the occurrence of the riots of 1915.

To shift the discussion to the area of politics, here too forces which were activated tended to show contrary results, at times submerging the factors of plurality and at other times highlighting and sharpening the differences between the social groups. In any event, as independence dawned, the picture which emerged was clear enough, the dominance of groupings structured on ethnic lines on the political plane. Antidotes for 'communalism' in politics were repeatedly sought and introduced by numerous administrators and constitution-makers — though there were also those who sought to profit from ethnic differences — but all to no avail.

The focus in politics was on constitutional advancement. When the Legislative Council was first established in 1833 its unofficial membership was so constituted that there was, in the eyes of the British, a *true* representation of the people through Burgher, Sinhalese and Tamil (and European) representatives. This perhaps set the trend for the leaders of the social groups to assume distinct postures in politics, though at the early stages the representatives acted with a sense of unity. The legislature was re-structured at various times. Thus representation was given to the Kandyans and Muslims — with the entry of the Kandyan, the original Sinhalese representative was styled the low-country Sinhalese member — and later when the low-country Sinhalese representation was increased to two, the representatives began to be selected on caste grounds, from the *goyigama* and *karāva* respectively. These changes perhaps accurately mirrored the disintegration of the tentative unity of the English-educated. The caste fissures among the Sinhalese had plainly surfaced by the end of the nineteenth century. The ethnic differences had then yet to be openly revealed on the political plane — indeed, conscious attempts were made to rise above them: this was exemplified by the selection of a Tamil as the first president of the Ceylon National Congress, that initial vehicle and symbol of the nationalist aspirations of the English-educated. The smug self-congratulation of the leadership — what now of officialdom's ominous forebodings of breakdown of social harmony with the emergence of nationalist demands? — was not to last long. Politics, within and without the legislature, began to reflect more clearly the island's social pluralism.

The 1920s saw separate and distinct political demands being put forward by the respective political groups, each designed to safeguard and further purely sectarian interests, though there was no failure to air protestations of 'national interests' at the same time. The setting for these should be noted: the emergence of territorial representation as the contentious next step in constitutional advancement. If territorial representation were strictly adhered to and the 'communal' principle abandoned, then it was obvious that the numerical superiority of a particular social group would be the deciding factor as to who would govern independent Srī Laṅkā. To the Tamils, Muslims and the Burghers this meant the Sinhalese, and to the Kandyans the low-country Sinhalese.

Among the social groups perhaps the clearest stance in politics was taken by the Burghers, who had throughout closely collaborated with the British and now, as others threatened to usurp their power and status, tended to intensify the collaboration, which estranged them further from the rest of society. Despite the collaboration, some Burghers had come forward in the later nineteenth century to articulate local opinion on constitutional issues, but now even this role was given up. The explanation for this is perhaps to be found in the different framework within which political agitation was now carried out: given a situation where numbers had a new meaning in politics, it is understandable that the Burghers were driven on to the defensive.

An equally defensive role in politics devolved upon the Kandyans. Faced with threats to their position as rulers, the British sought from the beginning to undermine the influence of the Kandyan aristocracy among their people. The danger, however, receded as the century advanced. With this there emerged a policy of consciously re-moulding the aristocracy as wielders of power and influence in society; much play was made with the view that they were the "natural" leaders of the Kandyans. This change is important in two respects. First, it marked the determination of the British to woo the Kandyans as a possible bulwark—a prop—to their rule. Secondly, it became the opening, albeit gladly seized, for the Kandyans to come forward as the countervailing conservative force in politics. In the background to these lay the essential development, the formulation of the separate Kandyan consciousness. Some of the ingredients which went into this have already been noted, and here it would suffice to emphasise one further factor: the creation of an institutional framework in which this identity could evolve. This stemmed from the public commitment the British made at the conquest of Kandy to safeguard the institutions and customs of the Kandyans. The commitment of the British here proved less than total, but some of the steps were of crucial importance, especially the fashioning of the Kandyan law as the personal law of the Kandyans — this became in the coming years the primary index to Kandyan identity.

Over the years, the Kandyans were to become increasingly disenchanted with the subordinate role they were forced to play in politics. Their position was well exposed when the elective principle was introduced. When the 'Educated Ceylonese' constituency was created, they formed only a minute percentage of voters. Far worse, when a beginning in territorial representation was made in the 1920s it was the low-country Sinhalese candidates who emerged victorious in the Kandyan constituencies. The Kandyans now took up the stance that they were being eclipsed in their own areas by the low-country Sinhalese, not only economically but also politically. Thenceforward the Kandyan position in politics was clear-cut: as some representative Kandyans demanded in 1925, "our entity as a separate and distinct community . . . [should] be recognised and maintained" in future constitution-making; the "Kandyan race" as a factor in politics had come into being.

The Kandyans and the low-country Sinhalese thus became divided, but there was one issue — the political rights of the Indian immigrants — which had the potential of bringing them together in the political field. From the Sinhalese point of view the issue at stake was not only the possibility of the Indians voting *en bloc* to ensure the victory of their candidates in the interior constituencies but also whether a people who had few or no roots in the island— 'birds of passage' was the oft-used phrase to describe the Indians — should be allowed a voice in politics at all. This issue was finally responsible for the forging of a shaky, but nevertheless useful, unity between the Kandyans and the low-country Sinhalese against the officials who were disposed to look at the political rights of the Indians much more favourably than the local politicians.

In the endeavour to win concessions from the British, the closest political collaboration had been established between the low-country Sinhalese and the Tamils. But events were soon to prove its tenuous nature, and it ended over the issue of territorial representation. Attempts at reconciliation failed, possibly because they were not made with the seriousness they deserved; and, in any case, the concessions offered by the low-country Sinhalese leadership were in no way designed to disarm the fears of the Tamils or to procure their confidence in the majority. Of great pertinence here is the shift in the thinking of the Tamils themselves as a social group: they no longer tended to view themselves as a majority community, to be bracketed with the Sinhalese — they had now become one of the host of minorities, though no doubt the strongest. With this the Tamils became an increasingly inward-looking group and the affinities between them and the Sinhalese began to be played down and the ethnic and cultural factors which had made them distinct were brought into sharp focus.

The picture which emerges in politics had a certain inevitability about it, especially given the obvious presence of social pluralism in other areas. It is well worth noting here that Srī Laṅkā was not the only ex-colonial country with a plural society that faced social dissension and tension as the transfer of power progressed.

Caste as a factor of social pluralism in the island remains to be considered. The Sinhalese caste system — Tamil castes would be considered below — was much more clearly rooted in the indigenous soil and although it did not develop free of Indian influences, it has emerged quite distinct from the Indian model, possibly through the impact of Buddhism. The very essence of the Sinhalese caste system was its flexibility: there was no rigid stratification on the basis of an immutable order of precedence of castes. In consequence, some noteworthy changes in the gradations of the hierarchy have been recorded over the years. Thus, the *navandannō* (artificers), who were the principal low caste in the mid-seventeenth century, lost their position to the *karāva* (fishers) within the next 150 years or so. Similarly, there have been changes in the role — this was possible because Sinhalese castes were of the 'functional' type — and consequently in the status of some of the lower castes. The characteristic of flexibility was demonstrated even more strikingly with the absorption of South Indian migrant communities into the caste system: the *karāva, salāgama* (cinnamon peelers), *durāva* (toddy tappers) and *navandannō* are all examples of this.

Whether caste could be considered as a factor of pluralism in the pre-colonial society is debatable. That a spirit of caste-exclusiveness pervaded society cannot be denied, but the degree to which this affected social relations is still not quite clear. On the basis of the present evidence it could be fairly concluded that caste was no great divide in society. The all-important factor many have been the "feudal" framework within which caste functioned: it was not the type of order which would have given rise to a fiercely competitive spirit in society. Quite apart from ritual interdependence, there was an important dependence of castes on each other in their normal activities. This perhaps is why inter-caste regulations were so subtle and equally why castes could not be distinguished strictly in terms of formally organised units. Caste endogamy was there and tabus of caste avoidance existed as well, but the latter did not cover the whole gamut of social relations, and significantly the Sinhalese had no category of 'untouchables'. Above all, there was also the fact of cultural homogenity.

This picture was bound to change with the arrival of the colonial powers. The Portuguese and the Dutch are known to have hesitated before overtly interfering with either the caste system or the "feudal" order, yet neither remained unaffected by their rule. A case in point is the *salāgama* a lowly caste in the conventional hierarchy which acquired a new status on the basis of its economic importance to the colonial powers: with cinnamon becoming the principal commodity of trade, its occupational role assumed hitherto unknown values. Both the Portuguese and the Dutch granted the *salāgama* extensive privileges —deemed 'unconscionable privileges' by the British later — and a whole institutional apparatus was created to maintain the caste as an exclusive group. The *salā-gama* were geographically concentrated and, aided by their newly won status and privileges, they developed a unity and aggressiveness which were later to stand them in good stead. During this period there were also opportunities for castes to shift from the traditionally ascribed occupations. The traditionally pre-eminent *goyigama* (farmers) were perhaps the best placed to accomplish this, but there were other castes who did not hesitate to exploit the new opportunities. Perhaps the classic example are the *kārāvā*. Fishing continued to be the main activity of the *karāva* but by the end of the Dutch rule they had established interests in new areas like trade and various activities which required artisan skills. Because of this type of involvement by castes like the *karāva* outside their traditional occupations at this early stage itself, they were able to achieve a headstart over the others and benefit greatly from the changes which took place under the British.

The British rule was the crucial period in the transformation of the Sinhalese caste system. Here a distinction between the littoral and the interior may be in order. In the low country, the caste system was repeatedly assaulted by the pervasive influences of westernisation. A new framework, different from the 'feudal' order which had sustained the castes, came into being. Caste became divorced from landholding and the state no longer had any stake in the ordering of the caste hierarchy or the maintenance of the caste system. Thus the *salāgama* were freed of the fetters which had bound them to the state economy. Caste claims began to be rejected in the recruitment to the administration. In the new economy, opportunities became available irrespective of caste status, and a similar avenue of mobility was opened up in education. All this meant that the formal indices of caste distinctions, in particular formal caste precedence, were gradually obliterated. This of course did not occur without opposition: at times the opposition came from dominant caste interests, invariably the *goyigama*, and at other times from the officials who were reluctant to relinquish a useful instrument of statecraft.

With these changes caste affiliations no longer had an inevitable link with occupations. The consequence of this should have been the disappearance of inter-caste regulations but it did not happen. Some regulations lapsed because they now had no functional value, but others were maintained intact by social sanction. Moreover, caste endogamy was in no way weakened; even the most sophisticated continued for the most part to abide by it. In the inter-caste relations the removal of the regulatory mechanism of the state was to have important results. This, it has been argued, paved the way for various castes to question the conventional hierarchical arrangement of castes. This was exemplified in the '*kara-goi* contest' which took place at the turn of the nineteenth century. The *karāva* was not the only caste which had the strength to contest the social pre-eminence of the *goyigama;* in particular, two other castes, *salāgama* and *durāva*, also entered the contest. A considerable polemical literature resulted and an entirely new mythology of caste origins was created. The *goyigama* dominance was challenged in more tangible ways too. Thus, on the economic plane there was a heightened competition. Again, the castes which competed with the *goyigama* were the *karāva, salāgama* and the *durāva*, no doubt a reflection of the headstart they had achieved previously. Theirs was not a concerted assault on the *goyigama;* neither did they unite with the *goyigama* to overthrow the Europeans from their position of economic primacy: competition among them was the key characteristic of whatever they did.

In the religious sphere too there is a welter of evidence indicative of a competition among the castes. The *karāva, salāgama* and *durāva* alike sought to vitiate the exclusive claims maintained by the *goyigama* since Kandyan times to enter the *sangha* (clergy) — by means of establishing new *nikāyas* (sects) governed by rules of organisation more suited to their aspirations. This was, in a sense, not only an anti-*goyigama* move but also a stroke at the dominance of the Kandyans in the Buddhist hierarchy.

Given this background, it was inevitable that caste would become a factor in politics too. The primary issue at stake, when a contest developed, was the right of the *goyigama* to sole representation of the Sinhalese in the legislature. A truly superb opportunity of not only contesting the *goyigama* claims but also of eclipsing them arose with the creation of the 'Educated Ceylonese' electorate. The electoral contest, when it came about in 1911, turned out to be one between a *karāva* and a Tamil, but this did not eliminate the caste factor; the *goyigama* voted, almost *en bloc*, for the Tamil candidate, activated by anti-*karāva* sentiments, and thereby ensured his victory. By this time even the colonial government, which had never doubted the propriety of nominating only *goyigama* Sinhalese representatives to the legislature, was forced to recognise the strength of the anti-*goyigama* forces — recognition that was publicly acknowledged by the appointment of a *karāva* to the legislature. Caste conflicts in politics did not thus abate but continued, so much so that in the future constitution-making weightage was given to castes; despite the calls to subsume caste sentiments in the 'national interest', they continued to be an indelible feature in politics.

On the whole, the castes of the interior remained less affected by modernising forces than those of the littoral. Thus, the primacy of the Kandyan *goyigama* was not challenged; there were no emergent castes comparable to the *karāva, salāgama* and *durāva*, the principal strength of whom lay in the low country. The competition that was faced by the Kandyan *goyigama* came from the low-country castes which had made incursions into the interior. Thus in the economy both the *karāva* and the *salāgama* played a noteworthy role, and in electoral politics the *karāva* won some notable victories. That these were more galling to the Kandyan *goyigama* than the competition of the low-country *goyigama* there is no doubt. The caste distinctions took longer to be relaxed in the Kandyan areas, and the inter-caste regulations had a greater hold here than in the littoral. In fact, there was even the survival of the old order in pockets in the Kandyan provinces because of the retention by the British of the old landholding pattern in relation to Buddhist temples and *devalēs* (shrines of gods); those who continued to receive land from these institutions were obliged, for the greater part, to carry on with the ascribed occupations of the 'feudal' order.

The Tamil caste system has received scant attention from scholars. It was distinct from the Sinhalese system in that it was more closely patterned after the Indian model. Thus there was in the hierarchy a priestly caste, Brahmins, who possessed secular powers with a religious basis. It had none of the flexibility of the Sinhalese caste system. Not having the influence of Buddhism, Tamil castes received supernatural or sacred sanction, which made them all the more rigid. The distinctions were sharp enough, not only between the 'clean' and the 'unclean' castes — a distinction absent among the Sinhalese — but also within the main classifications. The spatial distribution of caste settlements within villages and the inter-caste regulations, as well as caste endogamy, therefore assumed a greater meaning in the Tamil society. To what extent caste distinctions mattered was amply illustrated in the restriction of entry to Hindu temples to particular castes.

It is generally agreed that the Tamil caste system was hardly affected by the rule of the colonial powers. Considering the impression of modernising forces like education upon Tamils, this is indeed surprising. The reasons for this have yet to be properly explored but it may partly be explained by the close connection of Hinduism with the caste system at the practical as well as the doctrinal level. The consequence of this was that the hierarchical dominance of the *vellalas* (farmers, approximating to the Sinhalese *goyigama*), who also held a commanding numerical superiority, was never effectively challenged by the other castes. As it turned out, the *vellala* proved to be the main beneficiary of the new opportunities that were opened up by the British too.

SELECT BIBLIOGRAPHY

Arasaratnam, S., *Ceylon*, Englewood Cliffs, N. J. (1964).

Farmer, B. H., *Ceylon: a Divided Nation*. London: Institute of Race Relations (1963).

Kearney, R. N. *Communalism and Language in the Politics of Ceylon*, Durham, N. C. (1972).

Leach, E. (ed.), *Aspects of Caste in South India, Ceylon and North-West Pakistan*, Cambridge University Press (1960).

Ludowyk, E. F. C., *The Story of Ceylon*, London (1962); 2nd. ed., 1967.

————— , *The Modern History of Ceylon*, London (1966).

Nadaraja, T., *The Legal System of Ceylon in its Historical Setting*, Leiden (1972).

Pieris, R., *Sinhalese Social Organization: the Kandyan Period*, Colombo (1960).

Roberts, M., 'The Rise of the Karawa', *Ceylon Studies Seminar*, 1968/9 Series, No. 5 (mimeographed paper).

Ryan, B., *Caste in Modern Ceylon*, New Brunswick (1953).

Tambiah, S. J., 'Ethnic Representation in Ceylon's Higher Administrative Services, 1870-1946', *University of Ceylon Review*, XIII (1955), 113-34.

————— , 'The Politics of Language in India and Ceylon', *Modern Asian Studies*, I (1967), 215-40.

University of Ceylon, *History of Ceylon*, Vol. I, S. Paranavitana ed., Colombo (1959 and 1960); Vol. III, K. M. de Silva ed., Colombo (1973).

Wriggins, W. Howard, *Ceylon: Dilemmas of a New Nation*, Princeton (1960).

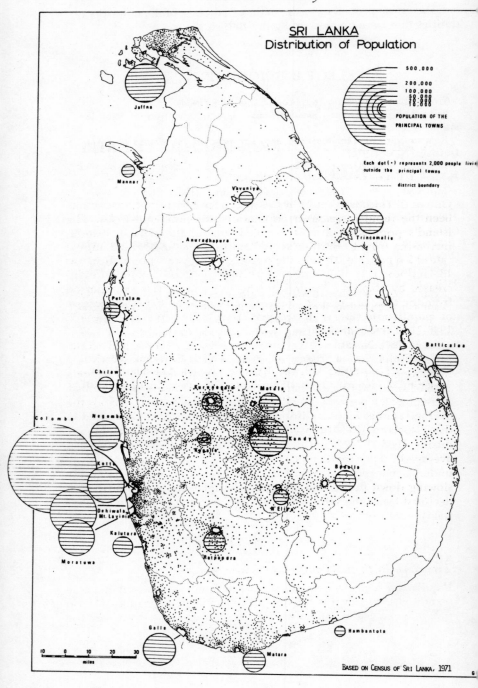

SRI LANKA
Distribution of Population

POPULATION OF THE
PRINCIPAL TOWNS

Each dot (·) represents 2,000 people living
outside the principal towns

.... district boundary

BASED ON CENSUS OF SRI LANKA, 1971

4

A REVIEW OF DEMOGRAPHIC TRENDS

by N. Balakrishnan and H. M. Gunasekera

One of the most striking features of Srī Laṅkā's recent history has
been the rapid increase in population since the mid-1940s. The
island's population almost doubled during the period 1946-71,
increasing from 6.6 million to 12.7 million — at an average annual
rate of 2.6 per cent. In 1974 the country's mid-year population was
13.4 million. It is significant that while the country's population increased by about 4.2 million during the seventy-five-year period
from the time of the first nation-wide census in 1871, the increase
of population during the subsequent twenty-five-year period,
1946-71, was 6.1 million (see Table 1).

Since the beginning of the 1940s there had been a marked acceleration in the rate of growth of Srī Laṅkā's population, which was
maintained until the mid 1960s. During the two intercensal periods
1946-53 and 1953-63, population growth recorded an average annual
increase of 2.8 per cent. In all the previous intercensal periods the
average annual increase did not exceed 1.6 per cent. Compared to
the 1940s and 1950s the rate of increase of population was lower
during 1963-71 — 2.3 per cent per annum — and during 1970-2 it
averaged 2.0 per cent, and currently the annual increase is slightly
under 2.0 per cent. Thus since the mid-1960s there has been definite
slowing down in the rate of population growth, as the birth rate
declined faster than the death rate, which came to be more or less
stabilised at low levels.

I

Trends in Birth Rates and Death Rates

Population increase depends on two factors, viz. natural increase
(excess of births over deaths) and international migration. Migration increase — associated with the arrival of Indian labour with the

Table 1.   POPULATION OF SRĪ LAṄKĀ

Census Year	(1) Total population	(2) Intercensal Increase	(%)	(3) Natural Increase	(4) Migration Increase	(5) 3 as % of 2	(6) 4 as % of 2
1871	2,400,380						
1881	2,759,738	359,358	(14.9)	119,792	239,566	33.3	66.7
1891	3,007,789	248,051	(8.9)	144,260	103,791	58.1	41.9
1901	3,565,954	558,165	(18.5)	225,406	332,759	40.4	59.6
1911	4,106,350	540,396	(15.1)	356,147	184,249	65.9	34.1
1921	4,498,605	392,255	(9.5)	319,410	72,845	81.4	18.6
1931	5,306,871	808,266	(17.9)	656,990	151,276	81.3	18.7
1946	6,657,339	1,350,468	(25.4)	1,280,916	69,552	94.8	5.2
1953	8,097,895	1,440,556	(21.6)	1,328,199	112,357	92.2	7.8
1963	10,582,064	2,484,169	(30.6)	2,513,248	−29,079	101.2	−1.2
1971	12,711,143	2,129,079	(20.1)	2,208,061	−78,982	103.7	−3.7

Sources: Department of Census and Statistics:: Census data, *Ceylon Year Book*, 1970; *The Population of Srī Lanka*, Colombo, 1974.

development of the plantations — significantly contributed to Srī Laṅkā's population growth during the many decades prior to independence. Until the beginning of the twentieth century, migration increase constituted over 50 per cent of the increase in total population. Thereafter it declined substantially and during the periods 1931-46 and 1946-53, on account of the increasing restrictions placed on immigration, migration increase amounted to only 5-7 per cent of the total increase in population. Since the mid-1950s net migration has had a mild negative effect on population growth because of the repatriation of Indian immigrant labour. Srī Laṅkā's "population explosion" of the 1940s and 1950s has been almost entirely due to natural increase brought about by high fertility and sharply reduced mortality.

The island's demographic profile showed a substantial and spectacular change during the late 1940s. Although the country's crude death rate had tended to decline in the earlier periods, the decline recorded during the late 1940s — largely on account of the successful malaria eradiction compaign[1] and improved medical and health facilities-was very marked and dramatic. Srī Laṅkā's crude death rate was around 21 per thousand of population during 1943-5; it had dropped sharply to 14 per thousand — a reduction of 33 per cent — by 1947. Thereafter it declined gradually to 8.6 per thousand in 1960 and to 7.5 per thousand in 1970 (see Table 2).

The country's crude birth rate, in contrast, remained at high levels for a considerable time—a situation aptly described as one of a 'primitive birth rate with a modernised death rate'[2]. During the 1940s and 1950s a substantial decline in mortality was accompanied by very little change in the birth rate, which remained consistently at a high level. The widening gap between the crude death rate and birth rate is shown by the fact that between the first decade of the present century and the 1950s the average crude birth rate declined only slightly from 38.1 to 37.6 per thousand. For the same period the average death rate dropped substantially from an average of 28.9 to 10.7 per thousand. With the beginning of the 1960s, however, the crude birth rate showed a more steady decline; during 1961-3 it averaged 35 per thousand and then dropped to 30 per thousand during 1970-2. Currently (mid-1975) it is around 28 per thousand. The decline in the birth rate in recent years has been attributed to increasing age at marriage among women (and the resultant fall in the proportions of married women in the youngest age groups) and a decline in marital fertility among females, more particularly marked in the 30-44 age group.[3] The present trends, characterised by a declining birth rate and a death rate that has already reached low levels with little likelihood of any major chan-

ges, indicate a new phase in Srī Laṅkā's demographic transition.
During the post-independence period the infant and maternal
mortality rates have also recorded a sharp decline. The infant
mortality rate of 141 (infant deaths per 1,000 live births) in 1946
dropped to 67 in 1956; in the years that followed there was a gradual
fall in the rate, which declined to 48 in 1967. Similar trends were

Table 2. VITAL STATISTICS

Year	Births per 1,000	Deaths per 1,000	Rate of natural increase (%)	Deaths under 1 year of age per 1,000 live births	Maternal death rate per 1,000 live births
1941	35.6	18.3	1.8	129	15.3
1942	35.8	18.1	1.8	120	14.4
1943	39.5	20.8	1.9	132	13.3
1944	36.1	20.8	1.5	135	13.7
1945	35.9	21.5	1.4	140	16.5
1946	37.4	19.8	1.8	141	15.5
1947	38.6	14.0	2.5	101	10.6
1948	39.7	13.0	2.7	92	8.3
1949	39.1	12.4	2.7	87	6.5
1950	39.7	12.4	2.7	82	5.6
1951	39.8	12.7	2.7	82	5.8
1952	38.8	11.8	2.7	78	5.8
1953	38.7	10.7	2.8	71	4.9
1954	35.7	10.2	2.5	72	4.6
1955	37.3	10.8	2.6	71	4.1
1956	36.4	9.8	2.7	67	3.8
1957	36.5	10.1	2.6	68	3.7
1958	35.8	9.7	2.6	64	3.9
1959	37.0	9.1	2.8	58	3.4
1960	36.6	8.6	2.8	57	3.0
1961	35.8	8.0	2.8	52	2.6
1962	35.5	8.5	2.7	53	3.0
1963	34.1	8.5	2.4	56	2.4
1964	33.2	8.8	2.4	57	2.8
1965	33.1	8.2	2.5	53	2.4
1966	32.3	8.3	2.4	54	2.2
1967	31.6	7.5	2.4	48	1.7
1968	32.0	7.9	2.4	50	1.8
1969	30.4	8.3	2.2	53	1.5
1970	29.4	7.5	2.2	51	1.2

Source: Administration Report of the Registrar General (1965);
Statistical Pocket Book of Srī Laṅkā (1973).

observed in the maternal mortality rates as well (see Table 2). A better indication of mortality level is given by the expectation of life at birth. In this respect there has been considerable improvement over the years. The life expectancy for males increased from 46.8 years during 1945-7 to 57.6 years in 1952 and 64.8 years in 1974. For the same periods female life expectancy increased from 44.7 to 55.5 years and to 66.9 years respectively. It is important to note that female life expectancy has exceeded that of the male since about 1962-4, which is a reversal of past trends.[4]

Future Population Trends

It has already been observed that international migration has ceased to be a factor in Srī Laṅkā's population growth. This trend is most likely to continue in the future years as well, with net migration having a slight negative effect on population growth on account of the implementation of the programme of repatriation of persons of Indian origin in Srī Laṅkā. No further significant changes could also be expected in the death rates,[5] as they seem to have stabilised at low levels. Therefore the growth of the country's future population would depend mostly on the trends in birth rates.

A recent official publication[6] provides estimates of future population of Srī Laṅkā based on "high", "medium" and "low" projections for the period 1971-2001, using different assumptions about future fertility trends. According to the high projection, which forms the upper limit, the country's population could nearly double itself, increasing from 12.7 million in 1971 to 24.7 million in the year 2001. The medium projection, assuming a gradual decline in fertility — and could therefore represent "the most probable future population" — gives an increase of 70 per cent, from 12.7 million to 21.7 million, during the thirty year period. Even the low projection, which is based on the assumption of a very rapid decline in fertility, shows an estimated increase of population from 12.7 million to 19.3 million by the year 2001, giving nearly a 52 per cent increase for the period.

Table 3.   POPULATION BY AGE (IN THOUSANDS)

	1946	(%)	1953	(%)	1963	(%)	1971	(%)
All ages:	6,657	(100.0)	8,098	(100.0)	10,582	(100.0)	12,711	(100.0)
0 – 14	2,478	(37.3)	3,215	(39.7)	4,390	(41.5)	4,998	(39.3)
15 – 24	1,322	(19.8)	1,471	(18.1)	1,907	(18.0)	2,607	(20.5)
24 – 64	2,626	(39.4)	3,127	(38.6)	3,837	(36.2)	4,557	(35.8)
65 +	229	(3.4)	284	(3.5)	448	(4.2)	549	(4.4)

Source: Census data, *Statistical Pocket Book 1973; Ceylon Year Book 1970.*

The demographic 'revolution' associated with high birth rates and sharply reduced death rates has resulted inevitably in an age structure in which a preponderance of persons in the relatively young age groups in the total population is the most noteworthy feature. Children under fifteen years, as a proportion of total population, increased from 37 per cent (2.5 million) in 1946 to 40 per cent (3.2 million) in 1953 and 42 per cent (4.4 million) in 1963; thereafter the proportion fell to 39 per cent in 1971 (4.9 million). Persons in the older age groups, sixty-five years and over, constituted a very much smaller proportion in total population — between 3.4 per cent and 4.4 per cent during 1946-71. Persons falling within the broad working age group 15-64, as a proportion of total population, declined from 59 per cent in 1946 to 57 per cent in 1953 and 54 per cent in 1963; in 1971 this proportion increased to 56 per cent. The age structure of the population had resulted in the rise in the dependency ratio[7], which increased from 68.6 in 1946 to 76.5 in 1953 and 83 in 1963 — significantly higher than what could be observed in some of the other less developed Asian countries.[8] In 1971, however, the dependency ratio has dropped to 78, reflecting the impact of declining fertility trends in the 1960s.

Population Distribution and Density

The distribution by districts of population and density for the census years are shown in Table 4. The largest concentrations of population are to be found in the districts of the south-west littoral and central regions of the island — these areas also roughly coincide with the agroclimatic region known as the wet zone (with an average annual rainfall of more than 75 inches). These districts comprise little less than 40 per cent of the country's total area but account for about three-quarters of its total population. The district of Colombo itself (the island's principal administrative and commercial centre) has nearly 20 per cent of the island's population with only 3 per cent of its total area. The rest of the country — the northern, north central and eastern regions — is in general more sparsely populated. These districts cover approximately two-thirds of the country's total area and have within them only about one-third of the total population. According to the 1971 census, most of the districts of the wet zone had populations of over 500,000. In the dry zone, all districts, with the exception of Jaffna, had populations of less than 500,000; some of them had populations of less than 200,000.

Between 1946 and 1971, Srī Laṅkā's overall population density increased from 263 to 509 persons per sq. mile, one of the highest in Asia today. Population density varies considerably as between districts, ranging from the highest density of 3,374 persons per sq.

Table 4.   POPULATION BY DISTRICTS (THOUSANDS)

	Area sq. miles	Population 1946	Population 1971	Increase 1946-71 (%)	Density (persons per sq. mile) 1946	Density (persons per sq. mile) 1971
Srī Lankā	25,332	6657.3	12711.1	91.8	263	509
Colombo	808	1420.3	2672.6	88.1	1,758	3374
Kalutara	624	456.6	731.8	60.2	732	1180
Kandy	914	711.4	1187.2	66.8	779	1299
Mātalé	770	155.7	316.3	103.1	173	411
Nuvara Eliya	474	268.1	453.2	69.0	566	956
Galle	652	459.8	737.4	60.3	705	1142
Matara	481	351.9	588.2	67.1	732	1223
Hambantota	1,013	149.7	341.0	127.7	148	341
Jaffna	998	424.8	704.3	65.7	425	730
Mannar	964	31.5	77.8	146.9	33	81
Vavūniyā	1,467	23.2	95.5	311.6	16	67
Batticaloa	1,016	203.2	258.1	161.2	73	271
Amparai	1,048	−	272.8		−	237
Trincomalee	1,177	75.9	191.9	152.8	72	190
Kurunägala	1,844	485.0	1028.1	111.9	263	558
Puttalam	1,172	43.1	379.8	107.6	47	331
Chilaw		139.8			533	
Anuradhapura	2,808	139.5	389.2	296.4	35	141
Polonnaruwa	1,331	−	163.8		−	125
Badulla	1,089	372.2	616.3	116.8	114	566
Monarāgala	2,785	−	191.4		−	70
Ratnapura	1,250	343.6	661.7	92.5	275	529
Kägalle	642	401.8	652.1	62.2	626	1016

* In 1946 and 1953 Badulla included Monarāgala and Batticaloa Amparai. In 1963 and 1971 Puttalam included Chilaw.

Source: *Statistical Abstract 1970-71*, Dept. of Census and Statistics.

mile (1971) in the Colombo district to the lowest of 67 persons in the Vavūniyā district. Many districts in the south-west and central regions have densities of over 1,000 persons per sq. mile. Compared to these densely populated areas, districts in the north (excluding Jaffna), north-central and eastern regions have much lower population densities of less than 300 persons per sq. mile. The dry-zone districts of Anurādhapura, Polonnaruwa, Vavūniyā, Mannar and Monarāgala have the lowest densities, some of them less than 100 persons per sq. mile.

During 1946-71 population in all districts increased considerably, although the rate of increase in the sparsely populated districts of the dry zone has been much higher than that of the densely populated districts in the wet zone. The relatively thinly populated areas such as Anurādhapura, Vavūniyā, Mannar and Trincomalee, have recorded a population increase of more than 100 % although the size of populations still remains small. On the other hand the densely populated districts of the south-west and centre, with a few exceptions, recorded population increase of less than 100%. Apart from the natural increase of population in all districts — which showed some variations as between districts — internal migration was a contributory factor in the population growth of the dry zone districts. The major colonisation and land settlement schemes there opened up a substantial area of hitherto unused and jungle land for agricultural activities from the 1930s onwards. This has contributed to the movement of population away from many of the densely populated wet-zone areas, where the pressure on land became more acute with the swift growth of population.

Srī Laṅkā's population growth intensified the pressure on land, which came to be felt more acutely in the wet zone districts where most of the available agricultural land had already been brought under use by the beginning of the twentieth century for the development of the plantations. For the island as a whole density in terms of agricultural land increased from 1.56 persons per acre in 1946 to 2.23 in 1962.[9] Taking agricultural land and rural population, the number of rural persons per acre of agricultural land increased from 1.34 in 1946 to 1.81 in 1962 to 2.02 in 1969. Snodgrass has also estimated that between 1871 and 1921 "peasant population" per acre of cultivated land remained more or less around 1.8 But thereafter it increased from 1.8 (1921) to 3.1 in 1959.[11] Population density in terms of thousands per acre of land (in 1962) in the wet zone was about six times that of the dry zone, indicating that the mounting pressure of population on land came to be felt more acutely in the wet zone areas — resulting in higher incidence of landlessness and adverse effects on the size of cultivated land holdings.

Srī Laṅkā's population is still predominantly rural; the proportion of rural population amounts to 78 per cent of the total. Between the two population censuses of 1963 and 1971, both of which adopted a uniform definition of urban areas, the ratio of urban population increased from 19.1 to 22.4 per cent. Available evidence shows no marked trends towards urbanisation in Srī Laṅkā during the past two decades or so. It is estimated that the proportion of urban population defined to include towns with a population above 2,000 increased in 1946-71 from 20.5 to 22.1 per cent. Urban population, considering only towns with a population over 20,000, increased from 11.5 to 15.8 per cent during the same period![2] As the country's economy underwent no significant structural changes, the drift of rural population to urban areas did not become a marked feature. Internal migration to towns was minimised for other reasons as well: there was the movement of people to the dry-zone areas, following their development through the government-sponsored colonisation and land settlement schemes; government socio-economic policies and programmes directed towards the rural areas — with a substantial social welfare element — also helped to prevent any significant movement of people away from the rural areas.

Ethnic Groups

The social composition of the country's population is a heterogeneous one, embracing different "racial" or ethnic groups, each possessing some distinctive characteristics based on language, religion and historical antecedents. The Sinhalese, with the highest concentration in the south-west coastal areas, form the majority community, accounting for 72 per cent of the Island's total population (see Statistical Appendix). They are largely Buddhists. The Srī Laṅkā Tamils, mostly Hindus, constitute a significant minority community, forming 11 per cent of the total population. They are distributed along the north and east coast with a heavy concentration in the Jaffna region. Together with the Indian Tamils, who are found predominantly in the estate areas of the central region, the Tamil population amounted to 20 per cent of the total in 1971. The number of Indian Tamils showed a marginal increase between the censuses of 1963 and 1971 while that of Indian Moors had declined owing to their emigration to India.[13] Ethnic differences between the Sinhalese and the Tamils became more marked in the country since the mid 1950s resulting in communal antagonism and political rivalry.[14]

The Moors in the country fall into two groups: the Srī Laṅkā Moors and Indian Moors — the latter being numerically very small. Of the 853,000 Moors in 1971, the Indian Moors amounted to 29,000 and the Srī Laṅkā Moors to 824,000 — the proportion of the Srī Laṅkā Moors in the total population being 6.5 per cent. The Moors, whose home language is mostly Tamil, have been able to preserve their ethnic identity largely though their religion, Islam (this also holds true for the Malays). The Srī Laṅkā Moors are spread throughout the country, but their largest concentration is on the east coast. All other ethnic groups —comprising the Malays, Burghers and Eurasians, Europeans, Veddhas and others —together form less than 1 per cent of the total population. The Malays, who have nearly doubled

during the past twenty-five years, numbered 43,000 in 1971, constituting 0.3 per cent of the total. The Burghers and Eurasians, who
are of mixed Srī Lankān and European ancestry, amounted to 44,000
in 1971, also forming 0.3 per cent of the total population. Many of
them have recently emigrated to other countries, mostly Australia.

The Veddhas in Srī Lankā are an aboriginal group whose ancestry, according to legend, is traceable to the pre-historic inhabitants
of the island. They live mostly as hunters, jungle-dwellers or no-
mads in the very remote eastern parts of the country. The number
of Veddhas recorded in the censuses had declined steeply from
about 5,000 in 1931 to 400 in 1963. The 1971 census does not give the
Veddha population separately as it has been grouped with others.
The declining number of the Veddha community partly reflects
the difficulties of enumeration and partly its increasing assimila-
tion with the other ethnic groups.

Literacy

Much educational progress has taken place in Srī Lankā since the
introduction of the Free Education Scheme in 1944. This has contributed to a high rate of literacy (defined as ability to read and
write). Between 1946 and 1971 the literacy rate in the population of
ten years and over increased from 65 to 78 per cent. For the male
population the rate of literacy increased from 78 to 85 per cent
during the same period; for the female population it rose from 53
to 71 per cent. The highest rate of literacy — nearly 90 per cent —
is to be found in the age group 10-24, a good indication of the extent
of educational expansion. Nearly 89 per cent of the population
over ten years are found to be literate in the urban sector, while in
the rural sector the rate amounted to 84 per cent.[15]

II

Impact of Population Growth

The rapid rise in Srī Lankā's population since the mid-1940s has
undoubtedly been a major factor in the country's socio-economic
scene throughout the entire post-independence period. Although
Srī Lankā did not have the highest rates of population increase in
the Asian region, it is probably true that it had to sustain a high rate
of population increase for a longer period than many of the other
less developed countries.[16] Srī Lankā's "population explosion"
created considerable socio-economic pressures in the context of a
socio-political system with a pronounced bias towards "social welfare", to a higher degree than in many other Asian countries.

The pressures of population growth were felt more directly or acutely in the field of public expenditure on (mostly free) social services such as education, health and food subsidies, which formed the cornerstone of social welfare policy and to which all governments in the post-independence period were strongly committed. Until the 1950s, under conditions of relative prosperity, largely due to a comparatively favourable foreign exchange situation, the socio-economic pressures arising from population increase were found to be more easily manageable. However, in the 1960s, with a relatively poor economic performance in general and a deteriorating foreign exchange situation due to stagnant export earnings and a sharp fall in the terms of trade resulting in reduced "import capacity", the impact of population growth came to be felt more acutely on both the domestic and foreign exchange resources of the country. The rapid growth of population in an economy which is heavily dependent on imports — particularly food imports — combined with food subsidies, notwithstanding the modest increase in domestic food production, inevitably created considerable pressures on the country's foreign exchange resources and balance of payments. And "the fundamental contrast between fast population growth and slow growth of export earnings"[17] emerged as the salient characteristic of the post-independence period.

The Ten Year Plan (1959) summed up the dilemma of development policy as follows: "A sizeable proportion of the resources for investment have to be devoted to meeting the social needs of the rising population in the way of school buildings, houses, sanitation systems, and so on. Investments in these fields compete with investments in the directly productive spheres and result in an allocation of resources unsuited to the needs of maximum growth. Such a maldistribution of resources would itself have a cumulative depressing effects on the level of future investment. Ceylon is clearly facing problems of this sort. Not only does the consumption needs of a growing population tend to depress the rate of investment but the social services, education, health and housing themselves make increasing claims on investment resources".[18]

Successive governments since Independence have been committed to maintaining more or less constant per capita expenditure on a wide range of social services — education, health, subsidised food and other transfer payments. The swift increase of population combined with a gradual rise in the unit cost of such services contributed to the rapid expansion of social welfare spending in the budget. In what emerged as the conflict between social welfare policies and development oriented policies,[19] the demographic pressures played a significant role. The data on government expenditure (see Statistical Appendix) shows that the total social welfare expenditure increased substantially in the 1950s and 1960s. During the period 1954/5-1970/1, the total social services expenditures increased by nearly 320 per cent, exceeding the rate of increase of total government expenditure. The relative share of government expenditure going into social welfare services increased from 34 per cent in 1954/5 to 45 per cent in 1964/5. As a proportion of the GNP (at current prices) the expenditure on social services, largely associated with population increase, rose from 6 per cent in 1954/5 to 13.5 per cent in 1964/5.

Labour Force and Employment. The rapid increase of population in the context of a relatively stagnant economy aggravated the employment situation in recent years. The available data from the censuses and from sample surveys on labour force, employment and unemployment are neither systematic nor easily comparable over different periods since they lack uniformity in definitions, concepts and coverage. However, they may be sufficient to enable us to deal with some of the broad trends.

The full impact of population increase on the labour force or the economically active population was delayed to some extent on account of the very nature of the demographic change that resulted in the rising proportion of young persons below the working age group, which led to a swift increase in the school-going population. Snodgrass[20] has estimated that during 1946-60 the labour force increased by 2.2 per cent per annum while population increased by 2.7 per cent per annum; the labour force also fell as a proportion of total population from 37.7 per cent in 1946 to 35.4 per cent in 1960. For the subsequent period as well, estimates of the labour force derived from sample surveys showed low overall labour force participation rates.[21] These trends reflected changes in the age structure in the population, as well as in age-specific participation rates. During 1946-63 the proportion of working-age population had declined.

The age-specific participation rates for both the youngest age groups (10-14) and the older age groups of sixty-five and over had also declined; and the decline in participation rates had closely followed the decline in the proportion of the working age population during 1946-63.[22] It is expected, however, that in the near future the share of the working-age population could increase significantly (the proportion had already shown an increase in 1971 (see Table 3) due to channging participation rates among the young age groups and females. In this context one could also expect a future rise in the overall labour-force participation ratio. A survey in 1973 showed a higher overall labour force participation rate of 35.1 per cent, which is possibly an "indication of a reversal in the trend of labour force participation rates".[23]

From the available estimates no accurate comparison could be made between increase in the country's labour force and that of employment during the past two decades. However, it is possible to get some idea of the existing gap between the two. During 1946-71 the country's labour force (employed and unemployed persons) increased from 2.6 to 4.2 million — an increase of 60 per cent. Employed population, however, increased from 2.5 to 3.6 million — by 44 per cent — during the same period. Of the total increase of about 1.1 million in employed population during this period, nearly 45 per cent was accounted for by agriculture (mostly domestic sector), forestry and fishing, which still account for little over 50 per cent of the total employed work force in the country. It is more likely that the gap between employment and labour force widened in the 1960s. According to one estimate,[24] the country's labour force increased between 1946 and 1953 on average by 54,000 every year; between 1953 and 1963 the increase averaged 62,000 per annum. During 1963-71 the average increase annually has been much higher — around 110,000. Data based on labour-force projection, linked to medium projection of population, suggested an annual increase of about 150,000 for the period 1971 to 1981.[25]

The available data on unemployment, though not very reliable, indicated that during most of the 1960s the number of unemployed had been around 400,000-450,000 or about 10-12 per cent of the labour force; it is difficult to say whether there has been any marked increase in unemployment during this period. The ILO Survey of 1959/60[26] reported total unemployment to be between 340,000 (low estimate) and 450,000 (high estimate), varying between 10.5-12.8 per cent of the labour force. The Consumer Finance Survey of 1963[27] estimated unemployment as 455,000 or 13 per cent of the labour force. Again the 1968 Labour Force Survey reported an unemployment figure of 450,000, about 12 per cent of the labour force. The number of unemployed reported in the 1969/70 Survey[28] amounted to 546,000, or close to 14 per cent of the labour force The most recent estimate from the 1973 survey gave a much higher unemployment figure 793,000 or 17 per cent of the labour force.[29] The above estimates, though not easily comparable, do suggest an overall increase in unemployment[30] since the end of the 1960s. The rising trend in overall unemployment seems to be consistent with both the relatively poor economic performance as well as the rise in the numbers entering the labour force in more recent years.

The presence of substantial open unemployment has become a major national question in Sri Lanka today. This is likely to remain the most difficult and intractable problem for many years to come. What is perhaps more disturbing about the country's unemployment situation is that it is concentrated for the most part among the youth with relatively higher educational attainments. According to the data from the Socio-economic Survey (1969/70) summarised in Table 5, of the total of openly unemployed, amounting to 546,000, about 83 per cent are in the 15-24 years age group. The unemployment rate for this age group was about three times as high as the all-island rate for all ages. The unemployment rate for females in this age group is higher (40 per cent) than for males (33 per cent), indicating that young females are entering the work force in larger numbers. In terms of numbers, most of the unemployed are concentrated in the rural sector, although the actual rate of unemployment is slightly higher in the urban than in the rural sector. The rate of unemployment seems much higher among the females in both the rural and urban sectors.

The educational attainments of the unemployed population showed that only 6 per cent of the total had no schooling. About 45 per cent had completed schooling in the middle grade (about 8-9 years of schooling); another 27 per cent had obtained GCE(O) level or higher qualifications (ten or more years of schooling). Considering the educational level of the unemployed in the young age group 15-24 it is found that nearly 75 per cent had attained an educational level up to and above middle school. With regard to unemployment and educational levels, the situation indicates a definite "disharmony between educational output and the employment market", implying that the chances of obtaining employment tend to diminish as the educational level of the labour force entrant increases, even though there is a strong positive relationship between better jobs, educational levels and income levels.[31] The slow rate of economic growth and inadequate employment opportunities in the context of a rapid expansion in the numbers coming out of the country's educational system, as well as a certain "structural mismatching"[32] of expectations of educated youth and employment opportunities, have all combined to produce a serious and complicated unemployment situation among the country's youth.

Population Policy and Family Planning

Until recent years, Srī Laṅkā, lacked any clear population policy despite the rapidity with which its population has increased. Political inhibitions arising from ethnic sensitivities had prevented

Table 5. COMPOSITION OF UNEMPLOYED POPULATION (15-64 YEARS)

All ages	No. unemployed Both sexes		Unemployment Rate (as % of labour force)			Educational level (%distribution)			
	No. in '000s	% of total	Both sexes	Male	Female	No. schooling	Primary	Middle school	GCE(O) and above
Urban	115.7	21.1	17.8	13.7	21.3	2.0	18.0	52.0	27.4
Rural	379.1	69.4	14.6	10.9	28.0	4.0	19.8	45.6	30.6
Estate	51.1	9.4	7.5	10.9	3.5	24.4	52.0	20.8	2.8
All-island	545.7	100.0	13.9	11.4	21.2	5.5	22.5	44.6	27.4
Selected Age Groups									
15-24	457.0	82.6	35.6	33.6	40.3	4.6	22.1	46.8	26.5
25-35	69.5	12.7	7.4	5.2	14.4	2.3	18.8	42.2	36.7

Source: Preliminary Report of the Socio-Economic Survey 1969-70, Department of Census and Statistics.

political parties and governments from making any definite commitments on this question. The attitudes to family planning and
population control have been influenced to some extent by the fear,
however unfounded, that differential rates of population increase
between the different ethnic groups might upset the existing ethnic
proportions in the population.[33]

Family planning as an organised programme at a semi-official
level began with the activities of the Family Planning Association
founded in 1953, the efforts and activities of which the government
supported with an annual grant. By 1958, when its grant was raised
to Rs. 75,000, the Association had begun to use the facilities and
personnel available in the government medical institutions for its
family planning work. In that year an agreement was signed between the Srī Laṅkā and Swedish governments to initiate a Pilot
Project on family planning. This was designed to investigate the
attitudes towards family planning, the response to, and acceptance
of, the different methods of family planning, and to train staff for
family planning work.

In 1965 the government made its first significant official policy
statement accepting family planning as an integral part of the
maternal and child health services falling within the work of the
Ministry of Health. Immediately after initiating the National Family
Planning Programme, the government adopted a series of measures
to extend and popularise birth control on an island-wide scale.
External assistance for the programme was received from the Swedish
International Development Authority. With the official acceptance
of family planning, an organised programme of family planning
work came to be integrated with the maternal health care programme under the Department of Health. In 1966 the government
also set a target of reducing the crude birth rate from 33 per thousand
to 25 per thousand over a period from 1966-75 through a national
programme of family planning work. Family planning programmes
sought to achieve the objectives of limiting births as well as that of
improving the health of the population, particularly mothers and
children.

In the year before the 1970 general elections the government
thought it advisable, for political reasons, to slow down the impetus
of the National Family Planning Programme because of opposition
to such activities from various groups. Although it did not become
a serious political issue, various groups expressed disapproval of
the Family Planning Programme aimed at limiting births on the
grounds that it would upset the existing ethnic balance of the population to the disadvantage of the majority community.[34] The publi-
city given to the Family Planning Programme was reduced to a

minimum, and the monetary incentives given to certain categories of family planning personnel were dropped.

The United Front government which came to power in 1970 was initially cautious in its attitude to the National Family Planning Programme. However, by the time its Five-Year Plan (1972) came to be submitted, a more positive statement emerged supporting family planning and birth control. The Five-Year Plan commented that "the strain on resources imposed by the present rate of population growth would almost be intolerable" and therefore urged that very high priority be given to the diffusion of family planning facilities among the mass of the adult population.[35]

Despite the problems arising from ethnic fears and those arising from social and religious prejudices, it appears that there is strong motivation for family planning, which is becoming increasingly accepted among many sections of the population. This is particularly evident among the middle classes due to considerations of both maternal and family health and the desire for smaller families for economic reasons. To the country as a whole the likely benefits accruing from reduced births would be felt mostly in the long run. A recent study has estimated that possible savings in the government budget, on education, health and food subsidies over a thirty-year period, resulting from a rapid decline in fertility on account of a more comprehensive and intensified family planning programme, would be at least fifteen times the cost of such a programme.[36] Although such estimates could be subject to a wide margin of error. the likely savings could be substantial, and this alone would justify an expanded family planning programme.

It is insufficiently realised that many government social welfare programmes, though not all directly pronatalist, tend to have "a dampening effect on the restrictionist population policy".[37] Most welfare programmes, extended mainly to the lower income groups, are an integral part of the anti-poverty measures. However, it may be necessary to redesign them so as to be more consistent with the objectives of family planning and population control.

REFERENCES

1. Estimates by Peter Newman (*Malaria Eradication and Population Growth*, Ann Arbor, University of Michigan, 1965) give "60 per cent of the credit for the acceleration of population growth to malaria control and 40 per cent to other causes", quoted in D. R. Snodgrass, *Ceylon, An Export Economy in Transition*, Homewood, Ill. (1966), p. 88.
2. Joan Robinson, 'Economic Possibilities of Ceylon', *Papers by Visiting Economists*, Planning Secretariat, Colombo (1959), p. 39.

3. UN-UNESCO-WHO, *Family Planning Evaluation Mission to Ceylon,* 1971, pp. 13-16. Also see C. H. S. Jayawardene, "The Declining Birth Rate in Ceylon", *Modern Ceylon Studies,* Vol. 1, No. 2, 1970, Peradeniya, pp. 246-55.
4. Department of Census and Statistics, *The Population of Sri Lanka,* 1974, Colombo, Table 2-22, p. 28.
5. S. Selvaratnam and S. A. Meegama, 'Towards a Population Policy for Ceylon', *Marga,* Vol. 1, No. 2, 1970, Colombo.
6. *The Population of Srī Laṅkā,* op. cit, Table 61, pp. 90-2.
7. $\dfrac{\text{Persons 0-14 years plus persons 65 years and above}}{\text{Persons 15-64 years}}$ X 100
8. See Sultan S. Hashmi, 'Constraints in Economic Development: The Problems of Population Growth in South Asia', in *Economic Development in South Asia,* edited by E. A. G. Robinson and M. Kidron, Macmillan, London (1970), p. 14.
9. *Ceylon Census of Agriculture,* Dept. of Census and Statistics, Vol. 1, Table 1, p. 29. The total extent of agricultural land increased from 4,267,398 acres in 1946 to 4,666,553 in 1962 — by 9.3 per cent; total population increased by 57 per cent during the same period from 6,657,339 to 10,443,000. Assuming that during 1962-72 the annual acreage increase averaged 30,000, compared to the figure of 25,000 for 1946-62, the total extent of agricultural land area for 1972 would amount to 4,966,553 acres. On this basis the density in terms of agricultural land works out to 2.60 persons per acre in 1972.
10. G. W. Jones and S. Selvaratnam, *Population Growth and Economic Development in Ceylon,* Colombo (1972) p. 193, Table 51.
11. Snodgrass, op. cit. p. 48, Table 2-8.
12. Godfrey Gunatilleke, "The Rural-Urban Balance and Development: The Experience of Sri Lanka", *Marga,* Vol. 2, No. 1, (1973), Colombo, pp. 45-6. Also see G. W. Jones and S. Selvaratnam "Urbanisation in Ceylon 1946-63", *Modern Ceylon Studies,* Vol. 1, No. 2 (1970), Peradeniya, pp. 199-211.
13. Most of the Indian Tamils resident in the country were made non-citizens by the citizenship laws introduced shortly after Independence. By 1964 c. 134,000 Indian Tamils, less than 10 per cent of the total, had gained Sri Lanka citizenship. In 1964, by the terms of an agreement reached between Sri Lanka and India, it was decided that 525,000 "stateless" persons of Indian origin in Sri Lanka would be repatriated to India and 300,000 persons would be given citizenship in Sri Lanka — over a period of fifteen years. The position of the remaining 150,000 was left undecided at the time. In 1974 another agreement was signed between the two countries, according to which half the remaining number would be given Indian citizenship and the other half Sri Lanka citizenship.
14. See Robert N. Kearney, *Communalism and Language in the Politics of Ceylon,* Duke University Press, North Carolina (1967).
15. Department of Census and Statistics, *The Socio-Economic Survey (Preliminary Report) 1969/70,* Colombo, 1971, *p. iii.*

16. Gamini Corea, 'Ceylon in the Sixties', *Marga*, Vol. I, No. 2 (1971), Colombo, p. 2.
17. International Labour Organisation, *Matching Employment Opportunities and Expectations — a Programme of Action for Ceylon*, Geneva (1971), p. 39.
18. *The Ten Year Plan*, The Planning Secretariat, Colombo (1959), p. 15.
19. On this see *Welfare and Growth in Sri Lanka*, Marga Research Studies-2, Marga Institute, Colombo (1974).
20. Snodgrass, op. cit., pp. 99-100.
21. See Jones and Selvaratnam, *Population Growth and Economic Development*, op. cit., pp. 167-8.
22. R. K. Srivastava, G. W. Jones and S. Selvaratnam, *Labour Force Projection for Ceylon, 1968-1998*, Ministry of Planning and Employment, Colombo (1970), p. 8.
23. Central Bank of Ceylon, *The Determinants of Labour Force Participation Rates in Sri Lanka, 1973*, Colombo, 1974, p. 25.
24. S. Selvaratnam, 'Impact of Population Growth on Employment and Training in Sri Lanka', *Report of the National Management Seminar on Population and Family Planning*, Colombo, 1972, p. 30.
25. *The Population of Sri Lanka*, 1974, op. cit., p. 97.
26. 'A Survey of Employment, Unemployment and Underemployment in Ceylon,' *International Labour Review*, March 1963, pp. 248-57.
27. Central Bank of Ceylon, *A Survey of Consumer Finances*, 1963, Colombo, p. 55.
28. *Socio-Economic Survey* 1969/70, op. cit., p. vi.
29. Central Bank of Ceylon, *Labour Force Participation Rates*, op. cit., p. 143.
30. The estimates quoted above deal with "open" unemployment referring broadly to persons without work who are available or looking for work. Needless to say, the distinction between open unemployment and underemployment is not always clear-cut and the measurement of underemployment involves many conceptual and practical difficulties. The 1959/60 ILO Sample Survey estimated that 19 per cent of the rural labour force and 11 per cent of the urban labour force in the country were found to be underemployed in the sense of working less than 40 hours per week and willing to work for more hours. The 1973 Survey of Labour Force Participation Rates, undertaken by the Central Bank, which adopted a somewhat broader definition reflecting both partial and ineffective or inefficient labour use, estimated that "about 30 per cent of the workers are underemployed".
31. R. K. Srivastava and S. Selvaratnam, 'Youth Employment in Ceylon — Problems and Prospects', *Marga*, Vol. 1, No. 4, 1972, Colombo, pp. 39-40.
32. ILO, *Matching Employment Opportunities. . . .*, op. cit., p. 21.
33. *Family Planning Evaluation Mission to Ceylon*, op. cit., p. 18.
34. Op. cit., p. 10.
35. *The Five Year Plan 1972-76*, Ministry of Planning and Employment, Colombo (1971), p. 21.
36. Jones and Selvaratnam, op. cit., p. 226-7.
37. O. E. R. Abeyaratne and C. H. S. Jayawardene, *Family Planning in Ceylon*, Colombo (1968), p. 142.

PART II

5

THE ECONOMY IN 1948

by L. A. Wickremeratne

I

In Srī Laṅkā, as elsewhere in South and South-east Asia, political independence did not necessarily bring about changes in the existing economic structure. To some extent, this was due to the reluctance of the new political leadership—heirs to the withdrawing *raj*—to make changes in economic systems with which their own interests were identified. However, in a wider and possibly less controversial sense the absence of immediate change may also be ascribed to the difficulties in changing—much less dismantling— economic systems that had taken firm root during the colonial period.

In Srī Laṅkā in particular the period of British rule witnessed the emergence and firm establishment of an export economy which revolved principally around the production of three crops — tea, rubber and coconut. The strength as well as the weakness of the economy arose from this central fact. In terms of export earnings the most important of these products was tea, the cultivation of which had been taken up by European capitalists following the dramatic collapse of the coffee industry in the late nineteenth century. Over the years, but particularly in the period preceding the grant of political independence, the susceptibility of tea to world market conditions had been amply illustrated. In the 1920s it was becoming evident that the world supply of tea was rapidly outstripping demand. Not only had supplies from the principal tea-producing countries — India, Srī Laṅkā and the Dutch East Indies — increased, but supplies from newer countries had also aggravated the problem. In the circumstances it became increasingly clear that there had to be some agreement among the producing countries with a view to restricting overall production. The need to do so became all the more evident with the onset of the great depression in the

131

beginning of the 1930s. Consequently, by a scheme which came into effect in April 1933, the principal tea-producing countries decided to regulate production for a period, in the first instance, of five years. However, the International Tea Control Committee, which supervised the scheme, decided in 1936 to extend the existing arrangements for a further period of five years from April 1938. By a subsequent decision the scheme was extended to cover the period of the war. These decisions were given effect locally by the promulgation of various ordinances, beginning with the Tea Control Ordinance no. 11 of 1933.[1]

The outbreak of the Second World War brought other problems. Because of the wartime restrictions on trade there was a great insufficiency of fertilisers. Available stocks had to be shared with rubber and coconut estates. The problem of replacing depreciated machinery and stock was another characteristic wartime difficulty with which the producers had to contend. Not surprisingly, therefore, when in 1942 the tea-controlling authority decided to increase the quota of tea which Srī Laṅkā could export from 239 million lb. to 314.4 million lb.; the producers were quite unable to increase output. Indeed even by 1945 Srı Laṅkā was able to export only 229 million lb. of tea which was slightly less than the pre-war figure of 235 million lb. which had been actually exported in 1938. By 1946, however, there was an appreciable increase when Srī Laṅkā exported 290 million lb. of tea.[2]

Moreover, during the war Srī Laṅkā had been compelled to sell all its tea to the United Kingdom at fixed prices. Although the contract prices were revised from time to time to take account of the rising cost of production, it is significant that when the contract system was done away with, tea prices markedly increased.[3] In the years immediately preceding independence, therefore, the most important development was the restoration of the free market in tea. There was also the not unreasonable prospect that Srī Laṅkā might benefit from an overall increase in the international demand for tea.

Rubber too had undergone remarkable vicissitudes. As in the case of tea, at the beginning of the 1920s the production of rubber outstripped demand. Efforts which were made — principally at the insistence of the Rubber Growers' Association in London — to regulate the international production of rubber were only moderately effective because of the reluctance of the Dutch East Indies, which produced about 25 per cent of the world's rubber supply, to cooperate. However, as a result of the depression of the early 1930s when rubber prices fell to unprecedently low levels, the production and export of rubber were regulated by the International Rubber

Restriction Scheme. Thus the International Rubber Regulation Agreement came into force in 1934 and was intended to last five years. In Srī Laṅkā under this scheme the planting of new areas under rubber was entirely prohibited.[4]

However, the outbreak of war and the resultant enormous demand for natural rubber witnessed a dramatic swing of the pendulum in the other direction. The restriction scheme was done away with, and instead the producer was to be encouraged to increase his output to the maximum level. As with tea, Srī Laṅkā contracted to sell its rubber to Britain at fixed prices. There was, however, a widespread feeling among rubber producers in Srī Laṅkā that the fixed price of 11d. per lb f.o.b., which had been decided on by Britain, was too little considering both the enhanced demand for rubber and the scarcities in world supplies, not to mention of the increases in the costs of production in the war period. Agitation on this score resulted in an increase in the price of rubber to 14d. Britain, however, stoutly resisted the continuing demand for further increases in price. In lieu of a price increase, however, Britain offered to repay costs of capital replacement to all producers willing to "slaughter-tap" their rubber trees, helping thereby to increase output. The end of war saw the predictable fall in prices, which was further accentuated when the British government terminated the contract agreement in 1946.[5]

To mitigate the dramatic fall in prices, the Srī Laṅkā government had perforce to offer to buy locally-produced rubber at a guaranteed floor price well above world prices. This apart, efforts were made within the industry to "rationalize" production, by effecting reductions in costs—through technically superior methods of production — and by getting rid of uneconomic holdings. In spite of these changes, the atmosphere remained one of unrelieved gloom.[6]

The fortunes of the coconut industry — which, in terms of the size of individual holdings and ownership, differed strikingly from both the tea and rubber industries — was on the whole less dramatically influenced by external conditions. War saw notable increases in most types of coconut products. On the other hand, a factor which certainly helped the coconut industry in the immediate post-war period was a five-year agreement entered into with Britain in 1946. Britain agreed to purchase almost all the copra and coconut oil which Srī Laṅkā produced. Although the agreement guaranteed a market for coconut products during the five years, the Srī Laṅkā government was quick to see the disadvantage — the widening gap between the contracted price and rising world prices. To offset the disadvantage, the Srī Laṅkā government imposed an export duty on coconut products in January 1947.[7]

Traditional Agriculture

While export earnings from tea, rubber and coconuts constituted, as it were, the life-blood of the economy, creating the surpluses for investment and expansion, the traditional agricultural sector lagged behind. Functionally the traditional agricultural sphere was geared to the production of rice, the staple food of the population. But because Srī Laṅkā could not produce sufficient to feed a growing population, rice had been customarily imported in annually increasing quantities. Lack of development in this sector was the long-term result of a multiplicity of factors like a perpetuation of a traditionally poor technology, the fragmentation of holdings, agricultural indebtedness and, above all, the market factor: as regards the last-named, there was little movement in the price of rice, due largely to the influx of imported rice, which by and large determined the price of rice in local markets. Moreover, compared with returns for investment in the more organised plantation sector, investment in paddy cultivation yielded poor results. Small wonder then that in the period 1930-46 there was little increase in the acreage of land under paddy. In 1926 the paddy acreage was estimated at 834,000. In 1945, when an attempt was made by the Department of Commerce and Industries to synthesise the data collected by various censuses of paddy production since 1930, the total acreage under paddy was estimated at 856,000 acres.[8]

If prices were a disincentive, the outbreak of war gave the government the best possible pretext for intervening on behalf of the producer. Thus in 1942 the Internal Purchase Scheme was introduced. This implied the offer to the producer of a guaranteed price of Rs 2.50 per bushel. In October 1943 the guaranteed price was increased to Rs 6.00 per bushel. Significantly, there was strong pressure when the war ended for the retention of the scheme as well as for the restriction of rice imports to Sri Lanka by means of a quota system, to ensure that "the local produce finds a market at economic prices".

Prompted by wartime exigencies, the government took other measures to step up production of rice. In 1942 it was stipulated that in the plantation sector every estate of over 35 acres should bring under food production 24 per cent of the total acreage if it were a tea estate, or 12 per cent of the acreage in the case of other estates. The Food Production (Estates) Ordinance No. 2 of 1945, however, gave the estates the option of obtaining exemption from the requirement by the payment of Rs. 10 per acre annually. More conventionally attempts had been made to expand the area of paddy cultivation since the 1930s by large-scale irrigation projects and colonization schemes in the dry zone like the Parakrama Samudra and Minneriya schemes.[9]

In spite of the efforts and the mood of urgency engendered by the war, Srī Laṅkā had perforce to continue importing her requirements of rice simply because local production could not match consumer requirements. During the war-years while rice imports remained at about half of what had been imported in 1939, by 1946 rice imports were steadily rising.

Looking ahead in 1948, the new independent government announced that it would strive to achieve self-sufficiency with regard to rice as well as subsidiary foodstuffs. Although the need for "intensive and scientific cultivation" was spoken of, it was evident that the new government had pinned its real hopes on the dramatic development of the dry zone as the principal means of achieving its declared objectives.[10]

The emphasis on agricultural development was not entirely unexpected. What particularly brought out the undiversified character of the economy in 1948 was the absence of a genuinely independent industrial sector. Using the term industrialization in a rather extended sense, there was no doubt that the industrial activity of Srī Laṅkā was centred almost exclusively in the preparation for export of tea, rubber and coconut products, as well as in meeting the engineering and mechanical requirements implied in this process. In a more conventional sense, however, one finds that the history of industrial development in Srī Laṅkā was indeed a chequered one. Although an Industries Commission was appointed in 1922 and recommended that the manufacture of certain items like soap, glass, paper and cement could be undertaken as government rather than as private ventures, its proposals were ignored. With the advent of the Donoughmore Constitution and the enhanced political power which Ceylonese began to enjoy, a Ministry of Labour, Industry and Commerce was established. It did little more than survey the potentialities for industrial development, although it did make some headway with regard to the establishment of cottage or rural domestic industries.

A more positive step was the establishment in 1938 of a separate department for industries — the Department of Commerce and Industries. It was hoped that factories would be set up for the production of items such as plywood for which local conditions seemed satisfactory and that steps would be taken for developing ancillary facilities for industrial development like the establishment of training and research centres.

However, in effect little was achieved. Partly because it was not wholly interested in doing so, the government also failed to impress private enterprise with its enthusiasm for industrial undertakings. In any event the idea of industrial ventures was new, and reluctant Ceylonese investors were more interested in "safe investments" in the plantation sector and in land in general. Above all, Srī Laṅkā was able to import its requirements in industrial capital and consumer goods, and in view of prevailing import policies, there was little market inducement for beginning industrial ventures.

Conversely, therefore, when the outbreak of war resulted in severe restrictions of imports there was a more favourable climate for industrial development. Even so, it was the government rather than private enterprise which took the initiative. In the period 1940-5 the government established no less than fifteen factories which attempted to produce certain industrial goods which it was not possible to import. Some — like the leather, plywood, coir, paper, glass and steel rolling factories — were successful and their profits enabled the government to cover the losses which it had to incur on account of the failure of, for example, the ceramics and acetic acid factories.

Predictably, with the resumption of imports after the war the entire sphere of government-run industries was put into jeopardy[11] But in spite of this and an intimidating array of theoretical odds against a programme of industrial development, there was the feeling that industrial development was necessary for Srī Laṅkā. "We cannot depend on agriculture alone", observed the Srī Laṅkān Ministers in the State Council at the end of the war," to provide the minimum standard. . . . for our rapidly increasing population." Specifically — in responding to immediate post war pressures — there was the belief that if industrial projects were taken in hand, provision could be made for employment opportunities for the Srī Laṅkān who were being discharged from military service at the end of the war.[12]

The structure of the National Income reflected the relative strength of the various sectors of the economy. As might be expected the export sector was the real bedrock of the national income, its contribution in 1947 being 33.8 per cent. The value of locally-consumed commodities and services — in which were included the traditional agricultural sector as well as industries — amounted to 25.5 per cent, while trade in general, other than exports, accounted for 11.1 per cent. The contribution of the other sector such as transport and the professions was in fact negligible. Significantly, in spite of an apparently substantial increase in the national income during the war, the relative positions of the different sectors in the national income structure had altered little in the period 1938-47.[13]

Lack of fundamental change was also evident in the continuation of the strong import bias of the economy. Certain factors made it inevitable that Srī Laṅkā should expend the bulk of her export earnings in imports. First, there was the absence of an industrial sector capable of producing a variety of consumer items as well as the intermediate and capital goods necessary for a subtained industrial effort. Secondly, the undeveloped potential of the traditional agricultural sector—in spite of heavy investment which had been made — implied that Srī Laṅkā had to import all its food requirements. The steady growth in population and possible increase in the world prices of Srī Laṅkā's food imports were likely to make the dependence more burdensome.

At first, however, there was little to warrant misgivings. Indeed, from 1926 to 1942 the terms of trade had been consistently favourable except in 1932. After 1942, however, the export index did not rise appreciably because the British government, which began the system of purchasing the major exports of Srī Laṅkā in bulk, paid prices which were clearly lower than the continually rising world market prices. On the other hand, on the side of imports — although many consumer imports had been severely curtailed — war-time needs implied their expansion in other directions and at prices over which Srī Laṅkā could exercise no control. Moreover, apart from the expansion in both the scale and volume of imports — the banned consumer imports excepted — Srī Laṅkā had to pay more for imports because of enhanced freight and insurance charges due to the war.

The unfavourable nature of the terms of trade was made all the more evident after 1943. In contrast to the export index — which, as in the previous year, settled at about 155.0 — the import index steadily increased until it had reached 309.0 by the end of 1945. It was true that by 1945 the export index had risen appreciably to reach a level of 198.0. As against this gain, however, the import index had increased to 334.0.[14]

The overall position was clearly reflected in the balance of payments. It has been shown that until the outbreak of war Srī Laṅkā enjoyed a favourable balance of trade in the sense that there was an excess of "visible" exports over imports. The position remained unaltered because until 1939 there was little fluctuation in the general pattern of exports and imports. But in spite of this Srī Laṅkā's overall balance of payments during the same period was unfavourable; because of the foreign capital invested in the economy, the "invisible" items in the balance of payments necessitated heavy payments of dividends and interest. There were remittances to Europe of a general nature as well as those made to India periodically by Indian immigrant labourers.

The outbreak of war changed this position. For one thing, there was a tendency for imports to fall because of the basic non-availability of supplies from abroad. Secondly, there was also an appreciable increase in "visible" exports. Thirdly, there was no change in remittance payments arising from the foreign capital investments. Finally, there was the sizeable military expenditure of the Allies in Srī Laṅkā during the war.[15] However briefly it may have lasted, this situation, enabled Srī Laṅkā to build its external assets, which were Rs. 275.1 million at the end of 1939 and had increased to Rs. 1,259.9 million in 1945.

Conversely, the end of war merely implied the restoration of the pre-war trends in the balance of payments. Apart from the effect of a heightened demand on the side of the "invisible" payments, more basically the balance of trade too deteriorated. On the export side, although the wartime restrictions on exports were done away with, the export industries — especially rubber, which was in disarray due to difficulties like lack of machinery and the effects of "slaughter-tapping" of one sort or another — could not immediately increase output levels. Besides the prices which the export staples fetched in world markets tended to fall in the long run, although in the immediate aftermath of the war there was at first a tendency for prices to pick up — at least, to levels well above the prices which Britain had enforced by means of the contract agreements. The long fall in prices was most spectacularly evident in rubber exports. In the case of tea, the end of the era of restrictions on shipping space there was brought about a marked tendency for world prices and supplies to outstrip demand.[16]

The situation was worse on the side of imports. The abandonment of wartime restrictions on imports, increased consumer demand and the need for restocking in general all contributed to a dramatic rise in imports. The result was that by 1947 there was a substantial adverse balance of payments situation. The deficit was met by drawing on the foreign assets which Srī Laṅkā had accumulated during the war. Consequently, in 1946 and 1947 in particular Srī Laṅkā's external assets dropped by Rs. 49.6 million and Rs. 263 million respectively![17]

The import-export bias of the economy also influenced the prevailing revenue structure. The reserves of the government of Srī Laṅkā were derived principally from indirect and direct taxation. In the period before 1948, the older and more important component of the revenue structure had been the indirect taxes, which consisted of import and export duties. In terms of the relative contribution to revenue, the more important of the two were the import duties. The revenue from import duties, which was Rs. 36.2 million in 1925, had increased to Rs. 51.9 million in 1938 and to Rs. 166.7 million in 1946. The rather sharp increase in import duty revenues between 1938 and 1946 may be ascribed to a 10 per cent surcharge on imports of articles other than food and to a higher rate of surcharge on the import of luxury goods.[18]

The revenue from export duties was less important. From Rs. 11.5 million the export duty revenues had increased to Rs. 83.1 million in 1946. After 1947, however, there was a notable increase when export duties rose to Rs. 136.7 million in 1947 and to Rs. 148.7 million in 1948. This sharp rise was due to a decision of the Srī Laṅkā government to increase the export duties on tea and coconut products.[19]

Although traditionally in terms of revenue the direct taxes were comparatively less important, the period 1932-48 witnessed several significant charges in this sphere. Mention must inevitably be made of the introduction of income tax, which had first been recommended by the Taxation Commission in 1928 but which became law only in 1932 due to strong opposition to the measure in the Legislative Council. The Income Tax Ordinance not only impinged on Srī Laṅkāns whose incomes exceeded Rs. 4,800 but made both non-Srī Laṅkān residents as well as companies liable for payment of income tax. Income tax revenue, which was Rs. 8.6 million in 1932, had increased to Rs. 61.8 million by 1947.[20]

Another noteworthy innovation was the excess profits duty, introduced as a war-time measure in 1941. Originally concerned with profits made by business in general this tax was extended in 1942 to cover agricultural and mining enterprises. Revenue from the excess profits duty, which was Rs. 5.1 million in 1941, had increased to Rs. 41.5 million in 1945.

The contribution made to revenue by other items of direct taxes such as estate duties, stamps, licences and tolls was negligible. In spite of this, revenue as a whole had increased from Rs. 132.7 million in 1939, when the war began, to Rs. 540.6 million in 1947.[21]

Political independence saw not so much a change in the revenue structure — which was inconceivable without a fundamental change in the nature of the prevailing economy — but rather a series of adjustments designed to augment government revenues. First, following the example of India, the excess profits duty was done away with and a new profits tax was adopted. Its distinctive feature was that it embraced categories such as the professions which the excess profits duty had excluded. Secondly, the income tax payable by companies was increased from 20 to 25 per cent. Thirdly, stamp and estate duties, which had not been revised for years during the colonial period, were increased. Finally there was a substantial increase in import duties, especially on luxury goods.[22]

II

To complete our survey of the economy of Srī Lankā in 1948, one may draw attention to the sphere of government expenditure, which above all reflected the emerging patterns of thinking involving the polarities of economic development and social *welfare-ism*. In the pre-independence period (1925-47) three spheres of government current revenue expenditure stood out, both in terms of their percentage relationship to total current revenue expenditure and because, in one way or another, they impinged on the economic development of Srī Lankā. These were, first, expenditure on utility services; secondly, provision for the "development of national wealth"; and thirdly, the money spent on social services.[23]

Prior to the Donoughmore Constitution, when Srī Lankāns had little voice in the disbursement of national expenditure, the emphasis was clearly on the expansion of utility services as opposed to either the social services or the expenditure on account of the development of national wealth. Indeed, until 1931 expenditure on the last item amounted to only 7.5 per cent of total current revenue expenditure. The percentage spent on social services was about 18.6. By contrast, the government spent 40 per cent of its current revenue in utility services.

In the Donoughmore period, which witnessed a substantial devolution of administrative and financial powers upon the Sri Lankan political leadership, there was a perceptible shift in emphasis. Expenditure on social services consistently outstripped that on utility services. During the war the shift was made even more evident. The climax was reached in the period 1947-8, when over 50 per cent of current revenue was devoted to social services expenditure. By contrast, expenditure on utility services remained broadly unchanged, and there had also been a moderate increase in expenditure in developing national wealth.[24]

It is possible to read several meanings into these figures. For example, in terms of economic development the sharp contrast between expenditure on social services, as opposed to the more fruitful investment in development, implied the absence of economic planning and a scale of priorities. On the other hand, the bias in the disbursement of current expenditure resources must also be understood in the prevailing context of the Donoughmore period and the grant of universal adult franchise, by which a hithertoaloof élite Srī Lankān political leadership was made responsive to popular needs. One should also bear in mind that there was a background of economic distress and social tension, ushered in with the economic depression which hit Srī Lankā in the early 1930s. In the circumstances the government of Srī Lankā prompted largely by the country's élite leadership, took upon itself a great part of the burden of relieving economic distress by direct state action.

The most visible effect of the depression of the early 1930s was widespread unemployment. As early as 1931, therefore, the government began schemes to provide relief work for the unemployed. Under schemes, which in fact were largely confined to Colombo, useful work was done in the construction and repair of roads, canals, flood protection embankments and swamp reclamation work.[25] Meanwhile the general principle of aiding the poor which antedated this period was put on an established footing when in 1939 the Poor Law Ordinance was enacted. The implied principle was that whereas it was the obligation of the central government to relieve the able-bodied poor, the local authorities were expected to bear the burden of poor relief for the non-able-bodied. In effect, the Ordinance was confined to the three municipalities of Colombo, Kandy and Galle, although provision was made for its extension to the areas covered by urban councils and village committees.[26]

Moreover, the government took upon itself the obligation of providing a free mid-day meal to all schoolchildren in vernacular schools. In elementary English schools the free mid-day meal was to be provided for "necessitous children" on condition that their number did not exceed 25 per cent of the total number attending the school concerned. Although the local authorities were expected to contribute towards the scheme on a percentage basis, in fact, the cost of the scheme was borne by the government.

Other notable developments in this period were the institution of a milk feeding scheme under which free milk was supplied to all children between the ages of two and five as well as to expectant and nursing mothers, the enactment of legislation to compel employers in the private sector to provide certain statutory benefits to workers, and finally the decision to give more generous assistance to voluntary organisations like the social service leagues and friend-in-need societies.[27]

Two specific areas of government involvement and expenditure — education and health — require special emphasis. Indeed the prevailing view of social welfare, with its implied overtones of equality of opportunity as well as the ideal of equitably distributing the national income, was best reflected in the sphere of education. In the 1930s the government, increasingly under the influence of Srī Laṅkān political leaders, decided to provide education without levying school fees to every child between the ages of five and fourteen. In 1945, taking the principle a stage further and conforming to the recommendations made by a special committee on education, education "from the kindergarten to the university" was declared "free".[28] Similarly, in the sphere of health, provision was made for free facilities in all hospitals and dispensaries which were in one way or another maintained by government.

Contemporary documents show that the social welfare investment was rarely if ever seen in a critical light — that a change in revenue resources might well make the obligations which the government had imposed on itself an almost insupportable burden. Instead the government took pride in its social welfare programme, drawing particular attention to the paucity of comparable facilities in most neighbouring countries.

Conclusion

In reviewing economic developments in the period immediately preceding the attainment of political independence in 1948, one is impressed by the absence of really fundamental changes in the economic structure. The Second World War was admittedly a notable catalyst. Yet the restoration of peace also saw a swift reversion to the prevailing patterns of economic normalcy.

As for the future there were three possible ways whereby a structural change in the economy might have been brought about: first, as a sequel to a major and lasting collapse of external markets of one or another of Srī Laṅkā's major export staples — a crisis comparable to that which followed the collapse of the island's coffee industry towards the end of the 1870s; secondly, by policies deliberately oriented to such a change; and finally — as the actual experiences of some countries in the post-colonial period demonstrated — resulting from popular pressures from below which a beleaguered ruling élite was powerless to resist.

REFERENCES

1. K. M. De Silva, (ed.) *History of Ceylon*, Vol. 3, Colombo (1973), pp. 431 ff. *Post-war Development Proposals*, Colombo (1946), pp. 3 ff; *Economic and Social Development in Ceylon, 1926-1954*, Colombo, (1955), pp. 2 ff.

2. B. B. Das Gupta, *A Short Economic Survey of Ceylon*, Colombo (1948), pp. 33 ff.
3. ibid.
4. *Post-War Development Proposals*, op. cit., p. 4. At the end of 1938 the participating countries were permitted to extend the area of rubber cultivation by 5 per cent. In Srī Laṅkā this was effected by a system of permits which the Rubber Controller issued.
5. ibid., also *Economic and Social Development of Ceylon*, op. cit., p. 4.
6. Das Gupta, op. cit., p. 36.
7. ibid., also, *Post-War Development Proposals*, op. cit., pp. 5 ff.
8. *Post War Development Proposals*, op. cit., pp. 10 ff; *Economic and Social Development of Ceylon*, op. cit., pp. 6 ff.
9. ibid.
10. *Six Year Plan for Ceylon*, Colombo, 1948, pp. 53 ff.
11. *Six-Year Programme of Investment, 1954-1960*, Colombo (1955), pp. 234 ff. *Six-Year Plan for Ceylon*, op. cit., pp. 59 ff. Also Appendix 'C'.
12. *Post War Development Proposals*, op. cit., p. 40.
13. ibid., p. 11. Also *Economic and Social Development of Ceylon*, op. cit., pp. 30 ff.
14. *Economic and Social Development of Ceylon*, op. cit., pp. 9 ff.
15. ibid., also *Post-War Development Proposals*, op. cit., pp. 16 ff.
16. ibid.
17. ibid.
18. *Economic and Social Development of Ceylon*, op. cit., pp. 15 ff.
19. ibid.
20. *Six-Year Plan for Ceylon, 1947-1949*, Colombo (1949), pp. 29 ff.
21. ibid.
22. ibid.
23. *Economic and Social Development*, op. cit., p. 19 and p. 123.
24. ibid.
25. ibid., pp. 20 ff. Also *Post-War Development Proposals*, op. cit., pp. 42 ff.
26. ibid.
27. ibid.
28. ibid.
29. ibid.

6

PLANNING AND ECONOMIC DEVELOPMENT

by L. A. Wickremeratne

Since the attainment of independence in 1948 Srī Laṅkā has had several official plans of development, culminating in the Five-Year Plan of the United Front Government in 1971. The rather impressive array of planning documents suggests that economic planning in Srī Laṅkā was a continuous process closely related to and derived from the development of the island's economy during the same period. However, in contrast to the successive Five-Year Plans in India, which at any rate gave a certain theoretical continuity to the planning process, planning in Srī Laṅkā was in fact a series of disjointed and sporadic exercises with individual plans often failing to survive their formal life-spans. Secondly, the basic discontinuity in the planning process was further underlined by the failure to evolve a planning machinery armed with an amplitude of administrative and even political powers and imbued with the will to set about the tasks of actually implementing the various planning proposals.

Although the planning process was marked by various elements of discontinuity, an unbroken thread runs through the background with which the planning processes were concerned — the economic conditions of the island. It is therefore the unity of the background which gives the history of the planning process in Srī Laṅkā a certain plausible coherence. Indeed, when on the one hand economic conditions deteriorated, there was on the other hand a corresponding reduction in the resources available for planning as well as a shrinking in the area of options available to the planning strategist.

Given these factors, two considerations — involving methodology — are relevant. First, it would be unrealistic to regard the planning process in Srī Laṅkā purely in terms of a study in implementation, matching actual performance achieved to the theoretical projections of, say, national income, investment and savings. If, on the other hand, planning in Srī Laṅkā is to be viewed as a gradual transition from an unplanned to a planned economy, it would be worthwhile to regard the various planning exercises — however mutually disjointed — as stages in the process of transition especially in terms of evolving concepts. Secondly, viewed in this light, periodization becomes inevitable, although the terminal dates of the periods may superficially suggest a deliberate correlation with political changes which Srī Laṅkā underwent in the post-independence period as a whole.

1948-1956

A rather theoretical and almost detached appraisal of the economic problems facing the country — and a corresponding lack of urgency concerning remedial policies and measures — characterised the major planning exercises during this period. This may be explained in terms of the background — the fact was that during this period, and in striking contrast to the periods which follow, Srī Laṅkā possessed reasonably ample resources.

In the study of this period one conventionally begins by referring to the Six-Year Plan of 1948. In spite of its impressive title, however, the Six-Year Plan was not so much an economic plan, possessing the conventional ingredients of a formal development programme, as an extension of the budget speech which the Minister of Finance J. R. Jayawardane, made in 1948 and which had evidently been conceived in the context of the recent achievement of political independence, and as a hopeful testament of economic aspirations.

Moreover, instead of the conventional marshalling of resources and an indication of how these resources were to be allocated during the planning period, the Six-Year Plan merely stated the sum of money which would be spent on certain major agricultural projects. In this sense the Six-Year Plan gave a theoretical sanction to the heavy investments which the government, whose policy antecedents extended well into the Donoughmore period, had already decided on making with regard to irrigation and colonization. It was made clear that the real hopes of economic development were centred in agriculture.[1]

Altogether the most noteworthy exercise of the period was the development plan of the International Bank for Reconstruction and Development Mission which visited Srī Laṅkā in 1952 at the

invitation of the government. It was a rather belated acknowledge-
ment that planning towards economic development was more
sophisticated and complex than had been assumed earlier. To some
extent the approach to planning during the period was best exemplified in the contemporary definition of the economic problems
facing Srī Laṅka. The I.B.R.D. mission laid stress on population
growth and its implications, pointing out that Srī Laṅkā had been
able to maintain reasonable economic standards, which compared
well with a number of neighbouring countries, owing largely to the
productivity of her export sector. But given on the one hand the
reality of rapid population growth and on the other the impossibi-
lity of assuming that the export sector could maintain its productive momentum indefinitely, the situation was bound to
change.[2]

The theme was reiterated in the Six-Year programme of investment which was published in 1954 and which was intended as a
sequel to the I.B.R.D. mission proposals of 1952. The Six-Year
Investment Programme remarked on the "exceptionally rapid
growth of population" and the deterioration of living standards,
adding significantly that the problem was already sufficiently well
recognised.[3] Nonetheless there was no corresponding sense of
urgency. There was rather the feeling that the problem of population was not one of immediate moment with which the government
had to come to grips. Indeed planning strategy did not really concern itself with the population aspect of the equation at all. Instead
there was an all too evident preoccupation with the development
of resources, and the specific objects of the development plans and
programmes of the period were expressed in conventional terms
of increasing national income, raising productivity and correcting
the imbalances derived from the existence of an undiversified
economy.

The I.B.R.D. mission asserted that Srī Laṅkā could without un-
due difficulty undertake a major development programme on the
resources which the government could marshal. First, there were
the domestic resources which really hinged on the expectation that
as in the period 1948-51 there would be annual budget surpluses
amounting in the aggregate to Rs. 100 million.[4] It was also suggested that domestic resources could be further augmented by increases
in taxation as well as by the reduction or elimination of food subsidies; even if allowance was made for the increases in government
expenditure arising out of compensatory adjustments of wages in
lieu of the abolished food subsidies, the aggregate domestic resources annually available for development would increase to
Rs. 150 million.[5] Next there were the external assets which Srī Laṅkā

could draw upon, which had been accumulated during the Second World War and during the period of the Korean boom. In 1951 these assets amounted to Rs. 1,185 million. Although admittedly a considerable proportion of the external assets would have to be set aside for eventualities such as a deterioration in the terms of trade, it was possible to assume that Rs. 80 million could be earmarked for development purposes.[6] There was also the possibility of receiving foreign aid of the sort Srī Laṅkā was already obtaining under the Colombo Plan and which would enable the country to meet the rather complex technological demands imposed on it by a modern development programme. In sum, the I.B.R.D. mission concluded that even if no special effort were made by the government, it was possible to marshal ample resources which would permit an annual investment of about Rs. 250 million during a six-year period of planned economic development.

The strategy of financing the Six-Year Programme of Investment (1954-60) did not, in effect, materially differ from that of the I.B.R.D. mission. It was clearly stated that the calls of development could be met out of "domestic resources and within the confines of sound budgets", provided that during the period the terms of trade, which had been consistently favourable to Srī Laṅkā, would not deteriorate. On the other hand a feature of the Six-Year Programme of Investment was the confident assumption that even if there was a downward trend in export earnings, Srī Laṅkā need not resort to foreign aid and foreign loans. In any event, apart from considerations of covering the shortfalls caused by adverse external trade conditions, resources from abroad supplementing purely domestic resources were likely to expedite the phase of development envisaged in the programme of development.

A notable feature in planning during this period was the favoured place of agriculture *vis-à-vis* industrial development. In 1950, when the Colombo Plan was being mooted, the Srī Laṅkā government proposed to make an investment of Rs. 1,359 million for overall development, of which Rs. 503 million was set aside for agricultural development. The projected investment for industries amounted only to Rs. 75 million. Although in 1952 these figures were revised, the relative proportions were retained on a more extended scale with Rs. 900 million being earmarked for agriculture and Rs. 200 million for industry. For its part the I.B.R.D. mission maintained the *status quo*. Thus out of a projected investment of Rs. 1,600 million, the investments in agriculture and in industry were Rs. 460 million and Rs. 75 million respectively. In much the same way the Six-Year Programme of Investment gave pride of place to agricultural development, proposing an expenditure of

36 per cent of the total investment outlay of Rs. 2,529 million on agriculture as opposed to a 4.42 per cent on industry.

The modest scale of industrial development may be attributed partly to the absence of a reasonably large industrial sector which absorbed heavy investment. Indeed, by the beginning of the 1950s the government was tending to the view that state industries were "a drain on public resources", and by 1951 the closure of a number of existing industries was envisaged while others were to be handed over to co-operative societies. By 1954 the major government industrial ventures were confined to a handful of ventures like the cement factory (at Kankesanturai), a leather factory, the paper factory (at Valaichenai) and a plywood factory (at Gintota).[9]

To some extent, however, the situation reflected the absence of a clearly understood policy on industrial development. The I.B.R.D. mission, for instance, declared that given the conditions in Sri Lanka the initiative in industrial development must necessarily be taken by the private sector, which however had to be encouraged to do so. It believed that the government had hitherto followed a rather ambivalent policy on the role of the private sector; while numerous inducements to private industrialists such as loan facilities, underwriting loans and protective tariff policies were offered by the state, yet by virtually monopolosing industrial activity, the government had in effect discouraged private sector participation.[10] The importance of a clearly defined policy was emphasised, as a means of attracting the local entrepreneur who was traditionally partial to investment in land, and who fought shy of investment in what were at best purely hypothetical industrial ventures.[11] This had no bearing on foreign capital investment.

The Six-Year Programme of Investment was equally emphatic on the role of the private sector in industrial development. First, the development of certain small-scale industries — to produce goods in replacement of these which were being imported — necessarily involved in participation of the private sector. Secondly, certain large-scale industrial ventures which the programme urged, like the setting up of tyre-producing and fertiliser industries, also implied private sector participation. Thirdly, although certain industries like the cement factory were to be maintained as state enterprises, the programme visualised the time when such enterprises could be handed over to the private sector.[12]

In terms of priorities, what were to be the relative roles of agriculture and industry? The position of the I.B.R.D. mission was certainly unequivocal. Although it conceded that industrial advance was necessary for "balanced economic development", the mission took care to point out that in Sri Lanka industry must remain secondary to agriculture. Moreover, it cautioned that industrialisation was not a panacea for economic ills or a means of solving the unemployment problem.

While the Six-Year Programme of Investment, sharing this view, declared that Srī Lankā was "eminently suited for agricultural rather than industrial development", it was nonetheless recognised that it could not necessarily hope to solve its problems purely in terms of an agricultural strategy, and that industrialisation was an essential prerequisite of a more evenly balanced economy.[13]

But whatever the distant hopes of industrial development might be, emphasis during this period both in planning and in government activity was clearly centred on agriculture. In the over-all agricultural development strategy there was, as might be expected, a notable emphasis on the agricultural export sector, especially on increased yields in the existing acreage of land under tea, rubber and coconut, rather than on physical increases in the area under cultivation.

While the export agricultural sector was basically well organised, reflecting both a heavy capital investment and a traditionally well established large-scale entrepreneurship, the development of the traditional agriculture was correspondingly a more complicated matter owing to the absence of organised entrepreneurship and basic infra-structure facilities. The objective in this sphere was also twofold — to effect a qualitative change in production by the adoption of better cultural techniques, and to expand the area of cultivation principally by means of irrigation and colonization schemes. The policy was not a new one and had its roots in the 1930s. But a notable feature during this period was the growing emphasis on multi-purpose irrigation schemes such as the Gal Oya scheme implying unprecedentedly high levels of capital investment and technology.

1956-1965

Between the publication of the Six-Year Programme of Investment in 1954 and the establishment for the first time of a planning council in 1956, the inherent weakness of the island's economy — the dependence of its key exports on world market conditions — had been amply demonstrated. Although in 1954-5 there had been almost boom conditions because the key agricultural exports — particularly tea — had fetched high prices, 1956 saw a sharp reversal of this trend which continued in the following years. While this was not new, the fluctuations in export earnings — with their adverse effects on the balance of payments, savings and investment — demonstrated more effectively than ever before the need for a fundamental structural change in the economy. Moreover, the growth of Srī Laṅkā's population (at 2.6% per annum one of the highest in the world) the implications of its growth for the cost of consumer goods and, above all, its effect on employment stressed the need to achieve rapid economic development. Significantly the three major planning exercises of this period — the Interim report of the Planning Council published in 1957, the Ten-Year Plan of 1959 and the Short-Term Implementation Programme of 1962 — gave the population factor paramountcy in defining the economic problems facing the country.

It had been the practice of successive government to maintain a system of social welfare expenditure, characterised principally by schemes of "free" secondary education and health facilities and the subsidisation of the major items of food which were imported for mass consumption. Rice, for example, was sold to the consumers for less than the prevailing world market prices, and the government customarily bore the cost of the difference. It was clear that with increases in population the burdens which the state would be called upon to bear on account of this policy would increase. Apart from the financial burden *per se*, burgeoning social welfare costs implied that the resources which the government could direct towards purely developmental purposes had to be diverted to non-productive ones.

Possibly the most significant implication of the population problem was its impact on employment. The basic question was whether the economy could grow sufficiently fast to absorb the actual increases in the workforce. Workforce projections showed that, given the rate of population growth, by 1981 the addition to the workforce would total about 3.7 million, implying thereby that 100,000 persons would have to be found employment each year during this period.[14] Economic development had not only to be rapid but had to give priority to the employment problem, which had far-reaching political and social implications for the future.

In a sense the problems of fluctuating export earnings, diminishing foreign exchange resources, balance of payment difficulties and the implications of population growth — especially as regards employment — predetermined the objectives of planning during this period. The Ten-Year Plan as well as the Short-Term Implementation Plan placed emphasis on the objectives of providing greater employment, achieving equilibrium in the balance of payments and diversifying the economy. Moreover, both programmes — reflecting as they did the political views of the new government which came to power in 1956 — declared that the achievement of a socialist society was the ultimate object of planned economic development.

Both in terms of the magnitude of the investment outlay and the methods to be adopted in finding the implied resources, the Ten-Year Plan was conceived on an ambitious scale. The outlay projected amounted to Rs. 13,600 million. The annual expenditure on development was projected to increase from Rs. 692 million in 1959 to Rs. 2,050 million in 1968. The bulk of the investment was to come from government sources and amounted to Rs. 8,377 million. Private investment was to contribute Rs. 4,369 million of the balance. Government resources were to be obtained largely through the budget by anticipated surpluses of current revenue over expenditure.[15]

The investment outlay of the Ten-Year Plan had been based on certain fundamental assumptions. Possibly the most important of these was the expectation of a progressive and consistent growth of government resources during the period of implementation of the plan. The progressive escalation of the actual investment outlay was basically related to this assumption. Secondly, it was also assumed that the government would make a genuine effort to restrict expenditure; and thirdly, steps would be taken to obtain additional resources by means of a more broad-based system of levying income tax, or, in lieu of an "universal income tax", a compulsory development levy.[16]

It was in this context that the Ten-Year Plan — in spite of the political milieu from which it was derived — expressed scepticism about heavy expenditure being devoted to education and health. In fact the tendency in the preceding years for current government expenditure to increase faster than current revenue was attributed to this factor.[17] In the same breath — but surely more circumspectly — the Ten-Year Plan also cast doubts on the expenditure incurred annually in the subsidy on rice, and added that whatever might be the decision regarding the subsidy's future, it was at least important that "the scale of the financial costs of subsidies should be recognised".[18] However, in spite of the emphasis on domestic resources, the Ten-Year Plan also pinned its hope on obtaining foreign resources. Thus in the projected outlay of Rs. 13,000 million, the value of the anticipated foreign aid loans totalled Rs. 1,275 million.

By contrast the Short-Term Implementation Programme had to settle for a smaller scale of operations because the country's financial position had perceptibly deteriorated between 1959 and 1962. The Plan proposed an investment outlay totalling Rs. 2,005 million. However, the total resources available for the period 1961-4 — the specific period of the plan — amounted to only Rs. 1,218 million. The expectation was that taxation and savings would help towards reducing the gap especially if, as urged, new taxes were adopted. Emphasis was placed on obtaining foreign assistance which would —

apart from considerations of covering shortfalls — expedite the implementation of the overall development proposals envisaged in the Short-Term Implementation Programme. Consequently, the possibility that Srī Laṅkā would be in a position to muster foreign resources, in one form or another, amounting to Rs. 375.6 million was a feature of the Programme.[19]

However, the really distinctive feature in planning during this period was concerned with a significant change in the assumptions underlying the allocation of these resources. The *raison d'etre* of planning was the attainment of a distinct and reasonably rapid shift towards industrialisation and the achievement thereby of a structural change in the economy, with industry taking the place of agriculture as the leading sector in the economy.

Thus during the period covered by the Ten-Year Plan, the total investment on industry and allied spheres amounted to 41 per cent with 22.9 being devoted to agriculture. The share of industry and power, which was 15.1 per cent of the outlay in 1967, was expected to increase to 27.3 per cent of the annual outlay in 1968. By contrast, in the same period investment in agriculture was to diminish from 27.4 per cent to 22.5 per cent.

The significance of the structural change contemplated was reflected in the Gross Domestic Product. In 1957 the export staples — tea, rubber and coconut — accounted for 35 per cent of the Gross Domestic Product. It was anticipated that by 1968, as a consequence of the shift towards industry, the share of the export crops in the Gross Domestic Product would be reduced to 25 per cent, while the contribution made by industry would rise from 7.6 per cent to 13.7 in 1968.[20]

In the Short-Term Implementation Programme, too, there was no deviation from this broad pattern of investment. The difference was that the overall investment outlays involved were smaller. In this instance the emphasis on industrial development was particularly notable because the Short-Term Implementation Programme was conceived within the constraint of considerably reduced resources. Priorities and individual investment programmes were determined in particular by the lack of foreign exchange resources. On the other hand, industrialization — however carefully projects were selected in terms of prevailing exigencies — was essentially a capital-intensive process and it was to be expected that the capital costs of an accelerated industrial programme would be high.

Indeed much has been read into the emphasis on industry during this period. It has been pointed out for example that there was a S.L.F.P. government in the period 1956-64, whereas under U.N.P. rule, both in the periods 1948-56 and 1965-70, planning strategy was clearly centred on agricultural development. But far from being an implied dichotomy, both agriculture and industry were vital components of a single integrated development strategy. Thus agricultural development — involving the export sector as well as the traditional sector — was regarded as a precondition for the industrial spurt. The role of the export sector was particularly important and implied the maximization of its productive potential so that the surpluses from this sector could finance the heavy investments required for industrial ventures, especially with regard to the import of capital goods and raw materials.

Consequently in the Ten-Year Plan the basic aim was to increase the value of the output of tea, rubber and coconut by 32 per cent during the ten-year period by increasing output per acre by means of new high-yielding strains, schemes of replanting and rehabilitation, and, less significantly, by increasing acreage.[21] In fact the bulk of the investment for the export sector was earmarked for rehabilitation schemes and amounted to Rs. 351 million. Investment in buildings and machinery totalled Rs. 304 million, of which the share of the tea industry alone was Rs. 187 million. In terms of investment outlay the least significant was the object of increasing existing acreage, for which Rs. 85 million was to be spent.[22]

Although the Short-Term Implementation Programme reiterated the importance of the supporting role which the export crops were to play in achieving industrialisation, it was alive to the constraints imposed on the economy since 1959 and was therefore more cautious concerning the magnitude of the investment outlay involved in expanding the export sector. Moreover, the Short-Term Implementation Programme sounded a note of scepticism about the wisdom of depending on tea, rubber and coconuts alone as a means of earning export surpluses.[23]

Much hinged on the question of prices. With characteristic optimism the Ten-Year Plan had argued that falls in the price of tea were a temporary phenomenon reflecting purely cyclical movements, whereas the long-term trends governing the tea market — characterised by increases in population and in incomes in the tea-consuming countries — were basically favourable. The Short-Term Implementation Programme, on the other hand, found that not only with regard to tea but with rubber and coconuts as well, there had been a decline in prices despite increases in investment and output.[24] Consequently the feasibility of developing the export potentials of a wide variety of minor export crops like cocoa, cardamons and cinnamon was urged.[25]

The non-export or traditional agricultural sector was also closely involved in achieving the initial momentum towards industrialization. The fact was that a significant percentage of the agricultural products consumed locally had necessarily to be imported from abroad. This implied the expenditure of foreign exchange resources which might have been utilized for more productive investments. In 1957 the total value of the goods imported to Srī Lanka amounted to Rs. 1,713 million, of which as much as Rs. 646.9 million were spent on importing agricultural goods for consumption, with rice imports alone accounting for Rs. 254.9 million. Although Srī Lanka would not be able to substitute all agricultural imports with local production, the Ten-Year Plan aimed at achieving self-sufficiency, not only in rice and subsidiary products like chillies and potatoes, but also in dairy products, sugar and tobacco. The Ten-Year Plan therefore earmarked as much as Rs. 1,874.5 million for the development of the traditional agricultural sector. The bulk of the resources was specifically devoted to the development of irrigation facilities and the extension of colonization schemes. The need to develop the potential of the dry zone was also emphasized. While the investment in developing the export agricultural sector would rise by 47 per cent in the period 1957-68, the percentage increase in the traditional agricultural sector in the same period was in the region of 236 per cent. [26]

However, by the time of the Short-Term Implementation Programme there was growing disillusionment about the heavy expenditure involved in developing the traditional agricultural sector. For one thing investment had really centred in irrigation and land development. Although investments in these spheres and increased over the years, the results achieved in terms of the extent of land made irrigable, or in terms of the amount of land alienated, had not been commensurate. A major factor which had increased the capital costs of irrigation and colonisation schemes was the continuation of a policy — begun in the 1930s when the dry zone lands were being opened up for the first time and substantial inducements therefore had to be made to induce people to settle there as colonists — of providing a wide array of social service amenities such as housing, sanitary facilities, schools and hospitals. In the major colonization schemes over 30 per cent of the expenditure had been accounted for in terms of what the Short-Term Implementation Programme characterized as a "heavily built-in social service component".[27] Moreover, although the schemes had been conceived on a large scale and were basically of a capital-intensive nature, the government could not hope for immediate returns because the period of gestation was long and, in the case of certain schemes, almost fifty years would elapse before they yielded any economic returns.

In an interesting critique of past policies the Short-Term Implemention Programme pointed out that Srī Laṅkā could no longer afford the luxury of such large investments. Planning had to be sufficiently effective to reduce costs, ensure faster returns, and in general relieve the government of having to bear the entire costs of colonization settlement. It was urged that the colonists themselves should be made to bear some of the costs involved.[28]

The shift towards industrialisation was not, however, based negatively on a growing scepticism about the heavy investments in traditional agriculture. In spite of numerous theoretical objections to a programme of industrial development, industrialisation *per se* seemed increasingly to be an attractive proposition. To begin with, there was the question of raw materials — hitherto, as far as Srī Laṅkā was concerned, the most formidable conventional objection to industrialisation. Indeed the view had long prevailed that industrialisation should be put off until a systematic and comprehensive national survey was made of raw material potential, or that — as the I.B.R.D. mission had suggested in 1952 — Srī Laṅkā should confine industrialisation only to those industries for which raw materials were known to exist. On the other hand, planning in the post-1956 phase was characterised by a sense of urgency no doubt engendered by an awareness of deteriorating economic conditions and hence a dimunition of the options available to the economic planner.

In the circumstances the case for industrialisation rested on the strategy that both the raw materials and the machinery for industry could be obtained from abroad by utilising the export earnings of the agricultural sector, provided that production in this sector could be sufficiently enlarged to augment export earnings, and provided too that a really determined effort was made to utilise export earnings not for consumption purposes as in the past but for productive economic investment. Consequently the Ten-Year Plan envisaged a massive increase in the production of the major staples, with an increase exceeding 100 per cent in tea production alone.

The problem of markets was also germane to industrialisation. In countries like Srī Laṅkā the problem was not the size of the potential internal market for industrial goods — the physical limits of the internal market being likely to expand with the growth of population — but the more real consideration was the low purchasing power of the mass of the people. In the circumstances the functional role of agricultural expansion was to provide a market for industrial goods, by helping to achieve increases in the real income levels of the mass of the people. The increases in real income effected by this technique had, however, to be of a substantial order because a merely marginal increase in incomes would tend—in a situation where *per capita* incomes were admittedly low—to increase the demand for agricultural products rather than for industrial goods.

But the creation of an internal market for industrial goods was not wholly dependent on the agricultural sector. In 1957 the value of industrial goods used in Srī Lankā for purposes of either consumption or development had totalled Rs. 1,543 million. Local production had accounted for only 15 per cent of this amount, the remainder being met by imports. This suggested the viability of a policy of import substitution, an effort to produce some of these imported industrial goods locally, especially chemicals, petroleum products, paper, cement, iron and steel—thereby releasing valuable foreign exchange resources for obtaining the capital assets which would help to develop industrialisation a stage further.[29] Finally, and admittedly at a more hypothetical level, there seemed to be possibilities of external markets, largely in the South-east Asian region.

One is inevitably impressed by the contrast between the assumptions of planning on the one hand and the actual performance of the economy on the other. Changes in the Gross National Product are admittedly a good index. There had been an increase in the GNP of 4.8% in real terms in 1960; a drop to 2.4% in 1961; and a slight recovery to 4% in 1962. Industrial production had in fact been stimulated by the rather stringent import restrictions which Srī Lankā had to enforce on account of balance of payment difficulties. In 1963, on the other hand, the increase in the GNP was only 1.8%, caused by a fall in production both in the domestic and the export sectors. In 1964, despite increases in output in both sectors, the GNP in real terms increased by only 1.9%; in 1965 the increase was 2%.[30]

There was little doubt that the overall economic growth achieved by Srī Lankā during this period was wholly inadequate, especially considering the fact that during these years the population of the island increased annually by about 2.4%. So that in effect there was no real improvement in the GNP in *per capita* terms.

The prevailing economic malaise was also reflected in the deterioration of Ceylon's external payments situation. After 1957 there had been a striking dimunition in external reserves. In 1958-60, in particular, the annual loss in external reserves amounted to Rs. 173.5 million. Faced with the problem, the government resorted to measures of an unprecedented nature. To begin with, the volume of imports was drastically reduced. By 1961 an elaborate machinery of import quotas and licenses was introduced. The government also resorted to increases in the duties on imported goods in an effort to reduce the quantity of imports. Consequently, 1961-2 saw massive contractions in the range of imported goods. This affected well over 30 per cent of the goods which had customarily been imported. As a result of these measures there was an appreciable improvement in Srī Laṅkā's balance of trade position, although an increase in export values was also a factor in the improved situation.

However, developments in 1963 and 1964, which saw further expansion in the scale of import reduction, showed that the overall effectiveness of this policy could easily be vitiated by two factors over which Srī Laṅkā had relatively little control. Although it was contended that long-term external liabilities were "a normal phenomenon in most developing countries" and that for Srī Laṅkā such liabilities helped to protect its external reserves, some concern was expressed during this period both to ensure that these resources were legitimately utilised strictly for developmental purposes, and over the burden of repayments in the future. In 1962 the Central Bank cautioned that "repayment of the liabilities when they fall due will constitute a corresponding burden of payments and external resources". The prognosis explicitly stated on this occasion was that such difficulties would be felt acutely by 1964.

By 1965 the overall position had certainly become more serious.[32] Although imports had been drastically cut — and indeed for part of the year the very issue of import allocations had been suspended — the country had been compelled to increase foreign exchange expenditure because of increases in the imports of essential foodstuffs. There was also a sharp decline in production in the domestic sector, especially with regard to paddy. On the other hand external liabilities had increased. The government had negotiated a standby loan from the IMF for Rs. 142.8 million, and with the aid of the IBRD had obtained pledges for foreign commodity aid worth Rs. 50 million.[33]

In these circumstances, the policy of stringent import restrictions as originally conceived impinged only on consumer goods, although as the foreign exchange position deteriorated the apparatus of import quotas and licenses imperceptibly extended itself to the productive sectors of the economy, particularly private sector industries which had to contend with problems of supply shortages and the implied deterioration of capital stock.

1965-1970

During this period planning was based on a dual strategy involving a "recovery programme" and a long-term development perspective. Although the phrase "recovery programme" was some what

extravagant and had propagandist overtones, the problems that
confronted the U.N.P. led National Government, which came to
power in 1965, emphasised the absence of any notable degree of
economic growth in the previous period. In particular, stress was
laid on the probability that the whole complex machinery of import
restrictions and the lack of foreign exchange had engendered a climate unfavourable to economic development. Consequently, the
phrase "recovery programme" was synonymous with the kindred
phraseology of restoring "the momentum of activity in the economy" and dealing with "the chronic monetary and fiscal imbalances of the previous years".[34]

Institutionally, too, the object was to break away from the past,
first by the creation of a planning machinery which Srī Laṅkā had
hitherto lacked. Although the Ten-Year Plan had seen the establishment of a National Planning Council as well as a Planning
Secretariat in 1962, these institutions had been superseded by a
Cabinet Committee on planning under the Prime Minister and a
Department of National Planning. Gradually, however, the planning machinery had fallen into disuse so that by 1965 "the planning
organisation itself had virtually ceased to function as the focal point
of development policy".

With the change of government in 1965 a new Ministry of Planning
and Economic Affairs was established under the Prime Minister. In
addition, there was a Cabinet Policy Co-ordinating Committee —
much less unwieldly than the Cabinet Committee on planning in
1962 — a Department of National Planning, as well as two distinct
Departments, of Foreign Aid and Plan Implementation respectively.

Secondly, also from an institutional point of view, a distinctive
feature of planning during this period was the determination to
avoid past precedent, especially the production of yet another formal, long-term "macro plan" involving a five- or ten-year period.
It was observed that the drafting of such a plan, which would "fully
absorb the energies and resources of the planning organisation for
a lengthy time, was not an immediate priority in the existing situation". Instead a number of detailed and well integrated plans involving different ministries and spread generally over a five-year
period were to be drawn up. This approach was also a reaction to the
fact that development plans in the past had been of a purely "aggreg-
ative character" and had been vitiated by the absence of institutionalised efforts to translate the plan into the more detailed programmes.[35]

But notwithstanding these considerations and the urgency of the
"recovery" strategy, planning during this period reflected the
existence of a long-term perspective of growth, although not in the

guise of a formal long-term plan. The aim was to achieve an annual 5 per cent increase in the National Income — the minimum growth-rate if Srī Laṅkā were to come to terms with population and un-employment. Although, theoretically, a higher growth rate would have seemed desirable, a 5 per cent growth rate was what Srī Laṅkā might reasonably hope to achieve in view of the difficulties of mobi-lising resources and the fact that development efforts could easily be cancelled out by adverse trends in the terms of trade.[36]

Specifically it was on agricultural development rather than on industry that planning in this period relied to achieve the break-through in growth. The rationale was twofold: first, that in a pre-dominantly agricultural economy the overall rate of growth was unavoidably determined by the growth rate in the agricultural sector, and secondly that the greatest potential for growth was centred in the agricultural sector — a conclusion strikingly at vari-ance with the scepticism with which agricultural development had been regarded in the period after 1962.

Growth potential in the agricultural sphere was centred in three distinct areas. First, it was reasoned that as far as domestic agricul-tural crops — particularly paddy — were concerned, the existing trends of production reflected not the maximum output possibili-ties but rather a traditionally undeveloped one, with low production technology. It followed, therefore, that by the adoption of a more scientific and production-yielding technology the existing situation could be transformed. The essence of development strategy in this respect was to achieve the transformation as rapidly as possible. In fact, one-third of the projected investment in the traditional agricul-tural sphere was earmarked to effect the implied qualitative improve-ment in the existing acreages of land under paddy cultivation. The investment was to take the form of fertilisers, inputs of pesticides and weed-killers, adoption of higher yielding strains and better culture practices.[37]

Secondly, since the planned increases in output could not be achieved exclusively in terms of intensifying production in the ex-isting areas under paddy cultivation, there was the need for, as well as the possibilities of, expanding the area of paddy cultivation es-pecially by means of irrigation. Purely theoretical considerations concerning heavy investment and a doubtful cost-benefit ratio did not weigh seriously in planning strategies. Still it was recognised that when irrigation schemes were contemplated there was a good deal of room for "rationalization of investment decisions". For example, it had to be decided in terms of priorities, costs and returns whether it was more profitable to concentrade on "integrated river basin schemes" such as the Mahavāli Ganga Diversion Scheme, or alternatively to take in hand a multiplicity of "smaller scale self-contained works". Similarly, with regard to colonization schemes there was considerable room to effect changes in the pattern of settlement with a view to securing "a more dynamic agriculture than in the past and . . . a higher return per unit of investment".

Apart from the Mahavāli Diversion Scheme which, in terms of the investment involved and development potential, surpassed any project so far undertaken, the government decided during this period on other multi-purpose schemes like the Uda Walawe Scheme, a major land reclamation scheme and a scheme intended "for the residual development in the Gal Oya Valley". In all it was planned to bring under cultivation 60,000 acres of new land by means of the major irrigation schemes as well as an additional 40,000 acres through medium-scale irrigation works. It was also expected that a fairly large acreage of new land would also be made available for paddy cultivation under village irrigation schemes.[38]

Finally the development of subsidiary food crops was also a major part of the strategy of developing the potential of the traditional agricultural sector. As in paddy production, the purpose was to make the country self-sufficient in subsidiary crops like chillies, potatoes and onions, on which large sums of money were being spent annually. In emphasising the role of subsidiary food crop development, it was observed that "the future development of agriculture in Ceylon need not continue to be based on one or the other of the polarities which have hitherto been familiar — plantation agriculture and subsistence farming". A distinctive feature with regard to planning during this period was the policy that private entrepreneurship should also take part in the development of the traditional agricultural sector: various inducements were held out to induce the private sector to do so. Overall, the investment in the agricultural sector — including the export agricultural sector — for the period 1965-70 was approximately Rs. 1,506.55 million.

The projected investment in industrial development during the same period was Rs. 930.1 million. Although in strict relation to the period 1965-70 agricultural development had pride of place, the ultimate object of planning strategy in this period — looking well into the future — was that industry rather than agriculture would be the predominant sector in the economy. In this respect at any rate there was a broad conceptual continuity with the planning objectives of the earlier period. The rationale implied in agricultural development was that it would assist in the transformation of the economy, both by releasing the resources being spent on agricultural imports and by creating a domestic market for industrial products.[39]

The change was reflected in the relative growth rates as well as in the structure of the Gross Domestic Product envisaged. Planning strategy was aimed at achieving a 9 per cent annual growth rate in industry, which would thereby grow faster than the annual growth rate of 6 per cent for the domestic agricultural sector. Consequently, the share of agriculture in the GDP was expected to fall between 1965 and 1971 from 41.4 to 39.7 per cent. On the other hand it was envisaged that the share of industry in the GDP would increase from 14.1 to 18.1 per cent.[40]

How did these work out in practice? By 1967 it was evident that substantial gains were being made in paddy production; in 1966, the island produced 45.7 million bushels; this reached 55.1 million bushels in 1967, and touched a record of 64.6 million bushels in 1968. In 1969, paddy production increased at a more moderate 2.0 per cent rate, and aggregated 65.9 million bushels. By 1970, as much as 76.8 million bushels were produced, representing an increase of 16.5 per cent.[41]

The increases were, no doubt, the result of the intensive food production drive which the government maintained during this period and which saw the adoption of better cultural practices, an overall improved technology, and increases of inputs like fertiliser. Indeed in its review of agricultural developments in 1968, the Central Bank commented that the provision of credit facilities to the farmer and the operation of a fertiliser subsidy scheme had resulted in a considerable increase in the use of fertiliser, and that well over 30,000 tons of fertiliser had been used in 1968 alone.[42] This apart, increases in public investment in agriculture had resulted in extensions of irrigation facilities in overall improvements in the agrarian situation in general.[43]

There had been similar increases in output with regard to subsidiary foodstuffs, especially red onions, chillies and potatoes. These increases were particularly evident after 1968. The incentives adopted to achieve this were twofold. First, there was the provision of credit facilities for the production of subsidiary foodstuffs. Secondly, there was also the inducement of unprecedently high prices following the government decision in 1967 substantially to reduce the imports of subsidiary foodstuffs like red onions, chillies and potatoes.[44]

The expansion of the domestic agricultural sector was significant. First, it enabled Srī Laṅkā to offset, to some extent, a very perceptible downward trend in the export sector which characterised this period. Secondly, the expansion of production in the domestic agricultural sector enabled the government to make headway with regard to the ultimate object of import substitution in agriculture.

After 1966, when rice production began to expand, the amounts of rice imported to Sri Lanka were progressively reduced. By 1968, for example, rice imports had fallen from its 1966 level of 494,000 tons to 344,000 tons.

The expansion of the domestic agricultural sector was reflected in increases in the GNP. In 1967, the GNP at constant prices reflected an increase of 4.9 per cent. More spectacularly, in 1968, there was an increase of 8.3 per cent. Even after allowing for population growth of about 2.2 per cent in that year, the rise in *per capita* real product was 6.1 per cent which was described as "the highest growth rate so far achieved". The year 1969, however, witnessed a lower rate of growth — due primarily to a decline in export incomes — when the GNP at constant prices rose by 5.7 per cent. Finally, in 1970 there was an increase of 4.1 per cent in the GNP.[46]

However, the significance of these developments was largely overshadowed by a worsening balance of payments problem, which attracted much attention during this period. The crux of the problem, which had first become apparent at the beginning of the 1960s, concerned adverse movements in the terms of trade. Between 1947 and 1970, the total volume of Sri Lanka's exports rose by as much as 60 per cent, but the value of these exports increased by only 10 per cent. The net result was a dimunition of Sri Lanka's capacity to sustain her import requirements. The corollary to the downward trend in export prices was a rise in the prices which Sri Lanka had to pay for imports due to a multiplicity of factors — such as increases in freight charges — which were clearly beyond its control.

It has been pointed out that if the prices of exports and imports had remained at the pre-1960 levels, the sheer increases in the value of exports would have enabled Sri Lanka to obtain the resources necessary for a major development effort. In the event, however, the worsening terms of trade made the more basic consideration of financing the resource gap a major preoccupation. In the absence of external assets Sri Lanka had to resort increasingly to foreign aid to meet the problem.

The problem was not a new one and indeed transcended the individual periods delineated in this chapter. In 1965-70, however, the adverse trends were more apparent than ever and forced the government to rely increasingly on foreign borrowings, thereby increasing the overall magnitude of the foreign debt.[47]

1970-1973

The predominent feature in planning during this period was the emergence in November 1971—with appropriate fanfare and trappings—of the Five-Year Plan which spelled out the development programme of the United Front Government. Two features, above all, determined the perspectives of the Plan. There was the overwhelming election victory which the S.L.F.P. and its Marxist allies in the United Front Coalition had achieved in the general election in May 1970. The implied ideological commitment to socialism was put fairly unequivocally.[48] More specifically, there were the characteristic references to the need to remove disparities in incomes and living standards, as well as the predictable onslaught on privileges. In short, the Five-Year Plan was determined to keep faith — in the picturesque phraseology which it had coined — with "the egalitarian yearnings which propelled the government into power".[49] Secondly, although the connection was not explicitly stated in the Five-Year Plan, it was evident that the insurrection which took place in Srī Laṅkā in April 1971 and in the ensuing months had left its mark on the Plan. Indeed the short-lived uprising was as much a protest against the tardiness of economic growth in post-independence Srī Laṅkā as a clarion-call to youth to set up a genuinely egalitarian socialist society.

Thus the heightened electoral hopes which had been aroused by the United Front Coalition during the 1970 general election, in which economic issues were sharply silhouetted — as well as the trauma of the insurrection — brought home the necessity of achieving economic development of a significant order and of doing so as quickly as possible.

But planned economic growth which implied — as in the case of Srī Laṅkā — structural adjustments to the prevailing economy was by definition a long-term process. The tardiness of economic development in the past was as much a result of such constraints as the product of indecision and lack of energy in pursuing the ends of economic development. Consequently, a dilemma on which the Five-Year Plan hinged was the reconciliation of the long-term growth perspective with the need to achieve quick results, especially with regard to employment.

In other ways too the Five-Year Plan reflected the background in which it was conceived. The events of 1970-1 were also widely construed as an indictment on planning. For one thing, planning had failed to bring about reasonably rapid economic growth. Secondly, it was criticised on the ground that its strategy had been conceived in the rarified atmosphere of secretariats, with no institutional provision to ensure a broad-based popular participation in the implementation of the planning process. Predictably, therefore, the Five-Year Plan criticised past planning exercises and was determined that with the advent of the United Front Government there would be a definite break with existing planning traditions, especially with regard to popular participation in the planning process.

But in spite of the disavowal of the past, there were notable similarities between the Five-Year Plan and its predecessors, especially regarding the crucial directions in which economic development had already been oriented. In a sense, given the conditions of Srī Lankā, development strategies necessarily implied a continuation of major objectives like diversification of economic growth, import substitution and expansion of production.

The theme of continuity was most evident in the agricultural sector, which was significantly described as the sector in which the growth potential was greatest. As in previous plans, the expansion of the export agricultural sector received predictable emphasis. Output in tea and rubber were to be achieved by effecting qualitative improvements — the adoption of newer and higher-yielding varieties, replanting and, in the case of rubber in particular, the abandonment of poor holdings.[50] With regard to the export agricultural sector as a whole, an annual growth rate of about 2.8 per cent was envisaged during the period 1970-6 with the coconut industry significantly achieving a higher growth rate of 3.5 per cent.

The Five-Year Plan hoped to diversify the agricultural sector so that tea, rubber and coconuts would no longer be the sole export earning spheres in the economy. Diversification was to be achieved by developing the potential of the so-called minor agricultural exports, as well as by the creation of a new export sector.

Elements of continuity were also evident in the traditional agricultural sector. The Five-Year Plan which acknowledged that there had been in fact a sustained increase in paddy cultivation, envisaged in turn massive increases in output for the period 1970-6.[51] As much as 80 per cent of the increase was to come from existing paddy lands, and the balance from lands the cultivation of which would be made possible by the extension of irrigation facilities. Apart from major irrigation schemes, the Five-Year Plan made provision for a number of medium and minor schemes. In all of them, irrigation facilities were to affect as much as 400,000 acres of paddy land out of a total area of almost 800,238 acres.[52]

Apart from the continuing and inevitable emphasis on irrigation, the Five-Year Plan, like its predecessors, also pinned its faith on qualitative improvements — better culture practices, the use of fertilisers on a large scale and inputs of pesticides — to achieve the planned increase in output. Thus by resorting to strategies in rice production which were essentially part of the conventional agricultural development strategy in previous periods, the Plan sought to make self-sufficiency in rice production a practical reality. It visualised that by 1976 Srī Laṅkā would be able to produce as much as 97 per cent of its total rice requirements.

As in the previous plans, import substitution was the key to a strategy of developing subsidiary food crops. The Plan pointed out that much foreign exchange was being spent on importing food-stuffs such as chillies and onions which could be produced locally.[53] In fact the bulk of the projected investment in the agricultural sector during 1972-6, which totalled Rs. 3,000 million, emphasised the importance of the conventional spheres of agricultural development.[54] Thus:

		Rs. Millions
I.	Export agricultural sector	540
II.	Traditional agricultural sector including provision for subsidiary foodstuffs	1,354
III.	Investment in providing facilities for development of II (equipment, storage, milling etc.)	255
	Total	2,149

The Five-Year Plan also emphasised other dimensions in agricultural development. Instead of the preoccupation with paddy cultivation which had hitherto bulked large in the peasant's economic horizons, it envisaged a broadening of the agricultural sphere in two directions. First, the small-scale agriculturist was to be encouraged to take in hand the cultivation of products like mulberry, sunflower, manioc, kenaf and cotton, which would provide the raw materials for industry and help to augment peasant incomes.[55] Secondly, products such as cashew, passion fruit, pineapples, cut flowers, cocoa were to be cultivated, all of which could be exported in ancilliary facilities, like effective marketing, could be provided.

Apart from the diversification of the traditional agricultural sector, there were two rather distinctive institutional features in the agricultural plan. First, the Five-Year Plan urged the necessity of effecting some kind of land reform with a view to changing the balance in property relations in agricultural areas, which were weighted heavily in favour of a class of landowners on whom land utilization had hitherto entirely depended. Secondly, the Plan also urged that some kind of statutory step should be taken to ensure that owners of land would put it to effective and maximum economic use — the penalty for neglect being the compulsory acquisition of estates.

These needs were theoretically met by two measures enacted in 1972. The Land Reform Act No. 1 of 1972 created a Land Reform Commission, imposed a ceiling on agricultural land which individuals could own, and vested the excess lands in the Land Reform Commission. Its sister enactment, the Agricultural Productivity Act No. 2 of 1972, defined the objectives and duties incumbent on owners of agricultural land, gave the State considerable power to confiscate land which had failed to conform to the government norms of production, and finally defined the powers of Agricultural Productivity Councils as an institutional device to achieve prduction with regard to land which came into the hands of the State.

Meanwhile, in the industrial sphere also, given the constraints under which industrialization had to be achieved, there was little room for manoeuvre, much less for a significant change in industrial policies. Nevertheless the Five-Year Plan put its emphasis on a labour-intensive approach to industrialization as opposed to capital-intensive industries, which it claimed had been emphasized in the previous period.[56] To some extent the distinction was exaggerated, because, in the conditions of Sri Laṅkā and the obvious difficulties of importing expensive industrial plant and equipment — a difficulty which had been evident since the beginning of the 1960s — there was in fact no reliance on a capital-intensive approach to the virtual exclusion of an intensive use of labour. Even more fundamentally, the choice of industries as well as the timing of industrial development programmes was often governed by "the logic of developmental programmes", which had little relation to the question of labour intensity. The Five-Year Plan conceded that emphasis would be on a labour-intensive approach "selectively supplemented by capital-intensive investments". More reasonably, the Plan claimed that the small-scale industrial sector had not been adequately developed in the past although such industries needed less foreign resources, had a relatively high employment potential, and were capable of considerable import substitution.[57]

In all an investment outlay of Rs. 2,240 million was proposed in industrial development during the Five-Year period. Basic industries like steel, cement and chemicals were — partly due to considerations of scale and technology — to be developed as public sector industries. There was also to be private sector participation to produce essential consumer goods as well as "a wide range of goods for export". Private sector investment, together with investment in a third and new sector — co-operative enterprises, was to amount to Rs. 1,000 million.[58]

Above all, industrial growth was also to cause a significant change in the sectoral composition of the GDP in the period 1970-6. The contribution of the industrial sector was to increase from 13 per cent in 1970 to 16 per cent with an annual growth rate of 10 per cent. The share of the agricultural sector, on the other hand, was to reflect a fall from 36.3 per cent to 33.7 per cent despite an annual growth rate of 4.9 per cent. In thus emphasising the growing preponderance of industry, the Plan was in harmony rather than at variance with past planning strategy.[59]

In spite of such broad similarities, the Five-Year Plan was in some ways rather distinctive. The vexatious problem of employment was an obvious example. Conspicuously woven into the development plans for industry and agriculture was this problem, which was characterised by the high rate of population growth, the inability of the economy to absorb the resulting increases in the work-force and the penchant among educated youth for white-collar employment. Sectorally the majority of the unemployed were in rural areas. Clearly the rural economy with its bias for paddy cultivation was not capable of absorbing a growing work-force. In the circumstances, rural youth who were also educated looked to white-collar employment, to which they felt they were entitled because of their education but which to all intents and purposes was almost unobtainable.[60]

Implied in the Five-Year Plan was a distinction between the expansion of employment as an incidental corollary to economic development on the one hand, and employment expansion which was the result of a deliberate employment-oriented development strategy. The diversification of the agricultural sector is best understood in this context. The planned production of subsidiary foodstuffs, the encouragement of agricultural products for export, as well as the production of suitable raw materials for industry, implied an expansion of employment in a sector in which traditionally the amplitude of employment opportunities had depended solely on paddy cultivation.

By way of a parallel strategy the Five-Year Plan also emphasised the importance of bringing about an attitudinal change with regard to employment by means of educational reforms. It was pointed out that the education system as it existed had been geared to "desk-type occupations" and that it had placed an unwarranted and misguided emphasis on examinations and degrees as opposed to "the development of skills so necessary for economic development". Moreover the Plan also argued that, by means of a wage structure which needlessly rewarded desk-type occupations at the expense of possibly more productive manual work, society had contributed to the perpetuation of prevailing attitudes.[61] Apart from attitudinal and egalitarian considerations, the Five-Year Plan also urged changes in the prevailing salary structure as a means of enabling the government to increase the number of its employees.

As shown by the first three years' (1972-4) working of the Plan, however, the actual performance of the economy seems to have lagged far behind the desired targets. The observed average annual growth rate of the Real National Product, for example, has only been 3.1 per cent, slightly more than half of the 6.0 per cent growth rate aimed at by the Plan. Similarly, although the Plan expected to bring about a significant reduction in the rate of unemployment in the economy, the unemployment rate has actually soared during this period. In contrast to an estimated 14.0 per cent (546,000 persons) in 1969-70, the unemployment rate in 1973 was 18.1 per cent (743,000 persons).[62] Achievements in domestic savings and financing of the Plan were also modest. The Plan's target was to increase the economy's average rate of saving from 12.5 per cent to 17.0 per cent over the period 1972-6. In the three years under consideration, however, the average rate of saving was only 13.0 per cent. Likewise, even though the Plan aimed at gradually reducing the country's dependence on foreign resources for development, by the end of 1974 the reliance on foreign aid seemed to have increased. A substantial proportion of the deficit in the government's budget for 1975, for instance, was expected to be financed with foreign assistance.

In contrast, however, certain targets of the Plan such as those set for the export of precious stones and for exchange earnings from tourism were realised in less than three years. These achievements, however, were marginal compared to the major targets of the Plan. Nevertheless, in fairness to the Plan it must be pointed out clearly that the successful implementation of the Plan was thwarted by unanticipated constraints. These related mainly to the foreign trade sector of the economy which still stands as its mainstay. Particularly disastrous was the phenomenal rise in the prices of essential imports in these three years. The import price index rose from 158 in 1972 to 370 in 1974. The index for food and drink alone rose from 173 to 451 while that of intermediate goods rose from 152 to 386. In 1974 with a fourfold increase in the price of oil, many other essential imports had to be cut down in order to save foreign exchange to meet the mounting expenditure on oil imports.[63]

In view of this drastic change in the nature of exogenous factors against which the Five-Year Plan was prepared, the position at the end of 1974 was that a major revision of the Plan was being undertaken by the government.

In the industrial sphere there was little more than the general enumeration of the principle of private sector participation. On the one hand the Plan referred to the need to tap "the initiative and the skills" of the private sector in industry, leaving to the private sector the tasks of producing essential consumer goods and goods for export. On the other hand, with equal or more emphasis, the Plan spoke of setting up "collective and co-operative forms of ownership" in industry as well as of "mixed enterprises" in industry between the government and the private sector.

Over and above the lack of evidence of positive inducements to private enterprise, the Plan leaves unanswered the rather more basic question of the private sector's role. It scarcely needs to be emphasised that the expansion of state economic activity and increasing socialisation of the means of production would mean a shrinking of the sphere of organised entrepreneurial capitalist enterprises.

Indeed, because of the latent dichotomy it is likely that every decision concerning private enterprise participation would give rise to sharp ideological differences in policy-making between those who see an extension of private enterprise, however slight, as a betrayal of cherished principles and those who, in viewing the question more pragmatically and in terms of economic development, would welcome and encourage private enterprise.

Moreover, it is evident that the Five-Year Plan, as well as the policies of the United Front Coalition, have above all affected those sectors of the economy which have hitherto made the largest contribution to the national wealth thereby causing a slowing-down of economic activity. To redress the balance, following the liquidation of the old economic order, the Plan looked to the creation of new spheres of economic activity such as the agricultural co-operative enterprises which, presumably inspired by the ethic of socialism, were to bring about quick and dramatic increases in production to more than compensate for the inevitable but transitional retardation of economic development. To what extent and — equally important — how fast the hope would be realised is a moot question. It may well be possible that the new sectors would take longer than is generally admitted to become viable economic alternatives to the old order which they displace. The longer the delay, the greater would surely be the danger that the Five-Year Plan might fall between two stools.

To conclude — in reviewing more than twenty five years of economic development in Srī Laṅkā after political independence, it is evident that, far from being an excrescence, planning has become increasingly important in policy-making. This may well have been an integral part of the increasing general popular awareness of economic problems in a climate of deteriorating economic conditions.

However, it is possible that — precisely because of popular awareness of economic problems — exaggerated and unreasonably hopeful expectations could be placed in the efficacy of planning in general, as well as in a particular planning exercise — such as the Five-Year Plan — as the panacea for Srī Laṅkā's prevailing economic ills.

REFERENCES

1. See, *The Six-Year Plan for Ceylon,* issued by the Department of Information (n.d.), pp. 45 ff.
2. *The Economic Development of Ceylon* (Report of a mission organised by the International Bank for Reconstruction and Development), Colombo (1952), Part I, pp. 1 ff.
3. *Six-Year Programme of Investment (1954-1960),* Colombo (1955), pp. 3 ff.
4. ibid., pp. 55 ff.
5. ibid., part II, pp. 34 ff.
6. ibid., part I, pp. 57 ff.
7. ibid., pp. 23ff. *The Economic Development of Ceylon,* Part, I, pp. 70 ff.
8. ibid., pp. 23 ff. *The Economic Development of Ceylon,* Part I, pp. 70 ff.
9. *Six-Year Programme of Investment,* op. cit., pp. 234 ff; *The Economic Development of Ceylon,* Part II, pp. 251 ff.
10. ibid.
11. ibid.
12. *Six-Year Programme of Investment,* op. cit., p. 237 ff.
13. ibid.
14. ibid., pp. 14 ff.
15. *The Ten-Year Plan,* op. cit., pp. 68 ff. Also pp. 107 ff.
16. ibid.
17. ibid.
18. ibid., p. 119.
19. *The Short-Term Implementation Programme,* Colombo (1962), pp. 40 ff.
20. *The Ten-Year Plan,* op. cit., pp. 69 ff. Also p. 82.
21. ibid., pp. 169 ff.
22. ibid., pp. 169 ff.
23. *The Short-Term Implementation Programme,* op. cit., pp. 102 ff.
24. *The Ten-Year Plan,* op. cit., p. 168.
25. *The Short-Term Implementation Programme,* op. cit., pp. 102 ff.
26. *The Ten-Year Plan,* op. cit., p. 75, Also pp. 235 ff.
27. *The Short-Term Implementation Programme,* op. cit., pp. 118 ff.
28. ibid.
29. ibid., pp. 29 ff. and pp. 345 ff. Also, *First Interim Report,* Colombo (1957), pp. 11 ff.
30. Central Bank of Ceylon, *Annual Reports* (1960-5).
31. Central Bank, *Annual Report* (1961), pp. 4 ff; (1962), pp. 10 ff.

32. Central Bank, *Annual Report* (1965), pp. 9 ff.
33. ibid.
34. *The Development Programme, 1966-67*, Colombo (1966), pp. 1 ff.
35. ibid., pp. 3 ff. Also see article 'Recent Approaches to Planning in Ceylon' by Lal Jayawardane in *Economic Development in South Asia*, London (1970), edited by E. A. G. Robinson and Michael Kidron, pp. 392 ff.
36. *The Development Programme, 1966-67*. op. cit., pp. 5 ff.
37. ibid., pp. 7 ff and pp. 23 ff.
38. ibid.
39. ibid., pp. 26 ff and 35 ff.
40. ibid.
41. See, Central Bank of Ceylon *Annual Report* (1965-70).
42. Central Bank of Ceylon, *Annual Report* (1968), pp. 16 ff.
43. ibid.
44. Central Bank, *Annual Report* (1967)., p. 13; (1969), p. 24.
45. Central Bank, *Annual Report* (1968), p. 6.
46. Central Bank, *Annual Reports* (1965, 1966, 1967, 1968, 1969 and 1970).
47. Central Bank, *Annual Report* (1970), pp. 11 ff.
48. *The Five-Year Plan*, Colombo, 1971, p. 1.
49. ibid., p. 000.
50. ibid., pp. 41 ff.
51. Possibly out of political and polemical motives the Five-Year Plan took care to assert that the increase in paddy cultivation had occurred over "the past fifteen years", whereas in fact the "sustained increase" had been a conspicuous feature of the period 1965-70.
52. *Five-Year Plan*, op. cit., p. 38.
53. ibid., p. 45.
54. ibid., p. 39.
55. ibid., pp. 16 and 33 ff.
56. ibid., pp. 13, 15 and 59 ff.
57. ibid.
58. ibid., pp. 64 ff.
59. ibid., p. 28.
60. *Five-Year Plan*, op. cit., p. 16.
61. ibid., pp. 17 ff.
62. Central Bank of Ceylon, *The Determinants of the Labour Force Participation Rates in Sri Lanka, 1973*, Colombo (1974).
63. Data from Central Bank, *Annual Report* (1974).

7

FOREIGN TRADE OF SRĪ LAṄKĀ

by H. M. Gunasekera

I

Introduction

Foreign trade has played, and continues to play, an important role in the economy of Srī Laṅkā. In the one hundred years from 1840 — forty years after Srī Laṅkā became a British colony — up to the Second World War, foreign trade was the single most dynamic force in her economic development. The dominance of the export sector in this development was so complete that the economy of Srī Laṅkā in these years was typical of an 'export economy'.[1] The rise of the coffee plantations in the three decades after 1840 — followed later by tea, rubber and coconut estates — established a modern sector in a hitherto primitive economy. This sector catered solely to an export market. The characteristic features of a modern economy — such as specialisation and production for a cash market, the use of capital, a wage earning labour — all came into being with the increased flow of international trade arising out of the growth of the plantations. Besides catering to foreign markets, these plantations and their ancillary activities such as trade, insurance, transport and communications depended largely on foreign entrepreneurship, foreign capital and immigrant labour. As a result, the modern sector grew quite independently of the traditional domestic peasant economy, and injected little dynamism into the latter. Nevertheless, with the growth of plantations, an economy developed which was largely dependent on foreign trade for a substantial portion of its requirements such as food and other manufactured consumer goods, raw materials and capital goods. Thus in 1948 when Srī Laṅkā became a politically sovereign nation, 34 per cent of its Gross National Income was derived from exports and an equal percentage of the national income was being spent on imports.

172

In more recent years the foreign trade sector has stagnated. Income from exports has ceased to grow particularly because of falling prices. On the other hand, the aim of economic policy has centered upon the development of the industrial and peasant agricultural sectors, both of which were neglected during the growth of plantations. As a reaction to the 'lop-sided' growth of the colonial export economy, economic policies of the post-independence era have sought to develop a more diversified economy less critically dependent on foreign trade. Yet foreign trade continues to be dominant in the economy, the very effort of diversifying the economy being dependent largely on the foreign exchange proceeds derived from exports from the plantation agricultural sector.

The export of goods still contribute a substantial proportion of the national income. For example, in the period 1972-3 the value added in the export sector (at constant prices) came to about 23 per cent of the GNP. On the other hand, the country's standard of living and the level of economic activity depends heavily on imports, because a substantial part of the required consumer goods — particularly food, raw materials and capital goods — is imported. A significant proportion of the country's work-force is employed in the foreign trade sector. In the period 1969-70, for example, 22 per cent of the gainfully employed labour force was in the plantations.[2] The proportion would be higher if we add those employed in the activities ancillary to plantation agriculture, such as processing and packing, trade, insurance, transport etc. The government derives about 40 per cent of its tax revenue from levies on imports and exports.[3]

II

Main Characteristics of Srī Laṅkā's Foreign Trade

The most striking characteristics of Srī Laṅkā's foreign trade is the high degree of specialisation of its exports. This may be illustrated in terms of the ratio of specialised exports to the National Product and the ratio of specialised exports to total exports. As may be seen from Table 1, the average contribution from the export of commodities to Srī Laṅkā's real National Income (at 1959 prices) in the period 1971-4 was 18 per cent. The three commodities — tea, rubber and coconut products — alone contributed as much as 16 per cent. In the same period these commodities accounted for 79 per cent of the foreign exchange earnings from all merchandise exports.[4] Because merchandise exports fetch 90 per cent of all Srī Laṅkā's export income — the balance of 10 per cent being contributed by the export of services — tea, rubber and coconut products constituted the source of 71 per cent of total export earnings for Srī Laṅkā in this period.

Table 1.

COMPOSITION OF SRI LANKA'S EXPORTS

Commodity	% of National Income		% of merchandise exports	
	1950-3	*1971-4*	*1950-3*	*1971-4*
Tea	17.0	11.0	48.0	49.0
Natural Rubber	9.0	4.0	26.0	19.0
Coconut Products	6.0	1.0	16.0	11.0
Minor Exports		1.0		10.0
(agricultural)				
Minor Exports	1.5		5.0	
(industrial)		1.0		10.0
Re-exports				
	1.5	0.3	5.0	1.0

Sources: Central Bank of Ceylon, *Annual Reports*; Department of Census and Statistics, *Statistical Abstract.*

The high degree of commodity concentration becomes still clearer from the fact that more than half the merchandise exports consist of a single item — tea. Furthermore, both tea and natural rubber are produced mainly for export. In the period 1971-4 more than 90 per cent of the total output of these commodities was exported. Of the three main exports, only in the case of coconuts is a substantial proportion of the output consumed domestically. In recent years, owing to the importance of this commodity in local consumption, an increasing share of its output (about 65 per cent in the period 1971-3) has been absorbed by the local market.

Table 1 also shows that Srī Laṅkā's exports are predominantly agricultural, industrial goods accounting for only about 5 per cent of merchandise exports. This in turn reflects the still primarily agricultural nature of Srī Laṅkā's economy. In 1974, the manufacturing sector contributed only about 13 per cent of the total value added in the economy whereas the agricultural sector's contribution came to 33 per cent.[5] The contrast is even greater in terms of the relative shares of the labour employed in these sectors. In 1969 the manufacturing sector employed only 11 per cent of the workforce while the agricultural sector employed 50 per cent.[6] Srī Laṅkā's economy has failed so far to break away significantly from the pattern of resource allocation common to all export economies — namely specialisation in a few primary products for export.

In very recent years, however, there has been a slight change in the high degree of commodity concentration shown in Table 1. These changes have occurred in the early 1970s particularly due to the special efforts of the Srī Laṅkā government to diversify the export base. Thus the share of tea, rubber and coconut products — known as the traditional exports — in export income fell from 84 to 72 per cent between 1971 and 1974, while that of the "non-traditional exports" increased : minor agricultural exports increased from 6.6 to 11 per cent while — industrial products — petroleum products, precious stones, garments, batik, sea foods, footwear, cement, wood products, fatty acids and edible fats rose from 3 to 17 per cent.[7]

In contrast, Srī Laṅkā's imports are more diversified and include a significant proportion of manufactured goods. This is, of course, to be expected in a country specialising in the production of a few commodities for export. The composition of Srī Laṅkā's imports by major categories is shown in Table 2. The table shows that almost

Table 2.
COMPOSITION OF SRI LANKA'S IMPORTS

Category of Imports	% of total imports	
	1950-3	1971-4
Food and drink of which	47.0	44.5
Rice	18.0	10.8
Wheat Flour	8.0	13.8
Sugar	5.0	10.5
Textiles	10.0	2.7
Intermediate goods ⎱	38.0	29.3
Capital goods ⎰		17.0

Source: Central Bank of Ceylon, *Annual Reports.*

half the imports consist of three main food items — rice, wheat flour and sugar. These three items are basic necessities in the consumption pattern of the people of Srī Laṅkā. Rice is the staple diet and wheat flour is its closest substitute, while sugar is the complementary item that goes with tea, the main beverage consumed. The entire requirements of wheat flour are imported because wheat cannot be grown locally. Rice imports came to 30 per cent of total consumption in 1970-2 and sugar to 94 per cent in 1970-1. The country is dependent on imports for a substantial portion of its rice requirements because the domestic sector was neglected until recently. During the last few years, however, an effort has been made to make Srī Laṅkā self-sufficient in this commodity, and consequently its import coefficient fell from 46 to 25 per cent in the period 1961-72.

Table 2 shows that 46 per cent of all imports consist of raw materials and capital goods. In 1973-4 the import component of the gross domestic capital formation was 17 per cent while the import component in the raw material usage of the industrial sector was 72 per cent. Imported capital goods consist of items such as building materials, transport equipment, plant and machinery. Fertiliser, petroleum products, chemicals, yarn and thread, coal and tea chests are the major items of raw material imports.[8]

The crucial importance of imports for the survival of Srī Laṅkā's economy is succinctly expressed in the following statement of an International Labour Organisation mission which visited Srī Laṅkā:

The country has become so integrated to the world economy that it needs a big range of imports for production as well as consumption. Its farmers now rely on imported fertilisers and machinery; the industrial sector is still more heavily dependent on imports, and yet Ceylon's market is small and to produce many of these requirements for itself would imply under-sized firms and high costs.

Position in the World Market

Compared with the total of world trade — i.e. the average of all the world's exports and imports — Srī Laṅkā's foreign trade is insignificant, although — as we have seen — it is quite significant from the point of view of the domestic economy. In 1972-3 Srī Laṅkā's external trade was only 0.12 per cent of the total world trade — which is hardly surprising for a small, underdeveloped economy like that of Srī Laṅkā. This is also true of individual items of exports and imports, except for tea. In 1969-70 Srī Laṅkā's natural rubber exports were only 5 per cent of the world total, and the corresponding figure for coconut oil exports was 11 per cent. The most important single import item was rice, of which Srī Laṅka's imports constitute about 5 per cent of world total.

The position is quite different as regards tea. For many years Srī Laṅka has been the second biggest supplier of black tea in the world, India being the first. In 1968-70 Srī Laṅkā supplied about 32 per cent of the total world export of such tea. Since black tea accounts for about 90 per cent of the world's tea exports, including green tea, Srī Laṅkā is the source of about 30 per cent of the total volume of the entire world's tea exports. Under the tea supply restriction scheme currently in operation, Sri Laṅkā's export quota for 1973-4 was 31 per cent of the global quota, while India's was 32 per cent.[9]

Despite its relatively large share of the world tea market, Srī Laṅkā has no control over the price of tea. This is because of the severe competition faced by Srī Laṅka's tea in the world market, both from other tea suppliers and from close substitutes such as coffee, cocoa, soft drinks and fruit juices.[10] Moreover, an excess supply has prevailed in the world tea market as a whole in recent years, and is likely to continue in the forseeable future.[11]

The Regional Distribution of Trade

The distribution of Srī Laṅkā's external trade by trading blocs and other groups and by individual trading partners is given in Table 3, which shows that developed countries account for nearly half the total. The underdeveloped countries account for about one-third and the Soviet Area for about one-fifth, while the share of trade with Africa and Latin America is negligible.

Table 3

THE DISTRIBUTION OF SRI LANKA'S TRADE AMONG TRADING
BLOCS, REGIONS AND INDIVIDUAL COUNTRIES

Region or Country	% of trade in 1972	
	Exports	Imports
(a) *By trading blocs and regions*		
Developed countries	52	43
Less Developed countries	27	35
Soviet Area	21	22
Middle East	13	4
Asia including Japan	21	34
Africa	1	2
Latin America	0.8	—
U.S. & Canada	10	9
The Commonwealth	28	28
European Economic Community	23	18
(b) *By Individual Countries*		
U.K.	14	11
U.S.A.	7	7
India	0.5	5
People's Republic of China	8	5
U.S.S.R.	4	1
Japan	4	8
Pakistan	8	4

Source: International Bank for Reconstruction and Development, *Direction of Trade — Annual 1968-72, p. 524.*

In terms of individual countries, the most important single trading partner of Srī Laṅkā is the United Kingdom. This situation is a heritage from the colonial past. During the period of growth of plantation agriculture, Srī Laṅkā was a British colony. It was only natural that the trade, growing out of plantations mostly owned by British investors, had to be with the mother country whose own economy at that time was geared to importing primary products and exporting industrial products. In recent years, however, the United Kingdom's relative importance as a trading partner of Srī Laṅkā has been declining. Its share of Srī Laṅkā's total external trade, which in 1949 was 27 per cent, was only 12 per cent in 1972. Among the other important trading partners are the United States, the People's Republic of China, Japan, India, Pakistan and the Soviet Union. The relative importance of China, the Soviet Union and Japan has been increasing in recent years while that of India has fallen.

The growth of trade with these new trading partners — China, the Soviet Union and other countries in Eastern Europe and the Middle East — has been the main reason for the United Kingdom's declining importance as a trading partner. Thus, for example, although the United Kingdom is still the largest single buyer of Srī Laṅkā's tea, the exports have fallen since 1953, when it bought 118 million lb. or 35 per cent of Srī Laṅkā's tea exports; in 1972 it bought only 74 million lb. or 18 per cent. Over the same period tea exports to the Middle East, Pakistan and Eastern Europe increased from 46 million lb. or 14 per cent to 132 million lb. or 34 per cent. Exports of rubber to the United Kingdom has also fallen, while they have increased to the Soviet bloc, which in 1953 imported only 10 million lb. or 3.6 per cent. Exports to China have increased from 29 million lb. or 32 per cent to 118 million lb. or 41 per cent. The import restrictions which have existed in Srī Laṅkā for the last fourteen years have been partly responsible for the declining importance of its traditional markets.[12] These restrictions have led particularly to a reduction of industrial inputs for which the United Kingdom was formerly an important source. Thus in 1970-3 the United Kingdom accounted for only 11 per cent of Srī Laṅkā's imports as compared to 22 per cent in 1950-3. The decline in importance of India as Srī Laṅkā's trading partner has also been mainly due to import restrictions — which cut down the importation of several subsidiary foodstuffs that have traditionally been imported from India.

Bilateral Trade Agreements

The main instrument through which Srī Laṅkā has established and expanded trade with new partners such as China, Eastern Europe and Middle Eastern countries has been bilateral trade agreements. In 1973 Srī Laṅkā had twelve such agreements.[13] The value of trade conducted through these channels (i.e. average of exports and imports) in the same year was Rs. 58 million or 22 per cent of the country's total trade. The first of these agreements was the Srī Laṅkā-China rubber-rice agreement signed in 1952 for five years. This agreement has been renewed from time to time, and still continues on a more diversified commodity base.[14] Several similar agreements were signed after 1956 when Srī Laṅkā first established diplomatic relations with the Communist countries. In more recent years, due to the continuing balance of payments problems, Srī Laṅkā has attempted to make greater use of these agreements to expand its trade.

III

The Balance of Payments — Recent Trends

Srī Laṅkā's balance of payments has been in a chronic state of imbalance in the past two decades or so. For the entire period of eighteen years, 1957 to 1974, there has been a basic surplus only in 1965 and 1971-3 (see Table 4).[15] Even these surpluses have been mostly marginal and were achieved only through strict import and exchange controls; they could hardly be considered a sign of improvement in the basic underlying factors. While the import capacity has been declining due to falling export earnings and the rising unit cost of imports,[16] the demand for imports has been high due to the increasing requirements of a development-oriented economy characterised by a 'population explosion', a 'revolution of rising expectations' and limited import substitution possibilities. The resulting shortage of foreign exchange has been the greatest problem of the economy in recent years. The government has tried to overcome this problem mainly by slashing the amount of imports through non-price rationing methods like import quotas and exchange control. But the basic disequilibrium in the balance of payments continues because the long-term measures such as a proper exchange rate policy and reallocation of resources needed to remove such a disequilibrium have not been undertaken.

Table 4 shows that the basic deficit has been mostly due to an adverse trade balance, i.e. an excess of merchandise imports over merchandise exports. Hence it is necessary to examine the behaviour of merchandise exports and imports during this period so as to understand the factors behind Srī Laṅkā's current foreign exchange problem.

Table 4
SRĪ LAṄKĀ'S BALANCE ON BASIC TRANSACTIONS 1955-74

Item	1955	1956	1957	1958	1959	1960	1961	1962	1963	1964
Trade balance	415	196	−95	−89	−185	−210	−87	−143	−161	−193
Net invisibles including transfer payments	−92	−114	−100	−64	−23	−10	−7	3	−7	33
Balance on current account	323	82	−195	−153	−208	−220	−94	−140	−168	−160
Net private long term capital	−50	−49	−41	−15	−6	2	−8	−2	5	1
Net official long term capital	8	9	23	23	15	20	19	40	75	7
All net long term capital	−42	−40	−19	8	9	22	11	38	80	8
Basic balance	281	42	−213	−145	−199	−198	−83	−102	−88	−152

Item	1965	1966	1967	1968	1969	1970	1971	1972	1973	1974
Trade balance	−13	−344	−335	−380	−746	−316	−287	−255	−298	−1227
Net invisibles including transfer payments	72	54	47	25	−51	−36	71	59	137	328
Balance on current account	59	−290	−288	−355	−797	−350	−216	−196	−161	−899
Net private long term capital	−3	−16	−7	−11	−10	−2	2	1	1	12
Net official long term capital	37	153	167	235	285	186	402	291	194	253
All net long term capital	34	137	160	224	275	184	404	290	195	265
Basic balance	93	−153	−128	−131	−522	−166	188	94	34	−634

(a) Provisional
Source: Central Bank of Ceylon, *Annual Reports 1972 and 1974.*

Data on export value quantity and prices for this period are given in Table 5. In particular, column 1 of the Table gives us an idea of the long-term behaviour of export income in terms of foreign exchange. The column, which gives these values in terms of SDRs[17], indicates that the income from merchandise exports has fluctuated between 400 million and 410 million between 1955 and 1965 and slightly declined thereafter.[18] It is clear from these data that at any rate export income has not tended to increase in these years.

Table 5
SRĪ LAŃKĀ'S EXPORTS 1955-74 *(a) (b)*

Year	Export Value (1)	Quantity Index (2)	Price Index (3)
1955	400	86	134
1956	372	81	125
1957	351	79	120
1958	341	84	118
1959	372	82	122
1960	377	87	122
1961	360	90	112
1962	370	97	109
1963	360	93	109
1964	371	102	111
1965	410	105	113
1966	352	96	107
1967	347	100	100
1968	352	103	117
1969	322	98	117
1970	342	102	118
1971	327	99	117
1972	296	97	118
1973	343	98	137
1974	431	85	213

(*a*) Value in Millions of SDRs. Conversion rates used are as follows: 1955-67, 1 SDR – Rs. 4.76; 1968-71, 1 SDR – Rs. 4.95; 1972, 1 SDR – Rs. 6.78; 1973, 1 SDR – Rs. 7.63; 1974, 1 SDR – Rs. 8.05.

(*b*) Base year for indices – 1967.
Source: Central Bank of Ceylon, *Annual Reports.*

This state of stagnation in the total foreign exchange earnings from merchandise exports has been brought about by falls in the price of tea and rubber and in the export quantity of coconut products. Income from tea exports was more or less constant in 1955-65 but somewhat declined thereafter, despite a considerable rise in the export quantity. The average price of a pound of tea exports declined from 63 to 40 SDR cents (approximately 37 per cent) between 1955-7 and 1971-3.[19] Because tea contributes nearly half of all Srī Laṅkā's export earnings, the adverse effect of this price decline on the import capacity has been large indeed.

Rubber export income has faced a similar situation. Here too the income has been constant, in spite of a 50 per cent rise in the quantity of exports, because of a drastic fall in the price. The average price of a pound of rubber fell from 33 SDR cents in the period 1955-7 to only 21 SDR cents in the period 1971-2. Since rubber contributes another 17 per cent of Srī Laṅkā's export income, the decline in rubber prices has also been a major contribution to the constancy of the country's foreign exchange earnings. However, the situation could have been worse had it not been for a significant increase in the export quantities of these two items, which partly offset the impact of the price decline.

Stagnation in the earnings from coconut product exports also helped to prevent an increase in export earnings. But here the forces at work were different from the precedingī it was a case of declining export quantity in the face of rising prices rather than one of declining prices and rising quantities. Income from this source increased slightly from 46 million SDR in 1954-8 to 49 million SDR in 1964-8 and was only 36 million SDR in 1969-73. The quantity index showed a decline from 136 to 63 and the price index increased from 83 to 138 (1967 = 100).[20] Thus supply inelasticity has prevented Srī Laṅkā from capitalising on the only price increase in her major exports. The failure of coconut exports to rise with rising prices has been due to increasing domestic demand which, confronted by a stagnant supply, has encroached upon potential exports. In the period 1955-7 to 1971-3, domestic consumption of coconuts increased by 624,000 nuts, whereas production increased by only 225,000 nuts. The balance was met by a fall in exports as a result of which the share of exports in total production fell from 56 to 36 per cent.

The only category of merchandise exports in which foreign exchange earnings increased during this period was the minor exports group, the proceeds from which increased by 150 per cent due to increase in both quantity and price. However, this favourable behaviour did not succeed in greatly improving the trade balance because of the small base of these exports. Even after this high increase, the absolute value of these exports came to only 60 million SDR or 20 per cent of merchandise exports in 1971-3.

The discussion has so far been limited to the supply side of the merchandise account. The adverse trade balance has been due to factors both on the supply and the demand sides. On the demand side the contributing factor has been a high import bill. The data on different categories of imports for selected years in the period 1955-73 are given in Table 6. In looking at these indices we should remember that the period in question falls into two sub-periods

Table 6

SRI LANKA'S IMPORTS AND
TERMS OF TRADE 1955-74 (a) (b)

Year	Value	Quantity Index	Price Index	Terms of Trade Index (c)
1955	311	98	83	149
1956	331	109	83	162
1957	371	116	88	151
1958	360	118	81	136
1959	411	136	83	145
1960	421	133	83	148
1961	377	107	82	136
1962	400	108	77	142
1963	393	93	85	129
1964	412	114	105	105
1965	404	86	100	112
1966	423	118	98	109
1967	418	100	100	100
1968	475	101	126	93
1969	536	108	134	88
1970	471	102	140	84
1971	449	90	150	78
1972	318	88	158	75
1973	347	79	209	65
1974	572	56	370	58

(a) Base year for indices −1967.
(b) Values are in millions of SDRs.
(c) i.e. $\dfrac{\text{Export Price Index}}{\text{Import Price Index}} \times 100$

Source: Central Bank of Ceylon, *Annual Reports.*

depending on whether import control measures existed or not: 1955-60 when the flow of imports was generally free and the years after 1960 when they were under strict quantitative controls.

As may be seen from the table, the quantity of imports in the earlier period increased significantly while in general import prices fell. Therefore in these years the import bill increased due to an increase in the quantity of imports. The increase in the demand for imports in those years resulted from a number of factors. Because of two export booms experienced by Srī Laṅkā — the rubber boom of 1950-1 and the tea boom of 1955 — the consumption levels went up permanently, thus increasing the aggregate consumption expenditure.[21] The aggregate level of demand was further increased by spiralling government expenditure financed mostly through deficit budgets. In the period 1950-1 to 1960-1 total government expenditure increased from Rs. 969 million to 2,005 million and the budget was in deficit except for 1953-4 and 1954-5. The deficit, which was only 58.5 million rupees in 1950-1, increased to 491 million in 1960-1. These budget deficits resulted in large-scale net additions to the economy's aggregate demand since they were financed mostly by directly inflationary methods. Moreover, rapidly increasing population also tended to add to the pressure of demand for goods and services. Since most of the goods demanded were not produced at home and could not be so produced cheaply enough, the excess aggregate demand increased the pressure on the balance of payments.

On the other hand, in the period after 1960 the main factor responsible for the high import bill has been the increasing import prices. The import quantity index shows a 60 per cent reduction in this period. This reduction was brought about by stringent import control measures which were introduced after 1960. The value of imports however, has not shown a clear tendency to fall. In some years it has even increased. This was particularly seen in 1974 when import quantity was 30 per cent below the previous year's level but the value of imports was 36 per cent higher.[22] The increase in import prices, taken together with the decline in the export prices, may be considered as the single main factor responsible for Srī Laṅkā's balance of payment disequilibrium in recent years. We have seen that the prices of main exports began their decline after the boom of 1955. Import prices began to rise only in 1960, but Srī Laṅkā's commodity terms of trade have been declining since 1955. Table 6 shows that the terms of trade index which was 156 in 1955-6 was only 62 in 1972-4 — much less than half of what it was earlier. The declining terms of trade have led to a fast shrinking import capacity of Srī Laṅkā. Table 7 illustrate this situation for some selected years since 1960.

Table *1*

IMPORT CAPACITY OF SRI LANKA—1959 PRICES

(Rs. Million)

Year (1)	Exports (2)	Terms of trade effect (3)	Net capital inflow (4)	Net factor payments (5)	Capacity to import (6)	Actual imports (7)	(6) as a % of (7) (8)
1960	1,777	-11	2	-44	1,724	1,939	90
1964	2,060	-316	2	-34	1,712	1,870	91
1966	1,928	-505	-12	-36	1,375	1,740	80
1967	2,002	-667	-2	-45	1,288	1,442	82
1968	2,022	-784	-3	-29	1,206	1,430	90
1969	1,951	-811	-3	-58	1,079	1,577	70
1970	2,083	-916	-	-84	1,083	1,383	78
1971	2,014	-955	-	-70	989	1,227	80
1972	2,006	-970	-1	72	963	1,131	85
1973	2,155	-1,170	-2	-44	939	1,093	86
1974	1,961	-1,143	-1	-25	792	1,033	71

Source: Central Bank of Ceylon, *Annual Reports.*

Even in the period after 1960, the balance of payments deficit may be attributed partly to the lack of effective and suitable government policies. The expansionary monetary and fiscal policies and the resulting deficit budgets continued unabated even after 1960. Import substitution policies followed by the government seem to have followed the wrong system of priorities. Instead of an all-out attempt to make the country self-sufficient in foods which accounted for 50 per cent of the import bill, import substitution was encouraged in industries producing goods classified as luxuries and banned from being imported. Such industries were not only highly import-intensive but, by being mainly for the satisfaction of local demand, constituted a source of net drain on scarce foreign exchange.

The adverse effect on Srī Laṅkā's balance of payments due to declining terms of trade and expansionary monetary and fiscal policy at home may have been at least partly mitigated by an inflow of long term private investment. But, as may be seen from Table 4, the net flow of such capital has been outwards rather than inwards for most part of this period.

There were several ways in which the resulting disequilibrium could have been remedied. Among these were adjustments in the exchange rate, import and exchange controls, export promotion and import substitution, and the use of foreign resources in the form of loans and grants. As may be seen from the discussion in the next section, the policies followed were a mixture of all these measures. Nevertheless, it is clear that there has been an increasing reliance on foreign aid and loans in these years as a method of financing the balance of payments deficit. The country's net external debt has increased from Rs. 223 million in 1960 to Rs. 2,922 million in 1974. This increase has led to the emergence of a debt servicing problem of a substantial degree. In 1960 foreign debt servicing expenditure amounted to only Rs. 33 million or 1.6 per cent of the total earnings. By 1974 however, the amount had increased to Rs. 683 million or 18 per cent of export earnings.

IV

Trade and Exchange Rate Policies

Srī Laṅkā's recent trade and exchange rate policies have been determined largely by three main factors: the foreign exchange problem, a policy of rapid economic development and a persistent desire to protect the living standards of domestic consumers of whom a large majority are low income earners.

The foreign exchange problem with which the country has grappled for nearly two decades has led the government to impose stringent import control measures. Until 1959 imports were generally free from control and were subject only to nominal revenue duties. This free trade situation could not be continued for long due to recurring balance of payment deficits, which by 1959 had become a heavy drain on the foreign exchange reserves of the country. Hence in this year highly protective tariffs were imposed on several luxury and semi-luxury imports. Since the foreign exchange situation continued to worsen despite the tariffs, Draconian measures were taken in January 1961 to halt the drain on foreign assets. These included exchange control, individual licensing of imports and complete banning of the import of forty-nine luxury items. Henceforth more and more items were gradually brought under individual licensing until 1965 when all imports had been brought under such regulation. Quotas were fixed on all imports that were permitted. Under the currently existing regulations all imports are subject to individual licensing and quotas. Only imports of goods classified as essential are permitted. The list of such items has become restricted over the years due to increasing scarcity of foreign exchange and the availability of certain items through local production. As a result, present imports consist of the barest minimum of foodstuffs, drugs, textiles, raw materials and capital goods. The overall quotas of these imports are determined in terms of a foreign exchange budget prepared by a Foreign Exchange Budget Committee under the supervision of the Ministry of Planning and Employment.

In addition to the exchange and import controls, a dual exchange rate system exists in Srī Laṅkā. Under this system imports of certain indispensable imports such as basic food items and drugs are allowed at the official exchange rate, while all other imports are subject to a higher rate, which at the present is 65 per cent above the official rate. Foreign exchange earned from tea, rubber and coconut is converted into rupees at the official exchange rate, while earnings from all other exports are given the benefit of the higher rate. This dual exchange rate is some kind of a compromise solution to a dilemma faced by the policy-makers: the continuing foreign exchange problem suggests the existence of a fundamental disequilibrium in the balance of payments for which a general devaluation of the rupee seems necessary; on the other hand, such a devaluation would increase the prices of imports and lower the living standards of the domestic consumers, most of whom are already on the verge of poverty.[23]

As part of the strategy of economic development and solving the balance of payments problem, the government has actively pursued a policy of export promotion and diversification and import substitution. The import substitution policy has been successful mostly in the case of subsidiary foods such as potatoes, onions, chillies and eggs. An increasing proportion of the country's rice requirements has also come to be produced domestically.[24] A certain amount of import substitution has taken place also in the industrial sphere, particularly due to the existence of a captive market created by severe import controls. But such industries are highly import-intensive and have suffered from a shortage of imported raw materials.

In recent years the government has actively encouraged the expansion and diversification of exports. The Five-Year Plan of 1972-6 envisaged an increase in exports of Rs. 700 million, 80 per cent of which was expected to come from exports other than tea, rubber and coconut. If these expectations are realised, the share of tea, rubber and coconut products in merchandise exports should have fallen from about 85 per cent to about 65 per cent at the end of the plan period. Towards this end, the government has provided various incentives such as subsidies, credit facilities, fiscal incentives, guaranteed prices and marketing facilities. An export promotion secretariat has been set up to co-ordinate all export promotion activities. Particularly noteworthy is the Convertible Rupee scheme started in 1972 under which certain categories of exporters were allowed to credit 25 per cent of their net f.o.b. export earnings to convertible rupee accounts. This scheme has particularly helped to boost gem exports. There was a spectacular increase in these exports in 1973 when their value shot up from a mere Rs. 12 million to Rs. 141 million. Other minor exports increased from Rs. 216 million to Rs. 346 million. The share of non-traditional exports (i.e. those other than tea, rubber and coconut products) increased from 12 per cent in 1972 to 19 per cent in 1973 and to 29 per cent in 1974.[25] However, it is too early to judge whether a breakthrough has been made towards a significant degree of export diversification. In the last two years the proportion of traditional exports in the total export income has tended to be lower than it would otherwise have been, due to the poor performance of export quantity particularly in tea and coconuts. Even in the case of non-traditional exports, despite the noteworthy increase in recent years, there are very few signs of buoyancy and sustained growth. The export of precious stones, for example, which increased from Rs. 12 million to Rs. 141 million in 1973 alone, declined to Rs. 109 million in 1974.

V

Conclusion

In conclusion, foreign trade will continue to play an important role in the economy of Srī Laṅkā. Its small size makes it inconceivable that the country will be able to achieve economic development by concentrating on the domestic market alone. What is needed is a shift of emphasis from traditional exports, for which the world demand has deteriorated, into new lines of exports with better future prospects.

REFERENCES

1. Export economies were the overseas areas opened up by Europe and United States in the nineteenth century as sources of raw material supply. The principal activity of these countries was production of primary products—food and raw materials—for export. See J. V.Levin, *The Export Economies: Their pattern of development in Historical Perspective*, Cambridge, Mass. (1960), Chap. 1; D. R. Snodgrass, *Ceylon: an Export Economy in Transition*, Homewood, Ill. (1966), Chap. I; H. C. Wallich, *Monetary Problems of an Export Economy: the Cuban Experience 1914-1947*, Cambridge, Mass. (1950).

2. Department of Census and Statistics of the Government of Srī Laṅkā, *Socio-Economic Survey 1969-70*, Colombo, Srī Laṅkā Government Press (1970), Table 25, p. 38.

3. The Central Bank of Ceylon, *Annual Report* (1973), Colombo, Table 36.

4. There have been some changes in this pattern in the last few years. These are discussed at the end of the present section.

5. Central Bank of Ceylon, *Annual Report* (1973), p. 23.

6. Department of Census and Statistics, op. cit., Table 24, p. 37.

7. Note, however, the conclusion in Section IV below.

8. International Labour Office, *Matching Employment Opportunities and Expectations: A Programme of Action for Ceylon*, (2 vols.) Geneva (1971), Vol. I, p. 56.

9. To arrest the decline of tea prices due to excess supply, a tea supply restriction scheme is currently followed by the producer countries under the aegis of the Food and Agricultural Organization. This came into effect as a result of the Mauritius Tea Agreement of 1969, whereby a global quota of tea exports for a given year initially agreed upon is then divided among individual countries in accordance with their relative importance in the world market for the commodity.

10. For an excellent analysis of the factors affecting Srī Laṅkā's tea export trade see N. Jeyapalan and A. S. Jayawardana, 'Some Aspects of the Tea Industry', *Central Bank of Ceylon Monthly Bulletin* (June, August, October 1967 and March 1968), especially parts III and IV.

11. *F.A.O. Agricultural Commodity Projections, 1975 and 1985*, Rome (1967).

12. See the section below on trade and exchange rate policies for a discussion of these restrictions.

13. With Bulgaria, China, Czechoslovakia, German Democratic Republic, Hungary, Poland, Rumania, North Korea, Egypt, Syria, the Soviet

Union and Yugoslavia. See Central Bank of Ceylon, *Annual Report* (1973), p. 258.

14. For a detailed analysis of Srī Laṅkā's bilateral trade agreements up to 1967, in particular those with China, see Elaine Gunawardena, 'Bilateral Trade Agreements of Sri Lanka with Special Reference to Rubber' in *The Central Bank of Ceylon Bulletin*, May 1967.

15. A basic deficit is a deficit which takes into account the balances on basic transactions — goods and services, transfers and long term capital movements.

16. See Table 7 below.

17. (SDR=Special Drawing Rights of the IMF.) The rupee value of these earnings shows a small increase for this period. But it should be noted that the rupee values do not depict the behaviour of foreign exchange income from exports correctly because the exchange rate of the Srī Laṅkā rupee changed several times recently, beginning with the November 1967 devaluation.

18. In 1974 however, these earnings have risen to an unprecidently high level. But the Balance of Payments was in deficit because, as we shall see, the import prices also rose to an abnormally high level in this year.

19. It should be noted however, that both tea and natural rubber prices have recovered in the last two years. The average price of tea exports rose from 36 to 44 SDR cents in 1974 while that of rubber rose from 14 to 32 SDR cents between 1972 and 1974. In the case of tea it resulted from a decline in the world supply due to the oil crisis and drought in some countries, while in the case of rubber the improvement was brought about by a scarcity of petroleum based inputs for synthetic rubber. We have however, been concerned with the long-term behaviour of these exports.

20. The quantity and value of coconut exports for the period 1971-3 are heavily biased downwards by the unusually low exports for 1973. In this year coconut exports were restricted by the government because of a large fall in the output caused by a drought. Such restrictions were considered necessary in order to assure an adequate supply of this commodity for domestic consumption.

21. See Snodgrass, op. cit., pp. 118-21 and 183-7.

22. Although import prices have been rising continuously since 1960 the increase in 1974 was phenomenal. This year alone import price index registered an 80 per cent increase over the previous year. The increase in the prices of essential imports such as rice (200 per cent) flour (100 per cent) sugar (70 per cent) petroleum products (400 per cent) was so high that the even a drastic reduction in imports of essential foods failed to prevent the emergence of a huge Balance of Payment deficit. The oil price hike was particularly disastrous in this respect. While the import bill on oil more than doubled its share in the total imports shot up from a mere 2 per cent in 1972 to 20 per cent in 1974.

23. The rupee was devalued by 20 per cent in November 1967 following the (14 per cent) devaluation of the pound sterling. Hence the rupee was devalued only by 7 per cent in terms of sterling, which was hardly sufficient to reflect the scarcity value of foreign exchange at the time.

24. See Gamini Corea, "Economic Planning, the Green Revolution and the 'Food Drive' in Ceylon" in Wilfred L. David (ed.), *Public Finance Planning and Economic Development: Essays in Honour of Ursula Hicks*, London and Basingstoke, Macmillan 1973, pp. 273-303.
25. Central Bank of Ceylon, *Annual Report (1973)*.

8

INDUSTRIAL POLICY AND DEVELOPMENT SINCE INDEPENDENCE

by N. Balakrishnan

At the time of independence (1948) the Srī Laṅkā economy remained predominantly an "undiversified agricultural export economy".[1] ed predominantly an "undiversified agricultural export economy". It was sustained largely by the production and export of tea, rubber and coconut products and, to a smaller extent, by the indigenous subsistence peasant sector engaged mainly in paddy cultivation. At the time there was little industrial activity other than the processing activities associated with export products, which had traditionally been treated as part of agricultural production. Snodgrass[2] estimated that in 1950 manufacturing (excluding the processing of exports) accounted for only 4 per cent of the Gross Domestic Product (GDP) at current factor cost. Manufacturing together with mining, construction and electricity, gas and water (the secondary sector) accounted for nearly 12 per cent of the GDP. Agriculture, forestry and fishing amounted to 50 per cent of the GDP, while the value of tea, rubber and coconut products together accounted for 37 per cent. The pattern of sectoral employment showed that while agriculture accounted for 59 per cent of the total estimated employment in 1950, the secondary sector (including manufacturing) accounted for only 10 per cent of the total.

Evolution of Industrial Policy in the 1950s

Political independence in Srī Laṅkā brought to the forefront many issues and problems relating to the country's future economic development. These mostly centred around the vulnerability of the country's economy due to its 'openness' and substantial dependence on a narrow range of primary products, the need to diversify the economy and to reduce external dependence for basic consumer requirements. Such considerations gave considerable importance

192

to the development of domestic peasant agriculture. A modest role, however, was also assigned to industrialisation.

The official policy towards industrial development during the first few years after independence was very much a continuation of the policy of the post-war years under the State Council Administration. The Executive Committee for Labour, Industry and Commerce[3] in the State Council Administration outlined the industrial policy in terms of 'basic' industries and 'non-basic' industries assigned to state and private enterprise respectively. Although the outlay earmarked for industries was relatively small, the development programme outlined by the government after independence (which merely provided a broad framework for the allocation of capital expenditure from the budget), included plans for the reorganisation of the wartime factories and the establishment of new factories by the government for the production of such items as cement, steel, paper, caustic soda, vegetable oil, textile and sugar. The policy of reserving what were considered basic industries for state ownership remained unchanged. In fact, however, not much progress was made in the reorganisation of the old factories, which continued to suffer heavy financial losses. In 1952 most of the new factories scheduled were still at the planning stage and a few of them were under construction. But at this time there began a significant change in official policy, deviating from earlier commitments towards the role of public enterprise in industrial development. The recommendations of the World Bank Mission (1952)[4] and the adverse findings of the Commission on government industrial undertakings contributed to much of the change in policy.

The state factories set up during the Second World War and which continued in the post-war years became increasingly uneconomical as most of them incurred substantial losses. The Commission set up in 1951 to investigate government commercial undertakings expressed the view that "industrial activities of the government have suffered from a great deal of original sin . . .; in most cases there appeared to have been a certain lack of planning and preliminary investigation in respect of industrial activity.'[5] The Commission also found the management of state factories as government departmental concerns to be inefficient. The Commission's recommendations led to the closing of some of the wartime factories; plans were made to transfer others to semi-independent public corporations or co-operatives. Following the recommendations urging greater private enterprise participation and partnership between government and private capital, the government initiated moves — through the provisions of the State Sponsored Corporations Act of 1955 — to transfer government undertakings to private enterprise, involving initially varying degrees of government participation and eventually complete withdrawal of government ownership. The latter, however, did not materialise because of a change of government in 1956.

The World Bank mission team, which reported on the development prospects of the Srī Lankā economy, did not favour large-scale industrial programmes through the public sector. The mission found the existing state enterprises unprofitable and badly managed. It recommended that "for the present, Ceylon's main industrial growth should be centred on the development of numerous small or medium-sized industries, rather than a few large-scale ones. . ."[6] Considering the smallness of the domestic market and the shortage of capital and technical skills, the mission took the view that at that stage no substantial industrialisation could be sustained; it therefore recommended small-scale industrialisation through private enterprise. Further, the mission felt strongly that the development of domestic agriculture and expansion of basic infrastructure facilities should receive priority in government development efforts. The World Bank mission's views and recommendations came to be reflected substantially in the government's subsequent Six-Year Programme of Investment, which spelled out the new policy as being the policy "to help the private sector to help itself". The government policy indicated "a shift of emphasis from the large-scale to small-scale industries and a shift in the role of the state to that of a promoter rather than of sole entrepreneur".[7] The Programme, which covered the projected capital expenditure of the government over the six-year period, gave very low priority to industry, allocating to it only 4 per cent of the total, while agriculture received 36 per cent, public utilities 33 per cent and social services 16 per cent out of the total projected expenditure. The extremely low share assigned to industry implied that the private sector was expected to participate substantially in industrial development.

By 1957 there had been a significant shift in industrial development policy particularly regarding public sector participation. The change of government in 1956 gave added importance not only to industrial development but also to the public sector's role in it. The increased commitment to a programme of rapid industrialisation (within a 'mixed economy' framework) also seemed to reflect the growing awareness of unemployment that emerged in the wake of the 'population explosion' of the post-war years. Besides, the era of prosperity enjoyed by the export sector was ending, and the inability of this sector to sustain the rest of the economy became even clearer. Hence, efforts had to be taken to develop the domestic industrial and agricultural sectors — the latter had already received much attention in the earlier period. The shift of policy towards more industrialisation with considerable public sector participation was clearly reflected in the Ten-Year Plan formulated by the government in 1958, which embodied a well-reasoned and balanced formulation of policy favouring "the creation of a sizeable industrial sector".[8] The strategy of industrial development formulated in this Plan took into account the productivity criterion, structural diversification and, above all, the employment question.[9] It argued the case for industrialisation in terms of both the domestic market — based on import substitution — and prospective export markets. The projected sectoral allocation of investment revealed the basic pattern of priorities envisaged in the Plan. Of the total investment outlay estimated for the Plan-period (Rs. 13,600 million for both public and private sectors), industry received 20 per cent, agriculture 23 per cent, transport and communications 14 per cent and social investments 26 per cent. The considerable importance given to industrialisation (and public sector participation in it) was also largely endorsed by the foreign economists who came to advise the government at the time the Ten-Year Plan was drawn up.[10]

Government policy on industrial development, both in the public and private sectors, came to be clarified in 1957 in a significant policy pronouncement.[11] Broadly three categories of industries were listed. The first one dealt with a group of basic industries such as iron and steel, cement, chemicals, fertiliser, mineral sands and salt; this group was reserved exclusively for the public sector. In the second category there were about twenty industries — textiles, tyres and tubes, acetic acid, ceramics, vegetable oil refinery, glass etc. — for both government and private enterprise, with possibilities of joint participation. The third group comprised a large number of light consumer-goods industries left entirely for the private sector. This demarcation did not remain rigid, as subsequent revisions and changes occurred particularly in the second category where public sector involvement became greater. The third group remained more or less the same and it was in this area that most of the private sector activities came to be concentrated during the late 1950s and the 1960s as the country experienced for the first time a rapid growth of manufacturing industries aimed at import substitution.

Balance of Payments Problems and Import-Substituting Industrialisation

Government attempts to promote private sector industrial development in the 1950s through numerous tax incentives and other promotional efforts did not produce encouraging results. The private sector was still largely tied up with the traditional outlets such as processing of export products, commerce, service activities and real estate, associated principally with the country's export-import trade. Besides, fiscal incentives on their own in the context of liberal imports and "the absence of a supporting policy of vigorous protection"[12] proved inadequate to induce substantial private sector participation in new industrial ventures. However, the situation changed at the beginning of the 1960s when higher tariffs and import restrictions were introduced—not as conscious policy but mainly as a result of a deteriorating balance of payments. This largely contributed to private sector participation in industrial development to an extent hitherto unknown. Import-substitution policies in agriculture and industry, although advocated for some time past, received added urgency and significance in the 1960s as the country's balance of payments began to worsen. Such policies were intended, against the background of poor performance of exports, to reduce dependence on substantial imports of food and manufactured goods so as to relieve the pressure on the balance of payments and to release additional foreign exchange resources for more pressing development-oriented needs.

Balance of payments difficulties began to dominate the country's economic scene from about 1957 onwards — and the problems became increasingly severe later — due to unfavourable prices abroad for major exports, declining terms of trade and a high level of domestic consumption partly induced by expansionary government budgets. Imports were allowed relatively freely in the 1950s and until 1961, the resulting balance of payments deficits were financed very largely by drawing upon the country's external assets. This inevitably led to a rapid depletion of the country's external assets, and thereby posed a serious threat to the economy by the early 1960s. Reacting to such a situation, the government abandoned the hitherto relatively liberal import and foreign exchange policies and introduced a system of rigid import restrictions from 1961 onwards. The imposition of quantitative restrictions on imports, covering initially manufactured consumer goods and later extended to intermediate goods, as part of the balance of payments policy, provided the basic impetus to import-substituting industrialisation in the 1960s.

Import restrictions, which led to reductions in a wide range of manufactured goods, some of which were totally banned, created a protected and potentially profitable market with the virtual elimination of outside competition. Thus private industry responded well to what amounted to a ready-made domestic market and the prospect of attractive returns, partly helped by tax concessions and relatively cheap credit.

During the years roughly between 1959 and 1963 — the initial or "easy phase"[13] of import substitution — the country witnessed the growth of a large number of consumer goods industries, largely based on imported inputs, catering to local demand. In the early stages not only was the quality of products poor, but in many cases production involved only a minimum conversion of imported inputs. Government approvals for setting up new industrial ventures were granted freely and somewhat indiscriminately without due consideration of the foreign exchange costs involved, particularly in the initial period. During the first phase, many of the import-substituting industries in the private sector began to concentrate on those very items which were earlier restricted or banned on the grounds of being non-essentials and luxuries.[14] Evidently, the early phase of import-substitution in industries, particularly with regard to the private sector, "lacked careful planning and clearly defined priorities".[15] In the later years, no doubt, a more strict and rationalised approach came to be adopted both in the approval of new private sector industries and in the foreign exchange allocation for raw material imports as the country's foreign exchange situation became increasingly difficult.

Public Sector Industry: State Industrial Corporations
Since the latter part of the 1950s the commitment to the development of public sector industries became more firmly established, principally through the state industrial corporations. The enactment of the State Industrial Corporations Act of 1957 (which replaced the State-Sponsored Corporations Act of 1955) provided for the reconstitution of the existing state enterprises as well as for the establishment of new corporations to promote the development of large-scale and basic industries in the public sector. Under the new provisions the existing public corporations were reconstituted and several new concerns were started in the early 1960s; the latter trend continued more or less uninterruptedly thereafter. The period 1958-63 witnessed the first phase of a rapid growth of several state industrial corporations (as well as other state corporations). By 1963 there were fourteen state industrial corporations engaged in production in such fields as cement, textiles, sugar, paper, chemicals, oils and fats, ceramics, mineral sands, plywood and leather. At the end of 1967 the number of public corporations in the industrial sector went up to twenty-one. By 1974 there were twenty-five state industrial corporations — all except one in production — under

such principal groups as food and beverages; textile, wearing apparel, and leather; paper and paper products; wood and wood products; chemical, petroleum, rubber and plastic products; non-metallic mineral products; basic metal products; fabricated metal products, machinery and equipment. Investment in state industrial corporations increased from Rs. 953 million in 1968-9 to Rs. 2,346 million in 1974, the latter representing about 43 per sent of the total investment in all the state corporations.[16] These figures being at current prices, partly reflect the steep rise in the price level that has become more marked in recent years.

From the very inception many industrial as well as other corporations in the state sector have been troubled by several problems such as management inefficiency, technical deficiencies in planning, over-staffing and defective pricing policies. These have contributed in many undertakings to very poor economic results. Explicitly or implicitly, public sector enterprises (including industrial ones) have been associated with many objectives reflecting both growth and 'welfare' considerations. They have become the chief instruments furthering state ownership and social control in the economy; they are expected to function as a 'leading sector' promoting capital formation and long-term development. At times they have also been looked upon chiefly as employment outlets and enterprises providing goods or services to the public at relatively low prices.

In the early years political pressures seem to have contributed to the maintenance of low selling prices by some industrial and other state enterprises.[17] During the early stages the state industrial corporations were not altogether free from the influence of 'subsidy-pricing', largely inherited from the other public sector enterprises providing basic services, where the consumer had long been subsidised against rising costs and prices. As one writer suggested, "the public sector industries have suffered owing to too close an association with the concept of 'public service' with insufficient concern for the concept of an independent commercial corporation".[18]

State industrial corporations in many cases also suffered from the problems inherited from initial errors such as technical faults in selection, planning and location of projects.[19] Although the public sector industries have contributed somewhat towards a greater regional spread of industries, their selection and location have not entirely been free from political considerations. For many years after the beginning of operations, several industrial corporations could not function as economically profitable units and tended to become a burden on the economy. The Naylor Report

(1966),[20] which surveyed the eighteen state industrial corporations then existing, highlighted several of the deficiencies in organisation, location, quality of staff, planning and project evaluation, marketing arrangements, labour management and pricing policies.

Since the mid-1960s considerable attention has been given to measures for improving the overall efficiency of state corporations. These were aimed mainly at achieving a high level of management efficiency and of capacity utilisation, and the adoption of more realistic pricing policies, abandoning the earlier subsidy-type pricing particularly in commercial and industrial undertakings. Moreover, in view of the substantial contribution made by the government to the state corporations, it was urged that they should generate sufficient surpluses to make a significant net contribution to the government budget. However, progress in this has been extremely slow in the industrial corporations. In a recent official publication it was estimated that in 1970/1 the industrial corporations as a group showed a profit of Rs. 38 million before tax. This expressed as a percentage return on 'government contribution' (government grants, plus government loans, plus foreign grants), which amounted to about 80 per cent of the total investment, came to only 4.1 per cent; profits after tax as a percentage return on government contribution amounted to only 2.6 per cent.[21]

The data assembled in the Central Bank annual reports for the years 1972-4 show a slight improvement. For the public sector industrial corporations as a group, the average rate of return (before tax) on capital employed in production varied between 3 and 9 per cent during 1972-4; and return on total investment ranged between 2 and 4.3 per cent during the same period. Recently some individual corporations have recorded a rate of return of 15-20 per cent on capital employed in production. Despite a noticeable improvement in the economic performance of some industrial corporations in recent years and their contribution to foreign exchange savings, many enterprises still suffer from such problems as "excess machine capacity, a surplus workforce, absence of forward planning, deficient management and excessive outlays on overheads".[22] Operating below full capacity output levels — in some cases only about 50 per cent of the annual estimated capacity levels — has been common in many state industrial corporations. Some of the deficiencies already referred to, as well as market limitations for certain products and scarcity of raw materials due to foreign exchange difficulties, have all contributed to underutilisation of capacity output levels in many enterprises.

Exchange Reform (1968), Import Liberalisation and Manufacturing Industries

During the late 1960s, some of the measures taken by the government had a favourable impact on the economy in general and on industrial development in particular. During this period many sectors of the economy recorded notably higher growth, contributing to a better overall performance.[23] Concerted and vigorous action in agriculture produced substantial gains resulting in higher income generation in the domestic agricultural sector, with a favourable impact on industrial activity. Further, the mobilisation of additional external resources and the partial liberalisation of imports, along with the reform of the exchange rate system, gave a much needed inducement to expansion in many sectors including the industrial sector.

By the time a new government came to power in 1965, the country's foreign exchange situation had become critical. By the mid-1960s outlays on almost all imports, other than essential food imports, were curtailed, and exchange allocation had been brought under strict rationing within the framework of 'foreign exchange budgeting' through import quotas and licensing. This meant that industries had to suffer shortage of raw materials, machinery and spares, not to mention the delays and uncertainties inherent in a system of quotas and licensing. The shortage of raw materials, which affected private sector industries worst, resulted in considerable underutilisation of capacity in the industrial sector. Under the circumstances the new government concentrated, as a first step, on measures to ensure fuller use of existing capacities by providing adequate imports of raw materials and other investment goods. This was brought about largely through additional external resources and partial import liberalisation, coupled with a significant reform of the exchange rate system involving the introduction of the Foreign Exchange Entitlement Certificate Scheme (FEECS).[24]

Already in 1967 the Srī Laṅkā rupee had been devalued, and the FEECS involved a further 'selective devaluation', intended to bring the rupee value of selected categories of imports much nearer to the scarcity value of foreign exchange. The change was also expected to provide incentives for 'non-traditional' exports, including manufactured and minor agricultural ones (the country's traditional or major agricultural exports did not come within the FEECS). Under the new arrangements an important part of the import bill relating mainly to intermediate and investment goods was placed under the Open General Licence (OGL) scheme, to be allowed freely subject to the FEECS. Of the total imports the proportion allowed under the OGL increased from 10 to 15 per cent during 1968-9. The OGL imports were mostly raw materials and machinery and spares for industry and allied sectors. The value of letters of credit opened with the banks — a necessary condition — for OGL imports showed that 75-80 per cent went for intermediate and capital goods imports.

The liberalisation of imports allowed under the OGL led to a marked increase in intermediate and investment goods imports supported by increased external assistance. Despite the problems and some abuses that resulted, the OGL scheme undoubtedly gave a big boost to industrial expansion. Higher growth rates, never achieved before or since, were recorded in the manufacturing sector in 1968 and 1969. Although the OGL scheme was suspended in June 1970 by the new government, the pace of industrial activity was maintained for a good part of 1970, also because of the stocks built up in the previous years. During 1968-9 manufacturing output in real terms (on value added basis) showed an average annual increase of 9.5 per cent, the highest on record. In 1968 and 1969 manufacturing output excluding processing activities associated with the three major exports recorded an average annual increase of 12.7 per cent.[25] Increased availability of imported raw materials leading to better capacity utilisation contributed to much of the growth in the industrial sector during 1968-70.

Pattern of Industrial Development

According to national accounts data (see Table 1) manufacturing output as a proportion of Gross National Product (at constant prices) increased gradually from an average of 11.6 per cent during 1960-2 to nearly 14 per cent during 1970-2; the proportion declined slightly in 1973-4. The share of manufacturing in the country's total output is still relatively small. Manufacturing together with mining and construction amounted to 16.5 per cent of the GNP in 1960; this proportion increased to 20 per cent in 1970. Manufacturing output in real terms has nearly doubled within the decade 1960-70 during which the manufacturing sector recorded an average annual increase of 6.3 per cent; in 1971-3 the annual increase averaged 2 per cent. In 1974 manufacturing output declined by 4 per cent over the previous year.

There are no adequate statistics on industrial employment. There is some difficulty in interpreting the census data relating to the gainfully employed persons, classified by major categories, partly because of a residual category (5-8 per cent of the total employed work-force) which has not been adequately classified. The data from this source[26] showed that manufacturing employment increased from 312,900 in 1963 to 347,400 in 1971 — by 11 per cent;

Table 1

MANUFACTURING AND GROSS NATIONAL PRODUCT AT CONSTANT (1959) FACTOR COST PRICES

Year	Manufacturing (value: Rs. mn.)	% change (over previous year)	GNP: (value-Rs. mn.)	Manufacturing/ GNP (%)
1960	728	6.7	6289	11.5
1961	746	2.5	6425	11.5
1962	798	6.8	6710	11.7
1963	853	6.9	6900	12.3
1964	901	5.6	7363	12.2
1965	937	3.9	7551	12.4
1966	1008	7.6	7818	12.9
1967	1052	4.4	8210	12.8
1968	1154	9.7	8901	12.9
1969	1261	9.3	9301	13.5
1970	1332	5.6	9686	13.7
1971	1379	3.5	9779	14.1
1972	1400	1.5	10,030	13.9
1973	1417	1.2	10,382	13.6
1974	1359	−4.1	10,730	12.6

Source: Central Bank of Ceylon, *Annual Reports.*

there was hardly any change in the proportion employed in manufacturing in relation to the total employed work-force — it remained around 10 per cent. Employment in manufacturing, mining and construction together increased by 16 per cent from 409,290 in 1963 to 475,100 in 1971. The increase in industrial employment (manufacturing, mining and construction) during this period amounted to only 15 per cent of the total increase in the employed work-force.

Industrial production in Srī Laṅkā is still dominated by the private sector, which accounts for 75-80 per cent of the total, and which embraces a relatively small number of large-scale and well-organised factory industries and a substantial number of small-scale units consisting of workshops, cottage industries, and handicraft production. Tentative estimates in the recent ILO Mission Report[27] showed that in 1968 public sector industries accounted for 17 per cent of the total value added in the industrial sector, including mining and quarrying. Private large-scale industries (factories employing more than twenty persons) contributed 50 per cent of the total value added, while private small-scale industries accounted for 33 per cent of the total. As regards employment, the small-scale sector has considerable importance as it provides the bulk of employment in the industrial sector, as much as 65 per cent of the whole.[28] Public sector industry and private large-scale industry provided nearly one-third of the total employment. In employment terms state industry is relatively insignificant, providing less than 10 per cent of the total in the industrial sector as a whole.

It is evident that capital-intensity (in terms of fixed capital per person employed) is much higher in public-sector than in private-sector industry, and in turn is significantly higher in private large-scale industry than in the small-scale sector. Public-sector industry as a group required nearly five times as much capital per worker as private large-scale industry. Compared to large-scale private industry, the small-scale workshop type of industry is less capital-intensive and the non-workshop small-scale industry is the least capital-intensive of all. In some areas of large-scale manufacturing there has been a tendency to adopt capital-intensive techniques indiscriminately, contributing to excessive capital-intensity.[29] Price distortions with regard to capital and foreign exchange (due to market imperfection and over-valued exchange rate), forms of technical assistance and technical advice from abroad, labour management problems and the desire for modern technology, all seemed to have contributed to a high level of capital-intensity in several industries to an extent unwarranted by the country's basic resource endowments. Such trends have also emerged in many other developing countries in recent years with adverse implications for employment generation.[30]

Statistical data on industries presented by the Central Bank in its annual reports, although incomplete, provide useful information on the broad aspects of industrial development during the past decade or so. The gross-value of industrial production (on the basis of the number of reporting units, which varied somewhat from year to year) increased nearly five-fold from Rs. 847 million in 1965 to Rs. 4,094 million in 1974 at current prices; in the case of the state industrial corporations, value of production increased from Rs. 424 million in 1969 to Rs. 1,074 million in 1973. Because of the sharp rise in the prices of raw materials in recent years, the value of industrial production given at current prices tends to give an inflated picture of the true increase in production. This tendency has become more marked in recent years, with the domestic price level taking a sharp upward turn. There are no data measuring the value of industrial production in real terms. Fragmentary evidence indicated that in 1973 in thirteen major manufacturing corporations in the public sector the value of industrial production declined by 2.1 per cent in real terms, while measured at current prices it increased by nearly 19 per cent.[31] In the private sector as well, the increase in the value of industrial production during the last few years could be attributed mainly to price increases. On the basis of national accounts data, it is found that the value of manufacturing output increased by 41 per cent in 1970-3 and by 22 per cent in 1973-4 at current prices; measured at constant (1959) prices the increase for 1970-3 amounted to only 6 per cent and in 1974 it actually declined by 4 per cent compared with the previous year.

According to the classification of industrial production in terms of the principal groups (see Table 2), the food, beverages and tobacco group is the dominant one, accounting at present for 35 per cent of the total value of industrial production. This group, together with textiles, wearing apparel and leather products, accounted for 50-55 per cent of the total value of industrial production. Before 1967, the proportion of these two groups together was even higher, amounting to an average of about 66 per cent. The relative importance of these two groups in the value of total industrial production has declined over the years. The other important group consists of industries producing chemicals, petroleum, coal, rubber and plastic products, which contributed about one-quarter of total industrial production in 1970-3. Compared with the previous years, there has been a noticeable increase in the relative importance of this group. Output of industries producing fabricated metals, machinery and transport equipment together represented about 12 per cent of the total value of industrial production. The share of this group in total production also showed a small increase over the period.

The classification of industrial production in terms of major economic categories such as consumer goods, intermediate products and investment goods provides some useful information on the broad trends in the country's industrial structure. The share of consumer goods in the value of total production, which averaged about 65 per cent during the early 1960s had dropped to 50 per cent by the 1970s. Although — with a large component of food, beverages and tobacco products — they still form the bulk of industrial production, their relative importance declined during the 1960s. On the other hand, there was an increase in the relative share of intermediate and investment goods. Intermediate products averaged 26 per cent of the value of total production in 1962-4, increased to 34 per cent during 1966-7 and 38 per cent in 1971-3. The relative share in total production of investment goods showed only a marginal increase, its share increasing from an average 8 per cent in 1962-4 to 12 per cent in 1971-3. On the whole, these trends reflected a favourable shift away from the production of consumer goods, indicating the beginning of an important structural change in industrial development.

One of the basic features of Sri Lankā's industrial structure is its

Table 2. VALUE OF INDUSTRIAL PRODUCTION BY PRINCIPAL GROUPS (*Rs. million*)

	1965	1966	1967	1968	1969	1970	1971	1972	1973
No. of Firms	1381	1394	1830	1804	1962	1853	1897	1626	1415
Food, beverages and tobacco	415.5	389.9	422.3	609.6	461.8	684.5	743.0	798.7	919.6
Textile, clothing and leather products	171.5	178.9	177.1	224.3	267.1	282.7	306.2	394.5	420.8
Wood and wood products including furniture	5.2	6.5	10.4	16.9	18.0	21.2	26.6	30.7	43.0
Paper and paper products	29.3	33.8	34.7	54.6	62.3	65.0	70.3	79.1	101.0
Chemicals, petroleum, coal, rubber and plastic products	125.3	137.2	136.7	203.3	249.8	439.2	530.0	563.8	543.4
Non-metallic mineral products (except petroleum and coal products)	40.2	32.5	69.5	92.8	123.3	138.8	176.4	172.9	190.0
Basic metal products	—	—	—	27.3	28.8	38.9	58.6	67.5	53.2
Fabricated metal products, machinery and transport equipment	58.7	69.8	102.0	167.1	226.2	256.1	273.5	304.8	347.1
Manufactured products not elsewhere specified	1.3	1.7	1.5	2.7	9.5	18.6	23.1	30.4	33.2
Total	847.0	850.3	954.2	1398.6	1626.8	1945.0	2207.7	2442.4	2651.3

Source: Central Bank of Ceylon, *Annual Reports.*

continued heavy reliance on imported raw materials, which makes it difficult to sustain the pace of development in the context of an acute foreign exchange shortage. It is estimated that imported raw materials accounted for approximately 75 per cent of the total value of raw materials used in industrial production during 1968-73.[32] There appears to have been no basic change in the position, although certain sub-groups have increased the local component of raw materials used in production. In 1972 four major industrial groups — basic metals; chemicals, petroleum, coal, rubber and plastic products; machinery and transport equipment; and certain other categories of manufactured products — accounted for more than 80 per cent in value of imported raw materials used in production.[33] As the organised manufacturing industry is largely geared to the use of imported inputs the pace of industrial development is heavily determined by the availability of imported supplies. Inevitably, the restricted foreign exchange allocation and the sharp rise in the prices of raw materials had not only affected industrial production in recent years but also contributed to the high cost of production of several manufactured products at home.

A significant fact about the country's industrial structure that evolved in recent times is that a very high proportion of the industrial units — especially in the private sector — came to be concentrated in one region, the Western Province, more particularly in close proximity to the metropolis. The readily available infrastructure facilities and easy access to markets and, partly, the unplanned nature of the early phase of import substitution industrialisation, have contributed to this development. The industrial units in the Western Province accounted for about 80 per cent of the total number, and about 90 per cent of the total value of industrial production.[34] The lack of basic supporting facilities in the other regions has prevented any significant regional spread of industries. The institutional devices adopted by the government to overcome these difficulties and to promote small and medium-sized industries in different parts of the country seem to have resulted in a certain amount of regional dispersion of industries; most recent policy measures are further aimed at avoiding the social problems arising from urban concentration and spreading the benefits of industrialisation to the less developed parts of the country.

Problems and Policies in the 1970s

Import-substituting industrialisation, which began in the late 1950s by concentrating on consumer goods industries and later shifting partly to intermediate and investment goods industries, entered its most difficult phase at the beginning of the 1970s. By that time the pace of development had started to slow down, largely because of the increasing difficulties relating to imported raw materials and other inputs.

Already during the late 1960s two basic needs had begun to dominate official policy — namely, to concentrate on the greater use of available domestic raw materials and to re-orient industrial production towards export markets. In the 1966 official policy statement, the following types of industry were listed as priority areas for investment: those likely to stimulate agricultural development, those based primarily on indigenous raw materials and those with export potential.[35] The introduction of an export incentive scheme in 1966, the attempt to attract foreign investment geared to production for export markets and the introduction of the FEECS to promote "non-traditional" exports (minor agricultural exports and industrial exports), all signified the efforts to diversify exports and develop industries with export potential. When the new government assumed office in May 1970, its basic industrial policy aims with regard to utilisation of indigenous raw materials, development of agro-based industries and promotion of export-oriented industries broadly reflected a continuity of policy that was already apparent in the late 1960s. These goals became the more urgent as the country's export earnings stagnated, import prices escalated (leading to a more pronounced downward trend in the terms of trade) and the foreign exchange scarcity impinged more heavily on the country's industrial sector.

The industrial policy of the government which took office in 1970 was outlined at the start to achieve, among other things, the following objectives: development of basic and heavy industries within the public sector; greater employment creation and location of industries in the less developed regions; maximum use of domestic resources in industries; maximum support for export-oriented industries; and the development of technology consistent with basic factor endowments.[36] Such basic policy objectives have been given more definite emphasis in the Five-Year Plan of 1972-6.[37]

This Plan, with an estimated total gross investment outlay of approximately Rs. 14,820 million shared in roughly equal parts between the private and public sectors, aimed at achieving an overall average growth in the economy of 6 per cent per annum during 1972-6. The basic projections in the Plan implied that the average investment ratio would be stepped up to about 19 per cent compared to the pre-plan overall average ratio of 17 per cent. According to the sectoral composition of planned investment, Rs. 2,240 million — 15 per cent of the total — was assigned to the development of the industrial sector, both private and public. In this proposed allocation the public sector took a larger share amounting to 55 per cent of the total outlays assigned for the industrial sector as a whole. Of the total public sector investment outlays envisaged for the Plan period (Rs. 7,040 million), the proportion allocated to the industrial sector amounted to 18 per cent. Of the total investment outlays indicated in the Plan for the private sector (Rs. 7,780 million) the expected share of investment in industrial activities amounted to 13 per cent. The gross value of industrial output at 1970 prices has been estimated to increase at an average rate of 8.6 per cent per annum and that of value added by 10 per cent per annum during the Plan period. As for employment creation, the industrial sector is expected to generate additional employment of about 165,000 during the Plan period, which would account for 20 per cent of the total estimated additional employment (810,000) expected during the five years. Much of the increase in employment in the industrial sector — about 75 per cent — was expected to be generated in the small-scale sector in areas such as textiles, wood products, light engineering, tobacco products and mining and quarrying.

The industrial development policy and programme envisaged in the Five-Year Plan strongly emphasised the utilisation of idle capacity in both private and public sector industries. It has been estimated, perhaps over-optimistically, that about 75 per cent of the increased output in the public industrial sector would be realised from the fuller utilisation of capacities that already exist. With a policy strongly committed to state ownership of large-scale, basic and capital goods industries, the private sector is expected to concentrate on other areas with the emphasis on small- and medium-scale ventures and with priorities assigned to industries using local raw materials, those with export potential and those biased towards labour-intensive techniques with greater employment possibilities. Employment generation, diversification of the rural economy, emphasis on low capital-intensity and minimum use of foreign exchange, labour-intensive technology, utilisation of local raw materials and dispersion of industries and regional development — these considerations provided the rationale for this emphasis on development in the small-scale industrial sector.

The creation and development of a "new export sector" based on industrial products is another key element in the Five-Year Plan's industrial programme. This represents an attempt to move away from the import-substituting industrialisation of the past. It is important to note that, of the total increase in export earnings originally envisaged to support the Plan effort, nearly 35 per cent was expected to come from industrial exports. The Plan was based on the somewhat optimistic assumption that the surplus capacity in the industrial sector could be successfully geared to an export market. Government policy measures provide numerous incentives and promotional assistance for export-oriented industries in the form of rebates on duty for imported raw materials, special allocation of foreign exchange, liberal tax incentives and other types of institutional support, in addition to the FEECS and the Convertible Rupee Accounts for non-traditional exports (including industrial exports). The official White Paper of August 1972 on foreign investment outlines the incentives offered to foreign capital in tourism, hotels and certain fields of industry, especially those producing for export markets, those which could utilise indigenous raw materials and those having "technology-producing" effects. There has been relatively little participation of foreign (private) capital in local industry, and it is unlikely that this situation will change substantially, despite some relatively recent joint ventures with foreign capital participation in industry. Ideological considerations have made government attitude towards the role of foreign (private) capital insufficiently forthright and unequivocal.

Srī Laṅkā's basic economic circumstances took an adverse turn after the Five-Year Plan was drawn up, partly due to externally induced factors. The Plan's implementation suffered seriously in many respects. The country's foreign exchange situation, already weakened by depressed export earnings in 1970-2 and a heavy external debt (debt-servicing amounted to 20-25 per cent total export earnings), was further aggravated by a sharp escalation in the prices of several imports such as essential foodstuffs, raw materials and crude oil. The Central Bank trade indices on imports (1967=100) showed that the all-imports price index increased from 140 in 1970 to 370 in 1974; the food and drink index rose from 130 to 451 and the intermediate goods index from 136 to 386. These trends inevitably resulted in a further fall in the commodity terms of trade—the index fell by 30 per cent in 1970-4. Although the rupee earnings of exports rose markedly in 1973 and 1974, the gains were largely offset by the sharp rise in import payments due to the impact of the world commodity inflation, which affected almost all imports. Furthermore, domestic food production, particularly in rice—the country's staple food—suffered a serious setback during the past few years, partly due to bad weather. The world food shortage and the steep rise in the prices of essential food imports resulted in restricted supplies. The country thus came to be caught up in a serious and unprecedented food crisis.

Amid such adverse economic conditions, the country's development efforts met with serious difficulties. The industrial sector, especially private industry, had to suffer severe shortages of imported raw materials and other inputs, following the suspension of the OGL and the re-introduction of import quotas, on account of cutbacks, delays and uncertainties in foreign exchange allocation as well as the escalation in the prices of these items. Inevitably, this adversely affected the performance of the industrial sector in general, notwithstanding some progress in new directions.[38] The manufacturing sector (in value added terms) showed the lowest growth in recent years — not to mention the negative growth in 1974 —averaging 2 per cent per annum during 1971-3, at constant (1959) prices.

In spite of some readjustment of industrial activity oriented towards the use of local raw materials, most industries, notably in the private sector, still rely heavily on imported intermediate products and raw materials, and foreign exchange constraints have persistently retarded activities in many fields of industry, resulting in low overall capacity utilisation. In 1974, the level of output in relation to the estimated capacity in the manufacturing sector remained around 40 per cent (though for a few industrial groups the percentage has been around 65-70), with 60 per cent of the existing capacity unutilised.[39] Apart from the major difficulties arising from shortages of raw materials, capacity utilisation was also affected by reduced demand on account of the very high prices of some categories of manufactured products resulting from high production cost. Increased capacity utilisation in the industrial sector is linked largely with adequate supplies of imported inputs. In this respect no significant improvement could be expected on account of both the rigid limits on foreign exchange allocation and the high prices of most industrial raw materials and other products of intermediate use in the world market.

REFERENCES

1. B. B. Das Gupta, *A Short Economic Survey of Ceylon*, Colombo (1948), p. 9.
2. D. R. Snodgrass, *Ceylon: An Export Economy in Transition*, Homewood, Ill. (1966), Tables 5-2 (p. 101) and 6-3 (p. 128).
3. *Report on Industrial Development and Policy*, Sessional Paper XV (1946).
4. In his study of the evolution of development policy in Sri Lanka during the 1950s, H. M. Oliver, Jr., remarks that during 1954-6 government policy on industrial development "went far towards adopting the programme recommended by the International Bank Mission with its emphasis on private enterprise" (*Economic Opinion and Policy in Ceylon*, Cambridge University Press, London (1957), p. 83).

5. *Report of the Commission on Government Commercial Undertakings*, Sessional Paper XIX (1953), p. 23.

6. International Bank for Reconstruction and Development, *Economic Development of Ceylon, (Part I)*, Baltimore, Md. (1953), p. 27.

7. Planning Secretariat, *Six-Year Programme of Investment, 1954-1950/60*, Colombo (1955), p. 245.

8. National Planning Council, *The Ten-Year Plan*, Government Press, Colombo (1959), p. 27. The Plan did not become fully operational, partly due to the adverse foreign exchange situation and partly due to the unstable political situation at the beginning of the 1960s.

9. For an evaluation of development policy and planning in relation to employment objectives in Sri Lanka during the 1950s and 1960s see Birger Möller, *Employment Approaches to Economic Planning in Developing Countries with Special Reference to Ceylon*, Scandinavian Institute of Asian Studies Monograph Series No. 9, Stockholm (1972).

10. See, *Papers by Visiting Economists*, Planning Secretariat, Colombo (1959).

11. *Administration Report of the Director of Industries*, 1957, pp. 32-5.

12. G Corea, 'Ceylon in the' Sixties', *Marga*, Vol. I, No. 2, Colombo (1971), p. 15.

13. H. Myint, *Southeast Asia's Economy: Development Policies in the 1970s* (1972). Myint refers to the "easy phase" of import substitution as one in which domestic industries expand rapidly to take over the ready-made markets for the imported consumer goods which have been shut out by protection and quantitative restrictions (p. 59).

14. International Labour Office, *Matching Employment Opportunities and Expectations — a Programme of Action for Ceylon (Report)*, Geneva (1971), p. 104.

15. Development Policies in Ceylon 1966-71, *Economic Bulletin for Asia and the Far East*, Vol. XXIII, No. 1 (June 1972), p. 30.

16. Central Bank of Ceylon, *Annual Report* (1974), Colombo, p. 76.

17. IBRD — IDA, *The Foreign Exchange Problem of Ceylon*, Ministry of Planning and Economic Affairs, Ceylon (1966), p. 47.

18. A. S. Jayawardena, Public Sector Industrial Enterprises in Ceylon, *Industry and Research*, Industrial Development Board, Colombo, p. 109.

19. For a recent contribution on the technical aspects of industrial planning in Sri Lanka, see N. D. Karunaratne, *Techno-Economic Survey of Industrial Potential in Sri Lanka*, Industrial Development Board of Ceylon, Colombo (1973).

20. G. W. Naylor, *Report of the Reconnaissance Mission to Ceylon in connection with State Industrial Corporations*, Ministry of Planning and Economic affairs, Colombo, 1966.

21. Ministry of Finance, *The Economy of Ceylon: Trends and Prospects*, Colombo (1971), Table XII, p. 50.

22. *Annual Report* (1973), op. cit., p. 17.

23. During 1967-9 the GNP (at 1959 prices) recorded an average annual growth of nearly 6 per cent.

24. The scheme, introduced in May 1968, created a dual exchange rate system — in the form of the official or non-FEEC rate and the FEEC

rate — for foreign exchange transactions. The FEEC rate placed an additional rupee cost on selected import payments and conferred an additional rupee gain on selected export and invisible earnings. The FEEC rate was originally fixed at 44 per cent on the official rate; it was later raised to 55 per cent and again to 65 per cent more recently.

25. Central Bank of Ceylon, *Annual Report* 1969, p. 28.
26. Dept. of Census and Statistics: *Statistical Pocket Book of Ceylon,* Colombo, 1970, Table 18, p. 37, and 1973, Table 18, p. 25
27. Op. cit., Table 19, p. 105.
28. Adopting a somewhat different classification, M. V. Divatia (Industrial Structure of Ceylon, in *Industry and Research,* op. cit., p. 80) estimated that in 1965 the unorganised or non-factory sector accounted for 68 per cent of the total estimated employment of 403,400 in manufacturing industries. Employment in the organised or factory sector amounted to 127,200 or 32 per cent of the total.
29. See B. Hewavitharane, Choice of Techniques in Ceylon, in *Economic Development in South Asia* (Proceedings of a Conference held by the International Economic Association at Kandy, Ceylon), ed. E. A. G. Robinson and Michael Kidron, London (1970), pp. 438-44.
30. For a summary treatment of the issues involved see "The Labour Absorption Problem", in G. M. Meir, *Leading Issues in Economic Development* (2nd ed.), Oxford University Press (1971).
31. *Annual Report* (1973), op. cit., p. 55.
32. Many public sector industries have a high component of local raw materials. Of the sixteen manufacturing corporations coming within the purview of the Ministry of Industries and Scientific Affairs, "the local content of raw materials in terms of value exceeded 27 per cent in respect of twelve corporations, while in seven corporations it was over 69 per cent", Ministry of Industries and Scientific Affairs, *Review of Activities of Corporations, 1970/71,* Colombo (1971), p. 34.
33. Central Bank of Ceylon, *Annual Report* (1972), p. 43.
34. Ibid., p. 30.
35. Ministry of Finance (Budget Supplement), *Economic and Social Progress, 1965-69,* Colombo (1969), p. 34.
36. See Ministry of Industries and Scientific Affairs, *Industrial Policy Statement* and *A New Industrial Policy,* Colombo, (1971).
37. Ministry of Planning and Employment, *The Five Year Plan 1972-76,* Govt. of Ceylon, Colombo (1971).
38. Recent incentive and other supporting measure taken by the Government in the field of export diversification and promotion seem to have had a favourable effect. Non-traditional exports (including industrial exports) averaged 25 per cent of the total commodity export earnings during 1973-4. This is a significant departure from the past, when the country's traditional exports of tea, rubber and coconut products together accounted for 90 per cent of one total export earnings. The rupee earnings from 'selected industrial exports' increased from Rs. 229 million in 1973 to Rs. 509 million in 1974. The bulk of this increase came from petroleum products including marine bunkers and aviation fuel.
39. Central Bank, *Annual Report (1974),* p. 56 and 66.

9

PLANTATION AGRICULTURE

by Gerald Peiris

Introduction

The term "plantation agriculture" usually connotes the large-scale cultivation of crops for commercial purposes. It is considered an export-oriented mode of production the development of which in the tropics and the sub-tropics was associated with European colonisation and investment. In Srī Laṅkā, however, this term is commonly used to refer to the production of a variety of crops on both large and small units, mainly though not exclusively for trade. It thus includes tea, rubber and coconut — three of the major crops in the country — and several minor crops like cacao, cinnamon, citronella, pepper and cardamom. When reference is made to these crops collectively as plantation crops or "commercial crops" (the two terms are often regarded as synonymous) it must be remembered that among them there are wide differences in circumstances relating to their origin and growth in Srī Laṅkā, their relative scales of operation and levels of technology, their organisation of production and marketing, and their degree of dependence on internal and foreign trade. It must also be borne in mind that during the recent past there has been increasing commercialisation in certain spheres of agricultural activity normally regarded as falling exclusively within the "subsistence" or "peasant" sector, and that no clear demarcation is possible between some of the "commercial crops" and the so-called "subsistence crops". Perhaps the only distinguishing feature common to the crops which were introduced as plantation crops is that their production caters, in varying degrees, to market demand outside the country.

Plantation agriculture occupies a vitally important position in Srī Laṅkā's economy, contributing about 29 per cent to the Gross National Product (GNP). Approximately 25 per cent of the gainfully employed work-force is in this sector. The value of its exports

213

account for about 90 per cent of the total export earnings. Plantation crops cover an aggregate extent of some 2.3 million acres, which represent roughly 58 per cent of the area under permanent agriculture. In the post-war era, as Snodgrass has shown, it is largely the economic surplus generated by this sector that provided for the growth of the other sectors of the economy

Tea is pre-eminent among Srī Lankā's plantation crops. It employs a work-force of about 680,000, and in recent years its exports, valued at over Rs 1,000 million per annum, have represented approximately 60 per cent of the country's total export earnings. Its direct contribution to government revenue in the form of export duties, company taxes and income tax may be estimated as accounting for about 18 per cent of the total revenue.

In terms of the value of output, contribution to export earnings and size of the work-force, rubber ranks second among the plantation crops, representing on the average, in each case, approximately one-third to half that of tea. The importance of the rubber industry also lies in the fact that its output forms one of the few important raw materials of large-scale modern industry produced in the country.

Coconut, though usually reckoned the third most important plantation industry in Srī Lankā, is in many ways more significant to the economy than rubber. During the recent past it has contributed in value about 16 per cent to the total output of the agricultural sector and 18 per cent to that of the manufacturing sector. The total work-force supported by coconut in Srī Lankā, including those in coconut-based manufacturing industries, is approximately 110,000. Since coconut forms an important item in the local diet (with average *per capita* consumption estimated at 125-130 nuts per year), about a half of the coconut produced in the country goes for domestic consumption. Yet the main kernel products—copra, oil and dessicated coconut — feature collectively as the third most important exchange earner, contributing on the average about 17 per cent to total export earnings. Further, while coconut fibre and shell charcoal are prominent among the country's minor exports, numerous other products derived from the palm and by-products of coconut-based industries cater to a variety of local needs. The government earns about 6 per cent of its revenue from the coconut industry and allied sources.

With the exception of pepper, a commodity of which about 45 per cent of the total output is estimated to be consumed locally, the minor plantation crops cater largely or exclusively to the export market. However, the aggregate value of such exports represent less than 2 per cent of the total value of the country's exports.

Although they are thus insignificant in the context of the entire economy, they assume some importance regionally in areas where they are grown, and periodically at times of high price. As in the mid-country districts of Kandy and Mātalē, minor plantation crops could form an important source of subsidiary income to peasants. These crops are important also because of their potential to provide the base for certain small and medium-scale processing industries and in the scope which some of them present for crop diversification.

Structure of the Plantation Sector

Units of production in plantation agriculture are often classified into two groups — estates and smallholdings. Such classifications are usually based on an arbitrary size criterion which, in the available statistical sources, varies from time to time, country to country and crop to crop.

The relative importance of estates and smallholdings varies widely among the different plantation crops of Srī Laṅkā. Tea is overwhelmingly an estate crop in which holdings of less than 10 acres cover only 17.4 per cent of the total acreage. In rubber, smallholdings assume some importance. Units of less than 10 acres account for nearly one-third of the total acreage of this crop. There is a preponderance of small units in coconut in which holdings under 20 acres represent about 64 per cent of the total acreage. There is similar variation among the minor plantation crops. Cardamom is produced almost exclusively on large units. In cacao, cinnamon and citronella, both categories of production units are roughly of equal importance. Pepper is always grown as a mixed crop, and the bulk of its production is derived from estates. Cloves and nutmeg are produced as mixed crops on smallholdings and home gardens.

In the literature on plantation agriculture, the dichotomy between estates and smallholdings is often reckoned as embodying something more than a mere difference in size or scale of operation. The estate is perceived as a highly capitalised, regimented and exploitative form of agricultural organisation which is typically a 'foreign enclave' controlled by a city-based managing agency which represents its owners, and operated by a large wage-earning labour force under the direction of a functionally integrated hierarchy of supervisory and technical personnel. These features are considered to make high costs and a rigid cost structure salient characteristics of the estate sector, and to motivate estates to economise on labour so as to cut to the minimum costs per unit weight of produce. Smallholdings, in contrast, have been visualised as an integral part of the peasant sector where all aspects of production are carried out individually or communally by the owners themselves. Hence it is frequently asserted that labour, a major item of cost in plantation agriculture, represents for the smallholder opportunity costs rather than money costs. Following from this, it is claimed that since (or where) labour is freely available to the smallholder, he seeks to maximise productivity per acre with a high labour input. It is further believed that owners of smallholdings (who are also usually held to be subsistence agriculturists) can transfer their labour from one avenue of production to another when market conditions warrant or demand such a transfer, thereby providing the small-holdings sector with a degree of flexibility which the estate sector does not possess.

The roots of some of these notions could be traced to the 'dual economy' model developed by Jan Boeke and others[1] in relation to society and agriculture in the Netherlands East Indies (Indonesia) during the early part of this century. Many others have since tacitly accepted, elaborated or worked within the framework of this model. Hence, in most writings on plantation agriculture, the contrasting attributes highlighted above have been seen as characteristics of the typical estate and the typical smallholding. Indeed attention has rarely been paid to implications of variations from what is generally assumed to be the norm.

Convenient though this division is, it tends to conceal certain differentiations that exist within each class of production unit. These differentiations are specially relevant to the situation in Srī Laṅkā. The typical estates of the dual economy model form only a part of the estate acreage in the country, and are more conspicuous in tea than in the other plantation crops. A large segment of the estate acreage is under private individual ownership. The estates within this segment are relatively small and are operated under the personal supervision of the owners themselves with considerable economy in overhead costs. In rubber and coconut, as well as in much of the low-grown tea, the estates draw a majority of their work-force from the local village population, and thus have a measure of flexibility in their labour input. These could be distinguished from the "foreign enclaves" typified in dual economy notions. Smallholdings, too, exhibit similar variations. There is no doubt that the "typical" peasant-owned, owner-operated units constitute a part of the smallholdings acreage. But here again evidence from diverse sources seem to suggest that in Srī Laṅkā, particularly in tea and rubber, a large share (probably a major share) of the smallholding acreage is in units owned by persons whose main occupations lie outside subsistence farming. Small-holdings of cash crops often represent in Srī Laṅkā the savings and investment of business and professional classes or acquisitions and inherited property of a wealthy minority of the rural population.[2] Such 'non-peasant' smallholdings are worked with hired labour, and on them costs of production are comparable to those on the individually owned estates. From the presence of these features one can infer that certain widely accepted generalisations on estates and smallholdings in plantation agriculture relating to such aspects as costs and relative flexibility require considerable qualification and modification when applied to plantation agriculture in Srī Laṅkā.

The composition of the plantation sector in terms of the size of its units of production has changed somewhat during the past two decades. In the main plantation crops, the smallholding sector has grown at the expense of the estate sector. Tea estates of over 100 acres, which covered 81 per cent of the total acreage under this crop in 1950, now account for about 69 per cent. The estate acreage in rubber has similarly dropped from 53 to 46 per cent. This change is due largely to fragmentation of estates into small units, a process accounted for by both private speculation in the land market in the form of buying, subdividing and selling of large blocks of land and acquisition of estates by the government for peasant settlement and village expansion schemes in certain densely populated parts of the country.

With the progressive implementation of the Land Reform Law of 1972[3], the increasing importance of smallholdings in Srī Laṅkā's plantation agriculture, a trend of the past, is likely to continue into the future, probably at an accelerated pace. This law has fixed a ceiling to the extent of land which an individual may own and has facilitated the vesting of land in excess of the stipulated ceiling in the Land Reform Commission. On the basis of changes that have been taking place since the passing of the Land Reform Law, it seems probable that a part of the land so vested in the Commission (it has been reported that by April 1974, the Land Commission had taken formal possession of about 400,000 acres of land previously under private ownership) would be alienated to peasants in the form of small units.

As a phenomenon of the post-independence era, changes that have occurred in the ownership pattern of plantations in Srī Laṅkā are quantitatively more significant than those relating to size composition discussed above. One such change has been the progressive transfer from foreign to local ownership of an increasing share of the capital assets in plantation agriculture. Between 1950 and 1970, the percentage share of the total acreage owned by non-citizens of Srī Laṅkā has fallen from about 69 to 31 per cent in tea

and from 37 to 14 per cent in the rubber. This process of 'Ceylonisation' could be attributed to such factors as restrictions placed on
the transfer of profits abroad and the increasing burden of direct
and indirect taxation placed on plantations — factors which have
reduced the attraction of the plantation sector as an area of foreign
investment. There has also, at various times since independence,
been a fear of nationalisation of foreign-owned estates, which may
have contributed to the withdrawal of foreign capital from Sri
Laṅkā's plantations.

Yet another incipient structural change within the plantation
sector which might become significant in the future is the emergence of public and cooperative ownership of plantations. The
State Plantation Corporation, instituted in 1959, at present owns
about 40,000 acres of land and is described as the largest single
owner of plantations in the country. Several other institutions have
been set up recently to promote co-operative farming on some of
the estates taken over by the government under the Land Reform
Law of 1972. Most of these institutions aim at establishing co-operative projects of the communal type with a high degree of integration and devoid of private ownership of land among the project
participants.

Comparative Advantages and Disadvantages

The tea plantations of Sri Laṅkā cover about 600,000 acres. Tea is
almost entirely confined to the wet zone where it is grown from near
sea-level in the districts of Galle and Mātara to elevations of over
6,500 feet in the interior. While the tea acreage at lower elevations
accounts for only a small fraction of the total area devoted to agriculture, the crop becomes virtually a monoculture in certain higher
parts of the Central Highlands.

Since the early 1950s the annual exports of tea from Sri Laṅkā
have increased from about 300 million to about 450 million lb. In
the mid-1960s Sri Laṅkā became the foremost source of tea supply
to the world market and has since accounted for 30-35 per cent of
all tea entering international trade.

Sri Laṅkā's tea industry depends more on external markets than
do tea industries elsewhere — the internal market absorbing only
about 5 per cent of the tea produced in the country. But since Sri
Laṅkā already has a higher level of *per capita* tea consumption than
the other developing countries, the potential of the internal market
for further expansion is believed to be less than that of the other
tea-producing countries like India, Bangladesh, Tanzania and
Kenya, where the prevailing low levels of consumption are expected to rise with increasing income.

The main tea-growing areas of Srī Laṅkā possess certain advantages over many of the other such areas of the world. Special weather characteristics and some carefully maintained harvesting and processing practices have enabled the highland tea districts of Srī Laṅkā to maintain a reputation of excellence for the quality of their produce in some of the principal tea markets of the world. Furthermore, certain difference between the country's 'high-grown' and 'low-grown' teas in flavour, colour, strength, pungency and infusion have made it possible for the tea produced in Srī Laṅkā to cater to a variety of consumer preferences and requirements in tea blending. In addition, because the tea districts have contrasting annual patterns of rainfall and hence diverse seasonal cycle of flush and slack production, the country as a whole maintains a more uniform output of tea throughout the year than its rivals. Yet another comparative advantage which the local tea industry shares with the older tea producers of Asia is the high level of skill acquired by its labour force. According to an FAO report,[4] the labour forces in Srī Laṅkā and some other tea-producing countries of Asia have developed standards of plucking which are difficult to equal in Africa, where the labour is largely migratory and the plucking gangs are largely composed of juveniles.

Despite these advantages, however, recent conditions in the international tea market have not favoured Srī Laṅkā's tea industry. Since the Second World War, there has been an enormous increase in the supply of tea to the world market, where the tea industry as a whole faces fierce competition from other beverages. While improved cultural practices such as the use of chemical fertiliser and high yielding cultivars has led to increased supplies from the older tea-producing countries in Asia, new sources of supply have emerged as vast extents of land have been brought under tea in parts of East Africa. The resultant increase in the supply of tea to the main consuming countries has depressed prices.

Factors other than increased supplies also appear to have contributed to low tea prices which have prevailed in recent times. It has been convincingly argued in certain writings[5] that diverse market manipulations by a few large firms wielding a high degree of control over various aspects of tea production and marketing have depressed the price which the producers have received. It has been shown that the ramified commercial interests of these firms cover such key aspects of the industry as production from the newly emergent sources of tea, the bulk purchase of tea from many of the primary markets in producing countries, shipping and insurance of tea in transit, its storage at warehouses in consuming countries and blending, packaging and retail distribution. It is said that the manner in which these firms exercise their control is often at variance with the interests of the older tea-producing countries.

During the past two decades, in the traditional tea markets (the most important being the United Kingdom) the lowering of prices has been more marked than elsewhere. It is mainly in these markets that Srī Laṅkā's tea has enjoyed a reputation for high quality. In the new tea markets, particularly those of the Middle East, where low quality teas produced at relatively low costs appear to be acceptable to the consumer, the price differences between different teas do not reflect a similar preference for high-cost, superior quality teas. The net impact of these features has been a drop in the relative demand for quality teas, the supply of many of which has traditionally been Srī Laṅkā's speciality.

Rubber occupies about 565,000 acres located largely in those parts of the wet zone below a height of 1,000 feet. The principal rubber growing areas of Srī Laṅkā form a rough crescent that girdles the Central Highlands to its west, south-west and south. Outside this, there are several smaller patches of rubber falling into the districts of Colombo, Kurunāgala, Kandy, Mātalē, Badulla and Monarāgala.

In this crop, unlike in tea, the country possesses no special advantages *vis-à-vis* the other natural rubber-producing countries, in relation to either the physical setting or tradition and practices. Though some of Srī Laṅkā's rubber lands are comparable physically to the best rubber areas of South-east Asia, excessive rainfall in the rubber areas in the south-western parts of the island reduces the average number of possible tapping days per year to a considerably lower level than in some of the major rubber areas of Malaysia and Indonesia. Srī Laṅkā's rubber is also worse affected by diseases associated with the fungus *Phytophthora palmivora*, which is endemic to rubber grown in some of the ultra-wet parts of Asia. In most aspects of cultivation and processing, the standards maintained by Srī Laṅkā appear to be on a par with those of the other rubber-producers. But the local average yield is lower than that of Western Malaysia. Furthermore, despite some slight recent improvement in the quality of the rubber produced in Srī Laṅkā, about 60 per cent of the country's rubber output is still in the form of Ribbed Smoked Sheet (of which only a quarter falls into the category of Grade 1 sheet), which fetches lower prices than other forms of raw rubber such as latex crèpe, coagulated latex and block rubber.

Srī Laṅkā produces about 325 million lb. of rubber per annum, of which approximately 96 per cent is exported. Supplies of rubber from the country have amounted to about 5-6 per cent of the total quantity of natural rubber entering the world market. Since natural rubber itself now accounts for only about 33 per cent of the total global supply of new rubber (natural and synthetic), Srī Laṅkā,— although fourth in importance among the natural rubber-producers of the world—is a relatively insignificant supplier of rubber.

The price of rubber in the world market has always been prone to marked short-term fluctuations. Though factors that determine the price of rubber at any given time may be diverse, it is mainly short-term imbalances between supply and demand that cause the price curve to oscillate. However, in the post-war period, because of the progress achieved in the field of synthetic rubber manufacture both in improvement of quality and reduction of costs, the long-term price trends of natural rubber have come to be largely determined by the supply price of synthetic rubber which has constantly been on the decline. Hence, during the past two decades or so, despite the short-run volatility of the price of rubber, its long-term trend has been downward.

The local rubber industry has been the beneficiary of a bi-lateral trade agreement between Srī Laṅkā and the People's Republic of China, initially negotiated in 1952 and under which China has purchased annually 30,000 to 55,000 metric tons of sheet rubber (about 60-95 per cent of the country's sheet output) at premium prices. During the first five years of the pact, the average price paid per lb. of rubber by China was around 35 cts. higher than the average price obtained for sheet rubber shipped from Srī Laṅkā to other destinations. Subsequently, for each consignment of rubber to China, Srī Laṅkā continued to receive prices 5 to 8 cts. per lb. above the average f.o.b. price prevailing at Singapore. In addition, China since 1957, has given aid grants totalling about Rs 100 million, specifically for use in Srī Laṅkā's Rubber Rehabilitation Programme.

The assured market and premium prices for the bulk of rubber produced in the country have of course been only marginal advantages. The rubber industry of Srī Laṅkā has shared with the other natural rubber producers of the world the twin problems of declining prices and encroachment into their markets by the synthetic rubber industry, both of which have been persistent long-term trends in the post-war period. The current setback to the synthetic rubber industry, a consequence of the petroleum crisis, has caused a slight improvement in the market conditions for natural rubber, and has generated some optimism among producers of the latter. Whether the current position would be temporary or a complete reversal of earlier trends is still premature to judge.

The area covered by coconut in Srī Laṅkā is about 1.15 million acres. Though coconut is cultivated up to elevations of 2,000 feet or more in the wet zone, it is essentially a lowland crop. It is the most important commercial crop in the western lowlands north-east of Colombo and along a narrow coastal strip in the south-west and south. In the dry zone, too, coconut is grown in certain localities where—due either to geological and edaphic peculiarities or to the presence of artificial reservoirs—the groundwater remains perennially close to the surface.

Coconut is a smallholders' crop the world over. The industry as a whole is less well organised than most other plantation industries and, though the potential exists for a high level of per acre productivity under well-managed conditions, the average level of productivity in coconut is substantially lower in terms of value than in other plantation crops. In Srī Laṅkā the value added per acre of coconut is reported to be about a quarter of that of tea and half that of rubber. Yet coconut is seldom an intensively cultivated crop anywhere in the world, and the standards of productivity per acre maintained by Srī Laṅkā's coconut industry are comparable to those prevailing elsewhere. For example, the overall average yield obtained in Srī Laṅkā, which is around 2,500 to 3,000 nuts per acre per year compares favourably with that of the Philippines which has been estimated at about 2,550.[6]

During the past two decades the total output of coconut in Srī Laṅkā has fluctuated between an estimated 2,000 to 3,000 million nuts per year.[7] The annual fluctuations in output have been attributed largely to vagaries of weather to which coconut is said to be more sensitive than the other plantation crops.

Srī Laṅkā is the second largest supplier of coconut oil and dessicated coconut to the world market, and ranks third in copra. In the world market, these coconut products compete with a variety of oils and fats. Coconut oil, which meets about 6 per cent of the world's demand for edible oils, ranks seventh among them. Although most other products that compete with coconut have been flowing into the world market in increasing quantities since the Second World War, this has not had adverse long-run effects on the price of coconut products. In fact, since the late 1960s the prices of coconut products, though subject to short-term changes, have generally been buoyant.

On the basis of various estimates, the area covered by the minor plantation crops of Srī Laṅkā could be placed at about 90,000 to 95,000 acres. Cocoa plantations covering some 25,000 acres are found mainly in areas of intermediate elevation and moderate rain in the districts of Kandy, Matale and Kurunāgala, where certain other crops like pepper, cloves and nutmeg — whose aggregate "effective acreage" has been estimated at about 6,000 acres — are also concentrated. Cardamom occupies about 11,000 acres in the wetter parts of the Central Highlands. About 95 per cent of the island's total cinnamon area (36,000 acres) is found scattered in the lowland and wet zone. The dwindling acerage covered by citronella plantations (at present, about 16,500 acres) is concentrated in the southern parts of the country bordering the dry zone.

The export of minor plantation crops since the early 1950s shows diverse trends.[8] Annual exports of cocoa have recorded a decline from over 50,000 tons in the early 1950s to below 30,000 tons in the early 1970s. Citronella exports, which for the most part remained between 1 to 2 million lb. in the 1950s, soared to a peak of 3 million lb. in 1962 and thence dropped the following year to about half a million lb., at which level it has remained. Cinnamon exports, which ranged from 40,000 to 55,000 cwt. in the years before 1965, rose gradually to reach a peak of 80,000 cwt. in 1972. More or less the same trend is seen in cardamon which recorded its highest export figure of 4,000 cwt. in 1970. Among minor export crops, cloves and nutmeg show the sharpest year to year fluctuations. During the past twenty years, the former has ranged from 150 to 5,500 cwt. and the latter from 500 to 5,000 cwt. Among the main causes for these diverse trends and fluctuations of exports are vagaries of weather, neglect of plantations during prolonged spells of low price (particularly important in cocoa and citronella), speculative stock-piling by dealers and exporters (more significant with less perishable commodities like pepper, cloves and nutmeg) and fiscal concessions granted by the government to exporters of these commodities (exports of cinnamon, cardamom and cloves have shown clear responses to the introduction of the FEECs scheme).

A characteristic common to all Srī Laṅkā's minor plantation crops is low yields. Where statistical comparison is possible, it is seen that the local average yields always compare unfavourably with those obtained by the respective major producers abroad. Besides this, in cocoa, cardamom and citronella, under which the land is invariably mono-cropped, the average per-acre productivity is considerably lower than that of tea and rubber. This is largely due to relatively low standards maintained in the cultivation of these crops. A frequently observable pattern of utilisation of land under most of the minor plantation crops is that while there is a bustle of activity in the form of fertilising and weeding during spells of high price, normally the land remains in a semi-neglected state.

Both the strength and the weakness of the minor plantation industries of Srī Laṅkā lie in the fact that they are relatively insignificant suppliers to the world market. In the supply of such commodities as cocoa, cloves, cardamom, pepper and nutmeg, Srī Laṅkā is completely overshadowed by the world's major sources of supply. This implies that a substantial increase in supplies from Srī Laṅkā is unlikely to create a glut and a consequent lowering of prices in the world market. When stated as an advantage, this fact requires immediate qualification. First, this advantage is to some extent offset in the long run because the physical potential for producing these crops exists in many parts of the tropical world, and because economic possibilities for diversifying commercial agriculture are not unique to Srī Laṅkā. In fact, many other ex-colonial, monolithic, export-oriented agricultural economies have shown during the recent past much the same desire as Srī Laṅkā for diversification of exports and the creation of new sources of foreign income. Secondly, the advantage of being a small supplier is reduced by the notoriously volatile nature of the prices of these commodities in the world market, over which an insignificant supplier like Srī Laṅkā exercises no influence. This price instability is caused more by changes occurring at the respective major sources of supply rather than by changes in demand in the market. In cocoa, for example, when supplies from the disease-affected plantations of West Africa shrank in 1956, the price soared to £467 per ton to fall once again, with the recovery of African cocoa in the early 1960s, to less than £200 per ton. Similarly, in cardamom and cloves, although consumption levels in their main markets have been remarkably stable, convulsive price movements have occurred corresponding to changes in the supply levels from India, Guatemala and Tanzania in the former, and from Zanzibar and Indonesia in the latter commodity.

Challenges and Responses

As shown in the foregoing discussion, tea and rubber have witnessed a general decline of prices during the past two decades. In addition, there has been a weakening of Srī Laṅkā's competitive position with regard to tea. While the market *milieu* has thus become increasingly unfavourable, there has been a steady increase in the costs of some of the main inputs in both these industries. Since the late 1940s, wage rates in the plantation sector have more than doubled. Capital costs and costs of materials like fertiliser and fuel have also risen substantially. Hence the cardinal problem which the tea and rubber industries have been facing in recent times may be summed up as that of maintaining overall costs per unit weight of produce at levels that are remunerative to the producer in the face of declining prices. For the less efficient producer of these commodities, there has clearly been a struggle for survival.

Field operations on tea and rubber plantations are labour-intensive (the average man-equivalents per acre of tea and rubber in the country are *ca.* .89 and .27 respectively). The data on recurrent costs in tea and rubber production show that over 60 per cent of the cost per lb. of the finished product is accounted for by labour costs on plucking in the case of tea and tapping in rubber. While labour is thus a major item of cost, the nature of operations involved in the production of these commodities seems to give scope for raising the output per worker (without a comparable increase in wages) by increasing the productivity of the land. Specifically, if the tea bushes and the rubber trees are made to yield higher, then the costs of plucking and tapping, taken as a component of the final costs per unit weight of produce, could be brought down. The existence of an inverse relationship between yield per acre and cost per pound in both tea and rubber provides empirical evidence for this possibility. It is towards such a lowering of costs that much of the development effort in the tea and rubber industries of Srī Laṅkā has been directed during the past two decades.

Raising the yields of tea and rubber has, of course, been important from another point of view. As shown earlier, these crops are Srī Laṅkā's principal sources of foreign income. Thus efforts to increase their output may in fact be looked upon as efforts directed towards increasing the foreign exchange earnings of the country.

In this, however, the position of the tea industry during the past decade or so has been somewhat more complex than that of rubber. Between 1950 and 1965 local tea production and tea exports rose by about 60 per cent. If this rate of increase had continued after 1965, there was a strong possibility that it would have created (or substantially added to) a glut of tea in the world market and thereby a lowering of its price. Because of this, despite Srī Laṅkā's desire to retain its important position as a supplier of tea and the need to increase the foreign income derived from tea, there was a reluctance then to pursue a policy of unrestrained expansion of tea output. However, by the early 1970s it was becoming apparent that, making allowance for the usual short-term fluctuations in output, the production trends of the pre-1965 period had not continued, and that the shortfall in the supplies from Srī Laṅkā to the international market was being filled by the other tea-producing countries. Thus it has become imperative once again for Srī Laṅkā to emphasise expansion in the output of tea.[9]

In the post-independence period, there have been certain internal adjustments within the tea and rubber industries of Srī Laṅkā to deteriorating market conditions and to increasing costs. If data relating to the triennial periods 1948-50 and 1970-2 are taken to represent the differences between the early years of independence and the present, the average yield per mature acre can be seen to have increased from 542 to 791 lb. in tea and 369 to 674 lb. in rubber, leading to an increase in the total output from 301 to 473 million lb. in the former and from 222 to 324 million lb. in the latter. It would also be seen that these increases in yield and output were obtained without comparable expansions in the workforces of the two industries. In the period under review, while the tea output increased by 57 per cent, the estimated total number employed in tea plantations increased by only about 15 per cent. Rubber output increased by 46 per cent, and the size of the workforce seems to have stayed more or less constant. The increased labour productivity which these figures represent has enabled tea and rubber to achieve some economy in costs. In the face of steadily rising wage rates of labour and costs of other inputs, the available data suggest that tea estates have maintained average costs per lb. at a more or less constant level while rubber estates have succeeded in lowering costs by about 18 per cent.

The progress achieved by the tea and rubber industries in the form of higher yields, higher production and constant or lower costs is due largely to the spread of improved methods of cultivation. Through research conducted at specialised institutes both in Srī Laṅkā and abroad, improvements and innovations relating to cultivars, planting techniques, fertiliser usage, disease control, soil conservation, harvesting and processing were made available to the producers. The state provided various inducements to promote the spread of these improved methods. Except at times of low price, a majority of producers have responded effectively to such inducements.

The rapid expansion in the output of tea particularly in the period before 1965 was due largely to increased use of fertiliser. Though precise statistical data on fertiliser usage in tea are not available, there is evidence to suggest that between the early 1950s and the mid-1960s, there was roughly a twofold increase in the amount of fertiliser consumed by the local tea industry.

The efforts to improve conditions in the tea industry have not had a uniform degree of success among its different classes of producers. Since 1952, there has been a state-sponsored programme to assist the smallholdings sector, which has generally been regarded as the weaker sector of the tea industry. Among these programmes were free distribution of seed, supply of fertiliser at subsidised prices, financial assistance for soil conservation and as debt relief, advisory services, establishment of smallholders' colonisation schemes, and the setting up of smallholders' co-operatives, both to channel governmental assistance and to facilitate the disposal of produce. These programmes were first intended for holdings of less than 10 acres, but were broadened in 1958 to cover those of between 10 and 100 acres.

On the whole, the results of these programmes have fallen short of expectations, particularly among smaller size groups. An evaluation survey conducted in 1964 on units of less than 10 acres revealed that smallholders' co-operatives had been able to enrol only 2-3 per cent of the total number of tea smallholders in the country, and 44 per cent of the units which had received aid of some form were still in a neglected state.

The response of medium-sized holdings to the programmes referred to above have been somewhat more satisfactory. Nearly 75 per cent of these units had received aid under the fertiliser subsidy scheme, and over 50 per cent had obtained assistance for soil conservation.

In 1959 a programme of replanting was introduced to the tea industry. This programme was specially intended for the estate sector, and has involved the payment of subsidies to tea growers for replacing old low-yielding tea with vegetatively propagated high-yielding strains and for the proper upkeep of the land so replanted. The tea growers' initial response to this scheme was poor and the extents replanted each year fell far below the target figure of 5,000 acres. However, since 1963 when the scale of governmental assistance was enhanced, the scheme gathered momentum, and, at the end of the first ten years of its implementation, replanting operations had begun on some 47,000 acres of tea land. In all these it is seen that the estate sector of tea has been far more responsive to innovation and change than the smallholdings sector.

These improvements in conditions in the tea industry are confined to tea cultivation. In tea processing, the achievements of the past two decades are far less impressive. In the highland tea areas, particularly on large estates, there have been continued efforts at quality control and quality improvement through finer plucking. But in the light of an apparent change in consumer preferences, as reflected in the declining price premia of quality teas, the benefits of an excessive preoccupation with quality seem dubious. Perhaps more important is the fact that efforts to modernise tea processing have hitherto made little headway in Srī Laṅkā. There has been a programme aimed at lowering processing costs by making factory operations more efficient and by the use of modern machinery all of which has already gained wide acceptance in some of the other major tea-producing countries. Attempts have been made to popularise 'unorthodox' processes of tea manufacture which give quick-brewing teas that are increasingly popular in most tea markets.[10] Efforts have also been made to introduce new processes for producing 'instant' teas that would have the capability of competing with other instant beverages in the world market. By and large these attempts have so far met with only meagre success.

Srī Laṅkā, as well as some of the other major tea-producing countries, has been conscious of the various factors that have contributed to the general lowering of tea prices in the world market during the past two decades. In this, as shown earlier, the unrestrained expansion in the supply of tea has been the most important factor. There has accordingly been some interest during the recent past among certain tea producers in reaching an international agreement for the control of tea supplies to the world market. Since Srī Laṅkā's dependence on the fortunes of the tea industry is greater than that of the other major tea-producers, she has been in the forefront of the search for such an agreement. Periodical meetings of representatives from tea-producing countries held under the aegis of the FAO during the late 1960s culminated in a loose short-term agreement between tea-producing countries collectively to control the global supply of tea with each of them supplying less than a specified quota. This agreement has not had an impact on tea prices, but it engendered some hope that a more rigid long-term agreement on control might soon become a reality. But it has become increasingly apparent that the suppliers of tea to the world market lack the community of interests which could form the foundation for such collective action.

Reference was made earlier to the competition which tea faces from other beverages and to the high degree of control which a few international commercial firms exercise on the tea markets of the world — factors which have also been responsible for the falling prices of tea. Some steps have been taken to combat the effects of these factors. Among them is the state-sponsored Tea Propaganda Campaign whose organisational network has spread to many cities in the developed world. The promotion of tea consumption through propaganda is by its very nature costly, and its exact effects cannot be assessed. The 'instant tea' project, which has hitherto met with little success is yet another measure which has been aimed at popularising tea consumption. As an attempt to reduce Srī Laṅkā's dependence on the traditional channels of tea marketing, the government has been encouraging the export of packeted tea through a system of preferential export duties. Though in recent years the volume of tea exported in this form has gradually risen, it still represents only about 5 per cent of the total of tea exports.

The progress seen during the past twenty years in Srī Laṅkā's rubber industry is due largely to the success of a rehabilitation programme which has been in continuous operation since it was introduced in 1953. In the period before its introduction the local rubber plantations, in comparison to those of the other major producing areas of Asia, were in a run-down state. Yields were low and costs were high. A Commission of Inquiry[11] which investigated Srī Laṅkā's rubber industry in the late 1940s found that about one-third of the total rubber acreage was operating uneconomically, and drew attention to the urgency of concerted action to rejuvenate the local plantations. It was on the recommendations of this Commission that the Rubber Rehabilitation Programme came to be based.

The principal feature of the programme was a replanting subsidy scheme which envisaged the annual replacement of about 3 per cent of the total area under rubber in the country with high yielding bud-grafts and clonal seedlings of rubber. The scale of governmental aid granted through the subsidy has been greater for small units than for large ones. At various stages since the launching of the scheme the subsidies were increased as compensation for rising costs of replanting. The scheme had various checks to ensure the maintenance of specified standards of replanting by those receiving the subsidies.

During the twenty years following the introduction of the programme, about 305,000 acres had received assistance under the replanting scheme. Neither in the rate of replanting nor in the performance of the replanted rubber do there seem to be major differences between estates and smallholdings. A little over half the area in each sector of the industry has so far been replanted. As for performance, though comprehensive and reliable statistical data are not available, it appears from estimates of average yields for the entire replanted area and from results of a sample survey conducted on replanted smallholdings that the average yield obtained from mature replanted rubber in both sectors of the industry would be about 800-1,000 lb. per acre per year. A noteworthy difference in response to the scheme among the different classes of producers is that variations in the price of rubber have affected the replanting rates on large estates much less than on small estates and smallholdings. While the large estates seem to have maintained a more or less uniform pace of replanting irrespective of price variations, the other classes of producers have tended to slow down their rates of replanting during periods of low prices.

The replanting scheme has undoubtedly raised yields, lowered costs and generally strengthened the competitive position of Srī Laṅkā's rubber industry in the world market. However, similar replanting programmes have been in operation elsewhere; and, it would be pertinent to attempt a general comparison of Srī Laṅkā's scheme with those of the others. From the meagre and fragmentary data available, it appears that the performance of the local replanted rubber has hitherto been superior to that of Indonesia, Thailand, South Vietnam and India, but distinctly inferior to that of Western Malaysia, which stems not from the comparative rates of replanting but from the choice of cultivars. In Srī Laṅkā an overwhelmingly large proportion of the replanted acreage has been planted with PB 86 clones. This clone, though considered reliable and a moderately high yielder of latex, is a poor yielder when compared to some of the modern clones (specially those of the RRIM 600 series) which have been more extensively used in Malaysia's replanting programme.[12] This implies that, given similar wage rates and similar costs of materials, the ultimate lowering of cost (per pound) through replanting is potentially more substantial in Malaysia than it would be in Srī Laṅkā.

Besides replanting, there have been certain other improvements in Srī Laṅkā's rubber industry. As in tea, fertiliser usage seems to have increased. Some effort has been directed at quality control in processing. The fact that the proportion of the total output of raw rubber falling into superior grades is slightly higher now than in the early 1950s probably results from this effort. There have also been some recent attempts at promoting the manufacture of various types of high-priced raw rubber such as coagulated latex and block rubber. The consumption of rubber by the local manufacturing industries has risen from 156 tons in 1950 to 5,005 tons in 1971. Rubber has continued to increase in importance as a barter commodity in the country's bi-lateral trade agreements.

For coconut, the main challenge has been that of raising the level of productivity of the land under its cultivation. This could be considered vital from several points of view. The crop covers nearly a quarter of the country's total cultivated area and occupies some of its most densely populated parts where there is acute pressure of population on developed agricultural land. According to a survey conducted in 1956, in the island as a whole, the maximum extent of new land which could be made available for coconut was about 50,000 acres. The implication seems to be that any substantial increase in the total output of coconut would have to be derived from the existing acreage by applying more fertiliser and by replacing old plants with high-yielding varieties. Further, there is the proven potential for raising the present levels of productivity through improved agricultural techniques which are both simple to apply and which give good returns on investment. There is also considerable scope for increasing the overall productivity of the land under coconut by mixed cropping and catch cropping which would partly alleviate the problem of food scarcity in the country. Above all, domestic consumption of coconut has been increasing rapidly, and hence, despite the relatively high prices of the recent past, there has been a general decline in the foreign exchange earnings from this industry.

Data relating to such aspects as extent, output, employment and costs in the coconut industry covering the post-war period, though obtainable from official sources, are probably less reliable than the parallel data for tea and rubber. Treating the data available at face value, it could be said that in coconut, unlike tea and rubber, no clear and significant trends of improvement are visible. On the contrary, in 1973, there was an unprecedented drop, estimated at about 35 per cent, in the total output of coconut compared with that recorded for the previous year.[13] In 1974 there was an increase of about 5 per cent over the 1973 crop. This was still much below the level attained in 1972 or even earlier.

During the past two decades, there have been state-sponsored research programmes, subsidy schemes and various other extension services for coconut. The establishment in 1972 of four statutory boards vested respectively with the promotion of research, cultivation, processing and marketing in the coconut industry and a Coconut Development Authority to regulate the functions of the four boards signifies increased government attention to this industry. But, on the whole, efforts to improve conditions within the coconut industry appear to have had little impact on its yield, costs of production and general production trends so far.

Among various schemes for development of the coconut industry the most important one so far has been the fertiliser subsidy scheme, which has been in operation since 1956 and under which the government has borne half the cost of fertiliser supplied to coconut growers. From an estimated annual consumption of 10,000-12,000 tons of fertiliser before the introduction of the scheme, the amount of fertiliser used for coconut increased to about 60,000 tons by the mid-1960s. Data on the issue of permits under the scheme suggest that the acreage receiving the subsidy rose steadily from 1956 to 1963 and remained more or less constant thereafter. It is probably the impact of this increase in fertiliser application (coupled with favourable weather conditions) which was reflected in the peak production figure reached in 1964. In spite of this increase in the total amount of fertiliser used, a large majority of coconut smallholders still seldom if ever use fertiliser, and only a small fraction of the total coconut acreage is systematically and regularly fertilised. In 1971, for example, only about one-third of the total extent in units of over 50 acres and one-ninth of the extent in units of under 50 acres made use of the fertiliser subsidy.

The record of replanting coconut has also been unimpressive. On a large majority of plantations in the country, yields have been on the decline due to the age of trees. Replanting coconut does not involve, as an initial step, the removal of the old stand and therefore a loss of income until the new plants reach maturity. Liberal assistance has also been given by the government to those who undertake replanting. Despite these factors, the rate of replanting on coconut land during the past has been lower than in both tea and rubber.

Problems that are encountered in attempts to increase the efficiency of the coconut industry differ from those relating to tea and rubber. It was noted that the estate sector forms only a small part of this industry. This implies that those who possess the capacity, unaided by the government, to invest in improved agricultural practices and whose efforts are guided primarily by motives of profit maximisation, form a minority among owners of coconut land. Both the multiplicity of producers and the low incomes of the overwhelming majority of them make the task of externally inducing the spread of improved techniques in the coconut industry immensely more complex than is the case with tea and rubber. Furthermore, the production costs of coconut are low, and the prices that have prevailed in the past two or three decades have always been high enough to enable even the less efficient producer to operate profitably. This has meant that, unlike in tea and rubber, even for the marginal producer of coconut there has been no question of a struggle for survival. As a consequence of these factors, the coconut industry as a whole has been less progressive in the adoption of improved agricultural practices than the other major plantation industries in the country.[14]

Statements of government policy and plans and programmes of economic development of the past decade or so have repeatedly emphasised the need for safeguarding the economy of Srī Laṅkā from the vulnerability which stems from its over-dependence on the three staple export products. Diversifying export agriculture by increasing the relative importance of the minor plantation crops has been an important aspect of the overall strategy of development, particularly since the early 1960s.

Among various government programmes of the recent past relating to these crops were those involving both direct assistance to producers in the form of financial subsidies for planting, replanting and fertiliser purchase, and indirect inducements through special fiscal concessions granted to exporters. The initiation of the Mid-country Crop Diversification Programme in 1971 by the Ministry of Plantation Industries may be seen as a systematic and co-ordinated intensification of attempts to facilitate the rapid growth of this sphere of production. However, these attempts, in their totality, have had little impact hitherto either on the position of the minor plantation crops in the country's economy or on their general trends of production.

Efforts to promote the minor plantation industries have always faced certain handicaps which are all basically related either to their very insignificance in the economy or to the uncertainty of their prospects in the world market. Research, advisory services, credit and state-sponsored marketing facilities for producers of these crops either do not exist or are very poorly organised. In the world market, neither long-term demand nor trends of supplies from other sources (including synthetic substitution) can be forecast with any certainty. These are coupled with the low income of a majority of the producers of many of these crops and the smallness of the income which such crops generate for the economy. Hence, despite the widely acknowledged desirability of diversifying export agriculture and the somewhat ostentatious commitment to bringing about diversification, these factors have tended to inhibit investment and effort on minor plantation crops both by the government and by individual producers.

Addendum — Land Reform and Plantation Agriculture

Reference has already been made to the early stages of implementation (i.e. up to early 1974) of the Land Reform Law promulgated in August 1972. A communique issued by the Ministry of Agriculture and Lands in August 1974 claimed that 560,000 acres had been acquired under the provisions of this law.[15] About 60 per cent of this area was under tea, rubber and coconut. Subsequently, in October 1975, a further extension of land reform was seen in the enactment of the Land Reform Amendment Law which provided for the takeover by the Land Reform Commission of all lands owned by public (sterling and rupee) companies. The total extent of company-owned plantation land vested in the Commission under the provisions of this law is reported to be about 410,000 acres.[16]

The current land reforms have thus paved the way for major structural changes in the plantation sector of Srī Laṅkā. The aggregate area acquired from the private sector through these reforms includes 72 per cent of the total tea acreage, 34 per cent of the rubber acreage and 10 per cent of the coconut acreage.

It still remains uncertain how the acquired land will finally be apportioned out by the Land Reform Commission to different types of alienation and settlement. By early 1974 a part of the land had been alienated to three types of farm organisation. The related data, which cover about 40 per cent of the extent acquired under the reform law of 1972, show that about half the area has been blocked out for re-distribution in small allotments to peasants on an individual basis, and the remainder handed over in large blocks either to public corporations to be operated as estates or to various state-sponsored agencies for setting up co-operative farms.[17]

Although in the preliminary alienations the peasant sector has thus been the principal recipient of land, it seems doubtful whether later alienations will maintain the same proportionate emphasis on a direct redistribution of land to peasants on an individual basis. Recent official statements have repeatedly maintained that the integrity of the economically viable large units taken over by the Land Reform Commission will be preserved. Such statements also indicate that where alienation to the peasant sector is deemed necessary, preference would be for commune-type co-operative farms rather than for small individually operated family farms.

REFERENCES

1. See, J. H. Boeke, *The Evolution of the Netherlands Indies Economy* (1946), Amsterdam; *Economics and Economic Policy of Dual Societies* (1953), Amsterdam; 'Social and Economic Needs' and 'Dualistic Economics', Royal Tropical Institute (ed.) *Indonesian Economics* (1969), pp. 69-74 and 167-214. J. Van Gelderen, 'Economics of a Tropical Colony', *Indonesian Economics,* op. cit., pp. 111-63.

2. S. J. Tambiah, chapter on 'Ceylon' in Lambert and Hoselitz (ed.) *Role of Saving and Wealth in Southern Asia and the West* (1963), UNESCO.

3. The Land Reform Law No. 1 of 1972 stipulated that the maximum extent of agricultural land which may be owned by any person in Sri Laṅkā could be 50 acres if such land did not consist exclusively of paddy land; or 25 acres if it did consist exclusively of paddy land. Certain categories of land were exempted from this ceiling. Among such exemptions, the most important (for the present study) is that of land under the ownership of joint stock-companies.

4. *Tea — Trends and Prospects,* Commodity Bulletin Series, 30, U.N./F.A.O. (1960), Rome.

5. N. Jeyapalan and A. S. Jayawardane, 'Some Aspects of the Tea Industry', Part II, *Central Bank of Ceylon Bulletin* (March 1968), pp. 19-63.

6. *The Coconut Industry of Asia,* ECAFE (1969), U.N., New York.

7. ibid.

8. Export figures given in this paragraph have been obtained from *The Ceylon Export Directory,* Market Research Company of Ceylon (1968),

Colombo, and from Reports Nos. 1 to 6 U.N.D.P./F.A.O. (1972 and 1973) relating to Agricultural Diversification and Minor Export Crops of Srī Laṅkā.

9. See, particularly, *Matching Employment Opportunities and Expectations — A Programme of Action for Ceylon* I, Report, II Technical Papers (1971), ILO, Geneva.

10. There is some controversy regarding the profitability of adopting unorthodox processes for the manufacture of tea in Srī Laṅkā. See D. M. Forrest, *A Hundred Years of Ceylon Tea, 1867-1967*, London (1967), pp. 250-2.

11. *The Rubber Industry of Ceylon*, Sessional Paper XVIII of 1947.

12. Rubber Research Institute of Malaysia, *Planters, Bulletin*, Nos. 107 (1970) and 112 (1971).

13. Central Bank of Ceylon, *Annual Report* (1973 and 1974), Colombo.

14. Plantation coconut is characterized by very low recurrent costs. See C. J. Piggot, *Coconut Growing* (1964), London. This is largely due to low labour requirements for upkeep and harvesting. H. Ruthenburg, *Farming Systems in the Tropics* (1971), London, estimates that in Srī Laṅkā labour requirements for these activities is in the order of .081 man-equivalents per hour.

15. See fn. 3, above.

16. Central Bank of Ceylon, *Bulletin*, October 1975, p. 780.

17. According to data obtained from the Land Reform Commission.

10

PEASANT AGRICULTURE

by L. A. Wickremeratne

It has been customary to view Srī Laṅkān agriculture in terms of the plantation sector on the one hand and the traditional or peasant agricultural sector on the other — the distinction being based on a number of well recognised factors, not the least important of which have been the scale of operations and the objectives of production. Although the plantation sector has long been the leading sector in the economy, a distinctive feature in economic development after 1948 has been the determination to take in hand the comparatively neglected peasant agricultural sector.

A multiplicity of factors brought about the change. First, political independence implied a greater responsiveness to the needs of the peasant sector. Secondly, dwindling external resources and the difficulties of obtaining essential foodstuffs — primarily rice and a number of subsidiary items — which had to be imported in increasing quantities emphasised the need to develop peasant agriculture and achieve as much import substitution in consumer agricultural imports as possible. Moreover, the emergence of planning and the strategies of balanced economic growth meant that the peasant agricultural sector had to play an active rather than a passive role within the economy. Finally, the cumulative effect of social changes and the shift of political power from urban to rural areas was that the peasant sector became a major factor in the arithmetic of national politics.

Above all, the patterns of land utilisation clearly showed that there had been in the past a very real under-utilisation of the growth potential in the peasant sector. The Agricultural Census of 1946 showed that out of a total land area of 15,997,964 acres, the area under agriculture in the plantation as well as in the peasant agricultural sectors amounted to only 4,267,398 acres. By 1962, when a fresh census of agriculture was taken, the extent of land under agriculture was 4,666,553 acres. Within the period the percentage of land that had been developed agriculturally, in relation to the total land area of the island, had increased modestly from 26.67 to 29.17 per cent. Although due allowance should be made for a considerable proportion of the land area of the island necessarily remaining unused because of the existence of large forest reserves, the pressures of population growth and urban expansion — especially in the wet zone — it was abundantly clear that the bulk of land resources in Sri Lankā remained under-utilised.[1]

This was shown more clearly in the dry zone where the physical area of the land was considerable and population density was much less. Of the total land area, no less than 10,663,864 acres were situated in the dry zone; yet the total agriculturally cultivated area in the dry zone amounted to only 1,557,193 acres. Moreover, the possibilities of physical expansion of cultivation in the dry zone were not limited, as in the wet zone, by competing claims for the utilisation of land.[2]

On the other grounds too the distinction between paddy cultivation in the wet zone and in the dry zone is basic to our understanding of peasant agriculture. To a large extent the distinction is based on rainfall and water resources. It is in the dry zone, which contains no less than 70 per cent of the land area, that the major paddy-growing areas in the island are found. The cultivation of paddy in this zone has been dependent on irrigation as well as on rainfall. The major season of cultivation is the *mahā* season, which extends from October to February or March and coincides with the North-east monsoon, which brings rainfall of about 75 inches to the dry zone. The less important cultivation season is the *yala* season from April to August, during which the South-west monsoon brings abundant rainfall to the wet zone, but hardly any to the dry zone. It therefore follows that the extent of paddy cultivation in the dry zone during the *yala* season depends entirely on irrigation.

In the wet zone, on the other hand, which occupies the South-west of the island and where there is rainfall of between 100 and 200 inches, the cultivation of paddy takes place in both *mahā* and *yala* seasons. Indeed, in the wet zone the problem has often been an excess of rainfall and floods rather than a lack of water. However, in certain areas, as in the drier portions of the hill country, the essentially rain-fed cultivation of paddy has to be supplemented by minor irrigation works, which have been little more than small anicuts built to divert water from streams.

A striking feature of paddy cultivation in the wet zone has been the limited land available for cultivation. Land use has been constrained by the fact that the wet zone is also the home of the planta-

tion crops. For example, in the Kandy District which occupies 914
square miles, the major plantation crops account for 70 per cent of
the total cultivated area. Paddy cultivation *per se* occupies only 15
per cent of the total area.[3] Apart from the plantation system, the
land available for peasant agriculture has also tended to be limited
by urbanisation and population growth.

Taking the island as a whole, however, the potential for the expansion of paddy cultivation appears to be considerable — at any
rate on paper — as the following table shows:[4]

Categories of land utilisation	Acreage (in thousands)
Total land area	15,998
Plantation crops	2,428
Peasant crops (paddy)	1,249
Peasant crops (other than paddy)	508
Forest	8,208
Grassland	1,053
Miscellaneous	2,552

In delineating the broad physical and institutional features of
the peasant agricultural sector, one must emphasise that paddy
cultivation in Srī Laṅkā has characteristically been an economic
enterprise of comparatively small holdings or units of production.
The 1962 Census of Agriculture revealed that the 1,135,000 acres of
land under paddy cultivation were divided into as many as 570,000
separate holdings distributed thus;[5]

Size group (in acres)	Percentage holdings in total	Percentage of total area
0 — 1	43	17
1 — 2½	31	26
2½ — 5	20	33
5 — 10	5	16
10 acres and above	1	8

Physical Growth and the Peasant Agricultural Sector

Because of the rather obvious possibilities of physically expanding the area under paddy cultivation, developments in peasant
agriculture for much of the period before 1948 were substantially
centred in the opening of new lands largely in the dry zone.

By the late 1920s the claims of the peasant sector began to receive support and strength by a perceptible shift in official policy. Sir Hugh Clifford, the governor of Ceylon at this time, favoured a policy of peasant colonisation with a view to creating an independent and economically prosperous class of peasant proprietors. The Land Commission, which was appointed in 1927 largely on the initiative of Clifford, urged that the development of the peasant agricultural sector should be the main object of government land policy.

But the real breakthrough in policy came in 1932 and coincided significantly with the control and administration of agriculture and allied government departments passing into the hands of the Ceylonese in the State Council, in particular with D. S. Senanayake becoming Minister of Agriculture and Lands. Under Senanayake's guidance planned peasant colonisation schemes in the dry zone became the order of the day. After 1932, and in contrast to previous practice, the government took upon itself the task of clearing the land allotted for the establishment of peasant colonies, and moreover bore the cost of providing numerous infrastructural facilities like hospitals, schools, roads and irrigation channels. No outright cash subsidies were paid to the settler or colonist, but instead he was exempted from the payment of irrigation rates for three years. By 1935, when the Land Development Ordinance was enacted, the land policies of the government had become crystallised: lands in the dry zone were to be given to selected allottees, in perpetuity, and with careful restrictions to prevent the fragmentation of land.[6]

In the context of the early 1930s, substantial inducements had to be given to attract peasants from the wet zone to the various colonisation schemes in the malaria-infested dry zone. Significantly, it was found that, in spite of a wide range of inducements and facilities, the actual pace of peasant colonisation in the dry zone was slow. Consequently in 1939, as well as in 1941, the amplitude of facilities was further extended for habitation, roads and water facilities.

Attitudes of scepticism towards the government's liberal land policies became evident in the 1950s, and more perceptibly in the 1960s, when economic conditions were rapidly deteriorating, and investment and expenditure in several sectors were being critically examined. The point of attack was that the gains from peasant colonisation schemes have not been commensurate with the vast expenditure involved.

In one sense, nonetheless, it is arguable that the record of achievements with regard to peasant colonisation has been impressive. A considerable amount of land has been alienated, and thousands of allottees have been settled. The 1962 Census of Agriculture revealed that in 1935-50 as much as 24,000 acres of land had been alienated annually, and that the subsequent rate of alienation of land was about 20,000 acres each year. These rates may be compared to the extent of crown land — 21,000 acres each year — which had been alienated during the period of the growth of the plantation sector in Srī Laṅkā, specifically between 1828 and 1900.[8]

On the other hand, it is equally possible to argue that in spite of the impressive physical expansion there has been no proportionate increase in agricultural production. It is possible that the land given to the individual allottee in the major colonisation schemes — initially about 8 acres of highland and lowland per allottee but subsequently more realistically reduced to 5 acres — was too generous and well beyond the capacity of peasant allottees to put to maximum use. The evidence suggests that in practice highland cultivation — which had great potential for development in the dry zone — was ignored, the colonist preferring to concentrate on paddy cultivation in the irrigable lowland portions of his allotment. It is apparent that, statistics notwithstanding, the actual area under cultivation did not therefore match the vast area of land that had been theoretically alienated in colonisation schemes.

Moreover, in spite of the generosity of government assistance in setting up colonisation schemes, supporting facilities — e.g. transport, marketing, agricultural extension services — did not spread commensurately. As a consequence, colonisation schemes became rather isolated pockets of economic activity.

More conventionally, colonisation ventures have also been criticised because of a presumed connection between economic production and the type of settler who became a colonist. It has been pointed out that in the selection of allottees, weightage was given to applicants who had no land and had large families to support, ignoring the equally relevant consideration of whether the applicants had any real aptitude for agriculture. In this sense experience has shown that peasant colonisation schemes of the classic type may not be an ideal solution to urban unemployment. Moreover, the sociological factor in the selection of potential colonists too has also received little or no attention so that many colonies did not became socially cohesive communities.[9]

Peasant Agriculture and Technological Change

Possibly the most cogent criticism of peasant agricultural growth through colonisation schemes has been that — although such an outcome was not clearly intended — physical expansion had been emphasised at the expense of intensified production by means of improvements in technology and cultivation practices. Policies of extensive and intensive cultivation were admittedly not mutually exclusive; however, successive agricultural censuses showed that there was after all a considerable acreage of land in Srī Laṅkā which had been cleared of jungle and brought under cultivation in the dry zone in particular, as well as in the wet zone. Although not all this land was always actually cultivated due to extraneous factors such as droughts and floods, the moral was surely that if the yield of rice per acre were increased, Srī Laṅkā could go a long way towards producing its own requirements in rice.

Coinciding with the scepticism that was being felt over colonisation schemes, Srī Laṅkā was as much influenced by the spectacular results achieved in the major rice-producing countries in Southeast and East Asia — notably Japan, Thailand and the Philippines — by the adoption of superior techniques in producing rice. The emphasis consequently shifted perceptibly in favour of intensified cultivation. A significant feature of intensive cultivation based on improved techniques was the introduction of high-yielding varieties of paddy. By the 1960s hybrid varieties of paddy were produced by crossing outstanding foreign varieties with the best local types.

Taking the island as a whole, it has been found that the new varieties had certainly contributed to an overall increase in yields. The *maha* season paddy yields, for example, had increased from 37.7 bushels per acre in 1959-60 to an average of 52.2 bushels by 1969-70.[10] A feature in the diffusion of high-yielding varieties has been the appearance since 1971 of "new high-yielding varieties" (NHYV) like BG 11-11 and BG 34-8, whose potential is thought to be even greater than that of the "old high-yielding varieties" (OHYV) like H4.

The spread of the high-yielding varieties of paddy has been as much a reflex of the success of agricultural extension work in popularising new techniques as it has been testimony to the willingness of the cultivator — usually considered too hidebound by tradition — to adopt new techniques. A Central Bank Survey conducted in 1969 showed that only a minority of cultivators thought that traditional varieties of seeds, to which they had been accustomed for generations, were superior to the new hybrid varieties.

An increase in the use of fertilisers was a significant aspect of the emphasis on intensive cultivation. Traditionally, fertiliser inputs in paddy cultivation had been confined to vegetable and organic manures. The rather rapid diffusion of high-yielding varieties stressed the importance of using chemical fertilisers. Figures show

that overall the use of chemical fertilisers in paddy cultivation
increased.[11] Thus

Year	Fertiliser (tons)
1954	9,400
1959-60	20,173
1961-2	38,782
1962-3	47,059

Because of the importance of chemical fertilisers in the strategies
of intensive cultivation, the government set up the Sri Lanka Fertiliser Corporation in 1964, which assumed the responsibilities of
distributing fertilisers.

But in spite of the overall annual increases in the use of chemical
fertilisers, the Agricultural Census of 1962 showed that as many
as 65.1 per cent of the cultivators did not avail themselves of the
facilities given by the government to encourage the use of fertiliser,
and that in 1962, during the *mahā* as well as the *yala* seasons, the
percentage of the area on which chemical fertilisers had been used
was only 33 per cent of the total area sown.[12] Surveys revealed that
many cultivators did not have the means of obtaining fertiliser in
spite of the subsidies offered by the government, that in any case it
was often not possible to obtain fertiliser in time when cultivators
needed it, and that those who used fertiliser did not use the quantities recommended by the Department of Agriculture. Above all,
the difficulties of supplying chemical fertilisers — which had to be
imported — increased in time with the mounting foreign exchange
problems of the country.

In much the same way, the use of weedicides and pesticides has
been restricted not so much because of the innate conservatism of
the peasant, as by the shortage of agro-chemicals. Traditionally
weeding is done by harrowing or by flooding the paddy field with
water — a clearly wasteful use of water — or by rooting out the weeds
manually. The resort to harrowing has invariably been dependent
in many areas on labour costs. At first — no doubt as a result of the
influence of Japanese methods of rice cultivation — mechanised
weeding was introduced in some areas. Rotary weeders as well as
hand operated seeders were used. The mechanical contrivances —
which required that the paddy seed should be planted in rows —
could not be manufactured in sufficient quantities. In any event
their use was not possible on all drained or boggy fields or in areas
where there was not sufficient water. In general, the use of chemical

weedicides — in so far as they have been available — has been more popular.[13]

A notable feature in the campaign for increasing yields in paddy cultivation was the efforts of agricultural extension officials to popularise transplanting — as opposed to sowing the paddy seed broadcast — as the ideal method of propagating paddy. Traditionally transplanting has been most popular in the districts of Kāgalla and Mātalē. Experiments as well as the experience of cultivators demonstrated repeatedly that the method of transplanting ensured higher yields. A Central Bank Survey on paddy cultivation conducted in 1966-7, covering twenty-two districts, showed conclusively that whereas the average yield per acre by means of broadcast sowing was only 30.7 bushels per acre, transplanting yielded an impressive 47.3 bushels per acre.[14] Nevertheless, successive surveys revealed that although the average cultivator willingly recognised the superiority of transplanting, in fact the traditional practice of sowing paddy broadcast widely prevailed.

A possible factor — often urged by the cultivators themselves — has been the lack of water. More plausibly, there have been difficulties in finding labour for transplanting which, by its very nature, is more labour-intensive than the alternative method of broadcasting. In areas where the cultivator is dependent fundamentally on family labour resources supplemented by *attān* or exchange labour, the cost of hiring labour — for which during the cultivation season there is great demand — becomes virtually a luxury which the average cultivator cannot afford. Moreover, available labour resources are invariably used first for the basic operations of tillage and threshing.[15]

The following table, based on a survey of paddy production during the *mahā* season of 1972-3, shows the relative importance of the two methods of paddy propagation in selected paddy-growing areas in Sri Lanka, on a percentage basis.[16]

	Hambantota	Polonnaruva	Elahara	Kurunägala	Kandy	Colombo
Transplanting	36.6	76.9	88.5	37.8	89.3	11.3
Broadcasting	63.4	23.1	11.5	62.2	10.7	88.7

A growing partiality for mechanisation has also reflected the changes in the traditional attitudes to the cultivation of paddy. In 1946 ploughing by the use of tractors was a comparative novelty. By 1962 the situation had changed appreciably. A number of factors helped in the spread of mechanisation. To begin with, when tractors were first becoming popular, foreign exchange difficulties, which would naturally have limited the import of tractors as well as spares, were not felt. On the contrary, "an undervalued foreign exchange rate for both tractors and fuel helped to boost the demand for tractors as a substitute for animal draught". Secondly, tractors were owned and hired by a class of comparatively affluent people at rates which were lower than the cost of labour or that of draught animals. Indeed in many areas in Srī Laṅkā tractor hire costs were initially even cheaper. Moreover, the reduction in the number of bullocks and buffalos because of the increasing demand for meat and the rising costs of hired labour ensured the lasting popularity of mechanisation, especially in districts where the physical setting — flat land and broad tracts of fields — were conducive to their use.[17]

In spite of this, however, the use of mechanisation has not been, and is not likely to be, universally resorted to. Variations in the use of mechanised *vis-à-vis* conventional types of draught power are in fact significant. For example, in the Hambantota district where there is perhaps a greater concentration of two-wheeled and four-wheeled tractors than elsewhere in Srī Laṅkā, as much as 93 per cent of the cultivators used tractors in the preparation of the land for paddy cultivation. By contrast, in the Kandy District 95 per cent of the cultivators used only buffaloes.[18]

The difference can largely be attributed to topographical factors. Apart from the existence of terraced fields of paddy, which make the use of tractors impossible in Kandy, more generally the fields are small and therefore more conveniently ploughed by buffaloes. Indeed, in a recent survey it became evident that among the principal reasons given by cultivators in the Kandy district for the predominance of the buffalo was that the soils were too boggy for the use of tractors and that the buffaloes achieved a better quality of work. By contrast, topographical conditions have been generally conducive to the use of tractors in the Hambantota district where, as in the allied dry zone districts like Ampārai, Vavūniyā, Hambantota and Batticaloa, there is often a scarcity of labour.

In the context of a worsening economic situation, scepticism has often been expressed about the dependence on mechanised traction, on the grounds that it consumes foreign exchange since spares as well as fuel for tractors have to be imported — apart from the possibility that mechanisation displaces labour. It has also been contended that since tractors are invariably owned and hired out either by the more affluent farmers or by entrepreneurs who have made a living out of doing so, the average cultivator has had to contend with a new class of oppressors. It has been said that "a new feudalism of technology has grown up around tractor-owners", to whom the average cultivator may well lose control and ownership of his land.[19]

The scepticism may be misplaced. Quite apart from foreign exchange difficulties, it is a moot point whether there would be a large-scale substitution of farm machinery for human and animal labour. With the rising cost of tractor hire — due to increases in fuel and spare parts costs — the balance may well be restored in favour of hired labour.

Institutional Incentives to Production

In Srī Laṅkā, as elsewhere in Southern Asia, the history of peasant agriculture has been closely intertwined with the intervention of the state. The average peasant has been unable to cope with the problem of production and marketing without external assistance.

Among a number of positive measures taken by the government to encourage the cultivator, the Guaranteed Price Scheme (GPS), which came into existence in 1942, deserves special mention. Until its scope was subsequently enlarged to cover a variety of peasant products, the GPS was originally concerned exclusively with paddy.[20] In concrete terms the government in 1948 stipulated a guaranteed price of Rs. 8 per bushel, regardless of the price of paddy prevailing in the free market. The idea was to offer the cultivator both a fair price and an assured market for his product. In 1951 this was raised to Rs. 9 and, more significantly, in 1952 to Rs. 12 with an undertaking, as an added inducement to the cultivator, that the guaranteed price would be maintained for five years. Indeed by 1952 the idea emerged that the GPS should be viewed not merely as an assurance of a fair price to the peasant agriculturist but also as a means of supporting him against the rising cost of living on account of which the more organised and articulate urban worker had already received protection by means of special living allowances. Subsequent increases in the GPS for paddy have been more spectacular: Rs. 14 (December 1967), Rs. 18 (November 1972), Rs. 25 (October 1973), Rs. 30 (March 1974) and Rs. 33 (July 1974). The increases took cognisance of the fact that the costs of paddy production—especially with regard to fertilisers, agro-chemicals and mechanised traction—had undeniably increased.[21]

In practice, however, limitations with regard to the purchase and storage of paddy have vitiated the effectiveness of the GPS and encouraged enterprising middlemen. Because Multi-Purpose Co-operative Societies — the agents for the purchase of paddy — have not been able to provide storage facilities and because of the inadequacies of purchasing points, the producer has often been compelled to sell his paddy to middlemen, who invariably resold it subsequently at higher prices. Moreover, producers have also been discouraged by the inability of the purchasing co-operative societies to pay ready cash for the paddy delivered.

Apart from the GPS, the introduction of crop insurance has been a significant inducement to the peasant agriculturalist. A pilot paddy crop insurance scheme was begun in 1958 in five paddy-growing districts, and covered about 25,000 acres. In 1962 the scheme was extended to cover 65,000 acres in eleven districts, and 1963 saw further extensions. Today 16 per cent of the total area cultivated with paddy has been covered by crop insurance.[22]

Although crop insurance with paddy has been compulsory, at any rate in those areas to which it has been extended, the low degree of peasant responsiveness bears testimony to the comparative novelty of the idea. For example, it has often been found that — possibly because the tangible benefits of a crop insurance scheme would be apparent to the cultivator only in times of crisis and crop failure — the payment of premia has been regarded as an unnecessary and vexatious taxation measure.[23] In order to overcome prejudice and win the trust of the peasant farmer, the government has worked a number of concessions into the crop insurance scheme. So far there has been no real appreciation of the benefits of crop insurance, and instead there has evidently been the expectation that insurance benefits should be provided by the government without reciprocal obligations on the part of the peasant agriculturalist.

The idea that the peasant should be assisted with credit facilities by means of government-sponsored institutions antedates the GPS as well as crop insurance. Production-oriented agricultural credit took three forms: first, short-term loans to cultivators for the purchase of seeds and fertilisers; secondly, medium-term loans, intended for the purchase of machinery, and thirdly, long-term loans for capital expenditure on storage, transport and rice-milling apparatus. The long-term loans, however, were not made available for the individual farmer directly, but were utilised by the co-operative societies to provide the infrastructural facilities on his behalf. In fact, the co-operatives — whether they be Co-operative Credit Societies or Multi-Purpose Co-operative Societies — have been the agents in the distribution and recovery of loans.[25]

Yet notwithstanding the existence of agricultural credit for a considerable period of time, actual performance has aroused misgivings. Theoretically, the effectiveness of schemes of rural credit of the type that has been in existence in Sri Lanka could be assessed in terms of certain broad criteria: first, the extent to which institutional credit has displaced, or made unnecessary, recourse to non-institutional credit sources usually found in rural communities;

and secondly, the extent to which the interests of the government — as the ultimate source of loans — have been safeguarded. Surveys have shown that many cultivators do not utilise the co-operatives to obtain credit. The inability to repay loans taken from co-operatives, procedural difficulties involved in getting loans and the existence of unpaid loans already taken from co-operatives have been among various reasons given by cultivators in the course of surveys for preferring non-institutional credit sources like the village moneylender to the co-operatives. In many areas it was reported that as many as a third of the cultivators were not even members of co-operative societies because they did not see how they could benefit from membership. Instead, many cultivators preferred to borrow from friends and relatives. This type of informal borrowing was always possible in the village society because of the extended family system, and was not thought of as a strictly commercial transaction. A survey on rural indebtedness in 1969 disclosed that friends and relations were the "most important sources of rural credit".[26]

Above all the government has been perturbed by the high rate of default in the repayment of loans taken from government sources. Whereas the loans granted by the government have increased from Rs. 4,356,000 in 1947 to Rs. 32,307,000 in 1966, the balance outstanding has steadily increased during the same period from Rs. 1,812,000 to Rs. 78,534,000. The high rate of default may be partly attributed to genuine difficulties in repayment but may also be due to an impression prevalent among peasants that somehow it is not necessary to repay government loans. By contrast, as surveys have repeatedly shown, loans borrowed from friends and relatives have been repaid promptly.[27]

Co-operatives have not brought any real pressure on the borrower for repayment of loans — an attitude which strongly contrasts with that of the private moneylender. In case of default the only sanction has been the forfeiture of future borrowing rights. It is, of course, possible that genuine difficulties have prevented peasants from repaying loans to the co-operatives; it has not been uncommon for them to plead crop failures as their principal reason for inability to repay loans. Indeed, it is debatable whether a loan intended and taken strictly for purposes of production could, in the context of smallholdings and subsistence farming, result ultimately in the creation of a marketable surplus over and above the needs of the farmer and his family.

However, even while one may make every allowance for the difficulties of the cultivator, the evidence suggests that default has often been due to his own rather negative attitudes. Having benefited

from a number of welfare measures, the peasant evidently feels
that it is the business of an essentially paternalistic government
to look after his interests. In other words, credit has been viewed
in the light of a further increment in social welfare — a view refurbished by the pledges given from time to time by responsible
politicians to get the state to write off these debts.

Institutional Reforms and the Peasant Agricultural Sector

As elsewhere in Asia, the state has been concerned in Sri Lanka
with bringing about certain reforms in the peasant agricultural
sector to eliminate institutional disincentives to production.
Changes in the tenurial conditions of the peasant have loomed
large in this strategy.

It has traditionally been a common practice among owners of paddy
land in Srī Laṅkā to rent their land to other cultivators in return
for a share of the produce. Over the years, the simple form of renting out the land — commonly described as the *andē* system of tenancy
— has naturally assumed a number of variations. In general, however, under the *andē* system the landlord provides collateral assistance to the cultivator by supplying seed paddy, manures, draught
animals and even the cost of fencing the land, and in return receives
as his share between half and three-quarters of the produce.

Variations in the basic *andē* principle involved have been determined by the demand for land. In areas where landlessness has
been great, the *andē* system has existed replete with certain rather
orthodox conventions which may have been derived from an essentially feudal ethos. Conversely, in the areas where there has been
no great pressure on land resources but where the owner of the land
has found it difficult to have his land cultivated — especially because
of difficulties in finding labour — share-cropping has existed shorn
of the extraneous attributes of orthodoxy, and the *andēkāraya* or
share-cropper has been able to insist on collateral assistance from
the landlord and to restrict the latter's demands to a strict half of
the crop.

The *andē* system of share-cropping has survived for a number
of reasons. Both the landlord and the tenant cultivator have had a
substantial stake in its perpetuation. Far from being a catalyst of
change, modernisation has contributed in some ways to the perpetuation of the *andē* system particularly from the point of view of
the needs of the land owing class. The spread of non-agricultural
vocations as part of the process of economic modernisation after
the beginning of the nineteenth century — like trade, mercantile
and government employment as well as professional openings —
affected the rural land owing class — who, however, were reluctant

to sever ownership and all connection with their lands, despite their preference for the new spheres of employment. Consequently, they resorted to the *andē* system which at least secured for them a share of the produce of the land, as well as continued enjoyment of the privilege of ownership.

On the other hand, from the point of view of the cultivator who has had no land of his own to cultivate or any means of doing so without getting into debt, to become a share-cropper has been the sole means of economic survival, in spite of the insecurity of tenure. In the wet zone, particularly, population pressures have allowed little land to become available for cultivation, and the landlords have often felt that they were conferring a great boon on the *andē-kāraya* or share-cropper. Moreover, quite apart from mutual economic necessity in the traditional *milieu* of the village, the landlord and tenant were not viewed as mutually antagonistic classes — as middle-class reformist legislators have viewed the relationship — but as two groups within rural society, often bound by ties of kinship. For example, even the landowner who had ample means as well as the opportunities of cultivating his own lands often felt that he should give some of his land in *andē* either to kinsmen or to other villagers because such behaviour was traditionally expected of him.[28]

However, with the enactment of the Paddy Lands Act in 1958, an attempt was made to regulate the traditional relations between landlord and the cultivator tenant. Typically, an official document of the time referred to the "condition of impecunious servitude and insecurity" of the tenant, as well as to the "interference and exploitation" by the landlord to which he was subject.[29] As for security of tenure, the Paddy Lands Act declared that tenancy rights were to be permanent, transferable and heritable. The rents which the tenant had to pay the landlord varied from district to district according to the Act. The Act's rent provisions were based on the principle of a fixed rent which did not change with the whims and fancies of the landlord, but at the same time provided incentive to the cultivator to produce more. Thus every bushel of paddy which the cultivator produced in excess of the maximum payable rent was legally his.

However, because of certain shortcomings in the law as well as official lethargy in implementing it, events soon demonstrated that under the Paddy Lands Act the tenant cultivator had neither security of tenure nor the advantage of fixed rents. On the contrary, evictions became common: in 1958-67 the number of evictions complained of by tenants who had attempted to pay the legally stipulated rent amounted to 23,000. In the next five years there were

12,400 recorded instances of evictions. Thus notwithstanding the Paddy Lands Act the old traditional rent of half the share of the produce was generally being paid, and payment of rent in general according to the Act was more the exception than the rule.[30]

In a sense this might have been foreseen. To some extent, no doubt, delays in dealing with complaints as well as the questionable success achieved in restoring tenure to cultivators who had been evicted produced a sense of frustration and helplessness among the tenant cultivators. More significantly, the tenant cultivator depended on the landlord not only for the land he cultivated — which was, after all, a means of livelihood in a context of landlessness — but, in the absence of acceptable alternative sources of income and of savings, to provide operating capital, obtain credit and even give employment to members of his family.[31]

Moreover, in the village context tenant cultivators as such have predominantly been friends, relatives or neighbours of their landlords. Recent research conducted by the Agrarian Research and Training Institute in the Kandy and Hambantota districts has brought out the basically informal and personal nature of the relationships. In the Hambantota district 84 per cent of the landowners who gave out land on *andē* were friends, relatives or neighbours of tenants, and in the Kandy district the percentage was 82. This may well account for the impression prevailing among tenant cultivators in both districts that they enjoy permanent tenancy rights, although in fact they dare not resort to paying the rents as prescribed by the Paddy Lands Act. In short the arrangements between landlords and their tenants have been aptly described as being of a "non-business type often arising out of social obligations on the part of better-off relations or neighbours towards their poorer ones".[32]

Be that as it may, if the strict legal position alone is considered it is evident that notwithstanding the Paddy Lands Act, relations between landlord and tenant in Srī Laṅkā remain unsettled. Indeed, in spite of radical reforms which have been rapidly introduced in other directions, the official mind has tended to think that "no acute tenurial problems seriously hamper the drive towards self-sufficiency", and that in any case what is more urgently required is to provide the average cultivator with infrastructural facilities such as credit, fertilisers and marketing opportunities. Because of this viewpoint, as well as an unwillingness to clash with vested interests, there has been no attempt to solve the tenurial problem by the radical remedy of expropriating paddy lands and by following a "land to the tiller" policy. Consequently even the Land Reform Act of 1972 — which expropriated all privately owned agricultural land over 50 acres in extent, other than lands coming within certain categories, partly for redistribution among the landless—exempted paddy land that was less than 25 acres in extent, thereby virtually preserving the *status quo* in the traditional peasant agricultural sector.[33]

Indeed, it may be asked, from a strictly economic point of view, whether the existing tenant-landlord relations, however stable sociologically, have not been a substantial disincentive to production. Recent researches have shown—especially in the Kandy district—that the landlord often does not provide the tenant cultivator with the necessary collateral assistance in the form of seed, draught animals, fertiliser and agro-chemicals, and that although the use of such inputs has not been entirely unknown among tenants, as a rule tenant cultivators use fewer inputs than owner cultivators. More fundamentally, there can be no denying that the obligation upon the tenant to pay as much as half his produce to the landlord could hardly be an incentive to produce more, particularly if the rents form a substantial portion of the expenses.[34]

A factor which has clearly been instrumental in perpetuating the *andē* system of landlord-tenant relations has been landlessness. Apart from the colonisation schemes in the dry zone, the state has endeavoured until recent time to tackle the problem largely in terms of village expansion schemes. It has been the practice to acquire "marginal" lands from estates for village expansion, the land being distributed among villagers. Since 1936 as many as 600,000 such lands have been alienated in this manner.[35]

We may consider next the Land Reform Act of 1972. Apart from imposing a ceiling of 50 acres on privately-owned land, part of the rationale of the Land Reform Act has been the acquisition of lands in excess of the ceiling and distribution among the landless. However, because certain categories of land were exempted from the ceiling—notably land owned by public companies and paddy lands under 25 acres in extent—a considerable amount of land which would otherwise have been made available for distribution among the landless has not come within the purview of the Land Reform Act. The total extent of land acquired by the Land Reform Commission amounted to 559,377 acres made up as shown on p. 252.

Apart from waste and uncultivated land which amounts to very nearly a third of the acreage vested, tea, rubber and coconut lands constituted nearly 60 per cent of the total extent of land acquired under the Act. Paddy land acquired constitutes a very insignificant proportion as very little of it was affected by the ceiling of 25 acres.

The pattern of distribution of the lands acquired under Land Reform—there is, however, no finality in this as yet, and there could be further changes—shows that a little over half (52 per cent) has

Type	Extent available in acres	Percentage of total land vested
Jungle, Patna and uncultivated land	182,257	32.6%
Tea	135,760	24.3%
Coconut	115,350	20.6%
Rubber	82,944	14.8%
Paddy	16,270	2.9%
Mixed Crops	14,513	2.6%
Cardamom	7,699	1.4%
Chena	1,861	0.3%
Abandoned tea and rubber lands	1,701	0.3%
Cinnamon and cocoa	1,022	0.2%

been given over to District Land Reform Authorities and the Land Commissioner for development. Another 35 per cent of the total area vested has been alienated to various co-operative agencies like the Up-country Co-operative Estates Development Board (*Usawasama*), multi-purpose co-operative societies, co-operative settlements, and special co-operative organizations. The State Planations Corporation which has been given many of the larger estates has so far received only 6 per cent of the total land acquired. The land so far alienated to individuals amounts to only 2 per cent of the total.

Finally, there is the question of fragmentation of land. Fragmentation of peasant holdings, closely linked with the problem of landlessness, has been an area in which the poverty and inadequacy of institutional solutions has been made most evident. Over the years, population increase, landlessness and inheritance laws have combined to bring about a situation in which the peasant holdings have long ceased to be viable operational units. In the strictly traditional agrarian set-up, the adverse effects of distributing the land equally among several sons were largely mitigated by the fact that to all intents and purposes the land was cultivated collectively among the co-owners. With the spread of concepts of individual property ownership rights, as well as with the creation of institutional devices that went with the maintenance of such rights, the adverse effects of fragmentation have been clearly revealed.[37]

In summing up agricultural developments in the period 1948-74, one is impressed by the general sameness of agricultural strategies pursued by successive governments: the *modus operandi* has consisted of encouraging the peasant cultivator to adopt less traditional and a more productive technology, the maximisation of institutional inducements to encourage production, and the removal of institutional obstacles which over the years have acted as a disincentive to the average cultivator. More recently, however, agricultural policies have also reflected a curious and puzzling amalgam of radicalism on the one hand and unwillingness to change the *status quo* on the other hand.

The genuinely novel element in recent agricultural policies has been the reluctance to develop the traditional agricultural sector purely on the conventional lines of creating a class of land-owning peasants. More perceptibly, the emphasis has been on the development of the traditional agricultural sector on the collective or corporate principle of ownership by the establishment of co-operative settlements and co-operative estate development boards. The strategy no doubt has been in ideological accord with the prevailing socialist sentiments, the ideals of collective ownership, and above all, basic egalitarianism. It is conceivable, however, that the prevailing orientation in agricultural policy would in time give the state a measure of control over the traditionally independent peasant agricultural sector.

REFERENCES

1. *Census of Agriculture 1962*, Vol. II, Colombo (1966). Also S. Selvanayagam, 'Agricultural Development in Ceylon: a study in the problems of the small farmers', in *The Journal of the National Agricultural Society of Ceylon*, Vol. 6 (1969), pp. 30 ff.
2. ibid.
3. *The Agrarian situation relating to paddy cultivation in five selected districts of Sri Lanka, Part 2, Kandy District*. Research Studies Series of the Agrarian Research Training Institute (hereafter, ARTI), Colombo (1974), p. 1.
4. P. Richard and E. Stoutjesdifte, *Agriculture in Ceylon until 1975*, Paris (1970), p. 45.
5. ibid.
6. Hishashi Nakamura, *The Rural Economy in the Wet Zone of Ceylon*, Institute of Asian Economic Affairs, Japan, n.d. B. H. Farmer, *Pioneer Peasant Colonization in Ceylon*, London (1957). P. C. Bansil, *Ceylon Agriculture a perspective*, Delhi (1971). V. K. Samaraweera, *'Land Policy and Peasant Colonization, 1914-1948'* Part IV, Chapter V, in K. M. de Silva (ed.), *History of Ceylon*, Vol. III, pp. 446-60.
7. The IBRD mission in 1952 pointed out that expenditure on such a lavish scale was something which the government could ill afford and evidently encouraged settlers to believe that it was obligatory on the part of the government to provide such facilities.
8. *Census of Agriculture 1962*, Vol. I, p. 29.
9. S. Narayanaswamy, 'New Approaches to settlements in Sri Lanka', Ceylon Studies Seminar, Peradeniya (1974).

10. K. Izumi and A. S. Ranatunga, *Environmental and Social Constraints on Paddy Production under existing conditions*, ARTI, Colombo (1974), pp. 1 ff. K. Izumi and A. S. Ranatunga, *Cost of Production of Paddy, Maha 1972-73*, ARTI Colombo (1974), p. vi, pp. 3 and 9. A. Akthar Kahn, *Small Farmer Credit*, ARTI Colombo (1974), p. 51. *Agrarian Situation . . . Kandy District*, ARTI, op. cit., pp. 74 ff. Also p. 79. *Agrarian Situation relating to Paddy Cultivation in Five Selected Districts of Sri Lanka* (Part I, Hambantota District), ARTI, p. x, also pp. 6 ff.

11. Nakamura, op. cit., p. 18. Also *Report on the Survey on Paddy Production, Central Bank.*, pp. 48 ff.

12. *Census of Agriculture*, 1962, Part III, pp. 37 ff. *Cost of Production of Paddy . . .*, Izumi and Ranatunga, op. cit., p. 13 ff. *Small Farmer Credit*, op. cit., p. 51. *Agrarian Situation relating to Paddy. . . .* (Hambantota), op. cit., p. xii. Also p. xviii.

13. Nakamura, op. cit., p. 19. *Census of Agriculture*, 1962, Vol. II, op. cit., pp. 39 ff. *Agrarian Situation . . . Hambantota*, op. cit. p. xiii. Also p. xviii.

14. *Cost of Production Paddy Survey*, Central Bank, op. cit., pp. 23 ff. Also Nakamura, op. cit., p. 17.

15. *Census of Agriculture*, 1962, Vol. III, op. cit., p. 36. *Cost of Production Paddy . . .*, Izumi and Ranatunga, op. cit., p. 3. *The Agrarian Situation . . . Hambantota District*, op. cit., p. xviii.

16. *Cost of Production of Paddy*, Izumi and Ranatunga, op. cit., p. 4.

17. Barbara Harris, "The Economics and spatial relations of traction and its implications for rural indebtedness in Hambantota District of Sri Lanka", Ceylon Studies Seminar, Peradeniya (1974). *Cost of Paddy Production Survey*, Central Bank, op. cit., pp. 18 ff. and 38 ff. *Census of Agriculture* (1962), Vol. III, op. cit., p. 33.

18. *The Agrarian Situation . . . Hambantota District*, op. cit., p. x. also pp. 5 ff. and p. 69. *The Agrarian Situation . . . Kandy District*, op. cit., pp. 10 ff. Also p. 73.

19. Barbara Harris, op. cit., p. 11.

20. K. Sunderalingam, 'Transport and Marketing in Sri Lanka with special reference to Agriculture', Ceylon Studies Seminar, Peradeniya (1974).

21. Nimal Sanderatne, "Agricultural Insurance in Peasant Agriculture: Sri Lanka's experience 1958-1973", Ceylon Studies Seminar, Peradeniya (1974), p. 5.

22. ibid.

23. ibid.

24. ibid.

25. R. G. G. O. Gunasekera, 'Institutional Credit to the Peasant Sector through Co-operatives', Ceylon Studies Seminar, Peradeniya (1974).

26. *The Agrarian Situation . . . Kandy District*, op. cit., pp. 45 ff. *The Agrarian Situation . . . Hambantota District, op. cit., pp. xi ff. Also pp. 41 ff. Nakamura, op. cit., pp. 59 ff Small Farmer Credit*, op. cit., p. 2, pp. 14 ff, pp. 29 ff and 56 ff.

27. Gunasekera, op. cit.

28. *The Agrarian Situation . . . Kandy District*, op. cit., pp. 36 ff. *The Agrarian Situation . . . Hambantota District*, op. cit., pp. 27 ff.

29. ibid.

30. ibid.
31. *The Agrarian Situation* . . . *Hambantota District*, pp. 30 ff. *The Agrarian Situation... Kandy District*, pp. 36 ff. Sanderatne, op. cit., pp. 9 ff. K. Izumi, *The Productivity of Land and the Economic Nature of Peasant Rent in the Paddy Sector of Sri Lanka*, p. 11.
32. ibid.
33. Sanderatne, op. cit., According to the most recent statistics only 1.38 per cent of the paddy holdings are 25 acres or more in extent; in all this amounts to around 11.5 per cent of the total acreage.
34. Izumi and Ranatunga, "*Environmental and Social Constraints*", op. cit., pp. 7 ff.
35. *Census of Agriculture* (1962), Vol. I, op. cit., pp. 37 ff. Also Sanderatne, 'Leading issues on Land Reform', op. cit., pp. 37 ff.
36. Sanderatne, op. cit., pp. 21 ff.
37. P. Ganewatte, *Fragmentation of Paddy Land*, ARTI Colombo (1974).

11

STATISTICAL APPENDIX

Compiled by N. Balakrishnan and H. M. Gunasekera

Table 1. INDUSTRIAL ORIGIN OF GROSS NATIONAL
(millions of rupees at constant factor cost prices)

Sector	1953a	%	1963b	%
Agriculture, Forestry, Hunting and Fishing	2,275.0	49.92	2,846.0	41.25
Mining and Quarrying	4.1	0.08	29.5	0.43
Manufacturing	216.1	4.74	853.0	12.36
Construction	392.2	8.6	271.8	3.94
Electricity, Gas, Water, and Sanitary Services	24.0	0.52	11.4	0.16
Transport, Storage and Communications	222.6	4.9	591.8	8.58
Wholesale and Retail Trade	403.4	8.84	875.1	12.68
Banking, Insurance and Real Estate	18.2	0.4	67.4	0.97
Ownership of Dwellings	316.6	6.96	227.2	3.29
Public Administration and Defence	257.8	5.66	365.1	5.29
Services	464.8	10.2	812.3	11.77
Gross Domestic Product	4,594.8	100.83	6,950.6	100.74
Net Factor Income from abroad	−37.8	−0.83	−50.9	−0.74
Gross National Product	4,557.0	100.00	6,899.7	100.00

(a) At 1953 factor cost prices. (b) At 1959 factor cost prices.
Sources: Central Bank of Ceylon, *Annual Reports.* D. R. Snodgrass,
Ceylon: An Export Economy in Transition, Homewood, Ill. (1966).

PRODUCT FOR SELECTED YEARS

1971b	%	1974b	%	% increase 1963-74
3,375.0	34.51	3,558.3	33.16	25.0
66.6	0.69	190.9	1.79	547.1
1,378.9	14.10	1,359.4	12.69	59.3
549.5	5.62	552.8	5.15	103.3
28.6	0.3	31.5	0.29	176.3
920.3	9.4	1,053.7	9.82	78.0
1,315.7	13.46	1,449.8	13.51	65.6
128.5	1.32	164.9	1.54	144.6
307.4	3.4	344.4	3.21	51.5
488.1	5.0	609.1	5.68	66.8
1,297.0	13.26	1,440.6	13.42	77.3
9,855.6	100.78	10,755.4	100.23	54.7
−76.4	−0.78	−24.9	−0.23	
9,779.2	100.00	10,730.5	100.00	55.5

Table 2. SECTORAL DISTRIBUTION OF GAINFULLY EMPLOYED PERSONS (CENSUS YEARS 1946-71)

Sector	1946 Total employed	1946 % of total	1953 Total employed	1953 % of total	1963 Total employed	1963 % of total	1971 Total employed	1971 % of total
Agriculture, Forestry, hunting and fishing	1,381,612	52.2	1,584,141	52.0	1,693,430	52.9	1,824,000	50.4
Mining and Quarrying	9,086	0.4	13,790	0.4	10,360	0.3	15,300	0.4
Manufacturing	259,799	9.8	303,038	10.1	312,900	9.8	347,400	9.6
Construction	—	—	56,686	1.9	86,030	2.6	112,400	3.1
Electricity, Gas, Water and Sanitary Services	—	—	5,280	—	10,470	—	9,400	0.3
Commerce, Banking and Finance	205,065	7.7	246,234	8.2	287,810	9.0	371,700	10.2
Transport, Storage and Communications	93,969	3.5	104,292	3.5	133,290	4.1	155,300	4.3
Services	382,665	15.9	482,073	16.3	495,270	15.8	488,100	13.5
Activities not adequately described	279,329	10.5	197,815	6.6	170,170	5.3	298,300	8.2
	2,611,524	100.0	2,993,341	100.0	3,199,730	100.0	3,622,000	100.0

Table 3. GOVERNMENT FINANCE: SELECTED DATA

(Rs. million)

		1954/5	1958/9	1964/5	1967/8	1970/1
(A)	Revenue	1,159	1,330	1,816	2,156	2,815
	% of GNP	21.6	22.5	24.2	21.8	23.8
(B)	Expenditure	1,031	1,744	2,247	2,871	3,899
	% of GNP	18.9	29.6	30.0	29.0	32.9
(C)	Net Cash Deficit/ Surplus	128	−414	−431	−715	−1084
(D)	Social Welfare Expenditure of which:—	350	582	1011	1269	1464
	Education	153	255	355	410	532
	Health	110	149	167	221	266
	Food Subsidy	36	146	447	579	614
	D as % of Total Expenditure	33.9	33.3	44.9	44.2	37.5
	D as % of GNP	6.4	9.8	13.5	12.8	12.4

		1960	1962	1964	1966	1968	1970	1972
(E)	Public Debt (net):	1,913	2,689	3,436	4,268	5,689	7,237	9,448
	Internal Debt	1,690	2,430	3,063	3,747	4,651	5,686	7,096
	External Debt	223	259	373	521	1,038	1,551	2,352

Source: Central Bank of Ceylon, *Annual Reports.*

Notes: (i) Government Expenditure and Revenue refer to fiscal years (October-September). Expenditure includes all items that enter into the computation of the net cash deficit/surplus; excludes contributions to public debt sinking funds and direct repayments of public debt from revenue and special payments to international financial organisations as well as certain extrabudgetary items.

(ii) GNP data used — which are at current factor cost prices — refer to calendar years (1955, 1959, 1965, 1968 and 1971).

(iii) Public Debt outstanding at end of period — September for all years and December for 1972, which covers a period of 15 months from October 1971 to December 1972. External debt figures have been adjusted to take into account the devaluation of 1967.

(iv) Social welfare expenditure includes education, health, housing and other special welfare services as well as food subsidy.

Table 4. MERCHANDISE EXPORTS, IMPORTS, AND TERMS OF

Year	EXPORTS			
	f.o.b. value		*Quan-tity index*	*Price index*
	Rs. million	*SDR million*		
1950	1,412	300	75	121
1951	1,783	374	76	146
1952	1,410	299	77	113
1953	1,495	314	79	115
1954	1,724	362	82	128
1955	1,893	400	86	134
1956	1,772	372	81	125
1957	1,669	351	79	120
1958	1,624	341	84	118
1959	1,773	372	82	122
1960	1,796	377	87	122
1961	1,706	360	90	112
1962	1,763	370	97	109
1963	1,708	359	93	109
1964	1,767	371	102	111
1965	1,909	400	105	113
1966	1,674	352	96	107
1967	1,650	347	100	100
1968	1,976	352	103	117
1969	1,909	322	98	117
1970	2,016	342	102	118
1971	1,931	327	99	117
1972	1,898	296	97	118
1973	2,617	343	98	137
1974	3,472	431	85	213

Source: Central Bank of Ceylon, *Annual Reports.*
For the computation of SDR values, the
following conversion rates were used:

	SDR	Rs.
1950-67	1	— 4.76
1968-71	1	— 4.95
1972-	1	— 6.78
1973	1	— 7.63
1974	1	— 8.05 (provisional)

TRADE 1950-74 (*Indices 1967 = 100*)

	IMPORTS			Terms of Trade
c.i.f. value		*Quan-*		
Rs.	*SDR*	*tity*	*Price*	
million	*million*	*index*	*index*	*Index*
1,173	246	82	73	165
1,545	324	93	93	157
1,707	360	93	93	122
1,633	344	94	93	125
1,384	295	87	86	149
1,478	311	98	83	162
1,576	331	109	83	151
1,764	370	116	88	136
1,713	360	118	81	145
1,958	411	136	83	148
2,006	421	133	83	148
1,794	377	107	82	136
1,906	400	108	77	142
1,869	393	93	85	129
1,960	411	114	105	105
1,922	403	86	100	112
2,018	423	118	98	109
1,985	416	100	100	100
2,356	475	101	126	93
2,655	536	108	134	88
2,332	471	102	140	84
2,218	448	90	150	78
2,153	318	88	158	75
2,644	347	79	209	65
4,603	572	56	370	58

Table 5. SRI LANKA'S EXTERNAL RESOURCES GAP (1956-74)

	1956	1957	1958	1959	1960
Total foreign exchange earnings (goods and services)	2,086	1,995	1,956	2,056	2,050
Total import payments (goods and services)	2,032	2,217	2,164	2,309	2,323
Total capital payments	99	92	29	75	36
Total current and capital payments	2,131	2,309	2,193	2,384	2,359
External resource gap	−45	−314	−237	−328	−309
Methods of Financing the Gap					
Project aid	6	23	22	16	20
Commodity aid	—	—	—	—	—
Grants	28	27	55	44	53
Private Capital	40	21	25	18	14
Change in bilateral trade balances	—	—	—	—	—
Short term credits	—	—	55	48	—
Suppliers Credit	—	—	—	—	—
Bank Borrowings	—	—	—	—	—
IMF drawings	—	—	—	—	—
Oil facility drawings	—	—	—	—	—
Change in external assets (increase is indicated by a minus sign and decrease by a plus sign)	−25	236	60	199	193
Other loans and lines of credit	—	—	—	—	—
Special Drawings Rights	—	—	—	—	—
Other Errors/Ommissions	−3	+7	−26	+3	+30
Total	+45	+314	+237	+328	+309

Source: Central Bank of Ceylon, *Annual Reports.*

AND METHODS OF FINANCING (*Rs. million*)

1961	1962	1963	1964	1965	1966	1967	1968	1969
1,937	1,992	1,924	1,955	2,116	1,885	1,866	2,231	2,178
2,072	2,173	2,135	2,192	2,121	2,237	2,200	2,615	3,021
37	12	17	86	121	189	80	265	392
2,109	2,185	2,152	2,278	2,242	2,426	2,280	2,880	3,413
−172	−193	−228	−323	−126	−541	−414	−649	−1235
19	40	82	78	77	76	34	40	89
−	−	−	−	−	107	178	255	272
41	37	44	76	64	63	46	28	46
19	10	9	7	2	6	17	9	9
16	−14	39	19	−69	30	80	42	18
28	7	8	39	26	2	7	84	185
−	−	−	−	−	−	−	−	176
−	−	−	−	−	−	57	−	227
54	54	−	−	110	144	123	213	77
−	−	−	−	−	−	−	−	−
10	28	42	111	−89	122	−131	−14	86
−	−	−	−	−	−	−	−	−
−	−	−	−	−	−	−	−	−
−20	+31	+3	−6	−6	−18	−12	−22	+18
+172	+193	+228	+323	+126	+541	+414	+649	+1235

Table 5. SRI LANKA'S EXTERNAL RESOURCES GAP (1956-74)
AND METHODS OF FINANCING (_Rs. million_) _(Continued)_

	1970	1971	1972	1973	1974[a]
Total Foreign exchange earnings (goods and services)	2,049	2,263	2,230	2,783	3,875
Total import payments (goods and services)	2,474	2,584	2,526	3,024	5,027
Total capital payments	656	1051	995	1,282	1,364
Total current and capital payments	3,130	3,635	3,521	4,306	6,391
External resource gap	−1,081	−1,372	−1,291	−1,523	−2.516
Methods of Financing the Gap					
Project aid	35	86	98	125	103
Commodity aid	263	260	304	210	328
Grants	75	105	100	83	254
Private Capital	8	25	10	6	12
Change in bilateral trade balances	−75	−57	−11	35	167
Short term credits	434	658	593	781	836
Suppliers Credit	85	58	52	240	429
Bank Borrowings	123	—	12	—	—
IMF drawings	57	83	163	137	106
Oil facility drawings	—	—	—	—	271
Change in external assets (increase is indicated by a minus sign and decrease by a plus sign)	−25	−96	−229	−125	−38
Other loans and lines of credit	33	—	13	14	32
Special Drawings Rights	78	63	62	—	—
Other Errors/Ommissions	−29	+6	+17	+17	+16
Total	+1081	+1372	+1291	+1523	+2516

[a]Provisional

Table 6. AREA AND YIELD OF PADDY

		Area Sown (acres)	Area Harvested (acres)	Production (thousand bushels)	Yield per acre (in bushels)
1964/5	Mahā	984,576	795,696	23,070	34.1
	Yala	470,773	446,935	13,182	34.7
1965/6	Mahā	1,050,066	1,007,070	30,739	35.9
	Yala	566,817	505,241	15,048	35.0
1966/7	Mahā	1,053,902	1,006,408	34,900	40.8
	Yala	582,529	560,559	20,017	42.0
1967/8	Mahā	1,146,958	1,077,853	43,509	47.5
	Yala	582,511	556,285	21,084	44.6
1968/9	Mahā	1,182,001	1,078,540	46,962	51.2
	Yala	527,151	460,885	18,898	48.2
1969/70	Mahā	1,191,473	1,115,225	49,492	52.3
	Yala	684,084	660,672	27,955	49.7
1970/1	Mahā	1,147,458	1,088,966	41,560	44.9
	Yala	646,153	625,379	25,335	47.7
1971/2	Mahā	1,186,038	1,035,491	42,327	48.1
	Yala	608,534	543,438	20,574	44.5

Source: *Statistical Pocket Book of Srī Laṅkā, 1973,* Dept, of Census and Statistics.
Mahā season: Crop sown from July to November (in Badulla and Monaragala, July to December).
Yala season: Crop sown from February to June (in Badulla and Monaragala, January to June).

Table 7. VOLUME INDEX OF AGRICULTURAL PRODUCTION
(base year 1962=100)

	1963	1964	1965	1966	1967	1968	1969	1970	1971
Tea	103.7	103.1	107.7	104.9	104.2	106.1	103.7	100.2	100.7
Rubber	101.1	107.2	113.8	125.9	137.7	142.9	144.9	152.9	135.9
Coconut	105.3	119.8	96.5	100.8	83.4	90.3	83.6	97.3	104.3
Paddy	112.2	105.2	75.6	96.2	114.4	137.4	137.2	161.3	139.3
Highland crops	120.6	130.3	114.9	118.7	132.4	151.2	141.6	157.2	153.4
Minor Export crops	104.2	95.5	78.5	96.1	70.1	106.3	111.6	102.5	104.5
Livestock and Livestock Products	114.0	120.9	108.9	97.4	125.9	129.4	163.1	177.7	182.0
Overall Index	104.2	109.8	99.6	103.0	109.4	117.2	120.6	129.2	125.9

Source: Revision of Volume Index of Agricultural Production, Dept. of Census and Statistics, Srī Laṅkā (1973).

Table 8. PATTERN OF OWNERSHIP:PLANTATION AGRICULTURE*

Type of Ownership	Tea (1972)		Rubber (1969)		Coconut (1952)†	
	Acreage	% of Acreage	Acreage	% of Acreage	Acreage	% of Acreage
Sterling companies (i.e. registered in U.K.)	158,147	26.46	80,335	11.90	6,827	2.87
Rupee companies (i.e. registered in Sri Laṅkā)	150,889	25.25	89,350	13.30	17,680	7.42
Non-Sri Laṅkān individuals and Partnerships	10,859	1.82	15,772	2.30	11,552	4.84
Srī-Laṅkān individuals and partnerships	260,135	43.53	488,508	72.50	197,670	82.90
Srī-Laṅkāns and Non-Sri Lankans jointly	4,085	0.68	—	—	—	—
Stated owned	13,530	2.26	—	—	2,015	0.85
Trusts	—	—	—	—	2,680	1.12
Total	597,645	100.00	673,965	100.00	238,420	100.00

Sources: Ferguson's Ceylon Directory (1973-4). Ministry of Plantation Industries, National Rubber Statistics of Srī Laṅkā, No. 1, 1973, p. 6, Table 3. Department of Census and Statistics, Census of Agriculture 1952.

*All public company estates, foreign as well as local, were nationalised under the Land Reform (Amendment) Act, 1975.
†This data refers only to coconut cultivation on estates, which in 1952 constituted approximately 30 per cent of the total acreage under coconut. (The 1952 Census of agriculture covered only 70 per cent of the total acreage under estates).

The total acreage under coconut given in the 1962 Census of agriculture amounted to 1,152,428 – which has changed very little over the years. It is estimated that of this, roughly two-thirds consist of small holdings – of 20 acres and below – almost all of which is under local ownership.

Table 9. COST OF LIVING INDEX — COLOMBO TOWN (1952 = 100)

	All items	Food	Clothing	Fuel and Light
Weights:	100.0	61.9	9.4	4.3
1960	103.5	100.8	95.1	102.7
1961	104.8	109.8	103.9	104.4
1962	106.3	100.9	108.2	105.6
1963	108.8	103.0	118.2	103.0
1964	112.2	106.4	127.2	103.2
1965	112.5	107.3	126.8	100.7
1966	112.3	109.1	117.0	95.9
1967	114.8	112.7	116.7	96.5
1968	121.5	121.2	120.1	103.2
1969	130.5	127.9	130.9	124.9
1970	138.2	136.6	137.3	136.1
1971	141.9	139.1	145.0	140.8
1972	150.8	147.5	163.4	145.4
1973	165.4	164.8	186.4	164.4
1974	185.8	189.7	204.6	221.0

Source: Central Bank of Ceylon, Annual Report (1974).

Note: The Cost of Living Index, the only available official price index, is inadequate to measure the extent of changes in the general level of prices in Srī Laṅkā. It is limited in coverage and the weighting is based on an out-of-date consumption expenditure pattern of the Colombo working class, which has not been revised since 1952. The Index also gives relatively greater weightage to items whose prices are either subsidised or controlled.

Rent	Miscel-laneous	Domestic Group	Import Group	Export Group
5.7	18.7	60	35	5
101.5	117.5	108.9	93.7	138.4
101.5	122.8	112.3	94.6	119.1
101.5	124.9	113.9	96.7	113.8
101.5	126.6	113.4	102.5	117.7
101.5	129.3	116.7	106.6	115.3
108.4	128.3	116.4	106.4	127.2
109.4	127.3	116.8	105.4	127.6
109.8	128.9	117.1	111.2	123.9
109.8	133.6	123.2	117.3	142.4
109.8	147.1	134.3	123.5	148.2
109.8	153.2	142.9	129.3	157.3
109.8	159.5	148.9	129.7	157.9
109.8	169.4	161.6	136.1	140.6
109.8	170.0	167.8	162.5	171.6
109.8	178.3	176.1	195.7	251.4

Table 10. MANUFACTURING INDUSTRY: FOREIGN PRIVATE
LIABILITIES AS AT 1967 BY COUNTRY OF INVESTOR AND
INDUSTRIAL CATEGORY *(Rs. Thousand)*

	Country of Investor					
Industrial Category	*U. K.*	*U.S.A.*	*Japan*	*India*	*West Germany*	*Others*
Food, Beverages, tabacco	72,320	1,245	1,022	—	5,228	335
Textiles	—	—	2,285	—	—	—
Chemicals	41,831	1,062	—	—	—	1,571
Leather/rubber	—	—	1,286	—	—	5,347
Non-Metallic mineral products	6,543	—	—	—	—	—
Base metals	1,430	98	—	220	—	534
Non-electrical machinery	58,745	1,343	—	742	—	—
Electrical machinery	1,016	—	1,401	—	—	—
Total	181,885	3,748	5,994	962	5,228	7,787
Percentage	88.5	1.8	2.9	0.5	2.5	3.8

Source: L.E.N. Fernando, Senior Economist, Central Bank of Ceylon.

Table 11.

GROSS DOMESTIC CAPITAL FORMATION AT CURRENT
MARKET PRICES
(Rs. million)

Year	Gross domestic capital formation	Private sector and public corporations	Government and public enterprises	Gross domestic capital formation as % of GNP at market prices
1960	977.7	675.0	302.7	14.60
1961	1,101.5	706.9	394.6	16.44
1962	1,080.4	677.0	403.4	15.44
1963	1,160.3	771.6	388.7	15.93
1964	1,113.1	777.2	335.9	14.31
1965	1,013.1	609.7	403.5	12.64
1966	1,195.1	841.8	353.3	14.34
1967	1,377.0	931.2	445.8	15.26
1968	1,699.2	1,168.2	530.9	16.12
1969	2,253.2	1,747.9	505.3	19.38
1970	2,554.9	1,769.8	785.1	20.16
1971	2,249.2	1,660.8	588.4	17.61
1972	2,117.6	1,776.0	341.6	15.51
1973	2,629.6	1,952.4	677.2	15.63
1974	3,139.7	2,268.3	871.4	14.77

Source: Central Bank of Ceylon, *Annual Reports.*

SOME SOCIAL WELFARE INDICATORS

Table 12 A. PERCENTAGE DISTRIBUTION OF POPULATION BY
EDUCATION

Education	1953[a]	1963[a]	1969/70[b]
No Schooling	41.6	36.6	17.5
Primary	46.8	39.3	44.6
Secondary	9.8	19.6	30.4
Passed GCE/SSC	0.9	3.4	6.6
Higher and Technical	0.9	1.1	0.9
	100.0	100.0	100.0

(a) *Survey of Ceylon's Consumer Finances, 1963,* Central Bank of Ceylon,
(Table 12, p. 35). (b) *Socio-Economic Survey 1969/70.*
Source: Dept. of Census and Statistics (Table 7, p. 10).

Table 12B. INCOME DISTRIBUTION OF SRI LANKA:
PERCENTAGE OF TOTAL INCOME RECEIVED BY EACH TENTH
OF INCOME RECEIVERS.

Decile	*Percentage of total income received*		
	1953	1963	1973
Highest tenth	42.49	39.24	29.98
Second tenth	14.16	16.01	15.91
Third tenth	10.39	11.46	12.65
Fourth tenth	7.94	8.98	10.56
Fifth tenth	6.31	6.82	8.75
Sixth tenth	5.71	5.55	7.10
Seventh tenth	4.37	4.57	5.70
Eighth tenth	3.56	3.56	4.38
Ninth tenth	3.56	2.70	3.17
Lowest tenth	1.51	1.17	1.80
Gini concentration ratio	0.50	0.49	0.41

Source: The Central Bank of Ceylon, *Survey of Srī Laṅkā's Consumer
Finances,* 1973.

Table 12 C.

INCOME DISTRIBUTION OF SRĪ LAŇKĀ BY
RECEIVING/SPENDING UNITS 1953-73

Income groups	1953		1973	
	% of units	% of total income received	% of units	% of total income received
Below 100	42.1	15.6	8.3	1.7
100 — 200	38.5	31.2	35.3	13.7
200 — 400	15.1	23.8	37.2	41.3
400 — 600	2.1	6.3	11.4	19.7
600 — 800	0.8	3.0	4.3	8.6
800 — 1,000	0.5	2.7	1.7	4.7
1,000 and over	0.9	17.4	1.8	10.4

Notes:

(a) Income is calculated on a monthly basis at current prices
(b) Average size of unit: 1953=5.0. 1969/70=5.8
(c) Number of income receivers per unit 1953=1.6. 1969/70=1.7

Sources: Central Bank of Ceylon, *Consumer Finance Survey 1953, and 1973.*

Table 12 D.
GOVERNMENT MEDICAL INSTITUTIONS AND PERSONNEL FOR SELECTED YEARS

Year	No. of Hos- pitals	No. of persons per hospi- tal	No. of beds	No. of persons per bed	No. of doctors and apo- thecaries	No. of persons per doc- tor/apo- thecary	No. of nurses	No. of persons per nurse
1950	263	29,194	19,959	400	1,350	5,690	1,165	6,530
1955	274	31,800	24,312	350	1,942	4,480	2,210	4,000
1960	289	34,240	29,816	328	2,280	4,380	3,232	3,600
1965	296	39,000	33,802	333	2,738	4,250	3,642	3,200
1970	328	39,000	37,753	331	3,157	3,900	5,542	2,260

Table 12 E.
NUMBER OF SCHOOLS, STUDENTS AND TEACHERS FOR SELECTED YEARS

Year	No. of pupils	No. of schools	No. of teachers	No. of pupils per teacher
1950	1,349,345	6,246	38,046	35
1955	1,677,008	6,755	49,184	33
1960	2,219,014	7,956	69,658	32
1966	2,565,891	9,560	90,515	28
1970	2,716,187	9,931	96,426	28

Source: Statistical Abstracts, Dept. of Census and Statistics.

Table 13.

POPULATION BY ETHNIC GROUPS, CENSUS YEARS

(Thousands)

	1946	%	1953	%	1963	%	1971	%
All Ethnic Groups	6,657	100.0	8,098	100.0	10,582	100.0	12,711	100.0
Low-country Sinhalese	2,903	43.6	3,470	42.9	4,470	42.2	5,446	42.8
Kandyan Sinhalese	1,718	26.0	2,147	26.5	3,043	28.8	3,701	29.1
Srī Lankā Tamils	734	11.0	885	10.9	1,165	11.0	1,416	11.0
Indian Tamils	781	11.7	974	12.0	1,123	10.6	1,195	9.4
Srī Lankā Moors	374	5.6	464	5.7	627	5.9	824	6.5
Indian Moors	36	0.5	47	0.6	55	0.5	29	0.2
Burghers and Eurasians	42	0.6	46	0.6	46	0.5	44	0.3
Malays	23	0.4	25	0.3	33	0.3	42	0.3
Others*	49	0.6	40	0.5	20	0.2	14	0.1

*Includes the Europeans and Veddhas.

Source: Department of Census and Statistics, *Population of Srī Lankā, 1974* and *Statistical Pocket Book 1973*, Colombo.

Table 14.
POPULATION BY RELIGION, CENSUS YEARS
(Thousands)

	1946	%	1953	%	1963	%	1971	%
All Religions	6,657	100.0	8,098	100.0	10,582	100.0	12,711	100.0
Buddhists	4,295	64.5	5,209	64.3	7,003	66.3	8,568	67.4
Hindus	1,320	19.8	1,611	19.9	1,958	18.5	2,239	17.6
Christians	603	9.1	724	8.9	885	8.4	987	7.7
Muslims	437	6.6	542	6.8	724	6.7	910	7.1
Others	2	—	12	0.1	12	0.1	8	0.1

Source: Department of Census and Statistics, *Statistical Pocket Book 1973,* Colomɒo.

PART III

12

POLITICS AND POLITICAL DEVELOPMENT
SINCE 1948

by A. Jeyaratnam Wilson

More than any other independent state in South Asia, Srī Laṅkā can claim to be a nation in a more complete sense than a mere geographical expression or an artificial administrative entity. Serious rifts between the different communities that constitute Srī Laṅkā society have, it is true, created unsettled conditions from time to time, but despite these and the differences that exist in race, language, culture, religion and caste, there remains a basic loyalty to the concept of a Srī Laṅkā nation. None of the country's ethnic groups or religious minorities has looked beyond the island for solutions to its problems. All insist that they have a stake in the country, and they seek to settle their differences within the national framework.

In a sense this striving towards the ideal of a Srī Laṅkā nation has been largely due to the path of moderation pursued by successive governments as well as by responsible political parties. The reason is not altogether altruistic but is one of expediency, if not of necessity. Cabinets in office face the risk of their majorities collapsing or being undermined if they stir the communal cauldron too much. Forces unleashed may not be controlled, and serious opposition from any aggrieved group can interfere with economic development, or even give 'ideas' to the armed forces. Political parties making a determined bid for power cannot afford to take up extreme positions, for there are minority pockets in a fair number of Sinhalese constituencies and these can be decisive in a general election. Hence, in framing policies, on matters connected with race, language or religion the national parties have attempted to work out compromises.

Governmental Structure and Governmental Development
The Electorate. The island's electorate is the oldest in South Asia.

Universal suffrage was introduced in 1931 and there have been nine general elections since then conducted in an orderly and constitutional manner. On five of these occasions governments were turned out of office. Only once, in March 1960, did the electors fail to make up their minds, but in every other case they ensured that they returned to parliament a party or a readily identifiable coalition with a clear mandate and an adequate majority to govern, notwithstanding the siren attractions of a multiplicity of parties.

However, despite these trends the political processes get distorted because of the way in which constituencies are demarcated under the electoral system. The balance is markedly in favour of the rural voter. The urban voter is at a disadvantage because the principle of one man, one vote does not prevail. For instance, at the general election of 1956, some thirty-eight constituencies had as many as 40,000 to 60,000 voters, while as many as twenty-five had between 5,000 and 25,000 voters. A new demarcation effected in 1959 counts the population of Indian Tamil estate workers in carving out constituencies in the plantation districts which are mainly in the Kandyan Sinhalese areas yet the vast majority of these Indian workers do not have voting rights.

This basis of electoral demarcation was primarily designed to provide weightage in representation to the backward and sparsely populated areas, in some of which the dominant population belongs to the minority groups. This would be a better way of ensuring representation for them than creating separate communal electorates. The latter, it was felt, would only emphasise divisive tendencies and thereby inhibit the growth of a unified nation. But the sum effect of this system has been to handicap radical and left-wing parties, of whose economic programmes and non-sectarian approaches to questions of language, religion, culture, race and caste the rural electors tended to be suspicious. Consequently the right-of-centre UNP had the lead in the general election of 1947; thereafter the centrist Srī Lankā Freedom Party (SLFP) went into competition with it. The continuous frustration and disillusionment that this system imposed on them led the left-wing parties in the 1960s to discard their marxist secularism and internationalist outlook for parochial goals in their quest for parliamentary recognition.

The electoral system also denies to the economic forces in the country adequate opportunities to obtain their fair share of representation. This again interferes with the proper functioning of parliamentary government. This is especially notable with regard to the wage-earning sections of the population, who (and this includes the disfranchised Indian Tamil workers) produce approximately half the national wealth, although comprising only about one-eighth of the total population. But they do not even have their proportionate representation in the House. In contrast the rural sector, where about 70 per cent of the total population is concentrated, produces less than half the national wealth but enjoys a highly disproportionate weightage in parliamentary representation.

Though the territorial (as opposed to the communal) principle is observed in electoral demarcation, in practice community, religion and sometimes caste are taken for granted when parties choose their candidates. Thus in the Ceylon-Tamil and Muslim majority areas in North and East Srī Laṅkā, only a Ceylon Tamil or a Muslim can hope to be returned to parliament, while in the south, except in those electorates specially carved out to help the Muslims, it is a Sinhalese who has the best chance. In certain constituencies, caste is an important consideration, and parties take account of this when making their nominations. No attempts have been made to get Sinhalese to contest seats in the Ceylon Tamil areas (except in a few marginal constituencies) and vice versa, so that 'race' is not the deciding factor. On a national basis, however, 'race' or religion can play a part in persuading the electors to prefer a particular party.

The period since 1956 has seen evidence of increasing politicisation of the masses—a process which began when universal suffrage was granted in 1931. More and more layers of the population have begun to interest themselves in the political processes because they see in these a method of finding solutions to the pressing problems of an underdeveloped economy and a multi-group society. Public meetings are well attended. There is a wide newspaper reading public and a variety of newspapers exist. Political leadership is consequently easily identified, which therefore makes the task of fixing responsibility much simpler, especially because political styles tend to be more individualistic than collegial.

Fortuitous circumstances made the parliamentary system a viable proposition. It was utilised, with some measure of success, during the last twenty-five years as a problem-solving mechanism. Its membership has changed considerably since 1947 when it was first constituted. Recruitment is more and more from the lower crusts, and members after 1956 have taken increasingly to speaking in Sinhalese or Tamil because they can be sure of a wider audience, judging from the large number of copies of *Hansard* that are sold when important debates take place in the House of Representatives. Parliament is regarded as a problem-solving device, the views of which the cabinet takes into account before arriving at decisions. More and more of the voting population is therefore interested in parliament, as is shown by the large numbers participating at general elections — 61.3 per cent in 1947, 74 in 1952, 71 in 1956, 77.6 in March 1960, 75.6 in July 1960, 82 in 1965 and 84.9 in 1970. The rural intelligentsia, the trade unions, the student population, the urban elements including the professional classes and commercial interests are interested in the process of decision making, for in Srī Laṅkā firm policies are still in the process of being evolved and most decisions are taken only after their possible political repercussions have been carefully looked into.

Party Competition. Inter-party rivalry based largely on socioeconomic lines took institutional shape in Srī Laṅkā, for the first time, with the approach of general elections in August-September 1947, under the newly-inaugurated Soulbury Constitution. Political activity had previously been mainly the pre-occupation of conservative communal organisations whose primary interest was to secure advantages for their respective communities in any proposed scheme of constitutional reform. Further, the preceding Donoughmore Constitution (1931-47) encouraged individualism of a corrosive kind, both at the legislative and executive levels, thereby inhibiting the emergence of a proper party system. The only national organisation concentrating its energies in the direction of independence for the country was the Ceylon National Congress, founded in 1919. But within a few years of its inauguration, the Congress transformed itself mainly into an organ of the low-country Sinhalese landed and commercial interests.

Despite these discouraging trends, the 1930s saw the beginnings of a left-wing movement — whose growth and development were held up by the outbreak of war in 1939. As a wartime measure, some of the left-wing organisations were banned by the colonial government. In course of time, the movement provoked opposition to itself from both indigenous as well as British and Indian agricultural and mercantile interests. The "moderates" coalesced in 1946 to form the right-of-centre UNP under D. S. Senanayake. In fact it had become necessary in 1946 for such a party to be organised to work the cabinet system envisaged under the Soulbury Reforms.

At the 1947 general election, only the UNP presented itself to the electors as a party making a serious bid for power. Its opponents on the left were seriously split. There were two Trotskyite groups, the Lanka Sama Samaja Party (the Ceylon Equal Society Party, LSSP) and its splinter, the Bolshevik Leninist Party, which later changed its name to Bolskevik Samasamaja Party (BSP), and the Moscow-oriented Communist Party (CP). In all, the left contested fifty-one out of ninety-five seats, but they were not united. In fact they clashed with each other in a number of constituencies.

There were fundamental differences between the UNP and the left-wing groups, and these prevented the proper working of the parliamentary system. The UNP realised that little purpose would be served in co-operating with the left-wing groups because the latter's views on parliamentary government were only too well-known. In fact, when the overall results of the general election indicated a possibility (though somewhat remote) of an alternate government to the UNP being formed, the parliamentary leader of the LSSP, Dr. N. M. Perera, declared that they were a "revolutionary party" and would therefore not serve in a "capitalist government", though he added that his party would assist those who might take office in an "alternative progressive government". The LSSP's indifference and doctrinaire attitude brought to nought any prospects of a united opposition being formed.

Furthermore, for almost three years all three left-wing parties would not agree on a leader of the opposition. The LSSP, as the largest party in opposition, favoured the idea but its splinter, the BSP, opposed it and the CP denounced it as a "reactionary British convention". Only after the BSP and the LSSP united in June 1950 did the opposition groups, with the exception of the CP, meet and elect Dr. N. M. Perera as their leader.

The nucleus of a democratic alternative to the UNP appeared only when S. W. R. D. Bandaranaike resigned his portfolio of health and local government in July 1951 and crossed over to the opposition. Bandaranaike helped to coalesce a layer of opinion — the rural middle-classes comprising *bhikkhus*, Sinhalese school teachers, *ayurvedic* physicians, petty shopkeepers as well as Sinhalese merchants — which had hitherto been neglected by both the UNP and the left-wing parties. In September 1951 he inaugurated the SLFP, and in it anti-UNP opinion in the country sensed the possibilities of an alternative government.

In addition to these opposition forces, there was a hard core of Tamil communal elements which ranged itself against the UNP in defence of the rights of the groups it claimed to represent. A majority in the main organisation of the Ceylon Tamils, the All-Ceylon Tamil Congress (TC), crossed over to the government in August 1948. Those in the TC who opposed this move formed a rival organisation, the Tamil Federal Party (FP), which was to play an important role after 1956. The other Tamil organisation, the Ceylon Indian Congress (CIC), represented the Indian Tamil workers.

Srī Laṅkā's first parliament was dissolved on 14 April 1952 and at the general election that followed the main contenders were the UNP and the SLFP. The left, with its sectarian quarrels, was hopelessly split. The SLFP emerged from the election as the only democratic alternative to the victorious UNP.

The SLFP's leader, S. W. R. D. Bandaranaike, had a different notion of the role of a parliamentary opposition from that of his marxist associates. Where the latter had conceived of strikes, mass action and extra-parliamentary struggles as forms of protest, Bandaranaike believed in persuading the electors—especially the rural intelligentsia—about the need for the cultural and economic regeneration of the Sinhalese masses. His liberal democratic approach was made evident when he declined to let his party get involved in the left-wing-organised *hartāl* (general stoppage of work) of August 1953 against the decision of Dudley Senanayake's UNP government to raise the price of rice. The *hartāl* was nevertheless successful to the extent that it brought about the resignation of Dudley Senanayake in October 1953. He was succeeded as prime minister by his cousin, Sir John Kotelawala.

To fight the general election of 1956, Bandaranaike joined forces with three other groups, two of which were campaigners for Sinhalese as the only official language throughout the island, while the third was marxist-oriented though committed to the same objective. This coalition, called the Mahajana Eksath Peramuna(People's United Front, known as MEP), entered into a no-contest electoral pact with the two leading marxist parties, the LSSP and the CP, in September-October 1955 and inflicted a crushing defeat on the UNP government of Sir John Kotelawala.

The defeated UNP accepted the verdict of the electors with good grace, and in opposition concentrated on exposing the inherent weaknesses of Bandaranaike's coalition of contradictory elements which was soon to split apart into a democratic socialist wing and a marxist wing. The UNP realised that Bandaranaike would be hard put to it to keep the extravagant promises he had made to the electors, and it therefore presented itself as the democratic alternative to his MEP government. An anomalous situation was created, however, when the leader of the LSSP, Dr. N. M. Perera, became leader of the opposition. The LSSP had had a no-contest electoral pact with Bandaranaike's MEP. It was the UNP which had come off second best in the polls, though it won only eight of the seventy-six seats it contested. The LSSP won fourteen but it contested only twenty-one constituencies.

The opposition in the 1956 parliament was a heterogeneous group and the contradictions within it were seen in the way the different groups voted on controversial bills.

The LSSP as the major opposition party preferred to organise a series of major strikes in the public and private sectors to embarrass the new government. This showed it up in a poor light to the rural masses, who came to believe that food and other shortages in the country were due to strikes by marxist-led dock workers. At the same time, however, the LSSP utilised parliament to expose the weaknesses and contradictions within Bandaranaike's coalition. Bandaranaike soon got enmeshed in the politics of the language problem through his attempts to placate the Tamil FP, which was now taking to extra-parliamentary forms of struggle. He had at the same time to appease the forces of Sinhalese extremism. The LSSP, which had advocated the recognition of both Sinhalese and Tamil as the official languages of the country, was not slow to seize the opportunity to tell the electors of the dangers to which Bandaranaike's language policies were exposing the country. In this, however, they did not meet with much success.

The UNP did not challenge the Prime Minister or his government in parliament. Instead they campaigned in the country and scored a success when *bhikkhus,* partly instigated by them, compelled the prime minister in May 1958 to renounce a pact he had entered into with the Tamil FP in July the previous year. Widespread disturbances followed this abrogation and an island-wide state of emergency was declared on 27 May 1958. From then on, the pattern was set for governments to resort to emergency rule whenever they were confronted with serious and embarrassing situations.

Bandaranaike's assassination on 26 September 1959 gave rise to a highly volatile situation—which ended, however, when his widow Sirima Bandaranaike, inheriting his charisma, led the SLFP to complete victory at the general election of July 1960. The general election held four months earlier in March 1960 had proved inconclusive; the largest single group—the UNP, led by Dudley Senanayake—failed to improve its minority position in the House. The LSSP, which had decided to tread the parliamentary path, made a determined bid for power at this election but came off badly. The disillusionment that seized its ranks after this débâcle gradually led it to content itself with becoming an appendage of the SLFP.

Sirima Bandaranaike's SLFP government held office for more than four years despite opposition from vested interests, from the Tamil Federalists and from the Roman Catholics who were dispossessed of most of their schools by legislation enacted in late 1960 and early 1961. There was also trouble from the LSSP on the trade union front. The government received its severest jolt when army officers unsuccessfully attempted to stage a right-wing *coup d'état* in January 1962.

By June 1964 the government was showing signs of collapse due to incompetence in its own ministerial ranks. To remedy this, the Prime Minister entered into a coalition with the LSSP. The UNP, fearing for itself, warned the electors of an impending marxist-inspired dictatorship and, as if to provide proof of this trend, the new coalition government announced its intention to nationalise the press. The right wing of the SLFP, led by Sirima Bandaranaike's own deputy C. P. de Silva, became increasingly apprehensive of the LSSP's presence in the government, and eventually crossed over to the opposition. The result was a defeat for the government at the division on the throne speech on 3 December 1964.

The general election which followed in March 1965 indicated that the electors preferred the UNP and its allies. A 'national government' under Dudley Senanayake was formed mainly comprising the UNP and the Tamil FP, along with five other minor groups. For a little more than three years the Prime Minister was able to keep the diverse and opposing elements in his coalition together, but in September 1968 the Tamil Federalists made their exit mainly because of their disenchantment with the Prime Minister's inability to keep his undertakings to them.

On the opposition side, however, the most promising development during 1967-70 was the decision of the two marxist parties, the LSSP and the CP, to form a United Front with the SLFP (the UF) under the leadership of Mrs. Sirima Bandaranaike. A Common Programme, which made some concessions to the socialist policies of the left but was mainly social democratic with an indigenous bias that is markedly Sinhalese Buddhist-oriented, was agreed on by all three parties in early 1968. It was this UF with its Common Programme that inflicted a crushing defeat on the UNP at the general election of May 1970.

Srī Laṅkā has been able with local adaptations, to work the Westminster model reasonably well although it lacks an expanding economic base and a well-defined bi-party situation, which are the conventional attributes of an ideal parliamentary system. The habits of toleration, a commitment to constitutional methods of agitation in essential matters, a measure of agreement over a fairly wide range of fundamentals and the presence of two clearly identifiable coalitions—one with a UNP bias and the other SLFP-oriented —are evidence of a Srī Laṅkā version of the Westminster model. Political discussion and debate are on a relatively high plane and the standards of comparison are with Britain, not with neighbouring India. Erskine May, Gilbert Campion, Ivor Jennings, Harold Laski and in recent times S. A. de Smith are not infrequently quoted in parliamentary debate. Besides, most of the upper layer of politicians both before and after independence have been men with an

English-oriented education, and therefore British practices not surprisingly have an uncanny attraction for them.

Most of the controversial issues in Srī Laṅkā politics — the Sinhalese-Tamil problem, the Indian Question, Buddhism, the Roman Catholic Church, non-alignment in foreign policy — have been settled on the basis of compromises to which the two major parties are more or less committed, though with differing emphases. The questions of democracy, dictatorship, marxism, the separatist ambitions of Ceylon Tamil parties, the path to economic development, etc. give rise to debate and rivalry between the parties, but the electors are discerning enough to know which of these are most pertinent at any particular time.

The Constitutional Structure. It had often been argued that it was not the sovereign people but an alien country, Britain, that devised a constitution for Srī Laṅkā. To some extent it could be said that the Ceylon (Constitution) Orders in Council, 1946 and 1947, which formed the basis of the constitution until May 1972, and which were the outcome of the recommendations of the Report of the Commission on Constitutional Reform headed by Lord Soulbury, published in September 1945, was a 'foreign product'. But the facts that the Soulbury Report was itself based on the Constitutional Scheme formulated by the Ceylonese Board of Ministers in September 1944; that the Ceylonese State Council also adopted a similar scheme early in 1945 with the difference that this provided for full independence (the Ministers' Scheme was framed within the limitations imposed by His Majesty's Government's Declaration of 26 May 1943 and therefore fell short of independence) and that a White Paper issued in October 1945 by His Majesty's Government with the Soulbury proposals as its basis was accepted by the State Council by an overwhelming majority of fifty-one votes to three — these facts were overlooked. The main work on the 1948-72 constitution was undertaken by D. S. Senanayake, the island's leading statesman who became Srī Laṅkā's first prime minister and the constitutional expert Sir Ivor Jennings, then Vice-Chancellor of the University of Ceylon. Jennings functioned as draftsman and advisor. Senanayake and his colleagues in the State Council wanted the Westminster model, and with Jennings's assistance they fashioned one, with modifications to suit local requirements.

Thus till 1972 Srī Laṅkā had a Westminster-style constitution, except that it was written and thus rigid, requiring a special process for the amendment of its various provisions while at the same time it contained certain restrictions on the powers of Parliament. The last-mentioned were mainly designed to protect the rights of minority groups from legislative discrimination, but there was often discrimination on the administrative plane.

Nevertheless there was a widespread conviction that the constitution was not designed to suit the genius of the people and it did show certain defects during the approximately twenty-five years of its working. From 1956 onwards serious efforts were made to alter its provisions, and change was finally effected after the UF rode to victory in 1970.

Two Englishmen, Sir Henry Monck-Mason Moore and Viscount Soulbury, held the governor-generalship in succession after independence — both being thus rewarded for their assistance in helping Srī Lankā to win independence. Two distinguished Sinhalese, Sir Oliver Goonetilleke and William Gopallawa, succeeded them. The former had a long and useful record of service as an administrator, negotiator and statesman, and during his tenure of office, he had to deal with extremely difficult situations, especially communal holocausts and serious trade union disputes. He was of great assistance to at least four of the five prime ministers who were in office during his seven-year term (1955-62). Often he exceeded the limits of constitutional propriety, but this was overlooked because of his invaluable expertise. William Gopallawa (1962-72), municipal administrator, diplomat and kinsman of Mrs. Sirima Bandaranaike, was the first Buddhist and first Kandyan Sinhalese to become governor-general (Goonetilleke belongs to the Protestant faith).

Some of the powers of the Queen were exercised by her, others delegated to her representative the governor general. All were exercised on formal or informal advice tendered by the Prime Minister. There is room for discretion, as in Britain, in the matter of granting a dissolution or selecting a Prime Minister from one or two eligibles. However, though Soulbury and Goonetilleke came in for criticism when using this discretion, their conduct nevertheless accorded on the whole with accepted British conventions.

The cabinet, whose collective responsibility was enshrined in the constitution, wielded authority with the Prime Minister, the leader of the largest group in the House of Representatives, as its head. The Prime Minister constitutionally held also the portfolios of defence and external affairs. He assigned the subject and functions of the various ministers, and appointed junior ministers who were called parliamentary secretaries.

Parliament was composed of the Queen and two Chambers, the Senate and the House of Representatives. The Senate consisted of thirty members, of whom fifteen were elected by members of the House of Representatives according to the principle of proportional representation on the basis of the single transferable vote and fifteen were appointed by the Governor-General on the advice of the Prime Minister. In the appointment of senators, the constitution provided that the Governor-General should endeavour to appoint persons who had distinguished themselves in public service or in professional, commercial, industrial or agricultural life, including education, law, medicine, science, engineering and banking. Senators held office for a term of six years from the date of election or appointment, but there was provision in the Consitution for one-third of the senators to retire every second year.

The House of Representatives consisted of 157 members. Of these 140 were elected from 140 single-member constituencies, eight from four two-member constituencies and three from one three-member constituency. The Governor-General was empowered to appoint not more than six members to the House after a general election to represent any unrepresented or inadequately represented interests in the island. In making these appointments the Governor-General acted on the advice of the Prime Minister. The term of the House was five years unless parliament were dissolved earlier.

In a difference of opinion or a conflict between the two chambers, the Senate had only a delaying power. It could delay money bills for only a month, and other bills for about one year.

The UF government of Mrs. Bandaranaike promulgated a new republican constitution in May 1972, resulting from the endeavours of a constituent assembly which it had convened in July 1970. The new constitution, while it regularised existing practices and removed features which were thought to impede the smooth functioning of government and the implementation of the popular will, had many of the characteristics of its predecessor in other respects. Nevertheless, it was claimed to be the result of the endeavours of the elected representatives of the people and therefore autochthonous.

The 1972 constitution provides for a unicameral legislature, special recognition for Buddhism, a statement of fundamental rights and directive principles of state policy. Some of the essential features of its predecessor which it retained are those relating to the position of the President though with certain modifications, the principles of cabinet government—the cabinet, however, being vested with greater power—and most important, the system of electoral demarcation with its bias towards the rural and sparsely-populated areas. The new constitution marks a break from the old in that it specifically does away with any implicit or explicit separation of powers. All powers are concentrated in a National State Assembly, though there is provision for a distribution of functions as between the executive, the legislature and the judiciary. The judiciary, however, will not have any right to pronounce on the constitutionality of legislation. That power is vested in a constitutional court of five judges appointed by the President on the advice of the Prime Minister for a term of four years.

The administration of the public services is vested in a State Services Advisory Board and a State Services Disciplinary Board with the cabinet of ministers having the controlling authority on essential matters. The middle and lower rungs of the judiciary are in the charge of a Judicial Services Advisory Board and a Judicial Services Disciplinary Board. Detailed clauses provide for the independence of judges.

The constitution makes various provisions for the use of the national languages. Sinhalese is declared the official language, but attempts are made to accommodate the language of the principal minority group, Tamil, in the administrative and judicial spheres.

Outside the constitution, there is an elaborate network of institutions providing for participatory democracy — divisional development councils, workers' councils, advisory committees in government offices and people's committees constituted on a territorial basis. Some of these have worked satisfactorily, while others have hampered administration or become corrupt and/or ineffective.'

The Government has also appointed a Political Authority from among its senior MPs to be responsible for coordinating developmental and other related activities in each of the twenty-two administrative districts into which Srī Laṅkā is divided. It is too soon to pass judgement on this innovation.

The Nature of Politics and Political Developments, 1947-1956 — the Dominance of the UNP.

The Electoral Structure and Political Leadership. During this phase the UNP were the main beneficiaries of the fact that the rural areas are the arbiters of Srī Laṅkā's political destinies. In terms of percentage distribution, the bulk of the country's population — at least 75 per cent — is rural and another 10 per cent or so live in the plantations, mostly disfranchised Indian Tamil labour. Two closely-knit communal organisations with an Indian Tamil leadership have continued to control this vote, the Ceylon Workers' Congress — by far the more influential — and the Democratic Worker's Congress, whose base is confined to specific areas.

At this time political leadership at the higher levels came from a relatively small category of landowners and professional men (mostly lawyers and doctors), as well as retired public servants, including school teachers, and some industrialists and business-men. There was also a very small group of whole-time professional politicians who generally form the top-rung leadership in all parties. The lower strata of the rural population hardly provided a recruiting base, though at the middle and lower levels some far-mers took an active interest in local government and constituency politics. However, even at these levels it was the big and small shop-keepers and traders, the local legal profession with a sprinkling of *ayurvedic* physicians and *swabasha* school teachers that formed the major component of local bodies and the constituency organisations.

Though the 67 per cent of Srī Laṅkā's population who are Bud-dhist have economic, social and cultural problems which were attributed to the neglect and oppression of centuries of foreign rule and the callous disregard of their problems by the westernised intelligentsia, the UNP gave low priority to their demands, and as a result the Buddhist movement tended to be alienated from the national political leadership. Furthermore, a majority (about half) of the Sinhalese population belonged to the *goyigama* (farmer) caste, though this is not to say that the other castes, especially the *karāvas* (fisherman) and *salāgama* (cinnamon peelers), are without influence. There are also depressed caste groups in the Kandyan Sinhalese areas which had some electoral influence. But because the *goyigama* Sinhalese Buddhists are the majority in the Sinhalese population, leadership at most levels is primarily from this layer. It is significant that until 1956 — i.e. during the first phase of UNP rule — this *goyigama* Sinhalese Buddhist leadership was drawn pre-dominantly from this caste while a section of the English-educated, westernised intelligentsia — especially from non-*goyigama* castes — provided a grudging allegiance to this leadership or recorded its dissent by voting for left-wing candidates both of the Trotskyist and Moscow-communist groups. Neither group of marxists was prepared to provide an alternative to the UNP, nor would the elec-tors have accepted them. But they nevertheless welcomed them as a vigilant and critical opposition to the UNP.

Traditionalism in its classic forms — especially an outward con-formity to the tenets of Buddhism, veiled casteism which placed a premium on *goyigama* Sinhalese Buddhists, distrust of the Ceylon Tamil middle class because of competition from them, and hostility to the presence of Indian Tamil traders and labourers in the island — characterised the conduct of this westernised intelligentsia at this stage. Coupled with this was an innate conservatism, manifest-ed in strong opposition to marxism, the trade unions and even any form of neo-liberalism.

This conservatism was also manifested in the belief that economic prosperity lay in trade ties with the West and in the improvement and diversification of agriculture. There was little attempt at economic planning. A six-year plan of development — a mere collection of the hopes and schemes of the various ministers — was drawn up for the period 1947/8-1953/4, but no serious steps were taken to set up any machinery of plan implementation. Even worse, the country's valuable sterling balances of some Rs. 1,260 millions were frittered away in an orgy of unplanned spending, mostly on imported consumer goods. The situation was saved when rubber prices boomed with the outbreak of the Korean War, but this was merely a repetition of the earlier record of wasteful expenditure. Later the release of rubber stockpiles by the USA caused a depression in prices. Disaster was averted when the Dudley Senanayake government (May 1952 — October 1953) entered into a rubber-rice agreement with China early in 1952; but adverse terms of trade continued unabated and when in July 1953 the Government took the drastic step of raising the price of rice (hitherto heavily subsidised by the state) from 25 to 70 cents a measure, widespread violence broke out in the wake of a protest *hartal* called by left-wing parties on 12 August. A number of deaths from police firing affected the health of the sensitive and inexperienced Prime Minister and he tendered his resignation in October of the same year, to be succeeded by his cousin Sir John Kotelawala.

D. S. Senanayake and his successors Dudley Senanayake and Sir John Kotelawala were conservative, pro-West and anti-marxist, and hoped that everything would be well if the surface of political life was kept unruffled. The defence and external affairs agreements concluded by D. S. Senanayake with Britain in November 1947 prior to the grant of independence, the imitation of the Westminster model in the constitution, the decision to remain within the Commonwealth and to accept the British sovereign as Srī Laṅkā's when India and Pakistan had decided in favour of republican status; the enactment of such legislation as the Public Security Act of 1947 and the Trade Union (Amendment) Act of 1948 which were directed against marxist-dominated working-class organisations; and the Citizenship Act of 1948, the Indian and Pakistani Residents (Citizenship) Act of 1949 and the Parliamentary Elections (Amendment) Act of 1949, all of which deprived the bulk of the Indian Tamil population of its citizenship rights and the franchise, reflected the basic political ideology of this conservative class.

The conflict between the UNP and its marxist opponents in the House of Representatives, the Trotskyist LSSP and the CP, grew sharper as it increasingly dawned on the UNP that the alternative to it would be a "workers' and peasants' dictatorship". In June 1950 Sir John Kotelawala, then a minister in D. S. Senanayake's cabinet, characterised the Opposition as one which did not believe in the democratic system, adding that "once they got in they would not get out. There is no guarantee you would ever have a chance to go to the ballot again." These fears seemed to be confirmed when at the general election of 1952 the LSSP put forward a fourteen-point "anti-imperialist and anti-capitalist programme" with a call for a *sama samaja* government — though how this could have been effected is hard to envisage, for the party was contesting only forty out of the ninety-five seats.

The UNP has persistently taken up the position that the marxists present a threat to democratic institutions, and that any alliance they may enter into with democratic parties can only be for the purpose of infiltrating and ultimately seizing power. This was alleged, for instance when the United Front of the CP and the Viplavakari Lanka Sama Samaja Party (VLSSP — Philip Gunawardena's breakaway group from the LSSP when the latter coalesced with its splinter, the Bolshevik Samasamaja Party, in June 1950) campaigned for a "democratic government" at the 1952 general election and in the constituencies supported the candidates of S. W. R. D. Bandaranaike's democratic socialist SLFP as against those of its Trotskyist rivals. The same charge was levelled when the CP and LSSP entered into a no-contest electoral-agreement prior to the 1956 general election with Bandaranaike's broad-based coalition of diverse interests, the MEP. The fact that Philip Gunawardena's marxist VLSSP was a constituent of the MEP, and the appointment of Philip Gunawardena and his party colleague William de Silva respectively to the two key portfolios of agriculture and industries when Bandaranaike formed his MEP cabinet in April 1956, seemed to cause uneasiness among the conservative middle-class elements at this time. The UNP harbours the same misgivings of a possible marxist takeover under the present UF set-up, where traditional marxist parties form a significant component.

The Tamil Problem. The UNP's attitude to the Ceylon Tamil minority during its first phase of political power was one of an attempt at reconciliation. The Tamils under the leadership of G. G. Ponnambalam's TC, after their relentless battle for balanced representation (that is, that half the seats in the popular house should be allocated to the minority communities and the other half to the Sinhalese majority) remained in sullen but uneasy opposition with the left-wing parties, after scoring notable victories in the Ceylon

Tamil majority areas of north Srī Laṅkā, at the general election of 1947. D. S. Senanayake, in his anxiety to indicate to Whitehall that he had secured the co-operation of the Ceylon Tamils, had included two uncommitted Tamil MPs in the cabinet he formed in September 1947. However, within a year of the formation of his government, Ponnambalam and a majority of his Congress crossed the floor. Some members of the Congress did not support this line and launched their own organisation, the Tamil Federal Party (FP) in December 1949. This new organisation made no impression until the general election of 1956 when it won a majority of seats in the Ceylon Tamil areas. The FP strongly objected to the legislation of 1948 and 1949 depriving Indian Tamils in Srī Laṅkā of voting and citizenship rights; it also opposed what it alleged was the planned state-sponsored colonisation of "the traditional homelands" of the Ceylon Tamils in the northern and eastern parts of the island with Sinhalese settlers, but despite these protests, colonisation went on apace. Owing to the prevailing harmony, there was no friction between Sinhalese and Ceylon Tamils in these frontier areas.

It was over the question of official status for the Tamil language that the cleavage between the two communities took place. D. S. Senanayake preferred to let time provide the solution, especially as the Tamil-medium schools were teaching Sinhalese as a second language to their children. Sinhalese would then have become the *lingua franca*, which would solve the problem of a unifying official language for the entire island. But there were other forces among the Sinhalese-educated intelligentsia which demanded an immediate imposition of Sinhalese as the only official language, hoping that such a step would give them an advantage over the Ceylon Tamils in the competition for jobs in the public sector. In 1954-6 the problem was how to allay the fears of the Ceylon Tamils and satisfy the aspirations of the Sinhalese. Sir John Kotelawala's maladroit handling of the situation soon brought it to crisis proportions. While on an official visit to the Tamil north in late 1955, he promised the Ceylon Tamils that he would make constitutional provision for parity of status for the Sinhalese and Tamil languages. There was strong opposition to this in the Sinhalese areas. The UNP's immediate political rivals in the SLFP, who had also stood for Sinhalese and Tamil as the official languages of the country, now capitalised on the situation by changing their stance to champion Sinhalese as the only official language — with a provision, however, for the "reasonable use" of the Tamil language. It was only a matter of months before the UNP (in February 1956) effected a *volte face* by accepting the position that Sinhalese alone should be the official language.

The Indian Problem. One of the most pressing problems that Srī Laṅkā had to deal with shortly after independence was the future of the Indians in the island. The UNP and the SLFP have been sensitive to Sinhalese opinion on this question, especially in the Kandyan areas. Many Sinhalese look on these Indians as a potential fifth column and the visible evidence of the exploitation of the Kandyan areas. The position has been complicated by the support the Indians receive from the political parties of the Ceylon Tamils, especially the Tamil Federalists, and from left-wing organisations — though for very different reasons. The Ceylon Tamils regard the Indians as an additional source of political strength to them, electorally speaking. The Sinhalese on the other hand would not like the two groups to combine into what they fear might well be a pan-Tamil movement, and the Kandyan Sinhalese in particular object to the inclusion of Indian Tamil voters in their electorates. Left-wing groups, however, look on the Indian workers as a potentially powerful component of their trade union movement if they could be weaned away from the two communal workers' organisations which now control them. At the general election of 1947, in about twenty constituencies, the Indian vote went to left-wing and anti-UNP candidates. The situation is further aggravated by the influx of illicit Indian immigrants from the south Indian coast and the recent emergence of a militant local Dravida Munnetra Kazhagam (DMK, Dravidian Progressive Front) organisation in the plantation areas.

The Indians for their part protest, with justification, that the majority of them do not know any other home besides Srī Laṅkā. One solution seriously suggested is to assimilate the Indian population by making it adopt the Sinhalese language and culture, but this is not feasible. The other solution is to persuade the Government of India to take back as many of them as possible. This, in fact, has been the strategy employed, with varying degrees of success, by all Srī Laṅkā governments up to date. Thus the Nehru-Kotelawala Pact of 1954 provided among other things that Indian Tamils who wished to qualify as citizens should learn "the language of the area", i. e., the Sinhalese language.

The Indian problem came closest to a solution when Mrs. Bandaranaike entered into a pact in October 1964 with the Indian Prime Minister of the time, L. B. Shastri. Briefly, this pact provided for (1) 525,000 Indians resident in Srī Laṅkā with their natural increase to be repatriated to India over a fifteen-year phased program; (2) 300,000 to be absorbed as citizens of Srī Laṅkā; and (3) the future of the remaining 150,000 Indians to be negotiated later by the two countries. It was finally resolved in 1974, when Mrs. Bandaranaike and the Indian Prime Minister Mrs. Indira Gandhi agreed to settle the question of these 150,000 Indians on a half-and-half basis.

Religion and Language. The attitude of the UNP governments of 1947-56 to the religious and cultural question was one of avoiding controversy. UNP ministers patronised Buddhist occasions, but took the position that Buddhism required no special protection or any specific constitutional guarantees. They held that what was important was freedom of worship—which, they alleged, was threatened by left-wing parties. Not even the criticisms of the unofficial Buddhist Commission of Inquiry set up by various Buddhist organisations in the country in 1954 could make the UNP aware of the magnitude of the Buddhist problem.

Their indifference was no better in regard to the demand that the national languages be given their due place in the administration of the country. The UNP no doubt had to take note of the difficulties of the English-educated public servants, but it did not even wish to make a beginning until it was too late. It made a faint claim that it stood for a gradual transition and that an overnight switch was impracticable. It had changed the medium of instruction in the schools to the mother-tongue, but evidence of its carelessness was seen in that, even as late as 1955, English was the primary language of debate and discussion in parliament.

To the Buddhist demand that all denominational schools should be taken over by the state the response was a stout refusal. The policy was laid down by D. S. Senanayake in July 1948 when he said that "the services of all people who are engaged in education should be utilised". He added that attempts were being made by some people to destroy missionary schools but that his government "had no intention of doing any harm to anyone".

During this phase, the UNP's alienation from the rural masses and the underprivileged urban classes was becoming increasingly apparent. While the party stood somewhat to the right of centre in politics, and had been responsible for establishing firmly the foundations of a welfare state, its leadership, especially at the top and middle levels, had only tenuous links with the ordinary mass of voters. This leadership looked on itself as being the natural rulers of the country, and since the opposition to it was disorganised and splintered, it tended to have the feeling of a monopoly of power. The party had the confidence of business interests, large sections of the middle classes, the administrative grades in the public service and the higher rungs of the Buddhist priesthood. It had fair support from all the minority groups, but it failed to penetrate the lower layers of society. However, one of its principal leaders, S. W. R. D

Bandaranaike, whose indigenous-style nationalism and neo-liberal attitudes to political, economic and social questions made him suspect in the eyes of the UNP top echelons, tried unsuccessfully to make the party aware of the dangers of the developing crisis. He sought to give expression to the needs and aspirations of those sections of the Sinhalese-educated rural and urban classes which were being tolerated only on the fringes of society—the neglected and underprivileged Buddhist monks, the Sinhalese small shopkeepers and petty traders, *ayurvedic* physicians, school teachers, novelists, musicians and artists, and the urban workers. In 1951, Bandaranaike resigned his portfolio of health and local government and crossed the floor of the House. Shortly afterwards he formed the SLFP, a centrist organisation, which immediately became the focal point of all interests dissatisfied with the UNP which were at the same time opposed to marxist solutions.

Bandaranaike had much fertile ground to operate on. The radicalisation of politics had been undertaken since the 1930s by young intellectuals returning from their studies abroad who had organised a left-wing movement in the urban sectors and plantation areas. These left-wing elements spoke in a modern idiom to the rural masses, the urban workers and the lower middle classes generally. Their economic programme sought social welfare benefits for the underprivileged and the improvement of the conditions of the working class. Much of the work of the State Council and the Board of Ministers under the Donoughmore constitution as well as of their ideological successor, the UNP, was a fulfilment of this left-wing programme. When this happened these left-wing parties became more or less urban-based organisations, concentrating on building a powerful trade union movement and appealing to the youth of the country in general and the young intellectuals in particular, and to the workers in the city and outskirts of Colombo. They proposed marxist remedies to the country's economic and social problems, but it is very improbable that their message was clearly understood, let alone accepted, by those whom they sought to indoctrinate. The serious ideological disputes that broke out among them with the resultant rifts and splinterings proved incomprehensible to the mass of voters. The electors who supported their candidates were mainly seeking to record a dissenting vote.

The left leadership failed to make any significant impact on the rural areas. To the people there it seemed politically too sophisticated, preaching alien and materialistic doctrines and unsympathetic to their national aspirations in regard to Buddhism, the Sinhalese language and Sinhalese culture. It is to this large area of society with its deep cultural frustrations and perennial social and economic discontent, neglected both by the Left and the UNP, that Bandaranaike successfully responded.

The general election of May 1952 came too soon after Bandaranaike's exit from the UNP for his SLFP to organise the passive protest forces languishing in the rural areas. But the economic difficulties that followed, particularly the attempt by the Dudley Senanayake government to raise the price of subsidised rice and the several cuts on the social services imposed by its successor, the government of Sir John Kotelawala, raised the political temperature.

Influential Sinhalese anti-UNP organisations of Buddhist monks, Sinhalese school teachers, unemployed senior school certified youths and an entire range of disaffected elements placed themselves behind a broad political coalition, the MEP, comprising the SLFP (the major component), the marxist-oriented VLSSP of Philip Gunawardena, and the Sinhala Bhasa Peramuna (Sinhalese Language Front) of W. Dahanayake. This front defeated the UNP at the general election of 1956.

1956 and after: the Dominance of the Bandaranaikes

The electoral victory of the MEP in 1956 is the dividing line in Srī Laṅkā's post-independence political development. It unleashed new forces hitherto held in check by a colonial-style bureaucracy and a sophisticated and far-removed political process. As a consequence, the governments in office after 1956, especially those headed by S. W. R. D. Bandaranaike (1956-9), his widow Mrs. Sirima Bandaranaike (1960-5 and 1970-) and Dudley Senanayake (1965-70), were obliged to be more responsive to entirely new layers of public opinion from the rural and urban areas. Government policies therefore ceased to follow any defined and predictable path. Instead, they are largely formulated on an *ad hoc* basis and on pragmatic considerations.

After 1956 there was a break with the previous near-*laissez-faire* economic doctrine of optimum opportunity for private commercial interests. Henceforth Srī Laṅkā had to move in the direction of a mixed economy with more and more emphasis on state control of the mercantile and production sectors. In the process, some of the supports of the UNP were knocked away. Thus the nationalisation of the port of Colombo and bus transport in 1958 by Bandaranaike's MEP government, of petroleum and insurance by Mrs. Bandaranaike's SLFP government and the dispossession of the schools of the Roman Catholic Church and Protestant missions in 1960-1 endangered the very foundations of the unp.

Some economic power now came to be dispersed among small industrialists and small and middle-rung Sinhalese traders, because of the imposition of severe import controls due to balance of payments difficulties. But the commanding heights of the economy nevertheless continued to remain in the hands of British and local big commercial combines.

There was also a wider distribution of rural credit facilities by the creation in 1961 of the People's Bank, branches of which were opened in various parts of the island. Peasant cultivators had already gained some security with the enactment of the Paddy Lands Act by Bandaranaike's minister of Food and Agriculture, Philip Gunawardena, in 1958. The nationalisation of the Ceylonese-owned Bank of Ceylon, the biggest commercial bank in the island, in 1961 was directed at assisting local enterprise to a greater extent than in the past.

More than anything else, however, the principle of planned economic development—in which the public and private sectors are defined and progress is measured on a timetable of achievement —came to be accepted. Bandaranaike established a national planning council soon after assuming office, and by 1958 a Ten-Year Plan of development was worked out by experienced economists from Srī Laṅkā, from the West and from communist countries.

Organised labour experienced a sense of relief under the MEP government. The trade union movement exploited the wide tolerance given to it to launch a series of mammoth strikes through the years 1956 to 1959. Many of these were politically inspired and were aimed at embarrassing the new government, for the LSSP at this juncture planned to be successors to Bandaranaike. The Prime Minister personally intervened to settle many of these strikes, making many concessions to the trade unions wherever possible. It was the MEP government which made May Day a statutory public holiday. This same policy of accomodating labour was continued under Mrs. Bandaranaike, though she at the same time strongly disapproved of unauthorised strikes.

The most significant outcome of the MEP victory of 1956 was that the rural masses and the Sinhalese Buddhist intellegentsia now came to grips with the realities of political power. Bandaranaike, who had reflected as well as articulated their needs and aspirations, found it difficult at times to hold the more militant sections in check. He was, however, ultimately successful in getting these new forces to adapt themselves to the built-in restraints of modern constitutionalism and the parliamentary system. However, important concessions had to be made to them. In June 1956 the Sinhalese language was declared by legislation to be the only official language throughout the island. A ministry of cultural affairs and a separate department of official language affairs were established. The

College of Indigenous Medicine was reorganised and a central institute of *ayurveda* was set up so that the indigenous systems of medical treatment would obtain their 'rightful' place in the health services of the country. The two premier Sinhalese seats of Buddhist learning, the Vidyalankara and Vidyodaya Pirivenas were granted university status. Finally, in the religious sphere a Buddha Sāsana Commission was appointed in February 1957 to make recommendations for the reform of the *sangha* (Buddhist clergy) and for "according Buddhism its rightful place in the country". There was opposition from the influential *siyam nikāya*, but the Commission nevertheless proceeded with its work. Bandaranaike however resisted the demand that all schools should be taken over by the state. He was under heavy pressure from the Roman Catholic Church. Further, having embroiled himself with the Tamils on the language question, he had no desire to add to his troubles. Buddhist groups, however, kept up a persistent agitation and achieved their objective when Mrs. Bandaranaike's SLFP government nationalised most of the schools by legislation enacted in late 1960 and early 1961. Some of the schools—much the better ones—were permitted under certain conditions to become private institutions, but they have had to labour under severe financial hardships.

The Roman Catholics at first resisted the take-over of their schools, occupying them and refusing to hand them over to the state. An ugly situation was averted, however, by the intervention of Cardinal Valerian Gracias from India, reportedly sent by Nehru to help break the deadlock. In return for certain assurances by the government, the Church called off its protest occupation of the schools. The Catholics hoped for some measure of relief for their schools when the UNP-led coalition of Dudley Senanayake won the general election of March 1965, but they were disappointed. They complained against the Senanayake government making the four *póya* days in the month, which relate to the changing phases of the moon and are of significance to Buddhists, obligatory public holidays in the public and private sectors instead of the usual sabbath days.

It was, however, the Ceylon Tamil problem that created the greatest difficulties for the post-1956 governments. Although in June 1956 Parliament passed the bill to make Sinhalese the only official language throughout the island, Bandaranaike realised the difficulty of effecting an overnight switch and therefore postponed by gazette notification its full implementation to January 1961. But trouble was to come from the Tamil FP. In August 1956 the FP met in convention at Trincomalee and demanded autonomy under a Federal constitution for the Ceylon Tamil areas, parity of status for the Sinhalese and Tamil languages and a satisfactory settlement of the problem of the stateless Indian Tamils in Srī Laṅkā. Tension mounted in the months that followed, and a crisis was averted when the Prime Minister and the FP entered into a compromise agreement in July 1957. Under this pact, Bandaranaike agreed to Tamil being an additional official language in the Ceylon Tamil majority northern and eastern provinces and to a scheme for devolving administrative powers to regional councils as a concession to the federal demand. Further, Bandaranaike agreed not to utilise the instrument of colonisation to disturb the Ceylon Tamil majority complexion of the northern and eastern provinces of the island.

This settlement may have brought about Sinhalese-Tamil reconciliation, but there was determined opposition to it from the UNP as well as from Sinhalese extremist forces. Delay in the implementation of its terms made the FP feel that the Prime Minister was not serious about his declared intentions, and drove it to launch a protest campaign against the sending of nationalised public transport buses with Sinhalese-lettered number plates to the Ceylon Tamil areas. This was followed by retaliatory acts in the Sinhalese districts culminating in a demonstration of Buddhist monks performing *satyagraha* on the lawn of the Prime Minister's private residence in Colombo and demanding the abrogation of his pact with the Federalists. The Prime Minister gave in to this demand. There then followed the communal holocaust of May 1958. In August of that year, however, the Prime Minister had the Tamil Language (Special Provisions) Act passed by Parliament, but though it was an important concession, it failed to satisfy Ceylon Tamil opinion.

Since then however, Bandaranaike's settlement with the Federalists has been the basis for negotiations to solve the Sinhalese-Ceylon Tamil problem. In April 1960, the FP secured such an assurance from Mrs. Bandaranaike and the SLFP, before it gave its votes to defeat Dudley Senanayake's minority administration. Failure by Mr. Bandaranaike to keep her pledges, the enactment by her government of the Language of the Courts Act in December 1959 which provided for legal decisions being given in Sinhalese even in the Tamil areas, and her government's determination to implement Sinhalese as the only language of administration throughout the island as from 1 January 1961, notwithstanding the protests of the Ceylon Tamil representatives in Parliament, led the FP once more to launch a massive civil disobedience campaign in the northern and eastern parts of the island during March-April 1961. On 17 April a state of emergency was once again declared to bring the Ceylon Tamil areas under control. The UNP for its part, because of its minority situation after the general election of 1965, used Bandaranaike's agreement with the FP as a basis for securing its support for the formation of a coalition government. Sinhalese pressure groups however again organised opposition to the implementation of that section of the agreement which provided for the setting up of district councils "under the control and direction of the central government", and forced Dudley Senanayake in mid-1968 to abandon his district councils bill.

The language provisions of Bandaranaike's agreement with the FP were, however, implemented by legislation enacted in January 1966. Dudley Senanayake and his Government argued that they were only implementing Bandaranaike's legislation of 1958. The SLFP and its left-wing allies, however, opposed this legislation, stating that it was contrary to their late leader's intentions.

The Problems of a Stagnant Economy. In economic policy the main trend since 1956 has been the emphasis on a mixed economy. The public sector has been strengthened largely at the expense of private enterprise. But though the latter has received a lower priority, especially under SLFP dominated governments, it has nevertheless received various incentives within the confines of its more restricted role in the economy.

Some of the problems of the economy prior to 1956 had stemmed from the fact that the island's trade was not sufficiently diversified. The situation changed with the election of 1956. Previously most of the traditional markets with the exception of the U.S.A. and China were in the sterling area. Srī Laṅkā did not even have diplomatic relations with the communist countries. But after 1956 trade ties were established with the U.S.S.R. and the other countries of Eastern Europe. The sterling area, however, still continues to be the major buyer of export produce, and a little over one-third of imports is from the countries of the Commonwealth, of which Britain again is the major supplier. Next to Britain, China is at present the principal trading partner.

Ceylonese enterprise was also hampered by the fact that it did not secure proper accomodation from the locally operating foreign-owned commercial banks. This explains why, in 1948, 90 per cent of the island's import trade was controlled by non-Ceylonese. Since then, governments in office, responding to pressure from local trading interests, have introduced various measures to help the indigenous trader. Trade established with a number of new countries is reserved only for indigenous traders, by whom alone imports of specified goods and exports to a number of countries can be undertaken. Added to all this, the Bank of Ceylon (established in 1939) and the People's Bank (established in 1961) have enabled more and more local traders to enter the field of commerce and industry.

There are, as has been seen in earlier chapters, serious balance of payments problems owing to adverse terms of trade — a situation which has not altered even with corrective measures such as the imposition of severe and rigid import and exchange controls. The volume of domestic resources available is simply not sufficient to meet the country's target rate of economic growth. External assets, short-term borrowings and aid from donor countries have therefore had to make up the shortfall.

In late 1967 and early 1968 steps were taken by the private-enter-prise-oriented 'national government' to ease the restrictions on imports and the use of foreign exchange to provide incentives to increase output and to exploit domestic resources on a more rational basis. The devaluation of the rupee by 20 per cent in November 1967, the introduction of a foreign exchange entitlement scheme in May 1968 resulting in a further depreciation in the exchange rate for a number of transactions, the placing of a considerable number of commodities under open general licence and the liberal-isation of procedures for the remittance of profits and dividends abroad had some favourable impact on the balance of payments. Foreign assistance was also obtained to help bridge the gap. This came in the form of commodity aid programmes and loans from the International Monetary Fund. However, the net foreign debt of the country more than doubled between 1964 and 1968. Foreign aid has been readily forthcoming even after the left-wing-oriented UF government took office in May 1970.

Foreign exchange earnings have declined considerably since 1970 and the question is how best to adjust the economy to prevent it reverting to a state of near-stagnation. Further, net payment for such services as remittances of dividends and profits, rise in interest payments on external borrowings and increase in private remit-tances of Indians being repatriated under the Indo-Ceylon agree-ments of 1964 and 1974 add to the existing difficulties. Besides, repayments have to be made to the International Monetary Fund. Import capacity to maintain economic growth has therefore been very much less since 1970 than in 1967-8. Import substitution, at the present rate of growth, will not be able to close the gap, especial-ly because the rate of growth has fallen sharply after 1970. Addi-tional financing from abroad provides the only interim solution.

Sri Lanka's economic dilemma lies in its rising population, at the disposal of which has been placed a whole range of welfare services, unequalled in Asia, which the country's resources can ill afford to

sustain. Between the censuses of 1946 and 1953, the population rose
from 6.7 to 8.1 million and at the census of 1963, it stood at 10.6
million. Ten years later it was 12.8 million. Though the annual
rate of increase declined from 2.8 per cent in 1953 to 2.4 per cent in
1968, partly because of the use of contraceptive devices and the
postponement of marriage by women, it is nevertheless expected
that if the present trends persist, the population will double itself
in twenty-nine years compared with the three score years and ten
that developed nations take to double their population. In effect,
the country retains a primitive birth-rate with a modernised
death-rate.

More pertinent to the economic problem is the relative youth of
the island's population. It is estimated that 52 per cent of the population is below nineteen years of age and 40 per cent is under fourteen. This implies greater dependence of the young on the old and
an additional strain on the nation's welfare system. Thus a survey
of consumer finances conducted by the Central Bank in 1953 revealed that every 100 employed persons had 203 dependants. A similar
survey in 1963 indicated a higher proportion, viz. 100 employed
persons to every 268 dependants. Because of the increase in the
number of dependants and growing unemployment the crude
activity rate for Srī Laṅkā had fallen from 35.6 per cent in 1953 to
31.7 per cent in 1963.

The high rate of population increase brings a corresponding increase in the work-force. The estimated work-force of 3.4 million
in 1956 is expected to have increased to about 7 million by 1981,
creating problems for the country in the field of manpower planning and employment. Further, in view of the undiversified and
ill-planned structure of secondary and higher education in the
country, labour is at a surplus in both the traditional and developing sectors of the economy; there is consequently unemployment
and under-employment. There is also a marked shortage of technically and vocationally qualified personnel. It is estimated that
about 100,000 school-leavers enter the labour market annually but
mainly in search of white-collar jobs.

Of the work force, it was estimated in 1963 that 13.8 per cent, or
approximately 4.4 per cent of the island's population, was unemployed—in this group is a large number of graduates. The problem of absorbing this growing unemployed and under-employed
work-force has still not been solved by governments in office.

About 60 per cent of the island's population of over 12 million
people lives within the south-west quadrant of the island, with
population densities of over 1,000 per square mile along the coastal
strip. Put another way, about 75 per cent of the entire population

lives and earns its livelihood within a radius of 80 miles from the capital city of Colombo, thus making it almost impossible for governments in office to effect any sizeable cuts in the social services without courting disastrous consequences either in the form of strikes and acts of violence, or electoral defeats unless of course they provide other compensatory benefits.

Expenditure on the social services has increased tremendously since independence — roughly, it has been about 35 per cent of total government expenditure. Most of the money has been spent on food subsidies, education, land redistribution schemes, public health, subsidised transport in the form of cheap bus and rail fares, housing and poor relief. It is argued that such expenditure is wasteful and a drag on economic development.

The overwhelming majority of schools are state-operated as a consequence of legislation enacted in 1960 and 1961 for the nationalisation of almost all the educational institutions, which were previously controlled by Roman Catholic and Protestant missionary organisations. Over 75 per cent of children between the ages of five and fourteen attend school. The literacy rate, if the 0-4 age group is excluded, is very high, about 85 per cent of the total population. State expenditure on education is among the highest in Asia. It averaged at a little more than 4.5 per cent of the estimated GNP between 1959 and 1968. An IBRD mission to Ceylon in 1966 reported that after Japan, Ceylon "had the best developed education system in Asia".

In the field of medicare too the state is very liberal. Hospitals and dispensaries are provided throughout the country and outpatient as well as inpatient treatment is provided free in all these institutions to patients who cannot afford to pay. Consequently the crude death rate today is only 8 per thousand of the population compared to 31.2 in 1921, and expectation of life at birth has increased from 32.7 in 1921 to about 65 in 1962.

It is, however, the rice subsidy which is the severest drain on the limited resources available to the country for economic development. This is in fact a double subsidy involving a guaranteed price for paddy to domestic producers much above the world market price, a free weekly ration (in November 1974) of 1 lb. of rice per person and an additional 1 lb. per person per week at a subsidised price. This double subsidy absorbs a considerable portion of all revenue, blocks public savings for public investment, increases the use of foreign exchange for imports of rice and discouraged until very recently the domestic production of substitutes for rice.

Rice in Srī Laṅkā is politics, and the 'National government' of Dudley Senanayake paid the price of a devastating electoral defeat at the general election of May 1970 for its decision in December 1966 to reduce the weekly ration of 4 lb. of rice per person at Rs. 0.50 per lb. to a free weekly ration of 2 lb. The succeeding UF Government retained the free weekly ration of 2 lb. while providing in addition 2 lb. per week at a subsidised price. This was in fulfilment of its electoral promise to make good the cuts imposed by its predecessor.

The gravity of these problems was highlighted with the outbreak of the insurrection of April 1971. The overwhelming victory scored by the United Front at the general election of May 1970 gave rise to a highly unstable situation. Expectations were raised especially among the large numbers of educated unemployed. The new government's efforts at providing solutions proved weak palliatives and the resulting frustrations were compounded by the fact of its Left component failing to implement the policies on nationalisation that were pledged in the UF's election manifesto and earlier in their Common Programme. To add to it all, the Government's leftward direction in domestic matters and its pronouncedly anti-West stance on foreign policy questions reduced the possibilities of foreign aid from the West. The inevitable climax came with the insurrection of youth in April 1971, sponsored and directed by the ultra-left Janatha Vimukthi Peramuna (People's Liberation Front).

The JVP demanded immediate nationalisation and solutions to the economic and unemployment problems. It concentrated its fire on the traditional Left within the UF government. The JVP leader, Rohana Wijeweera, ridiculed the socialism that the UF's Trotskyist Minister of Finance (Dr. N. M. Perera) was seeking to inaugurate "through the World Bank and the International Monetary Fund". He insisted that his party was "the only genuine and dedicated revolutionary party in the country" condemning in the process the LSSP's and CP's "shameful revisionism" and the Peking-wing CP's "opportunist maoism".

The JVP's objectives correspond to the principles of revolutionary marxism. Their program is epitomised in *the five lectures.* The first was on the subject, "Economic Crisis", the solution to this being the establishment of "the dictatorship of the proletariat" accompanied by "socialist industrialisation" and the "collectivisation of agriculture". The second, "Independence — a neo colonial stratagem", insisted that "political independence without economic independence was a sham". The third, "Indian Expansionism", explained the adverse consequences to the island of the devious methods of Indian capital and the "racist politics" they engage in to keep the Indian plantation workers isolated from their indigenous counterparts. The fourth criticised and condemned the politics of the traditional Left and was entitled "The Left Movement in Ceylon". The fifth, "The Path to Socialism in Ceylon" — also referred to by some of the JVP leaders as "The Path the Ceylonese Revolution should take" — explained that socialist revolutions did not have to follow a "uniform path" but would vary according to "the time, the place and the conditions peculiar to each occasion".

The movement drew its support primarily from the younger generation — the 16-25 age group from the higher forms in senior secondary schools and universities. A large number of school-leavers also provided a recruiting base. Many girls were active members. There was sympathy from government and state corporation employees as well as from sections of the Buddhist clergy. A noteworthy feature was the involvement in the insurrection of depressed caste groups in the central and southern districts of the island. The JVP's hard core, however, was not among workers or peasants, but among the middle and lower-middle classes and those with aspirations of entering that segment of the community.

The insurrection failed because it did not have substantial support in the countryside or from the urban workers. It was put down with considerable ruthlessness. Though in the first few days the Srī Laṅkā army was in serious difficulties, adequate military assistance soon came from Britain, the United States and India, as well as from the Soviet Union, Yugoslavia and Pakistan to enable the armed forces to recover from their initial setbacks. All the same, the insurrectionists left behind a trail of disaster putting back for several years the progress of economic development.

The widespread appeal of the JVP and its success in obtaining the support of the country's youth led the UF to think that, in order to survive electorally, it must move further to the left. This largely explains the radical changes put through in 1972 and 1973 — the ceilings on incomes, on ownership of land and houses, legislation for the state to appoint directors to public and private companies and provisions for the nationalisation or acquisition of not less than 51 per cent of any trade or industry where necessary.

The UF Government has, however, found it virtually impossible to handle the economic situation because of serious balance of payments difficulties and the burden of servicing the foreign debts incurred by successive governments to date. Consequently various restrictions have had to be imposed on the social services, and the main Opposition party, the UNP, has not been slow to exploit the situation. To save itself from further embarrassment, the Government has tended to become increasingly authoritarian, eroding in the process many of the freedom available to a democratic polity.

Conclusion

Sri Lanka has worked the Westminster model with local adaptations for well over twenty-five years while many of the post-World War II new states have opted for various forms of authoritarian rule. The singular achievement is that change followed a fairly settled path despite occasional disturbances and challenges to the constitutional order. The years 1948, 1956 and 1970 have been significant milestones in the island's progress from independence (1948) to political and social change (1956), to leftward socialist directions (1970). These changes, have no doubt produced turmoil but the system proved resilient enough to accommodate the periodical shocks.

The question arises as to whether the fairly long phase of parliamentary politics is approaching its end — evidenced already by what is known as rule by emergency decree. There are a number of possibilities — the abandonment of Parliament, foreign intervention, nation-breaking and/or revolutionary situations accompanied by endemic or sporadic violence. For the time being the two major political groupings led by the SLFP and the UNP provide a kind of shadowy stability. This cannot last for very long.

The SLFP-led UF Government has by its steady output of socialist legislation since 1970—especially in the area of land reform and land nationalisation—dammed the growing social resentment to some extent. Despite all these efforts, however, the Government has failed to find satisfactory solutions to the problems of unemployment and poverty confirmed by the many defeats it has suffered at parliamentary by-elections. The UF, however, strives to maintain itself as a party of the national bourgeoisie with support from the traditional Left.

In the present context, the UNP is the immediate alternative. The death of its leader, Dudley Senanayake, in April 1973 removed from the political scene a powerful charismatic personality. His successor, J. R. Jayawardene, the Leader of the Opposition, has given the party a refurbished image. He was involved in similar efforts in 1956, 1960 and 1965, and the results were seen in the party's successes at the general elections of March 1960 and March 1965. Jayawardene has rallied his party and there is every reason to believe that it will make a powerful impact at the general election scheduled for 1977.

FURTHER READING

Karunatilake, H. N. S., *Economic Development in Ceylon*, New York (1965).
Kearney, Robert N., *The Politics of Ceylon (Sri Lanka)*, Ithaca, N. Y. (1974).

Wilson, A. Jeyaratnam, *Politics in Sri Lanka,* 1947-1973, London (1974).

Wilson, A. Jeyaratnam, *Electoral Politics in an Emergent State: The Ceylon General Election of May 1970,* Cambridge University Press (1975).

Woodward, C. A., *Growth of a Party System in Ceylon,* Providence, R. I. (1969).

Wriggins, W. Howard, *Ceylon: Dilemmas of a New Nation,* Princeton, N. J. (1960).

NOTE   Valuable information on other source material is available in the bibliographical section of each of the above-mentioned references.

13

THE CONSTITUTION AND CONSTITUTIONAL REFORM SINCE 1948

by K. M. de Silva

Constitution-making was an inevitable concomitant of the process of transfer of power in South Asia. If the constitution under which the new Dominion of Ceylon began its political existence—the Soulbury constitution—was of British origin, in contrast to the autochthonous constitution drafted for India by her constituent assembly, it was also true that it was basically the constitution drafted for D. S. Senanayake in 1944 — and subsequently overwhelmingly approved by the State Council—modified to suit the needs of the changed circumstances of 1947-8. And these modifications, as we shall presently see, were few and not very substantial.

The most striking feature of this constitution was that it came closer to the Westminster model than most other Commonwealth constitutions. The draft scheme of 1944 provided for a cabinet form of government adhering to the principles of collective responsibility, a unicameral legislature, and a governor-general as head of state. Whether or not there was to be a second chamber was left for the future legislature to decide, by a simple majority. The Soulbury constitution took over the scheme but added to it a second chamber. The draft constitution incorporated a scheme of representation which, without compromising the territorial as against the communal principle, gave weightage to minority groups and to backward and sparsely populated areas. This scheme was adopted in its entirety by the Soulbury Commission (and has survived the supercession of the constitution of 1972).

The guiding principles behind the draft scheme of 1944 (and the Soulbury constitution) were: that Srī Laṅkā was a multi-racial democracy; and the commitment to the maintenance of the liberal concept of a secular state in which the lines between state power and religion were scrupulously demarcated. D. S. Senanayake placed himself in direct opposition to an influential current of opinion which viewed the Srī Laṅkā polity as being essentially Sinhala and Buddhist in character, and which urged that government policies should be fashioned to accommodate a far-reaching transformation to build a new Srī Laṅkā on traditional, 'ideal', Sinhala-Buddhist lines. Implicit in this latter was a rejection of the concept of a multi-racial polity, as well as the concept of a secular state.

The draft constitution of 1944 incorporated clauses which prohibited the legislature from introducing laws which discriminated against minorities. These provisions were introduced on the initiative of D. S. Senanayake as a gesture of generosity and reassurance to the minorities. They were incorporated into the Soulbury constitution (S.29[2]), and were the only serious limitation on the powers of the new parliament. In retrospect, the rights of minorities do not appear to have received adequate protection in the Soulbury constitution, but at the time of the transfer of power the constitutional guarantees against discriminatory legislation seemed sufficiently reassuring to the minorities, largely because of the trust and confidence they reposed in D. S. Senanayake. The constitution did not incorporate a bill of rights. It was a unitary constitution, surprisingly flexible in practice despite its apparent rigidity, and the courts—as in other Dominion constitutions—could review the constitutionality of legislation and the legitimacy of the use of power.

Finally, the link with the British crown was maintained in strict law, although it had no practical significance in the lives of the people or the affairs of the country. The existence of this link tended to obscure the true fact of the island's independence from subjection to Britain. Besides, this link, in contrast to the situation in most white Dominions, was without meaning for an Asian people.

Right from its inception, the Soulbury constitution came under attack. Left-wing critics of D. S. Senanayake's government were able to argue that the independence achieved in 1947-8 was spurious. The gibe of a "fake" independence, which they kept hurling at the government, evoked a positive response from a wider circle of the political nation than merely the left wing. This was because the Indian experience seemed to provide a more emotionally satisfying example than the process by which power had been transferred in Srī Laṅkā—independence granted from above (as in Srī Laṅkā) being regarded as much less satisfying to the spirit of nationalism than if it had been won after prolonged strife and untiring sacrifice.

The island's political leadership within the Board of Ministers took pride in the fact that the transfer of power was smooth and uneventful. Thus, the last British governor of the colony of Ceylon became the first governor-general of the new Dominion. If there was a parallel for this in the case of India and Mountbatten, there was a notable difference between the constitutional and legal instruments which conferred independence on Srī Lankā and the cognate process in the rest of South Asia—for India and Pakistan there had been Acts of Parliament, for Burma, a specially negotiated treaty, for Srī Lankā a mere order-in-council. Certainly, there was no qualitative difference in the nature of the independence achieved by Srī Lankā and that attained by India and Pakistan, and no meaningful difference in status was either intended by Britain or accepted by Srī Lankā's leaders; yet, inevitably, there were disadvantages in making the process of transferring power so bland as to be virtually imperceptible to those not directly involved.

Opposition critics focussed attention on the British origins of the new constitution, and the contrast with India's autochthonous constitution. The left wing, composed of the Trotskyist Lankā Sama Samaj Party (LSSP)[2] and the Communist Party (CP), urged the establishment of constituent assembly—as in India—to draft a new constitution for the island. This idea was first put forward by the LSSP who contended that ". . . an independent country or rather a country achieving independence after foreign subjection required to mark its independence by the framing of a constitution for itself — and that the proper instrument for so framing a constitution was classically the Constituent Assembly." It might have been expected, in these circumstances, that Srī Lankā would have departed very early, from the system of government it had inherited, and developed instead a political style appropriate to the conditions of its own society. Yet the inherited system remained intact without any significant modifications for twenty-five years after independence.

In analysing the causes for the long survival of the Soulbury constitution one needs to begin by dividing the years 1947-72 into two main phases with 1956 as the dividing-line, but with a subdivision in the latter period from 1965 onwards. The first phase, 1947 to early 1956, comprised the years of the UNP domination of Srī Lankā politics. During this phase there were no moves to amend the constitution in any significant way, much less to replace it with another. The 1952 elections had given the UNP government an effective two-thirds majority, which might have been used for such a purpose had it been so minded, but it was not, though there were occasional murmurs about the need for a republican status for Srī Lankā. The left wing, both within and outside parliament, persisted in its opposition to the constitution, but its power-base was not strong enough or wide enough to make this opposition more than symbolic or ritualistic. The emergence of the Srī Lankā Freedom

Party in 1951 did not initially strengthen the forces of constitutional reform, for the new party did not have the same dogmatic opposition to the Soulbury constitution as the left-wing groups. Indeed S.W.R.D. Bandaranaike, the founder of the SLFP, had been a member of the Board of Ministers and the cabinet at the time the constitution was negotiated and accepted. He had seconded D. S. Senanayake's formal motion introduced in the State Council on 8 November 1945, accepting the Soulbury constitution. The Federal Party, in the meantime, had set forth its proposal for a federal constitution, but it was not much more than a voice in the wilderness; its following among the Tamils was much less substantial than that of G. G. Ponnambalam, the acknowledged leader of the Tamils, who for much of this period was a member of the cabinet, and whose party the Tamil Congress was an integral unit of the government.

During the years 1956-72 the SLFP was the dominant force in Srī Laṅkā's politics, either ruling on its own or as the predominant influence in a coalition with left-wing parties. Bandaranaike's main concern at the time he became Prime Minister in 1956 was about limitations and curbs on Srī Laṅkā's sovereignty, which he was anxious to eliminate. However, he was concerned more with the defence agreements with Britain, signed at the time of the transfer of power than with the Soulbury constitution itself. Soon he was able to satisfy himself that these agreements were not detrimental to the country's status as a free and sovereign state (and it is significant that these agreements, for all the criticism they have been subjected to from time to time, have never yet been abrogated). At the Commonwealth Prime Ministers Conference in 1956, Bandaranaike secured the agreement of his fellow Prime Ministers for his country's transition to republican status within the Commonwealth. He was anxious, at the same time, to introduce amendments to the Soulbury constitution. On his initiative a Joint Parliamentary Select Committe on Constitutional Reform was set up on 2 November 1957 to prepare the basis of a new constitutional structure.[3] But the political instability of the last phase of his tenure of office as Prime Minister put paid to any prospects of introducing amendments to the constitution.[4]

Between 1960 and 1965 the SLFP took the view that the Soulbury constitution should be amended, and its election manifesto of 1960 spelled out the amendments desired: ".... a reconsideration of the position of the Senate, the definition of democratic and economic rights, and the establishment of a democratic republic..." Its manifesto of 1965 — which had the endorsement of the LSSP and CP (Moscow Wing)—reiterated the theme of a republic and the need to revise the constitution "to suit the needs of the country". The Federal

Party by this time was the predominant influence among the Tamil minority, but the federal constitutional structure they advocated was not a politically viable proposition.

The survival of the Soulbury constitution, without fundamental change, during this decade of SLFP-dominated governments can be explained on a different basis as well. The comparative flexibility of the constitution, and the lack of a bill of fundamental rights enabled the political structure to accomodate itself to a series of far-reaching changes, most if not all of which adversely affected ethnic and religious minorities. As early as 1948 the Ceylon Citizenship Act eliminated the vast bulk of the Indian plantation workers from the electoral registers by the simple device of defining the right to citizenship far more rigidly than under the Donoughmore constitution. It was thus demonstrated that the constitutional obstacle of Section 29[2] [b] would not operate as long as legislation was so framed that there might be a restriction in fact but not in legal form, and the restriction was made applicable to all sections of the community and not to a specific group. When S.W.R.D. Bandaranaike's Official Language Act was introduced in the House of Representatives in 1956, the Speaker ruled that it was not a constitutional amendment and therefore required only a simple majority. In 1960 the Roman Catholics found to their dismay that the constitution provided no protection for them in their campaign to preserve the *status quo* in education.

Equally important, nationalisation of local and foreign business ventures was facilitated by the fact that there was no provision in the constitution for just and expeditious payment of compensation. Thus there was no constitutional protection for special economic interests and property rights in general.

In 1963 Lord Soulbury[5] himself was afforded an opportunity of expressing his views on these developments.[6] He would not endorse a comment made by a senior Colonial Office civil servant that "the Soulbury constitution . . . had entrenched in it all the protective provisions for minorities that the wit of man could devise."[7] On the contrary, he argued that ". . . . in the light of later happenings — I now think it is a pity that the [Soulbury] Commission did not also recommend the entrenchment in the constitution of guarantees of fundamental rights, on the lines enacted in the constitutions of India, Pakistan, Malaya, Nigeria and elsewhere."[8]

It could be argued that if the constitution had provided more effective checks against legislation discriminating against minorities or indeed depriving them of privileges enjoyed during colonial times and continued after independence, pressure for fundamental amendments of the constitution, or for its replacement by an autochthonous constitution would have been impossible to resist. As it was, constitutional reform received very low priority in the 1960s from the SLFP.

The policy of the UNP in government and in opposition had been the revision of the Soulbury constitution; in particular, the party advocated that Srī Laṅkā should become a republic within the Commonwealth. But when in power (1965-70) it lacked the parliamentary majority (two-thirds of all members of the Lower House) necessary to amend the constitution.

It was during their years in opposition between 1965 and 1970 that the constituent parties of the present coalition government made a far-reaching re-appraisal of their stand on the question of constitutional reform. They came to the conclusion that a mere revision of the existing constitution was inadequate and committed themselves to a new policy of forming a constituent assembly which would derive its "authority from the people of Srī Laṅkā and not from the power and authority assumed and exercised by the British Crown and Parliament in establishing the present [Soulbury] constitution . . . nor from the constitution they gave us." This was no more—and no less—than the adoption by the present coalition government of the orthodox LSSP and CP attitude on an autochthonous constitution for the island.

The question naturally arises—how did the SLFP come to acquiesce in, and indeed enthusiastically endorse, this line of action? The answer, one suspects, lies in the judgements of the Judicial Committee of the Privy Council in London, in regard to Section 29 of the Soulbury constitution which related to minority safeguards. The Privy Council, in an *obiter dictum*, had held that this clause was an entrenched provision which could not be amended in any revision of the constitution.[9] To the SLFP—as the unabashed advocates of the Sinhala-Buddhist domination of the island—this would have been ample justification for accepting the view that a new constitution should be drafted and that a constituent assembly would be the best means of doing this. Its overwhelming electoral victory in May 1970 gave the present coalition the opportunity it sought to put these ideas into effect. One of their first acts after assumption of office was the summoning of a constituent assembly. The intention was quite deliberately to provide for the establishment of a free, sovereign and independent republic through an authochthonous constitution. And to underline the autochthonous nature of the new constitution, the constituent assembly consciously and consistently acted outside the framework of the Soulbury constitution; indeed its framers claimed that in "its essential procedures and entire functioning [it was] counterposed to the [Soulbury] constitution".[10]

The Minister of Constitutional Affairs, Colvin R. de Silva, had been a critic of the Soulbury constitution from the time it was introduced in 1947, and he now had the satisfaction of presiding over its supercession. More important, the new constitutional structure that emerged bore the imprint of his ideas, even though he was not always the predominant influence in this enterprise of constitution-making.

On 19 July 1970, when the Prime Minister, Sirima Dias Bandaranaike, moved that the Members of Parliament proclaim themselves the constituent assembly of the people of Sri Lanka for the purpose of adopting and enacting a constitution, her resolution was unanimously accepted and there was the appearance of a national consensus on the basic elements of constitutional reform. But the consensus was more apparent than real. A demoralised opposition confronting a government at the height of its very real popularity and prestige was too weak to do more than follow where the government led, even though it felt strong reservations about the process of constitution-making adopted by the government and the proclaimed aims of the new constitution. As will be seen later in this chapter, one of the most striking developments since then was the withdrawal of support by opposition parties to the new constitution. What began as a-national endeavour with popular support ended as a party affair with lukewarm public support.

In a broadcast on 10 September 1970 Colvin R. de Silva set out what the government considered the shortcomings of the Soulbury constitution: the existence of an entrenched clause (Clause 29) which safeguarded minorities against discriminatory legislation; the right of judicial review by the courts over the constitutionality of legislation passed by parliament; colonial-oriented administrative machinery; a bi-cameral legislature; and the inequality of the adult vote under the existing system of delimiting constituencies in the legislature with its weighted bias in favour of the rural areas and remoter parts of the country.

The new constitution eliminated all except the last of these—the system of delimiting constituencies passed almost unchanged into the new constitutional structure. Its survival reflected the realities of political power in Sri Lanka. Originally designed to swamp the radical urban vote, the system of delimitation has come to form the basis of the SLFP's hold on power—the rural constituencies. The urban areas have become, by and large, more conservative in outlook, while the rural constituencies have become correspondingly less so.

On the eve of its introduction in May 1972, Colvin R. de Silva claimed that "the new constitution not only marks a change in the status of our land and people but also has a foundation or root which is entirely different from the foundation or root of the constitution which will be displaced today."[11] His colleague in the cabinet and fellow Trotskyite, N. M. Perera, had been more restrained in his assessment of the processes of constitution-making; on 19 July 1970, seconding the Prime Minister's resolution for the convening of the constituent assembly, he declared. "We have had forty years of experience of limited political freedom but with a full franchise. We have in some ways utilised the valued portions of that experience. We would have to discard some of the institutions associated with the recent period of our history. We would have to modify others and also construct new institutions."[12] He concluded: "No one can build entirely a new constitution. All of us are circumscribed by our own past, by our social habits and inclinations."[13]

The salient feature of the new constitution is the establishment of a uni-cameral republican structure which may be described as a centralised democracy in which the dominant element is the political executive, which has few institutional checks on its use of political power. Colvin R. de Silva, guiding spirit of the new constitution, preferred to emphasise the role of the National State Assembly in the new constitutional structure "It constitutes the legislature; the executive is drawn from it, and made responsible and answerable to it; and the courts are of its creation. . . The legislative, the executive and the judicial functions are only three aspects of the single power of the people and that organic unity of the three aspects of power is carried into the organisation of the state."[14]

The conception of the National State Assembly as the vehicle of the sovereignty of the people finds final expression in the provision which denies to the courts the power or jurisdiction to pronounce upon the validity of the laws enacted by the Assembly. The functions of the courts are confined to the interpretation of the laws. A constitutional court[15] has been established whose duty is to participate in the process of legislation as the adviser to the National State Assembly on the question of whether any provision of a bill, or a bill itself, is unconstitutional. Its advice is made binding on the National State Assembly, which has to provide a special majority of two-thirds of its membership to override a decision of the constitutional court that the provisions of a bill are unconstitutional. The Speaker of the National State Assembly is bound by the decision of the Constitutional Court, and this decision is conclusive for all purposes. Though Colvin R. De Silva claimed this device of a constitutional court was "perhaps the novel feature of the constitution"; it had a striking similarity to the constitutional court under the Fifth Republic in France.

The new constitution brought the entire administrative structure of the country under the control of the Council of Ministers. The United Front government's tenure of office has been notable for a politicisation of appointments in the more sensitive and influential positions in the higher bureaucracy. This stems from the government's belief that committed men at the top are essential for the purposeful implementation of socialist policies. This process of politicisation has been accompanied by the establishment of institutional checks on the bureaucracy at a popular level, both within and outside it. The provisions relating to the bureaucracy in the new constitution are the logical extension of this trend; they gave legal and constitutional form to a fundamental departure from the British concept of an independent public service and to the introduction of a version of the American spoils system.

The new republic of Srī Laṅkā has a President as head of state but his position is perhaps unique in that he is nominated by the Prime Minister and not elected directly or indirectly.[16] In so far as he is the Prime Minister's nominee, there is no change from the position of the Governor-General under the Soulbury constitution except that it is clearly laid down in the new constitution that the President is appointed for a period of four years. There can be no doubt that nomination by the Prime Minister detracts from the dignity and authority of the President.

In two respects, both of crucial significance, the powers of the President under the new constitution are inferior to those of the Governor-General under the Soulbury system. First, there is the removal of the residuary powers which were vested in the head of state by the Public Security Act, and the vesting of almost all these powers in the head of the political executive. Secondly, the new constitution has incorporated as law some of the constitutional conventions relating to the powers and functions of the head of state. Under the Soulbury constitution these powers and functions were exercised in accordance with the constitutional conventions governing their exercise by the Queen in the United Kingdom. These British conventions have nowhere been authoritatively laid down, and constitutional lawyers sometimes hold contradictory views about them. In Srī Laṅkā difficulties and doubts have arisen in the past, especially over the obligation of the Governor-General as head of state to accede to a Prime Minister's request for a dissolution of parliament. The new constitution spells out the circumstances in which such a dissolution may be granted or refused. The initiative and discretionary authority of the head of state are thus substantially reduced.

The new constitution, unlike its predecessor, incorporates a chapter on Fundamental Rights and Freedoms, including: the equality of all persons before the law; the prohibition of discrimination in public employment on the grounds of religion, race, caste or sex; freedom of thought, conscience and religion; protection of life and personal liberty; freedom of speech, of peaceful assembly and of association; and freedom of movement and residence.

In practice, however, their effect is largely nullified by the wide-ranging scope of the restrictions on these rights and freedoms incorporated in Section 18(2) of the constitution, which reads thus:

The exercise and operation of the fundamental rights and freedoms provided in this chapter shall be subject to such restrictions as the law prescribes in the interests of national unity and integrity, national security, national economy, public safety, public order, the protection of public health or morals or the protection of rights and freedoms of others or giving effect to the Principles of State Policy set out in Section 16.

Section 16 of the constitution sets out certain Principles of State Policy, which bear a strong imprint of the government's political outlook and commitments—the realisation of the objectives of a socialist democracy. These principles are not justiciable, and the constitution in fact states that they confer no legal rights and are not enforceable in any court of law. The principles are set out, as in some constitutions, in order to guide the making of laws and the governance of the country. The differences between the new constitution and its predecessor are therefore vital. Nevertheless, though in little more than a formal way, it does resemble the Soulbury constitution and, through it, the draft constitution of 1944. The unicameral structure goes back to 1944, as does the system of demarcation of constituencies. The draft constitution of 1944 provided for a public service commission which would advise the Governor-General *only* on new appointments carrying an initial salary of at least Rs. 3,600 a year — in effect, the higher bureaucracy. The promotion, transfer, dismissal and disciplinary control of other officers was to be vested in the Governor-General, who could delegate any of these powers to any minister of state or public officer. The Soulbury constitution adopted this scheme. It was expected that progressively the Governor-General would act on ministerial advice over appointments to, and promotions in, the higher bureaucracy and disciplinary matters, or delegate powers to ministers, and in this way enable the ministers answerable to parliament to discharge their responsibilities. Section 106 of the republican constitution of 1972 follows similar principles in vesting such powers in the hands of the Council of Ministers and makes them clearly answerable to the National State Assembly for their actions in these matters.

The Republication Constitution of 1972 incorporates two pieces of legislation which were in fact some of the most important policy formulations of D. S. Senanayake himself, though they were outside the 1944 draft. Section 67 of the new constitution essentially retains the laws relating to citizenship enacted in 1948 and 1949 with their consequential amendments, while Section 134 inscribes into the new constitution the Public Security Act of 1947 with the amendments to it introduced subsequently.

Between 19 July 1970, when the constituent assembly first met, and 22 May 1972, when the new constitution was adopted, the political situation had changed to the disadvantage of the government. Had the new constitution been introduced in 1970 or early in 1971 when the government was still popular, it would have received enthusiastic endorsement. But 1972 was a different proposition. The remorseless pressure of economic decline — inflation, unemployment and falling output in every sphere of activity — combined with the near-civil war of 1971 had perceptibly eroded the popularity of the government and reduced its self-confidence. The insurrection itself had been a challenge to its credibility as a genuinely socialist government.

It was on 16 March 1971 that the first of the basic resolutions on the new constitution came up for discussion before the constituent assembly (these basic resolutions had been discussed first by a Steering and Subjects Committee consisting of political leaders and constitutional experts). The outbreak of the insurrection of April 1971 interrupted the work of the constituent assembly. But significantly it re-assembled in the second week of May almost as soon as the government had re-established its control over the districts which were centres of insurrectionary activity. Indeed the constituent assembly was at that time the most significant, if not the only, formal political activity permitted. With a curfew, emergency legislation and censorship in force, there was legitimate fear that the free exchange of ideas and organisation of public opinion on constitutional reform would be greatly impeded. To underscore its dissatisfaction with the government's decision to continue with the debates of the constituent assembly against the background of a formidable insurrection, the main opposition group—the United National Party—staged a well-publicised walk-out from the constituent assembly at its first meeting on 14 May 1971, but they returned to participate in the debates of the assembly next day.[17] They maintained that the possibility of obtaining a genuine national consensus on constitutional reform was seriously jeopardised by ignoring these obstacles.

The government sought to reassure its critics on this point by guaranteeing that existing restrictions would not apply to discussions and meetings on the constitution. But the situation in the country was not conducive to the organisation of meetings or the free expression of views. Thus critics could argue with ample justice that public participation in the process of constitutional reform was ". . . minimal, not because the public did not want to participate, but because the procedures were such as to make participation minimal".[18]

A referendum on the new constitution might have been some compensation for the lack of opportunities for free discussion on the constitution outside the precincts of the constituent assembly and for public participation in the process of constitution-making. Instead the government was satisfied with the adoption of the constitution by a majority (two-thirds) in the constituent assembly. Or a general election might have been held for the National State Assembly immediately after the inauguration of the new constitution. However, the ruling coalition gave itself an extended term of office to 1977, two years beyond the five-year term for which it had been elected in May 1970. This latter decision was crucial in the withdrawal of opposition support for the new constitution.

In June 1971 the constituent assembly resolved that the National State Assembly under the new constitution would go on for a period of six years after the constituent assembly adopted the new constitution. Since this latter body was no more and no less than the House of Representatives elected in May 1970, this would have meant that MPs elected in May 1970 would have a spell of eight years. This, the opposition urged, was a breach of faith with the people who had not been given any indication in May 1970 that they were electing a parliament for any longer than the normal five-year term provided for by the existing constitution. They argued that the government had no mandate for thus extending the life of parliament. Under strong pressure from opposition groups in the constituent assembly the government decided to reduce the term of the first National State Assembly to five years (all future ones would sit for a term of six years). But this revision, which was announced in the constituent assembly on 8 May 1972, did not satisfy the opposition. For the fact was that the government had used its overwhelming majority in the constituent assembly to give itself an extended term of life.

This action by the government is probably unprecedented in the annals of constitution-making in democratic states. In taking the decision the government demonstrated scant regard for any considerations of its own sense of public integrity. Its immediate effect was to give these proceedings a patently partisan outlook, ensuring thereby a substantial erosion of what national consensus there remained on constitutional reform. Dudley Senanayake, former Prime Minister and late leader of the UNP, declared that this unilateral extension of the government's normal term of office was one of the main reasons for his party's decision to vote against the adoption of the new constitution.

By the end of the June 1971 the Federal Party, the main political party of the indigenous Tamil minority, had made the crucial decision to boycott the constituent assembly as a protest against the failure to provide adequate protection for minority rights. The rift between the Federal Party and the government had emerged over the question of language rights. To the official resolution that "all laws shall be enacted in Sinhala. There shall be a Tamil translation of every law so enacted", the Federal Party moved an amendment that Sinhala and Tamil should be the official languages of Srī Laṅkā, the languages of the courts, and the languages in which all laws should be published. This amendment led to an acrimonious debate. The government argued that the amendment was tantamount to a total rejection of the existing position on the national language—a consensus achieved through the years since 1956—and a position which the Federal Party itself had come to accept. It added that this amendment would be totally unacceptable to the people.

On 28 June 1971 the Federal Party amendment was defeated by a vote of 87 to 13, upon which its members walked out of the constituent assembly, and did not return to participate any further in its deliberations thereafter.

That there was a consensus on language to which the Federal Party among others had given its tacit acceptance is incontrovertible. At the same time it is important to remember that clause 29 of the Soulbury constitution—that relating to minority rights—was an integral part in this consensus. Though the protection this clause afforded to the minorities was less comprehensive than its framers intended it to be, it nevertheless acted as a deterent against patently discriminatory legislation. The government scarcely concealed the fact that it was resorting to the device of a new constitution in preference to a reform of the old one partly, at least, because it afforded a means of eliminating Clause 29. Once this vital clause had been removed a significant element in the consensus on language had been unilaterally discarded to the detriment of the Tamil minority. Thus it was no longer possible to speak of a consensus on language which the Federal Party itself had come to accept, tacitly or otherwise.

If the Tamil minority was decisively alienated by this controversy over language rights in the new constitution, the sensibilities of other opposition groups were offended by the manner in which the state's propaganda machinery sought to make political capital out of this enterprise of a new constitution, and to identify it with the government parties alone. It was inevitable that the constitution would come to bear the ideological stamp of the political groups which formed the government, and every realistic opposition politician would have anticipated such an outcome; however, they had been given reason to believe that the government would treat it as a national and nation-building enterprise, but this was not to be. Thus the grant of Dominion status on 4 February 1948 was downgraded, and the celebration of national independence on 4 February was ostentatiously rejected for the future in favour of 22 May, Republic Day. The assumption of republican status was identified with the attainment of independence. Thus a national endeavour became a partisan affair, and the new constitution, far from bringing the people together,[19] ensured the perpetuation of ethnic disharmony, and aggravated political rivalries.

In the final phase of the constituent assembly's life it became clear that the UNP would vote against the adoption of the new constitution. On 22 May 1972, at the final sessions of the constituent assembly, Dudley Senanayake explained at length why his party was voting against the new constitution. He declared that while they were ". . . clearly and unequivocally . . . in full accord with the government that the new constitution should declare Ceylon a free sovereign and independent republic," the constitution contained too many objectionable and potentially dangerous features to merit their support.

Thus the establishment of the republic of Srī Laṅkā was the one feature of the new constitution which attracted support extending beyond the ranks of the government. And the new constitution, like its predecessor, started off with a large section of the political nation (a much larger section than in the case of the Soulbury Constitution) unenthusiastic about it if not vocally opposed to it, and quite definitely committed to its supercession or modification through far-reaching amendment.

These misgivings about the new constitution were given greater emphasis with two events that occurred since the introduction of the constitution, the first in December 1972—January 1973, and second in September 1974. The first of these was with regard to the constitutional court.

One of the most important ways in which the new constitution broke off from past constitutional practice was in the provisions which prohibited the ordinary courts from exercising the power of judicial review over legislation. Instead a constitutional court of five judges was established for this purpose. The judges are appointed by the President on the advice of the Prime Minister, and cannot be removed, once appointed, except in certain circumstances specified in Section 56 of the new constitution. Thus a constitutional court appointed during the term of office of one government or of one National State Assembly is vested with powers to sit in judgement over the acts of a succeeding National State Assembly because the terms of the office of the court and the Assembly overlap. The draft constitution (of 1971) sought to overcome this difficulty by providing for the constitutional court to go out of existence at the same time as the National State Assembly, but this was dropped in the final draft of the constitution. Thus there is the distinct possibility that the constitutional court could, like the American Supreme Court, thwart the popular will if a new government in office were not in command of a two-thirds majority.

The new constitution was hardly a year old when the first constitutional crisis erupted[20] — significantly, over the powers of the constitutional court. This was with regard to the Press Council Bill which was challenged before the court, the first bill to be so challenged under the new constitution. At this stage there was no procedure laid down for the purpose of these hearings and no precedents to go by. Under Section 65 of the constitution the court was required to deliver its verdict within fourteen days. The three members of the constitutional court who heard the appeal against the Press Council Bill took up the position that this fourteen-day rule was directory, that they were not bound by it and would instead have a full and complete hearing of the case. The government refused to accept this position; they held that the fourteen-day rule was mandatory, and that if the constitutional court failed to give its verdict on the Bill within this period, the National State Assembly had no option but to proceed with the debate on the Bill. The view of the constitutional court was that the duty of interpreting the constitution — to determine whether the fourteen-day rule was mandatory or not — was theirs and theirs alone.

At issue were two diametrically opposed views on the status of the constitutional court. The government held the view that the constitution did not recognise the theory of the separation of powers, and the National State Assembly was the residual source of all power and authority; the constitutional court was an advisory body and its function was to help the Assembly by testing bills for repugnancy. As against this, the constitutional court sought to uphold its right as the sole interpretive authority of the constitution. It was also upholding the principle of the independence of the judiciary from interference by the executive.

The crisis ended with the resignation of the three judges directly involved in testing the Press Council Bill for repugnancy, and three others were shortly afterwards appointed in their place.

The issues involved in the second event —that of September 1974 — were more complex and subtle, but not less controversial for that. The problem arose out of judicial construction of the clauses of the Interpretation Ordinance of 1972, and more specifically with regard to injunctions against the state. In eighteen cases the high courts of Kandy, Badulla and Ratnapura, as well as some district courts, had entertained applications for injunctions against the Minister of Agriculture and Lands for *mala fide* acquisition of property. The supreme court, by a majority of five to four, upheld the view taken by the lower courts in granting injunctions in these cases. Their decision was delivered on 3 September 1974. On 5 September government rushed amending legislation through the National State Assembly[21] to meet the situation created by this decision of the supreme court. What transpired on this occasion may be summarised as follows: when a majority of judges of the supreme court interpreted the legal construction of a law that had been passed, amending legislation was introduced —and passed —substituting what the legislature had intended to say in the first instance, and two ministers[22] maintained in the National State Assembly that the law must be held to say what the legislature had intended to say, namely that injunctions could not be given against the state.

In defence of the amending bill, F. R. Dias Bandaranaike, Minister of Home Affairs, Local Government, Public Administration and Justice, stated that its purpose was to make clear the intention of the legislature concerning injunctions. He pointed out that the amending bill, while ensuring the independence of the judiciary, would delineate the principle of the sovereignty of the National State Assembly in the process of law-making. A suggestion he outlined on this occasion was even more significant in this regard: viz. whenever there were doubts about the meaning of a law enacted by the National State Assembly, these could be settled by a committee of lawyer-parliamentarians.[23] Although this latter has not materialised, the fact is that with the Interpretation Ordinance (Amendment) Bill of 1974, the executive and the legislature were encroaching on a sphere of activity —the interpretation of legislation —which is the prerogative of the judiciary. To that extent it served once more to emphasise the point that the central feature of the new constitution was the dominance of the executive and the lack of meaningful institutional — and constitutional —checks on the exercise of its powers.

1. For discussion of this see K.M. de Silva, 'The History and Politics of the Transfer of Power' in K.M. de Silva (ed.), *History of Ceylon*, Vol. III, Part IV, Chapter VIII, pp. 489-533.

2. The Trotskyists were divided into two factions at this time — the Lanka Sama Samaj Party, and the Bolshevik-Leninist Party of India.

3. Joint Select Committees on Constitutional Reform were appointed during the administrations of Mrs. Sirima Bandaranaike (1960-5), and Dudley Senanayake (1965-70).

4. The only amendment secured was with regard to the law for the delimitation of constituencies. This amendment was introduced in 1959.

5. Soulbury had been Governor-General of Ceylon in 1949-54.
In a foreword to B. H. Farmer's book on *Ceylon, A Divided Nation* (O. U. P., 1963, for the Institute of Race Relations).

7. Cited in Soulbury's foreword to B. H. Farmer, op. cit. The extract was from Sir Charles Jeffries, *Ceylon — the Path to Independence*.

8. Soulbury's foreword to B. H. Farmer, op. cit.

9. See *Bribery Commissioner* vs. *Ranasinghe* [1964] in 66. *New Law Reports* 73.

10. Quite inconsistent with this, however, the government used the conventional method of a two-thirds majority, in the last quarter of 1971, to abolish the Senate and appeals to the Judicial Committee of the Privy Council.

11. Colvin R. de Silva, 'Why a New Constitution', *Times of Ceylon* (22 May 1972), special supplement.

12. See *Ceylon Daily News* (20 July 1970).

13. Ibid.

14. Colvin R. de Silva, in an interview published in the *Ceylon Oberver Sunday Magazine* (21 May 1972).

15. See below, pp.

16. As Professor A. J. Wilson has pointed out, "appointment by the Prime Minister is an unusual feature not to be found in any other constitution in the world." A. J. Wilson, *Politics in Srī Laṅkā, 1947-1973*, London (1974), p. 253.

17. The *Ceylon Daily News* (15 May 1971).

18. Seneka, 'The Restless Ecstasy of Power' in *The Times of Ceylon* (22 May 1972), special supplement.

19. In her address to the constituent assembly at its inaugural sessions on 19 July 1970 the Prime Minister declared that the new constitution must set the seal on the country's freedom, sovereignty and independence, and must be acceptable for the two-fold task of enabling the nation to complete its advance to a socialist democracy, and in a plural society, serve to build a nation "ever more conscious of its one-ness amidst diversity".

20. For discussion of this see the article entitled "Constitutional crisis over the Press Council Bill", *The Parliamentarian*, Vol. LIV (II) (1973), p. 96. See also A. J. Wilson, op. cit. n 93. on pp 324-5.

21. Introduced in the National State Assembly on 5 September, it was debated to a finish on the same day. The government moved the closure of the debate at 22 25 hours. The National State Assembly approved the bill by 86 votes to 15.
22. Colvin R. de Silva and F. R. Dias Bandaranaike.
23. F. R. Dias Bandaranaike's speech of 5 September 1974, in *Hansard* (Srī Laṅkā), Vol. II, No. 16: "... It may be we shall have to adopt systems by which the interpretation as to what parliament intended can actually be referred to parliament itself. A standing committee of lawyer-members, perhaps, would be able to advise the judges that they are out of tune and cannot get the right wave-length."

SELECT BIBLIOGRAPHY

Jacob, Lucy M., *Sri Lanka, from Dominion to Republic,* Delhi (1973).

Jennings, W.I. *The Constitution of Ceylon,* Bombay (1949).

    and Tambiah, H. W. *The Dominion of Ceylon: the Development of its Laws and Constitution,* London (1952).

Jupp, J., 'Constitutional Developments in Ceylon since Independence', *Pacific Affairs,* Vol. XLI, No. 2 (1968), pp. 169-83.

Wilson, A. J., *Politics in Sri Lanka, 1947-1973,* London (1974), Chapter V, pp. 189-225.

Wiswa-Warnapala, W. A., 'The New Constitution of Sri Lanka', *Asian Survey,* Vol. XIII, no. 12, December 1973, pp. 1179-92.

Wolf-Philips, L., 'Post Independence Constitutional Changes in the Commonwealth', *Political Studies,* XVIII (1970), pp. 18-43.

14

FOREIGN POLICY

by Vijaya Samaraweera

The Institutional Framework

The foreign affairs of independent Srī Laṅkā have throughout been the responsibility of the Prime Minister. The constitution which the country received at independence expressly provided for this: the Prime Minister was required to hold the portfolios of Defence and External Affairs. The conduct of external policy was thus brought within the very epicentre of the government — less, it may be argued, because of the intrinsic importance attributed to foreign policy at the time the constitution was drafted than because of the convention already established in the Commonwealth. In the new republican constitution no explicit provision has been made for the attachment of the external affairs portfolio to the prime-ministerial office, but the Prime Minister has continued to hold it, and this seems likely to be the precedent that will be followed in the future. Theory and constitutional practice alike require that the responsibility for external affairs, like other branches should be the collective responsibility of the cabinet, but only rarely has the cabinet been able to play a decisive role in the making of foreign policy. Individual cabinet members are of course known to have received the Prime Minister's ear, and because external policy has crucial ramifications affecting the functioning of their departments, some ministers would of necessity be consulted by the Prime Minister in policy formulation. However, it can be fairly concluded that successive Prime Ministers have tended to exercise a *personal* control and direction over the conduct of foreign affairs, though to varying degrees.

The parliament and its successor, the National State Assembly, have played only a minimal and largely unimportant role in the foreign policy process. This is perhaps a reflection of the place accorded to external affairs in domestic politics: it would be difficult indeed to conceive of a situation in which a government in power would be defeated in the legislature on an issue arising out of its conduct of foreign policy. The legislature has been by convention the forum for all Prime Ministers for the announcement of policy statements on foreign affairs, but these statements have never provoked the call for full-scale debates on foreign policy. For that matter, the throne speeches, in which the policy outlines of governments are stated at the beginning of each parliamentary session, have not evoked any lengthy or notable debates on foreign policy either. Even parliamentary questions on external relations have been rare. The expertise has been there, though no doubt in a highly limited way, and so the occasional critic of government policy has made himself heard, especially among those who are ideologically committed to an international stance in politics, but in general there has been a conspicuous lack of interest in external affairs among members of independent Srī Laṅkā's legislatures. Where individual members have been concerned about specific foreign policy issues, they have tended to choose not the legislative floor but public platforms for the airing of their views. In recent years an increasing number of parliamentarians have begun to travel abroad, some quite extensively, but this does not seem to have stimulated a new interest in foreign affairs among them.

While the conduct of foreign affairs has been largely the personal preserve of the Prime Minister, à key role in the actual formulation of policy has devolved upon official advisers and foreign affairs staff attached to the Ministries of Defence and External Affairs, which significantly is located in the same building as the Prime Minister's office. The principal adviser as well as the official directly responsible to the Prime Minister for the implementation of policy has been the Permanent Secretary (since 1972 the Secretary) to the Ministry. This official functioned in a dual capacity — he was also responsible for defence affairs — and with the increasing concern of governments with foreign affairs and the new emphasis on and commitments to defence, especially after the revolt of April 1971, his duties were found too unwieldly. An additional Secretary to the Ministry specifically in charge of external affairs was appointed in 1974. The number of officials assisting the Secretary has markedly increased over the years. At the time the ministry was created in 1948, the total home-based foreign affairs staff (excluding clerical officers) amounted to only seven but by April 1972 it had been increased to twenty-two. Various 'Desks' have been set up within the ministry, based on a regional and subject classification system — thus the Asia Desk, the United Nations Desk, etc. — so that in the despatch of day-to-day business a degree of specialisation within the office has been introduced. This reflects not only the extent to which Srī Laṅkā's relations with foreign countries have increased over the years but also a recognition of the complexities inherent in foreign affairs administration.

Since there is little doubt that the foreign affairs staff has notably influenced the conduct of Srī Laṅkā's foreign affairs, the way in which they have been recruited and the background from which they are drawn merit notice. Foreign affairs personnel — both locally-based and stationed overseas — are recruited on the basis of a periodical competitive examination open mainly to university graduates, which was common to both foreign service and civil service candidates. At the beginning the foreign service carried less occupational prestige than the civil service, but with the abolition of the civil service in 1963 and its amalgamation with the power-ranking administrative service, the foreign service has truly become the élite branch of the country's public service. More significantly, the transformation of the public service left the foreign service virtually unaffected until recent times. Consequently, the background from which the foreign service personnel has been drawn has remained largely unchanged: there has been no intrusion by the rural and semi-rural, government-schooled, *swabhasha*-speaking category of the educated. In the past few years the foreign service has been heavily criticised as being dominated by a small, self-perpetuating élite with ideals and values more attuned to the colonial era than to modern times. It is scarcely surprising that a high value was placed on a liberal education in the recruitment of foreign affairs staff and that the British Foreign Office was the chosen model for the service, but despite the public criticisms, it cannot be claimed that the foreign service has been tightly bound to the past. The present government, however, has been less than satisfied with the changes which have taken place by initiative from within the service. It has been looking beyond the exclusive service for overseas appointments, and the new Secretary in charge of foreign affairs has been recruited from outside the public service. The precise criteria adopted in choosing the new appointees are not known, though there is sufficient evidence that the emerging trend, as is already amply evident in the public service in general, is an extension of the political patronage system to an area which had hitherto remained untouched.

One further innovation introduced in 1974 merits emphasis, for it again reflects the mistrust of the "bureaucracy" manifest in the changes in the recruitment system: the creation of a "Foreign Policy

Advisory Committee" consisting of the Prime Minister's close personal advisers. Implicit in its appointment is the feeling, strongly held in some quarters of the government, that the inordinate influence exercised over Srī Laṅkā's external relations by a select group operating with a remarkable degree of freedom from domestic political, economic and social realities should be checked. It is perhaps premature to judge the impact of this committee on policy formulation — there have yet to be new departures in foreign policy — but the important fact is that the role played by officials in the conduct of external affairs has been publicly devalued.

Srī Laṅkā's diplomatic representation abroad has increased significantly. It no longer depends, as in the immediate post-independence years, on the facilities provided by Britain for representation in some countries. While continuing to have representation in the Commonwealth countries and in the power blocs, there has been an increasing emphasis on the relations with the emergent nations, partly due to ideological reasons: Srī Laṅkā has proudly identified itself with the Third World. Equally important has been the economic factor, the growing trade relations with these countries; this factor has in fact become so vital in external relations that there have been pressures for the gearing of representation abroad mainly as agencies concerned with trade and allied matters rather than as diplomatic and political outlets. Many of Srī Laṅkā's missions overseas have for long had trade *attachés*, drawn not from the foreign service but from the Ministry of Trade and Commerce at home, and the Trade Commissioner service has become a specialised branch of the country's representation abroad. The integration of the Trade Commissioner service with the foreign service has been mooted from time to time, but so far both services, each jealous of its own province and privileges, have succeeded in resisting it. The principal representatives of Srī Laṅkā abroad—high commissioners in the Commonwealth countries and ambassadors elsewhere —have been drawn from among the career diplomats attached to the foreign service as well as from political supporters of the government in power. Like many of the countries which look upon diplomatic representation as a channel for patronage, Srī Laṅkā has had its share of scandals and diplomatic *faux pas* arising out of the conduct of its non-career diplomats. More recently, especially with the increasing concern with the economic factor, the effectiveness of non-career representatives has been questioned and in some instances, especially at economically and politically sensitive stations, career diplomats have been appointed instead of non-career diplomats, and all representatives have been subjected to closer control from the home office. Thus, paradoxically, at a time when the role of officials in policy formulations has been devalued, their role in representation overseas has tended to be strengthened.

Domestic Sources of Foreign Policy

The geographical situation of Srī Laṅkā in the centre of the Indian Ocean has been an inescapable factor in the shaping of its foreign policy. The country's peoples have always been conscious of its strategic importance and its focal value for seaborne traffic — its long history as a colony could be considered by itself a sufficient index to its situational importance. Certain developments during and since the 1960s seemed at one point to have lessened this importance. With the closing of the Suez Canal the ports of Srī Laṅkā were no longer on the trade routes which traversed the Indian Ocean. The establishment of a Royal Air Force station at Gan in the Maldive Islands provided Britain and its allies with an alternate to the bases it had occupied previously in Srī Laṅkā. Moreover, as some tended to see it, the realities of nuclear strategy eclipsed the island's strategic importance. More recent events, however, have brought about a re-evaluation, and it is now clear that Srī Laṅkā's geographical location would continue to be meaningful within a world setting. The re-opening of the Suez canal will once again place its ports on the trade maps. Most important, with the increasing naval presence of the major powers, in the Indian Ocean, the island's naval facilities have acquired a new importance, and it has been alleged at different times that the Americans, the Russians and even the Chinese have cast a covetous eye on Trincomalee, the renowned natural harbour of Srī Laṅkā, as a possible base for their respective fleets. Western military analysts have introduced a further dimension to the island's strategic value by showing that submarines operating in the sea immediately south of Srī Laṅkā would be ideally placed for the launching of nuclear attacks on both the Soviet Union and China. In such a context it is no surprise that the government of Srī Laṅkā has constantly reiterated the non-alignment of its foreign policy and has begun agitating for the creation of a 'Peace Zone' embracing the Indian Ocean.

Being an island Srī Laṅkā does not share borders with any other country, but its close proximity to India has affected its conduct of foreign policy. The concept of 'Indian expansionism' has often surfaced, and official reaction to this has been somewhat ambivalent. Spokesmen for the Government have dismissed the idea as unworthy of serious consideration, yet some leading members of successive governments have also articulated the fear of this vast and populous country, which is perhaps due to history, since the island's early history abounds with South Indian attempts to establish dominion over its peoples. It is also partly due to the presence of communities within the island which have ethnic and cultural affinities with the inhabitants of South India. Moreover, there is a consciousness of the importance of the island for the defence of India: it could provide the point of entry through India's exposed southern flank. Indian governments have not been unmindful of the strategic value of Srī Laṅkā, especially during the Sino-Indian conflict and the successive Indo-Pakistan crises. Thus the deep suspicions aroused in India during the Bangladesh war over the landing in Srī Laṅkā of Pakistani air force planes flying to and from the east, despite the assurance of the Srī Laṅkā government that these flights did not involve troops or armaments, is understandable enough. Srī Laṅkā's relations with India are bound to be especially sensitive in the future as well, now that the power structure of South Asia has changed with the dismemberment of Pakistan.

Among the domestic determinant sources of Srī Laṅkā's foreign policy, the economic factor looms large. Specifically, the bent of different governments, especially those dominated by the Srī Laṅkā Freedom Party (SLFP), to pursue a properly conceptualised foreign policy has frequently been countered by the country's heavy dependence upon the vagaries of market conditions which are beyond its grasp. *This has been amply demonstrated by Srī Laṅkā's continued dealings with international monetary agencies. The politicians who in opposition decried government borrowings from institutions identified with the West, particularly with the United States, have been forced, once in power, to seek aid from those very agencies. Thus the role of institutions like the International Monetary Fund (IMF) and the International Bank for Reconstruction and Development (IBRD) as lending bodies has changed little whatever the political orientation of the government in power. Srī Laṅkā's retention of its Commonwealth membership can be viewed in the same light. The Commonwealth tie has been considered incompatible with the neutralist stance cherished by some politicians, but as members of governments they have been unable to overlook the advantages derived from it, ranging from assistance given under programmes like the Colombo Plan to trade relations on the basis of a common partnership in the sterling area. Thus the apprehension with which the present Srī Laṅkā government, which had a Trotskyite Minister of Finance till October 1975, viewed Britain's entry into the European Economic Community and its repercussions on the Commonwealth, becomes understandable.

---

*See Part II above for detailed discussions on Sri Lanka's economy.

To counter and lessen the traditional economic relations with the West, successive governments have established bilateral trade agreements with communist states. Srī Laṅkā has no doubt benefited greatly from these, but it has been discovered from time to time that some of these countries have resold trade items received from Srī Laṅkā in the open world market to their own advantage. Militant stances taken in international issues, primarily in order to emphasise Srī Laṅkā's Third World identity, have tended at times to harm the country economically. Thus the present government has acknowledged that the breaking off of relations with Israel has had repercussions on Srī Laṅkā's foreign trade. Conversely, though the government expected that due recognition for this gesture would be given by Arab states, it found to its great disappointment, and despite many urgings, that it received no special treatment from them during the oil crisis. On the other hand, governments have also realised that economic considerations would always impose limits on the militancy Srī Laṅkā could assume in international politics. Thus, despite periodic criticisms of South Africa, no government has so far made moves to sever the valuable economic ties there. The importance of the economic factor can also be illustrated by the constant attempts of governments to establish closer economic co-operation with India: misgivings in some quarters that intimate economic ties with India would lead to the drawing of Srī Laṅkā closer within the orbit of a country with territorial ambitions seem not to have carried weight.

Srī Laṅkā's population, with its plurality, has also influenced the conduct of external policy. The majority community, the Sinhalese, unlike the minority groups, do not have an ethnic or cultural focus outside the country, and have been able in consequence to take a strongly nationalist line in external affairs, unless of course the ideological commitments of particular individuals dictated otherwise. The position of the Tamils, the community next in importance numerically, has been different: leaders among them have sought with considerable success to carry the community with them in identifying with the Tamils of South India. The separatist movements in South India for the creation of a Dravidian state have given this development a pronounced political complexion. The attitude of the Tamils has brought in a particular perspective to the relations between the Sinhalese and the Tamils: the acquisition of a minority complex by the majority community, a factor compounded by the presence within the country of a sizable Indian Tamil population. Long a key issue in Indo-Srī Laṅkā relations, the political status of the Indian Tamils has now been resolved by agreements with India, but there has been no way in which its smooth operation could be guaranteed. Of the other communities, the Muslims are important in the present discussion. With their strong identification with co-religionists elsewhere and the crucial role they play in the political process in the island, often as voters who hold the balance in many constituencies, they have been able to extract gestures, if not concessions, in the formulation of foreign policy. Thus it is widely acknowledged that one of the factors which influenced the present government to break off relations with Israel was the need to conciliate the strongly pro-Arab local Muslim opinion.

The religions of the peoples of the island have had no marked influence as domestic considerations of foreign policy. Some Buddhist leaders, both lay and *bhikkhu*, have from time to time attempted to portray communist states as anti-Buddhist—the example usually quoted is Tibet under China—but it is doubtful whether they have ever succeeded in galvanising Buddhist opinion in a way which would have affected the conduct of foreign policy. Some Prime Ministers have drawn on the idiom of Buddhist literature to enunciate their external policies but this is not an indicator of an impact of Buddhist opinion. Of the other religious groups perhaps only the Roman Catholics merit notice in this context. In keeping with the stance adopted by the Catholic Church in general, much play was made by the local Catholics with the anti-religious theoretical bias of Marxists. It is arguable that this had an impact on the electoral process, but it is doubtful whether any governments have been guided by it in the formulation of their foreign policy. In any case, this factor is no longer important even in local politics.

There has been sporadic interest in foreign affairs among the wider public, but it is not possible to speak of an abiding concern with Srī Laṅkā's external relations among its peoples in general nor of a real understanding of the issues involved in foreign policy. 'Imperialism', 'colonialism', 'neo-colonialism' and the like have long been a part of the national political rhetoric, but the articulation of issues involving these concepts have invariably degenerated into a hashing and re-hashing of a number of clichés; and it is doubtful whether political leaders have succeeded in conveying a proper awareness and understanding of them to their audiences. Although foreign policy has an important bearing on the 'bread-and-butter' questions of the average voter in Srī Laṅkā—food and social welfare—the conduct of foreign policy as such has yet to emerge as a decisive issue at times of national polls. If any serious interest in foreign affairs is to be found in the country, it is largely among the English-educated professional groups. It is they above all who have access to the large literature on international affairs; neither the average Sinhalese and Tamil newspapers nor the few journals published in these languages devote substantial space to world events or their analysis. The literature distributed in the national languages by foreign missions in Srī Laṅkā have a limited circulation, and in any case are admittedly partisan. A significant number of 'friendship societies' concerned with both western and communist countries have flourished over the last two decades or so, but again their active membership has been drawn from among the intelligentsia. In fact, so close has been the interlocking of office-bearers of these societies — along a broad division between western and socialist organisations — that it has been cynically commented that office-holding in them has become a profession of its own.

Main Trends in Sri Lanka's Foreign Policy

Independent Srī Laṅkā inherited no distinctive foreign policy of its own. It was left to the new leaders to evolve a policy with the resources available to them at the time. The first Prime Minister, D. S. Senanayake, had admittedly acquired no wide-ranging experience in foreign affairs, though he had negotiated with India with consummate skill in the immediate pre-independence period on the status of the Indian Tamil population in the island. Senanayake has been heavily attacked by later critics for following Britain's lead in charting the course of Srī Laṅkā's external relations. In the context of his own times, his close association with Britain was understandable. Unlike India, whose leaders had been forced to follow a tortuous path to independence, Srī Laṅkā had negotiated its freedom from Britain, in a largely amicable way and to Senanayake, as to the other leading members of the new government, Britain was a safe and trustworthy ally. Added to this was Senanayake's own personal conviction that marxism, in its various forms, both within and without the country, posed threats to the independence of the young nation. Communist states, on the other hand, were not enamoured with Srī Laṅkā's posture in external affairs, and its repeated application for admission to the United Nations were consistently vetoed by the Soviet Union on the grounds that Srī Laṅkā was not truly an independent country, until a package deal between the major powers permitted its admission together with a number of other countries in 1955. Senanayake felt strongly about Srī Laṅkā's membership in the Commonwealth, and particularly about the material benefits which could be derived from it; it was during his premiership that the Colombo Plan was initiated, on the basis of a co-sponsorship by Srī Laṅkā and Australia at the Commonwealth conference held in Colombo in 1950. He kept Srī Laṅkā within the mainstream of the western-oriented newly independent nations. However, it is a mistake to characterise Senanayake's foreign policy as a slavish following of the western powers. In recognising China—Srī Laṅkā was one of the first states to do so—and, for example, in denying the Dutch landing rights for their aircraft and the use of its ports at the time of the Indonesian war of independence, and in mooting the plan which provided economic assistance to the newly-independent crisis-ridden Burma, he showed a capacity to act independently of the western powers and to take the initiative in international affairs when Srī Laṅkā's interests might demand it. Moreover, his ties with the western world did not preclude him, with the other leaders of the region, from advocating the concept of Asian solidarity and working towards its realisation at successive conferences of Asian statesmen. To Senanayake the greatest value of regionalism lay in the prospect of ensuring the security of the area, and he seems to have viewed this, from his own country's standpoint, as a viable alternative to dependence on Britain's military might.

Of Senanayake's policies his defence agreement with Britain, concluded at the time of independence, has attracted most attention. Under its terms Srī Laṅkā was to provide Britain with naval and air base facilities, and Britain in return guaranteed Srī Laṅkā's defence from foreign aggression. To Senanayake this was defence on the cheap; with no substantial standing army and without a navy or an air force, he saw reliance on Britain's military strength as the country's sole option. There is no doubt that Senanayake feared foreign designs on Srī Laṅkā, and although he cited the Soviet Union as the possible aggressor, his concern is more likely to have been with India. The defence agreement was sharply criticised by his opponents: to them, in particular to the politicians of the left, it exemplified his 'imperialist' connections and the illusory nature of Srī Laṅkā's independence.

In retrospect, it is arguable that the foreign policy of Srī Laṅkā's first Prime Minister lacked dynamism. However, the economy of the country had not yet come to its later beleaguered state. Also, foreign affairs never came high among Senanayake's interests — he was preoccupied for much of the time with agriculture — and once broad outlines were established, he was apparently content to leave the policy to run its course, unless specific issues demanded intervention. Not saddled with threats to his position as a leader of a political party and as Prime Minister, D. S. Senanayake was certainly not moved to involve himself actively in international affairs in order to bolster his image as a statesman within the country.

D. S. Senanayake's successor, his son Dudley, largely followed his father's policy during his short first tenure as premier. The orientation of foreign policy remained favourable to the west, and the younger Senanayake demonstrated the flexibility inherent in the policy he inherited by entering into a bilateral trade agreement with China in 1952, involving Srī Laṅkā's rubber and China's rice. This agreement was undoubtedly a landmark in the gradual movement of Srī Laṅkā's foreign policy towards a neutralist stance; from the Chinese point of view, it was also significant, because it signalled the re-entry of China into the diplomatic world of the non-communist states. The trade agreement of course did not immediately lead to intimate diplomatic ties. Its importance perhaps lay elsewhere, in the country's relations with the United States: it was at once a consequence and a cause of Srī Laṅkā's disenchantment with the policies of the Americans. The agreement came about only when Srī Laṅkā failed to obtain from the United States favourable terms for the sale of its rubber and the purchase of urgently needed rice. Once Srī Laṅkā moved to accept the better terms offered by the Chinese, the United States brought tremendous pressure to bear upon the Senanayake government to end these negotiations, in particular by threatening to cut off its economic assistance. This proved not to be the only occasion when the United States attempted to impose limitations on Srī Laṅkā's external relations by means of similar threats. On the first occasion, as later, Srī Laṅkā demonstrated its capacity to withstand such pressures,

In many respects, the tenure of the third Prime Minister of Srī Laṅkā, Sir John Kotelawala, who formed the third successive United National Party (UNP) government after independence, could be viewed as an aberration, in both his internal policies and external relations. The brash, extrovert Kotelawala acquired early a reputation for outspokenness. In keeping perhaps with the mood of the country, Kotelawala claimed to interpret international affairs in terms of the teachings of the Buddha; however, his intemperate language alone, apart from other factors, contradicted this claim. He was most vocal in denouncing marxists; the restrained voice of the perhaps much more deeply personally committed anti-marxism of the elder Senanayake was to be no guide. He carried Srī Laṅkā well into the western camp, choosing the United States rather than Britain as the principal ally. The commitments to Britain of course remained, and the British continued to be the mainstay of Srī Laṅkā's defence, though by now Srī Laṅkā had begun to build up its own armed forces. Kotelawala spoke proudly of the country's Commonwealth membership; unlike the Senanayakes, who viewed the Commonwealth more in pragmatic terms, he tended to stress the Crown's role in the Commonwealth ties—hence, his rejection of a republican constitution for his country. This has led some commentators to observe that Kotelawala was a monarchist at heart. His alignment with the west was no better demonstrated than when he permitted landing rights for American air force planes ferrying French troops for the Indo-China war. Kotelawala continued the policy of the earlier Prime Ministers and refused to establish diplomatic representation in the communist states. It is ironical, therefore, that it was during his premiership that Srī Laṅkā was admitted to the UN with the withdrawal of the Soviet Union's veto.

Kotelawala's period saw a greater activism in relation to Asian regionalism. By then a tradition of conferences of Asian leaders to discuss mutual problems had grown up—conferences were held in Delhi in 1947 and 1949—and the trend towards what has been described as 'the spirit of Bandung' had been established. Srī Laṅkā had participated in the first two conferences and had in fact played an important role in the 1949 conference, called the 'Indonesian conference' because it was summoned to discuss the Dutch-Indonesian issue. Before the meeting the Senanayake government had indicated Srī Laṅkā's stand on this by prohibiting the use of transit facilities in the island to the Dutch for their transports, and at the conference Srī Laṅkā contributed to the achieving of a consensus on the issue. Kotelawala was responsible for initiating the third conference of this series, the Colombo conference of 1954, which took place against the background of the issues arising out of Indo-China. Kotelawala's concern with communist threats was made clear when he advocated the adoption of a resolution on 'aggressive communism' in addition to the resolutions concerning 'colonialism' favoured by the majority of the delegates. Again, at the path-finding Bandung conference held the following year, at which not only Asian but also African nations were represented, he took up the same stance. Kotelawala has been accused of souring the meeting—Chou En-lai left the deliberations after one of his speeches—and of striving for headlines. In this there may be an element of truth, but his speeches struck a responsive chord among a number of the delegates present. There is little doubt that Kotelawala's image—and by association that of Srī Laṅkā—became well established internationally. At home his stance at Bandung further increased criticisms of his foreign policy, and there was even an unsuccessful no-confidence motion against him in Parliament.

Kotelawala's successor was S. W. R. D. Bandaranaike, who in 1956 formed the first of the non-UNP governments, his SLFP-dominated administration. His foreign policy has attracted wide attention and he has received acclaim as the man responsible for bringing Sri Lanka firmly within the camp of the non-aligned states. Bandaranaike has been the subject of much uncritical adulation, both for his external and internal policies, from those who inherited the party he founded. More recently, even scholars appraising his foreign policy have tended blandly to accept the claims of the propagandists. Bandaranaike undoubtedly carved a special niche for himself in the history of Sri Lanka's foreign policy, but the limitations of his policy should not go unheeded.

It is pertinent to draw attention to the particular ideology that Bandaranaike fashioned. From the time when he formed his party in 1951, he had sought to traverse the middle ground in politics, between the marxist parties and the right-oriented UNP from which he had broken away. More specifically, in relation to international affairs he argued that given a period of lessened tension in the world, the two extremes of capitalism and communism would disappear and a synthesised middle form would evolve. It was his opinion that countries newly emerged from colonial situations should strive for this middle ground by refusing to align themselves with either of the extreme ideological camps, and by borrowing and deriving from both the capitalists and the communists. Thus, the goal to be sought in foreign policy was 'friends of all, enemies of none', in other words, neutralism.

As Prime Minister, Bandaranaike sought to redeem his promises regarding foreign policy made while in opposition. Perhaps the most concrete step taken in this direction was the transfer of the military bases in the island from British hands to Sri Lanka. Since he broke away from the UNP and went into opposition, Bandaranaike had been most vehement in his criticism of Sri Lanka's defence agreement with Britain. He saw, like the elder Senanayake, that Sri Lanka lacked resources to make its own defence arrangements, but unlike the former Prime Minister, he held the view that distant Britain would be in no position effectively to stave off an attack on the island. Conscious of the Cold War climate, he felt that military association with Britain would inevitably lead to Sri Lanka's involvement in any wars between the power blocs; he did not fail to notice that Sri Lanka was easily accessible to both the Soviet Union and China. He saw complete neutrality as the answer to the island's defence problem; his model was Switzerland. It is clear, however, that the more pragmatic side of his character saw the inadequacy of this, which is perhaps why he was moved to advocate regional co-operation among the Asian states, in particular the drawing up of a mutual defence scheme involving India, Pakistan, Burma and Pakistan together with Sri Lanka.

The military bases were handed back to the Srī Laṅkā government in late 1957. The transfer took place amicably and indeed Bandaranaike himself took great pains to act without a 'spirit of hostility'; coincidentally, after the Suez débâcle, Britain was reviewing its own commitments east of Suez at the time. The original defence agreement itself was not formally repealed by either party. Bandaranaike — and Srī Laṅkā — drew immense psychological satisfaction from this step; he saw this as the completion of the island's independence and it proved crucial for the image which Bandaranaike was building for himself, both within and without the country.

After Bandaranaike became Prime Minister he lost no time in making clear his independent stance in international affairs. One of his first opportunities for doing so was the Suez Canal crisis. Srī Laṅkā was especially sensitive about the canal, for it was a vital link in its international trade network: 65-70 per cent of exports and 45-50 per cent of the island's imports are estimated to have passed through the canal. Bandaranaike condemned in no uncertain terms the Franco-British-Israeli invasion of Egypt and action in the Canal area.

Bandaranaike drew away from Britain but made no attempt to break with the Commonwealth. While in opposition he had tended to belittle the Commonwealth tie and dismiss it as tenuous and nebulous, but once in power his attitude seemed to change. Indeed, quite apart from the material benefits accruing from it, he argued that the Commonwealth was valuable because it could constitute itself as a third force between the power blocs and thereby play a role which he could cherish. He also stressed the common inheritance of democratic institutions as the cornerstone of the Commonwealth bond, and in this gave a reminder to the local left, who had applauded his stance against Britain, of the true direction of his ideological commitments. Whether or not Britain was mollified by these pronouncements is unknown, but Bandaranaike was careful to emphasise that his neutralism was not directed against the west. As he often commented, Sri Lanka felt closer to the United States than other countries because of their common adherance to a democratic way of life.

Bandaranaike's neutralist position was the basis on which he initiated the exchange of diplomatic representation with the communist states, beginning with the Soviet Union and China. He began developing cultural ties with them as well — specifically, lifting the ban imposed by Kotelawala in 1953 on the importation of literature from communist states — and sought to balance the aid given by the west to Srī Laṅkā by seeking technical and economic assistance from these countries. Steps were taken to improve trade relations with them and, following the rubber-rice pact with China, a number of bilateral trade agreements were signed. It is worth stressing that Bandaranaike's neutralism in relation to the Soviet Union and China was less consistent than in relation to the western nations. This was especially evident on two separate occasions. On the first, Bandaranaike showed a great reluctance to condemn outright the Soviet Union's intervention in Hungary. The language he finally chose expressed no more than mild censure and in no way matched the strong terms in which he condemned France, Britain and Israel for their action in Egypt; the contrast was particularly striking because the two events coincided. Secondly, he failed to take a stand on China's invasion of Tibet — which he professed to view purely as an internal affair of China. This drew heavy criticism from both his supporters and his opponents at home, for Tibet was an issue on which local Buddhist sensibilities were aroused. It is difficult to explain this apparent contradiction in Bandaranaike's policies, but he was not in a strikingly different position from a number of Afro-Asian leaders who were emerging as neutralists at this time: groping their way into establishing friendly relations with both the Soviet Union and China, they seem to have been especially careful not to offend the susceptibilities of these countries.

Bandaranaike clearly wanted a more affirmative role for Srī Laṅkā on the international stage, and in fact emerged as an Asian statesman of stature. Previous Prime Ministers had been concerned about the dominant role that India wished to play and did play within the region, and it has been argued that Kotelawala's particular posture at Asian conference tables was designed to strike a contrast to Nehru. Though Nehru's position internationally became stronger during his period of office, Bandaranaike showed no reluctance to work closely with him, and indeed Bandaranaike at times appeared to follow Nehru's lead on international issues. However, this was a period when not only Nehru and Bandaranaike but also a number of other Asian statesmen showed broadly similar opinions on the problems of the Third World. Thus Bandaranaike could range himself with such different figures as Nehru, Soekarno of Indonesia, Chou En-lai of China and Kishi of Japan, and in joint communiques and at conferences of Asian Prime Ministers condemned all manifestations of colonialism and militarism in the world, especially the nuclear stockpiling of the major powers.

In retrospect, Bandaranaike's foreign policy has taken on a special character of its own. Kotelawala's extreme stance on communism, and the obvious distaste with which his posture abroad was received at home, enabled Bandaranaike to emerge as a moderating influence in foreign affairs; his neutralism was placed in the best possible perspective not only because of its striking contrast with Kotelawala but also because of the rather dogmatic and doctrinaire views on international affairs held by the Left opposition. Both the Communists and the Trotskyites, though differing over details, saw international relations as essentially class relations, and their interpretation of world issues tended to be hamstrung on this. In the following years the positions taken on either side of Bandaranaike at this time became looser: the marxists became less doctrinaire, especially when associated with governing administrations, and the UNP, though still inclined to favour the west, lost no time in abandoning the extreme position taken by Kotelawala on international communism: the climate was being prepared for the broad consensus which was soon to be seen in some major areas in external relations between all political parties in the country.

The foreign policy of Sirima Bandaranaike, who came into power in 1960, was by her own admission a continuation of the policy of her late husband, S. W. R. D. Bandaranaike. However, her tenure saw a pronounced straining of relations with the west, particularly with the United States, and a marked strengthening of ties with China. Though it is possible to discern a shift in Srī Laṅkā's attitude to the United States from the beginning of the government of 1970 — for example, the Asia Foundation was asked to wind up its work in the island and the Peace Corps was removed — the actual turning-point in relations came in late 1963 with the enacting of the legislation for the nationalisation of the foreign oil companies in the island. The oil companies had British as well as American owners, but it was the United States which took stronger exception to the nationalisation. Negotiations between the United States and Sri Lanka on compensation for the assets of the nationalised companies ended in failure, and acting under the guidelines set up for the discontinuation of assistance to countries which pay no compensation for property taken over from American citizens, the United States cut off its aid programme to Srī Laṅkā. This of course did not deter the Srī Laṅkā government from pursuing its policies.

The increasing friendship between Sri Lanka and China during this period was reflected in many ways. There were mutual visits of Srī Laṅkā's leader and Chou En-lai to each other's countries, and in 1963 Srī Laṅkā entered into a maritime agreement with China involving reciprocal most-favoured-nation treatment in relation to seaborne traffic. The agreement came under heavy fire at home, and in particular the lack of specificity about references to commercial vessels in the agreement was quoted as an example of Srī Laṅkā being unwittingly drawn within the military ambitions of China. Again, during the Sino-Indian crisis in 1962, despite the pressure which was brought on her from within her party as well as outside, Mrs. Bandaranaike refused to name China as the aggressor.

Mrs. Bandaranaike began to participate actively in the growing deliberations of the non-aligned states of Africa and Asia. Thus, at meetings held at Belgrade in 1961, Colombo in 1962 (a meeting initiated by her) and Cairo in 1964, she identified herself and Srī Laṅkā with the participating nations and advocated non-alignment as a third force in international affairs, condemning the increasing penchant of the major powers to indulge in the development of nuclear arms. She envisaged for herself the role of a mediator in international disputes but her one conspicuous intervention, during the Sino-Indian war, achieved no significant results. During the period, Srī Laṅkā's trade relations with the countries of the Third World were intensified and a greater diversity was achieved in Srī Laṅkā's trade pattern.

The trends which began under Mrs. Bandaranaike continued to some extent during the premiership of her successor, Dudley Senanayake, who formed a coalition government dominated by the UNP in 1965. The vexed and long deferred question of compensation for the nationalized petroleum companies was settled soon after the installation of the new administration, and the United States resumed its economic assistance programmes to the island. There is no doubt that the possibility of a resumption of American aid was a strong motive in the initiation of negotiations for the settlement of this issue by the Senanayake government. Indeed, throughout his tenure in 1965-70, faced with an economy which was steadily deteriorating, the desire to create a favourable climate for the influx of assistance from the western nations to increase seemed to have weighed heavily with Senanayake. To a considerable extent he seems to have succeeded in his aims, for apart from the aid normally channelled by the donor countries and the borrowing privileges extended by lending institutions like the IMF, IBRD and the Asian Development Bank, an Aid Srī Laṅkā consortium was set up with notable success. The Senanayake government was of course heavily criticised for its dependence on aid and loans from the west, by the opposition, who saw these as the pawning of Srī Laṅkā's independence to western capitalists, and the opposition parties made a concentrated attempt to bring the aid and loan programme of the Senanayake government before the electorate as a key issue in the 1970 election. The renewed friendship with the west inaugurated by the Senanayake government was also designed to attract western capital badly needed to inject into a sick economy; this policy was less than successful from the government's point of view.

The normalising of relations with the west under Senanayake was accompanied by a cooling and indeed some straining of ties with China. It was not a substantial issue but the protests of a UNP government minister, acting in his capacity as president of the "Anti-Marxist Muslim World Brotherhood", at the alleged ill-treatment of Muslims in China during the Cultural Revolution and the imposition of a ban on some Chinese literature, which was then lost in the port of Colombo, created strain between Srī Laṅkā and China.

The visits to Srī Laṅkā of some unofficial commercial and sports delegations from Taiwan and the visit to Taiwan of an unofficial Srī Laṅkā trade team seem to have greatly incensed the Chinese, even though the question of formal diplomatic relations between Srī Laṅkā and Taiwan never arose. Despite the acrimonious tone of notes exchanged between Srī Laṅkā and China during this period of time, there was in fact no change in their mutual trade pattern or a withdrawal of Chinese aid to the island. For example, the Chinese renewed the rubber-rice agreement in 1967 and offered assistance in the establishment of a textile mill complex in Srī Laṅkā. The Srī Laṅkā government, for its part, continued unequivocally to support China's admission to the UN.

It is arguable that two countries in particular viewed this turn in Srī Laṅkā's relations with China with satisfaction. One was the Soviet Union. Until friendship with China took special overtones, the Soviet Union had loomed large among Srī Laṅkā's socialist friends, and its eclipse by China, especially with China's emergence as the leading aid donor to Srī Laṅkā among non-western countries, would not have been viewed favourably by the Russians given the deterioration of relations between the Soviet Union and China on the international plane. Senanayake did not elevate the Soviet Union into the status of a special friend of Srī Laṅkā, but in the somewhat melodramatic climate created at times by the existence in the background of disputes with China, it was able to re-assert its position in Srī Laṅkā's external relations. The second country which was specially concerned over the nature of Srī Laṅkā's ties with China was India, and in the context of the strain and tension between India and China and the importance of the island country for India's defence, it is not surprising that any extraordinary treatment of China by Srī Laṅkā was viewed with apprehension by its neighbour. The exceptional extent of coverage of Srī Laṅkā-Chinese relations in the Indian press during Mrs. Bandaranaikes' premiership and the fear of Srī Laṅkā becoming a military ally of China by some Indians during this period are thus explicable.

Under Senanayake, whether or not caused by the cooling of the special relationship between Srī Laṅkā and China, a new interest developed regarding the ties between India and Srī Laṅkā. There were mutual visits of the respective heads of state as well as the Prime Ministers, the broad interests which the two countries shared politically and culturally were repeatedly stressed, and the feasibility of closer economic co-operation between them in joint ventures was explored.

On a broader front, the Senanayake government continued the tradition of associating with other Third World states on international issues. On such diverse issues as Vietnam, Rhodesia, Czechoslovakia and the Arab-Israeli conflict, the government took a consistently non-aligned line.

It was inevitable that a change of emphasis if not direction in Srī Laṅkā's foreign policy would come about with the return of Sirima Bandaranaike as Prime Minister in 1970. Her new government, unlike her previous one, was formed as a coalition of three political parties, the SLFP, the Communist Party (Moscow) and the trotskyite Lanka Sama Samaja Party. Given the ideological differences between the coalition parties, differing views on the nature and form of Srī Laṅkā's foreign policy were likely to be expressed. There have been rumblings of dissent, and indeed strong criticisms, within the government parliamentary group on the conduct of external relations but in keeping with a marked trend since Srī Laṅkā became independent, Mrs. Bandaranaike has been able to assert herself and characterise the foreign policy of her government as *her* policy.

The new government indicated early that it intended to draw away from a western inclined posture and take a more militant line internationally when it gave diplomatic recognition to East Germany, North Vietnam, North Korea, the South Vietnamese Revolutionary Government and the Cambodian government-in-exile, and by cutting off diplomatic relations with Israel on the grounds that Israel refused to conform to the UN resolution on its occupied territories. There have been attempts to develop trade ties and economic co-operation with those countries with which Srī Laṅkā established relations, but no appreciable developments have taken place. The relationship with China was brought to the forefront once again by the Bandaranaike government, and there has since been a remarkable increase in Chinese aid to Srī Laṅkā. China has repeatedly granted interest-free loans, both for development and consumption purposes, as well as making outright gifts of industrial machinery and armaments, and its gift of the recently completed Bandaranaike Memorial International Conference Hall stands in Colombo as a clear symbol of the close relations between the two countries.

Neither the Soviet Union nor India has been happy over the drawing together of China and Srī Laṅkā, and caustic comments on it have appeared in both the Russian and the Indian press; for example, Russian commentators remarked on the priority given to the construction of the symbolic memorial hall rather than the more obviously needed textile mill promised by China, and both Russian and Indian newspapers have commented on the possibility of China using Srī Laṅkā as a base for operations in the Indian Ocean. The validity of the argument could of course be questioned, but the Srī Laṅkā-China friendship has been cited as a factor which operated in the background of the signing of the Indo-Soviet Treaty in 1971. The Srī Laṅkā government has yet to offer any detailed comments on this treaty, but there is no doubt that, together with the emergence of Bangladesh and the loss of a unified Pakistan, this treaty has caused grave concern in Srī Laṅkā. Once again, repeating a recurrent pattern, the political factor does not seem to have acted in an adverse way on Srī Laṅkā's economic relations, with both the Soviet Union and India. The Soviet Union has continued to give aid, though in some quarters in the government it is felt that the Russians have not helped the weakened economy of Srī Laṅkā in the way anticipated, and the prospect of closer economic co-operation with India has grown with the establishment in 1972 of a joint committee consisting of officials of the two countries.

The attitude of the Bandaranaike government towards the west has become progressively more moderate and restrained. While they were in opposition as well as at the beginning of the new administration, leading personalities in the government were vocal not only about the political role played by western nations on the world stage, but also about their 'economic imperialism'. For example, much play was made by them while in opposition of the conditions laid down by the IBRD for the loan given to Srī Laṅkā for the financing of the first stage of the huge Mahavāli Development Scheme, and in numerous statements and positions taken before 1970 it was clear that Mrs. Bandaranaike and her associates were intending, once in power, to reduce Srī Laṅkā's dependence on the west for direct economic assistance as well as for commercial borrowings. This intention has apparently not been realised, and apart from China, no other non-western state has markedly increased its scale of assistance to Srī Laṅkā. Srī Laṅkā has continued to solicit the international lending institutions associated with the west, and it is significant that the very IBRD loan agreement which was cited as an example of western rapacity has been retained by the Bandaranaike government without any material alterations in its terms. The reappraisal of the west was perhaps reflected in another significant shift of position. In 1963 the then Bandaranaike government refused the US Seventh Fleet permission to enter Srī Laṅkā's territorial waters, as well as protesting about its operations in the Indian Ocean, but more recently it has welcomed to Srī Laṅkā the US Pacific Fleet as well as the Soviet Pacific Fleet. Continuing a tradition begun by S. W. R. D. Bandaranaike, the present government has thrown its weight behind the UN as a peacekeeping body. In particular, it has attempted to get the UN to accept the proposal to declare the Indian Ocean a 'Peace Zone' so that it would be a 'power vacuum' where intervention by the major military powers would be outlawed. This idea has also been canvassed by Mrs. Bandaranaike outside the UN, at other international conferences, and her grave misgivings at the proposal for establishing an Anglo-American base at Diego Garcia becomes understandable in the context. The proposal has attracted the sympathy of a number of countries within the region but so far nothing concrete has been achieved.

To Mrs. Bandaranaike as well as to her associates, the vindication of her foreign policy came at the time of the April Revolt of 1971. There was of course a note of discord to begin with, Chinese complicity being alleged (this was dismissed by the government), and the implicated North Korean embassy being closed down on government orders, but a formidable array of countries with which Srī Laṅkā had established relations came to its assistance — Britain, the United States and India, which gave the more substantial immediate aid; the Soviet Union, Egypt, Yugoslavia and Pakistan, which gave aid on a somewhat smaller scale; and China, which for unexplained reasons did not respond immediately, but which subsequently gave Srī Laṅkā a generous loan to assist its recovery. Whatever interpretations are given by the Srī Laṅkā government, it is clear that to these diverse nations it was vital that Srī Laṅkā should not fall into the hands of an extremist group but should remain within the mainstream of non-aligned states.

Finally, we must briefly review the negotiations conducted by Srī Laṅkā with India on the status of the people of Indian origin in the island? This issue has dominated not only much of Srī Laṅkā's dealings with India but also the country's internal politics, and reference will be made here only to the ramifications which have a bearing on external relations. By successive legislation enacted in 1948 and 1949, provision was made for Indians who had migrated into Srī Laṅkā and made their homes there to acquire the right of citizenship. However, the qualifications for citizenship were so stringent that only a small proportion were able to avail themselves of the privilege; and since India refused to accept responsibility for those who failed to get citizenship, an issue arose of the first magnitude. Repeated negotiations between Srī Laṅkā and India on this matter broke down over the reluctance of India to accept the principle of repatriation because of the possibility of it becoming a precedent for other countries, in Asia and elsewhere, with populations of Indian origin. The first concrete agreement to resolve the problem was taken in 1954 when India agreed to provide facilities and Srī Laṅkā promised to provide inducements for the Indians to acquire citizenship in India. The Srī Laṅkā government interpreted this agreement by taking the position that all those who failed to become citizens of Srī Laṅkā would automatically be registered as citizens of India; the Indian view was that of the applications received, a proportion would fail to qualify, and therefore a third category—soon to be described as 'stateless'—would arise. These divergent interpretations remained inspite of further negotiations, and while Srī Laṅkā continued to grant citizenship to successful applicants, India did not take corresponding steps to encourage the taking up of the citizenship rights it was offering. The next important step, which also proved the most successful, was the agreement signed between the two governments in 1964. Under this, of the 975,000 Indians without citizenship rights in the island, 525,000 and their natural increase were to be repatriated to India and 300,000 were to be granted citizenship in Srī Laṅkā, both steps to be taken over a period of fifteen years. Again difficulties of interpretation arose, partly on the Srī Laṅkā government's side, because of internal pressures and partly because of the shifting of position by both governments. However, there was a determination, which both governments shared, that the issue should be resolved with finality, and the agreement is now in the process of being implemented without major differences. This of course does not rule out future difficulties, and in any case it is inevitable that the implementation would have to be phased over a longer period than was originally intended.

SELECT BIBLIOGRAPHY

Note: Very little original research, as would be evidenced by the list below, has been undertaken on the foreign policy of independent Sri Lanka. Writings of an overtly partisan political nature have been excluded, even though in some instances they have been by writers with good academic credentials.

Ceylon and World Affairs, I Ministry of Defence and External Affairs, Colombo (1960).

De Silva, K. M., 'The Transfer of Power—British Perspectives', *Ceylon Journal of Historical and Social Studies*, n. s. IV (1974) special double number on "Srī Laṅkā since Independence".

The Foreign Policy of Ceylon: Extracts from Statements made by the Hon. Prime Minister, S. W. R. D. Bandaranaike, Colombo, Information Department, n.d.

Jennings, W. I., *The Constitution of Ceylon*, Bombay, 1949, ch. XIII.

'The D. S. Senanayake Memorial Number', *Ceylon Historical Journal*, V, nos. 1-4, 1955-6.

Wilson, A. J., *Politics in Sri Lanka, 1947-1973*, London (1974), Ch. VI.

Wriggins, W. Howard, *Ceylon: Dilemmas of a New Nation*, Princeton, N.J. (1960) Chs. X and XI.

15

THE ADMINISTRATION AND THE JUDICIAL SYSTEM

by Vijaya Samaraweera

THE ADMINISTRATION

The Structure

The administrative organization in Srī Laṅkā is hierarchically structured.[1] At its primary — indeed its key — level are the ministries, the grouping together of a number of departments under a cabinet minister. The number of cabinet ministers, and therefore the number of ministries, has varied through the years, ranging from eight in the short-lived government of 1960 to twenty-two, the largest ever, in the government formed in 1970. The size of the respective ministries too has varied, depending on the extent and nature of the subjects and functions assigned to the ministers by the Prime Minister. With the government increasingly entering new areas of economic development and welfare services in the years since independence, there has inevitably been an increase in the number of departments of state (and more specifically in the setting up of public corporations owned and run by the state). Another feature in the ministerial system has been the grouping together of disparate subjects and functions under individual ministers. It is possible to argue, as the Salaries and Cadres Commission submitted in 1961, that subjects and functions could be allocated to different ministers according to a functional rather than a political rationale but it is clear that this would not be politically feasible. The shuffling around of ministerial duties during the course of a single government in power has been rare, but almost as a rule successive Prime Ministers have thought fit to strike new arrangements in the assignment of subjects and functions to ministers, so that some departments have

---

1. On the structure and process of the government see above, Chapter 12.

been brought under a remarkably varied number of ministries over the years. Thus between January 1959 and August 1960, Labour was assigned to four different ministers. This is no doubt an extreme example, but it reflects the discontinuity noticeable in the structuring of the administration at the primary level. Since unrelated duties have often been allocated to a single minister, it has rarely been possible fully to co-ordinate and integrate the work of the different departments within the ministries. There are exceptions to this, such as Health and Education, but even these ministries, though always having under them relatively cohesive groups of subjects and functions, took more than a decade after independence to achieve integration, and that in only a partial manner. The lack of integration, compounded no doubt by the growth in ministerial duties, has resulted in a significant increase in the number of officials attached to the ministries, and most ministries are said to have become top-heavy with no commensurate gain in efficiency. A further consequence of the absence of integration may be noted: the increasing importance of the Secretaries to the ministries (until the constitutional change in 1972 known as Permanent Secretaries) in the administration as the administrative heads of each ministry.

A defect inherent in the ministerial system is the splitting and separation of related and connected subjects and functions between different ministers. The cabinet, of course, is thought to provide an answer to this by ensuring co-ordination at the highest possible level, but in Srī Laṅkā, where the concept of strict cabinet responsibility is not highly developed and where from time to time governments have been formed by a coalition of parties with differing political commitments there has not infrequently been friction between ministers, and full and correct co-ordination between ministries has been rarely been achieved in practice. This has impaired the administration, and especially in the context of urgent developmental goals sought by successive governments in power, the problem has come to be one causing grave concern. An innovation by the government formed in 1970 therefore merits examination. The innovation concerns the appointment of a Co-ordinating Secretary attached to the Prime Minister's office. At present, the duties of this office are entirely concerned with the overseeing of the government's food production drive. It was intended that the Co-ordinating Secretary's office would cut across the ministerial divisions and bring to bear upon food production the full resources of the administration—it was to be the nerve centre in the implementation of a critical government policy. Unfortunately, it is not possible to make a proper evaluation of this interesting innovation because the work of the Co-ordinating Secretary's office has been clouded by political implications. Specifically, it has been looked upon as a means by which the Prime Minister has sought to enhance her position and powers within the general administration and has been cited as a prime example of the "presidentalisation of the Prime Minister's office".

It is a patent, and to some an unpleasant, fact that certain ministries, by the very nature of the duties allocated to them, have a closer and more extensive impact upon the wider public than others. Ministries handling subjects like home affairs, agriculture and land, internal trade and consumer supplies, irrigation and power, for example, have a greater direct bearing on the people than, say, ministries charged with subjects like cultural affairs and posts and telecommunications. Such ministries, in their organisation, reach down to village level. There is a further index by which the relative importance of ministries within the government can be gauged: by the size of their annual budgetary allocations and the personnel attached to them, factors of patronage which have always carried a premium in the context of the country's politics. By these criteria education and health, for example, constitute important ministries. It is arguable that the relative importance of ministries reflects the political stature and force of individual ministers within the government, though in Srī Laṅkā, as elsewhere, there are dangers in seeing this as an invariable yardstick in the measurement of the powerbalance among the politicians in control.

At the second level of the administrative hierarchy are the heads of the departments attached to the ministries. There is a plethora of designations for heads of departments — director, director-general, commissioner, controller, etc. Department heads rank equally in the structural arrangement, but some positions carry greater importance and prestige by virtue of the duties attached to them, and in the rules governing the public service there has always been a requirement, not always strictly adhered to by governments in power, that such posts should only be held by officers who have reached a certain level of seniority in the service. Each department is concerned with a limited sphere of government activity, mostly on an island-wide scale. Some of the departments have a long history, originating in the early days of British rule, while some others are relatively new creations, set up to take charge of new activities which the government has entered into or to handle separately certain functions which have become increasingly specialised over the years. In any case, there is some degree of overlapping between departments in their duties, and consequently they have overlapping structures. In general, two broad categories of departments can be identified: those concerned with purely regulatory functions of administration and those concerned with development policies. Departments are normally organised as self-contained units but they have sometimes displayed virtual autonomy and, unless there is strong direction at ministerial level, departments within a single ministry tend to work without mutual co-ordination. It has even been alleged that both heads of departments as individuals and their departments are moved by jealousies and consequently work at cross-purposes, making effective planning and the implementation of policies useless. It has been argued, not without reason, that lack of integration between departments is the legacy of the immediate pre-independent administration, for the Donoughmore Constitution operated in such a way that the departments were established as the principal administrative units. The answer to this problem — to make the ministry rather than the department the unit of administration — has been often touted, but there has yet to be any indication that this would be formally adopted by a government in power as a measure of administrative reform.

The ministries and the head offices of the departments attached to them are sited in the capital, Colombo. This marked concentration of the administration in one centre has its merits — Colombo after all is well served by a network of roads and railways and is the nexus of the populous south-western coastal belt — but the benefits that could be derived from a measure of dispersal, principally through the means of de-centralisation of the administration, have been widely recognised, and a number of steps have been taken over the years to achieve this.

The departments with an island-wide focus have regional headquarters at the administrative district capitals. Until about two decades ago, only certain departments had regional offices, but now, with rare exceptions, all departments follow this arrangement. Those departments whose functions touch the wider public more directly and more intimately, have lower units of administration, at the administrative level of the division and the still lower level of field officers. The extent to which these lower units of administration are supervised by the respective higher levels cannot be precisely determined. Public officers in Sri Lankā are notorious for their reluctance to move into the field, leaving their offices, and the view that lower levels are controlled and supervised only by means of "files" cannot perhaps be entirely rejected.

The vertical arrangement of the administration becomes complex at the district level through the supplementary administrative structure headed by the Government Agents and their office of *kachcheries*. The Government Agentships have a long history. Created early in the period of British rule at the

Table 1. THE ADMINISTRATIVE STRUCTURE.

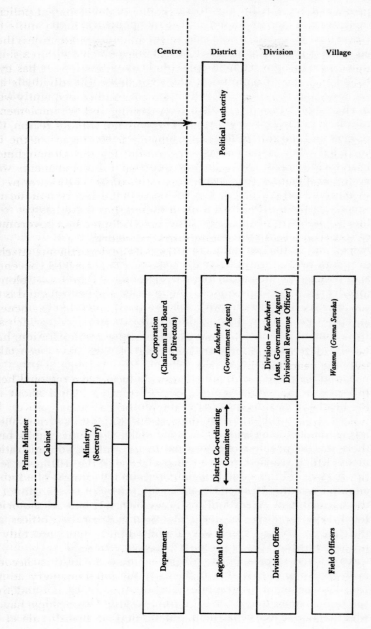

provincial level (with the increase in the number of provinces their numbers too increased, and at independence there were nine Government Agents), their role in the administration was reflected in the very designation itself, and it was most succintly described in a report of a government-appointed commission of inquiry published in 1948: "Communications were more difficult than they are now, and it was considered expedient to place a senior officer in charge of a Province with merely general instructions, leaving him free to direct every form of Government activity in it." The powers and the role of the Government Agents were considerably curtailed when departments were established at the centre with island-wide focus. Nevertheless, important functions remained vested in them, for the *kachcheries* continued to act in the capacity of regional offices of the central departments, quite apart from exercising the duties which were not taken over by the centre. Further curtailment of the role of the Government Agents and their office occurred with the setting up of regional offices of the departments, and in 1955 with the creation of twenty-one (later increased to twenty-two) administrative districts to cover the whole island, the area covered by the authority of a Government Agent was reduced to a district level (consequently the number of Government Agents was increased to twenty-two); this naturally affected the position and prestige of this official in the administration. By the 1960s the Government Agents had become a shadow of their former selves, but they continued to be responsible for a number of not-altogether unimportant duties especially relating to development programmes, and the place they retained in the administrative structure was reflected in the recognition of their office as equivalent in rank to the headship of a department at the centre.

Two major problems developed at district level, and it is interesting to note the measures which were taken to resolve them. First, there was the problem of co-ordinating the activities of the departments which reached down to district level and relating them to the responsibilities vested in the Government Agent. The device adopted was the District Co-ordinating Committee, consisting of the Government Agent and his immediate assistants at divisional level, representatives of departments functioning in the district, the chairmen of a representative number of local government institutions, and the MPs of the district constituencies. The committee was required to co-ordinate all government activities in the administrative area as well as to facilitate the implementation of the broad government programmes affecting the district. The key person in the committee at the beginning was the Government Agent, who functioned as its chairman, but in the years since the establishment of the committees in the mid-1950s, the MPs have played an increasingly dominant role within it. It is now generally recognised that the committees rarely accomplish their primary task of co-ordinating the work of the departments and that they have turned out to be the forums for MPs to agitate their particular interests; little wonder that their work has been characterised by sterile discussions.

The second problem is more fundamental and affects the administration and bureaucracy as a whole: to gear both these to serve the needs of the public more effectively. The public service in general has long been at the receiving end of a constant barrage of criticism from the politicians, especially as being backward-looking and insensitive to the common good, but there is no doubt that the greatest venom was directed against the Government Agents. Considering the image of the Government Agents which has hardly altered although their role in the administration has changed, this is not altogether surprising. For several years past, the idea has gained currency that the bureaucracy should be brought under 'political control' at all levels, in order to link the aspirations and needs of the public more effectively with the working of the administration. The association of MPs and representatives of the local authorities with the District Co-ordinating Committees was a first step in the direction of accomplishing this, but of far more significance was the appointment in late 1973 of a "Political Authority" in each administrative district to give immediate political direction and control to the work associated with the Government Agents and through them the broad programmes and activities undertaken by the administration in the area. The Political Authority is chosen and appointed by the Prime Minister from among the (government) MPs who have constituencies in a particular administrative district. Their powers and duties have not been clearly defined, neither is there any institutionalised device for exercising supervision over their work. It is perhaps premature to make any evaluation of the role of the Political Authorities in the administration, but some comments on their impact are in order. It is arguable that their creation has helped to enhance significantly the power and position of the Prime Minister within the administration, especially in the context of a government formed by a coalition of political parties (see Table 2). Political Authorities are directly responsible to the Prime Minister and not to the cabinet, or to the political parties to which they belong, or to the legislature. Secondly, there is no doubt that the appointment of these Authorities has led to the undermining of the authority of the Government Agents and the other officials at district level, whose morale by all accounts has deteriorated noticeably.

Table 2.

PARTY AFFILIATIONS OF POLITICAL AUTHORITIES, 1974

Political Party		No. of Political Authorities	Party strength in government
Sri Lanka Freedom Party	—	18[a]	95
Lanka Sama Samaja Party	—	1	18
Communist Party (Moscow)	—	1	6

(a) One SLFP Political Authority has been placed in charge of three administrative districts.

Much of course has depended upon the stance taken by the particular Political Authority. Some have acted in a spirit of co-operation rather than hostility and have thereby established a cordial relationship with the officials, but these are few. The majority, it seems, have looked upon the bureaucrats as 'enemies', and the period of transition has been fraught with major problems. If some reports are to be believed, most Government Agents have completely surrendered their initiative in the administration to the respective Political Authorities, who have emerged in every sense as the powers to be reckoned with within the districts. Thus it is no surprise that certain Political Authorities have been heavily criticised in public by other MPs, both government and opposition, of the district. Whether the innovation has endeared itself to the wider public cannot be easily answered.

At district level, the introduction of Political Authorities was coupled with another innovation, the 'de-centralisation' of the budget. Under this a previously pre-determined portion of the annual budgetary allocation made by the Ministry of Finance is set aside for the Political Authorities for capital expenditure in the district. The allocation for 1974 was Rs. 175 million (12.1 per cent of the allocation for development expenditure) and in 1975 Rs. 125 million (6.2 per cent). This idea was widely acclaimed, for it was looked upon as a way by which a certain amount of 'local' expenditure could be incurred realistically and flexibly without being rigidly tied to the budgetary allocations made at the beginning of each financial year, but the way in which it has been worked out has drawn heavy criticism. The money is disbursed largely at the personal discretion of the Political Authority — which, it has been argued, could lead to considerable corruption among the authorities, for strict financial accountability has not yet been introduced.

It was hoped that the Political Authorities, as the elected representatives of the people, would be able to assess the latter's requirements better than the bureaucrats, but the expenditure so far incurred for capital works has not reflected a consistently rational choice on their part. Moreover, quite understandably, this had led to friction between the Political Authorities and other MPs of the districts.

The Government Agents and the administrative structure immediately under them fall within the administrative purview of the Ministry of Home Affairs. Each administrative district is divided into a number of divisions which are in the charge of Divisional Revenue Officers or Assistant Government Agents who assist the Government Agent in his manifold duties. A division comprises a number of *wasama* under officials known as *grāma sēvaka* (lit. village servants). The administration, which is under the Home Ministry, thus reaches down to village level itself in an institutionalized form. It is important to note that until 1963, when the *grāma sēvaka* system came into operation, the village-level administration was not fully integrated with the general administrative structure. Previously villages had been under officials collectively known as 'Headmen', and they formed part of what was described as the 'traditional bureaucracy'. The Headmen were chosen primarily on the basis of their influence in the villages, and this perpetuated a system of values and order which ran counter the universalistic principles which governed the general administration. The need for integration of the village administration with the higher levels was repeatedly stressed, and the opportunities for nepotism and corruption provided by the Headmen system were a further reason for its final abolition.

The unity of the administrative structure so far described was provided by the Treasury, which functioned as the centre of administrative co-ordination, and which has been termed a 'super-department', an apt description of its position in the administrative structure. The main duties of the Treasury, which came under the Minister of Finance, were twofold: first, what could be described as 'book-keeping' duties, matters relating to the budgetary and financial arrangements of the government and administration and secondly, duties relating to the establishments and cadre. Under the first set of duties, in their financial estimates and disbursements all departments and ministries came under Treasury scrutiny, and this was undoubtedly a most vital task from the point of view of any government in power. Of the second set of duties, the most important was the management of the 'Combined Services', the personnel not attached to a particular department but who formed a common pool for service in the whole administration; within this category came the civil service, accountants, clerks and stenographèrs. In these duties, the Treasury was directly responsible to the Public Service Commission.

As an institution the Treasury was a legacy from colonial times, and its internal structure was revised several times after independence to suit changing needs. Nevertheless, it was heavily criticised time and again. It lacked adequate personnel to deal with its considerable duties, and of the criticisms made of it perhaps the most justifiable was that it adhered rigidly to rules and regulations in dealing with the departments and consequently slowed down their work. Whatever the criticisms, no government was moved to alter the structure and position of the Treasury radically until 1970. The new government formed in 1970 brought about a complete departure — not so much, it is now clear, because it accepted the validity of criticisms of the Treasury but for political reasons. A new Department of Public Administration was created and all the Treasury's duties relating to establishments and cadre were transferred to it. The Treasury now retains only its "book-keeper's" role.

The Public Service

It is no exaggeration to say that in the last two decades or so the public service has found itself in a beleagured state. Despite the changes introduced in its structure and composition, not always with due deliberation, and the good grace with which most public servants have accepted them, the public service as a whole has been constantly attacked for being insensitive and inimical to the developmental goals which are before the governments. "Break the power of the Bureaucracy" has for long been a key political slogan in the country, especially on the left, being directed first during the colonial era at the European-dominated Ceylon Civil Service, the élite cadre of the public service, and since then not only at those who inherited this position but also at those who man the middle rungs of the hierarchy. It would be tempting to dismiss this slogan as nothing but a cliché, but to do so it would be to ignore the political pressures which it brings to bear upon the public service.

In independent Srī Laṅkā, changes in the public service were slow in coming. A major explanation for this has been given: unlike many colonies, Srī Laṅkā found itself at independence with a largely indigenised public service (in 1947 only 21.7 % of the civil service was British), and the remaining expatriate personnel left within a few years. The civil service, which continued to form the key rung in the bureaucracy, had been deeply ingrained with the idea that narrow specialisation should be avoided and that a catholicity of experience should be its hall-mark, so that in the immediate post-independence period it was felt that the service would be able to adjust itself to the changing requirements of the administration without much strain. Specifically, from the Donoughmore era the service had become acquainted with social welfare and developmental tasks of administration, tasks which were to loom larger in the coming years. The question then emerges as to why not only the civil service but also the public service in general has been subjected to considerable changes over the last two decades or so. There is little doubt that a stage was reached when it became evident that a bureaucracy structured during colonial times, as if to serve colonial needs, was unsuited to a developing new nation. Equally important, perhaps, was the fact that over the years the public service became the prime focus of an overwhelming number of those who began to form the country's labour pool. Furthermore, though differing over the extent to which this was desirable, a striking consensus emerged among the political parties that the administration as well as the bureaucracy should be brought under "political control". The impact of this alone was momentous.

Among the structural changes brought about in the public service since independence, the most significant has been the abolition of the civil service and the creation of a unified administrative service. The civil servants had acquired over the years the characteristics of a virtual "caste". They were recruited, in strictly limited numbers, on the basis of a competitive written examination designed basically to test intellectual prowess. The other administrative officials, who have been suggestively described as forming the "supporting bureaucracy", were recruited on an *ad hoc* basis mainly through *viva voce* examinations. Once recruited, the civil servants were immediately marked out from the other officials by their separate and higher salary scale and by being appointed to much-coveted posts in the administration, which were reserved more or less exclusively for them. Further, unlike the others who were required to serve almost throughout their careers in the department to which they were originally recruited, the civil servants were freely transferable between departments and were thus able, in contrast to the rest, to acquire a wider outlook and expertise.

The need to eliminate the differentiation built up around the civil service and to establish a unified administrative service was stressed as early as 1953 by a government-appointed commission of inquiry, but it was a decade before concrete steps were taken: then all public servants within the category defined as administrative officials (209 civil servants and 821 other officers) were brought together to form the Ceylon (later Srī Laṅkā) Administrative Service. With the new scheme it was hoped that all officials in the administrative service would receive an equal opportunity of competing for entry into all administrative posts within the general administration, and thus transferability became a key feature in the service. Recruitment to the service was to be on a different basis. First, by open competitive examination, and the qualifications adopted for this pointed, as in the case of the former civil service, to an intake of young University graduates. To provide for mobility in the public service, 45 per cent of the recruitment was to be non-direct, 25 per cent on the basis of a competitive examination limited to public servants with ten years' service, and 20 per cent by promotion from the general clerical service. It is thus clear that though the civil service ceased to exist, a number of norms which governed the old élite cadre were adopted in the structuring of the new service. Indeed, in the first few years it was those who had previously belonged to the civil service who constituted the higher grades of the administrative service; the bias in favour of the ex-civil servants was exemplified in the fact that civil service cadets (recruits) were placed in the new Class IV together with non-civil service officers with up to eighteen years of service. It was inevitable that discord and discontent would appear in the new service on this count as well on other grounds, mainly relating to promotional prospects. The dominance of the ex-civil servants ended with the passage of time, and to provide for better promotional opportunities the administrative service was re-structured in 1971 into three classes (containing 100, 300 and 936 posts respectively) in place of the five classes originally established in 1965 (containing 20, 30, 60, 125 and 195 posts respectively).

The unified scheme did not absorb all officials who functioned in an administrative capacity in the administration. Certain officials whose duties required a degree of specialisation, such as those belonging to the departments of Inland Revenue, Customs, Police and Prisons, were kept out of the scheme and in each such case separate (closed) services were maintained. There were other categories of officials which by virtue of their professional or technical training and expertise formed separate services. Thus, for example, there has been an accountants' service since before independence and officers are drawn from it for accountancy duties in all departments and ministries. Similarly, a unified engineering service has been created embracing all engineering personnel in the public service, so that unlike previously these specialist cadres are not attached, on the basis of their original recruitment, to particular departments. All these officials and those of the unified administrative service come within the category described as "staff officers", and though they form only a small percentage of the personnel in the public service (see Table 3), it is on them that the running of the administration rests.

Table 3. PUBLIC SERVICE PERSONNEL, 1973.

Occupational Category	Number	Percentage of Total
Administrative, technical and professional officers of staff rank	12,935	5.5
Subordinate employees	122,430	52.1
Minor employees	68,659	29.2
Others	31,106	13.2
Total	235,131	100

Source: Annual Report of the Monetary Board to the Minister of Finance, 1973 p. 213. Note: Figures include temporary employees but not casual employees. 106,674 school teachers have not been included in the table.

Immediately below the staff officers are personnel who belong to intermediate grades, described as 'subordinate employees'. Within this category come a multitude of officials encompassing wide-ranging duties, and forming the majority of the public service. Some of these — policemen and various field officers associated with departments concerned with development work — are attached to the respective departments, but others, such as clerks and stenographers, belong to unified services. The hierarchical division between subordinate employees and staff officers is quite clear, though there are limited opportunities for those in the subordinate grade to reach the higher grade. At the lowest level are the "minor employees" recruited by each department separately and to this category belong the lower grades of office workers and skilled and unskilled labourers.

In recruitment and the control of the public service considerable changes have taken place in the recent years. The Ceylon constitution of 1948 created an independent Public Service Commission vested with authority over the appointment, transfer, dismissal and disciplinary control of all public servants, excepting the Permanent Secretaries who were appointed by the Governor-General. The constitution allowed the delegation of the powers of the commission which quickly availed itself of this facility and retained direct authority only over the civil servants and other officials drawing substantial salaries — in effect, this meant only about 6 per cent of the entire personnel of the public service. In the case of others, delegated officials exercised the authority on behalf of the Commission, with the Commission functioning as the appellate body. The constitution-makers hoped that the setting-up of an independent body to be concerned with the public service would shield the public servants from overt political interference and, in particular, would act as a safeguard against the introduction of measures inimical to the interests of the minority social groups in the country. It is doubtful whether the Public Service Commission ever succeeded in playing this intended role, and not long after its establishment, it was widely acknowledged to have become a mere "rubber-stamp" of the politicians in control and its abolition, with the enactment of the new constitution of 1972, was hardly bemoaned.

The constitution of 1972 brought into force entirely new provisions relating to the public service, and the cabinet of ministers was vested with the authority for the appointment, transfer, dismissal and disciplinary control of the public servants, now termed "state officers", and within these provisions were also brought the Secretaries to the ministries. In actuality this change cannot be looked upon as drastic; it merely gave constitutional force to what was by then normal practice. There was, however, a further provision which is of undoubted significance the exercise of the authority of the cabinet in relation to the public service was specifically excluded from the purview of the courts of law. To assist the cabinet in the exercise of its authority, the constitution provided for the setting up of two bodies, the State Services Advisory Board and the State Services Disciplinary Board.

Since independence, the public service has expanded dramatically from 109,854 in 1948 to 341,805 in 1973; well over 20 per cent of salaried individuals in the country are now employed by the government. The expansion of government activities and its entry into areas of the economy hitherto reserved to the private sector inevitably resulted in an increase in government personnel, but this alone does not account for the remarkable picture revealed by statistics on the public service. As a number of studies have shown, government employment carries significantly greater occupational prestige, and the pressure and competition to enter the service of the government has been great, especially over the last two decades or so when rapidly increasing numbers have entered the country's labour pool, and certain areas of government employment were expanded solely to absorb at least a proportion of this pool. The nature of the pressure for government employment can perhaps be gauged by a relatively recent trend—the foresaking not by choice but by compulsion of staff officer positions by university graduates, whose numbers have greatly increased, and their entry into the openings provided at subordinate levels.

The complexion of the personnel in the public service, especially at the higher levels, has also changed. In the early years after independence, the hierarchical division between the civil servants and other administrative officials and between staff officers and subordinate employees reflected not only a difference in the levels of attainment but also to a considerable extent a social difference, for the life-styles of the respective categories showed distinctive qualities. With the intake of the *swabhasha*-educated to higher positions since the early 1960s, one indicator of social difference, education in English, began to be removed, and in any case changing attitudes, within and without the public service, have resulted in the gradual disappearence of the elitist posture of the staff officers. Of great significance here has been the greater politicisation of the public service in general. At the highest level of the service, especially in the case of the Secretaries to the ministries, a practice has recently emerged of making appointments from outside the regular public service and this trend is likely to make the higher public service appointments entirely political and therefore changeable with the formation of every government. Most public servants now enjoy full political rights, and in recent years increasing numbers among them have begun to join political parties directly or party-sponsored trade unions. The increasingly pervasive influence of (government) MPs in the running of the administration, not only through their role as members of the District Co-ordinating Committees and Political Authorities but also through the utilisation of greater opportunities of patronage, such as in the appointment, transfer and promotion of public servants, has markedly devalued the prestige and the role of administrative officials—there is little doubt that what has been described by some political commentators as the "MPs' Raj" has come to stay, but it has yet to be closely evaluated.

There is a further factor which needs mentioning in relation to the changing face of the public service: the allegations of particularistic treatment in the recruitment and promotion of public servants. Immediately after independence, the cry was against the disproportionate representation of, and therefore the alleged domination of, the Tamils and non-Buddhists in the public service, and the cry became most vehement in the late 1950s and early 1960s when Sinhalese-Buddhist sentiments were militantly articulated. Now, however, accusations are directed at the Sinhalese-Buddhist majority for their discriminatory treatment of the minority social groups, particularly the Tamils. From time to time certain politicians and officials have been singled out and accused of giving favourable treatment to their own caste groups. It would be difficult indeed to sustain most of the charges made over the years, but the fact that allegations of favouritism have been made, and that demands have often surfaced for the allocation of quotas to different social groups in the intake to the public service, is ample evidence of the type of thinking that has emerged in the country in relation to the public service.

Finally, it is worthwhile highlighting certain general features of the public service in Srī Lankā. The salary structure of the service displays numerous anomalies. Examples could be cited of officials being entrusted with the same type of functions but being given different salaries. Moreover, the salary scales have been so structured that there is a bias in favour of the administrative officials as against those with professional or technical expertise. The bias has been now removed, though not entirely. Despite the recent efforts to increase the lowest salaries payable to government employees, there is a striking difference between the salaries of the minor employees and those of the staff officers in the highest grades. Promotions in the public service have been throughout based on seniority, though merit has not been completely ignored, and the Salaries and Cadres Commission of 1961, and reportedly its successor which submitted its findings in October 1974, recommended that greater weight should be given to merit than before in order to increase the efficiency of the service. Of course, in the context of greater politicisation of the public service, a cynic may comment that neither merit nor seniority but political loyalty constitutes the real criterion for the promotion of public servants. The public service, taken at its subordinate and staff officer levels, shows a marked predominance of administrative and clerical officials; despite the entry of the government into areas where much more than mere administrative ability is required of the personnel, the number of officials with professional and technical backgrounds forms only a small percentage of the entire public service, about 1.2 per cent. This is perhaps a reflection of the type of education provided in the country, for the opportunities of receiving a professional or technical training have been severely limited, in contrast to the opportunities for acquiring a liberal arts education. Much criticism has also been made of the tendency in the public service to use professionally and technically qualified personnel in capacities where only administrative skills are required. In the Health Department, for example, a government-appointed commission of inquiry reported in 1960 that the diversions of the medically qualified to administrative positions created a number of difficulties. For one, it depleted the urgently needed pool of doctors and for another it was found that the doctors lacked administrative training or experience and the administration therefore suffered. On the other hand, until recently, with rare exceptions, the administrative officials were not equipped with the proper management tools. An attempt has been made to remove this shortcoming with the government's establishment in 1966 of the Academy of Administrative Studies, which offers in-service training courses to public servants and provides opportunities for them to acquire a knowledge of new tools and techniques in administration.

THE JUDICIAL SYSTEM

A number of significant changes have been introduced in judicial administration, particularly since the new government was formed in 1970. None of these changes has yet been studied in any detail — indeed, the literature on the judicial system as it operated since independence is extremely sparse — and the review made here must necessarily be brief.

Many of the changes recently introduced have come into force with the Administration of Justice Law which became operative from 1 January 1974. Covering a multitude of subjects relating to judicial administration, this law was intended by its framers to usher in a "new era" in the administration of justice in Srī Laṅkā and specifically to break with the "colonial" system of judicature which was received as a legacy at independence. Clichés apart, there is no doubt that this law forms an important landmark in the island's legal history. It was subjected to wide discussion before enactment, both within and without the legislature, and some of its provisions aroused considerably controversy — indeed, even the constitutionality of the law was tested before the Constitutional Court and a few clauses found to be inconsistent with the constitution were altered. What is most significant is that the law was enacted by unanimous vote in the National State Assembly, which perhaps gave greater weight to the provisions it brought into force.

Under the administration of Justice Law an attempt was made greatly to simplify the courts structure in judicial administration. The earlier structure consisted of successive tiers of courts of law arranged in a hierarchical order; Rural Courts, Courts of Requests, Magistrate's Courts, District Courts, the Supreme Court, the two local Courts of Final Appeal, and the Court of Appeal (established with the abolition of the right of appeal to the Privy Council). Apart from these, there were two other courts of law concerned with specific and narrow areas of judicial administration, the Court of Admirality and the Election Courts.

Over and above the law courts functioning in Srī Laṅkā was the ultimate appellate authority, the Judicial Committee of the Privy Council in England, but this stage of appeal was removed before the new scheme came into operation. The new courts of law are also structured in a hierarchical fashion, but with less complexity: Magistrate's Courts, District Courts, High Courts and a Supreme Court. The Supreme Court now functions as the court of appeal and exercises only an appellate and revisionary jurisdiction, appeals from High Courts and District Courts being heard by a bench of three judges and appeals from Magistrate's Courts being heard by two judges. The Supreme Court consists of a Chief Justice and twenty other judges. The new High Courts are established in each of the sixteen judicial zones into which the island has been divided, and they have been empowered with the original jurisdiction which was exercised by the former Supreme Court. This includes the trial of serious crimes, the issuing of writs, the hearing of election petitions and admiralty cases, and the granting of bail and injunctions. In areas with low crime rates, arrangements have been made for the High Court judge to function as the District Court judge as well. The jurisdiction of the District Courts remained unchanged. As earlier, they possess unlimited civil jurisdiction and criminal jurisdiction over offences punishable with maximum penalties of five years' imprisonment or a fine not exceeding Rs. 5,000. In areas where civil actions are limited, the District Judges have been required also to function as Magistrates. The Magistrate's Courts, unlike previously, exercise both civil and criminal jurisdiction, civil jurisdiction being limited to actions not exceeding Rs. 1,500 in value and criminal jurisdiction to offences punishable by prison terms of at most eighteen months or by a fine not exceeding Rs. 1,500. Most magistrates are required to sit in about three circuit courts. District Courts and Magistrate's Courts are sited respectively in each of the forty districts and eighty divisions into which the judicial zones have been divided and sub-divided.

The institution of the new courts structure, unlike some of the other provisions contained in the Administration of Justice Law, did not meet with much opposition. Indeed, it was welcomed in some quarters as a meaningful step towards eliminating the delays which characterised the proceedings of the former complex structure. There was, however, one feature, the abolition of the second right of appeal, which aroused a great deal of criticism on the grounds that past experience had demonstrated again and again the need for the right for the correction of error on the part of the first court of appeal.

The judges of the new higher courts of law have been drawn mainly from the official bar, and of the Supreme Court judges only four have been recruited from the unofficial bar, a situation about which the unofficial bar has been less than pleased. The appointment of the judges and the inauguration of the new reforms occasioned once again widespread discussion on a crucial question, the independence of the judiciary. The constitution of 1972 had vested the authority for appointment, transfer, dismissal and disciplinary control of the judges other than those of the Supreme Court in the cabinet of ministers, and in the exercise of this authority two new bodies, the Judicial Services Board and the Judicial Services Disciplinary Board, became associated with the cabinet. Both these bodies derive their functions and duties from the cabinet. This change—control over judicial officers other than Judges of the Supreme Court was vested with the Judicial Services Commission, comprising the Chief Justice and two other Supreme Court judges—and the failure to embody in the new constitution certain other provisions which were contained in the constitution of 1948 relating to the standing of the judges of the Supreme Court aroused fears for judicial independence—though a clause covering "the independence of persons administering justice" was included in the new constitution. In 1973 there was a renewal of the discussion relating to the independence of the judiciary, centred on a specific clause in the Administration of Justice Law, under which the President of the Republic received the authority to direct any judge of the Supreme Court to discharge any "other appropriate duties". As it was pointed out, the President acts on the advice of the Prime Minister, and his directives are not subject to judicial inquiry or adjudication. The government would therefore be in a position, under this clause, to make any judge subservient to its bidding. The coupling of this clause with another, the right given to every court to exclude the public from its sittings, raised greater fears—namely that "secret trials" under "subservient" judges would become a possibility. Despite the strong criticisms of these clauses made by the legal profession, including the respected Srī Laṅkā branch of the International Commission of Jurists, no change was offered.

The Administration of Justice Law brought into force several new features in judicial proceedings. Non-summary proceedings in respect of serious crimes have been abolished, and the decision whether prosecution should be initiated or not now rests with the Director of Public Prosecutions, who would be acting on the basis of the investigations conducted by the police. The post of Director of Public Prosecutions was newly created, and he ranks equally with the Solicitor-General who continues to be concerned with civil matters. Both officials come under the direction of the Attorney-

General. Specific categories of cases continue to be heard before
juries, as before, but the qualifications for jurors have been changed
by shifting the emphasis from ownership of property to education
and employment. Women are now permitted to sit as jurors. To
expedite the disposal of cases, the courts have been given the authority to go into trial even in the absence of the person indicted, and
the opportunities for lawyers to obtain repeated postponements
of cases to suit their convenience have been severely curtailed.

A provision in the new law which created considerable controversy was the transfer of testamentary proceedings from the District
Courts to the Public Trustee. In fact, particular reference was made
to this provision when the constitutionality of the law was contested
by some applicants before the Constitutional Court; it was argued
that the Public Trustee was a state officer and not a judicial official,
and that the vesting in him as the competent authority of the granting of probate and letters of administration amounted to a virtual
creation of a court of law. The constitutional validity of this provision was upheld by the Constitutional Court, and it remained in
the bill to become law.

The Administration of Justice Law also abolished the distinction
which had been maintained since colonial times between the Advocates and Proctors, and created a single profession of Attorneys-
at-law. This provision, not surprisingly, was heavily attacked by
both the Advocates and Proctors and their respective professional
bodies, the Bar Council and the Law Society, who maintained that
the existing system was functioning satisfactorily and that therefore
no change as drastic as the one contemplated was necessary—the
so because the fusion was of more two categories which had acquired
substantially different training and skills. Again, no changes were
conceded. This reform of the legal profession was followed by
changes in the legal education system through another enactment,
and this too greatly perturbed the profession. The training of professional lawyers came within the purview of an independently
constituted Council of Legal Education under whose management
the Law College functioned. The new law changed the composition
of the Council of Legal Education, so that it now consists of the Chief
Justice, the Secretary to the Ministry of Justice, the Attorney-
General and four others appointed by the Minister of Justice from
the legal profession. At the time this law was placed before the
legislature, it was pertinently pointed out that with a majority of
direct ministerial appointees in the Council, the Council would no
longer have the standing of an autonomous body, and fears were
expressed that interference would be made on political grounds in
the process of legal education. The latter possibility arose in parti-

cular because the law gave the authority to the Minister of Justice to issue general or special directions to the Council regarding the exercise of its powers.

The enactment of the Administration of Justice Law was preceded by two equally — and in some respects more — important pieces of legislation. First, there was the Criminal Justice Commissions Law enacted in early 1972. This law was originally formulated to deal with an unprecedented event in the judicial administration experience of the country, the prosecution of hundreds of individuals for various offences connected with the April Revolt of 1971. It was clear that normal courts of law could not handle these cases without great strain, and there was a widely recognised need for a special apparatus. There was a further problem; the offences had taken place at a time when the regular law enforcement process had literally broken down and the real possibility arose that in numerous cases prosecutions would fail on technical grounds — i.e. grounds of failure to follow the investigatory procedures laid down. Certain modifications in respect of the admissability of investigatory procedures were therefore deemed necessary, yet when the draft legislation was finally presented before parliament, it became evident that its framers had gone far beyond the limits warranted by the extraordinary considerations which had been the basis of the new legislation. The legislation, as presented and enacted, provided for the establishment of special courts of law termed Criminal Justice Commissions under warrants issued by the Governor-General (later the President). Each such commission was to consist of a specific number of judges appointed by the Governor-General or President, and the Judges were required to try specific cases referred to them in the original warrant. The law laid down that three broad subjects could be brought before the commissions: offences arising out of the 1971 revolt, foreign exchange frauds and offences arising out of the widespread breakdown of law and order. Great concern was expressed in particular about the third subject, for it was felt, especially by some associated with the labour movement, that widespread breakdown of law and order could be interpreted as including trade union actions. The furore aroused by the powers granted to the commissions was great and sustained, and although it was largely unsuccessful, objections to certain provisions were carried — especially by a newly-founded umbrella organisation, the Civil Rights movement. Among the provisions heavily criticised was the failure to provide for the right of appeal from the decisions of the commissions, the powers vested in the judges of the commissions to regulate the court's proceedings — especially the discretion allowed to them to refuse oral submissions of lawyers appearing for the indicted — and the admissibility of certain types of evidence hitherto excluded in courts of law, especially confessions given to police officers.

The second law, the Interpretation Ordinance — also enacted in 1972[2] was in a sense an attempt firmly to establish a trend seen in the law-making of recent years. Most of the laws enacted since 1970 embody a clause to the effect that administrative action taken under the authority given by them may not be subjected to review before courts of law. The courts, however, following the precedents established in the English law, tended to take the view that administrative action was reviewable on certain narrow grounds. To obviate the difficulties which arose in consequence of this, the Interpretation Ordinance was enacted and the decisions of administrative officials taken under certain provisions were removed quite categorically from the purview of the courts and independent tribunals. The impact of this is immeasureable, especially because in recent years the government has firmly entered areas of activity which were hitherto left to private initiative. The economy in particular is now increasingly subjected to the regulatory control of administrative officials with large discretionary powers. The crucial question which has troubled so many is whether administrative action would invariably be guided by just and equitable principles. This is a question which looms large in the context of the factional politics prevalent in the country.

There is little doubt that in law-making and judicial administration a distinct and pronounced trend has emerged in favour of strengthening the position of the state at the expense of the individual rights which were hitherto enjoyed.

SELECT BIBLIOGRAPHY

Collins, C. H., *Public Administration in Ceylon,* London: Royal Institute of International Affairs (1951).

Hensman, C. R. (ed.), *The Public Services and the Public,* Community Pamphlet No. 3, Colombo (1963).

Jennings, W. I., *The Constitution of Ceylon,* Bombay (1949), Ch. XII.

Journal of Development Administration, I (1971) (Colombo, Academy of Administrative Studies; this journal was published in 1969 and 1970 as the *Training Digest*).

Kearney, R. N., 'Ceylon: The Contemporary Bureaucracy', in R. Braibanti (ed.). *Asian Bureaucratic Systems emergent from the British Imperial Tradition,* Durham, N. C. (1960), pp. 485-549.

---

2. For further discussion of this ordinance see above Chapter 13.

————, *The Politics of Ceylon (Srī Laṅkā)*, Ithaca, N. Y., and London (1973), Ch. II.

Nadaraja, T., *The Legal System of Ceylon in its Historical Setting*, Leiden (1972).

Ryan, B., 'Status, Achievement and Education in Ceylon', *Journal of Asian Studies* XX (1961), 463-6.

Wilson, A. J., 'Public Administration in Ceylon', in S. S. Hsueh (ed.), *Public Administration in South and South-East Asia*, Brussels: International Institute of Administrative Sciences (1962), pp. 199-240.

Wisva Warnapala, W. A., *Civil Service Administration in Ceylon*, Colombo: Government Press (1974).

PART IV

16

RELIGION

by K. M. de Silva and K. Malalgoda

INTRODUCTION by K. M. de Silva

There are in Srī Laṅkā four complexes of religion: the indigenous and traditional religious practices, Buddhism primarily and Hinduism, and two faiths, Islam and Christianity, the first of which was introduced by Moorish traders and was never in Srī Laṅkā aggressively expansionist, and the latter an impinging faith introduced in all its sectarian variety by the successive western powers who have had control over parts or the whole of the island. Christianity at various times has been militantly expansionist and an aggressively proselytising faith.

The statistics of religious affiliation in Srī Laṅkā today are as follows. The Buddhists with 67.4% are an overwhelming majority, while Hindus with 17.6% are the largest minority. The Christians constitute 7.7% (divided into Roman Catholics 6.9% and Protestants 0.8%) and the Muslims 7.1%, and all others 0.1%.

It was from the last quarter of the nineteenth century that the recovery of the indigenous religions and Islam from the pervasive pressures of an aggressive Protestantism began. By the turn of the century the tide had turned against Christianity, as the missionaries themselves realised. The new political consciousness, an extract from the World Missionary Congress in 1910 declared,

... is almost inevitably anti-British and pro-Hindu [in India], and in Ceylon, pro-Buddhist . . . The anti-British feeling develops into a determination to uphold all that passes under the name of Hinduism or Buddhism . . . [and] one of the most serious aspects of the Buddhist revival is the attempt to identify Buddhism with patriotism, and to urge upon people that loyalty to the country implies loyalty to the religion . . . [The Buddhist revival] is hostile to Christianity, representing it as alien, and Buddhism as national and patriotic...

This interaction between religion and politics, a notable feature of early twentieth-century Srī Laṅkā, was sustained throughout the agitation for independence, and indeed has gathered momentum since independence. Its impact on the balance of religious forces has been far-reaching and deeply significant. The Sinhalese-Buddhist majority is now in firm control in most spheres of life. The percentage of Christians has steadily decreased since the census of 1946 when it was 9.1; it was 9.0 in 1953, 8.3 in 1963, while in 1971, as we have seen, it showed a further decrease of 0.6 dropping to 7.7. The census of 1971 has shown that while the birth-rate of every other ethnic and religious group in the country had declined noticeably, that of the Muslims has remained at its previously high level. Thus it is likely that their position will improve to the point where in a decade or so they could overtake the Christians numerically.

While the stirrings in Hinduism and Islam, in the late-nineteenth century and early-twentieth century, had much in common with the processes of Buddhist resurgence, there were other features in these which set them apart from the Buddhist experience. The Islamic revival benefited greatly from the presence of a charismatic Arab exiled to Srī Laṅkā; the Hindu recovery was much more self-reliant and self-sufficient than the cognate process among the Buddhists and Muslims. Much more important was the fact that neither the Hindu nor the Islamic recovery in Srī Laṅkā developed any political overtones in the sense of an anti-British or anti-imperialist attitude. In contrast the Buddhist recovery was never wholly without political overtones.

BUDDHISM IN SRĪ LAṄKĀ
Continuity and Change
by K. Malalgoda

The problem of distinguishing between traditional and modern Buddhism remains a difficult one since the time that Bishop R. S. Copleston raised it in his *Buddhism: Primitive and Present in Magadha and in Ceylon* (London, 1892). In a curious way the old problem has reappeared in the two most recent books on Buddhism in Srī Laṅkā — Heinz Bechert's *Buddhismus, Staat und Gesellschaft in den Ländern des Theravāda Buddhismus*, Band I (Hamburg, 1966), and Richard F. Gombrich's *Precept and Practice: Traditional Buddhism in the Rural Highlands of Ceylon* (Oxford, 1971). Bechert was interested in modern Buddhism and Gombrich in traditional; each has, therefore, had to demarcate his area of interest, and in doing this, both have had difficulties.[1] Bechert, on his own initiative, changed his position with regard to one very important point: in 1966 he viewed Sinhalese-

Buddhist nationalism as a relatively recent phenomenon, but three years later he changed his mind and traced its origins as far back as the first century B.C.[2]

In terms of their professional training, Bechert and Gombrich have a similar background — in Indian philology. But in the two works referred to above both adopt new approaches: Bechert a historical one and Gombrich an anthropological one. The difficulties they have had to face in trying to distinguish between traditional and modern Buddhism are not altogether unrelated to the different approaches they had chosen.

The historical is clearly the better approach to this problem, but it does not automatically provide an easy solution. The Buddhist tradition in Sri Lanka is certainly very old, but it is by no means an uninterrupted one. The decline, loss, rediscovery and revival of tradition are recurrent themes in its long history. In the revivals of tradition, the consciousness of continuity has played a very important part, but consciousness and reality are two different things. The historian is thus faced with the problem of having to distinguish between continuities, discontinuities and transformations of tradition, and the problem is further complicated by the fact that, especially in recent times, revivals of traditional ideologies have been accompanied and supported by social processes which are quite new. The Sinhalese-Buddhist nationalism is particularly important in this regard because this ideology has sometimes been invoked as an explanation of communal conflict in the mid-twentieth century.

Tambiah, in his review of Arasaratnam's *Ceylon* (New Jersey, 1964), questioned the validity of this explanation by asking a series of perceptive questions:

Were the Sinhalese — Tamil frictions and riots inevitable in terms of an inexorable and unforgotten past characterised by rivalry and hatred between the two communities? Can one make a distinction between the 'actual past' and how that history has been interpreted in the twentieth century? Is the modern view of the past an enduring ordering of experience and memories by the Sinhalese and Tamils, or are we to locate the causes of current problems in the events of more recent history during which time interested politicians forged new historical myths or breathed life into ones long buried? . . . In brief . . . [are] the Ceylonese engaged in a modern battle being fought with traditional slogans and weapons, or are they waging a traditional war on a modern battlefield, or perhaps a combination of both?[3]

Tambiah focused his own attention on the social, economic and political changes initiated under colonial rule — changes which were on the whole 'progressive' in that they involved a widening of avenues for social mobility and an intensification of economic activity and political awareness — but which, in the absence of sufficient economic growth, led to an anomic disjunction between socially induced aspirations and the capacity of society to fulfil them, a situation in which "traditional cleavages and slogans become operative in the competition for prizes offered in a non-traditional context". He subsequently concluded that the position was "not so much that traditional wars are being fought in the twentieth century but that modern battles are being waged for modern trophies but with traditional slogans and revivalist dogmas".[4]

The same problem of having to distinguish between continuity and change, tradition and modernity, that the historian faces in the time dimension is tackled by the anthropologist in the spatial dimension, and his general inclination is to view villages as traditional and urban areas as modern.[5] But this simple dichotomy, rural/traditional *versus* urban/modern, can at times be very misleading. Villages, as Obeyekere himself has argued elsewhere[6], are not cultural isolates; they do, and did, have crucial links with urban centres, and these links constituted an essential part of their tradition. Historically, the Buddhist kingdoms from Anuradhapura to Kandy provided these (political and religious) centres; and after the decline of Kandy,[7] the religious centre gradually moved to the new political centre — Colombo — with the opening of new and influential monasteries and *piriveṇas* and the establishment of the headquarters of various Buddhist organisations (Buddhist Theosophical Society, Maha Bodhi Society, Young Men's Buddhist Association, etc.) in Colombo.[8] What the anthropologist observes in the villages, therefore, is a Buddhism that has come under the influence of, and been revitalised by, this new centre through *piriveṇas* and schools, teachers and preachers, pamphlets and journals, newspapers and books, etc.[9] While this makes the rural-traditional *versus* urban/modern dichotomy unhelpful, it is also necessary to point out that the new centre is only a structural approximation to the old centres provided by Buddhist kingdoms. Indeed from the point of view of ideal-typical traditional Buddhism, the end of the Buddhist kingdom was — to quote Mus — a "grave mutilation" which left only "a kind of rump Buddhist society".[10] For this reason, anthropological studies of contemporary villages cannot provide a complete picture of traditional Buddhism. They can only provide a partial picture which needs to be supplemented by historical studies of central — in contrast to peripheral or village — institutions.[11]

What does ideal-typical traditional Buddhism mean? This is

perhaps best explained with reference to the transformation of ancient Buddhism of which Weber wrote.[12] Weber was interested, among other things, in identifying the different social strata which had given different religions their characteristic features; and the stratum which gave ancient Buddhism its distinctive form, he argued, was the fellowship of monks who were held together by a common pursuit of (individual) salvation under the guidance of the Buddha and his teaching. The social origins of the monks as well as their lay supporters were principally among the privileged strata of urban patricians and merchant classes (or the 'bourgeoisie'); but the pursuit of salvation required withdrawal from active life in the world, and the monks themselves were mendicant, homeless and migratory. Consequently, ancient Buddhism was intellectual and contemplative (as against practical and active within the world), and asocial and apolitical in its orientation.

The transformation of this virtuoso religion[13] into a mass (or world) religion involved basically two things: first, at the level of belief and practice, making accomodations to meet the religious needs of the predominantly peasant laity; and secondly, at the level of religious organisation, developing links with secular authorities whose backing was necessary for maintaining unity and discipline within the order as well as for the propagation of Buddhism in different Asian communities. This transformation had already occurred in India by the time that Buddhism was formally introduced to Srī Laṅkā under Emperor Asoka's patronage, and it was this Buddhism that took root and developed there as the traditional religion of the Sinhalese.

Rahula has written a masterly survey of Buddhism during the first thirteen centuries of its history in Srī Laṅkā.[14] For the later centuries we have no works reaching the same degree of comprehensiveness though the main features of the subsequent history can be ascertained from several scattered sources. Our interest here, however, is not in the history of traditional Buddhism, but rather in features which might be considered as typical of it, and these features may be stated briefly as follows: a relationship of interdependence between the king and the order of monks; introduction of aspects of the socio-political order into the organisation of monastic life through a hierarchy of offices and monastic landlordism; structural and functional differentiation within the order of monks and the adoption by the majority of monks of learning and teaching (rather than practice) as their vocation; and the pursuit of more goals by Buddhists than that of release from *samsāra* (*nibbanic* Buddhism) — in particular, good rebirth within *samsāra* (*kammatic* Buddhism), and protection from misfortune and increase of good fortune during the present life (apotropaic Buddhism).[15]

While some of these features indicate departures from ancient Buddhism, others reflect not so much departures as accretions around it. The result, anyway, was a loosening of the logical consistency of ancient Buddhism,[16] leading to what Bechert has called "contradictions"[17] and Tambiah has termed "dialectical tensions".[18] The most important of these are: (a) the nature of the Buddha: unique historical figure as against one of a type of persons — the Buddhas — who appear successively at suitable intervals and who help in the release from *samsāra*; (b) the meaning of religious activity: release from *samsāra* as against good life in the world and good rebirth within *samsāra* (c) the nature of Buddhism: universalistic path to salvation as against particularistic national religion; the ideal of monkhood: (d) world-renouncer who seeks his own salvation and has no obligations to society as against positive social role with economic privileges, intellectual accomplishments, and spiritual, humanitarian and parish obligations towards society; and (e) administration of the affairs of the order: by monks themselves rather than with the initiative, support and participation of secular authorities.

These "contradictions" or "dialectical tensions" are important not merely in understanding the history of Buddhism but also the contemporary religious scene, including some of the recent debates and controversies over such issues as 'Vinaya Vardhana', 'political monks' and '*sāsana* reform'. That each side to these debates and controversies has been able to support its own position with cogent historical, if not canonical, arguments clearly indicates the deeply entrenched nature of 'contradictions' and 'dialectical tensions' in traditional Buddhism.[19] I do not propose here to go into these debates and controveries on which several others have commented.[20] I shall focus my attention rather on those changes which could be viewed as significant departures from the ideal type of traditional Buddhism.

Following Weber, we considered two criteria as crucial in the transformation of ancient Buddhism to traditional Buddhism: the relationship that it developed with secular authorities and the accommodations that it made to meet the religious needs of the predominantly peasant laity. If this analysis is valid, then a change in one or both of these criteria — i.e. a withdrawl of state patronage and/or changes in social stratification — can be expected to produce changes in traditional Buddhism. In Srī Laṅkā withdrawal of state patronage to Buddhism, as well as changes in social stratification, occurred under colonial rule.

The withdrawal of state patronage occurred in stages and over a long period. It began in the sixteenth century with Dharmapāla's conversion to Catholicism and his transfer of temple villages to the Franciscans, and his subsequent bequest of his whole kingdom to the King of Portugal. In the low country, the old politico-religious order was never restored — in fact, under the Portuguese as well as their colonial successors governmental machinery was used against Buddhism — though towards the end of the eighteenth century there were some monks and monasteries in the low country which received some support from the kings of Kandy. In Kandy itself, as is well known, there was no immediate withdrawal of state patronage to Buddhism after the cession of the kingdom to the British in 1815, but in stages it was made all the same.

When Buddhism was revived in the low country in the later eighteenth century under the influence of the Kandyan kingdom, the building of monasteries and providing sustenance for monks depended almost entirely on the support of local laymen (as there were no royal endowments in this region) and in particular of headmen. Some *goyigama* headmen gave the lead in this regard, and they were soon followed by headmen of other castes — *salāgama*, *karāva* and *durāva* — who were sufficiently wealthy and enthusiastic to help monks of their own castes to proceed to Burma and return with higher ordination which the *Siyam Nikāya*, established in Kandy, had refused to grant them. The upward mobility of these castes was a major change in social stratification which occurred under colonial rule, and though this change took place within the caste system, it led to a new situation in the religious sphere — in the form of monastic fraternities which were outside the control of the traditional politico-religious establishment. After 1815, the *Siyam Nikāya* establishment weakened even further, and gradually ceased to receive the political backing that it had traditionally enjoyed. The number of independent fraternities thus increased in the low country as well as in the Kandyan provinces; they were supported voluntarily (rather than through *rājakāriya*) by the laity — peasants and headmen as well as new social strata (entrepreneurs, lawyers, teachers, journalists, etc.) which had come into being as a result of the economic and social changes introduced under British rule. To be sure, the traditional religious establishment in Kandy continued to exist with its hierarchy of offices and monastic lands, though in a much weakened state due to lack of direct political support. But at the same time, there was also a new religious situation in the form of new monastic fraternities, autonomous in their own spheres; which, receiving no patronage from political authorities, depended entirely on the laity (who included a new and sizeable

'bourgeois' element) for their material support; and which in
fact were far more active and energetic than the demoralised traditional religious establishment. With these changes — which I have
examined in greater detail elsewhere[21] — in mind, Tambiah has
suggested that "modern Buddhism appeared as a reincarnation
of Weber's ancient Buddhism."[22]

Tambiah's hypothesis, which he himself calls 'unconventional'
is certainly an interesting one, and it is particularly useful in understanding—quite apart from the situation indicated above—the
growth and popularity of forest hermitages since the latter half of
the nineteenth century. But there are, to be sure, other aspects of
modern Buddhism which cannot be grasped adequately by viewing
them in this light. This would appear hardly surprising when one
considers the fact that ancient Buddhism is only one of the models
which are available to Buddhists. There are, in addition, two others —
diametrically opposed to each other, but equally important in their
direct and indirect influence on shaping the attitudes, organisations
and aspirations of the Buddhists—namely those of Protestant
Christianity and traditional Buddhism.

Obeyesekere introduced the term 'Protestant Buddhism' to
describe the changes brought about in Buddhism as a result of its
confrontation with Christianity.[23] In using this term; he emphasised
two points; (a) that it protested against Christianity, and (b) that
in doing this, it imitated many of the norms, practices and organisational forms of Protestant Christianity (as revealed, for example,
in the Society for the Propagation of Buddhism, Young Men's
Buddhist Associations, Sunday schools, Buddhist schools modelled
on missionary schools, Buddhist catechisms, etc.). A third feature of
the same process was the process of laicisation (also associated with
Protestant Christianity)—the increasing involvement of laymen in
roles of religious leadership and its concomitant—the displacement
of monks from some of their traditional positions of leadership.[24]

The success of the new voluntary associations and their activities
depended on this lay leadership which was recruited from the new
social strata referred to earlier and which had come into existence
under British rule. Their religious needs and interests, as much as
their economic bases, differed noticeably from those of the traditional peasantry, and Ames has already commented on some of its
consequences: criticisms of the conduct of monks and the religious
practices of villagers, lay meditation, doctrinal reinterpretations,
and the search for scientific proof for religious doctrines, etc. Obeyesekere drew attention to the tendency common in this leadership
to imbibe western norms and ideals and view them as traditional
Buddhist ones, and he referred in particular to Victorian morality.

The same tendency, if in a slightly different form, is also evident in the substantial body of apologetic literature on comparisons of Buddhism with science, democracy and socialism.[25]

Protestant Buddhism was a very militant form of Buddhism, and this militancy too, like many of its other characteristics, it acquired historically from missionary Christianity.[26] One result of this militancy was to dampen the optimism and aggressiveness of the Christians, as a result of the realisation by the latter that converting the whole population to Christianity was not a feasible ideal. From the late nineteenth to the mid-twentieth century, therefore, different religious groups competed with each other to protect and if possible extend their own interests within a broad framework of 'private enterprise' in religion, with the government taking a stand of formal neutrality. The right of each religious group to exist and to be involved in this competition was an implicitly accepted rule of the game. Despite their greater numbers, the Buddhists, as late starters as well as for other reasons, did not fare very well in open competition — not at any rate in spheres which were considered important by the lay leadership. In education, for instance, Christians continued to hold their supremacy with regard to both the number of schools under their management and the amount that they received in grants from the government for the maintenance of those schools. In the public service, business and professions, Buddhists remained under-represented in proportion to their numbers in the population. It was only natural in this situation that the model of traditional Buddhism had a special appeal for Buddhists, for it represented the pre-colonial past when Buddhism, instead of being just one among several competing religions, enjoyed a privileged position.

Of the different attempts to revive traditional Buddhism — which might be called traditionalist Buddhism — the most extreme was millennial in character, and restoration of Buddhist monarchy constituted an essential part of the millennium. There were several millennial episodes of this nature in the Kandyan areas in the nineteenth century, and beliefs and aspirations relating to the advent of a great Buddhist king in the 2500th year of the Buddhist era (1956 A.D.) persisted into the twentieth century in the form of the Diyasēna myth.[27] Other, more 'rational', attempts to revive traditional Buddhism have been necessarily more selective and limited in scope because they did not visualise restoration of Sinhalese-Buddhist monarchy, but they all sought to establish or re-establish connections with the government — colonial as well as independent. The fifth clause of the 'Kandyan Convention', in contrast to its other clauses, became a matter of concern and debate for a long time; and even in the low country, the various branches of the *Amarapura Nikāya*, which had originally rejected the right of secular authorities to regulate the affairs of the order of monks, eagerly sought formal recognition by the colonial government, just as institutions like Vidyodaya Pirivena solicited the friendship and patronage of colonial governors. This desire to be on good terms with the established political authority was probably one of the reasons why the Buddhist 'revival' of the nineteenth century did not develop into a political movement for national independence.

With independence, due to a new convergence of interests, traditionalist Buddhism became much stronger. To the lay leadership, as represented in particular by the All-Ceylon Buddhist Congress, government intervention appeared necessary as an easy solution to the frustrations of competition with non-Buddhists. To the monks, who had been left in the background not merely by the colonial government but also by the Buddhist lay leadership, and who had suffered a decline in status due to the rise of the lay intelligentsia, traditionalist Buddhism held hopes of regaining some of their lost social position. To the politicians, restoring Buddhism to its 'rightful place' provided a source of popularity and legitimacy, and since the mid-1950s the two major political parties have competed with each other to make political capital of this situation. The process of this new convergence of interests and dilemmas presented by it have been documented and commented on by others[28] and therefore need not be gone into here. It will suffice to note in connection with the analysis presented in this paper that traditionalist Buddhism—into which Protestant Buddhism easily merged—in fact involved a reversal of the conditions under which the latter had thrived. Instead of the separation of politics and religion, there was now a convergence of the two; and monks who had been pushed into the background reappeared in the limelight. If, as a consequence, several *ad hoc* bodies like the *Eksath Bhikshu Mandalaya, Eksath Bhikshu Peramuna* and the *Bauddha Jatika Balavegaya* have mushroomed since the 1940s, other more stable voluntary organisations which had been built over several decades with uncommon dedication and enthusiasm declined as a result of government intervention, for which the Buddhist leadership itself had agitated. The nationalisation of schools led to the extinction of organisations like the Buddhist Theosophical Society, and the Buddhist leadership thereby lost a good deal of their independent power, influence and patronage in the field of education. Within a few years of the elevation of Vidyodaya and Vidyalankara Pirivenas to university status, monks lost control over these institutions and the two new universities came to have very little continuity with their past except in their names. It is thus clear that not merely non-Buddhist organisations have had to suffer a weakening of their strength as a result of the ascendency of traditionalist Buddhism (which, in contrast to Protestant Buddhism, excluded free and equal competition between different religious groups) in the years after independence. Buddhist organisations perhaps even to a greater degree, have had to face a similar fate.

THE RELIGIONS OF THE MINORITIES *by K. M. de Silva*

HINDUISM

The recovery of Hinduism in nineteenth-century Srī Laṅkā began a whole generation earlier than that of Buddhism. In a sense Hinduism was in a more advantageous position from the point of view of resistance to missionary encroachment in that it was possible to draw on the tremendous resources of Hinduism in India. Nevertheless in the first half of the nineteenth century – and for that matter even later – the missionary organisations were much stronger in Jaffna and its environs than in most other parts of the island. There were fewer sectarian conflicts among the missionaries working in the north, and their network of schools was far more efficiently run. There was, besides, the fact that the state was less concerned with the possibility of riots and disorder following on the disturbance of the traditional Hindu religious pattern than with the reaction to mission work among the Buddhists.

The leadership in the Hindu recovery in Srī Laṅkā was given by Arumuga Navalar, and the structure of Hindu society in contemporary Srī Laṅkā has been largely influenced by him. The two dominant strands in his work were a concern to prevent conversions of Hindus to Christianity, and to preserve the orthodox form of Saivism. In both he was eminently successful.

As a counterpoise to the Christian missionary effort he organised Hindu schools for imparting religious and secular education, in which he was followed by a few eminent Hindu leaders of the nineteenth and early twentieth century, notably Sir Ponnambalam Ramanathan. The *Saiva Paripālana Sabhai* (established by Navalar) and the Hindu College Board of Management eventually came to control more than 150 schools (both primary and secondary) until the large majority of these were taken over by the state in the early 1960s.

The preservation of the orthodox form of Saivism had two aspects: the renovation and restoration of Hindu temples; and the publication of Saivite religious texts, in both of which Navalar was the pioneer.

Nearly all the Hindu temples in the Jaffna peninsula and the littoral had been destroyed by the Portuguese and the Dutch, and those that had survived were in a state of decay and dilapidation in the nineteenth century. The Hindu temples of Srī Laṅkā, unlike those in India, are of modest proportions and have rather slender resources for their maintenance. The latter is due partly at least to the fact that the restoration of the temples was not followed by a restoration of the lands that belonged to them in pre-colonial times. The restoration of Hindu temples has continued in contemporary Srī Laṅkā and is a prominent feature in Hindu life in all parts of the island. Among the Hindus the temple has been and still continues to be the centre of cultural activity in the villages, with the annual festival the most notable religious and cultural event of the year. While in recent times secular entertainment such as the cinema has tended to become a rival attraction to the cultural activities of the temples, the increasing popularity of the practice of holding wedding ceremonies in temples has undoubtedly helped to sustain the position of the temples as the predominant centre of cultural activity in the villages.

Perhaps Navalar's greatest contribution to the recovery of Hinduism was the publication of a large number of Saivite religious texts which have helped substantially to preserve the ideals and heritage of the Hindus in Srī Laṅkā primarily, and India as well. Some of these publications are still in use as texts for religious instruction in schools.

Hindus in Srī Laṅkā today are, with the exception of a few North Indian traders in Colombo, Saivites belonging to the Siddhanta school of Saivism which is dominant in South India. Although the Hindus generally consider the four *Vedas* as the source of all religious knowledge, the *Thirumurais* arranged into twelve sections form the most important body of sacred literature of the Tamil Saivites. The *Thirumurais* consist of the *Thevāram, Thiruvacakam* and the philosophical texts. The *Thevaram* and *Thiruvacakam* are collections of hymns of the Saivite saints of the sixth, seventh, eighth and ninth centuries A.D. written in simple, easily understood language. Every Saivite is taught selections from this collection both at his home and in his school (if it is a Hindu school). The tenets of Saiva Siddhanta, on the other hand, were formulated in the thirteenth and fourteenth centuries, in an archaic Tamil not easily understood by ordinary Hindus. Although the large majority of Hindus make no effort to study them, yet they have some elementary knowledge of the essentials of Saivism.

There have been no new developments or controversies in doctrinal matters in Srī Laṅkā Hinduism in recent times.

The crucial flaw in Navalar's work — and this became evident in the years after independence — was that he was not a social reformer. The Hindu revivalist movement which he led basically strengthened orthodoxy and did little to soften the rigours of the caste system. While the Sinhalese caste system had merely a social sanction, its Hindu counterpart had a religious one as well, and untouchability was very much a problem in Hindu society in Jaffna.

The *vellalas* among the Hindus were the equivalent of the *goyigama* among the Sinhalese, and like the latter were not a thin upper crust, but a substantial section if not a majority of the Hindus. They used the sanctions of Saivite orthodoxy to maintain their caste privileges at the expense of those in the lower rungs of the caste hierarchy. Because of the economic and political backwardness of the Harijan communities and because these latter were themselves divided on the basis of caste and had no organisation to mobilise their resources effectively for bargaining for their rights, the potential if not latent tensions in this situation did not emerge till after independence, in the late 1950s.

The attitude of the Buddhist Sinhalese to the Hindus was essentially ambivalent. Religious sentiment should have drawn them together because of the traditional links between the two religions in Srī Laṅkā society. Ethnic politics, however, was a divisive factor. After 1956 there was always an undercurrent of hostility to the Tamils: when the latter sought to rouse public opinion (especially international opinion) against the Sinhalese majority, their campaign for justice was vitiated by the orthodox Hindu resistance to the amelioration of the conditions of the Harijans. Sinhalese politicians and Buddhist activists diverted attention to the social evils of untouchability, to the great embarrassment of the Tamils.

But it would be unfair to attribute the positive improvement in the position of the Harijans in recent times to Sinhalese solicitude on their behalf, for that concern was never disinterested. It was largely owing to the efforts of the Tamil political leadership itself that the movement for the removal of Harijan disabilities was initiated — long before Sinhalese politicians and Buddhist activists interested themselves in the problem.[30] Substantial progress has been made since 1955: cafés and restaurants in urban areas (particularly) have permitted entry to Harijans; and more important — despite occasional and well-publicised efforts at resistance — one by one the large temples have opened their doors to them. Nevertheless there are still some areas in which the temple entry movement and the Harijan campaign for equality have not succeeded. The caste clashes of the late 1960s were largely politically motivated and embarrassed the government of the day and the political leadership among the Tamils alike. The most hopeful sign of all is that the youth of Jaffna are repelled by caste discrimination.

ISLAM

In contrast to Hinduism and Christianity, Islam has had a record of harmonious relations with the Buddhist Sinhalese both in the coastal areas and in the Kandyan region. In the latter they had been afforded a refuge against the vigorous hostility of the Portuguese and the harrassment of the Dutch. There the Muslims had been integrated into Kandyan society, though they retained their religious and cultural identity. In the early years of British rule the position of the Muslims of Srī Laṅkā improved considerably and they became in many ways a privileged group.

In the nineteenth century the Muslims, like the Buddhists and Hindus, faced the challenge of Protestant Christianity, but to a much greater extent than both the former, the Muslims were notable for a refusal to succumb to the blandishments of Christianity. This resistance persisted throughout the nineteenth century, but the survival of Islam in Srī Laṅkā had been secured, in a sense, at the expense of social and economic advancement. Since the education provided in the schools was primarily an English one, there was an attitude among the Muslims of Srī Laṅkā (natural to a conservative and cohesive community) of rejecting it because of the presumed danger of the impact of a foreign culture on Islam. Besides, education was not only in English but also largely Christian in content, and for that reason they were not prepared to endanger the faith of their children even at the expense of sacrificing the material benefits of an English education. As a consequence of this manifestation of zeal for their ancestral faith, by the third quarter of the nineteenth century the more enlightened Muslim leaders were profoundly disturbed to find their community sunk in ignorance and apathy, parochial in outlook and grossly materialistic.

The arresting of the decline in vitality of the Muslim community has been associated for long with the "charisma" of Arabi Pasha[31] who is believed to have jolted them out of their conservative seclusion. But much more important were the foresight and tactical skill of a local Muslim leader — M. C. Siddi Lebbe, a lawyer by profession and social worker by inclination — in helping to bring the community to accept the need for a change of outlook. Like Arumuga Navalar, Siddi Lebbe saw the supreme importance of education as a means to the regeneration of his community. The revitalising process initiated during this phase continued during the first half of the twentieth century.

Like every other ethnic and religious group in the country the Muslims found themselves called upon to define their attitude to the agitation for the transfer of power. The Sinhalese-Muslim riots of 1915 had been a traumatic experience for the latter, and this strengthened the trend towards collaboration with the British — which was any way quite strong among the Muslim leaders. There were occasional misgivings such as, for instance, after the First World War when the Khilāfat[32] movement in India had its repercussions among the Muslims in Srī Laṅkā, although the local version never developed the positively anti-British tone it had in India, and the Srī Laṅkā Muslims did not turn away from the traditional policy of association with the imperial power. Indeed, throughout the next two decades the Muslims formed part of a phalanx of minorities under Tamil leadership which accepted the need for collaboration with the British in return for the protection and consolidation of the rights of minorities as the price for accepting the transfer of power. It was not till the early 1940s that the Muslims broke away from them to support the Sinhalese leaders in their political campaigns for independence.

This policy of co-operation with the government of the day has been pursued by the Muslims after independence as well. And in this too they were, for the most part, a contrast to the Hindus and Tamils in general: they wished to remain an integral part of the Srī Laṅkā nation. There was no support from them for the agitation for a federal political structure; on the contrary they have been among the most vociferous critics of such a move.

What they have attempted to do is to safeguard, sustain and advance their distinctive cultural identity. They have sought and obtained state support for this in two distinct fields: the consolidation and recognition of the personal laws of the Muslims and in education. Here again, and more especially with regard to the former it was a trend which began from the earliest years of British rule.

The Muslim Marriage and Divorce Registration Ordinance 27 of 1929 (operative from 1937) set up a system of domestic relations courts presided over by Muslim judges (*qazis*) and explicitly recognised the pure Muslim law of marriage and divorce; and the same process may be observed in respect of inheritance in the Muslim Intestate Succession and *Wakfs* Ordinance of 1931. The provisions of the latter Ordinance relating to Muslim Charitable Trusts (*Wakfs*) was superseded by the Muslim Mosques and Charitable Trusts or *Wakfs* Act 51 of 1956, while the Ordinance of 1929 was repealed by the Muslim Marriage and Divorce Act 13 of 1951 (operative from 1954), whereby the *qazis* were given exclusive jurisdiction in respect of marriages and divorces, and the status and mutual rights and obligations of the parties concerned. The *Wakfs* Act of 1956 established a separate government department with a purely Muslim Executive Board. The personal laws of the Muslims have been preserved under the Republican Constitution of Srī Laṅkā.

It is in education that the greatest gains have been made, especially after 1956. The list of concessions won by the Muslims is remarkable. Special government Training Colleges have been set up for them. Arabic is taught in government schools to Muslim pupils by qualified *moulavis*, appointed by the Ministry of Education and paid by the state; Muslim children had the right—till 1974—to pursue their studies in any one of the three language media—Sinhalese, Tamil or English, a privilege enjoyed by no other group in the country. A new category of government Muslim schools has been established apparently in recognition of the cultural individuality of Muslims as distinct from the Tamils, whose language is the home language of the great majority of Srī Lankā Muslims. The usual practice had been to categorise schools on the basis of their language of instruction, and the Muslims formed part of the Tamil-speaking school population. In the new 'Muslim' schools the sessions and vacations are determined by the special requirements of the Muslim population. The establishment and expansion of these schools vitiates the non-sectarian system of state education which has been government policy since 1960.

No doubt the concessions made to the Muslim community have been introduced in recognition of the fact that in education they lagged behind the other ethnic and religious groups in Srī Lankā. Thus some special assistance from the state may be justified as a temporary measure, even though their previous handicaps were largely self-inflicted. But the sensitivity to the special Muslim indentity has no doubt been strengthened by the fact that a Muslim has been Minister of Education for over eight years in the period 1960 to 1974. And, more important, some Sinhalese politicians have not been disinclined to use state resources to build up the Muslims as a counterweight to the Tamil community in a game of checks and balances which is an intrinsic element in the process of government in a plural society — divide and rule.

CHRISTIANITY

The position of the Christian groups in Sri Lanka in the twentieth century can be viewed in terms of the transformation of a privileged group into a beleaguered minority.

The Christian missions had come to Srī Lankā as the apostles of a new faith and as critics of indigenous society, and in preaching their new ideas the missionaries had been fortified usually by an unquestioning faith not merely in their own rightness but also in the intrinsic depravity of many traditional customs and beliefs. This latter had given the Christian missionary movement its characteristic feature of cultural intolerance. There was a conscious attempt to undermine traditional customs and beliefs and to impose in their place the whole system of Christian values associated with the Victorian age. There was thus a seemingly contradictory position — the stronger the Christian faith the greater the prospect of the Christians becoming a privileged sect, viewing aspects of traditional life with contempt and disgust.

Moreover, Christianity was interpreted on western lines and in non-indigenous concepts. The missionaries imposed on their adherents in Srī Laṅkā the conventional forms of western Christianity almost in their entirety, oblivious to the potential value to Christian worship, of indigenous art forms such as music, drumming, dance and architecture. Christian churches in Srī Laṅkā were westernised — and the Protestants especially were anglicised — to the point where the soul-searching about the relationship between Christianity and nationalism which appeared in many parts of Asia and Africa at the end of the nineteenth century either did not emerge at all or did so a full generation later and on a more modest scale.

It was in the years after the First World War, however, that the missionaries working in Asia and Africa began to face up to the implications of the changes brought about by the rise of nationalism, when Christianity began to be viewed and resisted as an integral aspect of imperialism. And in Srī Laṅkā, as elsewhere in Asia and Africa, the missionary movement — both Protestant and Roman Catholic — responded to the new situation by seeking an accommodation with the forces of resistance by accepting the need to tone down the westernness of Christianity. And in so doing they went counter to the whole trend of missionary thinking and practice in the nineteenth century. The aim now was to make the missions and churches indigenous institutions less conspicuously under European leadership and direction. In Sri Lanka too this change of attitude became noticeable[33] but almost up to the grant of independence 'Ceylonisation' in religious affairs among the Christian groups working in the island was much more tardy than the equivalent process in the political and administrative spheres.

Part of the process of coming to terms with nationalism was the re-indigenisation movement — the revival of indigenous names, and dress, and the cultivation of the native arts and crafts among the Christians. In most Christian churches a Sinhalese prayer-book — a faithful translation from the English — had been the only concession to the indigenous culture, and no attempt had been made to adapt the form of worship to a national or truly Sinhalese form. The re-indigenisation movement proper was in the hands of the critics of the missionaries, and the missionaries in Srī Laṅkā at first rather self-consciously stayed aloof from it, but some of them sought to accomodate themselves to the changes inherent in this process. In this the Anglicans were always in the forefront, in the use of forms of worship natural to Srī Laṅkā, and in the adoption of traditional architectural forms in church building.

A third aspect of this trend was the tendency to establish an autonomous status for the Christian missions and churches, self-supporting, self-propagating and indigenous. This was a long-drawn-out process largely because of the practical and mundane problem of financial independence from the parent societies. The degree of independence achieved varied from mission to mission, but it would be true to say that before 1948 none were substantially self-supporting.

There are two other noteworthy points about these trends. Even in the attempt to make the missions and churches indigenous institutions — and this was so for all the Protestants — the articulate spokesmen of the new views were more often than not British missionaries rather than native Christians. Secondly, the re-indigenisation movement, such as it was, was essentially a Protestant one. The Roman Catholics lagged behind in this. It would seem as though the very nature of their organisation impeded them in the attempts to come to terms with nationalism.

At the same time, the Buddhist resurgence and the growth of nationalism led to a sober realism about the limits of evangelical activity. It was no longer a matter of expansion so much as consolidation, if not contraction. More important, the missionaries could no longer afford dissipating their energy in sectarian disputes among themselves. Sectarianism was common enough among the Buddhist *sangha* but that of the Christians was only meaningful in terms of western circumstances. At the turn of the century there had been little co-operation among the Christian groups working in the island. The greatest achievement of the World Missionary Conference held at Edinburgh in 1910 was the emergence of the first permanent instrument of Christian co-operation outside the Roman Catholic church. The impact of this began to be felt in Srī Laṅkā in the 1920s and after, and its influence fitted in neatly with the practical necessity to close ranks in the face of a resurgent Buddhism. This co-ordination of activity did not encompass the Roman Catholics, who stood aloof from the other Christian groups. There was also a great deal of friction which attended these well-intentioned efforts, but Protestant mission work as a whole was marked by increased co-operation and greater efforts at synchronising activities.

By the 1930s the political changes inherent in the new constitutional structure began to have their repercussions on the standing of religious bodies in Sri Lanka. There was a perceptible dimunition of the influence of missionary organisations in the island. Though the government still expressed a desire to maintain its neutrality in religious affairs, it had become politic to underline the sense of a special obligation towards Buddhism.

In retrospect it would seem that the inter-war period was the most decisive phase in the reconciliation of the Christian minority to a diminished role in the affairs of the country, if not yet the ready acceptance of the fact of Buddhism dominance. The policies, trends and tendencies evident at this stage proved to be exceptionally durable, and they were continued beyond independence with renewed vigour. That is not to say that there were no difficulties, and obstacles. Most of these latter centred on education and the schools, and the conflicts which emerged on this issue determined the pattern of relations between Buddhist majority and Christian minority both in the final phase of British rule and in the years after independence.

For too long education had been feared as a means of religious conversion, and demands for fundamental reform in education were inevitable. With the increasing devolution of political power and responsibility to the local political leadership, the mission schools organised on denominational lines came increasingly under attack. The principle of denominationalism was viewed with distrust if not hostility and the use of the educational process as a means of conversion to Christianity was effectively checked. In the 1940s an especially purposeful effort was made to give the island's educational system a new orientation, which was basically secularist, and the role of the state in education was considerably enlarged at the expense of the missions. The missionary resistance to these reforms — and more especially to the "free" education scheme — organised and led by the Roman Catholics succeeded in delaying their implementation and in softening if not eliminating some of the more far-reaching aspects which were regarded as being especially inimical to denominational interests.

The difference between the attitudes of the Roman Catholics and the Protestants over the education of their adherents' children needs to be explained. The Roman Catholics brought pressure on Catholic parents to send their children to Catholic schools, and the larger (and better) of such schools had a majority of Catholic pupils; there were no such pressures exerted by Protestant churches and in few, if any, Protestant schools was there a majority of pupils who were Protestants (even using the term widely to cover all Protestant denominations). Thus the Catholics' resistance to secularisation and state control of education was much stronger than that of the Protestants. The fact that the opposition to these reforms came mainly from the Catholics largely explains the irony of a situation where the bitterness of the Buddhists against the slights and neglect suffered at the hands of the Christians during the period of western rule should be directed at the Catholics rather than the Protestants who for the last century or more had enjoyed special favour if not a privileged position.

At the transfer of power the Christian minority was on the defensive. Section 29(2) (*b*) of the Soulbury Constitution seemingly offered protection against legislation discriminating against them and other minorities.[34] In general there seemed to be no reason to anticipate the introduction of such legislation from the political leadership of the day. The Christians for their part, as in the past, sought to define their position in terms of their minority identity, and to preserve their distinctiveness not only against other religious groups but also to the Srī Laṅkā polityi the commitment to reindigenisation was much more wholehearted, even though they did not entirely discard the elements of westernisation in their cultural identity; the trend towards an autonomous status, especially among the Protestants, became much more purposeful, and the Christian ecumenical movement made firm progress largely among the Protestant groups.

Nevertheless the tensions between the Christian minority — especially the Roman Catholics — and the Buddhists, which had erupted to the surface during the "free" education struggle, remained dormant. The Buddhist movement continued to view the Christian minority as a privileged group with a vested interest in the survival of the denominational system in education. Indeed the denominational schools were regarded as the source of Christian privilege, and it was at these that the attack was directed. By 1960-1 the Buddhist agitation succeeded in putting an end to the Christian dominance in the field of education. Once more it was the Roman Catholics who bore the brunt of the attack. They had opposed "free" education in the 1940s because it would break the bonds that bound the better schools to the Christian management and thus expose Christian children to the influence of Buddhist and secularist cultures. The take-over of schools was resisted in 1960-1 because it was felt that with the schools would go the last bulwark of the identity of Christians in the nation.[35]

The Roman Catholics discovered that section 29 (2) (*b*) of the Constitution gave them no protection against these pressures. But its proven ineffectiveness as a constitutional check on encroachments on the interests of the minorities did not make that clause any more palatable to Buddhist activists. They continued to regard it as an ostentatious concession to minority influence, and persisted in their agitation for its elimination.[36]

Buddhist-Roman Catholic relations reached their nadir in the early 1960s. But within a few years there was evidence of a change in attitude on the part of the Roman Catholics, and a greater readiness towards the acceptance of religious pluralism. The greatest single factor promoting change was the Vatican Council of 1963-5. In Srī Laṅkā this implied a greater readiness on the part of the Roman Catholics to seek an accommodation with the forces of nationalism and to tone down the occidental features of their church — in other words to adopt much the same attitudes in the organisation of their work that the Protestant groups had done more than a generation earlier.

REFERENCES

1. K. Malalgoda, 'Sinhalese Buddhism: Orthodox and Syncretistic, Traditional and Modern', *Ceylon Journal of Historical and Social Studies*, n.s. Vol. II/2 (1972), 156-69.
2. Heinz Bechert, 'Zum Ursprung der Geschichtsschreibung im indischen Kulturbereich', *Nachrichten der Akademie der Wissenschaften in Göttingen*, Philhist, Vol. K1 2 (1969).
3. *Bijdragen tot de Taal—Land—en Volkenkunde*, 112 (1966) 385.
4. S. J. Tambiah, 'The Politics of Language in India and Ceylon', *Modern Asian Studies*, Vol. I/3 (1967) 216.
5. See e.g. M. M. Ames, 'Ideological and Social Change in Ceylon', *Human Organisation*, Vol.XXII/I (1963), 45-53; G. Obeyesekere, 'Religious Symbolism and Political Change in Ceylon', *Modern Ceylon Studies*, Vol I/1 (1970) 43-63; and Gombrich, op. cit.
6. G. Obeyesekere, 'The Great Tradition and the Little in the Perspective of Sinhalese Buddhism', *Journal of Asian Studies*, Vol XXII (1963) 139-53.
7. K. Malalgoda, "Sociological Aspects of Revival and Change in Buddhism in Nineteenth-Century Ceylon", D. Phil. thesis, Oxford (1970), Ch. V.
8. During the last 150 years, the building of monasteries and *pirivenas* seems to have occurred at a prodigious scale in the Colombo district, for in 1959 this district—five centuries earlier a flourishing centre of Buddhism under the Kotte kingdom, but subsequently, victim of the ravages of the Portuguese and the 'anti-heathenish' laws of the Dutch — had more monasteries and *pirivenas* than any other district in the island. The total number in the Colombo district was 837, and within the ten administrative divisions of this district, the highest concentration (188) was in the most central (*Mudaliyar's*) division.

9. Some illustrations are given in the paper cited in footnote 1.

10. P. Mus. 'Buddhism and the World Order', *Daedalus*, 95 (1966), 821.

11. See also note 15, below.

12. Max Weber, *The Religion of India: The Sociology of Hinduism and Buddhism*, tr. and ed. Hans H. Gerth and Don Martindale, Glencoe, Ill. (1958), Ch. VII.

13. Weber's ideas on ancient Buddhism (first published between 1915 and 1917) were based on the work of early European orientalists whose research at the time was confined almost exclusively to Theravada sources. The classic exposition of this tradition of research was Herman Oldenburg's *Buddha: His Life, His Doctrine, and His Order*, London (1882).

14. W. Rahula, *History of Buddhism in Ceylon: The Anuradhapura Period*, Colombo (1965).

15. For brevity and convenience I have used this typology suggested by Spiro in his study of Burma, *Buddhism and Society: A Great Tradition and its Burmese Vicissitudes*, New York (1970), rather than other typologies suggested by anthropologists who have worked on Srī Laṅkā.

16. It is helpful, for purposes of analysis to assume logical consistency even if the actual situation was more complex (see note 13, above). What Weber himself wrote (op. cit., p. 206) was: "For our purposes it is advisable . . . to present early Buddhism . . . systematically, with regard to points important to us, stating the ideas in as close connection as possible, and disregarding whether in its original phases it contained this rational closure actually and fully—a question which only the expert can decide".

17. In the paper cited in note 13, above.

18. S. J. Tambiah, 'The Persistence and Transformation of Tradition in Southeast Asia, with special reference to Thailand', *Daedalus*, 102/1 (1973) 55-84.

19. It is hardly necessary to point out that the prevalence of 'contradictions' or 'dialectical tensions' is not a peculiar feature of Buddhism, but of every religion with a long, rich and varied tradition behind it.

20. See especially Ames, op. cit., Tambiah (1973) op. cit., Bechert (1966 and 1973) op. cit. and also his 'Theravada Buddhist Sangha: Some General Observations on Historical and Political Factors in its Development', *Journal of Asian Studies*, Vol. XXIX/4 (1970) 761-778, and Donald E. Smith, 'The Political Monks and Monastic Reform' in Donald E. Smith (ed.), *South Asian Politics and Religion*, Princeton, N.J. (1966), pp. 489-509.

21. 'Sociological Aspects of Revival and Change in Buddhism in Nineteenth Century Ceylon', Part I.

22. S. J. Tambiah, 'Buddhism and Third-Worldly Activity', *Modern Asian Studies*, Vol. VII/1 (1973) 8.

23. Obeyesekere (1970), op. cit., pp. 46-7.

24. 'Sociological Aspects of Revival and Change in Buddhism in 'Nineteenth-Century Ceylon', Ch. VII.

25. For comments on this literature, see Ames, op. cit., Bechert (1966) op.

cit., and Howard A. Wilson, 'An Anatomy of the Buddhist Renaissance in Ceylon in the Work of K. N. Jayatilleke', *Social Compass*, Vol. XX/2 (1973) 201-15.

26. This thesis has been elaborated in K. Malalgoda, "The Buddhist-Christian Confrontation in Ceylon, 1800-1880", *Social Compass*, Vol. XX/2 (1973) 171-200.
27. Details are given in K. Malalgoda, "Millennialism in Relation to Buddhism", *Comparative Studies in Society and History,* Vol. XII/4 (1970) 421-41.
28. See especially Bechert (1966), op. cit., W. Howard Wriggins, *Ceylon; Dilemmas of a New Nation*, Princeton, N.J. (1960), and Donald E. Smith, "The Sinhalese Buddhist Revolution" in Smith (ed.), op. cit.
29. I am greatly indebted to my colleague Dr. S. Pathmanathan for his generous assistance in the preparation of this section of the present chapter. But the views expressed here are mine and he must be absolved of any responsibility for them.
30. The Federal Party's first convention in 1951 had a list of basic aims which included "the regeneration and unification of the Tamil-speaking people of Ceylon by the removal of all forms of social inequalities and injustices, in particular that of untouchability. wherever it exists". Quoted in R. N. Kearney, *Communalism and Language in the Politics of Ceylon*, Durham, N.C. (1967), p. 100.
31. Arabi Pasha, the leader of the abortive uprising against the Western powers in Egypt in 1882, spent nineteen years of his life (1883 to 1901) as an exile in Srī Lankā. To the Muslims of Srī Lankā he was Arabi Pasha of Tel-el-Kebir, the hero of Egypt, and they welcomed him with great enthusiasm.
32. The Khilāfat or Caliphate, a movement among the Muslims sought to preserve the Turkish Khalifah (Caliph). Under Gandhi's leadership this movement temporarily united the Hindus and Muslims in India in the struggle against the British.
33. For example, the first Ceylonese Roman Catholic bishop was appointed in 1933; but the appointment of a Ceylonese Archbishop came only after independence.
34. For discussion of this, see Chapter 13, pp. 317-18.
35. See Father Paul Caspersz, 'The role of Sri Lanka Christians in a Buddhist Majority System', *The Ceylon Journal of Historical and Social Studies*, n.s., Vol. IV 1974, Special Number on *Sri Lanka Since Independence*.
36. See fn. 34, above.

NOTE ON FURTHER READING

The literature on Buddhism in Srī Lankā is substantial and only a fraction of it has been referred to in this essay. The interested reader should consult the relevant sections in H. A. I. Goonetileke's *A Bibliography of Ceylon*, 2 vols., Zug, Switzerland (1970). Several items which appeared since Goonetileke's general bibliography was compiled are listed in Frank E. Reynolds, 'Tradition and Change in Theravāda Buddhism: A Bibliographical Essay

Focussed on the Modern Period', *Contributions to Asian Studies*, IV (1973), 94-104. This issue of *Contributions to Asian Studies* was devoted to 'Tradition and Change in Theravāda Buddhism: Essays on Ceylon and Thailand in the 19th and 20th Centuries' and it contained three papers on Srī Laṅkā (by Heinz Bechert, Tissa Fernando and B. G. Gokhale). Published in the same year were: a special issue of *Social Compass*, XX/2 (1973) devoted to the 'Sociology and Social Anthropology of Religion in Sri Laṅkā'; an issue of *Daedalus*, 102/1 (Winter 1973) on 'Post-Traditional Societies', which has three papers on Theravāda countries (by Edmund Leach, S. J. Tambiah and Heinz Bechert).

Very few published works of any substance or quality on the minority religions of Srī Laṅkā have appeared recently. The Revd. James Cartman's work on *Hinduism on Ceylon* Colombo, (1957) is still the only monograph of any substantial value on the subject, while there has not been a single monograph or book on Islam in Srī Laṅkā. Published work on Christianity in contemporary Srī Laṅkā has not been very plentiful either. Two recent works may be mentioned: The Revd. W. J. T. Small (ed.), *A History of the Methodist Church in Ceylon 1814-1964*, Colombo (1973) and Father F. Houtart, *Religion and Ideology in Srī Laṅkā* , Colombo (1974).

17

EDUCATION

by C. R. de Silva

Background and Development up to 1948

Education in its widest sense connotes the totality of learning experience of any individual or community. However, in this particular survey attention will be concentrated on the formal system of education that obtains in Srī Laṅkā today, the recent efforts to remould its structure and content, and the interaction between such reforms and the social, political and economic scene in the island.

Education, in the sense of 'formal instruction and learning', has had a long history in Srī Laṅkā. Religious instruction for novices in Buddhist temples started well before the Christian era, and basic instruction in reading, writing and religion appears to have been given to interested laymen by Buddhist monks from about the same period. Thus from early times there was in the island a considerable literate lay public. Indeed, some of the older Sinhalese literary works were specifically written for literate laymen.

The traditional educational system was thus fashioned and controlled by the religious order and education generally was regarded as a means of religious edification. Education imparted at the temple had a strong academic or literary bias. On the other hand, technical skills such as those needed to construct the ancient irrigation reservoirs and canals were transmitted from generation to generation, either by traditional instruction given by father to son or by craft apprenticeships, both outside the system of temple instruction. The academic nature of temple education was strengthened because it met the contemporary need for literate officials who could maintain revenue and other records for purposes of administration. The system was also bolstered by a tradition that gave respect to an 'educated' man rather than to one who was merely 'wealthy' or able to get things done.

Colonial rule by the Portuguese and the Dutch in the lowlands during the seventeenth and eighteenth centuries did not markedly change the pattern of instruction. Religion continued to dominate education, though in some areas and for some periods the dominant creed became Catholic or Presbyterian Christianity rather than Buddhism or Hinduism. A few printed works became available, but they were not numerous enough to induce any real transformation of the method of learning which still depended largely on the memorizing and study of selected texts. Nor did British rule in the first half of the nineteenth century usher in any great changes in the educational sphere.

The English Evangelicals of the 1840s and 1850s considered education a legitimate activity of the state, but in terms of actual achievements on the part of the local colonial administration the results were limited. As late as 1870 there were only 156 government schools with a total enrolment of 8,736 and 229 private schools with a further 8,201 pupils. These figures, however, exclude the Buddhist temple schools which survived into the early twentieth century and indeed perhaps taught more pupils in 1870 than the western-type schools 'recognized' by the government.[1]

This was not surprising. The training of a few English-educated Ceylonese to assist in administrative tasks did not need a widely based eudcational system. Of course it is true that the Christian missionaries saw mass education through schools as a method of conversion, but none of the various denominations in the island had the resources to establish a widespread school structure on its own.

The situation changed after 1870. The educational reforms of that year in England strengthened the case for better educational facilities in the colonies, and the continuing success of coffee culture in the 1860s and the 1870s seemed to provide the necessary finances. Missionary organizations successfully campaigned for state assistance for maintaining and expanding their school systems. In 1869 a Department of Public Instruction was established, and in the following year the government decided to give grants-in-aid to private schools that conformed to certain minimum requirements. The results were spectacular. By 1879 already 372 government schools catered for 19,120 pupils, while 814 private schools had an enrolment of 55,944. Two decades later the total pupil enrolment had risen to 218,479.

The benefits of education were not, however, equally distributed. Although the south-west coastland and the Jaffna peninsula were fairly well provided with schools, the situation was very different in the interior parts of the island. Even in 1901 barely one-quarter of the children of school-going age were attending school, and of a total population of 3,565,904 as many as 2,790,255 were considered illiterate. Religion had also become a significant factor in the access to educational facilities. In 1868, for instance, 65 per cent of all children attending school were Christian and only 27 per cent Buddhist. Government policy after 1884, which left the development of secondary education virtually in the hands of religious bodies, would have further aggravated the situation had not the Buddhist, the Hindus and, to a more limited extent, the Muslims — stimulated by the contemporary religious revival — begun to compete with Christian missionaries in the establishment of schools. Despite these efforts, however, the other religious groups lagged behind the Christians in educational attainment for many years to come.

Table 1. LITERACY RATES BY RELIGION

	1901			1921	
	Male	*Female*		*Male*	*Female*
Christians	55.2	30.0		66.0	50.1
Buddhists	34.9	5.2		50.4	16.8
Muslims	34.4	3.3		44.8	6.3
Hindus	25.9	2.5		36.9	10.2

Source: Education in Ceylon; p. 529 (see footnote 1).

Perhaps the most glaring inequality, however, was between the opportunities available for those who studied in English-medium schools and those in schools which taught in Sinhala or Tamil. Schools of this first category were few in number — only 179 in 1912, rising to 197 in 1915 and 262 in 1928 — and they levied fees and were thus barred to a vast majority of the people. This explains why literacy in English — the key to the more lucrative professions, was limited to 2.6 per cent of the population in 1901 and to 6.3 per cent as late as 1946. Furthermore, secondary education was provided exclusively in schools which taught in English, and recognized secondary educational institutions proved an even more exclusive group — thirteen in 1915 and forty-seven in 1928. These led their students to more lucrative careers in government service or the professions. The *swabhasha*[2] schools by contrast were free and taught little beyond the Three Rs.

The first three decades of the twentieth century saw a steady expansion in the educational structure. Student enrolment figures continued to rise — to 441,372 in 1925 and to 539,755 in 1930. This was partly due to a government decision to enforce compulsory schooling from the ages of five to fourteen. The state programme of providing educational facilities to all areas had the effect of reducing regional inequalities, at least in the sphere of primary education. On the other hand, an increasingly vocal Buddhist and Hindu opposition to the extension of the Christian missionary school system led the Christians after 1920 to concentrate largely on improvements to existing Mission schools. Meanwhile the establishment of a University College in Colombo in 1921 to prepare students for external examinations of the University of London laid the foundations of tertiary-level education in the island.

Table 2. THE PROPORTION OF CHILDREN IN SCHOOL TO THE TOTAL POPULATION BY PROVINCE

	1879	1898	1930	1971
Western Province	1:21	1:10	1:7	1:4.3
Southern Province	1:68	1:12	1:8	1:4.2
Central Province	1:116	1:27	1:10	1:4.6
North Western Province	1:72	1:26	1:10	1:4.3
North Central Province	1:281	1:32	1:13	1:4.6
Northern Province	1:14	1:10	1:6	1:4.1
Eastern Province	1:20	1:15	1:10	1:5.3
Uva Province	—	1:53	1:20	1:4.9
Sabaragamuwa Province	—	1:33	1:13	1:4.6

Sources (for 1966): Education Centenary Volume; (for 1972 and 1973): Statistical Report 1974 (See footnote 11).

Throughout this period the content of education retained a strong academic bias. Many reasons may be adduced for this. British educational practice has traditionally favoured the separation of institutions giving general education from those which provided vocational training. Literary courses were less expensive as far as facilities to be provided were concerned, and the British grammar school tradition lent greater prestige to academic studies. Moreover, the English secondary schools in the island were regarded as models for the rest, and when they began to prepare their students for the examinations of British universities, the academic curriculum they adopted had great influence over the whole school system. The establishment of University College in 1921 did little to break this tradition, for University College itself prepared its students for examinations of a similar type, and its own requirements for admission were naturally on the same lines. Perhaps the most important factor, however, was the question of employment opportunities. The island had no developed industries to speak of, and the demand for trained personnel from the agricultural sector was minimal. On the other hand the 'liberal' education provided by the English secondary schools led to lucrative posts in the administrative services and to the professions, and the policy of 'Ceylonization' of the state administration — pursued vigorously in the second quarter of the twentieth century provided openings for a large number of those who were fortunate enough to obtain an education in English.

Thus agricultural, commercial and technical education made little progress. It was not that the shortcomings of the existing curriculum were not perceived. As early as 1841 a School Commission Report declared that 'the system of education in Ceylon was by no means sufficiently practical', but almost all efforts either to establish separate institutions to teach these aspects or to introduce them into the regular school curriculum failed. An early example of such efforts was the Colombo Agricultural College, established in 1884 to train teachers in agriculture in rural schools and superintendents for estates in areas not coveted by Europeans. The Director of Public Instruction of the time expected that this college would have a beneficial impact on paddy production by promoting the use of transplantation and a more efficient plough, but his hopes were not realised mainly because the employment opportunities available for trainees of the college proved so poor. Similar reasons led to the failure of a School of Agriculture set up in 1896 to train teachers and students in agriculture, veterinary science, forestry and dairy farming and of the various industrial schools which were established in the nineteenth century.

Efforts to integrate agricultural and industrial training into the general school curriculum also met with limited success. In 1901 a school garden scheme was initiated to make the *swabhasha* school 'a centre for practical and useful knowledge as well as mere book learning'. Elementary text-books on agriculture were published, and school gardens given a government grant after 1911. Yet by 1927 less than 30 per cent of the *swabhasha* schools possessed school gardens, and agricultural training was not integrated with the rest of the teaching in school. Even less successful was the effort to introduce industrial training in some primary schools after 1916.

There were some successes, however. The School of Tropical

Agriculture started at the Royal Botanical Gardens, Peradeniya, in 1916 and reorganised into two farm schools at Peradeniya and Jaffna in 1922, successfully provided a two-year course in English and a one-year course in Sinhala and Tamil. The Technical School (later Ceylon Technical College), established in 1894 in Colombo, trained students in engineering and surveying for several government departments and private establishments had in-service technical and craft training schemes on their own. These, however, barely counterbalanced the predominantly academic bias of the general school curriculum.

The constitutional advances of 1931, which introduced universal suffrage and placed the control of education in local hands, ushered in a period of unprecedented reform and experimentation. In the sphere of curricular reform perhaps the most significant experiment was that termed the Rural Scheme of Education. This involved the establishment of special schools for rural youths who had completed eighty ears of formal schooling. These schools were to attempt to impart an education directly relevant to the rural environment largely by means of practical work. For instance, the study of health and sanitation was pursued partly by the building of walls round open wells to prevent water pollution and other similar tasks. The school curriculum was organized round a study of the locality, health, vocational studies and aesthetic studies. By 1939 this scheme had spread to 246 government schools and seven aided ones, and teachers for these schools were being specially trained at four centres.

The scheme eventually collapsed chiefly because it failed to compete with the existing secondary schools which provided access to the more lucrative avenues of employment. Moreover, in the absence of adequate funds, equipment and expertise, the practical aspect of schooling quickly degenerated to the level of repetitive manual labour. However, the scheme itself was significant in that it was a pioneer effort to use education to check the migration of rural youth to urban areas and to find a meaningful role for them in the villages. Its view of education as a factor for social stability rather than as an avenue for social mobility was to rear its head again in more recent times.

Indeed the establishment of Central Schools in the rural areas was originally based on similar lines of thinking. They were supposed to provide practical instruction in agriculture, commerce, handicrafts and domestic science as well as a training in more academic subjects. Instruction was to be in English and by 1944 fifty-four Central Schools had been established. Once again, however, socio-economic factors began to influence the practical working of the scheme. Tremendous pressure from parents and politicians to model these schools on the lines of the existing urban English secondary schools resulted in the warping of the whole curriculum. By 1947 only twenty-seven of the fifty-four central schools still retained practical departments, and even in these schools the conventional liberal education had gained pride of place. Thus the Central School scheme failed in one of its major aims, but especially after the abolition of tuition fees consequent on the decision to grant 'free education', the Central Schools became one of the major avenues of advancement for the rural child.

The establishment of the University of Ceylon in 1942 may be regarded as yet another key educational development of this era of reforms. The University quickly established a reputation for the quality of its first degrees, and despite competition from the external examinations of the University of London its student enrolment rose from 904 in 1942 to 1,554 in 1947.

The provision of free education—meaning free tuition from the primary grades up to the University: another of the well-known reforms of this period—was less revolutionary than appears at first sight, for even before this measure was enforced, all schools teaching in the local languages were in effect imparting education without charging tuition fees. What really happened in 1945 was that those English secondary schools which had levied fees were given the option of either receiving government grants and abolishing fees except a maximum monthly facilities fee of Rs. 5.00 or continuing as unaided fee-levying schools. A vast majority opted to join the 'free education' scheme. Fees in the University were also abolished. 'Free education' became a significant measure largely in the context of its implications for later times.

Main Developments since 1948—the Growth of State Control

One of the noteworthy features of the education system since independence is the steady growth of the power and influence of the state Ministry of Education over almost all aspects of educational development in the island. In some ways it is possible to trace the development of state control over education to the era before independence. As late as 1931, for instance, only 1,498 of the 4,119 schools and only two of the twenty-one teacher training colleges had been directly run by the state. The situation had changed somewhat by 1947, when 2,880 of the 4,980 schools and most of the teacher training institutions were administered by the Ministry. Nevertheless it was the developments of the post-independence era that were most striking.

After the inception of the 'free education scheme' it was possible for the Ministry to develop greater supervision over assisted schools on the grounds that the Ministry bore the brunt of the expenses. The Education Inspectorate was gradually strengthened in the 1950s. The Ordinance No. 20 of 1947, which abolished fees in government and assisted schools, also stipulated that in schools registered after July 1947 the grant was to be paid only in respect of pupils whose parents professed the religion of the proprietor of the school. This effectively checked the expansion of the missionary school system while the extension of the system of state schools proceeded apace. The Education Act No. 5 of 1951 which brought all schools in the island within the purview of the Ministry of Education and which provided for the registration of all unaided schools was another step in the same direction.

More important than all these measures was the take-over of the vast majority of the private assisted schools in 1960-1. Buddhist pressure groups had been agitating for this for some time. They argued that it was unfair for the state, which obtained its revenue from a predominantly Buddhist population, to fund schools run by Christian missionary bodies to propagate their faith. They demanded that Buddhist children in Christian schools should be taught their religion as a part of the curriculum and when this was refused, a campaign was built up for the take-over of all schools by the state. Despite the bitter opposition of the Roman Catholics, the Srī Laṅkā Freedom Party Government of 1960-4 agreed to implement this demand. By the Assisted Schools and Training Colleges (Special Provisions) Act No. 5 of 1960 and the Assisted Schools and Training Colleges (Supplementary Provisions) Act No. 8 of 1961 the administration and ownership of these institutions, save those which opted to continue as non fee-levying schools and colleges, were vested in the hands of the state. All Training Colleges were handed over, and only thirty-eight of the assisted schools preferred to take the option. From then on 95 per cent or more of all students in primary and secondary schools came under schools directly managed by the Ministry.

Even the few schools that opted to continue as non-fee-levying institutions and the few others which had elected to stay outside the 'free education scheme' from 1945 were required to conform to Ministry directions. They were easily kept in line with state educational policy by an implicit threat of a complete take-over of schools. A clause in the Act No. 8 of 1961, which specifically prohibited the establishment of any school by a private individual, further safeguarded the position of the Ministry in this sphere. Finally the education reforms of the 1970s, which introduced the National

Certificate of Education Examination in 1975 at the end of the ninth year of schooling, is expected further to strengthen state control over education. According to present plans, only candidates from schools run by or recognized by the Ministry will be permitted to enter for this examination, and there will be no private candidates. This measure is expected to provide a death-blow to most private tutorial establishments which flourish by training candidates who have had to leave school after two unsuccessful attempts at the GCE "O" Level Examination.

The extension of the power and influence of the Ministry of Education can also be seen in the sphere of technical education. As a result of a recommendation of the report of the Commission of Inquiry on Technical Education in 1961 a new Department of Technical Education and Training was established under the Ministry of Education. This department was placed in charge of several training institutions which had hitherto functioned under other ministries. The Hardy Technical Institute of Amparai and the Basic Technical Training Institute which had operated under the Gal Oya Development Board and the Ministry of Transport respectively may be cited as examples of such institutions. In 1966 the Department of Technical Education and Training itself was merged with the Department of Education.

In fact, the expansion of the scope of the work of the Ministry of Education has largely meant the development of one particular department within the Ministry—the Department of Education. The other departments of the Ministry such as the Department of Examinations and the Department of Educational Publications were mostly confined to specific tasks so that by the late 1960s the Department of Education had become almost synonymous with the Ministry, especially as it occupied the same headquarters. By 1966 the department had become so unweildly that it was decided to divide it into regional departments, but the decentralisation is largely in routine matters and most important questions are still referred to headquarters. The whole structure of education in Srī Laṅkā is still closely controlled from the centre; indeed, it is one of the largest centrally controlled systems in the world.

The expansion of the power and scope of the Ministry of Education has had some beneficial effects. It has facilitated educational planning and promoted a more integrated view of the different aspects of education. On the other hand, on balance the adverse effects seem to have clearly outweighed these advantages. By 1968 the Education Department accounted for almost one-third of the total of 300,000 employees in government departments[3], and it swiftly developed into being a powerful instrument of patronage.

Inefficiency and dissatisfaction within the department continued, but in the context of restricted employment opportunities, criticism of the Minister of Education by government backbenchers also became noticeably muted. Probably the worst effects of the over-extension of the Ministry have been in its control over the Universities. The heavy-handed efforts of the Ministry officials to re-organise and rationalize the Universities have resulted in disaffection among a substantial section of the academic staff of the Universities without really solving any of the ills that had affected third-level education in the island.

Primary and Secondary Education

One of the well-known developments of the first decade after inde-pendence was a substantial advance in the number of schools pro-viding first and second level education. By 1960 there were 6,986 schools in the island, a substantial advance on the independence figure of 4,818. Pupil enrolment also rose from 1,400,000 in 1950 to 2,200,000 in 1960. The development of secondary education was particularly striking. The number of children in secondary schools rose from 65,000 to 225,000 during the decade in question, and this represented a significant broadening of the educational base of the country.

This factor has often been overshadowed at least in the public eye by another momentous change in the 1950s: the change of medium of secondary school instruction from English to Sinhala or Tamil. This change had been decided on before independence, but it was implemented only from 1953. By 1960 secondary education in schools in Srī Laṅkā was almost entirely in Sinhala and Tamil. There were exceptions. Science was taught in the higher forms in English for a few more years, and up to 1972 students whose mother-tongue was neither Sinhala or Tamil were allowed to be educated in English but by the early 1960s the transformation was largely complete.

It was perhaps unfortunate that the broadening of opportunities for secondary education coincided with the change in the medium of instruction. The same phenomenon occurred in 1960s in respect of University education, and in both cases it was often assumed that the difficulty the educated youth had in finding suitable employ-ment was due to the fact that he knew little or no English. While the small percentage with literacy in English has secured a definite advantage there is no adequate reason to conclude that the problem of unemployment of educated youth would have been of a different order of magnitude if the expansion in secondary level had occurred while English had remained the medium of instruction.

While the 1950s marked the development of primary and secondary education along lines generally determined in the previous era, the 1960s and the early 1970s were more a period of reform and re-organisation. The cost of education had risen from Rs. 105.6 million in 1950 to Rs. 227.5 millions in 1959/60 and it was to continue to rise steeply — to Rs. 472.4 millions in 1969/70 and Rs. 510.9 millions in 1971/2. By 1969 expenditure on education had accounted for 16.2 per cent of the national budget and 4.4 per cent of the gross national product.[4] On the other hand the result of this large outlay of money did not seem very encouraging. A socio-economic survey conducted in 1969 showed that of the persons in the 15-24 age group only 18 per cent of those with no education and 28 per cent of those with primary education were unemployed. In contrast 72 per cent of those who had been in Grade IX and X and 84 per cent of those who had been in Grades XI and XII had not found employment.[5] The reforms of this period can best be understood as a response to these two tendencies — rising costs and growing unemployment among school-leavers.

It is noteworthy that the measures taken to counter these tendencies show a strong underlying continuity despite changes of government in 1965 and 1970. In part this may be ascribed to the pervasive influence of the ideas contained in the National Education Commission Report of 1962, but it is undoubtedly partly due to the continued presence of the same group of administrators at the Ministry.

Of the economy measures the most important was probably the reduction of the duration of primary and secondary education from thirteen years to eleven. This was accomplished in two stages. In the period before 1964 primary education had commenced with children of five years of age (age of admission, 4-6 years) and consisted of six years of schooling. Secondary education continued for a further seven years. In 1964 primary education was reduced to five

Table 3. TOTAL SCHOOL ENROLMENT IN THOUSANDS

		1960	1964	1970	1972
Grades I — VIII		2,008	2,275	2,329	2,147
Grades IX — XII		225	345	351	480
	Total	2,233	2,620	2,680	2,627

Sources (for 1960, 1964): Education Centenary Volume; (for 1970, 1972): Adhyapana Sankhyalekhana Pilibanda Sankhyathi Sangrahya,1973.

years and from then on a minimum admission age of five was insisted upon. In 1972 the minimum admission age was raised to six, and secondary schooling was reduced by one year. The Education Ministry has somewhat unsuccessfully tried to defend these measures, particularly the second, as educationally desirable in themselves. What is clear is that they have contained school enrolment in an era of rapidly rising population and thus reduced increases in the cost of education.

The Ministry has of course denied that the 1972 reduction was an economy measure at all. It has argued that this measure should be taken not in isolation but in the general context of other reforms. In particular it has been argued that the utilization of the total capacity of schools located in residential areas for primary education and the conversion of urban centre schools into secondary institutions would increase enrolment of 6-10 year olds from 85 per cent in 1969 to 93 per cent in 1980. It is also anticipated that the dropout rate would be reduced by the practice of 'automatic' promotions except in Grades V and IX. The burden of the Ministry argument has been that, despite the rise in admission age and the reduction in the years of schooling, costs will rise on the whole as more children are likely to stay longer in school.[6]

The Ministry arguments need not be summarily dismissed. It is possible that the very high rate of repetition (20.9 per cent in Grade II and 18.1 per cent in Grade III in 1973) might be reduced at least to the level that obtains at present in secondary schools (6.7 per cent in Grade VII and 0.5 per cent in Grade VIII in 1973)[7] The number of schools devoting their whole space to primary education has increased rather dramatically from 712 in 1971 to 1945 in 1972.[8] But while these instances may show that the Ministry was not always guided by cost, it does not disprove that the reduction of the duration of schooling was an economy measure.

Finally, though it may be too early yet to judge, the evidence since 1972 gives the impression that, contrary to Ministry expectations, more children are dropping out of school. This of course may

Table 4. DROP-OUT RATES (%)

	Grade I	Grade II	Grade III	Grade IV	Grade V	Grade VI	Grade VII	Grade VIII
1972	—	5.3	5.3	6.4	7.3	9.3	4.7	8.4
1973	3.9	4.3	9.8	10.9	13.2	13.5	11.8	14.1

Source: Statistical Division, Education Ministry

be due to economic rather than educational reasons, but the total enrolment in state schools has dropped from 2,492,754 in 1972 to 2,475,433 in 1974, despite a rise in population.[9]

The 1960s also saw continued efforts to improve the content and level of education in various subjects, as well as changes in the total curriculum to make it less academically oriented. The former was best seen in the cases of science, English and mathematics. The reform of science teaching was touched off by problems that arose in teaching science in *swabhasha* at the early secondary school level in the late 1950s. In 1959 the Technical branch of the Education Department worked out a method of teaching and the sequence of lessons in a publication called *A Scheme for Teaching of General Science for Standards VI—VIII*. The first year was to be used to teach about 'water, air, the sun and ourselves', the second about 'the soil, getting work done, seeing and hearing', and the third about 'living things, tools we use, electricity, transmitting and transforming energy'. The scheme was subsequently revised and enlarged in 1963 and 1965 and specific course guides and pupils' texts were provided. Despite some shortcomings it was primarily responsible for maintaining the standard of science teaching despite a shortage of qualified teachers.

The programme for the improvement of the teaching of English has been noticeably less successful. In this case the provision of better pupils' texts could not really compensate for the inability to find teachers competent in English. In fact, the teacher shortage has compelled the education authorities to give up their earlier intention of providing instruction in English language from the third year of school. Since 1972 their policy had been to try to provide all secondary schools with English teachers and to review the position once this objective has been achieved.[10] The results of the English teaching programme on which a considerable sum of money was invested are still meagre. In the 1973 GCE "O" Level examination, 127,060 out of 240,669 school candidates sat the English paper and of them only 17,089 were successful.[11]

The introduction of 'new maths' was designed both to improve the quality of mathematics taught and to re-orient the curriculum. It proposed to eliminate the state of affairs that led four-fifths of the students to sit arithmetic rather than mathematics at their first public examination. In practice, however, the introduction of the new syllabus proved to be a lesson in how not to introduce changes. Although the teaching of 'new maths' was begun as early as 1969, the programme ran into difficulties and pupil texts for Grade VIII were published only in 1974. For a number of years, therefore, the students had to make an intellectual somersault from 'new maths' to old in Grade IX. Whatever the prospects in the future, the current effort on 'new maths' has so far achieved little to commend it.

On the other hand some progress was made towards the reduction of the imbalance between the different streams of students within school. Up to 1973 students have been placed in one of three streams — arts, science or commerce — after eight years of education. Due to the paucity of facilities for teaching science and the dearth of commerce teachers, the arts stream had accounted for 85 per cent of all GCE "O" Level candidates in 1964. During the 1960s and 1970s a crash programme of provision of science laboratories enabled the number of schools teaching science for this examination to rise from 125 in 1958 to 539 in 1967 and 847 in 1974. The number of schools preparing science for the GCE (Advanced Level) examination also rose, though less spectacularly, from 50 in 1958 to 146 in 1967 and 217 in 1974.[12] This has changed the proportion somewhat but even in 1974 the arts stream still accounted for well over half the total school enrolment.

Table 5. NUMBER OF CANDIDATES SITTING G.C.E. ('O' LEVEL) EXAMINATION

Subjects	Dec. 1966	1972	1973
History	83,303	103,662	102,126
Civics	81,985	102,570	99,993
Geography	60,931	108,077	129,896
Chemistry	31,463	84,374	80,925
Physics	30,334	82,060	99,320
Accounts	6,737	45,786	57,987
Shorthand/Typing	2,936	20,868	20,407
Needlework	6,101	17,643	21,693
Handicraft (Woodwork)	1,779	5,964	7,253
Handicraft (Metalwork)	311	2,015	2,363
Handicraft (Weaving)	1,580	6,961	8,743
Handicraft (Ceramics)	369	1,528	2,097
Total	175,273	374,113	419,054

Sources: (for 1966) Education Centenary Volume; (for 1972 and 1973): Statistical Report 1974 (See footnote 11).

Some effort was made to introduce a greater emphasis on practical work, especially in the early years of secondary school. In 1963 a Ministry circular directed that, of the thirty hours of weekly schooling, three were to be devoted to handicrafts, needlework or gardening, and a further one-and-a-half hours to arts and crafts. The trend was continued in the 1967 revision of curriculum for the first year of secondary school. It was then laid down that three hours should be kept aside for agriculture and 'work experience', and three more for arts, craft and needle work. Nevertheless if the applications for the GCE "O" Level examination as given in Table 5 are any indication, these subjects have failed to compete with the older and more academic disciplines. This is not difficult to explain. The more practical subjects led to posts at the craft level, while the more academic subjects had greater prestige and led rather to posts at the technician and professional levels.

The curriculum reforms of 1972 may be seen as yet another step in the road taken in the 1960s. These reforms were largely concerned with the early stages of secondary school — Grades VI — IX (11-14-year-olds). According to the new plan, all students will follow a common curriculum upto Grade IX, and this will consist of the following ten units — religion, mother-tongue, second language, mathematics, science, social studies, health studies and physical education, aesthetic studies (i.e. one subject like singing or dancing), pre-vocational subject I (e.g. agriculture, home science or commerce) and pre-vocational subject II (a regional or cottage industry). Students will be tested on all ten subjects at the National Certificate of General Education examination at the end of Grade IX, and will be selected for various types of higher education according to their performance. Only two attempts at the examination through the school will be allowed per candidate.[13]

A parallel revision of courses in Grades XI and XII was being discussed in mid-1974. The new plan envisages that 25 per cent of the time of all students in these courses would be used to learn four 'core' subjects, namely first language, English, elementary quantitative methods and management methods, and the cultural heritage and socio-economic environment of Sri Lanka. The remainder of their time was to be used to study three specialized subjects chosen from one of four curricular streams — bio-science, physical science, management and social science, and language and aesthetic studies. The details are still being worked out.

Several advantages have been claimed for this new system. In the first place it is pointed out — perhaps with some justice — that the compulsory provision of science at all schools at junior secondary level will tend to equalize opportunities and to reverse the predominance of the arts stream in later secondary and higher education. Much, however, will depend on ensuring that minimum facilities are available in rural schools. It has also been anticipated that pre-vocational subjects would instil skills useful in every day life as well as in learning a vocation. The objective in the introduction of pre-vocational subjects was to re-orient attitudes and encourage students to turn to skilled work in and around their environment rather than to indulge in an often fruitless quest for employment in a service occupation. This factor, together with the provision of education beyond the NCGE 'according to national needs' rather than 'according to the number qualified to continue', was expected to check the problem of unemployment among educated youth. Finally, it has been expected that the new scheme of education would inspire sufficient interest among parents to induce them voluntarily to share the cost of the new equipment needed.

This last expectation seems unrealistic in the present economic context when a large proportion of the population is adversely affected by inflation. Moreover, parents who have regarded schools as an avenue for a better life for their children are hardly likely to react enthusiastically to a system designed to encourage students to remain in their family setting and be self-employed. There is also the possibility that, without adequate equipment and qualified teachers, instruction in the pre-vocational subjects could easily degenerate into training at a craft level.

Indeed the question of re-training teachers should be an aspect to which more attention ought to be paid. The Ministry of Education has, in the last decade or more, devoted some 9 per cent of its total expenditure to teacher training. As a result the number of teachers following the two-year training college course has risen from 992 in 1944 to 5,697 in 1969 and 8,278 in 1972.[14] This is why, despite a vast increase in the number of teachers, the percentage of trained teachers in government schools rose from 29 per cent in 1937 to 43 per cent in 1969 and 50 per cent in 1972. However, with the present change a number of these teachers will have to be provided with short re-training courses enabling them to teach effectively subjects like new maths and social studies. The un-trained teachers will probably need more extensive guidance. There is evidence that the Ministry has recognised the problem, but unless it is solved satisfactorily the changes in the curriculum could well be limited to changes in nomenclature.

However, the most damaging criticism of the reforms of 1972 appears to be that they are too narrowly focused on the secondary school level and that their implications have not been properly worked out. A parallel reform of the primary school curriculum was started in 1974 only after the reforms in the junior secondary schools were well under way. The changes envisaged at the senior secondary level, while they represent a welcome broadening of education from the pre-reform practice of the study of four specialized subjects, seem to run counter to the increasing emphasis on practical work that has been a feature of reforms in the lower grades. The refusal to continue with vocational courses such as agriculture in the highest forms of the school and the continued testing of students mainly by theory examinations could well operate to retain and strengthen the 'academic bias' in the whole secondary educational structure.

The possible impact of these reforms on the fields of technical and higher education have also not been adequately examined. For example, it is very likely that with the introduction of science as a compulsory subject at the junior secondary level, the proportion of those studying science subjects after the NCGE examination would suddenly increase to well over 60 per cent of the total enrolment. This would in turn affect the pattern of admission to the university and the need for facilities within it. However, very little planning has been done on how to accommodate this changing ratio of admissions. In fact, even in 1972 an attempt was made to close down one of the four science faculties of the University of Ceylon.

By far the most important question has been as to whether suitable provision will be made for those who drop out at or before the NCGE examination level. The Ministry, in a pamphlet published in 1972, started that national service camps would be organised for this category to give them one year's training in some craft.[15] In August 1974 the Ministry announced plans to commence several such camps in rural schools, chiefly to provide a training in agriculture.[16] However, it seems unlikely that the Ministry will have either the personnel or the facilities to provide a training for a majority of school-leavers for many years to come.

University Education

The development of university education in Ceylon may be conveniently divided into three stages. The first, extending from the establishment of a university to about 1959, was one of relatively steady expansion. In contrast the years 1959-65 were notable for swifter unplanned expansion, especially in courses based on arts subjects. The third stage, extending from 1966 to the present, found a maturing university beset by government efforts to interfere in academic matters and to freeze university expenditure in a period of inflation.

The University of Ceylon was originally formed by the amalgamation of Ceylon Medical College, Ceylon University College and the science section of the Ceylon Technical College. The

original four faculties — arts, oriental studies, medicine and science — received an addition in 1950 when the engineering section
of the Ceylon Technical College was absorbed by the University as
a new faculty. Three years later agriculture and veterinary science
courses which had commenced in 1947 were organized into a
separate faculty.

During the period 1942-59 attention was concentrated upon the
development of undergraduate courses. Some of the energies of
the new university were also absorbed by the shift from its crowded
premises in Colombo to a new university park of 1,700 acres at
Peradeniya. The transfer took somewhat longer than expected.
Although the departments of law and agriculture and some students
of veterinary science moved into the new campus in 1949 and although the faculties of arts and oriental studies followed in 1952,
the buildings of the faculty of science were not ready till 1960 and
the faculty of engineering remained in Colombo till 1962. The
reason for the delay lay partly in the decision to establish a residential university, for this demanded the provision of halls of
residence as well as recreational and other facilities.

The shift to Peradeniya was thus still in progress when the end
of the period of controlled expansion came in sight. The swift
growth of secondary education in the 1950s was beginning to exert
pressure on university admissions. It was not that these developments were unforeseen. As early as 1956 the University Council
warned that 'the university cannot provide for all the students who
will be seeking admission in and after 1959, nor can its present
physical structure be expanded to meet the anticipated increase'[17]
but although the same report categorically stated that '. . . . to exclude students from a university education solely because of the
lack of resources is a misfortune to the country. . .', neither the University nor the Ministry of Education drew up any detailed plans
as to how the expanding student population was to be accommodated.

The result was a period of unplanned expansion — 1959-65 —
and measures were adopted to solve immediate problems with
little thought for the future. Two old seats of Buddhist learning,
the Vidyalankara and Vidyodaya Pirivenas, were converted into
universities in 1959. In the initial stages, however, the new universities were pre-occupied with the construction of buildings and the
recruitment of staff and their expansion in terms of student number was slow. In 1960/1, for instance, the total full-time enrolment
at Vidyodaya was 976 and that at Vidyalankara was only 654, all of
them reading for a first degree in languages, Buddhist studies or
other arts subjects.

Thus the University of Ceylon was forced greatly to increase its

Table 6. FULL-TIME STUDENT ENROLMENT AT THE UNIVERSITIES IN SRĪ LAṄKĀ–BY COURSE OF STUDY

Year	Arts, Oriental Studies and Development Studies		Science		Agriculture and Vet. Science		Medicine and Dentistry		Engineering		Other		Total
	Number	%	Number	%	Number	%	Number	%	Number	%	Number	%	
1942	396	43.6	165	18.3	—	—	343	37.9	—	—	—	—	904
1947	647	41.6	244	15.7	28	1.8	624	40.2	—	—	11	0.7	1,554
1952	907	40.6	272	12.2	47	2.1	877	39.3	110	4.9	19	0.9	2,232
1957	1,096	40.3	522	19.2	38	1.4	863	31.8	181	6.7	18	0.6	2,718
1959	1,379	43.9	527	16.5	36	1.1	963	30.2	242	7.6	49	1.5	3,196
1962	4,558	63.5	784	10.9	93	1.3	1,271	17.7	336	4.7	42	0.6	7,184
1967	10,922	76.4	968	6.8	180	1.3	1,601	11.2	616	4.3	—	—	14,287
1971/2	8,162	65.8	1,333	10.8	307	2.5	1,344	10.8	1,197	9.7	—	—	12,388
1973	8,067	65.1	1,395	11.3	361	2.9	1,315	10.6	1,247	10.0	—	—	12,387

Sources: (1942-59): *University of Ceylon Review*, Vol. XXIII, p. 146; (1962-73) Statistics Branch, Senate House, University of Srī Laṅkā. Figures for 1971/2 and 1973 include students at Katubedda.

intake, despite there being little or no preparation for this. It was
decided to establish a second science faculty at Peradeniya rather
than shift the faculty from Colombo, and this enabled a higher
science intake from 1960 onwards. In the same year the University
agreed to admit an extra 692 so-called 'non-residential students'[18]
in arts at Peradeniya. They were to be allowed to follow lectures and
use other facilities but were not provided with residence, and their
arrival raised the total intake in arts to 1,106. This experiment
proved rather unsatisfactory and in 1962 a second arts faculty was
hurriedly devised in Colombo. In the same year a second medical
faculty was set up at Peradeniya. In 1966 the faculties of arts, medicine and science of the University of Ceylon located in Colombo
were grouped together to form a new university, the University
of Ceylon, Colombo. This afforded scant relief to the problems at

Table 7.

FULL-TIME PERMANENT ACADEMIC STAFF — BY FACULTY

Year	Arts and Oriental Studies No.	%	Science No.	%	Agriculture and Vet. Science No.	%	Medicine Dentistry No.	%	Engineering No.	%	Total
1942	20	36	19	35	—	—	16	29	—	—	55
1947	46	47	27	28	—	—	24	25	—	—	97
1952	66	36	35	20	12	6	70	38	—	—	183
1957	80	35	38	17	16	7	79	35	14	6	227
1959	111	42	43	_	16	7	76	28	18	7	264
1962	104	42	52	21	20	8	58	23	16	6	250
1967	314	58	98	18	23	4	81	15	28	5	544
1971/2	455	49	175	19	47	5	129	14	130	14	936
1973	629	44	336	23	51	4	196	13	227	16	1439

Sources: (1942-62): University of Ceylon Review, Vol. XXIII, p. 129; (1967-71/2):
Statistics Branch, Senate House, University of Srī Laṅkā. Figures
for 1971/2 and 1973 include Engineering staff at Katubedda.
Figures for 1962 refer only to the University of Ceylon (Colombo
and Peradeniya). Veterinary Science staff have been included
under Medicine/Dentistry, and not under Agriculture and Veterinary Science, in 1973.

Peradeniya. During the mid-1960s, despite crowding twice or three times as many students into halls of residence as the latter were intended to accommodate, almost all students at Peradeniya were forced to find accommodation for themselves for at least one year of their stay on the campus. However, in view of the relative paucity of residential facilities in other universities, their counterparts continued to regard the Peradeniya undergraduate as a 'privileged' individual.

While all faculties of all the universities expanded during the decade 1958 to 1968 the expansion was greatest in the sphere of arts and oriental studies. In 1958, for instance, 436 students admitted for courses in Arts subjects formed only 49.2 per cent of total admissions. In 1965 the 5,345 Arts students admitted made up 84.1 per cent of all admissions. The number of students following science-based courses increased much more slowly from 450 in 1958 to 1,014 in 1965.[19] This was partly a reflection of the development of secondary education in the schools during the 1960s.

One impact of this development may be perceived by examining the ratio of permanent full-time academic staff to the number of students in each faculty. In the case of the faculties of arts and oriental studies in the University of Ceylon (Colombo and Peradeniya), this proportion rose steeply from 1:14.2 in 1958 to 1:56 in 1966. Though this ratio fell again to 1:14.1 in Peradeniya and 1:20 in Colombo by 1970, much of the guidance of students came to be entrusted to temporary assistant lecturers. The situation in certain departments within these two faculties was even worse than what is indicated by the figures, partly due to the imbalance of staff as between departments of the same faculty and partly due to problems relating to the medium of instruction.[20]

Table 8. ADMISSIONS TO UNIVERSITIES

Year	Total sitting	Total admitted	Percentage admitted
1945	754	289	38.9
1950	1,443	438	30.3
1955	2,061	658	32.0
1960	5,277	1,812	34.3
1965	31,350	6,359	20.3
1969/70	30,445	3,457	11.3
1973/74	36,236	3,533	9.7

Sources (1945-60): *University of Ceylon Review,* Vol. XXIII, p. 150; (1965-73) Statistics Branch, Senate House, University of Srī Laṅkā, Department of Examinations, Colombo.

The entry of students who had received their entire education in either Sinhala or Tamil in 1960 began an era when courses at universities had sometimes to be taught in three different languages — English, Sinhalese and Tamil. Because some of the senior staff who had been educated in English were unable to express themselves fluently enough in the national languages to conduct an undergraduate course, this raised problems. The formulation of technical terms in *swabhasha* and the contribution of articles for undergraduate reading in Sinhalese or Tamil to provide some sort of reading material for those not proficient in English took up some of the time of the younger teachers.

The situation was somewhat better in the faculties teaching science-based courses. In the first place, the conversion to *swabhasha* took a somewhat longer time, and up to the 1970s a vast majority of students in these faculties continued to follow their courses in English.[21] In the second place, the numbers they had to cope with were much smaller. On the other hand all the faculties had problems in recruiting sufficient staff to fill their cadre. The engineering faculty in particular found that salaries outside the university were so attractive and the work so interesting that some of their best graduates refused to stay on to teach. The duplication of the medical faculty also caused problems of staffing, especially at Peradeniya, while the science faculty found its meagre talents dispersed in Colombo, Peradeniya, Nugegoda (Vidyodaya) and Kelaniya (Vidyalankara).

In this context it is not surprising that much of the effort during the 1960s went into retaining and indeed, when possible, improving the levels of teaching in existing disciplines. A few new undergraduate courses in applied arts and applied sciences, such as commerce (Peradeniya), public administration (Vidyodaya), business administration (Vidyodaya), education (Peradeniya) and food science (Vidyodaya), were started in the 1960s but they involved only a small proportion of the student population. Once again all the authorities who should have been concerned with drawing up plans for the future — the Ministry of Education, the university authorities and even the departments of education in the various universities — paid little attention to this task.

The headlong expansion of universities, especially in the arts-oriented courses, began to meet with snags in the late 1960s. By 1965 the increasing output of the four universities in arts graduates had led to the rapid filling up of employment opportunities, and when the new Minister of Education, I.M.R.A. Iriyagolla, refused to recruit graduates to the teaching profession — preferring to employ larger number of lower paid pupil-teachers recruited after the GCE 'O' Level examination — the number of unemployed arts graduates rose swiftly.

The action of the Minister perhaps only highlighted what would have become obvious within few years anyway — that the universities were overproducing graduates of a certain type; but the emergence of a growing community of unemployed graduates had momentous consequences. As long as the products of the universities were in demand, the question of an economic return for money invested in the universities was not seriously raised, but with the spectacle of the products of the university roaming the streets in search of employment after completing their formal education, the universities themselves became subject to more critical evaluation. A new stage of university education was about to begin. Unemployed graduates created political problems, and the government sought to solve the issue by obtaining more direct control over the universities.

The third stage of university educational development perhaps began with the introduction of the Higher Education Act No. 20 of 1966. A key feature of the new system was the establishment of a National Council of Higher Education (NCHE), consisting of a chairman and eight other members nominated by the Governor-General 'from among persons of eminence in all walks of life', a representative of the Ministry of Education and the vice-chancellors of the four universities. This body was expected to advise the Minister on policy decisions relating to higher education. It also admitted students to all universities through a central agency for admittance according to the performance of candidates at the GCE 'A' Level examination, and virtually determined the recurrent government grant to each university. The 1966 Act also changed the earlier procedure of the election of the vice-chancellors from within the university. Henceforth a vice-chancellor was to be appointed by the Minister from a panel of three names forwarded by NCHE. These and other less important changes were seen by the academic staff of the universities as an attack upon 'university autonomy' and 'academic freedom', and from 1966 onwards relations between the academic staff and the Minister deteriorated, leading to an atmosphere of discontent within the universities. The situation was not improved by virulent public attacks on university dons by the Minister himself, but on the whole, although the Minister easily converted the NCHE into a pliant instrument, his control over the universities was limited by the provisions of his own Act and the steadfast resistance of the majority of university dons.

It was often alleged that the NCHE was unimaginative, slow

Table 9. NEW ADMISSIONS TO THE UNIVERSITIES 1964-74 BY COURSE OF STUDY

Course of study	1964	1965	1966	1967	1968	1969	1970	1971	1972a	1973	1974
Arts/Oriental Studies/ Development Studies (excluding law)	2,625	5,345	2,841	2,854	2,285	2,285	2,454	2,190	—	2,099	2,200
Law	12	35	25	34	29	52	48	49	—	44	50
Science	267	412	345	415	343	333	433	433	—	464	516
Medicine	260	260	230	231	227	229	247	221	—	255	263
Dental Surgery	25	27	25	27	25	21	41	49	—	49	49
Engineering	150	230	152	149	149	149	152	274	—	275	284
Agriculture	23	30	18	29	37	38	43	82	—	88	99
Veterinary Science	20	20	20	21	20	18	21	29	—	23	32
Architecture	—	—	—	—	8	4	18	13	—	23	23
Applied Science	—	—	—	—	—	—	—	—	—	17	—
	3,382	6,359	3,656	3,760	3,571	3,129	3,457	3,338	—	3,420	3,533

(a) No admissions.

Source: Statistics Branch, Senate House, University of Sri Lanka, Colombo.

to act and more a barrier than an aid to university development. It responded to the growing problem of unemployment among arts graduates by restricting the intake of arts students to the university to a maximum of 2,750 a year. It is perhaps true to say that the curricular reform that was stimulated in the universities in the late 1960s owed little to the NCHE. But the NCHE did serve as an organisation with an overview of the whole of university education, and one of the documents it produced — '*The Framework of a Plan for the Development of Universities, 1969-1978*'—remains the only effort made at planning university education to date.

The critics of the NCHE of course argued that the work of planning and co-ordination could have been much better handled by a University Grants Commission patterned on that of the United Kingdom. They also strongly argued that relating university output to employment did not necessarily mean the restriction of admissions. In the context of a university enrolment which, proportionately, was among the lowest in Asia, it was urged that a far better solution was to expand employment opportunities available for university graduates by the diversification of courses within the university and the change of employment policies without. Many university students and dons openly campaigned for the opposition United Front (UF) in the election of 1970, partly due to that party's pledge that if it came to power, it would restore university autonomy and provide for the expansion of university education by the establishment of three new universities.

Less than a year after the victory of the UF the new Minister of Education, Badi-ud-din Mahmud, introduced a bill to regulate higher education in the island. It seemed to provide for much that the university dons and students had campaigned for: a University Grants Commission to promote the growth and balanced development of universities as well as greater student and staff participation in the administration of the university. However, a few days after the Bill was tabled in parliament, the insurrection of April 1971 broke out. There arose a strong belief in government circles that university students had played a major part in organising the insurrection — a belief strengthened by the discovery of *caches* of arms in various halls of residence at Peradeniya and Vidyodaya, Nugegoda. The bill was withdrawn and the Minister reversed his policy of giving greater freedom to the universities.

However, it is open to doubt whether the insurrection was the sole or most important factor that led to a change of policy, for the Minister held to his course long after it was clear that university students and graduates had played a very minor role in the uprising. It was suspected in university circles that the bureaucracy of the Ministry of Education, which had greatly influenced the former Minister, had also gained Mahamud's ear and was strengthened by the support of some politically active dons. This suspicion was strengthened when a clear alternative policy was spelt out by the Minister himself in the press within two months of the withdrawal of the Bill. A committee on the re-organization of higher education appointed by the Minister obligingly reported recommendations on the same lines in July 1971, and with some modifications they became law as the Higher Education Act No. I of 1972.

The new Act united all existing universities and the College of Technology at Katubedda into a single university with five distinct campuses. It also laid down an elaborate system of elected committees and councils to ensure student and staff participation in the working of the campus — a system, so complicated that so far no attempt has been made to put it into operation. Instead the universities have since 1972 been administered under the transitional provisions specified in Section 85 of the Act — provisions under which a vice-chancellor appointed by the Minister of Education has almost unlimited powers in administering the university.

A sustained attack by academics and students on the new structure concentrated on several key points relating to both the Act itself and the policies implemented under it. It was argued that the central administrative agency of the single university would only add to costs and cause delay, that the re-organization of the universities should be entrusted to duly constituted academic bodies and not to an appointed vice-chancellor and his nominees, that the new structure set up barriers between disciplines which had hitherto been usefully studied together, that the setting up of rigid structures to provide vocation-oriented courses which catered for limited employment opportunities was unwise and wasteful, and that all the positive gains that were projected under the new scheme could have been achieved under the earlier multi-university structure.

The campaign eventually failed despite minor successes, and it left behind a legacy of bitterness against the Minister and the government in the campuses. Two years under the new structure was sufficient to show that the critics of the new system had anticipated its defects correctly. The new university authorities were mainly too pre-occupied with meeting immediate problems to plan for the future. The university even failed to develop a co-ordinated acquisition policy for its five campus libraries. Departments in one campus continued to recruit staff while lecturers in the same disciplines in other campuses were under-employed. A new campus established in Jaffna in October 1974 seems to have unimaginatively duplicated the pure arts and pure science departments already available on other campuses. Moves have been started to establish another new campus, possibly in Koggala in 1975. Nevertheless the university authorities do not yet seem to have planned for the construction of buildings and training of staff needed to accommodate the extra intake of science-based students that will probably be needed in 1977 in the wake of secondary school reform.

If the efforts to re-organize the universities led to the alienation of the academic community, the later changes in admissions procedure to the universities led to considerable disquiet among the Tamil minority in Jaffna. Up to 1969 university admissions were made on the basis of students' performance at GCE Advanced Level. In 1970, however, the exceptionally good performance of Tamil-medium students in the sciences led to the adoption of a procedure known as 'standardization'. Details of this scheme were not revealed, but its effect seemed to be that the Tamil-medium science students thenceforth needed to obtain higher 'raw' marks than their Sinhalese counterparts. Further resentment among the Tamil minority was caused by the application of the 'area quota' from 1973. According to this scheme, recruitment to the university from each area was according to a quota which was determined by its population. While the Ministry defended this scheme as one that would ensure equality of opportunity to those in rural areas, it was interpreted by the Tamils of Jaffna as an attempt to deprive them of their lead in scientific and technological education by unfair weightage.[22]

As might have been anticipated, the conflicts and frustrations in the universities have persuaded some of the more experienced and able dons to seek places more congenial for academic work. Further, the refusal since 1972 to grant funds for publications, the paring of research grants and the ending of subscriptions for scores of foreign academic journals have only meant that the university has added to problems such as shortage of paper which beset the local research worker. Sufficient energy seems to remain in the relatively youthful academic staff to ensure that the research output remains higher than ever, but unless steps are taken to remedy the current shortages in equipment, journals and books, research in many fields is bound to cease. This in turn would be certain to have unfavourable consequences on undergraduate teaching levels and further to postpone the long-delayed development of graduate studies in the island.

Other Post-Secondary Education

To some degree the pressure on universities for admissions was a reflection of the rather undeveloped nature of post-secondary education outside the university structure. In agriculture, for instance, although seventeen practical farms providing one-year courses have been set up since 1963, these can barely cope with 1,000 trainees each year. No important addition has been made since 1948 to the three schools of agriculture which provide a middle-level training.

Technical and commercial education has attained a somewhat higher level of development. The Technical College at Maradana and the Hardy Technical School at Amparai provide courses in commerce at all levels and training in technical skills at the craft and technician level. These institutes are supplemented by poly-technics at Galle, Kandy, Jaffna and Dehiwala and by Junior Technical Colleges at Badulla, Kurunägala, Kägalla, Anurādhapura and Ratmalana. The total admissions to all these technical institutes in 1973 amounted to 3,436 full-time and 3,727 part-time students.[23]

Other avenues of vocational training are few. The twenty-seven teacher training colleges cater largely to those already holding appointments in government schools. Although the increased emphasis on aesthetic studies should lead to an expansion in the Heywood College of Art, it would necessarily be a limited one. The relatively high fees levied by the Ceylon Law College and the rather technical nature of the subject have limited the output of lawyers to less than 200 a year. School-leavers are finding it increasingly difficult to enter colleges of nursing, and specialized courses organized by institutes and associations such as those in accountancy and librarianship are available only in a few urban centres.

Assessment

For a country at its present stage of development Srī Laṅkā on the whole has an extensive and well-organized system of education. Except in the plantations, where hardly 10 per cent of children of school-going age attend elementary school, the primary and secondary schools are fairly well distributed. The best of the island's university products have had no difficulty in competing with those of more developed countries. The existence of well over half a million licenced radio receivers seems to indicate that the radio could well be developed as a low-cost instrument of imparting education. The literacy rate had risen to 78 per cent by 1971.

Shortcomings are not difficult to find — for example, 45 per cent of students drop out of school by the end of the primary stage, and efforts at adult education are negligible. University enrolments are comparatively low. Inadequacies in equipment and of reading material in the national languages, as well as constant changes in university organization, have affected undergraduate standards. The shortage of newsprint and paper have curtailed the publishing trade. There has been an increasing tendency to use educational institutions to disseminate political propaganda. The non-sectarian system of state education has been vitiated by the establishment and expansion within the state school system of so-called Muslim schools with separate holidays and schedules of sessions. However the main question for the next few years seems to be whether existing standards and facilities can be maintained. The increase in the school-going population is expected to raise the cost of education by 1980 to Rs. 800 millions at current prices. Given the present growth-rate of the economy it is unrealistic to assume that this prediction will materialise. It seems that Srī Laṅkā might have to modify its much-vaunted practice of 'free education' if standards are to be maintained. However, the same coverage of education can be provided at different standards and therefore at varying costs. In the last analysis, the quality of education in Srī Laṅkā will depend largely on how much the island's government and its people are able or willing to pay for it.

REFERENCES

1. The material for the early part of this chapter has been derived largely from *Education in Ceylon: A centenary volume*, Colombo, Ministry of Education (1969), pp. 1339.

2. *Swabhasha* schools are schools teaching in the national languages, Sinhala and Tamil.

3. *Statistics of Personnel in the Public Service 1968*, Colombo, General Treasury (1968), p. 53.

4. J. Hallack, *Financing and Educational Policy in Srī Laṅkā (Ceylon)* Paris, UNESCO (1972), p. 75.

5. *Preliminary Report on the Socio-economic Survey of Ceylon 1969-1970*, Colombo, Department of Census & Statistics (1971), p. 48.

6. Hallack, op. cit., p. 95; *Adyapanaye Nava Maga*, Colombo, Ministry of Education (1972), pp. 2-5.

7. *Adyapana Sankyalekhana Pilibanda Sankhyathi Sangrahaya 1974*, Colombo, Ministry of Education (1974) (hereafter *ASPSS 1974*), Table 40. This publication is an annual statistical report. For a discussion of the school drop-out problem in Srī Laṅkā see *Matching Employment Opportunities and Expectations: a programme of action for Ceylon*, Geneva, ILO (1971), pp. 1329.

8. *Adyapana Sankyalekhana Pilibanda Sankhyathi Sangrahaya 1973*. Colombo, Ministry of Education (1973) (hereafter *ASPSS 1973*) Table 2.

9. *ASPSS 1973*, Table 5; *ASPSS 1974*, Table 2.

10. *Adyapanaye Nava Maga,* p. 15.
11. *Statistical Report: General Certificate of Education (Ordinary Level and Advanced Level) Examination 1972 and 1973* compiled by D. Percy Nanayakkara, Colombo, Department of Examinations (1974), unpaginated.
12. Information obtained from the Science division of the Education Ministry.
13. *Adyapanaye Nava Maga,* pp. 7-15.
14. *ASPSS 1973,* Table 16.
15. *Adyapanaye Nava Maga,* p. 17.
16. *The Sunday Observer* (11 August 1974).
17. *University of Ceylon: Fifteenth Annual Report of the Council* (Colombo), Ceylon University Press (1957), pp. 13-14.
18. This particular group of students was allowed to follow lectures and was provided other facilities available for internal students excepting residence at University Halls. They should be distinguished from those external students who registered for University examinations but were not eligible for tuition or the use of campus facilities.
19. *University of Ceylon Review* Vol. XXIII, April and October 1965, p. 151; Information from the Statistics Branch, Senate House, University of Sri Lanka, Colombo.
20. *Report of the National Council of Higher Education for the year 1966-67.* Colombo (1968), p. 74. *Report of the National Council of Higher Education for the year 1970-71,* Colombo (1972), pp. 113-14. The staff-student ratio at the University of Ceylon (Colombo and Peradeniya) in 1965 for the Department of Sinhala was 1:104 for the Department of Geography 1:98 and for the Department of Economics 1:98. By 1970 the ratios for the respective departments had fallen to 1:19.1, 1:18.2 and 1:31.3 at Peradeniya and 1:29.6, 1:25.4 and 1:52.9 at Colombo.
21. As late as 1969/70 only 299 out of 3,432 students in these faculties were taught in Sinhala and none in Tamil.
22. In 1969 the Northern Province, largely populated by Tamils, provided 27.5 per cent of all admissions to science-based courses. In 1974 under the district quota system its share was to be restricted to approximately 7 per cent. The change in the system has also adversely affected some low-country Sinhalese areas. Western Province, which provided 67.2 per cent of all admissions to science-based courses in 1969, provided only 27 per cent in 1974. The real beneficiaries appear to be the Kandyan Sinhalese, especially as the Indian Tamils—who have hardly any schooling facilities — help to swell quotas for Kandyan areas.
23. *ASPSS 1973* Tables 35 & 36.

SELECT BIBLIOGRAPHY

Education in Ceylon: A centenary volume, Colombo, Ministry of Education (1969).
Hallack, Jacques, *Financing and Educational Policy in Srī Laṅkā (Ceylon),* Paris, UNESCO, International Institute for Educational Planning (1972).

Jayasuriya, D. L., 'Developments in University Education: The growth of the University of Ceylon: 1942-1965' *University of Ceylon Review*, Vol. XXIII, Nos. 1 and 2, (April and October 1965), pp. 83-153.

Jayasuriya, J. E., *Education in Ceylon before and after independence 1939-1968,* Colombo (1969).

Non-formal education in Sri Lanka, Marga Research Studies I, Colombo (1974).

Uswatte-aratchi, G., "University admissions in Ceylon: their economic and social background and employment expectations", *Modern Asian Studies,* Vol. VIII, No. 3 [1974], pp. 289-318.

18

LITERATURE AND THE ARTS

by *Ashley Halpé and K. N. O. Dharmadasa*

LITERARY ACTIVITY IN THE INDIGENOUS LANGUAGES
by K. N. O. Dharmadasa

The story of the arts in Srī Laṅkā under British rule is part of the story of a culture with long-standing traditions adapting itself to modern conditions under the impact of western domination. On the one hand there were the adjustments in relation to changed economic and social conditions: from being functional, in a feudal society dominated by a religious ethos, to being a factor in a money-based secular society. On the other hand, there was the influx of new genres, styles, attitudes, etc., as a result of the impact of western literature. Modernisation in this sense, which occurred during the nineteenth and early twentieth centuries, had gone a long way when independence was achieved in 1948.

The most popular of the arts in the early twentieth century were the novel and the theatre, where although at the surface the impact of the west was quite marked, the indigenous response in essence embodied protests from the traditional culture against the encroachments of western culture. The propagandist enthusiasm of Piyadasa Sirisena (1875-1946) in the novel and John de Silva (1857-1922) in the theatre was the dominant factor in the arts of the Sinhalese during the early decades of the twentieth century. In the Tamil novel N. V. Tirunanasambanda Pillai (1886-1955) played a similar role.

By the late 1940s when independence was visible on the horizon the mood had changed considerably. In addition to the relaxed atmosphere of an era witnessing a mission being accomplished via Political negotiation rather than by protracted mass struggle, there was another factor in the Second World War affecting taste in the arts.

The poem was by far the most popular literary form of the late 1940s and the early 1950s. The poets of the Colombo School, as the prominent poets of the day were called, rejected the archaic idiom which had been handed down from medieval times and which was still used by the first generation of modern poets such as Piyadasa Sirisena, Ananda Rajakaruna (1885-1957) and G. H. Perera (1886-1948). They also ignored precision in grammar—one of the main concerns of the traditional poets. Nor did they deem it necessary to adhere to a special poetic diction. The new poets were not constrained in using contemporary spoken idiom in their compositions. There was also a marked change in the themes with which the new poets were concerned. In place of the didacticism and the nostalgic nationalism of their immediate predecessors, there was a variety of themes more attuned to the audience of their times: themes such as romantic love and criticisms of contemporary society.

The Colombo poets, nevertheless, continued the tradition in maintaining the prosodic framework which had been handed down from medieval times. Of the work of the Colombo School little has survived the test of time. This was largely due to their incapacity either to present a meaningful literary content or to mould a poetic diction charged with expressive power. Poverty of thought was often veiled in a facade of sentimentality and prosaic social criticism. To compensate for it, eroticism, sometimes descending to mere pornography, was employed. The trite sentiments expressed in a tinsel language, appropriately called 'sob words' by later critics, soon led to the Colombo School ending in a mass of cliché. A similar tendency towards escapism was found in the popular novels of the 1940, dominated by the figure of W. A. Silva (1892-1957). His works follow "the conventional pattern where the ideal hero and the heroine, in spite of every obstacle in their way, attain the desired end and live happily ever after while poetic justice is wrought on the villain."[1]

While the forces of this popular art were gathering momentum there developed, among a section of the English-educated élite, a move to establish more exacting standards in the arts, to develop a critical literature on the one hand, and to present creations of high artistic value on the other, so that the foundation of a truly modern Sinhalese literature would be laid. The most prominent pioneers in this effort were Martin Wickramasinghe (b. 1891) and E. R. (Ediriweera) Sarachchandra (b. 1914).

Wickramasinghe embarked on his literary career with a novel, *Leelā* (1914) and a collection of essays on literary criticism, *Sás-*

trīya Lēkhana (1919). He continued in this dual role as creative writer and literary critic to emerge during the 1940s as the founder of the serious novel and the pace-setter in highbrow literary criticism. His *Gamperaliya* (1944) is widely acclaimed as the first Sinhalese novel with a serious intent comparable in content and technique with great novels in modern world literature. *Gamperaliya* depicts the disintegration of traditional village life under the impact of the forces of modernisation. The gradual supercession of the traditional economic and social structure of the village by the commercial culture of the city is portrayed in the story of a leading family in a village of the southern littoral. The charm of *Gamperaliya* lies in its insightful and lyrical portrayal of the joys and sorrows of a bygone village life caught in a set of circumstances beyond its control. Seen in the perspective of the generality of the novels of the mid-1940s, Wickramasinghe's *Gamperaliya* was a complete breakaway, being so markedly unique in theme and technique.

Paving the way, as it were, for a work such as *Gamperaliya*, a critical survey of the modern Sinhalese novel and the short story was made by E. R. Sarachchandra in *Modern Sinhalese Fiction* (1943), tracing the history of modern Sinhalese fiction which began late in the nineteenth century and making a critical evaluation of individual works using the criteria employed by critics of contemporary English literature.

Another notable feature in these pioneering ventures in building up serious standards in the literary arts was the deliberate policy of inviting the attention of the English-educated class to the task of fostering Sinhalese literature. It was with this intent that Sarachchandra wrote *Modern Sinhalese Fiction* in English. He believed that the English-educated class was suited by training and by inclination to take on the responsibility of enriching Sinhalese literature and broadening its horizons.[2] This choice was logical as well as inevitable in a context where the traditional oriental education imparted under the *pirivena* system provided no training for the appreciation of modern literature, while the English education imparted in the best schools did not cater to the development of an interest in vernacular literature.

Several years earlier Wickramasinghe has started his campaign for high literary standards among the Sinhalese reading public. In his *Sāhityōdaya Kathā* (1932), *Vicāra Lipi* (1941), *Guttila Gītaya* (1943) and *Sinhala Sāhitayayē Nāgima* (1946) he evaluated the classical literary heritage using a set of critical criteria which was a synthesis of what could be considered best in the Indian and western traditions of literary criticism.

The effect of these pioneering endeavours was being felt by the end of the 1940s, especially in the emergence of a small but energetic group of literary artists and critics who took up the mission of freeing the arts from the throes of commercialism and establishing standards comparable to the best in other modern literatures.

Some noteworthy contributions to critical literature during this period were Wickramasinghe's *Sāhitya Kalāva* ('The Art of Literature', 1950) and *Kāvya Vicāraya* ('The Criticism of Poetry', 1954), Sarachchandra's *The Sinhalese Novel* (in English, 1950) and *Sinhala Navakathā* (1950)—both enlarging upon the theme earlier presented in *Modern Sinhalese Fiction*—and *Sāhitya Vidyāya* ('The Science of Literature', 1949), G. B. Senanayake's *Navakathā Kalāva* ('The Art of the Novel', 1946) and *Vicāra Pravēsāya* ('Approach to Criticism', 1954) and B. A. S. (Siri) Gunasinghe's[3] 'The New Note in Contemporary Sinhalese Poetry' (*Observer Annual*, 1950, pp. 70-5).

In the creative sphere, along with Wickramasinghe in the novel, a short-story writer of great promise emerged in the person of G. B. Senanayake (b. 1913).[4] His first collections of short stories, *Duppatun Näti Lōkaya* (1945) and *Paligänīma* (1946), were characterised by a mastery of technique and a sensitive delineation of the problems of everyday life. Like Wickramasinghe, Senanayake too played the dual role of creative writer and literary critic his *Navakathā Kalāva* (1946) and *Vicāra Pravēsāya* (1954) have already been mentioned. He followed these with a critical introduction to the great novels in western literature, *Batahira Srēsta Navakathā* (1955). In this manner it may truly be said that these pioneers had to create the taste by which they were to be evaluated.

Wickramasinghe followed *Gamperaliya* by *Yugantaya* (1948) which, along with *Kali Yugaya* (1957), comprise a trilogy. Beginning with the decay of the traditional social and economic system, the story is told of the rise of the bourgeoisie, with its urban base and entrepreneurial drive, culminating in the rise of the labour movement and socialist ideology and the emergence of hopes for a new social order.

These writers belonged to the English-educated élite, and through their writings, in English and Sinhala, they contributed greatly to the emergence of a new Sinhalese literary élite capable of synthesising and harmonising the features of the western and indigenous traditions. A considerable role was played by the University of Ceylon (established in 1942)[5] in the creation of this élite. Sarachchandra himself was a teacher in the University. He and several others such as E. F. C. Ludowyk[6] and B. A. S. (Siri) Gunasinghe were able to create among the undergraduates an outlook befitting the new movement in the arts, and the University became a disseminating centre of the new literary ideology. And the new generation of writers came to be termed the Peradeniya School.

In Tamil literature too there was, by the 1940s, a drifting away from the didacticism and traditionalist orientation characteristic of the works of the earlier period. On the one hand, with the emergence in the 1930s of journalistic literature — creating and thriving upon 'popular' taste — a spate of sensational and sentimental novels came to be produced, mostly appearing in serial form in newspapers and periodicals. On the other hand, a new literary movement arose by about the 1940s, led, as in Sinhalese, by a section of the English-educated élite who tried to propagate a better literary taste by drawing inspiration from the west. One of their special aims was realism, a concentration of attention on life around them. Thus K. Kanapathipillai (1903-68), at the time a lecturer in the University of Ceylon and later Professor of Tamil, wrote during the late 1930s and early 1940s, a number of plays such as *Udaiyar midukku, Murukan Tirukuhthālam* and *Nāttavan Nakaravalkkai* where the weaknesses of the upper strata in village and town were satirized. The most significant aspect of these plays was the use — for the first time in serious literary activity — of the colloquial Jaffna dialect. The novels of M. A. Selvanayagam, N. Nelliah and Illangayarkon too may be mentioned in this context.

By the mid-1950s, as a result of the flaring up of the national language issue, an unprecedented hostility had arisen between the two communities. Within the ranks of the Sinhalese-Buddhists, the largest ethno-religious community in the island, there arose a militant revivalist movement actuated on the one hand by the millennial expectations connected with the *Buddha Jayanthi*, which fell in May 1956, and on the other by the nativistic urge to guard and preserve the Sinhalese language and the Buddhist religion from the 'threats' of the Tamils and the Christians. In the midst of the revivalist enthusiasm of 1956 a general election was held and, by the decision of a vast majority of the electorate in the Sinhalese-speaking areas, the United National Party which had been in power since independence was replaced by the *Mahajana Eksath Peramuna*, which had pledged itself to uphold the rights of the Sinhalese Buddhists. That year also witnessed, by a remarkable coincidence, several momentous achievements in the sphere of the arts.

Wickremesinghe's novel *Virāgaya* (1956), because of the significance of its theme and its sophistication of technique, soon came to be hailed as the greatest work of Sinhalese fiction. It depicted the spiritual dilemmas of a sensitive Sinhalese youth brought up in a traditional Buddhist home when confronted with the problems of adulthood and its responsibilities which were made all the more complex by the processes of modernisation in society. The author uses first-person narrative to present the autobiographical notes of the 'hero' in impressionistic sequences rather than in a chronological order. *Virāgaya*, in theme and technique, came to exert a seminal influence on the novels of the years that followed.

Another outstanding artistic achievement of the day was Sarachchandra's *Manamē* (1956), a play in which the elements of drama in the folk tradition were utilised with remarkable dramatic concentration, theatrical craft and poetic sophistication to present a theme basic to the relationship between man and woman. *Manamē* was a complete breakthrough in the Sinhalese theatre and marked a turning-point in its history. The year 1956 also witnessed a breakthrough in Sinhalese film. Lester James Peries' *Rēkāva* (1956) was a bold attempt to escape from the melodramatic stereotype thriving under the shadow of Indian cinema, and to bring the Sinhalese film up to standards comparable with the best in the world.

These achievements in several spheres of art were truly acts of faith in the Sinhalese audience. No doubt a receptive atmosphere had been created by the preceding years of steady development of a taste in good art. By the mid 1950s the Sinhalese reading public had undergone a remarkable change from preceding decades. With the growing interest in Sinhalese literature of a section of the English-educated élite and with the spread of mass literacy in the wake of the educational changes launched in the 1940s and the subsequent expansion of higher education, a new Sinhalese literary clientele was created. It was an 'educated' clientele in contrast to the earlier one in that its artistic taste was moulded by the new literary movement pioneered by personalities like Wickremesinghe and Sarachchandra.

In the revivalist atmosphere of the post-1956 period there was a general efflorescence in the arts. Flowing from the activities of the new literary élite there were two main and potentially conflicting tendencies in aesthetic ideology: one oriented towards the west as was shown above, and the other going back to indigenous traditions. In the mid-1950s, with the Sinhalese-Buddhist revivalism of the *Jayanti* era, the atmosphere was charged with the emotional appeal of tradition and a resuscitatory zeal was manifest in all spheres of art.

The conflict between westernization and traditionalism was most dramatically enacted in the field of poetry. In the late 1940s and the early 1950s, there had emerged a new genre of poetry called *nisaṅdäs*, which disregarded the restrictions of traditional prosodic patterns. Arising as a reaction against the weaknesses of the poetry of the Colombo School the new genre was also inspired by the works of Eliot, Pound, Whitman and other contemporary western poets. G. B. Senanayake was the pioneer *nisaṅdäs* poet with several compositions included in his collection of short stories, *Paligānīma* (1946). The new form, however, became a major force in the fifties with Martin Wickramasinghe's *Tēri Gī* (1952). Senanayake's own *Rubaiyyāṭ* (1954) and above all Siri Gunasinghe's *Mas Lē Nāti Āṭa* (1956), the last being a revolutionary work in many ways: the subject matter, the sentiments and the attitudes as well as the language all appeared to suggest that the poet was determined to effect a complete breakaway from tradition.

These innovations drew virulent attacks from the poets of the Colombo School who described them as being 'anti-national' and 'imitative of the decadent west'; there was also much more serious criticism of *nisaṅdäs* which arose from among the ranks of the new literary élite itself. This was with regard to the necessity, on the one hand, of conforming to a prosodic pattern for the purpose of enhancing the poetic effect, and on the other, with regard to the desirability of basing new poetic images on traditional motifs.

Gunadasa Amarasekara, himself a writer of the new wave and a critic of *nisaṅdäs*, published *Amal Bisō* (1961) and *Gurulu Vata* (1962) to illustrate that a truly modern poetry could be presented using traditional metrical formulae and basing the poetic imagery on traditional usage. In these works he used, in place of the rhymed quatrain, each line containing eighteen syllabic instants — the metrical form to which the Colombo poets almost totally confined themselves — a variety of metres from folk poetry as well as from classical poetry. Moreover, in his attempt to express a modern sensibility through poetic images rooted in tradition he used myth and symbol occurring in folk and classical traditions, giving them new significance. The *nisaṅdäs* poets, for their part, maintained that this type of neoarchaism was a blind alley. They believed their innovations, having broken free from the need to adhere to a pre-ordained prosodic pattern or system of imagery, were truly capable of portraying the immediate social and psychological realities confronted by modern man and had endless possibilities for doing it in the future. The significance of this confrontation between the 'traditionalists' and the 'modernists' was that it marked the beginning of a division within the ranks of the new literary élite.

The charge that the new literary élite did not consider national tradition and its susceptibilities was raised most vigorously in the field of the novel. The controversy arose mainly with the publication of Gunadasa Amarasekera's *Yali Upannemi* (1960) and Siri Gunasinghe's *Hevanälla* (1960). In *Yali Upannemi* there was a frank portrayal of the hero's sex-life. And both novels were in essence criticisms of the puritanical social ethos and the personal frustration and unhappiness which it tended to bring about in the lives of sensitive young people. Provoked by these sentiments a virulent campaign arose against the new writers spearheaded by the poets of the Colombo School and the traditionalist Sinhalese-Buddhist elite.[7]

Apart from the campaign against the new literary élite there were indications that much of what they upheld was soon becoming a spent force. Thus, following upon *Virāgaya*, there was a series of novels in the same vein. For example, Sarachchandra's *Malagiya Āttō* (1957) and *Valmat Vi Hasarak Nudutimi* (1963), Amarasekera's *Yali Upannemi* (1960), *Depā Noladdō* (1961) and *Gandabba Apadānaya* (1964), Siri Gunasinghe's *Hevanälla* (1960), Madawala Ratnayaka's *Sita Nāti Baṁbalova* (1961) and K. Jayatilaka's *Parājitayō* (1960) and *Aprasanna Katāvak* (1962), in spite of being notable achievements in the craft of fiction, brought forth a monotonous array of 'anti-heros' caught in social, cultural and psychological circumstances beyond their control.

The free verse of the *nisaṅdäs* poets, after the impact made by Gunasinghe in *Mas Le Nāti Äṭa* followed by *Abinikmana* (1958) and *Ratu Käkula* (1962), seemed incapable of the same vigour. The bulk of the *nisaṅdäs* compositions that appeared in the late 1950s and early 1960s seemed attempts to be in the current fashion. Thus, except in the case of a few poets such as Wimal Dissanayaka (*Akal Wässa*, n.d.) and Mahagama Sekera (*Sakvā Lihini*, 1962) who in fact did not follow the *nisaṅdäs* form exclusively, no other poet seemed to make a significant contribution.

The school of neo-archaic poetry headed by Gunadasa Amarasekera faced a similar plight. Save for the publications of Amarasekera, and the few compositions included in the collections of Dissanayaka and Sekara already mentioned, there were no other notable contributions in this genre. As was prophesied by the *nisaṅdäs* poets, the neo-archaic poetry — with its limited stock of traditional metrical formulae, imagery and symbols — ultimately ended up being formalist, unreal and tiring. Thus one notices that towards the mid-1960s there was a dearth of poetry, as though the enthusiasm and experimentation of the preceding years had been spent and a dead-end had been reached.

The events of the 1950s had their own impact on the literary activities of the Tamils. The failure to obtain parity of official status for Tamil along with Sinhalese led to a sense of injury and alienation.[8] In the Tamil novels and short stories of the period there is a marked tendency on the one hand to emphasize solidarity within the ranks of the Tamil-speaking people and on the other to underline the identity of interests of the Tamil-speaking people with the other communities in Srī Laṅkā. As an example of the latter Illangeeram in *Tenralum Payalum* (1956), *Ingirānthu Enge*, *Nithiyē Ni Keel* (1962) and *Kālum Marakirāthu* (the latter two appearing in newspaper serials) depicted, as a protest, the lot of the socially disadvantaged among the Tamils, showing that their day-to-day problems were no different from those of their counterparts among the Sinhalese or the Muslims. In this context may also be mentioned *Thuraikkāran* (1959) by V. A. Rajaratnam and *Erikōlam* (1959) by S. Agastiar, both serialised in newspapers. The same tendency is evident in the short story — e.g. S. Ganeshalingam in the collections *Nallavan* (1956) and *Sangamam* (1961) N. K. Raghunathan in the collection *Naanum Naangalum* (1956) and Sitpi in the collection *Nilavum Ninaivum* (1959).

Tamil literature in Srī Laṅkā has traditionally been under the influence of South India. Under British rule there was a free flow of publications from Madras which were very popular with the local readership. The local Tamil journals were eager to publish works of South Indian writers, and Ceylonese writers were eager to get their writings published in South India. During the late 1950s however, due to foreign exchange restrictions, this interflow was seriously affected, but in a way the new situation opened up more opportunities for the local writers. An additional impetus for self-assertion was the declaration by a leading South Indian journalist that the short story writers in Srī Laṅkā were ten years behind their Indian counterparts. The sense of injury due to the circumstances in Srī Laṅkā and the provokingly condesending attitude of South India led to an intense effort to prove the authenticity and validity of local Tamil literature. Writers turned with a new introspective force to depict the inequalities and injustices in their *milieu.* In this context may be viewed the later novels of Ilangeeran and V. A. Rajaratnam and S. Ganeshalingam's *Neenda Payanam* (1965), *Mannum Mākkalum* (1970), K. Daniel's *Pancamar* (1972). In a similar vein several novelists portrayed the sufferings of the Indian plantation workers in Srī Laṅkā: for example, Kohilam Subbiah's *Thurattuppachchai* (1964), Dr. Nandhi's *Malaikkōlunthu* (1964) and Y. Benedict Balan's *Sonthakkāran.* Also S. Ganeshalingam, Dominic Jeeva, S. Ponnathurai, Thelivathai Joseph, N. S. M. Ramaiah and Paneerchelvam in the short story and C. V. Velupillai in poetry depicted the lot of the poor and the downtrodden under prevailing class, caste and economic systems.

A major factor which affected Sinhalese literary activity in the 1960s was the disintegration of the Peradeniya School, which had comprised the new literary élite. This was much more serious than the controversy between the *nisaṅdās* and the neo-archaic poets. The breakup of this group occurred with the "defection" first of

Martin Wickramasinghe and next of Gunadasa Amarasekara. Wickramasinghe's main contention was that the other writers of the Peradeniya School were insensitive to the cultural traditions — especially the Buddhist background — of Sinhalese society. He accused Sarachchandra and others of being imitative of "decadent" western and post-war Japanese literature and of promoting a nihilistic view of life with cynical disregard for the national tradition.[9] Amarasekara, writing a "confession" to a newspaper, declared that his own earlier work as well as the works of Sarachchandra, Gunasinghe and others of the Peradeniya School were imitations of western models and not based on the social reality of Sinhalese society.[10] Although Sarachchandra, Gunasinghe and several others answered these accusations,[11] the criticisms of the erstwhile stalwarts of the Peradeniya School tended to strengthen those that had already been made by others. It was easy now to portray the Peradeniya writers and critics as standing for mere self-interest in the guise of promoting high sensibility.

A factor which affected the spread and acceptance of this idea was the change that had meanwhile occurred in the reading public. In the mid-1950s during the heyday of Sinhalese-Buddhist revivalism Sinhalese was recognised by an Act of Parliament as the official language of the state. And on the culmination of a process set afoot in the 1940s, education up to university level came to be imparted in the *swabhashā* media, i.e. in Sinhalese or Tamil. In a situation highly charged with nationalist emotion there occurred simultaneously the neglect of English, the already existing window to world knowledge. Higher education expanded very rapidly and two new universities were opened in 1959 at the seats of traditional oriental learning — Vidyodaya and Vidyalankara — to be supplemented subsequently by the Second Arts Faculty of the University of Ceylon in Colombo. With this large class of mainly *swabhashā*-educated youth there emerged a readership whose intellectual horizons were limited by what was available in the *swabhashā* medium. The new *swabhashā* intelligentsia, faced with the task of reading for examinations in a highly competitive society where occupational opportunities were fast drying up, had neither the inclination nor the ability to appreciate serious literature, let alone keep contact with literature available in the English medium. To cater to this unprecedently large and mainly youthful reading public, there arose the sentimental novel of the 1960s, characterised by its invariable theme of a love story set in school, university or office. The titles of these novels display their content, e.g. *Golu Hadawata* ('The Dumb Heart'), *Mulu Hadin Mama Ayata Pem Kota* ('I Loved her with all my Heart'), *Adara Ganga Galana Dasa* ('The

Eyes from which flow the River of Love'), *Sanda Eliyen Sihina Mavā* ('Dreams of Moonbeams') and *Mamat Pem Kalemi* ('I, the Lover').

Alongside this tendency there has arisen another movement, again appealing to the youthful readership. It is a type of Marxist approach to the arts, demanding that art should be wholly devoted to the portrayal of the struggles of the common man. The major premise of this theory of social commitment is that during the late 1950s and early 1960s the Peradeniya School presented a bourgeois view of life imitating the decadent 'capitalist' art of the west and post-war Japan. The Peradeniya School is portrayed as an agent of a cultural imperialism pursued by the 'neo-imperialists'. The pornography, cynicism towards traditional religious and social values and the spread of a defeatist attitude to life, all presented in the name of realistic portrayal of contemporary social problems, are pointed out as part of this 'intrigue'. The new ideology was composed of several strands of thought: the traditional value system (nationalist and religious), the anti-western feeling and Marxism.

Since the establishment of the Department of Cultural Affairs in 1956, government patronage has been a major factor in the field of literature. It was effected through several autonomous bodies such as the *Sāhitya Mandalaya* ("Academy of Letters") and the Arts Council. In 1970 a separate Ministry of Cultural Affairs was created, and the machinery of state cultural patronage is centralized in the Sri Lanka Cultural Council which consists of the Minister, the Secretary to the Ministry and the Director of Cultural Affairs. The policy of the Ministry, it has been declared, is to take the arts 'to the people'. Moreover, it has brought its activities into line with the larger political, social and economic policies of the government. Thus at the annual literary day celebrations of 1973 the theme of the speeches and discussions was the utilisation of literature for national development.

Contemporary literature is largely a reflection of the dominant ideology. For example, A. V. Suraweera's *Heyyammāruwa* (1972), D. S. Ranawake's *Labu Mala Suvanda Nāta* (1972) and Madawala Ratnayaka's *Aluta Genā Manamālī* (1973) contain themes depicting the attempt of youth, inspired by socialist thinking, to transform the traditional economic and social structure. Martin Wickramasinghe, the veteran novelist, in his latest work *Bava Taranaya* (1973), presents a new biography of the Buddha. Therein the great teacher's transformation from a royal heir-apparent to a philosopher-mendicant is portrayed as having occurred largely due to his sympathy with the poor and the down-trodden in society.

The political concern is most markedly apparent in the new generation of poets: for example, Roland Abaypala in *Mā Vāni Bilindā* (1971), Berty B. Kudahetty in *Cinderellā* (1972), Parakrama Kodituwakku in *Podi Malliye* (1972) and Gunasena Witana in *Denō Dāhak Atara Hindagena* (1973) may be mentioned in this context.

The contemporary scene in Tamil literature is similar in many respects to that in Sinhalese. Since the restriction of the influx of South Indian publications the task of catering to the sensational and sentimental has been taken over by the local newspapers and periodicals. Bordering upon this taste were such works of light entertainment as *Kanayāli* (1972) by Ranjani, *Pūjakku Vanda Malar* (1972) by P. Paleswari and *Tikkul Viralai Vaittāl* (1972) by K. S. Anandan. A somewhat more realistic type of novel is found in *Nilakkuli* (1973) by Bala Manoharan, a love-story set in a new agrarian settlement, and *Vādei Kattu* (1973) by Sengai Aliyan, another love story set in a fishing village. A more significant work is S. Ponnathurai's *Chandangu* (1971) an attempt at a mirror-to-life portrayal of the life of a middle-class public servant working in Colombo, leaving his family at Jaffna — a typical arrangement with the Tamils. In poetry in the meantime a militant political stand is being taken: for example in the works of Ratnathurai, Dikwela Kamal, Anbu Jawaharsha, Maruthur Kani and Pena Manoharan one finds a passionate protest against the existing socio-economic set-up and a yearning for a new order based on socialist ideology.

In an economic crisis the prospects for literary activity do not seem promising at the time of writing. Rising prices of paper and printing have made literature a costly pursuit. The statistics are disheartening while the total number of books produced in 1970 was 1,566 it dropped to 900 in 1972, which happened to be the International Book Year. In May 1974 the price of paper rose by about 80%, and a further reduction in book production could well be expected.

In the context of these scarcities and restrictions the tendency has been for the strengthening of the officially-sponsored view of literature and art. Already a warning has been sounded by the poet Wimal Dissanayake of the danger of literature declining into a mere display of stereotyped slogans. But this has been a minority voice. A whole host of other voices were raised subsequently against it, some of them branding Dissanayake's misgivings as a covert attempt to bring back the 'anti-socialist' views of the Peradeniya School. It has been claimed that when literature is in the process of development towards 'socialist realism' the appearance of a propagandist type of work is quite normal, as had happened in Russia.

REFERENCES

*   I wish to thank my colleague S. Thillainathan for providing me with
    information on the recent trends in Tamil literature.

1. E. R. Sarachchandra, *The Sinhalese Novel,* Colombo (1950), p. 113.

2. See E. R. Sarachchandra, *Modern Sinhalese Fiction,* Mount Lavinia
    (1943), Introduction.

3. At this time Lecturer in Sanskrit at the University of Ceylon. A versa-
    tile figure he made significant contributions in the fields of poetry,
    the novel, film and literary and art criticism.

4. G. B. Senanayake, short story writer, novelist, poet and literary critic;
    for an assessment of his work see p. 437.

5. Established in Colombo, the University was subsequently shifted to
    a newly planned campus at Peradeniya in the early 1950s.

6. At this time Professor of English at the University of Ceylon, Ludowyk
    produced several plays, and as literary critic was a frequent contribu-
    tor to the press and journals.

7. For the views of these campaigners see V. Desabandhu, *Sahitya Kollaya,*
    Colombo (1961) and K. B. Sugathadasa, *Upan Da Sita Vikramaya,*
    Colombo (1965).

8. S. Thillainathan, 'Recent Trends in Ceylon Tamil Literature.' Paper
    presented at the Fourth International Conference Seminar of Tamil
    Studies, Jaffna (January 1974).

9. See Martin Wickramasinghe, *Navakathanga Ha Viragaya,* Colombo,
    1965, esp. pp. 231-64 and 'Navakathava Ha Gurukula Attukkansa-
    naya'. *Sri Lankadipa* (17 April 1967).

10. 'Gunadasa Amarasekarage Papoccaranaya', *Silumina* (7 June 1969).

11. See E. R. Sarachchandra *Asampurana Carika Satahan,* Colombo 1967,
    pp. 180-2; 'Martin Wickramasinghege Kama Sevanalle Nandedavilla'
    Rivirasa (7 March 1970) and 'Gunadasa Amarasekera's Literary
    Theories and Recantations', *Ceylon Daily News* (16 July 1969). Siri
    Gunasinghe, 'Stranger thán Fiction: Plagiarism', *Ceylon Daily News*
    (30 August 1969).

CREATIVE WRITING IN ENGLISH
by Ashley Halpé

A Ceylonese would surely write in Sinhala or Tamil if he could:
if he does not, it is because he cannot. He would be very much aware
that his familiarity with English and other European literatures,
his fluency in English and the attitudes and associations which have
accrued to him from these aspects of his experience are all ancillary
to the main currents of national experience and but remotely related—if at all—to the languages and literatures of his country.

But the accidents of history have made him English-speaking; English may even be his adopted mother-tongue. British rule brought "English" education to Ceylon, and the knowledge of English became increasingly attractive when it was seen that power, wealth and prestige were the rewards awaiting the "educated native". The attractiveness was enhanced by the ghastly inadequacy of government provision for education in Sinhala and Tamil. The first products of the system were curious hybrids, "speaking bastard English without the ability to understand it, and at the same time unable to write a decent letter in Sinhala"[1] though there were a few Ceylonese like Charles Ambrose Lorenz and James Alwis in whose hands the English language was a strong and flexible instrument. Alwis was quick to perceive the limitations in this and to turn to the steady cultivation of his own language. But few followed his example and the new class of government servants, planters, businessmen and professionals set themselves to ape the English in manners, dress, furniture, architecture and every possible aspect of life as well as language, with a fond devotion that was only matched by their gift for vulgarising the forms they strove to imitate. The familiar colonial sensation of inferiority was compensated for by the equally familiar contempt for things "native".

After nearly a century of mongrelization we have some interesting results. Srī Laṅkā's first Parliament after the grant of independence in 1948 consisted largely of members who rejoiced in such first names as Stephen, Lionel, Leslie, Solomon and even Cholmondeley; Percival and Montague were soon to join them. Its business was conducted in English, its rhetoric was passable Victorian, its repartee imitation Wilde. Students reading Sinhala at the University of Ceylon attended lectures on Sinhala literature by Sinhala lectures delivered in English; they even wrote their examination answers in that language. Remote villages were signposted in English and hapless seekers for redress were at the mercy of professional petition-writers whose productions were of the "most humbly beg" variety addressed to a "most gracious Honour's kind, merciful and sympathetic consideration"[2]

A few sensitive and intelligent spirits among the English-educated Ceylonese have been keenly aware of their grotesque plight and have sought to educate themselves and their class into a more natural relationship with their environment, their history and their languages. They have achieved notable successes as orientalists, archaeologists and historians; they were active in reform movements and in the political processes which brought full adult franchise and finally independence; they have contributed to the renaissance of Sinhala literature and drama and the emergence of contemporary

Ceylonese art through the practice of intelligent and sympathetic criticism.[3]

But when they turned to creative writing they came into a cruel inheritance. They would have come upon Eliot writing of "purifying the language of the tribe" or have encountered the Joycean persona hoping to "forge anew the uncreated conscience of his race". But their command of their "own" languages was at best meagre and largely utilitarian. English was, for them, much more than the "language of least compromise" (the choice made by many Indian writers)—it was the only language in which they were at home.

Nor was this all. Such a writer would know that the majority of his English-speaking friends were profoundly—and sometimes overtly—utilitarian—often so by virtue of the very English education they—and he—had received. At Srī Lankā's university campuses today not 5 per cent of the students fluent in English read Humanities the majority are to be found in the professional schools of medicine, engineering and law and in the Faculty of Science. Few of their parents would be able to name a living English novelist; most would turn gratefully from administrative reports and research papers to Agatha Christie or Wodehouse. Not less discomforting would be the performance of writers working in Sinhala, though in another sense: the easy bilingualism and adventurous reading habits of the best among them would be a reproach to his inadequacy in his own tongue.

The artist, of course, writes because he must, but the circumstances have always been unpropitious. In the work produced we see both the consciousness of the predicament and its unfortunate results. Often these are curiously mixed. In H. E. Weerasuriya's *The Trousered Harijan* Ronald de Silva begins by smiling indulgently at his "dear old superstitious mother" as he sets out for Colombo "to sit for the Government Clerical Examination".[4] At the end of the novel he is in "national costume" living in a "neat detached cottage nestling in a profusion of flowers under a grove of coconut trees" with a wife who is "only a village girl, old chap, quite ignorant of English customs and languages". Disillusioned in the ways of government office and small-town "good" society, he has found his Ranee in Anuradhapura. It is no coincidence that at the ancient capital "thoughts of old Anuradhapura and Lanka's past glory were balm to his bruised heart".[5]

Weerasuriya's patriotic, anti-Western position is quite clear. At the time the novel was written, it was an unusual and even courageous position for one of his class to take. But he is insidiously enslaved by the very values he rejects. The "dear old" in the first quotation could be in character, but would a conscious patriot who has taken to the national dress and married a village girl persist in such forms as "old chap"? If he did, the point would be ironic, whereas Ronald de Silva's change of heart is meant to be taken quite seriously. What we have, therefore, is the author's own modish affectation of a now dated slang: his own "westernness" has prevented him from seeing the incongruity. But along with his westernness there goes a slack and uncreative use of cliché-English which reveals that the contact with English culture has not developed a sensitivity to the nuances of the language—we have "balm for his bruised heart", a "profusion of flowers", "nestling", there is also the clumsy "English customs and language". Indeed the malady has gone so deep that de Silva's patriotism is sadly mixed with the vague landscape enthusiasm and anti-urbanism characteristic of the weaker post-Romantic literature of England. Despite the evident sincerity of Weerasuriya's intentions; his upbringing and education have been too much for him.

These tendencies and disabilities persist in much of the fictional writing in English that has appeared since. The wish to rediscover and express the forms and values of traditional Srī Laṅkā life is often in evidence. But this valuable impulse is often contaminated by mere escapism; "to run away from the rat-race of the city"[6] ". . . the need for a place of retreat had been nagging him for so long"[7] —these are characteristic expressions. One is not surprised to find that village life is not handled with any power of concrete evocation. In the quality of the response to Ceylonese life in fiction we perceive, too often, the limitations of English-speaking Ceylonese rather than a creative consciousness of their situation.

Viewed in this context, Punyakante Wijenaike's *Giraya* represents a notable advance on earlier fiction, including her own *The Waiting Earth* which was barely saved by the sincerity of her effort to chart the course of the relationship between Podi Singho and his wife Sellohamy. Set in an old Southern *valauwwa* whose inmates have been accustomed to power and wealth, *Giraya* is a steady presentation of corruption and decay, of a way of life sustained by vicious inbred pride and cruel repression. Abnormalities are fostered by such a life which lead to murder and suicide, but these are played down; the earlier scenes are far more disturbing in their revelations of evil through a snatch of conversation, a brief telling episode, a firmly caught image:

... Adelaine's voice is stretched high like a thin steel wire.

Old Loku's hands begin to shake. I watch in horror how they shake. Old Loku himself stands rigid, gazing down at his shaking hands as if they are not a part of himself.[8]

The narrative is cast in the form of a diary kept by the daughter-in-law, a poor but educated girl; nurtured in the very different *milieu* of the small cultivator, she has been to the university and is alive to the changes that are already taking place outside the *valauwwa*. This mode of presentation enables a unity of tone and develops a distinctive point of view which is enriched by her own involvement in the action. It is implied that she speaks Sinhala, unlike the family, and it is a further virtue of the novel that the language is on the whole a subtle recreation of the rhythms of Sinhala.

At times, however, there is an uncertainty of stance. It appears, for instance, in a desire to explain too much, as if to inform a non-Ceylonese readership, which interferes with the realization of a fictive life. Thus the English names of the months are provided in brackets; two exorcism rituals are described in language which lapses into the reportorial:

According to legend, the Black Demon Prince persecutes only women, young women . .
. . . and so the ceremony begins. Although it is the Black Prince who has caused the trouble yet the whole of the demon clan must be summoned and honoured, each in his own way . . .[9]

It is significant that the rituals do not help to realize further aspects of the meaning, but remain mere local colour. It is also unfortunate that while the murder of Adelaine can be taken as a logical culmination of the action, it is followed by thick-coming revelations and surprises, as of Lal's illegitimacy and homosexuality, which give the last few pages a distressing resemblance to melodramatic pulp fiction. One is thankful for the more reflective last page.

The lapse into the world of thriller fiction is far more damaging to another novel which has a very promising beginning — Raja Proctor's *A Fisherman's Daughter*. Proctor allows himself to rely on melodramatic surprises and coincidences, on trick and counter-trick and even an incursion of gangsters, to precipitate the crisis. The influence of cheap fiction is also to be seen sometimes in the language, in such sentences as "she kept fighting happy hands"[10], or in the affectation of a spasmodic telegraphic style to suggest urgency. Fortunately, important parts of the novel are free of these alarming characteristics. In the opening chapters the presentation of Valli's transition from orphanage to village is done with an unhurried sweep and a precision of observation that impart great imaginative reality to the action; later, we have the remarkable scenes of the search at sea for the body of the missing fisherman Peduru and the excellent handling of the tragi-comic scenes of the fisherman's funeral.

These partial successes hold out some hope for the future, for both *Giraya* and *A Fisherman's Daughter* are of recent date. Yet we have to note the much greater consistency and control of two works published half a century ago and therefore ouside the scope of this study — S. J. K. Crowther's novel *The Knight Errant* and J. Vijayatunga's *Grass for my Feet*. It has also to be recognized that the most powerful novel of Ceylonese life is no more Ceylonese than *A Passage to India* is Indian or than *Heart of Darkness* is African: Leonard Woolf's *The Village in the Jungle* communicates its English author's perception of terrifying possibilities latent in the human condition in terms of the exigencies of village life in the remote jungles of Srī Laṅkā.

It is relevant to refer here to the performance of the Sinhala novelists. In these novels we have sensitive explorations of human situations and values in terms of contemporary Ceylonese experience, which also have the incidental virtue of educating the Ceylonese reader into a more mature response to his environment. They have solidity and imaginative scope beyond anything achieved in the novels in English by Ceylonese.

A similar point must be made with regard to the short story. Many of these stories are completely adult performances which easily overshadow most short stories written in English. However, it would be possible to assemble a respectable anthology of the latter in which one could encounter a truth of experience which is both evocatively Ceylonese and significantly human: it would include, for example, Punyakante Wijenaike's *Retreat*, Godfrey Gunatillake's *The Garden* and Suvimalee Gunaratne's *The Golden Oriole*.

Some time before the publication of *The Garden* Godfrey Gunatillake, writing in *Community*, called the English current in Srī Laṅkā "a language without metaphor"; through the metaphorical mode, he wrote, "we become alive to our own feelings and respond to the world of eye and ear". Though he recognized that our English did contain metaphor of a sort, he characterized it as "derivative" and lacking in immediacy, being "created by the community which spoke it in a different climate". He went on to define some of the consequences for art:

I have still to read a piece of creative writing by a Ceylonese which gathers our landscape, vegetation, our domestic surroundings, the familiar intonations of our speech unobtrusively into an effective idiom, giving me the sense of here and now, the immediacy, which is the moving spirit in art.[11]

His own short story went a long way towards repairing the deficiency:

A shower earlier in the day had left behind a subdued washed sky, with

smoothed-out wisps of cloud. In the west, the colour flowed like honey where
the sky met the smudged margin of trees, but in the east, where the light
was fading, an aqueous blue paled gradually into a white translucence.
There was a refreshing hint of moisture in the air. A light wind blew now and
again, and the dried leaves of the jak tree which spread over the garden
fell one by one, with a soft rustle littering the beds. 'This darned jak tree,'
Prema said, 'you clean and clean, but the leaves keep on falling.[12]

There, as in a few stories that have appeared since and in the greater
part of *Giraya*, we have a language that is sensitive to the immediate
environment as well as to the resources of the chosen medium.

One would expect an examination of the drama to yield interesting evidence regarding the control of the language. It does so — but
of an entirely negative kind. The drama written in English has
been profoundly unserious — costume melodrama and trivial entertainment which does not merit even the sort of attention that can
be paid to the fiction. In such a lurid melodrama and mindless
comedy there is no hint of an art concerned for values and creatively
related to the language of a living community.

It is in the poetry that the idiom of Ceylonese creative writing
in English achieves greatest range and force. There the language
can bear comparison with the idiom of Ceylonese who write in
English as analysts of society, as political commentators, as literary
critics — as practitioners, in fact, of almost any form of intelligent
discourse. In such areas Ceylonese use the language skilfully and
even inventively — a fact of importance to any discussion of English
in Srī Laṅkā. Perhaps this is because in such discourse the language
is fundamentally a utility. Perhaps, too, their very endowment can
make the most educated minds confused and reluctant when it comes
to the business of artistic expression. They could be stultified by
their very sensitivity to a complex predicament.

Fortunately, they have not shut their lips on poetry. We have a
substantial body of lyric poetry and some satiric verse which is
rich and subtle in perception and idiom, rising to moments of remarkable power. This poetry has to be distinguished from a quantity
of inept and inane verse, hopelessly dated as to diction and content
or modish in the latest European manners, particularly common
in the pages of periodicals.

The most distinctive poetic voice is perhaps that of Lakdas Wikkramasinha, and his is also the poetry that is most consistently Ceylonese in its material. Image, incident and character of Ceylonese
provenance are creatively fused with the resources of the English
language:

My arms are shredded
plantain leaves. I parried the wind
in the hurricane. You laugh:

'Give him one more coconut shell of blood;
he'll run awhile.'

I am blinded by the rain.
I am like Kadawara, hung up on your
immaculate white walls —
a show of peasants' wit.[13]

The maturity of this poetry is evident in its range of tone; take, for example, the poised playfulness of

Exalted eagles drop to earth to chide the sparrow bird
They are clumsy at this level, incongruous, absurd.
The sparrows hop and wink, and chirp: 'But how could we have erred,
We who in spite of all you say are yet unembittered?'[14]

or the plangency of

Beauty is born of friendship, and those tears
Weren't vainly shed for the innocence we lost,
The beauty that in innocence we squandered.[15]

Often unspectacular — though quite assured — as to idiom and structure, this poetry is sincere, civilised and has no lack of inner fire: it is concerned with a culture of the sensibility which makes for finer and more wholesome living. It is in terms of such concerns that these writers, and the minority for whom they are the voices, can achieve a sense of community with other Ceylonese.

But it is at this point that one notes a restriction of range that makes even such distinguished poetry a minor achievement. These writers have yet to bring their sensibilities, fine as they are, to bear on the whole business of living in contemporary Srī Laṅkā.

Will they ever do so? After more than a century of writing in English by Ceylonese they are yet so far from achieving a total response that there is no sustained exploration of the world they ought to know best — the world of the English-educated English-speaking class — from the inside: this class has yet to produce a literature which successfully contemplates its own most profound experience. It may be that the malaise of colonialism has corrupted it too deeply for recovery. At the very least, the trauma of the awakening has not as yet been sufficiently coped with for self-awareness and self-criticism to merge with a recovered sense of personal worth and public function.

REFERENCES

1. *Administrative Report, Director of Public Instruction*, 1887, pp. 27-28D. I owe this reference to Dr. B. S. S. A. Wickremesuriya.
2. cf. J. Halverson. 'Prolegomena to the Study of Ceylon English' *University of Ceylon Review*, Vol. XXIV, Nos. 1 and 2 (April and October 1966), p. 73.

3. Scholars such as James Alwis, Ananda Coomaraswamy and Senarat
   Paranavitana, reformers such as Anagarika Dharmapala, and a great
   many politicians from the days of Ponnambalam Arunachalam, Ponnambalam Ramanathan and F. R. Senanayake to those of D. B. Jayatilaka, D. S. Senanayake and S. W. R. D. Bandaranaike (we could go back
   to include James Alwis). There is a valuable body of criticism of Sinhala
   literature and drama in English, though much of it appeared in newspapers. The first real recognition of the distinctive character of the new
   Sinhala drama appeared in English reviews.

4. H. E. Weerasuriya, *The Trousered Harijan*, p. 1.

5. op. cit., pp. 160, 161, 162.

6. James Goonawardene, *A Quiet Place*, p. 42.

7. James Goonawardene, *Call of the Kirala*, . 46.

8. Punyakante Wijinaike, *Giraya*, p. 60.

9. op. cit., p. 65.

10. R. Procter, *A Fisherman's Daughter*, p. 253.

11. Godfrey Gunatilleke, 'A Language Without Metaphor' in *Community*,
    Vol. 1, No. 2 (1954), pp. 55-69.

12. Godfrey Gunatilleke, 'The Garden' in *Sankha*, Vol. I, p. 68.

13. L. Wikkramasinha, 'The Mask' in his *Nossa Senhora Dos Chingalas*, 1973,
    p. 22.

14. Patrick Fernando, *Though her mind was rather small*.

15. Gāmini Seneviratne, 'The Second Coming', *Twenty-Five Poems*.

DRAMA, FILM AND MUSIC *

by K. N. O. Dharmadasa

DRAMA

After the nationalist theatre of the Tower Hall era, dominated by
the figure of John de Silva (1857-1922), the Jayamanne "formula"
play consisting of love triangles, disguises, abductions, murders
and scenes in courts of law gained the ascendancy in the Sinhalese
theatre. Enhancing the popular attraction of the Jayamanne plays
were songs with melodies borrowed from Hindustani films and an
invariable dash of clownish humour by a man and woman duo.

The movement for better standards of liberary and artistic taste
launched by a section of the English educated élite under the leadership of Martin Wickramasinghe and E. R. (Ediriweera) Sarachchandra had its effects on the theatre and the cinema as well. And it

---

* I wish to thank my colleagues Professor S. Vithianathan and S. Thillainathan for providing me with information on the developments in
  Tamil drama.

was the University of Ceylon which became the disseminating centre of a more refined and discriminating taste, as well as a workshop for experimentation in artistic expression, which was most vigorously developed in the theatre. As a counter to the semi-operatic Jayamanne melodrama a series of mainly straight plays, adaptations of classics from the Western theatre, were presented during the 1940s and early 1950s by the University Drama Circle. Most notable among them were *Kapuvā Kapōti* (1945), based on Gogol's *Marriage*, and *Veda Hatana* (1953), based on Moliere's *Le Malade Imaginaire*. Several original plays on the same lines such as Sarachchandra's *Bahina Kalāva* (1951) were also produced at the same time.

These early ventures of the University Drama Circle were confined to comedy. With Sarachchandra's *Pabāvati* (1953) an attempt was made to present a serious theme within the framework of a dialogue play. However, in *Pabāvati*, Sarachchandra included a narrator — a feature from the traditional folk opera called *nādagam*. This traditional feature did not fit into the form of the dialogue play. But Sarachchandra in his next experiment utilised the *nādagam* form in its entirety. This was in *Manamē* (1956), a remarkable achievement in theatrical craft, poetic sophistication and dramatic concentration, by which the element of drama in the folk *nādagam* form was adapted to the modern stage. In producing *Manamē*, Sarachchandra drew inspiration from the living theatrical traditions of other parts of the orient, the *kabuki* and *noh* of Japan and the Peking opera of China. The Sinhalese theatre, which had been in search of an identity, vacillating between the *nurti* operatic form transplanted from North India and the dialogue play borrowed from the west, appeared at last to have found one. In this sense *Manamē* was an epoch-making breakthrough.

With the success of *Manamē* the stylized form which it adopted seemed to be establishing itself as the truly national form of theatre, and there was soon a spate of plays in that genre. Drawing sustenance from traditional folk plays and ritual drama, Sarachchandra produced *Rattaran* (1958), *Elova Gihin Melova Āvā* (1959), *Vella Vähum* (1960) and several other plays, each of which made a notable contribution to the Sinhalese theatre. His *Sinhabāhu* (1961), using the same form followed in *Manamē* is regarded as the finest play of the early 1960s. In its lyrical richness and the dramatic intensity with which a tragic theme (the conflict between youthful ideals and parental authority) is presented, *Sinhabāhu* proved an unusually significant achievement. Other notable creations in the stylized form were Gunasena Galapatty's *Sanda Kinduru* (1957) and Dayananda Gunawardene's *Nari Bāna* (1961).

In the hands of lesser talents than these the stylised drama often deteriorated into a mere cliché-ridden formula, and the assembling of the trappings of stylization without much theatre to speak of. But the situation was saved by the innovative skills of talented newcomers, the most notable among whom was Henry Jayasena whose *Janēlaya* (1961) attempted to blend the forms of naturalist and stylised drama. *Janēlaya*, basically a naturalist play, utilized some features of the stylized form such as mime and song to heighten theatrical effect. It was also significant in being an attempt to portray a contemporary theme: the emptiness of the life-style of all strata of the bourgeoisie. In this it was an answer to the charge that since *Maname* Sinhalese theatre had been preoccupied with myth and folktale. A play with a similar structure was Galapatty's *Mūdu Puttu* (1962), an adaptation of Garcia Lorca's *Yerma*. Jayasena followed with *Kuvēni* (1963), a reinterpretation of a national legend.

In the search for novelty and experimentation, the dramatist of the late 1960s resorted frequently to translation and adaptation. Thus Sugathapala de Silva adapted Pirandello's *Six Characters in Search of an Author* as *Harima Badu Hayak* (1965) and Tennessee William's *Cat on a Hot Tin Roof* as *Hele Nägga Dōn Putā* (1966); Dhamma Jagoda adapted Tennessee William's *A Streetcar named Desire* as *Wes Muhunu* (1966); Henry Jayasena translated Brecht's *Caucasian Chalk Circle* as *Hunuwataye Kathava* (1967) and Chandrasena Dassanayake adapted Shaw's *Pygmalion* as *Mage Ran Kaṅda* (1969). This trend continues in Jayasena's translation of *Mother Courage* as *Diriya Mava*, Namel Weeramuni's translation of *Colombe* as *Nättukkāri*, and Sugathapala de Silva's *Mutukumāri*, based on *Irma la Douce*.

In 1969 Sarachchandra made another experiment with *Pēmatō Jāyati Sōkō*, an operatic drama using a highly classical language and melodies based on North Indian classical *ragas*. And perhaps for this reason it was not as popular as his earlier plays. Of late the most popular plays have been those conveying a message pertinent to contemporary social and political problems. Thus *Dunna Dunugamuvē* (1972) by Sugathapala de Silva, a dialogue play with the theme of the heroic stand of striking workers against an autocratic and scheming employer, and *Puslōdang* (1972) by Simon Nawagattegama, obviously a parody from an ultra-left point of view of the present government, have been very popular. The latter was banned, as was *Malavun Nägitiy* (1972), a theatre of cruelty with a theme reminiscent of the insurgency of 1971. Recently Nawagattegama's own *Subha saha Yasa* (1974), a naturalist play reinterpreting a phase from Sinhalese history, has been the centre of much controversy. While several critics have acclaimed it as a remarkable achievement in dramatic art, others more preoccupied with content than with form found fault with its apparently nihilistic philosophy.

It has been argued that such a stance is detrimental to the morale of a people engaged in a critical struggle for the establishment of a socialist society.

In Tamil drama during the 1940s there was a movement, as in Sinhalese, to propagate a better literary taste drawing inspiration from the West. Representative of this movement were the dialogue plays of K. Kanapathypillai, a lecturer in the University of Ceylon: his *Udaiyar Midukku, Murukan Tirukuththālam* and *Nattavan Nakara-valkkai* portrayed the weaknesses of the upper strata of society. These plays were significant in being the first serious literary works using the colloquial Jaffna dialect.

The search by the Tamils for national identity during the post-1956 period was manifest in the literary sphere. Thus in the theatre, as among the Sinhalese, there was a search for authenticity and distinctiveness in the folk dramatic tradition. S. Vithianathan modernised a traditional folk play in the same manner as Sarach-chandra did with *Manamē*. This was *Karnan Pōr* (1962). He followed it with *Ravanēsan* (1964), an original play in the same genre. *Karnan Pōr* and *Ravanēsan* were based on themes from the *Mahabharata* and the *Ramayana* respectively and in form they were dance dramas. Vithianathan's own *Nondi Nātakam* (1963) was another adaptation of a traditional play, this time with a humorous theme. As in Sinhalese the modernized folk drama was a success, and following these pioneering works there appeared a large number of plays in the same genre. But, many of them were mere exercises in form rather than good drama. A significant experiment in the genre was Mauna-guru's *Sankāram* (1969). In it the traditional formula was utilized to portray contemporary social problems.

Another tendency in the Tamil theatre of the period, which may also be an aspect of the search for national identity, is the extolling of Jaffna history and its heroes. A forerunner in this attempt was K. Kanapathypillai's *Cankili* (1954), presented at a time when the Sinhalese-Tamil conflict over the national language problem was reaching boiling-point. Mullai Mani's *Pantara Vanniyan* (1964) depicts the heroic saga of one *vanniyar* chieftain of the area. At the same time several other historical plays, this time with an all-island rather than merely Tamil focus, were produced such as *Kandi Rājan Nātakam* (1964), portraying the story of the last king of Kandy, and *Cingagirik-kāvalan* (1962), the story of King Kassapa of Sigiriya.

FILM

The Sinhalese film which emerged in the late 1940s inherited the characteristics of the Jayamanne plays, being mostly renderings into celluloid of their stage presentations. The influence of South Indian cinema with its formula of melodrama consisting of fights, songs, dances and low comedy was equally pronounced. Together they contributed to a deplorably low level of technical and artistic skill.

Lester James Peries's *Rēkhāva* in 1956 made a breakthrough to finer artistic standards; this was a bold attempt to escape from the conditioning to which Sinhalese film-makers and cinema-goers had been subjected from the inception of the industry. Instead of having a melodramatic theme enacted in stereotyped gestures by heavily made-up heroes, heroines and villains in an unreal background patched up in the studio, *Rēkhāva* for the first time realistically portrayed the life of a Sinhalese village; and the village character-types were drawn in a typical outdoor location. Rejecting as it did the conventional formula of the box-office hit, *Rēkhāva* was not an immediate financial success, but it had shown the way towards a truly Sinhalese cinema, original and catering to a more refined sensibility.

Lester James Peries followed *Rēkhāva* with *Sandēsaya* (1960 a story of Sinhalese resistance to the Portuguese, and *Gamperaliya* (1963), based on the epoch-making novel by Martin Wickramasinghe. *Gamperaliya* won the Critics Award and the Golden Peacock at the Third International Film Festival in New Delhi in 1965. In rapid succession he directed *Delovak Atara* (1966), *Ran Salu* (1967), *Golu Hadawata* (1968) and *Nīdhānaya* (1972), the last based on a short story by G. B. Senanayake. In the meantime several other films, following standards which made them at least comparable with the best in world cinema, have appeared under the direction of newer talent. They are Siri Gunasinghe's *Sat Samudura* (1967) and G. D. L. Perera's *Dahasak Situvili* (1969). These works cumulatively contributed to a refinement of taste among a considerable section of the cinema-going public, and demonstrated that it is possible to make a popular film which also reflects a finer taste. Other successful films of this high standard have been *Kurulu Bädda* (1961), *Sikuru Taruva* (1964), *Gätavarayō* (1965), *Sāravita* (1966), *Parasathu Mal* (1967) and *Tun Man Handiya* (1970). However, these are exceptions rather than the rule. The Sinhalese film by and large continues to be dominated by the influence of the box-office hits in India. Of late, the South Indian formula has been replaced by the North Indian with night club scenes, semi-nude heroines and a profusion of song and dance.

With the establishment of the State Film Corporation in 1972 holding the monopoly in import and distribution of films and raw material for film production, the potential has been created for the maintenance of more exacting artistic standards. The Corporation has decided to inspect shooting scripts before granting the raw material for production. It is hoped thus to control the quality of

films. How this unprecedented involvement of the state in decisions concerned with artistic taste will fare remains to be seen.[2]

MUSIC

In music, as in the other spheres of creative activity already discussed, the main theme has been, and still is, the search for a 'national'
idiom, identity and authenticity. Because traditional music had all
but disappeared by the beginning of the twentieth century, its resuscitation and revival were altogether more difficult.

In the early years of the twentieth century the *nurti* music which
used North Indian classical *ragas* evoked a considerable response in
Srī Laṅkā. And with the advent of the gramaphone, musicians
like Sadiris Silva, H. W. Rupasinghe and Don Manis Pattiarachchy,
who were well versed in North Indian classical music and created
original compositions based on classical *ragas*, established themselves
as the *avant-garde* in Sinhala music. Thus the emerging national
tradition in music had taken on a distinct Indian form.

The visit of Rabindranath Tagore to the island in the 1930s made
a profound impression on Sinhala musicians, and the immediate result was a strengthening of Indian influence, which was already pervasive. At about this time M. G. Perera had begun his campaign to
disseminate a knowledge of North Indian classical music by writing
several beginners' courses and by setting up an academy of music.
The *Gāndharva Sabhā*, another organisation with which he was connected, was launched in 1936, its aim being to foster the study of
North Indian, South Indian and Kandyan dance and music. Largely
as a result of the interest generated by the *sabhā*, music came to be
included as a subject in the school curriculum and a number of young
students went to India to study Indian classical music.

Tagore's influence also had other effects. It bore fruit in inspiring
young musicians like Ananda Samarakoon and Suryashankar Molli-
goda to develop a more genuinely indigenous national musical
tradition. Samarakoon was the first Sinhalese musician to explore
the possibility of using Sinhalese folk music for this purpose. During
the 1940s Munidasa Cumaranatunge, better known as a grammarian
and literary artist, advocated a national music based on traditional
verse prosodies; and Sunil Santha, who had returned from India
after a rigorous training in Indian music, proposed a mixture of
the traditional folk music with Western musical concepts such as
harmony. Thus the search for a national identity in music involved
a positive attempt to break free of the pervasive influence of classical
Indian music.

In the meantime the Indian influence had begun to affect popular
tastes in music as well. With the rise of the Sinhalese cinema and

its unabashed imitation of Indian models, the music of the Sinhala cinema was largely derived from Hindustani films. The vogue of the day was the borrowing of melodies from Hindustani films. Thus commercialised Hindustani music maintained its hold during the late 1940s and early 1950s.

But the revivalist wave of the mid-1950s, with its deep appreciation of folkways and folk tradition, was breaking the hold of Hindustani music on the Sinhala cinema. In this context arose Amaradeva's experiments in synthesizing Sinhalese folk music tradition with North Indian classical music. Several others such as Somadasa Alvitigala, Dayaratna Ranatunga, Piyadasa Atukorala and Dunstan de Silva have followed suit, and the borrowing of melodies from Hindustani films has almost ceased.

Though primarily a 'traditionalist', Amaradeva has used western musical concepts such as harmony and counterpoint in some of his compositions, especially those devised for films and ballets. It is in the work of Premasiri Khēmadāsa that the influence of Western music stands out most prominently. His compositions are modernistic in their appeal and because of their suitability for dramatic effects they have been greatly in demand among film makers.

The western influence on Sinhalese music is seen also in a brand of Sinhalese "pop" music, part of the pervasive youth culture of the urban areas. Though its popularity is spreading to the villages as well, it is at the time of writing a phenomenon of marginal significance within the wider context of the development of a national musical tradition.

PAINTING AND SCULPTURE

by Ashley Halpé

Anyone who stops by a *gokkala*[1] artist at work on a *pirith mandapaya*[2], who has seen a *bali*[3] painter constructing his diagrams or responded to the plastic and symbolic power of Ambalangoda masks must readily perceive the continuing strength of living tradition in the crafts of Srī Laṅkā. Some of these traditions survive under threat. One wonders how long the genuine mask-makers will resist the tourist trade that is already in full flood with 'devil masks' made in 'factories'; one notes that the full-scale performance of a *bali* ritual or a *Kohomba Kankāriya*[4] is becoming increasingly rare. However, in the *pirith* decorations, the increasingly traditional character of wedding ceremonial, and in the mounting of public ceremonials, there is evidence that continuity and vital new expression are still possible and actual to the Srī Laṅkā craftsman.

It has been very much otherwise in studio painting and sculpture. Here we see discontinuity and disjunction; there is every appearance of a total break. Modern Sri Lankan painting and sculpture have been distinctly occidental in provenance and the occasional incidence of oriental motifs has never had the character of a full-bodied organic evolution from Srī Laṅkān traditions of aesthetic experience. Between the monumental Buddha sculptures of the Anuradhapura period and the street-corner statues of present-day piety there is no valid relationship except in the abstract idea: the aesthetic and spiritual lack of relationship is too jarring to bear contemplation. And between both these and the 'Buddhist' sculpture of the modern studio artist there is perhaps a more absolute gulf. The latter is a pure act of personal expression that not infrequently affects the fractured syntax of Giacometti and Epstein; it is unable to participate in or contribute to the societal intuitions that inform artistic expression within the ambience of a living religion.

Thus it is possible to say that the work of Tissa Ranasinghe, perhaps the most important of Srī Laṅkā's sculptors, is essentially European. He has evolved a mature and sensitive idiom, but one would not be able to say on the evidence of style that the artist was Srī Laṅkān.

The situation is not essentially different with regard to painting. The content of most works is Ceylonese in a denotational sense, but the connotations not infrequently have a strong Romantic or Modern element while in the style the dialects of European painting of the last hundred years tend to dominate. Yet the syntheses achieved are frequently powerful, original and profoundly honest. This is perhaps most vividly the case in the perceptions bodied forth by Justin Däraniyagala. The consistent element of his work is its fused incandescent intensity, an intensity seldom achieved by other Sri Lankan painters and which draws together the varied forms — lyrical, satiric, tragic and surrealist — in which his genius finds expression. Latent in his work is an extremely precise calligraphy and a sure grasp of traditional values of form, tone and balance, but this grasp of the craft is tested to the extreme in the service of a restless and even tortured imagination. His most distinctive work conveys a disturbing sense of tragic irony.

Däraniyagala's utterance is frequently dark, oblique and massive. George Keyt's is usually light, graceful and eagerly communicative though there is always a redeeming force of Dionysiac commitment to the dance of life. His work clearly fuses the tradition of

Picasso with the mythology of Hinduism. India is also reflected in certain linear rhythms and ornamentations which curiously evoke sensations both of delight and firm objectivity, and in the predilection for earth colours, for shades of tropical green, for flaring blues, reds and yellows which recall the raiment and the skies of India (though with perhaps a memory of Matisse). To the western observer Keyt's work will often seem 'oriental' enough; but it is significant that he turned from a Post-impressionist pictorial vocabulary and the writing of surrealist poetry to the development of an iconography based on Hindu experience. The choice is even more significant when one remembers that he comes from an English-speaking Christian family of Dutch colonial ancestry. It is very much a case of an artist deliberately seeking a congenial tradition, rather than coming into his inheritance; the result is an organisation of highly eclectic material.

Keyt is a prolific painter. His characteristic style is so distinctive that his reputation is his greatest danger. Certain moods and motifs seem to assemble too easily into deft compositions which have to be called purely decorative. But at its best his painting conveys a sense of vibrant energies trembling for release from confidently definitive forms.

Superficially there is far more sobriety in the paintings of L.T.P. Manjusri, an art of muted tones and gentle rhythms without the fierce linear emphases and brilliant colours of Keyt. But as one contemplates the paintings one enters a maze of baffling symbols and extraordinary juxtapositions, the deeply surrealist expression of a prodigal imaginative life. Powerful tensions, as between sensuality and Buddhist sensibility, are tamed and ordered within these quiet designs. As in Keyt, the stylistic effect is highly eclectic, though the constituent elements are very different: here we see Buddhist imagery — sometimes Ceylonese, sometimes Tibetan — traces of western Surrealism and the arcane symbols of private fantasy. The strangeness of this invented world seems all the greater when one considers Manjusri's reputation in Ceylon as a copyist of temple frescoes, seeking — single-handed and single-minded — to achieve a complete record in the absence of a more sophisticated technology of preservation and record. It is as if the life-long contact with traditional art and thought (he was for many years a Buddhist monk) has only stimulated him into a non-traditional creative output.

Harry Pieris matured as an artist within the confines of one clear tradition — that of Western Europe. Schooled in the salons of London and Paris and equipped with a wide technical knowledge, the urbane glow of his pigments and his treatment of light place him in the direct line of descent from Rembrandt. He is best known in Srī Lankā as a portrait painter, but his landscapes too are of great evocative richness. In both landscapes and portraits — the latter are certainly his major works — the signs are of the sombre brooding of a percipient and quietly responsive sensibility. Sitters and landscapes are held in the gleam of subtle revelations.

The mystical lyricism of Ivan Peries could be called Romantic, but only if one pays due heed to the complex overtones of that word. His subjects are hardly ever overtly religious, but the quality of his meditation upon them always is. A principal characteristic of his work is a purity — even starkness — which beautifully controls the evident impulse to tender feelings. In his early work one sometimes sees the influence of Gauguin and Modigliani, but the chief debt is to an older master — El Greco. Later, after he settled in London, the pictorial elements remain faintly Srī Lankān, though so generalised as to make this of little import. The method reveals, in its frequent use of gesso, that the painter has gone further in his exploration of the traditions of Christian art.

A lively sense of Christian tradition informs two interesting sets of murals by Srī Lankān artists. In David Paynter's murals for the Trinity College chapel a deep commitment to the subject-matter transfigures an essentially academic style. A sense of the relevance of the subjects has led to the choice of Srī Lankān models and settings — the Crucifixion, for instance, is poised over a pandanus swamp. In Richard Gabriel's murals executed for the Roman Catholic church of St. Martin de Porres at Timbirigasyaya, the artist seems to have had no difficulty in adapting his distinctive idiom to the scope defined by his commission.

That idiom is a notable achievement — it is the closest thing we have to a style formed in response to the immediate environment. The images — a bull, a child on a tricycle — are often deliberately naive or primitivistic, through a rare humility before the object of meditation. But the meditation also flows into considerations of texture and form, producing subtleties which betoken an alert painterly sensibility. The textures he achieves are particularly fascinating.

A special concern for texture also characterises the work of Stanley Kirinde, another painter whose art is firmly rooted in everyday reality. Not that he is a realistic painter; his pictures are always carefully elaborated compositions in which line and colour flow in counterpoint to the natural forms of the represented objects.

Most of the painters mentioned above came together in 1943 with the encouragement of Lionel Wendt — pianist, photographer and indefatigable promoter of the arts — to form the '43 group. It was

this Group that established and created a taste for modernist painting in Srī Laṅkā and provided a focal point for young talent. (In
the specific field of Art Education one should mention here the
extremely valuable contributions of two great Chief Inspectors of
Arts, C. F. Winsor and W. J. G. Beling, and of Cora Abrahams'
Melbourne Art Classes. Indeed, Winsor and Beling also contributed in no small measure to the education of the country's painters
and public in developments in modern painting.)

This was not the first organization for the promotion of Art in
the country. The Ceylon Society of Arts had been formed several
generations earlier, but the Ceylon Society had developed marked
conservative tendencies which encouraged sterile academicism,
and it was the '43 Group that stimulated painting in Srī Laṅkā into
twenty-five years of adventurous experiment.

Recent exhibitions have shown that there has been no important
change in fields of force. Many interesting new painters have emerged, among them Senaka Senanayake, Jayantha Koliyawansa, S. H.
Sarath and Upasena Gunawardena, but modern Srī Laṅkān painting and sculpture continue to cultivate the territory staked out by
their earliest practitioners. One cannot but regret the lack of a more
fruitful interaction between Srī Laṅkān aesthetic traditions and the
art of modern Europe, but the consciousness of the different traditions has most often been partisan and divisive. It is especially
embarrassing to encounter the deliberate attempts at nationalist
revivalism, for such will-tormented Srī Laṅkān-ness has usually
been affected by persons whose sensibilities have a crudeness clearly manifested in the grotesque or tasteless formulations which they
call Art. But it is scarcely less embarrassing to find a practising artist
writing that 'the frescoes at Sigiriya make no positive contribution
to the experience of life' and rejoicing in a consciousness beyond
'the pale limits of the temple fresco, the decorative leaf design and
the ornamental facade'.

Of course few artists would say such things. But they all paint
and sculpt as if they are true. And yet no honest evaluation can
fail to find that the educative experiences and essential dynamism
of modern Srī Laṅkān art have been provided by the West, though
it is probable that these artists would scarcely have been able to
function if they did not have a sense of applying their exciting dis-
coveries to an unexplored subject-matter. One does not abjure —
one only rejoices in — a phase of development that has produced
valid and vital utterance. But just when it seemed that changes in
our culture were making possible a healthier sense of tradition, new
threats have appeared. Earlier, the problems had been the erosion

of aristocratic and monastic patronage and the shift of power to a westernized middle class, together with the complications inevitable in a colonial situation. Today the threats are bureaucratization and the transference of power to officials and politicians with a naive commitment to utilitarian modes of thought.

Glossary

accomodessans, lands granted for maintenance in lieu of salaries.
ande, a system of renting land to share-croppers
andekaraya, share-cropper
attan, exchange labour
ayurveda, indigenous system of medicine
bali, exorcism ritual
bhikkhus, Buddhist monks
Buddha Jayanti, the 2500th anniversary of the Buddha's death
Culavamsa, a continuation of the historical chronicle, the *Mahavamsa*
dagaba, (Buddhist) depository of holy relics
devale, shrine of Hindu Gods
Dhammadipa, island of Buddhism
durava caste, toddy tapper caste
fidalgos, Portuguese noblemen
gokkala, the tender leaves of the coconut palm
goyigama caste, farmer caste
grama sevaka, village administrative official
hartal, non-violent protest
Jayanthi era, the period centering around the *Buddha Jayanti* of May 1956
kabuki, a form of Japanese traditional drama
kachcheri, district administration centre
kammatic Buddhism, Buddhism aiming at a desirable birth rather than salvation from rebirth
karava caste, fisher caste
kohomba kankariya, a ritual dance drama
lascarins, native militia
maha season, cultivation season from October to March
Mahavamsa, a chronicle compiled about the sixth century A.D. giving historical information on ancient Sri Lanka
Mahayana Buddhism, Buddhism, the ultimate goal of which is attaining Buddhahood
moulavis, Arabic teachers
mudaliyars, high ranking indigenous officials
nadagam, an indigenous form of drama
navandanna caste, artificer caste
nibbanic Buddhism, Buddhism concentrating on the attainment of *nibbana* (salvation)
nikaya, sect of Buddhist monks
nisandas, a form of poetry free of traditional prosodic patterns and traditional imagery
noh, a form of Japanese traditional drama

467

nurthi, a style of music using Northern Indian classical *ragas*.

parinibbana, the passing away (death) of the Buddha

pirith mandapaya, a small pavilion constructed for a ceremonial recitation of Buddhist scriptures

pirivenas, Buddhist educational establishments primarily for monks

poya, full-moon day

raga, melodic structure

raj, domain or empire

rajakariya, traditional service obligation

Rajarata, literally the king's country, refers to the Northern plain of Sri Lanka

Ruhuna, the south-eastern plain of Sri Lanka

salagama caste, cinnamon peeler caste

samsara, the cycle of birth and rebirth

sangha, the community of Buddhist monks

sasana, the Buddhist establishment

sati, self-immolation of widows on the funeral pyres of their husbands (in India)

satyagraha, non-violent non-corporation

Sinhaladipa, island of the Sinhalese

stupa, see dagaba

swabasha, mother-tongue (Sinhalese and Tamil)

Theravada Buddhism, Buddhism the ultimate goal of which is attaining self-salvation

thugi, ceremonial killing and robbing of selected victims by gangs (in India)

tombòs, land registers

Tripitaka, the teachings of the Buddha

valauwwa, dwelling of a notable in the area

vedas, sacred religious texts of the Hindus

vinaya vardhana, a movement which emphasised discipline (among Buddhist monks)

wasama, the smallest administrative unit

yala season, cultivation season from April to August

Index

Abayapala, Roland, 445
Abhayagiri *stupa*, 34; *vihara*, 40
Abrahams, Cora, 464
Academy of Administrative Studies, 369
accomodessans, see land grants
accountants, 362, 430
accountants service, 364
acetic acid, 136, 195
Adams, F.D., 11
Adams Peak, 9
administration, 354-69; British, 62, 70, 71, 362; colonial, 57, 69, 76, 77, 404; decentralization of, 356; district level, 36; employment in the, 90, 93, 95, 96, 97; local, v, 36, 57, 63, 65, 72, 90, 318, 320, 354-69, 403; politicisation of the, 320, 363; recruitment to the, 95, 104, 362, 364, 407; village level, 361.
Administration of Justice Law, 369-73
advocates, 372
aesthetic studies, 408, 417, 430
Africa, 48, 51, 177, 346, 395; East, 219; West, 224
Afro-Asian leaders, 344
Agastiar, S., 442
Agrarian Research and Training Institute, 250
agricultural, extension services, 240, 241, 243; indebtedness, 134, 247, 249; settlements, 34
Agricultural census of 1946, 236; of 1962, 236, 238, 240, 242
Agricultural Productivity Act, No. 2 of 1972, 166
Agricultural Productivity Councils, 166
agriculture, iv, 18, 20, 24, 46, 121, 152, 194, 339; diversification, 192, 224, 294; export, 149, 153-4, 164; income from, 200; instruction in, 408, 419; investment in, 147-8, 152-5, 160-1, 165; irrigated, 23; large-scale, 45; mechanisation of, 242; peasant, 69, 70, 193, 236-53; plantation, 67, 68, 69, 70, 74, 131-3, 160, 213-34; sedentary, 18; subsistence, 44, 160, 216; traditional, iv, 69, 134-5, 153-4, 161-2, 164-7, 236-53
Agriculture and Lands, Minister of, 239, 327; Ministry of, 233, 355
Agriculture, Department of, 242
agro-chemicals, 242, 245, 251
Aid Sri Lanka Consortium, 346
air base facilities, 339
Air Force, Ceylon, 339; Pakistani, 335; Royal, 334
Alexander the Great, 31
Aliyan, Sengai, 445
All-Ceylon Buddhist Congress, 388
All-Ceylon Tamil Congress (TC), 285, 295, 296, 315
Alms Bowl, 45
aluminium, 25
Aluvihara, 34
Alvitigala, Somadasa, 460
Alwis, James, 447
Amaradeva, 460
Amarapura nikaya, 387
Amarasekera, Gunadasa, 440, 441, 443
Ambalangoda, 460
ambassadors, 333
American, air force planes, 341; oil companies, 345; spoils system, 320; Supreme Court, 326
Ames, (M), 386
Amparai, 244, 411, 430
Anandan, K.S., 445

469

Index